TEACHING THE TRADITION

D1713465

Teaching the Tradition

CATHOLIC THEMES IN ACADEMIC DISCIPLINES

EDITED BY

John J. Piderit, S.J.

and Melanie M. Morey

OXFORD
UNIVERSITY PRESS

OXFORD
UNIVERSITY PRESS

Oxford University Press, Inc., publishes works that further
Oxford University's objective of excellence
in research, scholarship, and education.

Oxford   New York
Auckland   Cape Town   Dar es Salaam   Hong Kong   Karachi
Kuala Lumpur   Madrid   Melbourne   Mexico City   Nairobi
New Delhi   Shanghai   Taipei   Toronto

With offices in
Argentina   Austria   Brazil   Chile   Czech Republic   France   Greece
Guatemala   Hungary   Italy   Japan   Poland   Portugal   Singapore
South Korea   Switzerland   Thailand   Turkey   Ukraine   Vietnam

Published by Oxford University Press, Inc.
198 Madison Avenue, New York, New York 10016

www.oup.com

Oxford is a registered trademark of Oxford University Press

Library of Congress Cataloging-in-Publication Data
Teaching the tradition : Catholic themes in academic disciplines / edited by John J. Piderit and Melanie M. Morey.
    p.   cm.
Includes bibliographical references and index.
ISBN 978-0-19-979530-7 (hardcover : alk. paper) — ISBN 978-0-19-979531-4 (pbk. : alk. paper)
1. Catholic universities and colleges—Curricula—United States.   2. Catholic Church—Education
(Higher)—United States.   3. Catholic Church—United States—Influence.   I. Piderit, John J.
II. Morey, Melanie M.
LC501.T435 2012
378'.0712—dc23
2011020040

1 3 5 7 9 8 6 4 2

Printed in the United States of America
on acid-free paper

Contents

Contents

Contributors

Jeffrey B. Adams teaches at Saint Michael's College in the undergraduate and clinical master's programs and is currently serving as department chair. His main interests are the psychology of religion and the social and clinical psychology interface, the latter leading to his recent publication "Bridging Psychology's Scientist vs. Practitioner Divide: Fruits of a Twenty-Five Year Dialogue," *Journal of Theoretical and Philosophical Psychology* 28 (2008).

Ed Block Jr. is professor of English at Marquette University. He has been editor of *Renascence: Essays on Values in Literature* since 1995. His most recent publications include "A Ransom of Cholers: Catastrophe, Consolation, and Catholicism in Jon Hassler's *Staggerford, North of Hope*" and "The Life and Death of Nancy Clancy's Nephew" in *Between Human and Divine: The Catholic Vision in Contemporary Literature,* (Catholic University of America Press, 2010).

Patrick McKinley Brennan is associate academic dean and holds the John F. Scarpa Chair in Catholic Legal Studies at Villanova University School of Law. In addition to more than fifty articles, essays, and book chapters, he is the coauthor of *By Nature Equal: The Anatomy of a Western Insight* (Princeton University Press, 1999) and the editor of two other volumes. His next book, *The Sovereignty of the Good: An Essay on Law, Authority, and the Church*, will be published by Oxford University Press.

Rev. David B. Burrell, C.S.C., Theodore Hesburgh Professor Emeritus in Philosophy and Theology at the University of Notre Dame, currently serves as professor of comparative theology at Tangaza College, Nairobi. His publications include *Knowing the Unknowable God* (University of Notre Dame Press, 1986), *Freedom and Creation in Three Traditions* (University of Notre Dame Press, 1993), *Friendship and Ways to Truth* (University of Notre Dame Press, 2000), *Learning to Trust in Freedom* (University of Notre Dame Press, 2009), and *Original Peace* (with Elena Malits, Paulist Press, 1997).

Paul J. Contino is Blanche E. Seaver Professor of Humanities at Pepperdine University. With Maire Mullins he coedits *Christianity and Literature*. He has co-edited and introduced *Bakhtin and Religion: A Feeling for Faith* (Northwestern University Press, 2001). His work has appeared in *Religion and Literature, Studies in the Novel, Renascence, Religion and the Arts, Commonweal, America, Christian Century,* and *First Things.*

Lawrence S. Cunningham now Emeritus, was the John A. O'Brien Professor of Theology at the University of Notre Dame. Cunningham's scholarly interests are in the area of systematic theology and culture, Christian spirituality, and the history of Christian spirituality. His recent publications include *Francis of Assisi: Performing the Gospel Life* (Eerdmans, 2004), *A Brief History of Saints* (Blackwell, 2005), and *An Introduction to Catholicism* (Cambridge University Press, 2009).

David Gentry-Akin is professor of theology at Saint Mary's College of California in Moraga. In addition to publishing numerous articles in *Horizons, Listening,* and several anthologies, he is the executive director of national conventions for the College Theology Society and serves on the Mission and Ethics Committee of CHRISTUS Health, a Catholic health system sponsored by the Sisters of Charity of the Incarnate Word.

Elaine C. Grose is an assistant professor of environmental studies and the science laboratory manager at Neumann University in Aston, Pennsylvania. Her most recent publication is *Ethical Responsibilities of Franciscan Educators toward Environmental Issues* (Valley Press, 2009). She also chairs the university's Care of Creation Advisory Committee.

Robert Kiely is professor emeritus of English at Harvard University. His books include *Beyond Egotism: The Fiction of James Joyce, Virginia Woolf and D. H. Lawrence* (Harvard University Press, 1980), *Reverse Tradition, Postmodern Fiction and the Nineteenth-Century Novel* (Harvard University Press, 1993), *Still Learning: Spiritual Sketches from a Professor's Life* (Medio Media, 1999), and *Blessed and Beautiful: Picturing the Saints* (Yale University Press, 2010).

Melanie M. Morey is the senior director for research and consulting at the Catholic Education Institute, Bronx, and assistant dean for assessment at St. Patrick's Seminary and University, Menlo Park. She is a contributor to *Catholic Women's Colleges in America* (Johns Hopkins University Press, 2002). Together with John J. Piderit, S.J., she has authored *Catholic Higher Education: A Culture in Crisis* (Oxford University Press, 2006) and *Renewing Parish Culture* (Rowman and Littlefield, 2008).

Angela Alaimo O'Donnell is associate director of the Curran Center for American Catholic Studies and teaches English, creative writing, and American Catholic studies at Fordham University. Her publications include three books of poems, *Moving House* (Word Press, 2009), *Waiting for Ecstasy: A Chapbook of Saints' Lives* (Franciscan University Press, 2009), and *Saint Sinatra and Other Poems* (Word Press, 2011). An essay, "Seeing Catholicly: Poetry and the Catholic Imagination," appears in *A Catholic Studies Reader* (Fordham University Press, 2011).

Glenn W. Olsen is professor emeritus of history at the University of Utah. He was the director of the Honors Program at Seattle University, and taught in the history and philosophy departments of Fordham University. He has been a visiting professor in theology at St. John's University in Collegeville, Minnesota, and in the University of Notre Dame Program of Liberal Studies. Among his recent publications is *The Turn to Transcendence: The Role of Religion in the Twenty-first Century* (Catholic University Press, 2010).

Rev. John J. Piderit, S.J., is president of the Catholic Education Institute, Bronx, which promotes new ways to strengthen Catholic education. He is a former president of Loyola University Chicago and taught undergraduate and graduate economics at Fordham University for twelve years. His most recent book is *Sexual Morality: A Natural Law Approach to Intimate Relationships* (Oxford University Press, 2011).

Oliver Putz received an MA and a PhD in biology from the Freie Universität in Berlin and an MA in theology from the Graduate Theological Union in Berkeley, California. He is currently working toward a PhD in philosophical and systematic theology at the Graduate Theological Union.

Rev. Thomas P. Rausch, S.J., is the T. Marie Chilton Professor of Catholic Theology at Loyola Marymount University in Los Angeles. His most recent publications include *Educating for Faith and Justice* (Liturgical Press, 2010) and *Pope Benedict XVI: An Introduction to His Theological Vision* (Paulist Press, 2009).

Jeanne Heffernan Schindler is an assistant professor in the Department of Humanities at Villanova University. Her interests are interdisciplinary, integrating philosophy, theology, and political science. She has published in such areas as Catholic social thought, democratic theory, and faith and learning. Her most recent major publication is an edited volume on *Christianity and Civil Society: Catholic and Neo-Calvinist Perspectives* (Lexington Books, 2008).

Rev. Paul A. Schweitzer, S.J., originally from New York and now a Brazilian citizen, is an emeritus professor of mathematics at the Pontifical Catholic University in Rio de Janeiro. He is a specialist in differential topology and a member of the Brazilian Academy of Sciences. He has a long-term interest in the relationship of contemporary science and Christian faith.

Charles Scribner III is an art historian and the author of *The Triumph of the Eucharist: Tapestries Designed by Rubens* (UMI Research Press, 1982), *Rubens* (Abrams, 1989), *Bernini* (Abrams, 1991), and *The Shadow of God: A Journey through Memory, Art, and Faith* (Doubleday, 2006).

Rev. Brian J. Shanley, O.P., has been the president of Providence College since 2005. Previously (1994–2005) he was a member of the faculty of the School of Philosophy at the Catholic University of America. He was the editor of *The Thomist* from 2002 to 2005. His main research interest is the thought of Thomas Aquinas.

Rev. Myles N. Sheehan, S.J., M.D., is a Jesuit priest and physician with training in internal medicine and geriatrics. From 2001 to 2009 he was senior associate dean for education at Loyola University Chicago Stritch School of Medicine. He is currently the provincial of the New England Province of the Society of Jesus.

Rev. William R. Stoeger, S.J., is a Jesuit priest, astrophysicist, and cosmologist who has been working for the Vatican Observatory in Castel Gandolfo, Italy, and Tucson, Arizona, since 1979. He has authored a number of papers in scientific journals on gravitational physics, black hole astrophysics, and cosmology, and has also been heavily involved in lecturing, writing, and organizing conferences dealing with important issues in science and theology, particularly divine action in light of the findings of the natural sciences.

TEACHING THE TRADITION

Introduction

John J. Piderit S.J., and Melanie M. Morey

RESEARCH SHOWS THAT senior administrators believe Catholic perspectives on academics, social justice, personal development, and religious commitment should be integrated into the Catholic higher education experience. In other words, these perspectives should permeate the regular functioning of Catholic colleges and universities. In a previous study, most administrators asserted both the centrality of integration as a goal and its often thin implementation. While presidents offered a more positive view, the majority of senior administrators reluctantly and with some disappointment admitted that the Catholic faith did not effectively function as an integrating factor throughout their institutions. These same administrators, however, affirmed their strong desire to help students integrate their academic and social commitments.[1]

The focus of this volume is academic integration, and its primary purpose is to assist faculty efforts to more fully integrate Catholic themes in their course work. It is also designed to support the many existing initiatives that promote Catholic mission, character, and identity at scores of Catholic institutions of higher education.

Collectively the chapters offer ways to understand the relationship between Catholic faith and a wide range of academic disciplines. Ultimately the goal is to reach students and help them appreciate how a Catholic perspective helps integrate insights from a variety of academic disciplines. Because most students more easily make connections when guided by informed and committed teachers, faculty members are the book's target audience. Therefore, the discipline-specific material is discussed in terms that presume familiarity with the content of the main undergraduate courses in the various disciplines. But the book also attends to how students experience academic integration in courses connected with their undergraduate majors. This volume may provide helpful orientation for doctoral students with an interest in linking study in their chosen academic field with important religious themes from the Catholic intellectual tradition. It may also be of interest to parents, themselves former students, who may well be products of Catholic education.

The material on Catholic themes presented here is broad enough so that it can be linked in a variety of ways to segments of individual courses covered in most academic majors. It is neither assumed nor expected that professors will develop entire courses focused on Catholic themes.

There are limits to what an undertaking this large can hope to accomplish. Because many Catholic colleges and universities have thirty or more majors, covering all academic disciplines in sufficient detail in a single volume is impossible. Two specific goals influenced which academic disciplines were included: approximating the pattern of undergraduate course selection and at least hinting at the feasibility of a similar approach to academic integration on the graduate and professional level.

Approximating the pattern of undergraduate course selection at most Catholic institutions requires that theology and philosophy be given special prominence. For this reason, three chapters treat theological issues and two chapters handle important issues in philosophy from a Catholic perspective. At most Catholic institutions, English literature attracts a large number of students; accordingly four chapters explore Catholic themes in poetry, drama, fiction, and narrative. Other chapters address a range of undergraduate disciplines. To suggest that professional graduate studies are fruitful areas for exploring connections with Catholic themes, chapters on law and medicine were also included.

Choosing some academic areas means omitting others. Essays on nursing, sociology, and modern languages obviously would be excellent. But, together with classical languages, theater, chemistry, molecular biology, various area studies, particular disciplines in business, some branches of engineering, and other academic fields, they await treatment in a future volume.

Chapter 1 is a personal introduction to theology. It responds to a need articulated by faculty who participated in Substantially Catholic, a series of faculty seminars focused specifically on linking particular academic disciplines with Catholic themes. In their evaluations of the seminar, a significant number of faculty suggested that participants would benefit from exposure to a theology primer, or a basic review of theology. Some participants admitted that although they had studied theology in college, for the past ten or fifteen years they neither had done much theological reading nor had they been exposed to theology in systematic lectures or presentations. They maintained that reading works that situated them in the proper theological framework would have been helpful. Chapter 1 serves this function.

Contributors to this volume were chosen both because of their extensive background in teaching and research in their own academic area and because of their familiarity with the relations of their secular academic discipline to Catholic themes. Prior to writing their own essays, contributors read the essays by Rausch (chapter 2) and Cunningham (chapter 3). These two lead essays served as a reference point for reflections on important Catholic issues related to each specific academic discipline, and references by contributors to Rausch and Cunningham are to their essays in this volume.

In order to make the essays as accessible as possible, authors were encouraged to emphasize religious themes and connections that are helpful to faculty teaching the regular array of undergraduate courses in their academic area. In lieu of extensive footnotes, authors were encouraged to list five significant books or articles that might be helpful to teachers seeking more relevant material to present in the classroom.

Catholic religious themes other than social justice are the focus of this volume. Social justice issues and concerns are a very important component of the Catholic tradition. Many Catholic colleges and universities devote considerable academic resources to assuring that these topics are covered well from a Catholic perspective in a variety of courses. Far fewer, however, are similarly successful in assuring that Catholic religious connections are made more broadly in the majors normally pursued by undergraduates. Using theological themes provides the type of academic integration senior administrators strive for in the policies they develop at their institutions. For this reason, contributors were asked to focus on Catholic religious themes rather than on social justice.

The main motivation for this volume is to expand the art and practice of academic integration that occurs at Catholic colleges and universities. Because theology is the core academic discipline in all Catholic colleges and universities, ideally theologians should interact on a regular basis with at least one or two faculty members in each academic department. Philosophy also plays a pivotal role in academic integration because good theology relies on a realistic and adequate metaphysics and epistemology.

A second concern at many Catholic institutions is the extent of the integration. The general norm in Catholic tertiary education is that students take three or four courses in theology and philosophy. Compared with the more than forty courses they take to qualify for graduation, these three or four specifically Catholic courses (or Catholic-"tinged" courses, in the case of philosophy) offer a limited basis for Catholic integration of all academic disciplines. The courses in theology may be substantial in content and very well taught, and those in philosophy may address issues that are important both for Catholic theology and for the ensuing Catholic tradition in philosophy. However, taken as a group, three or four courses do not constitute even a single Catholic-concentrated semester among the eight semesters undergraduates typically spend in college or university. If it is to have a lasting impact, the Catholic contribution has to be integrated more broadly into the curriculum.

The concepts and ideas students encounter in theology and philosophy should be reinforced by faculty teaching otherwise secular disciplines. If that is the case, students may gradually come to appreciate that a Catholic perspective offers a comprehensive view of how academics, social interaction, and civil society are related in foundational Catholic beliefs and thinking. This is especially true when it happens within a student's academic major. When students see how Catholic themes relate to some of the material they study in their major, two things are possible: first, this insight can provide them with a satisfying framework with which to understand their personal faith commitment; second, they can come to appreciate how faith, though quite distinct from reason, informs reason.

There is no one way to read this book. The natural place to begin is with chapters that treat the reader's own area of expertise or interest. But it might be even more useful to read the theological essays that provide the underlying framework for the book before gravitating to a specific disciplinary essay. Chapter 1, "Fundamental Catholic Theology," situates theology for a modern academic. David Gentry-Akin explains what theology aspires to do for academics and shows how theology is related to the personal story that each faculty member brings to bear on his or her discipline. Chapters 2 ("Catholic Anthropology") and 3 ("Perspectives in Catholic Theology") are the pivotal chapters for the entire volume. Most readers will encounter themes in these chapters that resonate with a large segment of material already present in undergraduate courses. After reading those, chapter 13, "Catholic Themes in Art and Music," by Charles Scribner III will be an exhilarating experience for many people. And from there, *à chacun son goût!*

With one notable exception, the disciplinary chapters focus on Catholic themes connected to materials studied at the undergraduate level. In chapter 9, a different perspective is introduced. Large sections of the essays by Robert Kiely and Paul J. Contino emphasize the particular approach these two teachers take in the classroom. While they have worked occasionally with one another, this chapter reflects their independent teaching in separate non-Catholic institutions, Harvard University and Pepperdine University. With respect to specific authors and artists, they discuss how they present "Catholic material" in the classroom. These teacher scholars offer personal and pedagogical reasons for proceeding one way rather than another. In a sense, this is a "how-to" chapter, in which particular attention is given to the way students react to various Catholic themes raised by their professor. The authors highlight specific points that are important to the literature and to which students are receptive. For this reason, it can be valuable to all teachers, no matter what their particular academic discipline. While the book emphasizes Catholic integration, Kiely and Contino demonstrate how they integrate religion, literature, and art in their courses and how they encourage their students to do likewise.

The Catholic intellectual tradition extends in time back to the earliest fathers of the Church and, eventually, even embraces insights of the great Greek and Roman philosophers who lived before Christ. It assumed a more institutional presence at the end of the twelfth century with the formation of universities, all of which were Catholic from approximately 1200 until the middle of the sixteenth century. Catholic colleges and universities today continue to contribute to and partially modify this tradition as they wrestle with various issues in theology, philosophy, and other disciplines.

Despite the tradition's long history, the phrase *Catholic intellectual tradition* is of recent vintage. Fifty years ago the term was not used regularly, even though the Catholic intellectual tradition existed and was presented in various ways in practically all majors offered at Catholic colleges and universities. In those days priests, sisters, and brothers made up a large part of the teaching staff. Their instruction and cultural formation in religious life or the seminary was steeped in the tradition. The religious connections were illuminating for the priests and religious, and in time became second-nature for them. These teachers also regularly helped their students see and understand the connections, taking it upon themselves to demonstrate to students how much of the secular material they were learning could be fruitfully understood within a broader, Catholic context.

The religious and priests were not required to do this. It just made sense to do it, and there was little need to name an activity that everyone took for granted. *Catholic intellectual tradition* is now a phrase that helps alert faculty at Catholic institutions to their responsibility to know how their subject can either illuminate part of Catholic theology or be illuminated by it. No one expects faculty at Catholic institutions to spend time in seminaries or motherhouses. Nonetheless for Catholic institutions to continue their tradition of providing Catholic academic integration, current faculty members need useful resources that help them make connections between Catholic themes and the so-called secular disciplines. This volume is intended to do just that.

This volume respects the academic departmental structure at universities while it also encourages Catholic colleges and universities to make theology and philosophy more structurally central to the regular academic functioning of the university. Modern universities do their academic work through individual academic departments, and many students establish important professional relationships with faculty members who teach in their major area of concentration. While the approach taken in this book accepts and endorses this reality, it also encourages further development. At least some faculty members in each secular department should work with in-house theologians and philosophers to identify themes that promote the Catholic mission and identity of their college or university.

Religious congregations of men and women played pivotal roles in the foundation of most Catholic colleges and universities. Many contributed to the development of these institutions as teachers, administrators, or assistants. Today, however, lay people fill most of these roles in practically all Catholic colleges and universities. Many of these lay people are Catholic, and even those who are not Catholic are often interested in how Catholic issues relate to their academic disciplines. That is why this volume emphasizes Catholic themes common to all Catholic institutions rather than charisms of particular founding congregations. Over the next fifty years all involved in Catholic education will have a significant opportunity to develop new ways to share the common Catholic intellectual heritage that has been a hallmark of these institutions since their foundation.

NOTES

1. See Melanie M. Morey and John Piderit, *Catholic Higher Education: A Culture in Crisis* (New York: Oxford University Press, 2006), 211–41, especially 212–13.

PART ONE

Foundations

1

Fundamental Catholic Theology

David Gentry-Akin

Fifty years ago a book such as this would have been unnecessary. Catholic colleges and universities swam in the ocean that was the Catholic tradition. Most of our students, faculty, and staff were Catholic. While only a few were trained as theologians, and while the level of religious literacy varied greatly, these institutions were like rivers that carried everyone along, the strong swimmers as well as the weaker ones. An ethos permeated these places, and people absorbed that ethos silently—through icons and images and through the good example of its religious virtuosi—as much as by way of any formal instruction in the Catholic faith.

The reality is different now. In many places our Catholic colleges and universities operate in a much more diverse environment. Very little can be taken for granted in these institutions regarding an understanding of the faith tradition that undergirds them, that provided the inspiration for their founding, and that has the potential to continue to guide them into a faithful and vibrant future. Many regard the diversity and pluralism that now characterize most of our institutions as a good thing, but they come at a cost. Something has been gained, but something has also been lost.

This volume is intended for college and university professors, Catholic and non-Catholic alike, with an interest in nurturing the religious character of their institutions through their own teaching, research, and service. In thinking about the contribution they want to make to the religious mission of their institution and how they are going to make it, it is important for faculty to make a personal inventory of their own religious background, commitment, and level of literacy. If they are Catholic, how much do they really know about the Catholic intellectual tradition?[1] And if not Catholic, how much do they really know about their own faith tradition and how it might converge with or diverge from the Catholic tradition? How much do faculty members really know about their students' level of religious literacy?

In this essay I begin by telling you a bit about my own story. I do this not to indulge myself, but rather to illustrate the fact that Catholicism, as a complex religious tradition, is about much more than doctrine. Stories, rituals, signs, and symbols communicate as much about Catholicism as does the doctrinal elaboration of its core tenets. To really get at this tradition, one must begin to understand what some have termed "the Catholic imagination." Of course an understanding of doctrine is necessary, but the experience and worldview that provide the foundation for the rational explication of doctrine is at least as important, if not more so.

The second part of the essay is a discussion of a few of the core ideas that shape the Catholic dogmatic and intellectual tradition: the Incarnation, the sacramental worldview, the mystical body of Christ, and Mary as the feminine face of God. Many more themes could, of course, be explored, and settling on just a few was a struggle. Nevertheless what follows is intended to help orient the reader to the riches of the Catholic tradition and what it offers to scholars in all disciplines who seek to make use of its rich resources in their disciplinary research and teaching.

A CONVERSION STORY

I was born and raised in Houston, Texas, in the 1950s. My mom had a deep, simple faith that might best be described as "evangelical," while my dad had no faith. I was raised with some basic religious ideas—about the universality of Jesus' love for all, for example—but with very little formal religious instruction. As small children, my sister and I occasionally went to Sunday school, and I still remember my teacher helping all of us to learn the song "Jesus loves the little children / all the little children of the world / red and yellow, black and white / they are precious in his sight / Jesus loves the little children of the world." That was a pretty radical message for that day and time, when our neighborhoods were still utterly segregated, and, other than my uncle's adopted Native American boys and Korean girls, I did not know any children of races other than my own.

I liked school, did well, and was appreciated by my teachers. In the 1960s children came to Texas from Mexico and other parts of Latin America, but there was no school program for them—no bilingual education program of any kind. These children were dropped into age-appropriate classrooms and were expected to learn to speak, listen, read, and write in English and to master the curriculum of the grade into which they were placed. Public school classes were large in those days, up to thirty-five students, and teachers had no aides or other assistance.

Because I was a good student and had a gift for teaching, my teachers enlisted me to help the new students who came to us from south of the border not knowing English. Each day between classes, when I had finished my own work, I would take two or three immigrant students into the hall or an empty classroom and work with them on reading in English.

In the sixth grade, two boys, Eduardo and Francisco, twins from La Paz, Bolivia, joined our class. Their dad had come to work for Humble (later Exxon) Oil Company. As I had done with my other classmates, I helped them to acquire the gift of English. But these boys would also give me a gift, a gift that would change the whole course and direction of my life.

Eduardo, Francisco, and I became friends and spent time together outside of school, playing and eating dinner at one another's homes. In particular we loved to ride our bicycles throughout the neighborhood. One of their favorite places to ride was on the grounds of St. Anne's Church and School. So on Saturdays we would frequently ride over to St. Anne's, where we could ride freely on the expansive grounds without having to worry about traffic.

Eduardo and Francisco, like most Latin American children of that era, were devoutly Catholic, so we never went to St. Anne's without the boys wanting to stop into the church for a moment of prayer. Because Catholicism was totally alien to me, on their first few visits to the church I waited outside. And there was no pressure coming from the boys; the very last thing on their minds was trying to convert me to Catholicism! But one day my curiosity got the better of me, and I went with them into the Church.

I can still remember my very first impressions. Houston is hot and very humid for at least six months of the year. The church, built in the Spanish Mission style, had thick stucco walls that kept it cool and dark inside. I remember following Eduardo and Francisco into the church and watching them dip their hands in the cool water in the bowl near the door. They took the water and reverently made the sign of the cross, something I had never seen before, and I remember thinking, "Oh, there is something special about this water." I admired the beautiful statues, some of which were so artfully crafted that they appeared to be alive: the Sacred Heart of Jesus, the Immaculate Heart of Mary, but also Mother Frances Xavier Cabrini and St. Thérèse of Lisieux, the Little Flower. We crossed the church to the main altar, which had a large gold box positioned at its very center. The boys genuflected. Again I thought, "Oh, there is something special in that gold box." The boys knelt, made the sign of the cross again, and prayed briefly. I remember the beautiful stained-glass windows relating stories from the Bible, most of which were unfamiliar to me. I remember how the bright sun shone brilliantly through the colored windows, casting shafts of color across the sacred space that seemed to envelop me when I passed by. I remember the intoxicating aroma of incense that had seeped into the wood and gave off a fragrance long after the incense had been burned. And then we left the building and went about our play.

That beautiful space, however, had captured my imagination, and I had to return. A week or two later, on a Friday afternoon after school, I rode my bike over to the church and went in, and just sat in the back of the cool, quiet, womb-like space, feeling a sense of comfort and safety that I could not put into words.

And then something else happened. A beautiful creature, dressed in a long black robe and veil and with her head enveloped in brilliant white linen, came into the back of the Church, genuflected, entered a pew, knelt, made the sign of the cross, and prayed for a few moments. Then she rose and ascended to the choir loft, where she proceeded to play the organ for an hour or so. I was having a total sensory experience—the sight of the altar, the statues, the stained-glass windows, the stations of the cross, the smell of the incense, the sound of the organ—and I felt transported to another realm, a realm that seemed to take me out of time, a realm that allowed me to escape, for a few minutes at least, from my troubled family situation and all the angst that came with adolescence. For a month or two I continued going to St. Anne's once a week or so and sitting in the back of the church, listening to the beautiful creature play the organ.

One Friday afternoon the beautiful creature—whom I later learned was a Sister of Divine Providence from San Antonio, Texas—entered the church as she always did. But instead of taking her usual pew, she walked up to the pew immediately behind the one in which I was sitting. She genuflected, entered the pew, and knelt down right behind me. I could feel the air move as she made the sign of the cross and said her prayers. But when she finished, she did not rise and exit the pew. Instead she tapped me on the shoulder, reached out her hand in friendship, and said, "Hello. I am Sister Georgine. Who are you?" I was both pleased by her gesture and a bit frightened. Who were these beautiful creatures? Were they human or divine? What did she want with me?

It soon became clear that Sister Georgine wanted nothing except to be my friend. She had seen this twelve-year old boy sitting in the back of the church week after week and had wondered who he was. As the music teacher at St. Anne's School, she taught every student, so she knew that I was not a student at the school.

Nor had she ever seen me at Mass, because I had never been to Mass and did not even know what Mass was.

A friendship blossomed between Sister Georgine and me. We would meet in church, and after she practiced the organ we would walk around the grounds of the complex, talking, and frequently we went to the convent for ice cream. Over several months of friendship, Sister Georgine never once asked whether I wanted to become a Catholic. It was clear that she had no agenda other than wanting to be my friend. I am quite confident that, even if I had never inquired about the Catholic faith, our friendship would have gone on indefinitely.

It was May, and the school year was coming to a close. My visits with Sister Georgine had become easy and comfortable, and one day she told me that the convent would be closing for the summer, that all of the sisters would return to San Antonio for summer school, their annual retreat, and community meetings. She wanted me to know because she did not want me to come looking for her and wonder why she had disappeared. She assured me that she would send me postcards from San Antonio over the summer and that she would return in August.

It was at that point that I told Sister Georgine that I wanted to become Catholic. After some conversation in which she ascertained the motives for this impulse and assured me that it was in no way a condition of our ongoing friendship, she arranged to take me to meet Father Francis Emmet Monaghan, a Basilian priest who was the pastor of St. Anne's. As Sister Georgine had, Father Monaghan took what felt like a very genuine interest in me, a kind of interest that I had experienced only from my mom and from a few teachers and relatives. Father Monaghan took time of out his busy schedule to conduct twice-weekly one-hour catechetical sessions with me all summer, taking me through a basic adult catechism. After each session I attended his 12:10 weekday celebration of the Mass, along with a handful of parishioners, and then quite often he would invite me back to the rectory for lunch, or slip a $10 bill to one of the retired parishioners attending the noonday Mass and ask him to take me out to lunch. I felt incredibly loved. I felt I had a community of people, beyond my selfless and hardworking single mom, to whom I mattered.

At the end of the summer Father Monaghan and I concluded that I was ready for baptism, and so I was baptized in a simple private ceremony, as was customary in those days, on August 10, the feast of St. Lawrence, deacon and martyr. Father Monaghan suggested that I ask Marie Smith, the sacristan in the church, to be my godmother. Marie was a war bride whose husband had been one of the American GIs who liberated France during World War II. In spite of Marie's rather pedestrian last name, she had a thick Parisian accent and was full of stories of the French church: the gothic cathedrals, the stories of Francis De Sales and Vincent De Paul and so many more.

Shortly thereafter a bishop from the Philippines was visiting, conducting fund-raising appeals for the missions in the Philippines, and Father Monaghan decided that it was an opportune time for me to be confirmed. A year or so later I went down to the local Catholic hospital to inquire about a part-time job. There I met the wonderful Sisters of Charity of the Incarnate Word, many of whom were, at that time, from Ireland. I worked at the hospital for several years and was greatly influenced by the sisters. From them I learned about the Irish church: St. Patrick, Our Lady of Knock, and the deep faith and incredible resilience of the Irish people.

Why have I devoted so many pages of an academic essay to tell a very personal story? Because although it is the personal story of a single individual, it also speaks volumes about the fundamentals of the Catholic worldview. You see, I absorbed those fundamentals before I learned a single line of Catholic doctrine and before I attended a single Catholic Mass. As essential as doctrine and worship certainly are, they became personally compelling only because of the particular and profoundly religious experiences that preceded and grounded them.

THE CATHOLIC IMAGINATION

Certain principles of the Catholic tradition can be drawn from the formative experiences that preceded my formal catechesis in the Catholic faith:

1. Catholicism is a global faith tradition that holds meaning for Latin American schoolboys, elderly French widows, Filipino bishops, and Irish nuns.
2. Places are sacred. God's presence can take possession of a place and make it sacred. St. Anne's, the church of my experience, is a beautiful structure created out of masonry and glass, and it is also the House of God and the Gate of Heaven, a meeting point between heaven and earth, a real physical place that holds and mediates God's presence in a real but mysterious way.
3. Material reality is holy. It is imbued with spirit and carries and communicates the holy, through bread and wine, through water and oil, and ultimately through human flesh itself.
4. Art and music are essential means by which God gives us a fleeting glimpse into the depths of his own beauty.
5. Catholics are connected to one another—in the United States, in Latin America, in Africa, the Philippines, in France, in Ireland, and elsewhere— and they must care for one another.

6. Humans deserve reverence and respect for their dignity and freedom and special regard for the mysterious workings of the Holy Spirit in their souls.

7. God is everywhere, and God's work goes on, not only in liturgies conducted in the Church, but also when people educate the young or care for the sick and dying. Catholics have a long history of founding schools and hospitals that care for those in need regardless of their faith tradition.

   This willingness to care for all without distinction emerges from an incarnational sensibility. Each person is a unique and unrepeatable manifestation of God's presence in the world. Secular humanism and contemporary notions of cultural relativism are not what inspire this commitment to the service of others. Nor is it based on some ideology of inclusivity or antidiscrimination.

8. This incarnational sensibility is expressed through a mystical approach to the human person and through a desire to alleviate human ignorance and suffering. Lives of deep prayer enabled the men and women who have historically sponsored Catholic institutions to see Christ in each person they encountered and to work ardently to relieve human misery because they understood that, when they ministered to people in need, they were indeed ministering to Christ.

All people are to be cared for without distinction because God is present in all, as the Letter to the Hebrews reminds us: "Do not neglect hospitality, for through it some have unknowingly entertained angels."[2] Catholic schools and hospitals were founded to meet a basic human need, often because no other institutions delivering comparable services existed in a given region. But even in those cases where other institutions existed, Catholic institutions were founded to provide a uniquely Catholic witness in a particular field of endeavor or a particular geographic area. A Catholic way of approaching human endeavors such as education and health care—a way that witnesses to consciousness of the spiritual dimension of every human activity—was what set these institutions apart. Day in and day out, evangelization was going on. Most often it was implicit; occasionally it was explicit. An anonymous quote often attributed to St. Francis of Assisi captures well what was happening in these institutions: "Preach always, and when necessary, use words."

Evangelization in the Catholic sense should not be confused with proselytizing. The Catholic approach is clear and unequivocal, but without coercion. Catholics were witnessing to their beliefs in how they lived and what they did, and they shared their faith with others when they were called upon to give an account of the reason for their hope.[3]

The demise of these institutions and the wonderful religious virtuosi who staffed them means that fewer and fewer people have been blessed with the kind of introduction to and foundation in Catholicism described in the preceding pages. The process of becoming rooted in the Catholic tradition, as with any religious tradition, begins with experience, which in turn leads to reflection on the experience. For example, reverently recalling their baptism and the presence of Christ in the Eucharist, Catholics use holy water to make the sign of the cross and genuflect before a tabernacle. Reflecting on these experiences leads to the development of doctrine—the nuanced formulations of the core beliefs that arise out of our religious experience. The process is a cyclical one in which experience, symbol, reflection, and doctrine mutually inform and build on one another. We have an experience. We use a symbol. We reflect on the experience and symbol. We develop a refined understanding as to what the experience means. That conceptual understanding becomes the doctrine that will then inform our interpretation of the next experience, and so on.

People begin with religious awe, then engage in religious practice. Only later do they learn through doctrine what the practice means. One is essential to the other. Practice without doctrine would devolve into superstition. Doctrine without practice would be mere formalism. And doctrine does not eliminate awe, but accentuates it.

Some have compared the mutual interaction of practice, experience, and doctrine to a child coloring in a coloring book. On each page are forms that are the same in every copy of the book that is published. The child's love of colors is the awe and the forms correspond to doctrine. But each child selects which colors to use in filling them in. By selecting the colors and actually coloring the forms (practice and experience), children appropriate the forms and make them their own. The child "practices" coloring in the forms, and in the process the forms take on meaning (experience) for the child. This process is analogous to that of appropriating religious doctrine.

Earlier forms of catechesis are sometimes criticized because they relied on the memorization of doctrine. In fact, however, the memorization of core doctrinal concepts and ideas provides a framework, a scaffolding that gives people a way of interpreting their experience, of making meaning out of experience. Committing a few core ideas and concepts to memory is a superb pedagogical strategy, because that template will readily come to mind when one tries to make sense of new or earlier religious experiences.

The Incarnation

Catholicism is a rich, varied, and complex tradition that can be examined fruitfully through many lenses: biblical, historical, systematic, philosophical, and sociological. Entire libraries are filled with the writings of scripture, the fathers and mothers of the Church, the ecumenical councils, the popes, theologians and scripture scholars, and the mystics and agents of social change. When all is said and done, however, there is one doctrine that is the cornerstone of the entire tradition and without which the tradition would crumble, and that doctrine is the Incarnation.

The mystery of the Incarnation is captured in a beautiful prayer that has been recited by faithful Catholics in some form or another from at least the fourteenth century: the Angelus. It consists of three scripture verses recited in antiphonal fashion, each of which is followed by the recitation of a "Hail Mary," with a final collect closing the entire prayer. The first verse—"The Angel of the Lord declared unto Mary, and she conceived by the Holy Spirit"—calls to mind God's intervention in the life of Mary. The second verse—"Behold the handmaiden of the Lord, be it done unto me according to your word"—recalls Mary's receptivity to God's intervention. And the third verse—"And the Word became Flesh, and dwelt among us"—calls to mind the miracle of the Incarnation, the idea that God, in the person of the Word, the Logos, the second person of the Holy Trinity, would deign to take on human flesh, that God would love us so much and identify with us so thoroughly that he would choose to become one of us, to take on all that it means to be human, including the very human experience of death itself. This is the Greek notion of *kenosis*, or self-emptying, about which Paul writes in his Letter to the Philippians, "He emptied himself, taking the form of a slave, coming in human likeness; and found human in appearance, he humbled himself, becoming obedient to death, even death on a cross."[4]

This miracle, celebrated at Christmas with the very tender scenes evoked by the Christmas crèche, is truly at the heart of the Catholic way of perceiving reality. In choosing to become human flesh, God is testifying to the depth of his love for lost and alienated humanity, but at the same time he is testifying to the noble dignity and vocation of the human person as *imago dei*, as made in the image of God. In the Incarnation of the Word, God makes a second dramatic act of faith in human nature—more dramatic than the act of creation itself—and in the promise of the human race. As St. Athanasius writes, "God became human so that the human might become god."[5] This notion of *theosis*, or "divinization," so familiar to the Eastern Church, is fully orthodox teaching in the Church of the West as well and has been attested to in the writings of St. Augustine and St. Thomas Aquinas. In the Roman liturgy, at Vespers on the Octave of Christmas, the first antiphon proclaims the famous text, "O admirabile commercium": "O marvelous exchange! Man's Creator has become man, born of a virgin. We have been made sharers in the divinity of Christ who humbled himself to share in our humanity."[6]

The Incarnation stresses the notion of identification that is at the core of the experience of love. I cannot really love another until I am able to enter sympathetically into his experience, to understand his perspective, his unique way of participating in the human condition. This "entering into" the experience of another, with all that it entails in terms of letting go of my own ego, is modeled for us in the Incarnation itself. It also becomes the pattern of Christian faith and holiness throughout the entire Christian era. This letting go, this emptying out of the self is what allows human beings to create room in their minds and psyches to be able to experience something of the reality of the other, to be able to receive the other, and ultimately to be able to receive the ultimate Other, who is God. The model of self-emptying found in Jesus, then, becomes a "school of holiness" for his followers. We seek to imitate his example, and the promise of the gospel is that the habitual practice of self-emptying ultimately carves out a space within each person that will be filled by something far greater than that which it replaces. It will be filled by God himself.

In the Incarnation God becomes human without ceasing to be God. In precise language, the faith claim is that Jesus is both human and divine. That is, he has both a divine nature and a human nature. This both/and approach is at the heart of the Christian way of understanding reality. It is what is meant by incarnational theology and spirituality. In any situation a person confronts a reality: the man or woman who is in need, who may appear at the most inopportune time, who strikes us as a nuisance or a source of irritation with whom we would prefer not to deal. However, this obvious, surface reality is not the whole story. There is a depth dimension, a dimension that is *more real* than the obvious, empirically verifiable, surface dimension available through sense experience. This depth dimension, however, is not accessible to a person unless he or she has cultivated an ability to perceive it. And this is precisely where prayer and mystical experience come into the picture.

As with the development of any habitual way of responding to reality, the more Christians cultivate receptivity to the depth dimension of our experience, the greater will be our openness to it. The more open we are, the greater our capacity to receive the gift offered by that depth dimension. And that gift is precisely the presence of God. People are able to discern the presence of God in their experiences only if their spiritual practice has helped them to cultivate an awareness of that presence in the many and varied ways in which it manifests itself.

This rich incarnational theology and spirituality give rise to the sacramental principle. Here the idea of the Incarnation, of God becoming flesh, is extended in space and time. God not only became human in the person of Jesus in first-century Judea, but he continues to inhabit created reality, most especially through God's Word in sacred scripture, through the bread and wine that become the Body and Blood of Christ in the Eucharist, and through other sacramental celebrations of key moments in the human journey. God is present in the sacraments of initiation, forgiveness, commitment, and healing. We also experience God in the natural world, through friendship and human love and through all of the efforts of artists, musicians, novelists, poets, and dramatists to reveal the depth dimension, to reveal the beauty, truth, and goodness that is, in fact, God's "inbreaking" in the midst of the human condition.

Once a person accepts the already quite amazing idea that God becomes flesh in the person of Jesus, the notion that God is present and revealed in the Word of scripture and the celebration of the Eucharist becomes a much less challenging thing to believe.

Intrinsically related to the sacramental view of reality is the notion that times, places, and objects can be sacred, that God's graceful presence is especially available to us at sacred moments and in sacred places. Think here of Midnight Mass at Christmas, the Great Easter Vigil, the feast day of a special saint, the birthday of a dear friend, or the anniversary of the death of someone we loved deeply. Think too of sacred places: the magnificent Gothic cathedrals of northern France, such as Chartres. Think of pilgrimages to Rome, to Lourdes, to Fatima, or even to a sacred place closer to home, such as the Shrine of St. Katharine Drexel near Philadelphia or the Basilica of St. Joseph on Mount Royal in Montreal. Think, for a moment, even of objects, such as relics, that have taken on a sacred character.

Modern Catholics sometimes make fun of an earlier preoccupation with relics because the naïveté that motivated such devotion strikes us as being old-fashioned. In fact, some relics were not authentic, some may have inspired superstition, and some became a source for very profane commerce. Still the root idea is a valuable one: the sacred is mediated by the physical. Devotion to a relic is not so different from wanting to hold on to an object that belonged to a deceased parent or spouse. Even a modern, very sophisticated person derives some comfort from being in proximity to an object that belonged to a loved one who is now deceased. In some inexplicable way, the proximity of the object used or cherished by that loved one makes us feel closer to him or her. This sense is genuine even though contact with the loved one in the very real and physical way that was possible before death is no longer available to us.

In the Catholic imagination, desire too is understood to be sacred. Marriage is a sacrament in which the sacramental element is actually the love between the spouses, a love that will be consummated not only in sexual intercourse but in acts of commitment and self-sacrifice that cannot be imagined at the time the commitment is made. This commitment is given liturgical embodiment and expression in the nuptial vows exchanged and witnessed by the priest and community. "In principle, if sexual attraction is a part of the human condition, if it has been created by God, however indirectly, and if human nature, however flawed, is still fundamentally good, and finally if sexual imagery is used both in the Jewish and Christian scriptures as a metaphor for God's love, how can one possibly deny its sacramental value?... The human love between a man and a woman is a sacrament, a hint, a revelation, a sign, a metaphor for Jesus' love for the Church and for God's love for God's people." While consummation of sexual passion is sacramental, desire itself is holy: "Consider Bernini's statue of St. Teresa being transfixed by the arrow of divine love. It dares to portray her ecstasy as orgasmic, as explicit a metaphor as one could imagine. The saint herself was not hesitant about the use of erotic vocabulary in her description of her relationship with God."[7]

The Mystical Body of Christ: Community and Hierarchy

The Catholic doctrine on the Church, or ecclesiology, is based on the doctrine of the Incarnation and the sacramental vision of reality that flows from it. The Church is much more than a merely human organization. For all its historical failings, for all its human sinfulness, for all its flaws and blemishes, it nevertheless is a divine reality. It is the very extension of the mystery of the Incarnation in space and time. According to the account in the Acts of the Apostles, the members of the infant Christian community huddle together, in doubt and uncertainty, after Jesus' ascension. Orphaned once with the death of Jesus, it now seems to them that, after the consolation of his postresurrection appearances to the community, they are to be orphaned once again. But, as Jesus promised, he sends the Spirit, the Paraclete, to be God's presence with his people until he comes again. The outpouring of the Spirit on the Feast of Pentecost is thus regarded as the birthday of the Church. With that outpouring of the Spirit, God comes to be with the infant Church in a new way, to inspire his people and give them confidence about how they should proceed in the absence of the physical and historical presence of Jesus.

The Church, then, is another sacramental reality, another way—after the miracle of Creation itself, after the historical event of Jesus' life, witness, death, resurrection, and ascension—of God's being *Emmanuel,* "God with us," of God's abiding presence with his people. As Jesus brought his followers the fullness of the revelation of God, and thus Jesus himself is the "sacrament of the encounter with God," so the Church becomes Jesus' way of continuing his presence in space and time.[8] With the aid and comfort of the Holy Spirit, the Church becomes the "sacrament of our encounter with Christ." Just as Jesus was, at the same time, both God and human, so the Church is, in some mysterious sense, both human and divine. In fact at the opening of the second session of the Second Vatican Council, Pope Paul VI referred to the Church as "a reality imbued with the hidden presence of God."

Many people have difficulty with this way of thinking about the Church. What about the sinfulness to be found in her members? What about all of the errors and mistakes and even crimes that have been committed by the representatives of the Church in history? The Church is an earthen vessel; it is the instrument through which God communicates his graceful presence to us even amid the sinfulness of its members and even its ministers. When regarded as a purely human reality, the Church is merely the sum total of its members and its leaders. To the extent that they are sinful, it will be sinful; to the extent that they are holy, it will be holy. According to Catholic anthropology, humans are graced *and* flawed at the *same* time. At every moment of our existence we have the choice to act out of the graced dimension of our humanity or to act out of our flawed nature as sinful humans.

Seen purely through the lens of anthropological or sociological analysis, this is the human reality of God's Church. And yet Catholics stubbornly persist in the conviction that the Church is "imbued with the hidden presence of God." Thus, at any point in time, the Church's ministers may inspire us by being instruments of "epiphanies" or manifestations of God's presence among us. And at any point in time, the Church's ministers, failing to be God's instruments, may disappoint their fellow Catholics. Criticism in such cases is justified. However, critics should remember that the dual capacity for grace and sinfulness exists in every Catholic, lay and clergy, because that dual capacity is at the very heart of the human condition. Graced and yet flawed, capable of great holiness and capable of horrible evil at the same time—the potential for either is always present in each believer, because, as creatures formed in God's image, all human beings are blessed with freedom, the freedom to make choices.

Many biblical and theological metaphors and images are used to describe the Church, but the mystical body of Christ is one with a distinguished history. This image of the Church is found already in the first century, in the writings of Paul. In his Letter to the Ephesians, for example, Paul says, "Christ is the head of the church, he himself the savior of the body." Using rich spousal imagery, Paul goes on to tell us, "Christ loved the church and handed himself over for her to sanctify her, cleansing her by the bath of water with the word, that he might present to himself the church in splendor, without spot or wrinkle or any such thing, that she might be holy and without blemish." Finally, Paul draws an analogy to a person's care for himself: "No one hates his own flesh but rather nourishes and cherishes it, even as Christ does the church, because we are members of his body."[9]

This same lavish theology of the church as the mystical body of Christ is also developed by Paul in 1 Corinthians, as well as in his letters to the Romans and the Colossians:

> There are different kinds of spiritual gifts but the same Spirit; there are different forms of service but the same Lord; there are different workings but the same God who produces all of them in everyone. To each individual the manifestation of the Spirit is given for some benefit. To one is given through the Spirit the expression of wisdom; to another the expression of knowledge according to the same Spirit; to another faith by the same Spirit; to another gifts of healing by the one Spirit; to another mighty deeds; to another prophecy; to another discernment of spirits; to another varieties of tongues; to another interpretation of tongues. But one and the same Spirit produces all of these, distributing them individually to each person as he wishes.[10]

Paul's ecclesiology, drawn from his image of the mystical body of Christ, makes it clear that the Church is a community, "a discipleship of equals."[11] At the same time, however, any well-functioning community needs order, and thus the Church is hierarchically structured, with an order of ministry that seeks to assure the good order of the community and its fidelity to the message of the gospel and the tradition of the Church.

Elsewhere in Paul's Letter to the Ephesians we read, "Living the truth in love, we should grow in every way into him who is the head, Christ, from whom the whole body, joined and held together by every supporting ligament, with the proper functioning of each part, brings about the body's growth and builds itself up in love."[12] Developing the teaching of the mystical body, the Second Vatican Council fathers write in the Dogmatic Constitution on the Church, *Lumen Gentium*

> Christ, the one Mediator, established and continually sustains here on earth His holy Church, the community of faith, hope and charity, as an entity with visible delineation through which He communicated truth and grace to all. But, the society structured with hierarchical organs and the Mystical Body of

Christ, are not to be considered as two realities, nor are the visible assembly and the spiritual community, nor the earthly Church and the Church enriched with heavenly things; rather they form one complex reality which coalesces from a divine and a human element.[13]

This principle of mediation is a constitutive dimension of the Catholic vision of reality. It essentially says that, although each person may have "a personal relationship with Jesus," that personal relationship is not enough. The rich spiritual and theological legacy that is Catholicism can help individuals grow in faith and deepen their relationship with God. But there is more to the faith than a personal relationship with the divine. The faithful are also called to share their gifts with the community and to be accountable for personal choices and their impact on the community. While personal prayer and meditation are valuable means of connecting with God, the most prized means of connection takes place in the weekly celebration of the Eucharist. Even the most private moments of faith—the manifestation of conscience to a priest in the sacrament of reconciliation—is in reality a communal event.

A well-functioning community requires order, and so, already by the middle of the first century, the community had begun to develop a hierarchical system of governance. As the apostles, who had known Jesus, died, they were replaced by the *episcopoi*, the overseers, who later were called bishops. As the Church grew, the bishops instituted the office of the presbyters, or elders, who eventually were called priests, to assist them in their work. Catholics are connected to this global reality through their communion with one another, with their pastor, who is ordained by their bishop, and with their bishop, who is appointed by the pope. Catholic life is even governed by laws, by *The Code of Canon Law*, which outlines the rights and obligations that come with incorporation into the Church, the Body of Christ, as well as the ways in which leaders at various levels of the hierarchy are to relate to one another, to those they serve, and to those to whom they are accountable. While law can degenerate into legalism, canon law is intended to be a help to the right ordering and healthy functioning of the community, and it is always to be interpreted in ways that are consistent with the spirit of the gospel, in ways that promote full human growth and the spiritual flourishing of God's people.

In sum, to be a Catholic is to be a personal believer and also a member of a worldwide community of believers spanning every race and tongue and stretching across the globe. Catholics experience community in the parish, in Catholic schools, hospitals, and social service agencies, in the diocese, and internationally, through their communion with the bishop of Rome, the successor of St. Peter and the Vicar of Christ.

Mary as the Feminine Face of God

No discussion of the fundamentals of the Catholic vision of reality would be complete without some discussion of the role of Mary in Catholic dogma and devotion. Our Protestant brothers and sisters largely eschewed devotion to Mary after the Reformation, ostensibly because of excesses in Marian devotion that, for many of the faithful, caused Mary to eclipse Jesus himself. After the Second Vatican Council, Catholics shied away from devotion to Mary. They had become increasingly uncomfortable with what seemed to some to be exaggerated claims and by the ways in which Marian devotion set Catholics apart from Protestants and seemingly complicated ecumenical dialogue. Indeed devotion to Mary at times suffered from excess, but Mariology and Marian devotion are essential to the Catholic heritage and should be recaptured.[14] In fact a great deal of important work has been done in an effort to reform devotion to Mary in ways that are consistent with the teaching of the Second Vatican Council. In the documents of Vatican II, for example, Mary is not given a document of her own, but is treated in chapter 8 of *Lumen Gentium*.[15]

Interestingly, important theological and liturgical work on Marian devotion was done after the Second Vatican Council, but it has received very little attention. Various popes have issued important documents on Marian devotion, and one scholar in particular deserves special mention for his work in writing some magnificent hymns in honor of Mary that reflect the waves of biblical and liturgical renewal that were affirmed by the Second Vatican Council. Father Lucien Deiss, CSSp, now deceased, composed an entire album of beautiful hymns published under the title *Joy to You, Mother of the Lord: 12 Songs in Honor of Our Lady*, but few American Catholics have ever heard or sung any of them.[16] This may well be because of a tendency after Vatican II to downplay devotion to Our Lady.

Nevertheless throughout most of the Church's history Mary has functioned as the archetype of the divine feminine in the Catholic imagination. In the Middle Ages the people of northern France began the construction of roughly five hundred Gothic cathedrals in a hundred-year span, and almost all of them were dedicated to Mary. Countless beautiful images of Mary have been created throughout Christian history. The medieval images, such as *Sedes Sapientiae* (Seat of Wisdom), have Mary seated regally on a throne—not unlike images of ancient mother goddesses—with the baby Jesus on her lap. One cannot help but wonder whether, to the people who created such images, Mary was not somehow more important than Jesus. And yet if the emphasis in such works is on the miracle of the Incarnation, of the Word becoming flesh, how else could this happen than by a mother giving birth to a child and showing him to the waiting world? As Andrew Greeley notes, the Mary metaphor in the Catholic imagination "represents the Mother Love of God, the generous and loving, life-giving power of God, the tenderness of God, the fertility of God, the nurturing of God.... [Mary] pushes the envelope of the Catholic imagination as far as it can be pushed by hinting that there is a maternal dimension in God as well as a paternal one and thus absorbs and purifies and transforms all the female deities who came before."[17]

The earliest doctrine about Mary is the doctrine of the *theotokos*, Mother of God, declared at the Council of Ephesus in 451. Again Protestants are sometimes shocked to hear Catholic references to Mary as Mother of God. "How could God possibly have a mother?" they ask. However, this doctrine is not so much about elevating Mary as it is about protecting orthodox Catholic teaching about the dual natures of Christ as truly God and truly human. If Jesus is correctly to be understood as God made human, then he had to have a mother, and by logical deduction, his mother would have to be, in some real sense, the mother of God. And while the doctrine protects the teaching about the dual natures of Christ, it also has the felicitous by-product of elevating Mary in the Catholic psyche.

Mary becomes the prototype for the truly human person who is genuinely open and fully receptive to the promptings of God's spirit in her life, the person who is so open to God that she becomes capable of holding God within her very person, of being able to bring God more fully into this world, by being able to share God, in the person of Jesus, with the waiting world. She becomes not only Mother of God, but Mother of the Church, and prototype for the Christian believer seeking to bring Christ to a broken, hurting, and fragile world. This beautiful hymn to Mary, written by an anonymous author, captures very well Catholic Marian theology:

Mary the dawn, Christ the Perfect Day;
Mary the gate, Christ the Heavenly Way!
Mary the root, Christ the Mystic Vine;
Mary the grape, Christ the Sacred Wine!
Mary the wheat, Christ the Living Bread;
Mary the stem, Christ the Rose blood-red!
Mary the font, Christ the Cleansing Flood;
Mary the cup, Christ the Saving Blood!
Mary the temple, Christ the temple's Lord;
Mary the shrine, Christ the God adored!
Mary the beacon, Christ the Haven's Rest;
Mary the mirror, Christ the Vision Blest!
Mary the mother, Christ the mother's Son
By all things blest while endless ages run. Amen.

Catholics do not regard Mary as being in any sense equivalent to God. Nonetheless she does serve as the feminine archetype of the divine, and numerous theologians have pointed out the way in which she reveals the "feminine face of God."[18]

CONCLUSION

All human beings thirst for a deeper, richer, fuller experience of life. This is increasingly difficult in a culture that seems oriented toward the superficial, toward depriving people of the time and space for reflection and of the opportunity for depth experience. And yet the future of any religious tradition, and certainly of the Catholic tradition, lies in helping people to find that time and those spaces for reflection and depth of experience that will ultimately lead them to an encounter with the absolute, with God.

In the Gospel of John Jesus said, "I came so that they might have life and have it more abundantly." The ongoing vibrancy of the Catholic tradition depends upon communicating to future generations a deep feeling for the tradition and for what it has to offer them in their quest to experience life more abundantly and authentically. College and university professors in all disciplines can facilitate these experiences for students by helping them to search for that depth dimension in all of their studies, in the beauty of math and literature, in the human drama as it unfolds in studies of history and culture, in the wonder of the natural sciences, and in the probing of the human condition that takes place in philosophy and theology.

My own introduction to Catholicism began a long time ago, with the wonderful religious experiences related at the beginning of this essay. I ultimately became a theologian and have spent many years studying the tradition that became such a transformative gift for me as a teenager. Studying the tradition is deeply rewarding, but I would argue that a tradition cannot be passed on through study alone. It must be experienced, loved, cherished, and communicated. In fact it is sometimes the case that nontheologian faculty members more powerful witnesses than Catholic theologians about how faith animates their lives. The lived reality of the faith shared will quite often touch students more deeply than the academic discipline of theology per se. For instance, when Sister Georgine prayed a few minutes before practicing the organ, she communicated volumes to me before she ever uttered a word.

As at other colleges and universities, faculty members at Catholic institutions are expected to be experts in their own academic disciplines. However, the Catholic mission can be fulfilled effectively only if a significant number of faculty members are willing to explore the riches of the Catholic intellectual tradition in light of the questions raised by their own disciplines. In order to do this faculty members do not need a second degree in theology; they simply have to be willing to model for their students the practice of faith seeking understanding, to reflect on the intersections between the Catholic intellectual tradition and their respective disciplines, and to make their classrooms safe zones in which questions of faith and the intellectual life can be seriously engaged and explored. If questions of faith are just as ghettoized and marginalized in the classrooms of Catholic universities as they already are in secular institutions, we have no hope of preserving what has historically made these institutions unique. Only by embracing the freedom offered by Catholic universities to confront all of life's most challenging questions through both faith and reason can a Catholic university education hope to provide the kind of personal and intellectual integration that has been the hallmark of Catholic higher education from its inception.

The teachings of the Church, and the theology that seeks to make those teachings intelligible and to contribute to their appropriation and development in each new generation, would have little meaning or relevance for me were it not for those very powerful, initial formative experiences that planted Catholicism in my DNA and led it to becoming the interpretative framework—the web of signs and symbols and stories and rituals and relationships—that would mediate the world to me and me to myself. Fundamentally it is the communication of this vision of reality that will make Catholicism meaningful to succeeding generations of young people. This vision of reality is one that has faith that life is worth living because it is imbued by the presence of the living God. It is one that calls us to strive to be our best selves for the love of God and others. It is one that brings joy and comfort in the midst of disappointment and sorrow. It is one that promises that the taste of life we experience in this world—as sacred as it surely is—is only a foretaste of the deeper life that we are destined to know with God in eternity. It is urgent that we find more effective ways of communicating this worldview to our young people if we want the tradition to be passed on and to have a future.

NOTES

1. The website of the Holy See, www.vatican.va, contains a wealth of information, including official translations of all papal and conciliar documents, as well as documents issued by various dicasteries. Periodicals such as *America* and *First Things*, as well as journals, such as *Logos: The Journal of Catholic Thought and Culture*, are also excellent resources for gaining a deeper understanding of the Catholic intellectual tradition and educational, cultural, social, and political implications. The website of the Catholic Intellectual Tradition at Sacred Heart University contains a wealth of further information on the tradition in an accessible, user-friendly format: http://www.sacredheart.edu/pages/234_the_catholic_intellectual_tradition.cfm.

2. Hebrews 13:2. All biblical references are to the New American Bible.

3. 1 Peter 3:15.

4. Philippians 2:7–8.

5. St. Athanasius, *De Incarnatione,* 54:3.

6. *The Liturgy of the Hours according to the Roman Rite*, vol. 1, *Advent and Christmas* (New York: Catholic Book Publishing, 1975), 477.

7. Andrew Greeley, *The Catholic Imagination* (Berkeley: University of California Press, 2000), 55, 56, 57.

8. The term was coined by the late Father Edward Schillebeeckx and used as the title of one of his most important books, *Christ: Sacrament of the Encounter with God* (New York: Sheed and Ward, 1987).

9. Respectively, Ephesians 5:23, 26–27, and 29.

10. 1 Corinthians 12:4–11. See a passage evoking a similar theology in Romans 12:4–8.

11. A term coined by the feminist Catholic biblical scholar Elizabeth Schüssler Fiorenza.

12. Ephesians 4:15–16.

13. Second Vatican Council, *Lumen Gentium, the Dogmatic Constitution on the Church*, ¶8.

14. See Thomas H. Groome and Michael J. Daley, eds., *Reclaiming Catholicism: Treasures Old and New* (Maryknoll, N.Y.: Orbis Books, 2010). It has a number of splendid chapters, including one on devotion to Mary by Ada Maria Isasi-Diaz, one on the Rosary by Thomas Groome, and one on the Angelus by Bishop Robert Morneau.

15. Documents of the Second Vatican Council. *Lumen Gentium,* no. 53, http://www.vatican.va/archive/hist_councils/ii_vatican_council/documents/vat-ii_const_19641121_lumen-gentium_en.html.

16. Lucien Deiss, *Joy to You, Mother of the Lord: 12 Songs in Honor of Our Lady* (Chicago: World Library, 1965).

17. Greeley, *Catholic Imagination*, 90–1.

18. See, for example, Leonardo Boff, *The Maternal Face of God: The Feminine and Its Religious Expressions* (New York: HarperCollins, 1987).

SELECTED READINGS

Cernera, Anthony, and Oliver Morgan, eds. *Examining the Catholic Intellectual Tradition.* Vol. 1. Fairfield, Conn.: Sacred Heart University Press, 2000.

Cernera, Anthony, and Oliver Morgan, eds. *Examining the Catholic Intellectual Tradition,* vol. 2, *Issues and Perspectives.* Fairfield, Conn.: Sacred Heart University Press, 2002.

Haughey, John C. *Where Is Knowing Going: The Horizons of the Knowing Subject.* Washington, DC: Georgetown University Press, 2009.

Rausch, Thomas P. *Being Catholic in a Culture of Choice.* Collegeville, Minn.: Liturgical Press, 2006.

———. *Educating for Faith and Justice: Catholic Higher Education Today.* Collegeville, Minn.: Liturgical Press, 2010.

What are humans that you are mindful of them?
mere mortals that you care for them?
Yet you have made them little less than a god,
crowned them with glory and honor. (Psalm 8:5–6)

2

Catholic Anthropology

Thomas P. Rausch, S.J.

THESE WORDS OF the psalmist express the Old Testament appreciation of the wonder of the human person as well as awe at the fact that God loves so deeply the men and women he has created. While postmodern culture, with its loss of transcendence, has reduced the God of the Bible to an abstract principle, an impersonal "Higher Power," or an energy field like "the Force" in the movie *Star Wars*—if indeed it leaves any room for the divine at all—the Judeo-Christian tradition has maintained from its beginning that God has broken the silence of the stars, speaking the divine word to initiate a relationship with human beings. In a word, God is personal. Indeed Christianity goes even further. It begins with the incredible claim that God has become flesh, entering our world in the person of Jesus. This has enormous implications, both for our understanding of the divine mystery and for how we view ourselves.

In this essay I'd like to explore the vision of Catholic theological anthropology. I will begin by considering briefly the gods of the nations and then more carefully the God of Christianity. Then I will consider four fundamental principles of Catholic theological anthropology, developing further the theological notions of the divine, creation, and the human. Finally I will ask, What is the life that God calls us to?

THE MYSTERY OF THE DIVINE
The Gods of the Nations

From time immemorial human beings have created gods in their own image or projected their insecurities and fears onto all-powerful others. Some worshipped natural forces or malevolent demons, the spirits of their ancestors, or the god of their individual city states. The inhabitants of ancient Mesopotamia and Canaan worshipped the god of fertility with elaborate rituals that involved sexual intercourse between the god and his consort, symbolized by the temple priests and priestesses, with all the worshippers joining in. The gods of Greek and Roman mythology were anthropomorphic figures who governed the heavens, the seas, and the underworld, or personifications of powerful forces such as love and war. The gods of Mesoamerica were often bloodthirsty deities whose cults involved human sacrifice with thousands of victims.

Some ideas of the divine were more philosophically conceived. Traditional Chinese deities mirrored the stratified, hierarchical nature of imperial Chinese society; many understand them today as manifestations of the one Dao, the ultimate principle of all things, though it remains impersonal. The ancient Greek philosophers also sought to identify the ultimate principle (arche) of all that is. For Plato, God was noûs, or intellect, eternally contemplating the forms, or the Idea of the Good which is their source. The God of Aristotle was a self-enclosed deity, described as pure thought thinking itself. It was neither a creator nor a personal deity, but a prime mover, posited to explain the world's motion. But these deities were not that different from other beings, only more powerful, or changeless, or eternal, the kind of deity so easily mocked or dismissed by the "new atheists," foremost among them Richard Dawkins, Sam Harris, and Christopher Hitchens. How different is the transcendent God of the Judeo-Christian tradition.

The God of Christianity

Most educated Catholics take for granted that our incredibly mysterious, complex universe and the life it sustains on our little blue and white planet floating in the vastness of space is the result of an evolutionary process extending over billions of years. From a scientific perspective, they assume evolution as a fact. At the same time, from the standpoint of theology, they believe that behind the evolutionary process lies a creative intelligence working out the divine plan in mysterious ways. As we read in John 1:1, "In the beginning was the Word" (logos). In other words, God is not an impersonal, philosophical principle, but intelligence, rationality, and ultimately person, a God of love who in Jesus, in the literal Greek of the Prologue, "pitched his tent among us" (John 1:14).

That God is personal is fundamental to religious experience of the Old Testament. The God of the patriarchs was Israel's earliest experience of God, not a local deity but the God of Abraham, Isaac, and Jacob, who traveled with this nomadic people. It was only considerably later in their tradition that they began to think of their God as a creator. The book of Genesis, which in its present form dates from the sixth or perhaps late fifth century BCE, begins with this creator God, who is seeking to enter into a relationship with humankind, symbolized by Adam and Eve. The book of Exodus shows this God revealing his mysterious name to Moses as "I am who am" (Exodus 3:14), a name mysteriously associated with existence or being itself, the source of the sacred name Yahweh. This mysterious God delivers the children of Israel out of bondage in Egypt and enters into a special, "covenant" relationship with them, expressed in the Decalogue, especially the first commandment, "I, the Lord, am your God, who brought you out of the land of Egypt, that place of slavery" (Exodus 20:2). As Israel became more aware of failure and sin, including the loss of the kingdom and exile, the prophets taught the people to look forward to a new intervention of God in their life.

Christians believe that hoped for intervention took place in the person of Jesus, the Word become flesh, the Son of God who came into the world to make the Father known. Raised as a Jew, formed in the Scriptures and traditions of his people by his parents and the village elders, Jesus proclaimed that God's kingdom or reign was at hand; to show this he healed the sick, drove out unclean spirits, and reached out to the poor and the marginal. Laying down his life in fidelity to his mission, he was raised from the dead "on the third day" and exalted to his Father's right hand. While belief in the divinity of Jesus is already evident in the New Testament, in the fourth and fifth centuries it became part of the Church's creedal confession, as did the doctrine of the Trinity. Thus the God of Christianity is not just revealed in history as Father, Son, and Spirit, but exists as a unity of three "persons," to use the technical term. In other words, God is not just personal but intersubjective; relationality or communion that makes love possible lies at the very heart of the Christian understanding of God.

How do we understand the mystery of the divine revealed in the story of Israel and in the person of Jesus the Christ? In the following section I will consider a number of principles that are fundamental to Catholic anthropology: God is transcendent and immanent, God's creation is both flawed and graced, grace builds on nature, and God always respects our freedom.

THEOLOGICAL ANTHROPOLOGY
God Is Both Transcendent and Immanent

The word *transcendent* means "beyond," "outside the world," "other," "beyond our ability to grasp or comprehend." In the Old Testament God's transcendence is often expressed by the word *holy*, for God cannot be seen face to face. God's presence is frightening or awe-inspiring. To see God's face is to risk death (Exodus 33:20; cf. Judges 13:22). If God is described in anthropomorphic terms in the early Israelite writings, particularly those of the Jahwist tradition, the Decalogue forbade representing God by images "of anything in the sky above or on the earth below or in the waters beneath the earth" (Exodus 20:3; cf. Deuteronomy 5:8). Even the holy name of God, Yahweh, was not to be pronounced. In the gospels, when God draws near on the mountain of the transfiguration (Mark 9:6 and parallels), Peter, James, and John are terrified. God "dwells in unapproachable light" (1 Timothy 6:16), blinding the eyes of our understanding.

The subsequent Christian tradition continued to stress the transcendence of God and its consequences for human knowing. St. Anselm of Canterbury (1033–1109) compared the light in which God dwells to the sun, blinding the human intellect. For Thomas Aquinas (1225–74), God was not one being among others but pure, self-subsistent Being itself, the sheer act of uncaused existence. In his final years Karl Rahner (1904–84) spoke increasingly about the incomprehensibility of God. Basing his argument on the teaching of Aquinas, he maintained that the disparity between the infinite being of God and the finite human intellect was so great that even in the beatific vision, the immediate vision of God to which we look forward in faith, God cannot be comprehended or understood. God remains mystery. We cannot experience God directly as we can things in the world. The incomprehensibility and transcendence of the divine suggests the need for revelation, some act of self-disclosure on the part of God, who reaches out to humankind.

There are a number of consequences of recognizing the transcendence of God. First, a sense for God's transcendence illustrates how futile our contemporary attempts to domesticate the divine actually are. We cannot reduce the awe-inspiring God of Scripture to something manageable, a God available when needed but not the One who can make demands upon us. We should be cautious about personal ideas of God that may be nothing more than the products of popular culture. God remains incomprehensible. Revelation "unveils" the divine mystery, but it does not dissolve it or take it away. In the final analysis our philosophical and theological efforts to understand God and God's power run head-on into this mystery. That mystery can be glimpsed but never dissolved. We are united to God, not by our ideas but by love, for God is love (1 John 4:8) and thus ultimately personal.

Second, if revelation speaks of the divine transcendence, it also teaches us that there is an immanent dimension to the divine mystery. The God who created us sustains us each moment in existence. In spite of our tendency to temporalize God's eternal present, creation is happening now. Thus God is nearer to us than we are to ourselves. God surrounds us like the air we breathe, like the waters that sustain the fish in the sea. God's presence is reflected in nature, disclosed in symbol, sensed in the human heart. Most of all, in the mystery of the incarnation Christians confess that God has spoken his eternal word into space and time and human history in the person of Jesus, the Word become flesh (cf. John 1:1–14). Not only is God immanent, in Jesus God has entered completely into our experience, even unto the death that each of us must one day face. In the beautiful words of Rabbi Harold Kushner, "Christianity introduced the world to the idea of a God who suffers, alongside the image of a God who creates and commands."[1]

Finally, because God can never be an object of our direct experience, our theological language, even when informed by Scripture, is always a "second order" language, removed by several levels from the graced experience from which it arises. Our theological language is limited by time and culture, dependent on analogies and metaphors drawn from our experience. We call God "Father," "Shepherd," "king," "Lord," the "ground of our being," or simply "Thou." Theological language must be comfortable with paradox. It recognizes that God is immanent and transcendent, incomprehensible and revelatory, beyond and in our midst. While Catholics and Protestants recognize that God is both transcendent and immanent, Catholics tend to stress God's immanence while Protestants place more emphasis on the divine transcendence.

Creation Is Both Flawed and Graced

Christians have always confessed that Jesus is the mediator of God's salvation, but how that happens and what exactly salvation means has been differently conceived and interpreted at various moments and places in Christian history. The doctrine of the Fall, the results of the sin of our first parents in the biblical story, tells us that creation is in some way damaged. Yet it is also graced. Grace is God's free self-communication, God's life present in the world, infusing our own.

While the church fathers of both Eastern and Western Christianity recognized the damage done to the descendents of Adam and Eve, the theological anthropology of the East, with its emphasis on the incarnation, tends to be more optimistic. The Eastern fathers saw creation as elevated and humanity restored, even divinized because of the Word's assumption of human nature. The Western fathers tended to place more emphasis on redemption, the cross, and the idea of satisfaction for sin, first introduced by Tertullian (ca. 160–220). The doctrine of original sin, formulated by Augustine (354–430), was to permanently stamp Western theology. He taught that the will was in bondage because of the sin of Adam and that Christ's death was a "propitiation" or "satisfaction" offered to God for the sins of humankind. In his powerful work, *Cur Deus Homo?* (Why did God become man?), Anselm of Canterbury (d. 1109) gave quasi-magisterial status to Augustine's teaching on satisfaction; Christ, the divine Son, alone could make satisfaction for the infinite offense against God's justice, thus restoring the order of creation. Or at least, this is how Anselm has been interpreted in the West. But if Anselm saw human nature as damaged by Adam's sin, it was not totally corrupted, a position that was followed by Aquinas. Like the Eastern fathers, the Catholic tradition has generally placed far more stress on the doctrine of the incarnation than on the redemption.

However, the perspective of the Reformation was quite different, with significant consequences for Protestant theological anthropology. The Reformation began with Luther's concerns over his own struggle to make himself righteous before God, with his justification. His discovery of Paul's teaching on justification by faith in his Letter to the Romans (e.g., 1:17) led to the foundational Reformation doctrine of justification by faith alone (*sola fide*). Thus from the beginning the Reformation emphasized the doctrine of redemption. Like Augustine, Luther (d. 1546) stressed the damage done to human nature by Adam's sin; in his view access to God was through grace alone (*sola gratia*), and his suspicion of the medieval Church's teaching on the mediation of grace through devotions, sacraments, priests, and saints led him to stress that we are saved through Christ alone (*solo Christo*). Because of Christ, God no longer looks on our sinfulness, but sees only the righteousness of Jesus. Our sins are "covered over," but sin itself remains, what the Reformation called "forensic" or declarative justification. Theology was to be based solely on Scripture (*sola Scriptura*).

Jean Calvin (d. 1564) was influenced by Luther, but his own view of the state of the human person prior to the grace of justification was in many ways more radical. Because of Adam's sin, human nature is "totally depraved" (see *Institutes* II, 1, 7). The intellect, blinded by sin, is unable to know God apart from grace, and the will is hostile to God. Calvin went so far as to teach that human beings cannot even cooperate with God's grace, carrying his argument through to its logical conclusion of double predestination. God determines from eternity who will be saved and who will be condemned.

If Protestantism, characterized by its insistence on the chasm between nature and grace, and hence on the priority of grace and the divine initiative, says *sola Scriptura, sola fide, sola gratia*, and *solo Christo*, Catholicism traditionally says *both/and.* Not Scripture alone but Scripture and tradition; not grace alone but grace and nature; not faith alone but faith and works as well as faith and reason.

On a much deeper level, Catholicism recognizes that creation and thus human nature have been both graced and flawed, that is, in need of God's salvation, from the beginning. While we can separate nature and grace conceptually, there is no nature apart from grace. Creation is ordered and stamped by the incarnation (John 1:3). At the same time, unlike fundamentalist Christianity, Catholicism presumes an evolutionary worldview; the human species has emerged from an evolutionary process "red in tooth and claw" and under a veneer of civility and self-restraint still possesses those primitive instincts. In the soul of the lover or the poet lurks that of the hunter who once had to struggle for survival. No one has expressed this better than Annie Dillard, who in her beautiful book *Pilgrim at Tinker Creek* describes the beauty of nature in Virginia's Blue Ridge Mountains, but with a vision that often drops beneath the peaceful surface of the creeks and grass of the meadows to see in the animal kingdom close up violence, horror, and death: "Every live thing is a survivor on a kind of extended emergency bivouac" and at the same time something created.[2]

This inheritance of our biological past is compounded by our all-too-human egoism, self-seeking, and refusal to acknowledge our Creator, which the Bible calls sin. Thus there is great wisdom in the doctrine of original sin. We are born into a world of damaged relationships; our families are often dysfunctional, our social environments scarred by self-seeking or violence, our cultures marked by prejudice against the weak or the different. Our freedom is limited by forces beyond our control. Because we are radically social beings born into concrete situations both flawed and blessed, we have solidarity in sin as well as grace.

From a theological perspective, the redemption is not some kind of later moment in this evolutionary process, an intervention or transaction on the part of Jesus to set things right, as many imagine it. Rather it is a confession that in the incarnation the eternal Word spoken forth in creation realizes perfectly what every person is potentially. We are flawed and graced, touched by sin but open to God.

Grace Builds on Nature

A corollary of the preceding principle is that grace builds on nature, working through it, elevating and perfecting it. Nature is not something to be transcended; Christianity honors it as the work of God's hands. We discover God, not by fleeing the world, but by becoming more fully involved in it, while salvation involves becoming more truly human.

As the Church moved beyond its roots in the mythopoetic language of the Bible and into the Greco-Roman world, its greatest Christological challenge was not giving expression to the divinity of Jesus, but insisting that God's Word had truly become a human being, something incomprehensible to the Greek mind. The early Church was engaged in a long struggle with Gnosticism and Docetism, reflecting the dualism of Greek thought that privileged spirit over the merely material. Gnosticism could not accept that the divine could take on flesh, with its nasty implications of materiality and corruptibility. It tended to reduce the Johannine Logos or Word to a lesser emanation of the divine, as with Arius, who coined the jingle, "There was a time when he was not," leading ultimately to Nicaea's confession that the only Son of God is "one in Being" (*homoousios*) or "consubstantial" with the Father. Gnosticism was inherently elitist; knowledge (*gnōsis*) did not come to all from experience through the senses, but only to the few through a kind of illumination. Salvation was a matter of escaping the entanglements of human existence, with its implied responsibility for ethical living. Docetism, a variant of Gnosticism, taught that Jesus only seemed (*dokeō* in Greek means "to seem") to have a real human body, only seemed to die, and that the bread of the Eucharist could not really be the flesh of our Savior Jesus Christ.[3] Such was the Greek distaste for the world of materiality.

But from the beginning the biblical creation narrative pronounced nature good (Genesis 1:1–2:4a). Man and woman are created in God's image and likeness (Genesis 1:27); thus every human person is sacred, an absolute value, from the unborn child in the womb and the migrant or homeless person on the streets of our cities, to the prisoner on death row. Catholicism's respect for life is rooted here. Catholicism sees grace working through Mary, in her conception (the Immaculate Conception) and in her parents (Sts. Joachim and Ann), preparing her to be the mother of God's Son. The humanity of Jesus has long been celebrated in Catholic art and devotion as an icon of God's love for humanity, from the traditional devotion to the Sacred Heart, with its roots in the Middle Ages, to Pope Benedict XVI today celebrating the image of the "pierced heart of Jesus." Thomas Aquinas spoke of all creation mirroring the goodness of God:

> [God] brought things into being in order that His goodness might be communicated to creatures, and be represented by them; and because His goodness could not be adequately represented by one creature alone, He produced many and diverse creatures, that what was wanting to one in the representation of the divine goodness might be supplied by another. For goodness, which in God is simple and uniform, in creatures is manifold and divided and hence the whole universe together participates in the divine goodness more

perfectly, and represents it better than any single creature whatever. (*Summa Theologica*, I, q. 47, a. 1)

A fascinating book, *The Sexuality of Christ in Renaissance Art and in Modern Oblivion*, shows how during the Renaissance many works of art focused on the genitalia of Christ, a way of showing that humanity in all its concreteness could be the bearer of the divine.[4] The body is the medium through which spirit expresses itself, as we intuit through sensitivity to body language. Human sexuality itself is sacred, even sacramental when expressed within the marriage covenant; it shares in God's gift of bringing forth new life and the love that will sustain it. Society is not some necessary evil, at best to be tolerated, but necessary for full human flourishing. Thus Catholicism's fundamental ethos, recognizing the social nature of the human person, is communitarian. Even the saints are still close to us; we are able to ask their intercession through the communion we share with them and with God (the communion of saints).

If grace builds on nature, there are important consequences for how we come to know and experience God. The doctrine of the analogy of being means that while God remains transcendent, there is an analogy, even communion between God's pure, absolute existence and the contingent beings in the world which grounds the possibility of a metaphysical knowledge of God's existence, though personal knowledge of God depends on revelation. When we review the history of Israel and that of the earliest Christian communities, it becomes evident that it was precisely in the events of the ordinary human lives of these peoples, in encounters both mundane and extraordinary, in tragedy and hope and self-transcendence, in examples of love, compassion, and self-sacrifice, that God's grace became transparent and the divine self-disclosure took place, most fully in the person of Jesus.

We do not encounter God directly; God's revelation or self-disclosure is always mediated by some experience in the world, some person, event, story, or natural phenomenon. The community discerns the divine presence and action through persons, events, and things; expresses it in language and story; and eventually formulates its religious teaching in doctrines. Catholicism's appreciation of the capacity of art and symbol to mediate a sense for the sacred is often referred to as its sacramental imagination. Grace deepens the artist's ability to evoke transcendent beauty; the expressive power of religious symbol, music and song, light and darkness can create a sense for the sacred, and the love of a spouse can lead one to experience the unconditional love of God.

Protestant theology, especially in its Reformed or Calvinist expression, sees a chasm between nature and grace because of sin. With the intellect blinded by sin, the Reformers insisted that only Scripture could give us knowledge of God.

Furthermore both Luther and Calvin were uncomfortable with the Catholic concept of the mediation of grace through popular devotions and the Church's sacramental system, seeing only the abuses in the Christianity of their day. In reaction they put far more emphasis on the transcendence of God. Countries influenced by Calvin's theology saw a widespread destruction of religious images, an iconoclasm that led to a "stripping of the altars." A Protestant pastor once told me he wanted to use candles on his communion table, but some parishioners objected because "that was Catholic."

The result of this overemphasis on the divine transcendence was what has sometimes been described as a "disenchanting" or secularizing of nature, pushing the divine presence out of the world. With such a chasm between the human and the divine, nature and grace, it was no big step at all to an atheistic naturalism. Nature became a closed system, without room for the immanent divine presence, particularly as the scientific method was assumed to be the only way to genuine knowledge. Thus for Newton's physics and Darwin's biology, God was no a longer a necessary hypothesis.

Though Catholic theology has also been heavily influenced by Christianity's Augustinian heritage, its anthropology has generally remained more optimistic, stressing human freedom, the transcendental reach of reason, and God's presence within nature and the human. In reaction to the Reformers, the fathers gathered at the Council of Trent (1545–63) insisted that while our justification was always through God's grace in Jesus, our human freedom was always involved; we have to cooperate with grace. While Catholic theology recognizes Scripture as a unique source of knowledge of God, it also argues with Paul that God's invisible power and divinity can be understood and perceived in the things he has made (e.g., Romans 1:20). God's existence can be known from God's works.

While Protestantism is generally reluctant to speak of a "natural," metaphysical knowledge of God, privileging the prophetic word of Scripture, Catholicism has a rich tradition of mystical prayer. It also has long insisted that faith and reason are complementary and must work in harmony. Aquinas rejected the medieval theory of a "double truth," one of philosophy, another of faith. In his 1998 encyclical *Fides et Ratio* (no. 44), Pope John Paul II reiterated that faith and reason are complementary forms of wisdom, though there have been unhappy moments when this complementarity has not been respected, as in the case of Galileo. More recently Pope Benedict XVI went so far as to say in his Regensburg lecture that the Septuagint, or Greek translation of the Old Testament, represents, not just another translation but an important step in the history of revelation which witnesses in the later wisdom tradition to an inner rapprochement between biblical faith and Greek reason or philosophical inquiry.[5] Even if reason cannot produce faith, the act of faith is itself rational. Throughout his career Benedict has stressed that this synthesis or complementarity of faith and reason is what distinguishes Christianity from other religions.

Another consequence of grace building on nature is that our salvation is accomplished, not by fleeing from the world as something evil, but by living lives of faithful discipleship within it. Catholicism is not comfortable with an individualistic doctrine of salvation, based on a "personal relationship" with Jesus without reference to our life in the world. Recent studies in Christology have rediscovered Jesus' preaching on the kingdom or reign of God, which those in his movement were missioned to proclaim and "enact," by healing, reconciling, and driving out oppressive spirits (Matthew 10:7–8; Luke 10:3–9). The Jesus movement became the Church. St. Paul tells us, "Work out your salvation with fear and trembling. For God is the one who, for his good purpose, works in you both to desire and to work" (Philippians 2:12b–13). Similarly in his "Spiritual Exercises," St. Ignatius of Loyola invites retreatants to consider "how God works and labors for [them] in all creatures upon the face of the earth" (no. 236). Each of us must enter into the mystery of our own lives, in all our weakness and vulnerability, for it is precisely there that God's grace is to be found. Grace works in us, not in spite of our humanity, but in and through it.

God Always Respects Our Freedom

In the book of Revelation there is a lovely verse in which the risen Jesus says, "Behold, I stand at the door and knock. If anyone hears my voice and opens the door, [then] I will enter his house and dine with him, and he with me" (Revelation 3:20). What is suggestive about this is the certain hesitancy it shows on the part of the risen Lord: he does not force his way in; he stands and waits for an invitation; he respects our freedom. This is another basic principle. One finds frequent illustrations of it in Scripture. In the gospels Jesus invites others to follow him; he does not force them. The rich man in Mark turns down an invitation to be in Jesus' company and goes away sad, "for he had many possessions" (Mark 10:22). One can see this theme again in the Easter stories.

When I was a child, I always wondered why Jesus did not appear to those who had arranged his crucifixion, Pontius Pilate and the members of the Sanhedrin. That would have shown them. But the Easter stories are much more complicated. A theme of nonrecognition runs through them. The disciples do not recognize the risen Jesus; they are frightened or think they are seeing a ghost (Luke 24:37). Thomas wants empirical evidence (John 20:25), and Mary Magdalene, who loved him, thinks he's the gardener (John 20:15). Some continue to doubt even as others worship him (Matthew 28:17).

These stories suggest a number of things. First, recognizing the risen Jesus is very different from knowing the earthly Jesus. Jesus' presence cannot be objectified. Second, Jesus did not appear to his enemies, but to those who loved him, to those who had opened their hearts to him and who had followed him in faith. The others had shut him out; he could not have appeared to them, for their hearts were closed. Third, the experience does not compel the disciples to believe. Like us, they have to be led to faith; in John Jesus shows them his wounds, in Luke he asks for something to eat as evidence and breaks bread with them. God always respects our freedom.

Today, when more people experience God as absent rather than as present and all-powerful, perhaps we can gain some insight into the mystery of a God whose apparent weakness in the face of our freedom reflects the sovereign creator's love for the creature. Few have expressed this more powerfully than Pope John Paul II: "In a certain sense one could say that confronted with our human freedom, God decided to make Himself 'impotent.'"[6] God's ability to renounce power for persuasion, so unlike our own, is the ultimate witness to his power, which is really benevolence rather than control. God who created us as free beings cannot *not* respect our freedom.

The implications of this are many. Our destiny remains in our own hands, so much does God respect our freedom. God does not force the divine will upon us, far less predestine us for salvation or damnation. God is always present, inviting us into a relationship, present in the midst of the human, empowering us with grace. God cannot force us to love him, any more than we can force another to love us. Love is always a gift. But we must open our hearts, cooperate with grace, and welcome the divine presence, living before God in reverence and awe.

THE LIFE TO WHICH WE ARE CALLED

What God offers, finally, is not just the forgiveness of sins or even eternal life, important as that it, but love, a sharing in the divine life as self-gift. This is what Catholicism understands by the good life, following Jesus, living in communion with the Triune God. There are many ways of expressing this in the Christian tradition. Western Christians have used the word *grace* to express our share in God's life. The theology of the Eastern churches speaks of the elevation of our human nature because of the incarnation, even of our divinization, or *theosis*. Pentecostals speak of the empowering presence of the Holy Spirit.

In one of the earliest Christian documents, Paul uses the Greek work *koinōnia* to express this sharing in the divine life. From the Greek root *koinos*, "common," *koinōnia* means "a sharing, participation, or partnership in something else." Appearing nineteen times in the New Testament, it is generally translated as "communion" or "fellowship." In various passages it is used in a soteriological, Eucharistic, and ecclesial sense; it describes our relationship with God in Christ, in the Eucharist, and with the Christian community.

First of all, God calls us to *fellowship* (*koinōnia*) with Christ (1 Corinthians 1:9) through our *partnership* in the gospel (Philippians 1:4), *partnership* in faith (Philemon 6), and *sharing* in his sufferings (Philippians 3:10). Paul's blessing at the church in Corinth, still used in our liturgy, reveals a Trinitarian dimension to our life in Christ: "The grace of the Lord Jesus Christ and the love of God and the *fellowship* of the Holy Spirit be with you all" (2 Corinthians 13:13). The author of 2 Peter uses particularly strong language, suggesting that through God's promises we "may come *to share* [*koinōnia*] in the divine nature" (2 Peter 1:4).

Second, there is a strong Eucharistic dimension to *koinōnia*. Paul tells us that by sharing in the bread and wine of the Eucharist we have a participation or communion in the body and blood of Christ, and become his body, the Church: "The cup of blessing which we bless, is it not a participation [*koinōnia*] in the blood of Christ? The bread we break, is it not a participation [*koinōnia*] in the body of Christ? Because the loaf of bread is one, we, though many are one body, for we all partake of the one loaf" (1 Corinthians 10:16–17). It is the Eucharist that makes the Church. The language of Scripture is of an intimate union with the risen Christ himself through sharing in the Eucharistic meal: partaking of the one loaf (1 Corinthians 10:17), recognizing him in the breaking of the bread (Luke 24:30–31) and, in John's more literal language, eating his flesh and drinking his blood (John 6:54–56). From the second century the Church used realistic language to describe Christ's presence in the Eucharist, including the language of physical change, finally adopting the philosophical language of "transubstantiation" at the Council of Trent to express this mystery. Trent taught that in the form of bread and wine we receive "the true body and the true blood of our Lord, together with his soul and divinity" (Denziger-Schönmetzer 1640); in other words, we receive not discrete body and blood, but the whole Christ, not some thing but someone. More popularly, Catholics speak of the "real presence" of Christ in the Eucharist.

The Eucharistic dimension of *koinōnia* is related to its ecclesial meaning. For Paul, life "in Christ" means being part of his body, the Church; it is profoundly ecclesial. Baptized into Christ, God dwells in us as Father, Son, and Spirit (John 14:23), which makes us collectively the People of God (1 Peter 2:10), the Body of Christ (1 Corinthians 12:27), and a Temple or dwelling place of God in the Spirit (Ephesians 2:22). To be in Christ is to be in the Church; one cannot be a Christian all by oneself. Communion with God in Christ means also that we are in communion with each other. Acts 2:42 uses *koinōnia* to describe the communal life of the primitive Christian community of Jerusalem. The author of 1 John uses it to describe the community's shared life with God and with each other:

> What we have seen and heard
> We proclaim now to you,
> So that you too may have fellowship with us;
> for our fellowship is with the Father
> and with his Son, Jesus Christ. (1 John 1:3)

This profound sense for communion in Christ and with one another led very early to the practice of invoking the intercession of the faithful departed, who because of their communion with Christ were still in communion with us here below. As early as the third century Christians were invoking Mary the Mother of Jesus in the prayer, "Sub Tuum Praesidium":

> We fly to your protection,
> O holy Mother of God;
> Do not despise us in our need,
> But free us from all evil,
> Most glorious and blessed Virgin.

While Protestants often object that such devotion to Mary and the saints is illegitimate because it is not "in the Bible," to Catholics it makes perfect sense because we and they share a common life in Christ. This is precisely what the "Communion of Saints" means. The doctrine of the Trinity expresses the Christian belief that the inner life of the one God is a communion of persons. Communion, or *koinōnia*, also describes one's relationship to the Church, as well as the relationships that link the local churches together into the Church Catholic, while "excommunication" describes the breaking or rupture of these relationships.

Thus without denying the reality of sin, with the damage, exploitation, even violence that it brings into our relationships and into our world, Catholics believe that we live in a world in which grace abounds. St. Ignatius of Loyola, in his final Contemplation for Obtaining the Love of God at the end of his "Spiritual Exercises," describes a God who is present in all things, giving us his gifts, dwelling in them, working and laboring in them. Because all these gifts and blessings descend from above, they reflect the divine glory. Consequently Ignatian spirituality can speak about "finding God in all things." Karl Rahner describes a God who is constantly reaching out to us, drawing us to a personal knowledge and love through a self-communication that is intimate, free, and unmerited. Andrew Greeley stresses that for Catholics grace surges all around us, disclosing itself in nature, stories, human love, and religious symbols. So abundant is God's grace, for those who have eyes to see.

NOTES

1. Harold S. Kushner, *When Bad Things Happen to Good People* (New York: Schocken Books, 1981), 85.

2. Annie Dillard, *Pilgrim at Tinker Creek* (New York: HarperCollins, 1974), 6–7.

3. Ignatius of Antioch (d. 110), *To the Smyrnaens*, no. 6.

4. Leo Steinberg, *The Sexuality of Christ in Renaissance Art and in Modern Oblivion* (Chicago: University of Chicago Press, 1996).

5. Pope Benedict XVI, "Faith, Reason and the University," September 12, 2006, www.vatican.va.

6. John Paul II, *Crossing the Threshold of Hope*, ed. Vittorio Messori (New York: Random House, 1994), 61.

SELECTED READINGS

Barron, Robert. *Bridging the Great Divide: Musings of a Post-Liberal, Post-Conservative Evangelical Catholic*. New York: Sheed and Ward, 2004.

Greeley, Andrew. *The Catholic Imagination*. Berkeley: University of California Press, 2000.

Johnson, Elizabeth A. *Consider Jesus: Waves of Renewal in Christology*. New York: Crossroad, 1990.

McCarthy, Timothy G. *The Catholic Tradition: The Church in the Twentieth Century*. Chicago: Loyola Press, 1998.

Rausch, Thomas P. *Catholicism in the Third Millennium*. Collegeville, Minn.: Liturgical Press, 2003.

3

Perspectives in Catholic Theology

Lawrence S. Cunningham

THIS ESSAY HAS a dual objective: to explore theology as a discipline in the university setting and to outline, albeit briefly, some core elements of Catholic theology. The first goal justifies theology as a bona fide academic discipline and the second one shows that theology serves an integrating function within a Catholic university. Although theology functions in quite different ways within the Catholic Church (as pastoral reflections by the clergy and hierarchy, as studies in a pastoral setting, etc.), the word *theology* in this essay, unless otherwise specified, refers to the academic study and teaching of theology within the context of a Catholic college and university.

This essay begins with the assumption that a Catholic college or university cannot be sustained as such without a robust department of Catholic theology (albeit with an ecumenical and/or interreligious component). That is so precisely because theology reflects critically on the truth proclaimed by Jesus Christ as it is guarded and promulgated by the Church. This essay critically reflects upon this assumption and offers reasons to substantiate it.

Historically speaking,[1] theology looked to two "books" as its basic resource: the book of nature and the book of revelation. In the former, theologians saw the cosmos as a sign of the creator God, and in the latter, theology accepted that God revealed His Self in human history. The Epistle to the Hebrews puts it beautifully: "In many and various ways God spoke of old to our fathers by the prophets but in these last days he has spoken to us by a Son whom he appointed the heir of all

things through whom also he created the world" (Hebrews 1:1–2). Those two elegant verses encapsulate God as Revealer through His Son as well as creation itself
coming forth from the Word.

A few years ago, looking over the past century of the history of theology, David
Ford, a theologian at Cambridge University, articulated twelve theses as a kind of
projective look into the new century. He had in mind theology in the context of
the British university. Here, in a somewhat abbreviated form, are those theses:

1. God is the One who loves and blesses in Wisdom.
2. Theology is done for God's sake and for the sake of the Kingdom of God.
3. Prayer is the beginning, accompaniment, and end of theology.
4. Study of Scripture is at the heart of theology.
5. Describing reality in the light of God is a basic theological discipline.
6. Theology hopes in and seeks God's purpose in the contingencies, complexities, and ambiguities of creation and history.
7. Theological wisdom seeks to do justice to many contexts, levels, voices,
   modes, genres, systems, and responsibilities.
8. Theology is practiced collegially, in conversation, and, best of all, in friendship and through the communion of saints; it is simultaneously premodern, modern, and postmodern.
9. Theology is a broker of the arts, humanities, sciences, and common sense
   for the sake of wisdom that affirms, critiques, and transforms all of
   them.
10. Our religious and secular world needs theology with religious studies in
    its schools and universities.
11. Conversation around scriptures is at the heart of interfaith relations.
12. Theology is for all who desire to think about God and reality in relation to
    God.[2]

Looking over these theses even in a cursory manner makes it clear that Ford is
thinking of theology in the classic formulation of St. Anselm of Canterbury, as
"faith seeking understanding." He presumes theology is, in effect, reflection on the
datum of revelation and its reception by a believer. His theses are both theocentric
and, implicitly, Christocentric in that he sees the end of theology to be about God
and reflection upon God's self-revelation in Scripture for the sake of the Kingdom.
Ford is not antagonistic to the discipline of religious studies (as thesis 10 makes
clear), but his understanding of theology is clearly within the community of faith,
while cognizant of the fact that formal religious studies aids in the understanding
of a whole range of human inquiry. For Ford (and my sympathies are with him),

theology is a discipline with a proper home in a Catholic university, and, if I read him correctly, it ought to be a linchpin discipline (see thesis 9) within the curriculum. Of course, he writes from a British perspective, which is far more tolerant of the study of theology in a state-supported university, whereas in the United States theology, as opposed to "religious studies," might well run into constitutional issues. A linguistic presupposition in this essay is that *university* is to be understood as a university under the auspices of the Catholic Church.

What does theology in the university wish to accomplish as a discipline and in relation to other disciplines? Theology is a rather recent arrival to the undergraduate curriculum of the North American university and college. An even more recent innovation is doctoral-level studies at Catholic universities. Such programs (apart from pontifical faculties) were first begun in the 1960s.

Most Catholic colleges and universities before Vatican II were more or less modeled on the old Jesuit *ratio studiorum*. Classics and philosophy were studied at the undergraduate level by lay students and also by those preparing to study theology at the professional level. Generally speaking, in the area of religion an undergraduate might take some courses on apologetics, but theology qua theology was not taught. Before the Second Vatican Council at my own university students took religion courses oriented mainly to apologetics. Our theology department is purely a product of the post–Vatican II Church.

That situation changed rapidly after Vatican II. Now, almost without exception, high-level theology is taught primarily in universities. It is also possible to major in theology at the undergraduate level, an innovation introduced during the past two generations.[3] Not all of this has been a blessing. For example, the contemporary major in theology does not presuppose a deep philosophical background, as it once did.[4]

Leaving aside theology as an integrating discipline (an observation made by Newman's lectures on the idea of the university), it is important to ask how theology sees its own aims. In an excellent work on fundamental theology Gerald O'Collins has mapped out three fundamental strands of contemporary theology: academic, practical, and contemplative. Borrowing from St. Anselm's definition, O'Collins notes, "We might contrast faith seeking scientific understanding with faith seeking social justice and with faith seeking adoration."[5]

Each of these strands, to be sure, is not hermetically sealed off from the others. Indeed when seen atomistically, each carries within it certain potential dangers. Academic theology can devolve into mere philosophical logic chopping, rather like what Johann Baptist Metz pejoratively calls "God talk." Practical theology, divorced from its roots in understanding, can easily elide into pious social work, and contemplative theology left to itself constantly runs the risk of anti-intellectualism.

While various approaches to theology may put special emphasis on a particular approach, theology, when done within an ecclesial community, cannot remain intellectually detached from that community, as if one were inoculated from any obligation to that community. Interestingly, the three ends of theology articulated by O'Collins are strikingly similar to the three essential functions of the Church as Pope Benedict XVI describes them in his first encyclical, *Deus Caritas Est:* proclamation and witness, worship, and service. The pope also insists this triad is symbiotic.

The theologian speaks from within the Church either to the Church or, as David Tracy famously argued, to the larger academic community or to the still larger general public. Thus the theologian has three publics: Church, academe, and society.[6] While the kind of speech used by theologians may need to be tailored to a particular public (one does not necessarily use church language for a nonchurch audience), the theologian must remain faithful to the task of seeking understanding of what is meant by faith. Finally, if theology is to locate itself within the academic community is must be rigorous enough to satisfy certain criteria established by the academic world.

Doing theology at a serious level at a university requires a number of ancillary skills. These range from the acquisition of the required languages to training in the hermeneutical and historical methods. Some knowledge of philosophy and literature is also needed, both to read, comment on, and judge the inherited tradition and to advance the teaching of the theological tradition, including some enlargement of that tradition. In other words, and this hardly comes as a surprise, theology as a field contains within it many subfields. Precisely because theology calls on many disciplines, it must be in dialogue with many disciplines within the academy.

THE HEART OF THEOLOGY

As St. Thomas Aquinas argued centuries ago, the proper subject of theology is God, but not God considered as an abstract concept but rather the God revealed in nature, in the Chosen People of Israel, and in Jesus Christ the Son of God. God as revealed by Jesus Christ in the Spirit is at the heart of the Christian faith.

From the late second century on it was the custom to ask potential converts three questions prior to their baptism. They were:

Do you believe in God the Father Almighty, Creator of heaven and earth?
Do you believe in Jesus Christ, His Only Son, Our Lord?
Do you believe in the Holy Spirit and the holy Catholic Church?[7]

To those questions the one to be baptized responded, "I do believe." Without that assent the person would be refused admittance to the baptismal waters. Very early in Church history the three baptismal questions were simplified into a declaratory creed we call the Apostles Creed. The Creed we say at Mass today (the Nicene Creed) is a nuanced elaboration of this interrogatory creed. It was used in the Church of Jerusalem, and in order to resolve important theological issues it was adapted by the bishops at Nicaea in 325. Everyone who has ever gone to a baptism today knows that those questions are still asked of both the parents and the god-parents, who "stand for" the infant to be baptized.

Those three questions are so elementary and so familiar to Catholics that it is easy to overlook their significance in articulating the fundamental doctrines of Catholic Christianity. Rather like the sign of the cross, they are affirmations of Trinitarian belief serving both as a creedal affirmation and as a form of prayer. It is worthwhile to examine those three questions in some detail to ascertain what is contained within them. After all, the Creed is the rule of faith against which fidelity to the Gospel is tested.

There is a long tradition of theological commentary on the Creed from the apostolic period down to the present. St. Augustine wrote a commentary on it, as did St. Thomas Aquinas. Twentieth-century theologians such as the Protestant Karl Barth and the Catholic Hans Urs von Balthasar have written books on it. The Catechism of the Catholic Church structures its opening section on the Creed. Pope Benedict XVI used the Creed as the organizing principle for his frequently re-printed *Introduction to Christianity,* which he published as a young theologian.

In an essay as limited as this I cannot gloss the short creedal interrogation in any depth, but it is possible to show that the baptismal questions, so simple at first glance, contain within them profound truths cherished by the Catholic theological tradition.

God the Father, Creator of Heaven and Earth

Christianity inherited from the witness of the Chosen People that in the entire world there is only one God, and this one God is the creator of everything. The Hebrew word *bara* (create) is used over a dozen times in the Old Testament but always in reference to the creative act of God. The Book of Genesis teaches that it was God who created the heavenly bodies, the sun, moon, and stars. This was an implicit rejection of the common pagan idea that these heavenly bodies were divine; in the biblical witness, they are simply creatures whose being stems from God, who speaks them into existence. Furthermore, as Genesis 1 insists, everything God creates is pronounced "good" by the creator. When our Creed insists that God created the earth, it is an implicit challenge to those who think the "earthly" is somehow unworthy or something from which humans need to be freed.

Both Judaism and Christianity resist identifying creation as divine; it is created. However, creation reflects the work of the creator. This is a critical affirmation because the Catholic theological tradition has always taught that we learn something about God from the sheer fact of creation. Some theologians have insisted that creation is a kind of primordial sacrament, a visible sign that mediates grace (God's love) to us. For that reason the Catholic tradition can praise God with the psalmist: "O Lord, how manifest are thy works / In wisdom you have made them all" (Psalm 104:24). St. Paul makes the same point more prosaically in his Letter to the Romans when commenting on the religious ideas of pagans: "Ever since the creation of the world, his invisible nature, namely, his eternal power and deity, has been clearly perceived in the things that have been made" (Romans 1:20). The First Vatican Council (1869–70) stipulated that part of Catholic faith is to hold that humans can come to knowledge of God through the use of their powers of reason.

The Old Testament rarely refers to God as "Father." However, the ancient Creed does so as a starting point: We believe in God the Father. There are at least two reasons for doing so. The first and most important reason is because Jesus saw his own relationship to God in this fashion. Jesus felt his relationship to God was radically filial. Even at the end of his life, while on the cross, he underscores this relationship: "Father, into your hands I commend my spirit" (Luke 23:46). Furthermore Jesus taught his followers to address their prayers to "Our Father." It is worthy of note that when the celebrant introduces the "Our Father" at the Eucharistic liturgy he does so with the words "We dare to say . . ." St. Paul explains that through Jesus, who is the son by his very being, God offers us the status of adopted sons and daughters: "God sent forth his Son, born of a woman, born under the law, to redeem those who were under the law, so that we might receive adoptions as sons" (Galatians 4:4–5). The Christian insistence on the paternal nature of God reflects the deep belief that God is not an impersonal force but One with whom humans can be in personal relationship.

Jesus Christ, Only Son and Lord

To say "Jesus Christ" is to give a title to the person who was known as Jesus of Nazareth. *Christ* is a Greek word translating the Hebrew title *Messiah*, meaning "the Anointed One." To say "Jesus Christ" evokes both the human and the divine mission of Jesus of Nazareth. The joining of *Jesus* with *Christ* places Jesus in a human time and place; the man Jesus was born in ancient Palestine two millennia ago. It also gives him a hallowed genealogy; this man named Jesus born of Mary was the Anointed of God, promised by the prophets of ancient Israel. The affirmation "Jesus is the Christ" means, further, that the Christ is not some celestial figure appearing as an angelic wraith but a fellow member of the human race. The implications of this affirmation—the Incarnation—are of profound significance for the entire history of Christianity, not only because it is the starting point for a new understanding of humanity but also because it offers a profound insight about the nature and dignity of every human being, since in the Incarnation divinity is implicated in the common race of men and women.

The Creed goes on to say that Jesus is the "only Son" of God. Behind that affirmation is the tacit denial of there being multiple incarnations. The Incarnation is a once and never again event. It is at the core of the Christian faith that Jesus is the definitive Son of God by nature. That is, Jesus in human form is the fullest revelation of the Father. As a human being, with friends, relatives, and followers, Jesus embraces the human situation and grants to those who believe in Him the status of sons and daughters by adoption, as St. Paul points out.

Finally, the Creed says that He is "Lord." The Greek word is *kyrios* and was sometimes used as an imperial title in antiquity; for example, the Roman emperor was *kyrios*. Christianity, however, insisted that ultimately there was only One Lord, namely, Jesus called the Christ. We might assume that this affirmation of Lordship is of only religious significance. However, in early Christianity it was a subversive term for Christ because it meant that there was only One Lord, and it was not the emperor. To proclaim the Lordship of Jesus Christ is to relativize all human claims to absolute human control. Those who suffered in the Roman persecutions learned at the cost of their lives what it meant to say that no human power could demand ultimate allegiance. That fact, hidden within the seemingly simple phrase "Jesus is Lord," has had far-reaching implications as later Christians tried to articulate the fine balance between the demands of gospel faith to one's citizenship in the world of politics and society. Finally, to say Jesus is Lord is to participate in the gift of faith. "No one can say 'Jesus is Lord' except by the Holy Spirit" (1 Corinthians 12:3).

The ancient baptismal creed did not stipulate the precise relationship between the Father and the Son. That task was left to subsequent Christians who had to answer vexatious questions about how faith statements of "Father Creator," "Son of God and Lord," and "Spirit of Truth, Love, and Life" can be harmonized without tearing apart the unity of God.

Holy Spirit

It is patently the case that Christians have always prayed with the invocation of "Father, Son, and Holy Spirit." Already in the New Testament Christians were commanded to baptize using that triadic language (Matthew 28:19), and St. Paul not infrequently invokes the same kind of language. Thus Paul could write to the church in Rome, "I appeal to you, brethren, by our Lord Jesus Christ and by the love of the Spirit, to strive together with me in your prayers to God on my behalf" (Romans 15:30). From the very beginning Catholics have prayed to the Father through the Son in the Holy Spirit, and Christians almost always open their prayers by saying "In the name of the Father, Son, and Holy Spirit."

The Hebrew scriptures use the same Hebrew word (*ruah*) to signify breath, wind, and spirit. God's breath made Adam a living creature. It was God's spirit or breath that gave vivid speech to the prophets, inspiring them to preach. God's breath or spirit vivifies even the dead bones in the famous scene of the prophet Ezekiel. Majestic Psalm 104 declares that God's spirit or breath is sent out to revivify the life of the earth.

In the New Testament the Spirit is also sent by God. When Jesus is baptized in the Jordan at the beginning of his public ministry there is a clearly Trinitarian cast in the description of that scene. Mark's Gospel is a succinct example: "And when he [Jesus] came up out of the water, immediately he saw the heavens opened and the Spirit descending on him like a dove and a voice came from heaven 'You are my beloved Son with whom I am well pleased'" (Mark 1:10–11). In John's Gospel, Jesus promised to send the Spirit as a helper (*paraclete*) to the disciples. The Acts of the Apostles says that on Pentecost Day the first followers of Jesus, the apostles, were filled with the Holy Spirit, who came upon them in tongues of fire as if in a roaring wind. Throughout his letters the apostle Paul identifies the Spirit as the dynamic force that makes a Christian active, generous, and loving, certainly not a person dead to faith.

It is the constant teaching of the Catholic Church that this Holy Spirit, which came down upon Jesus and subsequently was promised by Jesus to his Church, is the Spirit that vivifies us, makes us holy, teaches us truth, and guides us. Catholic spirituality fundamentally argues that the indwelling of the Holy Spirit given to us at baptism and strengthened in confirmation is the presence of God within us, helping us on life's way. Spirituality at its most basic is simply living in the Spirit.

Remember that the word *inspiration* means "breathing into" and most characteristically is understood as the work of the Holy Spirit. The Spirit inspired the sacred writers of scriptures, inspires those who seek to lead a Christian life, and is always present in our prayers and worship. During the Eucharistic prayer at the Sunday liturgy the celebrant calls down the Holy Spirit to make the gifts of bread and wine on the altar holy and acceptable to the Father.

In the *Summa* St. Thomas Aquinas says that every good thought and deed is ultimately a gift of the Holy Spirit because the Holy Spirit is the giver of truth. It would not be out of bounds to say that every good thing made by human hands, whether by craft or art or through music or literary composition or achievement in science, is a manifestation of the workings of the Spirit. Christian humanism has always taught that the true, the beautiful, and the good (the transcendental characteristics of being) point somehow to God. To that conviction we could also say that they come through the aid of the Spirit.

Finally, Catholicism insists that the Spirit dwells within and is a guide for the Church. It is not human cleverness or human energy or the exercise of power that keeps the Church true to the Gospel entrusted to it. Rather the Church knows that its perfection will come only at the end of history. What keeps the Church from failure or irrevocably losing its mission is the Holy Spirit who dwells within it. It is most fitting, then, that the Creed links the Holy Spirit with the Church when it asks whether the person to be baptized believes in both Spirit and Church.

Church

I noted earlier that creation itself can be understood as a kind of primordial sacramental sign. The early Christian writers frequently called Jesus Christ the Great Sacrament, the visible and efficacious sign from God that produces grace. Because the Church praises, preaches, and unites its members to Christ, the Church itself functions as a sacrament; it is a visible reality that gives grace. Thus Christ, the Great Sacrament, gives us the visible sign of the Church, which in turn offers grace through visible signs we call sacraments. The Church is a sign that points beyond itself.

The English word *church* derives from the Greek *kyriake,* that really means a church building. The New Testament word that we often translate as *church* really means an assembly (Greek *ekklesia*). The Creed draws upon this latter meaning. We express our trust in the assembly/church, which brings together the body of believers. St. Paul in 1 Corinthians uses the nice metaphor of the Church as a "body," with Christ as the head. By arguing that the foot cannot be indifferent to the hand, Paul insists that when we enter the assembly of believers through baptism (in the name of the Father, Son, and Holy Spirit!) we assume a mutual responsibility for each other as fellow adopted children of God. This assembly/church is not restricted to a historical moment; rather it is the assembly of believers wherever they are located and extending over time until everything is reconciled, when history comes to an end. That is why later creeds expanded the notion of the church/assembly by calling it the "Communion of Saints." The point is made very nicely in the Eucharistic prayer of the liturgy when we invoke the patriarchs, the Virgin Mary, the apostles, and the saints and pray for the living and the dead. They all form part of the Church.

There are many aspects of the Church that I could discuss, but my focus here is on one aspect of its essential task of preaching the Good News (evangelizing) to the entire world. This task is one aspect of catholicity: the Church is for the whole world.

From its beginnings Christianity was a missionary faith without any traditional boundaries. Jesus said that the Gospel was to be preached to "all the nations." Paul said that in the body of Christ there is neither Jew nor Gentile, slave nor free, male nor female. This egalitarian premise of early Christianity meant that as a principle everyone who would listen could receive the Gospel, and no one was a priori excluded from its assembly/church. The subsequent history of Christian missions, from their spread within the Roman Empire to present-day evangelizing, derives from this universalist spirit.

Calling peoples to enter the Body of Christ which is the assembly/church requires actualization in every age. The Gospel becomes incarnated in specific languages, customs, and thought patterns. A Byzantine icon of Jesus is not the same as a Renaissance painting of Him, just as architectural contours, musical modes, and literary expressions of faith vary in emphasis, style, and content. What they share is a common desire to enflesh the Gospel in particular ages and specific cultures.

One other truth can be adduced from the universal mission of the Church, and this truth is closely bound to other theological observations I have made. If the task of the Church is to call all people to recognize the universality of the Gospel message, of necessity the Church must have a care for the whole world. Catholic social teaching and Catholic mercy and compassion cannot be restricted to those who are members of the Church but should include the whole world. Its attention cannot be primarily on its internal activities; rather it must also look and plan outward. Catholicism must learn about the world it hopes to serve. This means theologians have a responsibility not to squirrel away its message; they are to put it in dynamic dialogue with all that sheds light on the human condition. One way for the Church to fulfill this responsibility is to dedicate itself to a broad agenda of teaching and research. What better place to accomplish this than in the university setting? For this reason it is said that the university is where the Church does (should do!) its thinking.

THE ENDS OF THEOLOGY

As I noted earlier, Gerald O'Collins identifies the three strands of theology as understanding, justice (or better, perhaps, compassionate love), and adoration. I also remarked that these three strands are symbiotic in the sense that they mutually enrich each other. Another perspective on theology emerges when the focus is not on the discipline itself but on the students who study it. What do we want the student to carry away from the study of theology, and how is that related to the larger task of a university education in general? Put differently, what impact should theology have on the generic Catholic student in the context of a university education? When the focus is shifted to the student, what is the *telos* of theology in a university setting? One possible response is that theology should build character in students. But is this sufficient? Do we aspire to do more than simply shape what the German reformers in the late nineteenth century called *Bildung* (the well-rounded person)?

John Henry Newman in his classic *Idea of a University* had an answer to that question. While it is commonly said that Newman saw the end of education as the cultivation of the gentleman (he did not envision women being educated in the university), some argue that what he really desired was that students become saints. Newman does have a long paean to the educated gentleman in his eighth discourse,[8] but when he finishes his lectures in Discourse 9 it is not the gentleman he holds up as a paradigm but the figure of St. Philip Neri. A charming sixteenth-century Italian, St. Philip Neri exuded joy and happiness in the Lord and in His Church. Cardinal Newman's true Christian gentleman is, like St. Philip Neri, one whose "weapons would be unaffected humility and unpretending love. All he did was to be done in that light, and fervor, and convincing eloquence of his personal character and his easy conversation."[9] In other words, the *beau ideal* of a Catholic education was to be the gentleman who was shaped by the holiness of life. Newman, in short, saw the end of education not in the light of what was produced by a university education but what he considered to be the final *telos* of life itself.

If Newman is correct, it follows that one reason theology is crucial for a Catholic institution of higher learning is to make holiness more intelligible and appealing. According to this view, theology's proper competence is to reflect upon, make intelligible, and provide reasons for holiness and for the role a university education plays in promoting it. Proclaiming the coming Kingdom of God announced in the Good News of Jesus Christ is also a call to holiness.

In short, holiness and its fruits are the ultimate *telos* of a Catholic education. For inquisitive minds, theology expands the horizon of holiness. Emphasizing holiness does not gainsay the need to prepare students for the "good life" (understood as Aristotle's *eudaimonia*). Nonetheless holiness requires students to move beyond the good life as understood by Aristotle. Emphasizing the shortcomings of the traditional, secular understanding of the good life, the sociologists Christian Smith and Melinda Lunquist Denton refer to is as "moral therapeutic deism."[10] For them, the true Christian good life is, in the final analysis, life with God according to the pattern given to us by the Word made flesh (John 1:14).

HOLINESS

The Hebrew word *qdsh,* which we translate as "holy" means, etymologically, that which is separate. However, the Hebrew word is most commonly ascribed to God to a degree that it almost becomes a synonym for God. That God is holy is to say, in effect, that God is not us, not creation, not anything except God. It is for that reason that the angels cry out in the famous words of Isaiah used during the Eucharist, "Holy, holy, holy is the Lord God of Hosts."[11] While it is true that the adjective *holy* is ascribed to people, places, events, cultic instruments, and so on, their right to be called holy is possible only because they stand in some kind of relationship to the source of holiness, who is God. There is no meaningful concept of holiness unless it is seen in relationship to the One who is holy: God.

The Bible makes a distinction between the holiness of God and holiness that derives from a nexus to God. In a discussion of clean and unclean animals, the Bible says, "You shall therefore make a distinction between the clean animal and the unclean and between the unclean bird and the clean; you shall not bring abomination on yourselves by animal or bird or by anything with which the ground teems which I have set apart for you to hold unclean. You shall be holy to me for I the Lord am holy and I have separated you from the other people to be mine" (Leviticus 20:25–26, NRSV translation). The calculus seems clear enough: things are holy for a holy nation because they belong to the Lord, who alone can say "I the Lord am holy."[12]

When St. Paul greets "God's beloved in Rome who are called to be saints" (Romans 1:7), our modern translation uses the word *saints* as a literal translation of the Greek for "Holy Ones" (Greek *hagioi*). Paul, drawing on an old usage, simply means that those who are followers of Jesus have, by that fact, been "set aside" by entering into a relationship with the God who is holy. That notion is expanded even more in his greetings to the community at Corinth: "to those who are sanctified [literally 'made holy'] in Christ Jesus, called to be saints [literally 'holy ones'], together with all those who in every place call on the name of Our Lord Jesus Christ" (1 Corinthians 2).

"Holiness" is that condition by which a person, place, time, event, instrument, or gathering is set aside by some connection to God. In this sense we speak of "our holiness": through Jesus Christ we are called by God to relate our world and activities to God. To the extent we respond in this way to Christ, we are holy. For the Christian the way of holiness is rooted in following Jesus Christ.

Unfortunately a modern tendency is to balk at holiness because the word is so otherworldly and redolent of images of saints whose lives seem beyond the experiences of "normal" people. Indeed *holy* is often used pejoratively in today's vernacular (e.g., "holier than thou" is not a laudatory description of a person). A salutary effort was initiated at the Second Vatican Council to counteract such an understanding when it proclaimed, in the fifth chapter of its dogmatic constitution on the Church, *Lumen Gentium*, that the call to holiness is universal. *Lumen Gentium* says, "It is quite clear that all Christians in whatever state or walk in life are called to the fullness of Christian life and to the perfection of charity and this holiness is conducive to a more human way of living even in society here on earth" (no. 40).[13] In the next section the document goes on to say that "the forms and tasks of life are many, but there is one holiness" (no. 41). The reason for that assertion is simple enough: all "forms and tasks" are related to the One who is holy by definition: God.

Vatican II insists there is one holiness because the source of holiness is God's own self. However, at a subordinate level the "forms and tasks of life" are many. Expressed more particularly, the form and task of the Carthusian monk differs from that of the married layman, just as the form and task of the vowed religious differs from that of a student under his or her tutelage. In fact the many ways of holiness are attested to in the roll call of the saints over history as well as the examples of holiness we see in men and women today.[14] There is One who is Holy and many ways to live connected to that One.

A controversial Christian claim in secular society is that the search for holiness is "conducive to a more human way of living." The search for the good life understood in the classical sense of *eudaimonia* is not wrong, merely incomplete. A fuller happiness or satisfaction lies in the ongoing graced attempt to live in relationship to the Holy One revealed in Christ. The notion that the good life is the graced life, that *eudaimonia* necessarily involves holiness, has an illustrious history in Catholic teaching. For example, in his *De Doctrina Christiana* St. Augustine taught that the ultimate thing to be enjoyed is life in the Holy Trinity. Similarly, relying on Scripture, St. Thomas Aquinas identifies the final end of a human being as the contemplation of God. Drawing upon Aristotle, Aquinas notes that the contemplative act is the most human thing we can do, as well as that which is most enjoyable.[15]

Of course, both Augustine and Aquinas are thinking of our final end. Until we reach that end we must live out the life God gives us. While every true theology has an eschatological thrust, a realistic theology must take into account life as it is lived. After *Lumen Gentium* insists on the call to universal holiness in chapter 5, drawing up its fecund metaphor of the Pilgrim Church, it describes us as a people under way to a destination not yet achieved. Being on the way, it is worth remembering, was the earliest descriptor for those who believed in Jesus. The Way was shorthand for the believing community.

This call to holiness should not be understood as an individual effort, as if each person were a detached monad. After all, *Lumen Gentium* is a document on the Church. Each Christian is called into the Christian assembly, the Body of Christ. This is the organic metaphor suggesting how Christians relate to one another and Christ. This is also the assembly where there is neither male nor female, Jew nor Gentile, slave nor free.

Theology understood as "faith seeking understanding" brings us closer to and more clearly connects us with God (which is to say, brings us closer to making us holy). Holiness also helps us to see how the various subdisciplines within theology might find a unifying coherence. It is only in the early modern period that the theological tradition splintered into subcategories. There was no such thing as a distinct tract in theology known as "moral theology" until the post-Tridentine manual appeared as a vade mecum for confessors.[16] Similarly the study of Scripture used to be an integral task for every theologian, not an activity reserved to the scriptural scholar. St. Thomas Aquinas, after all, saw his own task as that of an expositor of the Sacred Page. Finally, it was only within the world of the Catholic Counter-Reformation of the late sixteenth century that we began to find such terms as *ecclesiology* and *Mariology*. Even the word *patristics* (and its older cousin, *patrology*) is of modern origin.

Specialization is a fact to be reckoned with, not a situation to be lamented. Specialization is part of the modern academic landscape. Advances in knowledge, the discovery of new hermeneutical techniques, the greater ability to search vast databases, the study of languages used in Palestine at the time of Christ, the multiplication of monographs, the findings from recently discovered manuscripts—all these factors and many more contribute to increased specialization within theology. Long gone are the days when one could brag about mastering the whole of religious knowledge, as did Pico della Mirandola at the end of the fifteenth century, when he claimed to have read everything and reduced it all into one hundred theses or brief, summary statements.

SOME CONCLUSIONS

I have proceeded by steps in this essay, with the first step insisting that the study of theology in any Catholic university has a proper place in the education of students. Theology does not exist as a closed-off system of thought untouched by the concerns of other academic disciplines. Like the Church itself, theology both teaches and learns. As a discipline within the university it has at least three audiences: the university community itself, the Church, and the wider public.

Second, theology reflects upon the revelation of God, who reveals Himself in creation and in human history as recounted in the Bible. A normative synopsis of the beliefs of Christians is contained in the three questions posed to candidates for baptism. These questions and their affirmative answers best capture the Trinitarian character of God. In our prayer we pray "to the Father, through the Son, in the Holy Spirit."

Third, the ultimate end of a Catholic education in general and theology in particular is not merely the well-rounded person but the one who is in relationship to God. Holiness and not simply character or moral fortitude is the aim of both education and life.

An important claim of this essay is that theology plays a central role in a Catholic college or university. Because God is the fullness of knowledge, theology can learn from all disciplines, and all other academic disciplines can learn from theology. Because the overall aim of this volume is to elucidate how the Catholic intellectual tradition relates to various academic disciplines, certain points in this essay should be highlighted precisely because they constitute connection points between theology and other academic disciplines. The following five points may be particularly helpful to experts in other academic disciplines:

1. God reveals Himself in two ways: through nature and in the Old and New Testament. Both are important, but the fullest revelation of God occurs through Jesus Christ in the New Testament.

2. The three baptismal affirmations of belief are bedrock expressions of the Catholic faith. All Catholics, including Catholic theologians, affirm the truth and central importance of these statements.

3. God is the creator of heaven and earth. This means that everything that is owes its being, its existence to God. It also means that God reveals beauty, order, and whimsy in the way created beings interact.

4. Holiness means being connected to God. For Christians, the most important connection is through Jesus Christ. In addition, Christian academics serve the Church and increase their holiness by relating aspects of their teaching and research to God and to His revelation in Christ.

5. The Church is the community of people who praise God in Christ, who help make known the revelation of God, and who provide loving service to others.

Woven into all these reflections, of course, is the belief that because of the Incarnation the whole of humanity is touched by the presence of divinity "among us." An inescapable consequence is that Catholics have a responsibility to all humanity and to the entire created cosmos, because Christian faith comes to us as sheer gift.

The twelfth-century scholar Bernard of Chartres said that we are dwarves sitting on the shoulders of giants; because of the work of the giants who came before him, Bernard could see further. The metaphor is equally apt for theologians today as well as for Catholic scholars teaching and researching in other academic disciplines. Faculty members teaching at the university level are heirs to two millennia of thinkers who have passed on to us their reflections on the revelation of God in Jesus Christ. We are privileged to look at the signs of our times with the benefit of a tradition of prayerful reflection and meditative insight into God's gracious revelation to us. We affirm the ancient Truth and simultaneously seek new insights that speak to the world in which we live. To the degree that we do that faithfully, we are like the enterprising householder praised by Jesus for bringing forth things old and new (Matthew 13:52).

NOTES

1. The history of theology is a complex subject; the best overview still remains Yves Congar, *A History of Theology* (Garden City, N.Y.: Doubleday, 1968).

2. David F. Ford, *Christian Wisdom: Desiring God and Learning in Love* (Cambridge, U.K.: Cambridge University Press, 2007), 4. These theses were originally cited in the epilogue to David F. Ford, ed., *The Modern Theologians*, 3rd edition (Oxford: Blackwell, 2005), 761.

3. Currently the University of Notre Dame has more than two hundred theology majors.

4. The University of Notre Dame does offer a double major in theology and philosophy with a requirement of at least one year of a classical language (either Greek or Latin). It attracts a small but quite elite clientele.

5. Gerald O'Collins, *Retrieving Fundamental Theology: The Three Styles of Contemporary Theology* (New York: Paulist, 1993), 11.

6. David Tracy, *The Analogical Imagination* (New York: Crossroad, 1981).

7. The literature on the development of creeds is vast; the history of creedal development is well outlined in J. N. D. Kelly, *Early Christian Creeds* (New York: Harper, 1972).

8. John Henry Newman, *The Idea of a University* (Notre Dame, Ind.: University of Notre Dame Press, 1982), 136–61, with specific discussion of the gentleman at 159–61.

9. Newman, *The Idea of a University,* 179.

10. Christian Smith and Melinda Lunquist Denton, *Soul Searching: The Religious and Spiritual Lives of Teenagers* (New York: Oxford University Press), especially 162–3.

11. For an analysis, see Geoffrey W. Bromiley, ed., *The Theological Dictionary of the New Testament* (Grand Rapids, Mich.: Eerdmans, 1985).

12. I am grateful to Mark Nussberger for this point.

13. All quotations are from Austin Flannery, ed., *The Sixteen Documents Vatican II* (Dublin: Dominican Publications, 1996). Citations are to the paragraph numbers of the documents.

14. On the relationship of God's holiness and the various ways of holiness, see Donna Orsuto, *Holiness* (London: Continuum, 2006); Stephen C. Barton, ed., *Holiness Past and Present* (London: T. & T. Clark, 2003).

15. See Thomas Aquinas, *Summa Theologica,* I, IIae, q. 3.

16. For the history of this development, see John Mahoney, *The Making of Moral Theology* (Oxford: Clarendon, 1989).

SELECTED READINGS

Cunningham, Lawrence, and Keith J. Egan. *Christian Spirituality: Themes from the Tradition.* New York: Paulist Press, 1996.

Dulles, Avery. *The Craft of Theology: From Symbol to System.* Expanded edition. New York: Crossroad, 1995.

O'Collins, Gerald, and Mario Ferrugia. *Catholicism: The Story of Catholic Christianity.* New York: Oxford University Press, 2004.

Pelikan, Jaroslav. *Credo: Historical and Theological Guide to Creeds and Confessions of Faith in the Christian Tradition.* New Haven, Conn.: Yale University Press, 2003.

Ratzinger, Joseph Cardinal. *Introduction to Christianity.* 2nd edition. 1969; San Francisco: Ignatius, 2001.

4

Perspectives in Catholic Philosophy I

Brian J. Shanley, O.P.

CATHOLIC CHRISTIANITY HAS been involved in a dialogue with philosophy since its origins. In the seventeenth chapter of the Acts of the Apostles we find Paul of Tarsus engaged in a spirited disputation with certain Epicurean and Stoic philosophers. His resulting speech at the Aereopagus contains numerous allusions to popular beliefs derived from Stoicism. As soon as Christianity entered into the Greco-Roman world, it became a competitor to popular religion and academic philosophy as a comprehensive theory of meaning and a guide for conduct. Leaving aside the challenges of Greek religion, the Christian message has had to contend with competing philosophical claims to truth about the deepest questions of human life: What is human nature? What is its destiny? How does it achieve that destiny? What is right and wrong? What form ought human community to take? Who or what is God? Underneath all of these questions lies the most basic inquiry, posed to Pilate by Jesus: What is truth?

In the writings of St. Paul there is a fundamental ambivalence, if not suspicion, about the value of human inquiry into truth as it is related to what has been revealed by God and accepted by faith. In Romans 1:18ff, Paul argues, "All that may be known of God by men lies plain before their eyes.... His invisible attributes, that is to say, his everlasting power and deity, have been visible, ever since the world began, to the eye of reason, in the things he has made." Yet this knowledge has "ended in futility" and "plunged [us] into darkness" in the vanity of idolatry. Knowledge of God is both available in creation and hidden by sin, apparently setting up a dialectic of futility as a result of the fallen nature of the human intellect.

An even stronger judgment on the wisdom of this world is rendered in the first two chapters of First Corinthians, where Paul proclaims that God "has made the wisdom of the world look foolish...by the folly of the Gospel": "Christ nailed to the cross is a stumbling block for Jews and folly to the Greeks." He goes on to boast that the Gospel is not dependent upon argument or human wisdom, but the power of God.

In the wake of such passages in St. Paul there has been a strain in the Catholic Christian tradition arguing that human speculation, and especially philosophy, should be regarded with only the deepest suspicion as the product of minds darkened by original sin. According to this school of thought, divine revelation is a substitute, correction, and guide for all other modes of human inquiry. If God has revealed to us in Scripture all that is necessary for our salvation, then what is the point of human philosophical inquiry? Revelation is the royal road to all that we need to know.

The classic articulation of this position is the famous dictum of the second-century theologian Tertullian: "What has Athens to do with Jerusalem?...Away with all attempts to produce a mottled Christianity of Stoic, Platonic, and dialectic composition! We want no curious disputation after possessing Christ Jesus."[1] This early form of fundamentalism, or fideism, has recurred throughout the Christian tradition, particularly when the deliverances of reason appear to undermine the deposit of faith.

If fideism stands as one ancient option in the negotiation of the differences between faith and reason, the other extreme is represented by rationalism, by which I mean the prima facie assumption that what reason in the guise of philosophy (or science) determines as true trumps what is believed by faith, such that the latter must be reinterpreted in the light of the former. The primacy of reason over revelation was a rare claim in the Catholic Christian tradition during the premodern period, but it did emerge in the medieval debate over the proper interpretation of revealed truth in the light of Aristotelianism. I shall say more about this shortly. In the modern period, however, it has become the deepest philosophical problem: How can we reconcile what is revealed in Scripture and taught by the Church with what is known certainly by science or philosophy in any other manner appropriate to our dignity as rational beings except by reinterpreting faith claims to cohere with rational claims?

In between the dichotomous extremes of faith or/instead of reason and reason or/instead of faith, there is an alternative: faith *and* reason. The most important word of John Paul II's 1998 encyclical letter *Fides et Ratio* is the conjunction *and*.

It has been first the achievement of that conjunction in the premodern period and the struggle to maintain that conjunction in the modern and postmodern period that defines the Catholic perspective on the relationship between theology and philosophy. Therefore the structure of this essay follows the status of reason in the Catholic tradition. First, I will outline the premodern achievement of the harmony of faith and reason through an analysis of the seminal Catholic thinkers Augustine, Anselm, and Aquinas. Second, I will discuss the tensions that have imperiled that harmony in the context of modernity and postmodernity. Third, I will offer some observations about the revival of Thomism in the twentieth century. In all this I will be attempting to translate the fundamental teachings of *Fides et Ratio* into a more historical narrative.

THE PREMODERN HARMONY AND UNITY OF FAITH AND REASON

Despite Tertullian's suspicions of Greek philosophy, the Patristic period was marked by an ever deepening dialogue with the philosophical currents of the day, above all, Neoplatonism. Two fundamental and perennial uses of philosophy emerged in this era: (1) philosophical concepts were needed internally in order to articulate and analyze the truths of faith, and (2) philosophy was needed to defend the claims of faith to external audiences. While for Christians their faith was superior to philosophy in its claims to constitute an overarching wisdom, it needed philosophy as a tool in both its internal imperative to articulate a coherent worldview and its external imperative to defend itself against competing claims to truth. Faith without reason is unable either to articulate its own meaning internally or to dialogue with opposing points of view. It thus became apparent early on that theology needed philosophy in order to achieve its deepest tasks. The internal need for philosophy is evident in the early debates surrounding the identity of Christ and the identity of God. How Christ can be both divine and human entails a philosophical distinction between "one person" and "two natures." Similarly how God can be both three and one entails a philosophical distinction between "one nature" and "three persons." The external use of philosophy to defend the coherence of Christian claims is pervasive in Patristic thought, especially in Justin's *Apologies* and Origen's *Against Celsus*.

The culminating and defining moment of Catholic engagement with philosophy in the Patristic period comes in the thought of St. Augustine of Hippo (354–430). Augustine's conceptual approach to the relationship between theology and philosophy is rooted in the narrative of his own life as articulated in his spiritual autobiography, *The Confessions*. Inspired by Cicero's *Hortensius*, the young Augustine made the pursuit of wisdom his life's goal. He initially thought he had found wisdom in the teaching of Manichaeanism, a form of dualism and gnosticism stemming from the late third-century Persian teacher Mani. Manichaeanism was a form of dualism because it postulated two competing deities, the God of Light and the God of Darkness, presiding, respectively, over the realm of spirit and the realm of matter. It was a form of gnosticism because Mani held that the road to wisdom lies in accepting a hidden knowledge, or *gnosis,* available only to the elect. As Augustine would later recognize, his long attraction to Manichaeanism was its ability to provide an explanation for one of the most basic human questions: Where does evil come from? For Augustine, the Manichaean explanation gave an account of his own internal moral divisions. After nearly a decade's flirtation with Manichaeanism, he became disillusioned when he realized that the fantastic myths propagated by the religion could not be reconciled with what could be known of the cosmos through human reason. He then passed through a brief period of skepticism, followed by a life-changing encounter with the books of Neoplatonism, especially as espoused by Plotinus and a group of Catholic intellectuals gathered about Bishop Ambrose of Milan. Neoplatonism opened Augustine to a powerful alternative to Manichaeanism and an apparent road to true wisdom about the nature of the soul, the cosmos, and the divine. At the same time he was finding answers to his intellectual aspirations, he felt increasingly debilitated by the internal conflict between the carnal desires of his old way of life and the moral and spiritual aspirations consonant with a new life. Augustine turned to the epistles of St. Paul to make sense of his divided self, eventually culminating in his famous garden conversion, where in obedience to a child's voice he opens the Scriptures to Romans 13:13–14 and reads, "Not in riots and drunken parties, not in eroticism and indecencies, not in strife and rivalry, but put on the Lord Jesus Christ and make no provision for the flesh in its lusts."

Augustine's life's work as a theologian would be to use the heritage of Greek and Roman philosophy to articulate a robust vision of Catholic Christianity to both internal and external audiences. His mature reflections on the relationship between theology and philosophy reflect his own experience: if you want to find wisdom, you must first believe, and then you will be rewarded with deeper understanding. The truth about God, soul, cosmos, and human destiny could be found free of error in the fallen condition of human nature only by first believing the truth revealed by God in Scripture and taught by the Church. Once the truth is grasped by faith, it can be understood and pondered using the tools of philosophy. Throughout his career Augustine would recur to Isaiah 7:9: "Unless you believe, you will not understand." Only under the tutelage of revelation can human reason find the reward of understanding. *Credo ut intelligam*—I believe in order that I might understand.

In the Augustinian tradition, faith that flowers into theology, *intellectus fidei,* is the highest mode of human understanding. When it comes to the most important questions in life, autonomous human reason cannot be a reliable guide to ultimate truth because of the fallen condition of both intellect and will; the search for truth inevitably involves both what we want to know and what we love. Augustine argues, in a sense, that it is rational to believe because it is irrational to think that the only grounds to accept something as true are to have some kind of intellectual evidence. It belongs to the nature of the human condition to accept truths on the authority of someone else's testimony; belief is part of the fabric of human life. Belief is a reliable mode of coming to the truth about many things, but especially God. If God did not propose to us through revelation the truth about himself, we would never understand God. It is the gift of faith working in conjunction with the gift of love that opens the believer to the insight that will complete his quest for truth. The wisdom that Greek and Roman philosophers yearned for is available through faith.

The Augustinian synthesis of theology and philosophy, faith and reason, would provide the paradigm for Catholic thinking throughout the medieval period. It would find its culmination in the work of the Benedictine bishop Anselm of Canterbury (1033–1109). His most famous work, the *Proslogion*, begins with a prologue announcing that his aim is to find a single argument that would prove the existence of God with the attributes traditionally assigned to God. Lest his intentions be misunderstood, however, Anselm immediately makes it clear that the purpose of the argument is not to find rational grounds for belief, but rather to come to a deeper understanding of the truth of what is already believed: "I have written the following treatise, in the person of one who strives to lift his mind to the contemplation of God, and seeks to understand what he believes." The first chapter is a classic Augustinian reflection on the limitations of the human mind regarding the knowledge of God because of divine transcendence and human sin, and it ends with a prayer for guidance and illumination. The second chapter contains the most famous argument for the existence of God in the history of Western thought. It is predicated on the premise that the very meaning of the concept of God is "that than which nothing greater can be conceived." God must be the most perfect of all conceivable beings and indeed more perfect than the entire domain of all else that exists. As soon as one begins to think about God as "that than which nothing greater can be conceived," the concept of God has reality or existence in the mind. But such a being cannot exist only in thought and not also in reality, because then it would not be the greatest conceivable being since it would lack an obvious perfection: existence in reality. If God is the greatest conceivable being, then God must exist in reality as well as in thought.

The validity of this argument, called ontological because it relies on the meaning (*logos*) of the being (*onto*) of God, has been hotly criticized and debated throughout the subsequent history of philosophy. (One of the few things Aquinas and Kant agree upon, for example, is that it is not a cogent argument!) It is not my purpose to discuss its merits here. What is important in Anselm is the confidence that he displays in philosophy's ability to make logically intelligible, if not almost necessary, what is believed in faith. Even more than Augustine, Anselm is confident in philosophy's ability to demonstrate the internal logic of faith. Philosophical reason is faith's sure ally in unlocking the logic of faith. Faith has nothing to fear from philosophy.

It is worth noting also, as Robert Sokolowski has often commented, that Anselm's definition of God as "that than which nothing greater can be conceived" marks a distinctively Christian understanding of God in contrast with Greek philosophy. The implied premise in the definition of God is not just that God is greater than any other being, but that God is greater (*maius*) than everything else that is not God (the world): God would be perfect even without the world, such that God does not need to create in order to realize the fullness of the divine being. Creation is thus a sovereign free gift and choice of God, who is ultimately fulfilled not in creation, but in the inner life of the Trinity. Sokolowski argues that Christian theology is different from Greek religious and philosophical thinking primarily in the distinction between God and the world as possibly not having existed without any diminution of God's fullness. That there is anything other than God at all is thus sheer gift, resulting in a fundamentally different take on the relationship between God and the world than is found in Greek thought.

The Augustinian synthesis of theology and philosophy was severely tested in the thirteenth century as a result of the need to come to terms with the newly translated major works of Aristotle. Hitherto the West knew Aristotle largely through the lens of Neoplatonism and had direct access only to translations of some of his logical writings. Once the major systematic works of Aristotle on such topics as the natural world (*The Physics*), the nature of soul (*De anima*), the meaning of being (*The Metaphysics*), and ethics (*The Nicomachean Ethics*) were available firsthand in Latin, it was evident that his philosophy constituted a powerful and systematic articulation of the nature of things from a completely pagan perspective.

At the same time that Aristotle's works were being introduced to western Europe's newly burgeoning universities, the works of various Greek, Muslim, and Jewish thinkers who already had grappled with the relationship between Aristotle, Neoplatonism, and theology were likewise translated and studied. This influx of texts caused a kind of intellectual crisis, because there now seemed to be a naturalistic alternative to the Christian worldview. On some critical questions—such as whether the world was created, whether every individual has an immortal soul, and whether God's providence extends to everything—Aristotle seemed to argue for positions that were at odds with the revealed doctrines of the faith. Indeed the doctrines of Aristotle were considered subversive enough that a series of ecclesiastical prohibitions were issued with respect to the teaching of Aristotle. By the middle of the thirteenth century, however, the horse was out of the barn, especially at the center of Western university life, the University of Paris.

The roiling question of the day in Paris was not whether Aristotle's philosophy would be studied, but rather whether Aristotle's philosophy could be interpreted in such a way as to harmonize it with the doctrines of the faith. On the one side were traditional Augustinians, who looked upon Aristotle with deep suspicion. These suspicions were enflamed by certain professors in the Faculty of Arts (Siger of Brabant and Boethius of Dacia) who argued that a fair reading of Aristotle's philosophy put his conclusions at odds with revealed doctrines on certain neuralgic points. These professors are commonly called "radical Aristotelians" because they believed that Aristotle embodied the essence and epitome of philosophy such that any conclusion that he drew was philosophically compelling regardless of whether it could be reconciled with revealed doctrine. In between the extremes of traditionalist Augustinians and radical Aristotelians stood two figures who argued that Aristotle's philosophy, properly understood and shorn of its erroneous interpretive apparatus, could become a powerful ally to theology: the Dominican thinkers Albert the Great and the pupil who eclipsed him, Thomas Aquinas. As a result of the work of Albert and Thomas, Aristotelian philosophy became part of the fabric of Catholic theology ever after.

Aquinas's respect for Aristotle's achievement is reflected in the way he cites Aristotle in his texts as "the Philosopher." Aquinas wrote numerous commentaries on the major texts of Aristotle as a means of both assimilating his thought and teaching it to others. Scholars have debated his strategy regarding whether he is offering a pure interpretation of the text or is reading his own philosophical and theological views into Aristotle. Whatever the case, the Aristotle of these commentaries is a philosopher who is friendly to Christian theology. One of Aquinas's major works, the *Summa contra gentiles*, is an extended exercise in dialectical engagement with the entire inheritance of the classical worldview, but especially of Aristotle and his commentators. While it is too facile to say that Aquinas "baptized" Aristotle, it would be fair to say that he believed that Aristotle's philosophy could be a powerful tool for theology; his entire oeuvre is a testament to that conviction. Ultimately Aquinas synthesized Aristotelian philosophy with Augustinianism in a unique vision of his own that included strands drawn from both and filtered through his own original philosophical and theological mind.

Aquinas was primarily a theologian who used philosophy to achieve the Augustinian theological aim of faith seeking understanding (*fides quaerens intellectum*), but in an Aristotelian key. He conceived of theology along the model of an Aristotelian science that depended upon a higher science—God's own knowledge—for first principles. Theology was a kind of participation in God's own higher knowledge through faith that sought to articulate the meaning of all things in the light of what God had revealed. Theology treats fundamentally of God, then of creation (including human beings), in the light of their ordering to God as final end. It looks at philosophy as a penultimate form of human knowing that needs to be integrated into the higher form of knowing that is theology. Theology looks at the deliverances of philosophy as a partial manifestation of meaning that can be woven into the new whole that is opened up by revelation. In a classic text on the relationship between theology and philosophy, Aquinas writes:

> The gifts of grace are added to nature in such a way that they do not destroy it, but rather perfect it; so too the light of faith, which is imparted to us as a gift, does not annul the light of natural reason given to us by God. And although the natural light of human reason is inadequate to make known those things revealed by faith, nonetheless it is impossible that what is given to us in faith by God be contrary to what is implanted in us naturally. For one would have to be false, and since both of them are given to us by God, this would make God the source of error, which is impossible.... It is impossible that those things which belong to philosophy be contrary to the contents of faith, but rather they fall short of them. Philosophy bears certain likenesses to faith and also preambles to faith, just as nature is a preamble to grace. (*De Trinitate*, Q2, A3)

Aquinas was confident that theology and philosophy could complement each other because one and the same God was the source of revelation and the Creator of the human mind and nature. What God reveals through revelation could therefore not contradict what God made human minds to know about the world. Philosophy's quest to comprehend the world, understood as created by God, was ultimately meant to be woven into the new intelligibility of what God has graciously revealed. We can understand the gratuity of the supernatural order of grace and gift revealed by God only against the foil provided by what we can know philosophically of the world, ourselves, and God.

In the same text Aquinas goes on to say that there are three ways in which theology makes use of philosophy. The first is to prove what he calls the "preambles" to faith. The Latin term *preambula* literally means a "walking before," from which we derive a term that means a kind of introduction. So philosophy articulates a kind of introduction to theology by establishing a wide range of truths that theology presupposes. Aquinas thinks that there are many truths about God and the world that philosophy can establish and theology thus presupposes. A good example of the range of truths composing this category is found in the first three books of the *Summa contra gentiles*, where Aquinas argues for the existence of God, the nature of many divine attributes or properties, the creation of the world, personal immortality, the problem of evil, the meaning of human fulfillment, the nature of providence, and the basic truths of morality. Philosophy provides sure rational grounds for many of the truths of faith.

Central to Aquinas's vision of the way philosophy provides support to theology is a robust confidence in the capacity of metaphysics to articulate the meaning of being. Aquinas distinguishes between different human sciences on the basis of both what they study and how they study it. Two different sciences can have overlapping objects of study but from different points of view. Formally speaking, metaphysics studies what is common to things insofar as they are beings, or being as being, in distinction from other sciences which study things in terms of some other aspect of their natures (e.g., as matter in motion).

Metaphysics arrives at a knowledge of God as cause at the conclusion of its inquiry into the meaning of being. Aquinas thinks that there are multiple a posteriori arguments that begin with some contingent feature of the material world that requires us to postulate that God exists in order to provide the ultimate causal explanation of that feature of the world. What metaphysics then does is derive other divine attributes or properties based on the implications of what it means to say that God is the cause of the world. Aquinas argues that what philosophy can say about God is extremely limited and mostly negative because our minds are not adequate to grasp the nature of God. Metaphysics can ascribe to God some attributes that connote metaphysical perfection—goodness, wisdom, omnipotence— but it mainly articulates the imperfections that cannot be asserted about God: that God cannot have metaphysical parts, or be finite, or change, or be temporal. When metaphysics reaches its last conclusions about God, it has reached its natural *telos* as a form of human wisdom by articulating a coherent causal account of all that is.

When theology takes up the conclusions of metaphysics into its own domain as preambles to faith, it accepts them as a penultimate form of wisdom that needs to be integrated into the consideration of God that is proper to theology as a form of wisdom. If metaphysics ends with the conclusion that God exists under a causal description, theology begins with a believer's personal encounter with the living God in the act of faith. Aquinas understands faith to be the human response to

God's self-disclosure that elevates the person's mind to share in the intelligibility that reality has to the God who is truth. Faith is an acceptance and assent to God and what God reveals about himself and the world. Faith is not based on rational evidence. It begins with truths about God that are not knowable in any form other than by revelation: that God is Father, Son, and Holy Spirit; that Jesus Christ is true God and true man. And all the other truths of the faith can be known to be true only on the basis of revelation.

Theology's approach to God begins with what is unknowable about God through metaphysics. It uses this metaphysical knowledge to make sense of the deeper dimension of God disclosed by revelation. While an individual's act of faith in no way requires rational evidence—you do not have to be able to do metaphysics to believe—theology as the science of faith logically presupposes what has been concluded on the basis of metaphysics. When it comes to the truths about God that philosophy can demonstrate, these will be available as metaphysical conclusions only to a learned few. What philosophers might be able to know about God is accepted as true by most people through belief, and these two cognitional states are mutually exclusive: you cannot both know and believe the same thing in the same way at the same time because knowledge intrinsically involves evidence, while belief accepts something as true on the authority of someone else.

When theology deploys arguments from metaphysics in its own work, they take on a different character. Metaphysics has to prove that God exists before it can talk about God; theology does not. Arguments for the existence of God are not needed to justify theology's talk of God. It can therefore appear as something of a puzzle when Aquinas begins both of his great theological *Summae* by offering arguments for the existence of God. He does not do so in order to justify theology in the face of atheism or to satisfy the subsequent demands that emerge in the modern era for all truth claims to have evidentiary support. Rather arguments for the existence of God provide a natural foil for what is believed on the basis of faith; we can appreciate more the gratuitousness of the Trinitarian God's self-disclosure when it is profiled against the natural knowledge of God. Philosophical arguments for God also enable theology to locate the intersection of its claims with philosophy. For Aquinas, his arguments for the existence of God showed where the Christian God fits on the map of an Aristotelian universe; philosophical argumentation for God establishes the referent in reason for theology's discourse.

It is worth noting that Aquinas believed that philosophy does not supply only theoretical truths useful to theology, but that moral philosophy can provide overlapping support for revealed morality. If the paradigm of revealed morality is the Ten Commandments, Aquinas thinks that the content of the commandments can also be known on the basis of human reason. Fundamentally the goods protected by the Ten Commandments are basic human goods that can be known to be good on the basis of natural law. Natural law claims involve the thesis that there are basic human goods that can be identified rationally as necessarily contributing to human fulfillment. We naturally see that it is an imperative in our nature to seek the goods that will enable us to flourish and avoid the things that will impede our fulfillment. Reason and revelation converge on the most basic goods constitutive of human flourishing. This is not to say that Christian morality is reducible to what can be naturally known as good, because the demands of the Gospel do indeed go beyond what we can deduce from our nature's inclination to the good. It is rather to say that moral philosophy can provide rational support for some of moral theology's claims about the human good.

So while there is a limited domain of overlapping claims where philosophy can provide rational evidence for truths important to theology, Aquinas also thinks that philosophy provides theology with conceptual tools to explore the intelligibility of properly theological concepts. If the Trinity is the paradigm par excellence of a revealed truth about God, then Trinitarian theology requires philosophical tools in order to explore the intelligibility of a God who is both three and one. Aquinas's Trinitarian theology has to employ conceptual tools from philosophy to describe the inner life of God as characterized by knowing and loving. He draws on sophisticated analyses of human knowing and the role that concepts play in human thinking to describe how an inner Word can form within God that helps explain the procession of the Son. To explain the procession of the Holy Spirit, Aquinas has to explore the analogies found in how love emerges in the soul. In order to make it possible to say that God is both three and one, it must be possible to explain how person is distinct from nature and how relations make persons distinct without compromising the unity of the nature. Theology depends upon the concepts and grammar of philosophy in order to do its work. Philosophy cannot prove that God is Three-Personed, but it can help theology explain why this is a coherent claim. Theology without philosophy can only assert, not explain.

On the moral side, Aquinas took Aristotelian concepts to provide the explanatory tools for the most basic claims of Christian morality. Aristotle's *Nicomachean Ethics* is predicated on the claim that the goal of human life is a flourishing state—happiness—in which the human capacity for rational agency reached perfection and that the capacity for sustained excellent action depended on the development of virtue. Aquinas took those conceptual tools and transposed them into a theological key. Instead of philosophical contemplation as the dominant end of human life, it was the beatific vision of the Triune God that would constitute human fulfillment.

One of the most contentious features of Aquinas's thought is how or whether he maintains the integrity of a properly natural completion of human agency in the light of a supernatural end of fulfillment in God. Do human beings have two ends—natural and supernatural—or one end? The bulk of Aquinas's ethics is focused on virtue, but he has to transpose this also to allow for dispositions that are not merely the function of moral tutelage and repeated actions—the traditional acquired virtues—but dispositions that are infused by the grace of God: the theological virtues of faith, hope, and love and the infused moral virtues. This is likewise an area where expositors of Aquinas disagree, but there is no question that Aquinas saw Aristotle's moral theory as a rich conceptual tool for his own project in moral theology.

The third and final way philosophy helps theology is to defend theology from philosophical attack. Because God is the source of the mind, the world, and revelation, Aquinas assumes that philosophy can never provide a probative argument that would undermine what is believed to be true on the basis of revelation. This means that whenever philosophy purported to prove something that would contradict revealed teaching, Catholic thought could meet that argument on philosophical grounds rather than claiming a higher authority. Aquinas thought that when philosophy at the service of theology met a competing claim, one of two things would happen: sometimes philosophy could directly refute the contending claim by demonstrating its opposite to be true; more often, however, the task of philosophy would be to show the problems in the position that conflict with faith. For example, one of the most contentious issues in Aquinas's day was whether or not you could prove that the world had to have a beginning. There were proponents on both sides who thought they had probative arguments for their position. Aquinas used philosophy to point out the weaknesses in both sides of the argument: you simply cannot prove whether or not the world had to have a beginning. With philosophy (which was equivalent to science) unable to prove it one way or the other, the theological claim that the world began to be was immune from attack. According to the logic of this position, any theological claim that could be refuted by philosophy would have to be revised. There could be no real contradiction between faith and reason.

The medieval achievement of the harmony of theology and philosophy assumed that philosophy would always be a subordinate discipline, the "handmaid of theology." It was assumed that the findings of philosophy would always cohere with and support theological claims. A robust metaphysical realism could be marshaled into the service of theology, the queen of the sciences. This would all change in modernity, when philosophy would seek to be emancipated from the tutelage of theology to eventually become its bitter rival and antagonist. It would no longer be faith *and* reason, but reason *or* faith.

THE MODERN DENIAL OF THE HARMONY AND
UNITY OF FAITH AND REASON

Descartes dedicated his *Meditations on First Philosophy* to the dean and doctors of the Faculty of Theology at the University of Paris. In the dedication he states that the existence of God and the immaterial human soul were the two fundamental questions that needed to be established on the basis of philosophical reasoning rather than theological argument. The starting point for the inquiry into God was no longer the natural world, however, but the nature of mind. According to Descartes, mind is what is first knowable, then God, and finally the external world. Whether or not Descartes was sincere in his apologetic purposes, he inaugurated a new era of philosophy and its relationship to theology. By starting with consciousness rather than nature and by arguing that nothing should be admitted by the mind except what can be proven by rational evidence, Descartes was setting a new course for philosophy that would take it far from its previous role as the servant of theology. His ambition to provide a new foundation for an apologetic argument for God and soul, a new kind of metaphysics based on consciousness, and a philosophical foundation for the new modern science designed to master nature by laying bare its fundamental laws would fundamentally alter philosophy's relationship to theology and eventually set them at odds with each other.

Across the pond Hume would argue in his seminal *Inquiry Concerning Human Understanding* that all knowledge may be divided into two kinds: relations of ideas and matters of fact. The first kind of knowledge is what belongs to mathematics, such as the Pythagorean theorem, and results in certainty. The second kind concerns the empirical world; it is marked by sheer contingency because every matter of fact is possibly otherwise. Metaphysics and theology fit on neither prong of Hume's famous fork, and he spent a great deal of time demonstrating this in his *Dialogues Concerning Natural Religion*. There he turns his skepticism and empiricism on any rational argument for the existence of God. If all nonmathematical argumentation must be based on empirical grounds and no empirical grounds can warrant a necessary conclusion, then metaphysics and theology are no forms of knowledge at all.

Reacting to both Cartesian rationalism and Humean empiricism, Kant's *Critique of Pure Reason* was a conscious intent to effect a "Copernican revolution" in philosophy. Rather than assume that the mind conforms or corresponds to the world, the most basic assumption of any form of realism, Kant proposed that the world of objects conforms to the inherent structures of the human mind. The project of the *Critique* is to lay bare the pure or a priori structures of human consciousness whereby it processes experience. Human consciousness has common structural features or filters through which we organize the deliverances of the senses, most notably through causality. According to Kant, we can know nothing of the way the world is independently of human knowing, what he calls the *noumenal* world; rather we only know the way the world appears to human consciousness, the *phenomenal* world. Traditional metaphysical realism is obviously destroyed by the Kantian critique. Kant's critique makes a point of demonstrating that it is impossible to mount a valid argument for the existence of God; he believes that all such arguments covertly rely on some version of the ontological argument, which is fallacious because it treats existence as if it were like any other perfection when it is categorically different. Kant's destruction of metaphysics in general and natural theology in particular was motivated not by any hostility to Christianity (he himself was a believer) but rather because he wanted to protect the most basic premises of Christianity—God, freedom, and the immortality of the soul—from philosophical attack: "I have therefore found it necessary to deny *knowledge*, in order to make room for faith."[2] The human mind is naturally inclined to think about God both speculatively and practically, but it can know nothing about God.

Modernity's hostility to the premodern picture reaches a kind of apogee in Nietzsche. At the beginning of *Beyond Good and Evil*, Nietzsche identifies Platonism as the origin of all that is wrong in the Western tradition because it argues for an objective reality beyond the sensible world and anchors morality in that ultimate Good. Christianity is nothing but Platonism for the masses. One of Nietzsche's central claims is that there is no objective point of view; everything is a matter of perspective. There is no such thing as "truth" in the sense of an objective take on the way the world is; claims to objective knowledge amount to an attempt to privilege one perspective over another. Rather than being rational agents, we are driven by the unconscious will to power, by the desire to exert ourselves and make a creative impact on the world. Traditional morality is designed to constrain human creativity and represents not some objective good, but the collective self-interest of the masses. Superior human beings need to be the artists of their own lives, unconstrained by traditional moral values, living beyond what has traditionally been called good and evil. God is dead.

This brief description of the positions of some of modernity's most important figures is offered to illustrate the kinds of philosophical positions decried by *Fides et Ratio*. While modern philosophy in Descartes may have begun in the service of faith, it ended up independent and largely antagonistic. The traditional metaphysical claims that buttressed theology were denied on the grounds either that we cannot know the way the world is but only the way the world appears to us (idealism), or that we can know only what can be verified by empirical means (positivism). As philosophy lost its prior confidence that it could achieve a kind of comprehensive view of the whole, it became one among many other human disciplines with no privileged claim to knowledge. Insofar as it accepts the basic dictum of modernity—that knowledge is for the sake of power over nature—philosophy has become just another form of instrumental knowledge. In its apogee, Nietzsche, modern philosophy becomes a form of nihilism: nothing is true, nothing is good, make your own meaning.

FROM *AETERNI PATRIS* TO *FIDES ET RATIO*

While there were attempts by many Catholic thinkers to dialogue with modern philosophy, and while it is clear that modern philosophy impacted Catholic thinking, it is not unfair to say that the twin challenges of the Reformation and the Enlightenment produced a defensive mentality. As modernity raged outside, inside Catholicism theologians and philosophers continued to pass on the medieval inheritance in the forms of commentaries and manuals on the greatest Scholastic thinkers, especially Aquinas but also John Duns Scotus. *Thomism* is the term for the commentatorial tradition that arose in order to perpetuate the thought of Thomas Aquinas. During the modern period the thought of Aquinas gradually became the dominant strain within Catholicism, uniting even Jesuits and Dominicans. The culmination of this ascendancy was Pope Leo XIII's encyclical letter, *Aeterni Patris,* in 1879. Leo believed that the fundamental error of modern philosophy was its separation from theology. In response, he urged a return to the thought of Thomas Aquinas in order to recover a proper sense of the fundamental harmony of faith and reason. From that moment on, Thomism became the privileged school of thought within the Catholic Church and the antidote to post-Cartesian and especially Kantian thought. Leo believed that Thomism could both preserve the past tradition and absorb all that was true and good in modernity. The tension between preserving the tradition and dialoguing with modernity would mark the resurgence of Thomism in the twentieth century.

The resurgence of Thomism flowered first in France in the early part of the twentieth century. It was fueled mainly by the desire to respond to the challenges posed to traditional Catholic thought by the work of Maurice Blondel and Henri Bergson. Both Blondel and Bergson accepted the post-Kantian claim that religious faith cannot be justified by metaphysical proofs for the existence of God or by apologetic appeal to miracles. Rather the starting point needed to be located in subjective experience. For Blondel, the starting point was the dynamism of the will; for Bergson, the starting point was the living dynamism (*élan vital*) that pulsed through reality, graspable only by an intuition rather than a concept. The cumulative effect of Blondel and Bergson was to frame a problematic that would result in Thomism spending the bulk of its efforts in the following areas: a defense of epistemological realism and the intellectual value of concepts and propositions, a resulting defense of traditional metaphysics, and withering attacks on idealism.

The most influential figures to emerge out of this French ferment were Jacques Maritain and Etienne Gilson. It would be hard to overestimate their influence on Catholic philosophical thought in the era before Vatican II. Maritain, a convert to Roman Catholicism and Thomism, attempted to make Thomistic metaphysics more contemporary by arguing that it was grounded in an intuition of being that arose as a spontaneous response to an initiative of reality itself. This attempt to integrate Bergsonian elements into Thomism made Maritain's metaphysics suspect to some Thomists. Maritain insisted, however, that the intuition led to a true concept of being that could be the subject of a traditional metaphysics. In addition to numerous books on metaphysics, he resolutely defended realism and attacked idealism. In one of his seminal works, *The Degrees of Knowledge*, he articulated a vision of a hierarchical order of all human sciences, from the philosophy of nature, to metaphysics, to the ultimate form of wisdom that is theology. Maritain maintained that philosophy was formally autonomous from theology, but that individual philosophers needed the help of grace to avoid error on the basis of sin. His prodigious output ranged beyond metaphysics and epistemology to ethics, politics, and aesthetics. He seemed to be the very embodiment of the kind of Thomism called for by *Aeterni Patris* in his confident dialogue with modern thought.

One of the most important outcomes of *Aeterni Patris* was a tremendous upsurge of interest within Catholicism in medieval philosophy. Catholic historians of medieval philosophy were especially interested in proving that there was genuine philosophical progress in the medieval era and that it was not the Dark Ages. The picture of Aquinas that emerged from the renewed historical-critical study was of a richer and more subtle thinker than what had been distilled into Thomistic manuals of philosophy and theology. The rediscovery of the "real" Thomas Aquinas of history would be the greatest resource for a vibrant Thomism. While the recovery of the historical Aquinas was the collective work of many people, the most influential figure was doubtless Etienne Gilson.

Gilson was uniquely qualified to rehabilitate the legitimacy of medieval philosophy because he backed into it through a historical study of the influence of scholastic thought on Descartes. As Gilson began to study medieval thought in general and Aquinas in particular, he came to believe that the medieval period had been a time of extraordinary philosophical progress, not despite philosophy's subservience to theology but precisely because of its service to theology. One of Gilson's central and most controversial claims was that the medieval period embodied a kind of thinking that he called "Christian philosophy." To some, Christian philosophy was and is an oxymoron, but in *The Spirit of Medieval Philosophy*, Gilson narrates the history of medieval philosophy as a deepening insight into genuinely philosophical topics—being, causality, knowledge, language, free will, personhood, love, law, morality—precisely as a result of the guidance of theology. Christian philosophy was not some hybrid of theology and philosophy involving appeals to revealed premises, however; it was the way philosophy advanced historically past the Classical achievement precisely because it had been led to think through things more deeply as a result of the challenges to the human mind posed by theology. Gilson therefore read and articulated a vision of Aquinas as Christian philosopher par excellence. He insisted that because Aquinas was primarily a theologian, his philosophical insights could be understood only in a theological manner, by beginning with God and then moving to creatures. Gilson's claims set off vigorous debates on both Christian philosophy and the proper way to articulate the thought of Aquinas.

The central place in Aquinas's thought where Gilson was convinced of the direct effect of revelation on reason was in Aquinas's metaphysical analysis of the nature of God. Gilson held that Aquinas's identification of God's nature as identical to God's existence was a result of metaphysical meditation on the self-revelation of God in Exodus 3:14 as "He who is," or *Qui est*. As a result of this revealed doctrine, Aquinas articulated a unique metaphysical vision far beyond Aristotle and Neoplatonism (while drawing on both) that understood God to be unique because his essence was identical with his infinite act of existence (*esse* in Latin). In every other being there is a real distinction between that whereby the creature is what it is, its finite essence, and that whereby it is or exists (its to-be, or *esse*).

The primacy of the act of existence in Aquinas's doctrine of being is a philosophical insight engendered by theology. Gilson believed that the primacy of existence over essence, as act to potency, was Aquinas's crowning philosophical achievement and the key to vindicating Thomistic metaphysics in the postmodern context. In *Being and Some Philosophers*, Gilson's history of metaphysics, Aquinas's doctrine of the primacy of existence over essence represents a singular metaphysical breakthrough against the persistent temptation to privilege form or essence over existence. Gilson believed that even Thomists of the earlier era were guilty of neglecting this key insight. It is arguable that the most important advance in Thomism in the twentieth century was the recovery of a distinctive metaphysical vision inspired at least by the doctrine of creation if not by Exodus.

Gilson and Maritain disagreed on some points, but they were both resolutely opposed to any compromise with modernity on the question of the starting point of philosophy. They believed that if you started with Cartesian or Kantian consciousness, you were doomed to idealism. The majority view among Thomists was that there was no possibility of a realistic metaphysics if you began with subjective immanence.

Another group of philosophers believed that the viability of Thomism in the modern context depended upon accepting a modern starting point and then showing how it can lead to a genuinely Thomistic and theology-friendly metaphysics. The term for this movement was *Transcendental Thomism*, because its adherents shared the conviction that a transcendental analysis of the a priori conditions of human subjectivity could conclude to epistemological realism and a recognizably Thomistic metaphysics. Transcendental Thomism believed that an a priori analysis of human knowing and willing discloses some form of spiritual dynamism toward the Absolute. Rather than modern subjectivity being closed off solipsistically, it was open to the infinite.

The originator of transcendental Thomism was the Belgian Jesuit Joseph Marechal. Marechal argued that an analysis of the a priori conditions of the human act of judgment reveal that all finite judgments presuppose the horizon of the Infinite as a backdrop. The most influential transcendental Thomist was the German Jesuit Karl Rahner, whose work engaged a broader range of post-Kantian German philosophy. Rahner tried to ground his a priori analysis in Aquinas's epistemology. For Rahner, the act of judgment discloses a preconceptual grasp (*Vorgriff*) of Infinite *Esse*. Rahner believed that human beings were incarnated spirits with an a priori dynamism toward the Absolute, and he developed a transcendental theology that explored the deep fit between the striving of the human spirit and God's self-disclosure. The last great transcendental Thomist was the Canadian Jesuit Bernard Lonergan, whose complex thinking defines any brief categorization.

Since the Second Vatican Council, Thomism has remained the dominant strain in Catholic philosophy. The most notable development among English-speaking Thomists has been a deeper engagement with analytic philosophy. Once Thomists grasped that analytic philosophy was not bound to the dogmas of logical positivism, they realized that the study of Thomas could be enriched by a dialogue with analytic philosophy. The emergence of the philosophy of religion as a recognized discipline opened the door for metaphysics and natural theology to be debated again. In this domain the works of Norman Kretzmann, Eleonore Stump, and Brian Davies have been influential in making Aquinas accessible to and in dialogue with current problematics. Some, like John Haldane, would even argue that there is such a thing as analytical Thomism, though not everyone would agree that these words belong together. Aquinas's ethical thought has also been retrieved into the modern conversation, notably through the works of Alasdair MacIntyre.

One could argue that the philosophical ideas of Aquinas have never been more involved in the philosophical conversation of the day than at present. The same could not be said in theology. It is important to note that while Aquinas remains the guide and paradigm for Catholicism insofar as he integrated faith and reason into a powerful synthesis, Thomism is not binding on Catholic philosophers in a doctrinaire way. John Paul II made that clear when he said in *Fides et Ratio,* "The Church has no philosophy of her own nor does she canonize any one particular philosophy in preference to others." The encyclical notes that many other philosophies have contributed to the project of articulating the meaning of an overarching Christian wisdom. The dialogue that began on the Aereopagus continues to this day.

NOTES

1. Tertullian, *On Prescription against Heretics*, chapter 7.
2. Kant, preface to the second edition of *The Critique of Pure Reason*.

SELECTED READINGS

Gilson, Etienne. *The Spirit of Medieval Philosophy.* Notre Dame, Ind.: University of Notre Dame Press, 1993.

McCool, Gerald. *From Unity to Pluralism: The Internal Evolution of Thomism.* New York: Fordham University Press, 1992.

Rist, John. "Faith and Reason." In *The Cambridge Companion to Augustine*, edited by Eleonore Stump and Norman Kretzmann. Cambridge, U.K.: Cambridge University Press, 2001.

Shanley, Brian J. *The Thomist Tradition.* Dordrecht, The Netherlands: Kluwer Academic, 2002.

Sokolowski, Robert. *The God of Faith and Reason.* Washington, DC: Catholic University of America Press, 1995.

5

Perspectives in Catholic Philosophy II

David B. Burrell, C.S.C.

THE RELATION OF philosophy to theology in Catholic higher education is at the core of the Catholic intellectual tradition. In recent years the distinguished phenomenologist Karol Wotyla, in his encyclical as Pope John Paul II, *Fides et Ratio*, details how reciprocal the two disciplines must be in order to fulfill their respective roles adequately. Highlighting some features of that reciprocity, I first explore philosophy's need for a perspective of faith to pursue its legitimately autonomous goals, then I show how faith's need for philosophical foundations finds traction in the openness of Thomas Aquinas to philosophy done in diverse cultural settings.[1]

PHILOSOPHY IN NEED OF FAITH TO BE ITSELF

Relating the respective disciplines of philosophy and theology in Catholic institutions of higher learning has proven difficult in the modern era. We need to show why that is the case in order to renew connections inherent to them both. The culprit turns out to be the timing of Leo XIII's 1879 encyclical *Aeterni Patris*, meant to wean Catholic students of philosophy from the lure of modern rationalism to the rich vein of thought represented by Thomas Aquinas.[2] Although the intention was to return to the central part of the tradition, the resulting Thomism favored the same "need for certitude" that had drawn Catholics to Descartes. As a result, the

Thomist teacher who emerged in Catholic institutions could easily be caricatured as providing answers to questions the students never asked!

This type of Cartesian Thomism was regularly presented as rational inquiry untrammeled by revelation (theology). Theology was based primarily on revelation, and its philosophical foundations were not critically explored. Part 1 of the *Summa Theologiae* was split into two treatises, *De Deo uno* (questions 2–26) and *De Deo trino* (27–43). These two sections were followed by questions treating *creation*, which were regularly placed with the earlier ones from *De Deo uno*, since "all divine action *ad extra* is to be attributed to the one God."

This sharp separation of theology and philosophy characterized the teaching of Aquinas until the rise of the *ressourcement* movement and the resulting *nouvelle théologie*, which shaped reflection at Vatican II and beyond. The result is that Thomists trained in the baroque manual tradition, often unwittingly reinforced by *Aeterni Patris*, were prone to link Vatican II with the eclipse of Aquinas.

In one sense an improperly dichotomized Thomism did fade away after Vatican II. But in the 1950s and 1960s the study of Aquinas made significant advances. This movement was inaugurated by the contextualizing work of pioneering scholars like Chenu, Grabmann, and others who were sharply critical of manual Thomism. The revisionists showed that manual Thomism distorted the fruitful modes of inquiry launched by Aquinas. The distortions, they showed, had arisen not from Aquinas but from a tendency among commentators to delineate sharply between philosophy and theology in his work.

Apologetics was offered as a salient justification for treating philosophy and theology apart from one another. In this view Aquinas's philosophy was a stepping-stone to bring unbelievers closer to Christian faith. Yet as Josef Pieper, a universally respected commentator on Aquinas, has shown, no such gap between philosophy and theology can be found in Aquinas. A central issue for Aquinas was understanding creation as a free act of God, who cannot be constrained.[3] Despite Pieper's findings, Catholic colleges and universities in Europe and the United States confirmed this misleading gap in the structure of their academic departments. The Europeans neatly maintained separate faculties of philosophy and theology, while in Catholic institutions in the United States departments of philosophy, on the one hand, and theology or religion, on the other, emerged during the past century.

For these cumulative reasons, this essay explores the resurgence of the study of Aquinas since the virtual demise of manual Thomism and illustrates the rich interaction between philosophy and theology. Besides those already mentioned, a proper *silsala* (chain of authorities) might well begin with Pieper and Bernard Lonergan. Their work on Aquinas suggests that he was no more a manual Thomist than Jesus was a Christian! For if Pieper called into question the easy demarcation of philosophy from theology by identifying free creation as the "hidden element" in Aquinas's philosophy, Lonergan demonstrates this by focusing on questions rather than answers, much as Aquinas himself did.

A POSTMODERN AQUINAS

Aquinas's customary way of introducing hermeneutics in relation to early conciliar decrees is telling: "If these are meant to be answers, let us first determine what the questions were to which they were proposed as answers." By contrast, manual Thomism as taught for much of the twentieth century proved to be *modernist* in that it strove to offer a philosophy useful in providing answers to queries made by any inquiring mind.[4]

Once Pieper reminded the philosophical community that Aquinas's philosophy was already predicated on the hidden premises of free creation, the suspicions of secular philosophers were aroused. Whatever the faults of manual Thomism, it was a philosophy that heretofore had been a rather neutral vehicle of reflection. When Pieper's writings became known, secular philosophers gradually turned away from it as they perceived that Thomism was already embedded in faith.

This bit of historical awareness leavens my suggestion that an Aquinas fruitful for us today would better be dubbed "postmodern." To justify this contention, recall a primary tenet of the postmodern reaction to modernist goals. For postmodern philosophers, hermeneutics reigns and the framework in which statements are to be interpreted is crucial. Therefore, key figures must be read in their context if they are to be assimilated to ours. And when that context involves faith, we need to learn how to enter into it rather than simply bracket it. In engaging faith we should recall John Henry Newman's claim that any broad academic inquiry demands faith of some sort.

Medieval philosophy was done in the context of theology. Modernism called for a sharp separation of philosophy from theology. And postmodernism emphasizes context and perspective in interpreting both texts and reality. The claim made in this essay is that postmodern inquiry is closer to a medieval dialectic of faith and reason than it is to the stark dichotomy of faith and reason demanded by modernism. Maintaining the dialectical relationship enables us to recognize how Aquinas's strategies usually involve faith as an ingredient to knowing, indeed, a distinct "mode of knowing."

Negotiating the standard *faith/reason* polarity requires the mediation of *culture*; so reading in context will inevitably privilege language as more basic than logic. This strategy allows thinkers to come alive, as philosophy becomes inquiry. By raising issues arising in culture, philosophy in this mode employs the *manuductio* (taking by the hand and leading on) that Thomas Hibbs delineates so carefully in *Aquinas, Ethics, and Philosophy of Religion: Metaphysics and Practice*.[5]

A similar logic/language distinction appears in a disagreement Aquinas has with Maimonides. Aquinas points out that from *logic* alone the claim that "God is just" is ill-formed. In a technical sense, using logic alone we finite beings cannot say or know anything about the infinite God in himself. On the other hand, drawing upon the *language* we properly use when we pray to God in the Psalms and elsewhere, we acknowledge God as just. That is, the language of prayer "imperfectly signifies" that God is just. Somewhat counterintuitively, the way we *use* our language reveals that in some instances we are referring to a direction rather than to a precise spot on some map. To use another example, we talk about God as the "creator of heaven and earth" without knowing precisely what "creator" means or what "heaven and earth" means, although admittedly we have a much clearer idea of earth than of heaven.

Olivier-Thomas Vénard reminds us that the desire for logical clarity and the attempt to address the infinite call for poetical constructions. Poets regularly fracture syntax to make a point, even if good poets do so adroitly, since they respect the syntax they fracture.[6] Vénard's careful delineation of the poetics embedded in Aquinas's chiseled constructions allows a contemporary entrée into a postmodern Aquinas. My quarter-century-old *Aquinas: God and Action* invoked Wittgenstein to provide similar postmodern access to Aquinas.[7]

To see how postmodern hermeneutics allows a positive evaluation of philosophers who take religious terms and realities seriously, allow me to sketch a framework that reorients the standard way we construct the history of philosophy.

Regularly teaching a course in ancient and medieval philosophy has led me to identify quite clearly the salient difference between two philosophical periods or approaches. The telling difference is the concern with the existence of a free creator. The ancient philosophers of Greece and Rome did not address the issue of a creator of the universe. By the turn of the first millennium, however, Jewish, Christian, and Muslim thinkers converged in their efforts to find a place for a free creator in the apparently seamless Hellenic philosophy they inherited.[8]

If we can say schematically that the presence of a free creator divides medieval from ancient philosophy, what marks the subsequent transition to modern philosophy? Many things, of course. But if one continues to focus on the larger issues with an eye to highlighting major differences, one important goal of modern philosophy was to eliminate the theological overtones of the scholastics. The moderns therefore proceeded by avoiding reference to a creator. This posed a large difficulty, since the creator was a bit large to overlook. So rather than deny God as creator, the moderns (postmedievalists) tended to deny the relevance of God as creator.

This is evidenced in Enlightenment fascination with "the Greeks," even though the Greeks were more a construct for the moderns than they were a historical group. Aristotle had managed quite well without a creator, and he was certainly a reliable authority.

Still speaking quite schematically, we can characterize modern philosophy as postmedieval and interpret *post-* as including a note of denial of a creator, whether this was an outright denial or an implicit denial by neglect. Such a denial had consequences for the philosophical agenda of the moderns. The modern philosophers had to compensate for the absence of a creator. In particular they needed grounds for certainty. Increasingly these philosophers sought a firm foundation, an unassailable starting point for their philosophy. They found this in "self-evident" propositions or "sense-data" or in whatever.

These unassailable starting points eventually proved to be illusory. Once this happened, we entered a postmodern world. Once we realize our presumptions regarding philosophy itself are inherently linked to such strategies, as Rorty presumes they are, then we inevitably regard a postmodern context as one in which anything goes.

If modern philosophy is seen as postmedieval, then postmodern philosophy should be read as post-postmedieval. And while the *post-* prefixes may not connote the same sort of denials, we are directed to a sense of postmodern that bears affinities with medieval inquiry. Put more positively and less schematically, both medieval and postmodern inquiry are more at ease with starting points that lack firm foundations. This accords with Gadamer's contention that any inquiry whatsoever rests on fiduciary premises.

In practice this postmodern approach means that faith may be regarded as a way of knowing. Such a contention would prove startling to Descartes, though he might be somewhat assuaged by the simultaneous assertion that faith, like any other way of knowing, is ever in need of critical assessment. The attempt to completely separate faith from critical thinking is a failed endeavor. But this account of the role of creator and faith in the development of philosophy enables us to see both where philosophy wandered from firm moorings and what direction we should set for ourselves. For Catholic philosophy in particular, we have seen how the desire for firm foundations led manual Thomists to align themselves more closely to Descartes and the context of modernity than to Aquinas himself, since they sought a metaphysical way to attain the certitude that Descartes had postulated epistemologically.

Due to the close alignment of a misplaced manual Thomism with the Cartesian project, the failure of the Cartesian project also means that Thomism as interpreted in the nineteenth and twentieth centuries is no longer viable. If there can be no viable epistemology without metaphysics, a postmodern ethos can show that there is no way to move to the level of metaphysics without a critical faith. So even on modern terms, an authentic turn to Aquinas effectively displaces us to a medieval world. The difference is that Catholic philosophers now have to justify explicitly, not necessarily prove, what thinkers like Aquinas could simply presume.

Like cultural displacement, historical displacement brings us face-to-face with our own unwitting presumptions. It also allows us to question the presumptions of the distinct historical period, assess their potential fruitfulness, and consider the possibility of adopting others. Note the Gadamerian premise here. Presumptions there will be; historical or intellectual displacement merely brings us face-to-face with another set of them. But the new presumptions illumine our old presumptions as lacking justification. In fact the former presumptions become formal assumptions, needing validation or change.

By focusing on the linguistic turn in medieval discourse, Vénard carries out his inquiry into the subtle ways Aquinas employs the language available to him. Vénard notes that Aquinas draws upon the language of "speculative grammar," developed in the previous generation of Anselm, Abelard, and Peter Lombard. Drawing upon Aquinas's own practice and highlighting some hitherto unnoticed clues, Vénard sketches a semiology that Aquinas himself had not explicitly developed.

So the conceit of "postmodern" allows us to appreciate more fully the singularity of Aquinas as a medieval philosophical theologian who has proved to be accessible and appealing to contemporaries of nearly any age.

A telling example of the linguistic turn undertaken by Aquinas can be found in the way he has recourse to two Islamic philosophical theologians, Avicenna (Ibn Sina) and Averroës (Ibn Rushd), together with a Jewish thinker immersed in the Islamicate, Moses Maimonides. Aquinas addresses a central theme in Jewish and Christian revelation, the free creation of the universe by the one God. This is a central tenet of Christian revelation. For Aquinas the challenge was to articulate that faith proposition with the tools available from a Hellenic philosophy that acknowledged no such origination. Aristotle, Plato, Parmenides, Plotinus, and other Greek philosophers did not speak of *creatio ex nihilo*.

Aquinas's conviction that we can at best "imperfectly signify" matters so arcane as *creatio ex nihilo* naturally urged him to seek help from thinkers in cognate traditions—no matter what each may have thought of the other's faith tradition in practice. To be sure, Greek philosophy had a prevailing account of the origination of the universe. Plotinus in particular had expanded Aristotle's matrix of causes to include a "cause of being," by emanation from the One. Yet it remained unclear whether "emanation from the One" could be said to be free, as both the Bible and the Qur'an demanded. Indeed one early Islamic philosopher enamored of Aristotle, al-Farabi, modeled that emanation from the One on the pattern of logical deduction. But if it was a logical deduction, then it would be *necessary*. However, as Plotinus and others described the emanation, nothing entailed necessity. In fact Aquinas's teacher, Albert the Great, had adopted an emanationist picture of creation quite wholeheartedly, and Aquinas himself had no difficulty offering a lapidary definition of creation as "the emanation of all of being from the singular cause of being." In sum, emanation was open to being free or necessary, but some argument for one or the other approach was required.

A picture or cursory definition of emanation falls far short of a philosophical account. To address this issue, Aquinas had recourse to Moses ben Maimon's account of creation as a free act of the one God. In turn, Moses ben Maimon found support for his position in al-Ghazali, to whose work Aquinas had no access. So while Aquinas's avowal of creation as free reflected the biblical narrative, philosophical support for this position derived from a Jewish thinker (Maimonides) formed in Islamic culture (the "Islamicate," as Marshall Hodgson expressed it). Because Maimonides was likely familiar with the impressive philosophical theologian al-Ghazali, Aquinas's mature reflections on this singular and expressly ineffable relation of free creatures to a free creator already represented an interfaith, intercultural achievement. In the case of a free creator, Aquinas relies on an expressly ineffable relation to ground his metaphysical view of the origins of the universe. This Thomistic account is far from a rational, modernist account of origins. Indeed it is more properly termed a postmodern explanation, inherently dependent on faith assertions.[9]

Much as John Paul II in his *Fides et Ratio* challenged a modernist account by presenting faith and reason in a dialectical relationship, my reading of Aquinas does the same. Until the late twentieth century Aquinas scholarship had all but neglected his dependence on Islamic and Jewish thinkers, perhaps because the scholars themselves were from northwestern Europe. But immersing myself in the culture of Jerusalem and Cairo provided me with a fresh look not only at Jerusalem (Maimonides) and Cairo (al-Ghazali) but also at Paris and Naples. The Thomistic cultural context I saw was primarily Christian and Greek, with a touch of Judaic and Islamic thought. Responding to the Dominican order's request to establish a house of studies, Dominic decided to locate it in Naples, which had an Islamic connection. Naples was part of the kingdom of the two Sicilys, and it is where translations from Arabic of key philosophical texts had already been commissioned. Naples would enable Aquinas to become more familiar with the philosophical thinking of Islam. Indeed some of this cross-cultural awareness is reflected in his later works. That he died a few years after moving to Naples meant that incorporation of Islamic thought into his writings was limited, though he included enough insights to suggest that eventually he would have attempted a broader synthesis.

Cross-cultural sharing continues in the Church, which has to wrestle with a postmodern environment. In the wake of John Paul II's exploratory encyclical *Fides et Ratio*, one of my confreres then serving as rector of a Catholic seminary in Africa was invited to Rome for a global consultation on the complex relations between faith and reason. His African perspective and his esteem for the Church emboldened him to add culture to the diptych of faith and reason. He brought back to Africa a triad: reason, culture, and faith. When he mentioned his modification to me, I thought of the American philosopher Charles Sanders Peirce. Peirce notes that any polarity is ever in danger of becoming just that, a contrast of opposites. Eventually a third pole is needed, since the third facet requires greater nuance and elucidation of the other two poles.

Beyond greater nuance, adding culture to faith and reason eventually requires a keen ear for analogous language. Indeed it is surprising that a person so respectful of culture as Karol Wotyla should apparently elide it in his binary treatment of faith and reason. Perhaps Pope John Paul did so for the practical reason of communicating effectively to millions of Catholics and non-Catholics. However, he understood the importance of culture. In the chapter in the encyclical detailing the interactions between theology and philosophy, he took note of the importance of culture: "Reason itself, in accord with which Christians experience their faith, is soaked in the culture of the place nearest to it, and in its turn ensures that with the progress of time, its own nature is bit by bit transformed" (no. 71).[10]

A final argument for a postmodern Aquinas notes his propensity to seek illumination from apparently alien sources, that is, sources deemed unfriendly or antagonistic. Aquinas was certainly conscious that Aristotle could be read many ways. Not willing to restrict too severely the understanding of the Gospel, Aquinas realized that diverse faith traditions might well offer interpretative schemes more able to express the rich legacy of their scriptures regarding a key issue like a freely created universe. He was a pioneer in doing comparative work among the Abrahamic traditions. If, as I have indicated, a propensity to comparative or cross-cultural study is distinctively postmodern, Aquinas himself should be regarded and even welcomed as an interlocutor with us in our contemporary inquiries.

FAITH NEEDS PHILOSOPHY TO SEEK UNDERSTANDING

Nothing illustrates theology's need for philosophical strategies more saliently and ironically than Professor Ratzinger's homecoming address at Regensburg as Pope Benedict XVI in September 2006. He sought to elaborate a recondite thesis about the way Christianity had relied on reason from the Hellenic world for its early development, so rendering a coveted place for the role reason can (and must) play in developing any religious tradition. Unfortunately the pope used the harsh remarks of a Byzantine emperor facing a siege by a Muslim army to highlight the more positive role played by reason in Christianity. What was intended as a bold and illuminating contrast came across to the public as a condescending putdown.

The way a faith tradition needs philosophical strategies to become "faith seeking understanding" (Augustine) or to develop a critical theology is best illustrated in the works of Robert Sokolowski. A phenomenologist, Sokolowski introduces the role of "distinctions" to illustrate how resolving questions surrounding the incarnation of divinity in Jesus delineates the unique relation of creatures to their creator. Once properly understood, Jesus' incarnation offers the key to a coherent grasp of free creation.

Sokolowski uses strategies developed by Hellenic philosophers to elaborate the connection between the incarnation and free creation. It is certainly remarkable that it took the fledgling Christian movement four centuries to respond to its central faith question concerning Jesus: Who and what is he? At least one cynic must have wondered how convincing a religion can be that requires four centuries to get its message straight! Moreover the long-standing quest for clarity regarding Jesus doubtless overshadowed more explicit reflection on the first article of the creed: "I believe in God, the Father almighty, creator of heaven and earth." Sokolowski observes, "The issue the Church had to settle first, once it acquired public and official recognition under Constantine and could turn to controversies regarding its teaching, was the issue of the being and actions of Christ." Yet Sokolowski goes on to insist:

> [While] the Council of Chalcedon, and the councils and controversies that led up to it, were concerned with the mystery of Christ, . . . they also tell us about the God who became incarnate in Christ. They tell us first that God does not destroy the natural necessities of things he becomes involved with, even in the intimate union of the incarnation. What is according to nature, and what reason can disclose in nature, retains its integrity before the Christian God [who] is not a part of the world and is not a "kind" of being at all. Therefore, the incarnation is not meaningless or impossible or destructive.[11]

According to Sokolowski, the discussion in the Church of how the Word became flesh brought greater clarity to God's apartness from the world:

> The same distinction [between God and the world] was also emphasized as a background for the Trinitarian doctrines and for the controversies about grace. . . . Thus many of the crucial dogmatic issues raised in the relationship

between God and the world, and the positions judged to be erroneous would generally have obscured the Christian distinction between the divine and the mundane.[12]

Creation comes first temporally and thematically in God's transactions with the world. But the way we understand the founding relation between God and the world also affects how we articulate any further interaction. For were the One who reached out to us in Christ not the creator of heaven and earth, the story would have to be told in a vastly different (and inescapably mythic) idiom. In fact the true doctrine of creation can unfortunately turn mythic if Christians are so preoccupied with redemption that creation is simply presumed as its stage setting.

The narrative of Incarnation and redemption captures the lion's share of the tripartite creed associated with the initiation rites of baptism. Coming first in the creed, creation appears to some thinkers less a foundation and more a preamble, something less important that leads up to the central mysteries of incarnation and redemption.

Although Christians are inclined to move quickly past creation to the "real revelation" of Jesus as the Christ, appreciating the act of creation as well as the ineffable relation between creatures and creator requires considerable philosophical acumen. Some more timid theologians prefer to finesse the issue by neglecting it or by not granting it careful analysis. Yet as Sokolowski reminds us, we cannot afford to do this since the interaction among these shaping mysteries of faith is at once palpable and mutually illuminating.

Neither should Christians treat the Hebrew scriptures as a mere preamble to their revelation of God in Jesus. The God whom Jesus calls "Abba" is introduced in the Hebrew scriptures, and there one learns how God interacts with the Jews, his chosen people. Furthermore the primary hermeneutic for the New Testament is the Hebrew scriptures. The early Church quickly understood the structural parallels between the creation story and redemption in Christ. The story of creation shows that God had loving plans for Adam and Eve, plans that were partially frustrated by their disobedience, which was a false imitation of God's freedom. But the initial missteps of man and woman are reversed through God's saving initiative, which begins with Abraham in Genesis 12.

CREATION EX NIHILO

By the time Aquinas engaged these issues, a third Abrahamic voice, reflecting a new scripture, clamored. Far more lapidary than what is stated in Genesis is the account in the Qur'an: "He says 'Be' and it is" (6:73). Yet the pattern of salvation and redemption is repeated in the account by the Prophet. The heart of the drama turns on Mohammed's God-given recitation. Allah's identifying Himself with "the Creator of the heavens and the earth" (2:117) assures us that we are not trafficking with an Arabian deity but with a God with the same role as that ascribed the Christian Creator of heaven and earth.

As is clear from the brief outline given above, the forces conspiring to elaborate the Christian doctrine of creation were at once historical and conceptual, scriptural and philosophical, with discussions from other faiths shaping the context.[13] Both Jewish and Christian readings of Genesis had taken the equivocal language in Genesis about preexistent stuff as part of the inherently narrative structure of the work. In interpreting the narrative, both Jews and Christians agreed that God created the universe ex nihilo. That is, God was so powerful that he could create without needing anything to work on, as it were. He could both subdue all things and bring all things into being. Consequently the philosophical task is to articulate sheer origination, while the theological goal is to show this action to be utterly gratuitous.

If creator and creation are to be what the Hebrew scriptures presume them to be, neither stuff nor motive can be presupposed. Here is where what Sokolowski identifies as "the distinction" proves so critical: creation can be creation only if God can be God without creating. No external incentive or internal need can induce God to create, and if God had not created he would still be God.

ESSENCE AND EXISTENCE

Aquinas's capacity to integrate philosophical with theological demands is displayed in the initial article in the *Summa Theologiae*. The subject is creation, and the overarching question to be addressed is "Must everything that is have been caused by God?" (I, 44, 1). Relying on his identification of God as that One whose very essence is to exist, Aquinas shows why one must "necessarily say that whatever in any way *is*, is from God." For if "God is sheer existence subsisting of its very nature (*ipsum esse* per se *subsistens*), [and so] must be unique,...then it follows that all things other than God are not their own existence but share in existence" (I, 3, 4). God is not being in the sense of another being, more powerful, intelligent, creative, and focused than all other beings combined. Rather God is *esse*, which means "to be." Aquinas invokes the Neoplatonic distinction between *essential* and *participated* being to give everything but the creator the stamp of *created*. Very little, if anything, is said here about causation or how God brought the world into existence. Nonetheless the basic philosophical elements for an adequate account of creation and a unique type of causation are in place.

Aquinas poses the question of causation in explicitly Aristotelian terms: "[Is] God...the efficient cause of all beings?" Following his "for and against" style in the *Summa Theologiae*, Aquinas first gives reasons justifying God as efficient cause and then raises all types of objections to this view. One objection notes that Aristotle presumed that some "natural necessities" have always existed. Aquinas continues stating the objection: "Since there are many such [natural necessities] in reality [such as spiritual substances and heavenly bodies that carry no principle of dissolution within themselves], all beings are not from God." For the Greeks and Hebrews, the firmament was where the stars were located. Stars and heavenly bodies did not deteriorate. The objection notes that many people presume such natural necessities have existed and will exist forever.

Aquinas deftly handles this objection of preexisting spiritual and heavenly bodies and their like. He simply invokes the primacy of existing: "An active cause is required not simply because the effect could not be [i.e., is contingent], but because the effect would not be if the cause were not [existing]" (I, 44, 1, ad. 2). So according to Aquinas, even "necessary things" require a cause for their very being. Other than being itself (God), something cannot simply be. It requires a cause.

This position is a radical revision of Aristotle and is based on a distinction made by the Islamic philosopher Avicenna's interpretation of Aristotle. For Avicenna, essence is quite distinct from existing, and Aquinas incorporated this into his explanation. What something does is not the same as that it exists. Aquinas points out that all beings, including spiritual beings and heavenly bodies, have both being (*esse*) and a way of being (*essentia*). All such beings must be caused.

Aquinas was seeking a way to understand created being by using Aristotelian metaphysics, which had been translated into Latin perhaps only fifty years before Aquinas was born, when Spanish scholars translated the text from Arabic versions. Aristotle had enormous prestige throughout the Middle Ages, and Aquinas wanted to use Aristotle critically. That is, provided the Aristotelian arguments were compelling for Aquinas, the "givens" of Aristotelian philosophy could be transformed to explain how a free creator is possible.

Expressed in a way that elucidates a point to be made later, the *being* that Aristotle took to characterize substance must become for Aquinas an *esse ad creatorem* (an existing in relation to the creator). This is another way of saying that "all things other than God are not their own existence." For Aquinas this must be true in the radical sense that creatures receive their *esse* from God. It must also be true in the more attenuated sense that their being (*esse*) is not their own, in the sense of belonging to them by right or by being the kind of thing (*essentia*) they are. (Aristotle's view was that necessary beings had their own *essentia*.) Everything other than God receives its being from the creator as a gift. Yet such derived or participated things are no less real than Aristotle's substances, since for all beings there is no other way to be, except to participate in the *ipsum esse* of the creator. So the nature of the creating act depends crucially on our conception of the One (*ipsum esse*) from whom all that is (individual *esses*, so to speak) comes.

The One (God) is most properly identified simply as "He who is" (*Esse*). What God does (his *essentia*) is exist or be (*esse*). For God, essence and existence (*essentia et esse*) are the same, and this is true for nobody and nothing else. God is unique in being, unlike any other being. In view of this, the characteristic act of the One is "to produce existence [*esse*] absolutely . . . which belongs to the meaning of creation," defined as "the emanation of the whole of being from a universal cause" or "universal being" (I, 13, 11; I, 3, 4; I, 45, 5; I, 45, 1; I, 45, 4, ad. 1). The proper effect of the One (or Being or *Esse*) is the very existence of things (I, 45, 5).

For Aquinas, one implication of this unique form of causation is that "creation is not a change, except merely according to our way of understanding, [since] creation, whereby the entire substance of things is produced, does not allow of some common subject now different from what it was before, except according to our way of understanding, which conceives an object as first not existing at all and afterwards as existing" (I, 45, 2, ad. 2).

So creating is not a process answering the question *How* does God create? God creates intentionally, that is, by intellect and will, though these are identical in God. Because of the simplicity and unity in God's creating, Aquinas has no difficulty adopting the metaphor of emanation to convey something of the act of creation. God consents to the universe coming forth from God, the One whose essence is simply to-be (I, 19, 4, ad. 4).

The revelation of God's inner life as Father, Son, and Spirit allows Aquinas to say more, while respecting the absence of process or development in God. For it is *divine* revelation that directs us to "the right idea of creation. The fact of saying that God made all things by His Word excludes the error of those who say that God produced things by necessity" (I, 32, 1, ad. 3). The act of creating is not a mere overflow (or emanation) from this One whose very nature is to-be. It is rather an intentional emanating and so a gracious gift. Yet the mode of action remains utterly consonant with the divine nature, hence the natural metaphor of emanation.

The other metaphor invoked by Aquinas is that of the artisan: "God's knowledge is the cause of things; for God's knowledge stands to all created things as the artist's to his products." The implication is that "natural things are suspended between God's [practical] knowledge and our [speculative] knowledge" (I, 14, 8, and ad 3). The deft way Aquinas employs Aristotle's distinction between *practical* and *speculative* knowing here allows him to utilize the metaphor of artisan critically, and so avoid pitting divine and human knowing against one another.

God causes free beings, such as men and women, to exist. Since God's knowing brings things into being and sustains them, we need not worry whether God's knowing "what will have happened" determines future contingent events. God's knowing "what will have taken place" is not propositional in character. God knows what God does; the model is practical knowing.

For the sake of our students, who fret about how God can already know what a free person has not yet decided to do, it is helpful to take a cue from Aquinas's strategy regarding God's practical knowledge of singulars. God's divine knowledge extends as far as divine activity, for God does not work mindlessly. We can have no more determinate model for divine knowing than this.[14]

The artisan metaphor for creation might lead one to suspect that the product could subsist without any further action on the part of its maker. To correct this false impression, emanation is needed to remind us how Aquinas has radically changed Aristotle's schema by introducing a creator and the act of creation. The very being (*esse*) of creatures is now an *esse-ad*, "a relation to the creator as the origin of its existence" (I, 45, 3). Aristotle's definition of substance as "what subsists in itself" can still function to distinguish substance from accident. But now the being (*esse*) inherent in created substances proceeds from another. This other is the source of all being who alone subsists eternally as the One whose essence is to-be.

Because Aquinas introduces being (*esse*), substances must now be denominated "created substances." Since individual beings can exist only in relation to God (*Esse*), the four causes Aristotle uses are no longer sufficient to understand the situation of created substances. The causes used by Aristotle are efficient, final, formal, and material. The two primary contenders to explain activity by created substances are efficient and final causes. They fail, however, since an efficient cause without something to work on would be unintelligible to Aristotle, while trying to fit the creator into Aristotle's formal cause would directly foster pantheism, as Aquinas notes (I, 3, 8). So a "cause of being" must be *sui generis*, as we shall see, confirming "the distinction" of creator from creation.

Each created substance enjoys a "non-reciprocal relation of dependence," which is also a unique type of relation, best characterized by the borrowed expression *nonduality*.[15] The practical knowing involved in God's creating will be more like *doing* than *making*. This suggests James Ross's prescient image of the "being of the cosmos like a song on the breath of a singer," although it is important to emphasize that "God's causing being can be analogous to many diverse things without ever possibly being the same as any one of them."[16]

FREE CREATION AND GOODNESS

The previous discussion reveals the philosophical thickets into which the assertion of faith that God freely creates the universe can lead us. And rightly so, since that affirmation grounds Christianity and all other Abrahamic faiths. Indeed both al-Ghazali and Moses Maimonides staunchly resisted allowing any necessity into creation. In their time emanation proceeded almost automatically from the Creator, and they rejected this. They worried that creation by necessity would preclude the very possibility of revelation. Nothing short of a free creation can ground a free revelation, and with it, a free human response to the One from whom all that is comes forth.[17]

Aquinas also enlists Neoplatonism to offer a philosophically coherent account of the creator as the One causing being, allowing him to insist that "the proper effect of the first and most universal cause, which is God, is existence itself (*ipsum esse*)" (I, 45, 5). Yet because creation comes about through an agent thoroughly intentional and free, Aquinas also insists that "what God principally intends in created things is that form which consists in 'the good of order of the universe' (*bonum ordinis universi*)" (I, 49, 2).

In the Aristotelian system, all substances consist of matter and form. Calling the "good of order of the universe" a "form" is an accommodation to Aristotelian terminology, as is calling the creator "the efficient cause of all being" (I, 44, 1). Yet the stretch of concepts must begin somewhere. In Aquinas one notices the transformation of concepts in the ways he employs these concepts; his use of language is what counts.

Language has its own dynamics. In Aquinas, mention of "good" invites a discussion of "evil," and his section on the distinction of creatures concludes with an illuminating discussion of "the distinction between good and evil." Using his normal method of raising objections to his ultimate position, Aquinas confronts the Manichaean argument "We should postulate some supreme evil which of itself is the cause of evils [since were one to] allege that evil has an indirect cause merely, not a direct cause, ... it would follow that evil would crop up rarely, not frequently, as it in fact does" (I, 49, 3, obj. 5; I, 48–9). His response is forthright:

> As for the reference to evil being present in the majority of cases (*in pluribus*), it is simply untrue. For things subject to generation and decay, in which alone we experience physical evil, compose but a small part of the whole universe, and besides, defects of nature are minority occurrences in any species. They seem to be in a majority only among human beings. For what appears good for them as creatures of sense is not simply good for them as human, that is

as reasonable beings; in fact most of them follow after sense, rather than intelligence. (I, 49, 3, ad. 5)

This sharp exchange can be parsed as Aquinas countering the claim that there is more evil than good in the universe by means of a distinction. Despite cataclysms, miscarriages, and other "defects of nature" in the natural world, there is manifestly more "physical" good than evil in creation. Here his faith perspective is reinforced by his Aristotelian cosmology, as it would be buttressed even more by the intricacies unveiled by modern science.

The human world, however, reflects the opposite state of affairs, to which Aquinas assigns a cause here, which he explores later in the *Summa Theologiae* (I–II, 77, 85). What might well startle us, however, is the matter-of-fact assertion that our human, cultural world displays more evil than good. He would have had no truck with modernity's claim about human perfectibility, so he hardly needed the chastening of the twentieth century to disabuse him. However, he did feel the need to account for our role in systematically distorting creation. Our experience with the way claims of human perfectibility have distorted the natural environment of humans could expand exponentially on his. Yet ironically, the hubris peculiar to humans can in part be traced to his quaint earlier claim that "things subject to generation and decay... compose but a small part of the whole universe."

Our modern culture does not recognize various forms of nonhuman intelligence and is loath to acknowledge restrictions on human freedom. But such a universe bereft of limits and intelligences, whether they be identified as heavenly bodies or as angels, can only position unrestricted human beings at its pinnacle. This leads us to interpret the mandate in Genesis "to increase and multiply and subdue the earth" as licensing us to transform the natural world to serve our needs. Aquinas's lapidary explanation for this propensity of ours, that most of us "follow after sense rather than intelligence," recalls the "good of order of the universe." Aquinas also notes that the human tendency to acquiesce to the senses rather than follow the lead of the intellect contravenes our given nature, since "what appears good for them as creatures of sense is not simply good for them as human."

Aquinas is trenchantly realistic. Part of his realism is that he also understands the glory of man and woman, and he depicts a marvelous picture of the universe. Humanity is firmly placed by God within the "good order of the universe," not merely within the good order of human society. Included in a vast world of nature, humans dwell at the point where the material and the spiritual dimensions of that universe intersect. An awesome picture indeed. Much of this Aquinas could glean from his Aristotelian cosmology. However, humans as resulting from a free act of God's creation and as participating in the being of God are insights only available through faith.

As we have seen, an arresting feature of Aquinas's account is the way he links *being* with *good*. Here we need to turn to the celebrated *Liber de causis*, an Islamic adaptation of Proclus, published in Arabic as *al-kitab al-Khaîr* (Book of the Pure Good), on which Aquinas commented.[18] Aquinas found in this manifestly Neoplatonic text an idiom for expounding the elusive category of "cause of being" to explicate the act of creation.

A good way to pose the central question is this: How is it that the One, whose proper effect is things' very being, effects that? Proclus says, "The first cause infuses all things with a single infusion, for it infuses things under the aspect (*sub rationem*) of the good." Aquinas concurs, reminding us that it had already been shown that "the first cause acts through its being, ... hence it does not act through any additional relation or disposition through which it would be adapted to and mixed with things." Moreover "because the first cause acts through its being, it must rule things in one manner, for it rules things according to the way it acts." The following Proposition 21 links this "sufficiency of God to rule" with divine simpleness, "since God is simple in the first and greatest degree as having his whole goodness in a oneness that is most perfect."[19] Hence Proposition 23 can assert, "What is essentially act and goodness, namely, God, essentially and originally communicates his goodness to things."

With such a One there can be no anxiety about control. The simile the proposition on divine rule elicits is that "it is proper for a ruler to lead those that are ruled to their appropriate end, which is the good." Thus to "infuse things under the aspect of the good" is precisely to bring all things to be in a certain order, inherent in their very existing. This means there is nothing "external" about divine providence, no imposition by God. God freely creates and humans freely act. Indeed the initial diversity comes from the first cause, who "produces the diverse grades of things for the completion of the universe. But in the action of ruling...the diversity of reception is according to the diversity of the recipients."[20]

Original order comes from the One, and in ruling "effortlessly" the One adapts itself to the order established in creating. Another way to express this is that the creator, in acting, always acts as creator. According to Aquinas, *creating* and *conserving* are the same action, differing only in that conserving presupposes things present. This perspective eliminates any putative conundrum about God compelling free human beings to do things.

The One (or God or Being) does not have a *manner* of acting, since he does not have a "disposition." The best we can do is to remind ourselves that Being ever acts by constituting the order that inheres in each existing thing, in the measure that it is. Since order is a consummately analogous term, we can never be sure we have detected the originating divine order in things. We can be sure that such an order exists and that it is inscribed in the very being of things. However, we may be uncertain about specific aspects of the order for certain animals or things. But we can use our intellect to discover more. Crude classifications—such as inanimate, animate, intentional—can be supplemented by refined mathematical structures and symmetries (as in DNA). Each stage of inquiry or analytic tool serves our innate desire to unveil the activity present in these infused "goodnesses" that constitute our universe. Moreover to grasp something of that constitutive ordering is to come closer to its source, "because every knowing substance, insofar as it has being more perfectly, knows both the first cause and the infusion of its goodness more perfectly, and the more it receives and knows this, the more it takes delight in it, [so] it follows that the closer something is to the first cause the more it takes delight in it" (*De Causis*, 130 (116), 138 (123)).

Indeed every intellectual inquiry that seeks to understand, and so to some extent unify, what we encounter—from scientific to anthropological study—is probing this pervasive *goodness* as the creator's legacy. Understood in the context of a loving creator, every academic discipline explores the manifold ways in which God's goodness is revealed in creation.

All is not light or delight, of course, because we cannot hope to *know* "the first cause and the infusion of goodness." Indeed the most important thing we can know about the first cause is that it surpasses all our knowledge and power of expression: "our intellect can grasp only that which has a *quiddity* participating in 'to-be' [while] the *quiddity* of God is 'to-be itself.'" This is why Aquinas concurs that "the first cause [*Esse*] is above being, inasmuch as it is itself infinite 'to-be.'" Yet "what belong to higher things are present in lower things according to some kind of participation." Therefore, we can be said to share, as beings, in this inaccessible One.[21]

CREATOR AND CREATURES: A NONDUALITY

What Aquinas explores finds resonance in other ancient cultures. In an Indian framework, Sara Grant explores the relationship between the eternal Self and what appears to be non-Self:

In India as in Greece, the ultimate question must always be that of the relation between the supreme unchanging Reality and the world of coming-to-be and passing away, the eternal Self and what appears as non-Self, and no epistemology can stand secure as long as this question remains unanswered....A systematic study of Sankara's use of relational terms made it quite clear to me that he agrees with St. Thomas Aquinas in regarding the relation between creation and the ultimate Source of all being as a *non-reciprocal dependence relation*; i.e., a relation in which subsistent effect or "relative absolute" is *dependent on its cause for its very existence as a subsistent entity*, whereas the cause is *in no way dependent on the effect for its subsistence*, though there is a *necessary logical relation between cause and effect*; i.e., a relation which is *perceived by the mind* when it reflects on the implications of the existence of the cosmos.[22]

Her final observation about a "necessary logical relation" is quite compatible with regarding creating as a free action of the creator. Its import is intended to capture Aquinas's identification of "creation in the creature [as] nothing other than a relation of sorts to the creator as the principle of its existing."[23]

The very existence (*esse*) of a creature is an *esse-ad*, an existing that is a relation to its source. Since the Other is the cause of being, each thing that exists-to the creator also exists in itself. That is, derived existence is no less substantial when it is derived from the One-who-is. Every individual being exists as a being-to as well as in itself. Because the individual being exists in itself, it can be examined without taking note of its being-to. That is, one can talk about existing things without explicitly referring to their source because their *esse-ad*, being-to, does not appear. This simply reminds us how unique a nonreciprocal relation of dependence must be; it characterizes one relation only, that of creatures to creator.

If creator and creature were distinct from each other in an ordinary way, the relation, even one of dependence, would have to be reciprocal. For example, a child depends on parents, and this characterizes the relationship for both parents and child. But God is Being itself and is complete in Himself; he has no relationship with humans, although they have an *esse-ad* relationship to him. This nonreciprocal relationship might suggest that God is remote and uncaring, but as we shall see, the opposite is the case.

The One must cause in such a way as to be present in each creature as that to which the creature is oriented in its very existing. In that sense, this One cannot be considered as *other* than what it creates in an ordinary sense of that term. Similarly the creature's *esse-ad* assures that it cannot *be* separately from its source.[24] Every individual participates in One. This is the obverse of pantheism, which sees the One contained in individual beings. Indeed to avoid such infelicities of imagination Grant has recourse to Sankara's sophisticated notion of nonduality to call our attention in an arresting way to the utter uniqueness of the "distinction" that must indeed hold between creator and creation but that cannot be pictured in any contrastive manner.[25]

As we have seen, Aquinas does not feel any compunction at defining creation as the "emanation of all of being from its universal cause [*emanatio totius entis a causa universali*]."[26] Indeed once he had emptied the emanation scheme of any mediating role, he could find no better way of marking the uniqueness of the causal relation of creation than using the term *emanation* to articulate it.[27] Once the scheme has been gutted and confined to communicating *esse*, the creator is not imagined over against the universe. The One is not an entity exercising efficient causality on anything-that-is, in a manner parallel to causation within the universe.[28]

Yet as Grant has underscored, the intimacy of the creator-creature relation means that we need not search for the God who sustains us; we need only learn how to "sink into" the sustaining activity of the One who creates us freely so, out of nothing other than love. In time and with practice, prayer can become a connatural posture of resting in the One who sustains us. That will be our way of exercising the "being toward the creator" that we can now recognize as our very being, an existence conceived gratuitously and sustained lovingly. Indeed once we appreciate the gratuitous origin of our very being, prayer emerges as spontaneous gratitude.

While the all-important "distinction" preserves God's freedom in creating, which the emanation scheme invariably finesses, we must nevertheless be wary of picturing that distinction in a fashion that assimilates the creator to another item within the universe. Harm Goris has shown that close attention to the uniqueness of the creator-creature relation, with its attendant corollary of participation as a way of articulating this *sui generis* causal relation, can neutralize many of the conundrums that fascinate philosophers of religion.[29]

CONCLUSION

Although it may seem that invoking Sankara's hybrid term of nonduality strays far from Aquinas, in fact nonduality is genuinely Thomist. Aquinas helped himself to various ways of expressing the inexpressible: the "distinction" as well as the "relation" between creatures and their creator. Both prove to be foundational to any attempt to grasp our transcendent origins as gift. Bible and Qur'an conspire to highlight the creator's freedom; philosophy proves helpful in finding ways to think both creature and creator together.

NOTES

1. See commentaries in *Restoring Faith in Reason: A New Translation of the Encyclical Letter Faith and Reason of Pope John Paul II*, edited by Laurence Paul Hemming and Susan Frank Parsons (London: SCM Press, 2002), as well as my "Philosophy" in Gareth Jones, ed., *Blackwell Companion to Modern Theology* (Oxford: Blackwell, 2004), 34–46.

2. *Aeterni Patris* is available on the Vatican's website, www.vatican.va/holy_father/leo_xiii/encyclicals/documents/hf_l-xiii_enc_04081879_aeterni-patris_en.html.

3. Josef Pieper, "The Negative Element in the Philosophy of St. Thomas," in *The Silence of St. Thomas: Three Essays* (1957; South Bend, Ind.: St. Augustine's Press, 2002).

4. The theology of Aquinas was definitely not "modernist" in the sense of Pius X's *Pascendi*.

5. Thomas Hibbs, *Aquinas, Ethics, and Philosophy of Religion: Metaphysics and Practice* (Bloomington: University of Indiana Press, 2007).

6. Oliver-Thomas Vénard, *Litterature et theologie: Une saison en enfer* (Geneva: Ad Solem, 2002); Oliver-Thomas Vénard, *La langue de l'ineffable: Essai sur le fondement théologique de la métaphysique* (Geneva: Ad Solem, 2004).

7. David Burrell, *Aquinas: God and Action* (Scranton, Pa.: Scranton University Press, 2009).

8. Our semester break at Notre Dame neatly demarcated "ancient" from "medieval," so over the break I asked students in my course to read Genesis 1–3, an easy assignment!

9. I have elaborated this intercultural exchange more fully in David Burrell, *Knowing the Unknowable God* (Notre Dame, Ind.: University of Notre Dame Press, 1986).

10. Hemming and Parsons, *Restoring Faith in Reason,* 115.

11. Robert Sokolowski, *God of Faith and Reason* (Washington, DC: Catholic University of America Press, 1995), 34–6. For a dramatic account of the sinuous journey to Chalcedon, see Thomas Weinandy, *Does God Change?* (Still River, Mass.: St. Bede's, 1985).

12. Sokolowski, *God of Faith and Reason,* 37.

13. For an explicitly interfaith appraisal, see the articles in David B. Burrell and Bernard McGinn, eds., *God and Creation* (Notre Dame, Ind.: University of Notre Dame Press, 1990). For a narrative sketch of the interaction among the chief medieval protagonists, see Burrell, *Knowing the Unknowable God;* David Burrell, *Freedom and Creation in Three Traditions* (Notre Dame, Ind.: University of Notre Dame Press, 1993).

14. St. Thomas Aquinas, *Summa Theologiae,* I, 14, 11. See Burrell, *Freedom and Creation,* 105–19 n11 for my extended treatment of these issues.

15. See Sara Grant's comparative study of Aquinas and Sankara for this creative proposal to find a positive way to express the relation attendant upon "the distinction": *Towards an Alternative Theology: Confessions of a Non-dualist Christian* (Notre Dame, Ind.: University of Notre Dame Press, 2002).

16. James Ross, "Creation II," in *The Existence and Nature of God,* ed. Alfred Freddoso (Notre Dame, Ind.: University of Notre Dame Press, 1983), 128.

17. This is the burden of Burrell, *Freedom and Creation,* n11.

18. Proclus was a fifth-century AD Greek Neoplatonist. For an annotated English translation of the commentary, see Vincent Gualiardo, Charles Hess, and Richard Taylor, eds., trans., *Commentary of the Book of Causes* (Washington, DC: Catholic University of America Press, 1996).

19. *De Causis,* 123 (110), 123–4 (111), 134 (111), 125 (112), 126 (113).

20. *De Causis,* 134 (118), 137 (122), 137 (123).

21. *De Causis,* 51 (47), 52 (43), 52 (17), 51 (47), 30 (17).

22. Grant, *Towards an Alternative Theology*, 39–40.

23. St. Thomas Aquinas, *Summa Theologiae*, I, 45, 3.

24. See my exchange with Tom Flint in Burrell, *Freedom and Creation*, 112, especially n33.

25. Kathryn Tanner develops a sense of transcendence that is expressly "noncontrastive," illustrating that suggestive category through the history of some key questions in philosophical theology: *God and Creation in Christian Theology* (Oxford: Blackwell, 1988).

26. St. Thomas Aquinas, *Summa Theologiae*, I, 45, 1.

27. See Burrell, *Knowing the Unknowable God*, 86–91.

28. As in William Hasker's treatment of the issues in *God, Time, and Knowledge* (Ithaca, N.Y.: Cornell University Press, 1989).

29. Harm Goris, *Free Creatures of an Eternal God* (Leuven, Belgium: Peeters, 1996).

SELECTED READINGS

Hadot, Pierre. *What Is Philosophy*? Cambridge, Mass.: Harvard University Press, 2003.

Kerr, Fergus. *After Aquinas: Versions of Thomism*. Oxford: Blackwell, 2002.

Rocca, Gregory. *Speaking the Incomprehensible God: Thomas Aquinas and the Interplay of Positive and Negative theology*. Washington, DC: Catholic University of America Press, 2004.

Sokolowski, Robert. *God of Faith and Reason*. Washington, DC: Catholic University of America Press, 1996.

Wisnovsky, Robert. *Avicenna's Metaphysics in Context*. Ithaca, N.Y.: Cornell University Press, 2003.

PART TWO

The Catholic Intellectual Tradition
in the Humanities

"Poems...become stepping stones in one's slow pilgrimage...small Virgils leading the soul's Dante around the spiral of hell and paradise."
—DENISE LEVERTOV, "Poetry, Prophecy, Survival."

6

Poetry and Catholic Themes

Angela Alaimo O'Donnell

THE POETIC AND the religious have long been considered analogous impulses of the human imagination. Both involve the use of finite methods and materials to gesture toward the infinite. Both entail the attempt of human beings to articulate what cannot be understood purely through the exercise of our considerable powers of reason. Both require the creation and employment of language that is but half understood, full of the possibilities of analogy and metaphor, rife with implication and ambiguity, singularity and multiplicity, play and paradox—yet invested with a power and authority that commands attention and assent. Both bring us into the presence of mystery and require us to dwell there a while without "irritable reaching after fact and reason," a state of intellectual and spiritual being described by Keats as "negative capability,"[1] and one essential to the engagement of the transcendent.

This ancient association between the poetic and the religious is a fortunate circumstance for the professor and student of literature in a Catholic university. Faculty teaching poetry in Catholic institutions are likely to discover the degree to which the engagement of art and the leap of faith are mirror images of one another. They in turn may lead their students to the realization that the parallel paths of faith and art may, paradoxically, meet.

Poetry, often subsumed under the category of English or literature, is one of several academic disciplines that form the core curriculum of most Catholic colleges and universities, yet it exists in a fundamentally different relationship to other academic majors. While the disciplines of the liberal arts, including history, philosophy, theology, and the sciences, each represent a body of knowledge and a vantage point from which to view and understand the cosmos and our place in it, poetry constitutes a distinctive *mode* of perceiving, articulating, and knowing. In fact it is a disposition or a *way of being* in the world, and, as such, is a particular challenge to master and to teach. Though a student may acquire the terminology to describe, analyze, and evaluate a poem, may read and memorize the work of exemplary poets, and may learn the various periods of literary history along with the theories and practitioners of poetry that flourished therein, an understanding of poetry itself—*how* poetry means in addition to *what* poetry means, in the words of John Ciardi—is a much rarer and more elusive accomplishment.[2] In his essay "The Figure a Poem Makes," Robert Frost describes this tension between poetry and scholarship:

> Scholars and artists thrown together are often annoyed at the puzzle of where they differ. Both work from knowledge; but I suspect they differ most importantly in the way their knowledge is come by. Scholars get theirs with conscientious thoroughness along projected lines of logic; poets theirs cavalierly and as it happens in and out of books. They stick to nothing deliberately, but let what will stick to them like burrs where they walk in the fields. No acquirement is on assignment, or even self-assignment. Knowledge of the second kind is much more available in the wild free ways of wit and art.[3]

Frost's description of the poet's unsystematic approach to acquiring knowledge (characteristically cavalier as it is) suggests one reason that poetry is, in some ways, subversive of the more conventionally academic disciplines in the curriculum. Comprehending *how* poetry means requires its reader to think like a poet rather than like a scholar, to deviate from the straight rule of logic that has been imposed upon the student from his earliest years of schooling and follow the more intuitive, associative, and involuntary inclinations of the human mind. It requires an engagement that goes beyond the intellectual, one that is imaginative and spiritual in nature. It requires a giving over of the self, a surrendering of the habitual certainties about language, about the world, and about ourselves that make the terrain of our daily lives familiar and safe. In fact it requires an acquiescence to commence a journey that will take the reader to a place he or she hasn't been.

Denise Levertov, a poet who began her long career as an agnostic but who gradually came to faith and finally converted to Roman Catholicism late in life, credits the practice of poetry with her spiritual transformation. Like Dante, whose *Divine*

Comedy depicts his own personal spiritual journey from darkness toward enlightenment, Levertov looks back at the pattern of her pilgrimage to find that poetry has served as both her pathway and her guide from the desolation of doubt toward the consolation of belief.

Seen in the light of Levertov's theologically charged image, poetry makes powerful claims upon us, both as writers and readers. It is a radical call to play a role in our own salvation history, a call analogous to the angel Gabriel's invitation to Mary at the Annunciation, Christ's call to each of his disciples, "Follow me," and Jesus' call to Lazarus to come out of the cave of death. The destiny the reader or poet is called to may not seem as grand as the one that beckons Mary, Lazarus, and the Twelve, but it nonetheless constitutes a call that comes from beyond the self and promises challenge and change. These are precisely the risks that education and formation at a Catholic university insists each student take: hear the call, accept the challenge, change.

In his powerful meditation on the nexus between art and religion, *Real Presences,* George Steiner confirms the high level of engagement the experience of poetry requires and the effects it produces:

> In a wholly fundamental, pragmatic sense, the poem, the statue, the sonata are not so much read, viewed, or heard as they are *lived.* The encounter with the aesthetic is, together with certain modes of religious and of metaphysical experience, the most "ingressive," transformative summons available to human experiencing. . . . . The shorthand image is that of an Annunciation, of a "terrible beauty" or gravity breaking into the small house of our cautionary being. If we have heard rightly the wing-beat and provocation of that visit, the house is no longer habitable in quite the same way it was before.[4]

Steiner introduces yet another metaphor to describe the effects of the encounter with art, one that connects nicely with Levertov's image of the journey: the small house of our being, no longer habitable after a genuine aesthetic experience, requires the inmate to set out in search of a larger, more capacious place to dwell.

To engage a poem imaginatively requires entering into an experience. Thus each poem issues an open invitation to student and reader. There are, of course, as many invitations as there are poems, and theoretically any good poem will serve to initiate the journey. A number of poems, however, accomplish this task particularly well in a Catholic academic context. These poems constitute an informal canon, a core group of poems that sound religious themes, both subtle and obvious, calling the reader out of a state of ordinary perception. Most important, the poems are grounded in certain metaphysical presuppositions that are foundational to Catholicism and resonant with the broader Judeo-Christian tradition.

Among these presuppositions, four are particularly important. First, creation is graced, albeit deformed by the presence of sin. Second, the physical world is incarnational in the sense that it embodies the immanence of the God who created it. Third, language possesses a unique power to express divine immanence and transcendence. Fourth, the act of making a poem imitates God the creator, thus manifesting one of the primary ways we are made in the image of God. These presuppositions can be expressed in language that is humanistic or theological, but employing the latter allows for engagement of terminology, as well as ideas, grounded in the Catholic tradition.

FINITUDE AND INFINITUDE

A key aspect of poetry that resonates with Catholic tradition is its commitment to giving access to the visionary through the engagement of the real. Poets convey truths that are universal, transcendent, and eternal as they are embodied in the concrete particulars of the ordinary, transient, material world we all inhabit. William Lynch demonstrates this point authoritatively in his study *Christ and Apollo: The Dimensions of the Literary Imagination:* "The first and basic image of the literary imagination is the definite or the finite, and not the infinite, the endless, the dream."[5] Lynch focuses on the Incarnation as the central manifestation of God's presence in the world in the definite, finite person of Jesus Christ. The story of Christ's life is familiar to us in all of its finite detail: his birth to a young Virgin named Mary and her husband, Joseph, in the town of Bethlehem; his thirty-three-year earthly sojourn in the regions of Nazareth, Galilee, and Jerusalem; his baptism and recruitment of disciples; his miraculous ministry of preaching and healing; his betrayal by Judas in the Garden of Gethsemane; his trial and torture at the hands of Pontius Pilate; and his death by crucifixion at Calvary.

This is a life as rife with particularity as our own—full of names and places, location and duration, circumstances of key events such as the wedding at Cana, the storm on the Lake of Galilee, and Christ's conversation with the Samaritan woman at the well. Indeed God is in the details, revealing Himself to us in the the specifics we need to understand any language, the parlance of particularity. Christ Himself spoke the language of the definite, conveying truths about the Kingdom of God in parables and stories of individual people in very particular situations—the Prodigal Son, the Good Samaritan, the woman in search of her lost coin—and in concrete images evident in the natural world: the Kingdom of God is like leaven, like a mustard seed, like a pearl of great price.

Yet in the midst of all this finitude of fact and image is the implied infinitude of promise and possibility. It is through finitude that God expresses His infinitude: the one life of the one Man contains the pattern of all our lives; the single Death redeems all the dead, and the single Resurrection resurrects us all. Thus the word and the image delineate and individuate even as they gesture upward, toward the Infinite and the All. This is precisely how poetry works.

GOD IN ALL THINGS

Among the clearest demonstrations of the complex workings of infinitude in finitude is the work of the Catholic convert and Jesuit poet Gerard Manley Hopkins. Taking his cue from his spiritual mentor, St. Ignatius of Loyola, Hopkins recognizes and celebrates the presence of "God in All Things." For Hopkins, every aspect of creation bears the imprint of its Creator, expressing God's singularity, energy, and sheer delight in the fact of existence. The most seemingly ordinary creatures and objects are fired from within by their own unique identity and purpose, each proclaiming its "inscape" or its this-ness.[6] Every thing is important and worthy of the poet's and the reader's attention for its own sake. But it takes on even greater significance when seen as a means through which God communicates His own boundless being to us. In his sonnet "As Kingfishers Catch Fire," Hopkins articulates this principle of uniqueness in the highly condensed language and fractured syntax characteristic of his work as he attempts to say the unsayable:

> Each mortal thing does one thing and the same:
> Deals out that being indoors each one dwells;
> Selves—goes its self; *myself*, it speaks and spells,
> Crying *What I do is me: For that I came!*[7]

Every object and creature in the material world is endowed by the Creator with a finite form and purpose, and the performance of that purpose is cause for celebration. Yet while the creature is wholly itself, it also bodies forth an aspect of the infinite God who made it. This fact is most evident, the poem reminds us, in human beings, who are made in the image of God:

> For Christ plays in ten thousand places,
> Lovely in limbs, and lovely in eyes not his
> To the Father through the features of men's faces.[8]

Hopkins's devotion to the definite is thus an echo of the infinite God's, and his poems become his means of expressing that principle through finite example after finite example.

In his sonnet "God's Grandeur," Hopkins celebrates the infinitude of God manifested in nature, despite seeming evidence to the contrary, demonstrating the presence of invisible grace in the visibly flawed world.[9] "The world is charged with the grandeur of God," the speaker insists, even as he acknowledges that "all is seared with trade; bleared, smeared with toil; And wears man's smudge and shares man's smell." Though it be hidden from the human eye, "there lives the dearest freshness deep down things." In the concluding lines of the poem, the promise of God's redemption takes the form of a nurturing dove, the traditional image of the Holy Spirit, who "broods" over the "bent" (notably, not "broken") world, incubating the earth and waiting for it to hatch. For Hopkins, the earth's rebirth is as inevitable as resurrection, for all things are possible with God.

Teaching Hopkins's poetry to Catholic students is a revelatory experience. Many of them are familiar with aspects of Catholic spirituality that are foundational to Hopkins's vision, yet few have heard them articulated so vividly, sensually, and imaginatively. Here is a mind that has taken ownership of these articles of faith, internalized them in his heart and fertile imagination, and created a series of linguistic artifacts attesting to the beauty of these beliefs as well as their truth. His joy and wonder are absolute and contagious, giving voice to a simultaneous affirmation of art and faith.

Hopkins's work demonstrates the link between the religious and the poetic both in the content of his poems and in their form. The imaginative vision he creates is of immanence and transcendence, of a finite world charged with infinite significance, all embodied in a language that is entirely unique in English poetic tradition, characterized by his particular and peculiar devotion to a loose and lively poetic line which he describes as "sprung rhythm." He makes heavy use of sonic devices such as assonance, consonance, and alliteration, which produce extraordinary and varied musical effects (euphony, cacophony, and onomatopoeia). His densely textured diction and syntax build lines and stanzas rich with ambiguity, serendipity, and paradox. These very particular qualities of craft and style further demonstrate the operation of finitude in poetry, embodying in their very form the sense the poem conveys.

THE POET AND THE SAINT: A PARADIGM OF PARTICULARITY

In his study *The Analogical Imagination,* David Tracy explores the intricate connections between the religious and the artistic impulse. He does so succinctly in his discussion of the production of "a classic," a work of art that conveys the universal reality of our common human experience compellingly and with great particularity:

> The artist, the thinker, the hero, the saint—who are they, finally, but the finite self radicalized and intensified? The difference between the artist and the rest of us is one of intense degree, not one of kind. The difference is one where the journey of intensification—a journey which most of us fear yet demand—is really undertaken. The journey into particularity in all its finitude and all its striving for the infinite in this particular history in all its effects, personal and cultural, will with the artist be radically embraced. The insistence upon taking the journey of intensification into particularity, if aligned with the luck of talent, the discipline of craftsmanship, and the gift of imagination will yield the possibility of the production of a classic.[10]

Tracy's recognition of the relationship among the artist, the thinker, the hero, and the saint is striking. Their associated modes of living may seem very different, yet he finds in each of these personalities a common pattern. Each and all exhibit the willingness to undertake a journey into personal particularity, to work within the finitude of given circumstances in order to discover fully and intensely their identities, their inscape or this-ness. And in living that finitude fully the artist, the thinker, the hero, and the saint gesture beyond it in acts of infinitude. Christ again is the perfect model of this; embracing his life as Jesus of Nazareth, preacher, healer, and baptized Son of God, in a great symbolic act of art he transforms the finite materials of bread and wine into his own flesh and blood, and thus Himself into infinite Eucharist, capable of feeding and transforming all mankind. The work of the ordinary artist differs from this in degree, not in kind.

Another striking observation in Tracy's analysis is his straightforward listing of the conditions necessary for the artist's work to flourish: the luck of talent, the discipline of craftsmanship, and the gift of imagination. Two of these essentials, talent and imagination, seem to come from outside the artist, unbidden, which lends them a complexity and air of mystery. On the other hand, the discipline of craftsmanship seems simpler because it is a conscious choice on the part of the artist and well within his or her control. It is instructive to explore each of these conditions in conjunction with poems that readily demonstrate their importance to the poets who cultivate them, beginning with the most simple and moving in the direction of the more difficult.

CRAFTSMANSHIP

A key aspect of poetry that invites the reader to undertake or to continue his or her poetic pilgrimage is craft. From our earliest years of infancy and childhood—if we were lucky—adults read and recited nursery rhymes to us, told us folk tales, and sang us songs. Our response to those rhymes and songs was almost certainly sheer delight. Five-year-olds will dance in a ring, repeatedly declaiming the words to "Ring around the Rosie," to the point of exhaustion because they are infatuated with rhythm and rhyme. The first sound we heard in utero was our mother's heart-beat, steady, omnipresent, and absolutely predictable. Once born into the world, that comforting pattern was replaced by the chaos of the world and all its noise. Is it any wonder we spend the rest of our lives in search of rhythm? Why else do we flock to the ocean and take such pleasure in watching as waves pound the beach, hour by hour? Why else do we seek out and listen to music almost obsessively, iPod ear buds in place in case we should have a moment of (relative) silence we can fill? Our bodies operate according to complex patterns of rhythm—inhalation and exhalation, systole and diastole, intake and elimination, waking and sleep—so much so that we might think of ourselves as flesh-and-blood metronomes, each keeping our own good time. Perhaps our incarnational identity as creatures of rhythm is in part responsible for the almost physiological response we have to rhythm and rhyme.

Because it is primarily through the ear that we perceive craft, poetry is consid-ered a sister art to music as well as a kind of music. But unlike in music, the melody and harmony of poetry are created entirely through words, not with notes sounded by a voice or instrumentation. The music of the poem is composed of its rhythms and its rhymes, and it is evident in excellent poetry of every kind, whether formal verse or free. Achieving this music and putting it in the service of meaning requires work on the part of the poet—labor that alternately can seem insurmountable and tedious, compulsive and impossible, a source of pain and a source of delight.

There are many poems and prose pieces that address the subject of craft thoughtfully and well. Among those that work most effectively for students new to poetry is Seamus Heaney's poem "Digging." The poem begins with the poet as a young man sitting at his writing desk, a "squat pen" resting in his hand, or, more precisely, "between [his] finger and [his] thumb." Outside, below his window, his father digs in the garden, ably lifting and heaving the damp, heavy soil on their farm in Northern Ireland. Immediately Heaney sets a scene ripe with dramatic possibility: the young son working primarily with his head, his pen, a symbol of the labors of learning; the father working with his back and his spade, a symbol of rural labor; the young son undertaking work that is solitary and of his own choosing, the father doing the work inherited from his own father and grandfather; the young son viewing the father from a vantage point that is superior both literally and metaphorically, and the father working below, unconscious of his son's presence.

From this beginning, with its promise of elevating mental over manual labor, the speaker takes an unexpected turn. Rather than congratulating himself for his successful avoidance of the well-trodden path, he allows the song and rhythm of his father's digging (musically described as "a clean rasping sound" made when "the spade sinks into gravelly ground") to take him back to childhood memories of his father and grandfather as young men accomplishing their labor with precision and power. The speaker recalls his own smallness beside the larger-than-life figure of his father and acknowledges the pleasurable sensations and results of his work: the "bright edge" of the spade, his father's expert posture described with great precision in words that sing with assonance and consonance—even the potatoes dug from the ground are transformed into beloved objects by the child's sense of wonder. This memory prompts his sudden recognition of the strength and dedication of the generation of men before his father's. Heaney then continues his narration, the events in his memory tinged with rising pride as well as elements of the Celtic tall tale.

The speaker describes his grandfather's work as craft: "nicking" and "slicing neatly" suggest an artist's eye for symmetry and elegance, "heaving sods" suggests the muscle required, and the repetition of "digging" and "down and down" emphasizes his tireless determination to find and claim "the good turf." These are all qualities that the young poet has inherited from his forebears, he discovers, only he finds himself engaged in digging of a different sort.

> The cold smell of potato mold, the squelch and slap
> Of soggy peat, the curt cuts of an edge
> Through living roots awaken in my head.
> But I've no spade to follow men like them.
> Between my finger and my thumb
> The squat pen rests.
> I'll dig with it.[11]

Instead of the "good turf" of Ireland, he digs within his own mind and memory, unearthing what needs to be brought to light, held in the hand, kept as common property by members of the tribe. Heaney often speaks of the importance of communal memory and the role that falls to poets to uncover, articulate, and eternize historical events, people, and circumstances that might be otherwise lost.

The final affirmation that concludes the poem arrives as an epiphany and brings us back full circle in echoing the opening lines, with their emphasis on the pen as image and symbol of his craft. Here Heaney takes ownership of the principle of "this-ness" that his brother poet (and fellow Catholic) Hopkins asserts in "As King-fishers Catch Fire", "What I do is me: for that I came!" He has discovered the gift he is endowed with, along with the finite form and purpose his life's labors are to take and accomplish. Yet equally important is the speaker's recognition that he writes poetry not only because he possesses something that his forbears lacked ("the luck of talent" and "imagination" in Tracy's terms; we might add "an education" to the list as well), but also because he lacks the strength, skill, and grace of "men like them." His "digging," then, is a form of homage to those generations who have made it possible for him to make this radical choice, again in Tracy's terms, to undertake the journey of intensification and reach for infinitude with finite means. It is the discipline of labor and craftsmanship that connects the young man to his forbears in an elemental and essential way. Ultimately the poem speaks to and resonates for all readers, regardless of background, nationality, or personal history. It does so in terms of the universal themes of labor, generational difference, and self-definition and by means of a careful attention to craft that manifests a reverence for the finitude common to us all.

IMAGINATION

The discipline of craft is very often considered antithetical to another essential quality the artist must possess and exercise: imagination. The latter term is associated with the original spark or initial inspiration wherein the idea for the poem or work of art is first conceived. Imagination is seen as a quickening of the mind that comes unbidden from some mysterious source within or outside the self. Craft, on the other hand, is associated with the practical business of technique, habit, and procedure, all of which can be controlled, to some extent, by the exertion of the artist's will. Seen in this way, craft is what must take over after the initial act of imagination occurs.

It is more helpful, however, to think of the shaping process that begins after the initial conception as another phase of the imaginative act that continues indefinitely. Wordsworth, for example, defined poetry as beginning with "the spontaneous overflow of powerful feelings" and ultimately becoming articulation of "emotion recollected in tranquility."[12] The poem originates with impulses so strong they are difficult to communicate, but they cannot become a poem until the poet is able to engage in the rational process of putting words to them. Thus, in the complex process of creation, imagination works in concert with reason, impulse in concert with will.

Even so, it is the initial moment of inspiration that writers and readers alike find fascinating, most likely because of the mystery that surrounds the origins. There are many approaches to this concept, but two poems are especially helpful in enabling students to see the range of possibilities: Denise Levertov's "Caedmon" and Czeslaw Milosz's "*Ars Poetica?*"[13] Both poets are Roman Catholic, Milosz by birth and Levertov by conversion, and, as such, both are conversant with Church teaching and tradition. However, as their poems demonstrate, they engage that tradition in markedly different ways as they attempt to account for the origins of the imagination.

Levertov's poem recounts the key incident in the life of Caedmon, the Anglo-Saxon poet credited with composing "Caedmon's Hymn," one of the earliest extant poems in Old English (ca. 737). The Venerable Bede describes Caedmon's life and the circumstances of the poem's composition in his *Historia Ecclesiastica*.[14] Caedmon, who worked as a herdsman at Whitby Abbey, would sit at table with the monks and laborers as they recited verses and accompanied themselves on the harp. Before the harp was passed to him, Caedmon, being inarticulate and thus incapable of verse, would retire to the barn to sleep among the animals he cared for. According to the story, the sleeping Caedmon was visited one night by a man who urged him to sing of Creation. In the course of the dream he recited his now famous hymn of praise. The following morning Caedmon recalled the poem he had created in his dream and also found he was able to improvise additional lines. His superiors at the monastery regarded his new gift as a commission from God, and Caedmon embarked upon a new life as a vowed religious and as a poet.

Levertov retells this familiar tale, but instead of employing third-person narrative, she creates a dramatic monologue, thus allowing the formerly ineloquent Caedmon to tell his own story and thereby reveal much about the nature of the transformation that occurs within him. The speaker's recounting of the events that forever changed his life is disarmingly simple and homely, yet also musical in its way, entirely appropriate for a former herdsman turned poet. He begins with his sense of isolation from "all others," who seem to speak with a natural grace. Their talk is a means of reinforcing their life together, imaged as a communal dance from which "Clodhopper" Caedmon is excluded by virtue of his clumsiness. Caedmon describes his self-imposed isolation even in the midst of his fellows: "Early I learned to / hunch myself," the unusual inversion of subject and adverb an unconscious expression of his attempts to hide himself, and the word "hunch" foreshadowing the refuge he will seek among the "warm beasts," himself "dumb" among the dumb creatures he considers kin.

Yet Caedmon's life among the animals is not without wonder. Like Hopkins and Heaney, poets who see and celebrate the goodness of the natural world, the speaker perceives the beauty of his fellow barn-dwellers. His description is a blend of sound, tactile sensation, and sight. His is also a knowing vision, one that encompasses both fire and flesh, energy and matter, the light and the darkness:

> I'd see by a twist
> of lit rush the motes
> of gold moving
> from shadow to shadow
> slow in the wake
> of deep untroubled sighs:
> The cows
> munched or stirred or were still.

Though he is like the cows in some ways, and feels he belongs in the barn more than in the mead hall, he knows himself to be radically unlike them as well, an intuition that leads him to the simple yet profound expression of the universal sense of alienation familiar to all human beings: "I / was at home and lonely / both in good measure." Unlike the animals, who rest easy amid the security of the herd, the speaker knows himself to be separated from them, as well as from his own human tribe, and finds this isolation amid unconscious creatures to be a burden. Yet he abides his condition patiently, as if waiting for some intervention.

Caedmon's intervention arrives much as Mary's does in the Annunciation, with the appearance of "the sudden angel" who instantaneously transforms him and his destiny. The "feeble beam" by which Caedmon formerly viewed the barn's dark interior has now become a conflagration, "a forest of torches, feathers of flame, sparks upflying." This line calls attention to itself as the longest in the poem and the most energetic, containing as it does three different descriptions of the same scene. We see and hear the loosening of Caedmon's previously tied tongue in this breathless catalogue of images. In addition, the sudden proliferation of alliteration constitutes an imitation, in small, of the primary formal element and sonic device that characterizes Anglo-Saxon poetry. Most important, the sudden inspiration Caedmon receives is carried not by wind (as is traditional and is also implied in the word *inspiration* itself) but by means of fire. He feels as if his lips have been touched by "the hand of fire" and his tongue "scorched," the latter image suggesting perhaps the tongues of flame that appeared over the heads of Christ's disciples at Pentecost when they received the gift of tongues from the Holy Spirit. The previous image is likely an allusion to the vision of Isaiah wherein an angel touches his lips with burning coals, thus purifying him from his iniquity and enabling him to respond affirmatively to God's call for a new prophet. Like Isaiah before him, Caedmon receives the gift of prophecy, the ability to perceive the truth and to speak it so that others might hear. Levertov thus both narrates and dramatizes the transformative power of the imagination, a gift that can make prophets of ordinary people.

Levertov's poem integrates the religious and the artistic impulse so completely it is impossible to separate them. The gift of imagination comes from a divine source, which changes Caedmon from what he once was and sets him on a new course in life. In the poem's final image, his gift restores him to the human community he once felt separate from and he joins "the ring of the dance."

In marked contrast to Levertov's celebratory vision of the source and workings of the imagination, Milosz offers a darker and more sobering account in his poem "*Ars Poetica?*" The question mark he includes in the title is the first indication of the poet's radical uncertainty about the origins of this supposed gift and its significance. The poem goes on to challenge the view that poetry comes from God:

> In the very essence of poetry there is something indecent:
> a thing is brought forth which we didn't know we had in us,
> so we blink our eyes, as if a tiger had sprung out
> and stood in the light, lashing his tail.
> That's why poetry is rightly said to be dictated by a daimonion,
> though it's an exaggeration to maintain that he must be an angel.

Poems do indeed come from a place beyond the artist's control, but that place seems to be situated inside the self rather than outside. At the same time, Milosz concurs with the tradition that attributes the poetic impulse to a supernatural source, but he revises it in an essential way: poems may come from the Devil as easily as from God, and in fact the former source seems more likely than the latter. Thus the process of writing is less like an Annunciation and more like demonic possession. Milosz's image of the poem as "a tiger . . . lashing its tail" suggests the brute, unpredictable power of the imagination and what it produces, making it as much a cause for terror as for joy. Further his description of what it is like to be a poet borders on the terrifying:

> What reasonable man would like to be a city of demons,
> who behave as if they were at home, speak in many tongues,
> and who, not satisfied with stealing his lips or hand,
> work at changing his destiny for their convenience?

The multitude of voices and languages roiling around inside the poet's mind creates a chaotic, Babel-like image, as opposed to the image of Pentecost implied in Levertov's poem. The "demons" who occupy his imagination have "stolen" his lips. Again this image is very different from the purified lips of Caedmon and Isaiah we encounter in Levertov's work. They have taken his hand as well, rendering the poet a ventriloquist of sorts, mouthing and writing the dictates of not one demon but many. "What reasonable man" indeed would choose such a vocation? Milosz asks. The implied answer, of course, is none, suggesting a divorce between reason and the imagination, confirming a long-held view that poetry provides us with a kind of revelation wildly beyond the purview of science and philosophy and nullifying the possibility of the poet's having a choice in the matter.

Toward the end of the poem, Milosz ventures to articulate the value of the poetic imagination for the artist in possession of it:

> The purpose of poetry is to remind us
> how difficult it is to remain just one person,
> for our house is open, there are no keys in the doors,
> and invisible guests come in and out at will.
> What I'm saying here is not, I agree, poetry,
> as poems should be written rarely and reluctantly,
> under unbearable duress and only with the hope
> that good spirits, not evil ones, choose us for their instrument.

The challenge that the poet faces is one of integrity, despite the disintegrating forces at work both internally and externally. The imagination requires a radical openness that leaves the artist vulnerable to visitation by many spirits. He or she cannot admit only the "good" ones, like the angel who visits Caedmon. To the contrary, the poet is required to be faithful to his vocation, to write (if only "rarely and reluctantly"), to endure the "unbearable duress" that comes with these visitations, and to be hopeful that the "evil" spirits do not choose him as their "instrument." The poem concludes on this ambiguous note, for though the poet asserts the virtue of hope, he also tacitly acknowledges the reality that evil spirits will—and do—occupy the imagination and use him as a means of conveying their dark truths or distortions.

Milosz's sobering view provides a necessary corrective to the mostly celebratory view of the poetic imagination evident in Levertov and Hopkins, for the truth is complex and ultimately mysterious. Milosz has a tragic vision, shaped by his life amid the grim realities of twentieth-century Europe, including World War II and the Holocaust. Is it any wonder he reminds us that poetry must bear witness to suffering, that it must speak of spiritual desolation as well as consolation, in order to be true to human experience? Granted, Hopkins and Levertov also acknowledge human suffering in their poems. Hopkins does so most famously in his "terrible sonnets" that dramatize his own bouts with desolation, and Levertov in her poetry of witness written in response to war. But their characteristic impulse is to emphasize the grace they see in nature, whereas Milosz's tendency is to emphasize the presence of disorder or sin and its consequences. To return to the metaphor of the journey with which this essay begins, the soul on pilgrimage must pass through Hell and Purgatory before it can approach the precincts of Paradise.

THE LUCK OF TALENT

Implicit in both Levertov's and Milosz's depictions of the imagination is the idea that the poet does not choose his or her vocation but is chosen. Poets are marked, somehow set apart from others, and they are aware of their special status. Surely one of the distinguishing marks of the potential poet is talent. Of the trinity of conditions Tracy cites as necessary to the flourishing of a poet, "the luck of talent" is the most foundational and yet the most elusive. The use of the word *luck* suggests that talent is an inheritance, a birthright. It also implies that there is a good deal of chance involved in whether one receives this gift or is aware that one has received it. Unlike craftsmanship and imagination, talent seems to be almost biologically based. It is a condition of one's constitution having to do with the complex operation of the mind and body, as opposed to a discipline one develops with conscious intent or a mysterious visitation that originates outside of and transcends the self.

Talent is typically defined as a capacity or ability to perform a particular task. For the poet, the form this would primarily take is a facility with words—the ability to see, hear, comprehend, and use them in extraordinary and inventive ways. In addition, the poet would need to have an ear attentive to pattern, cadence, and the music words create when placed in relationship to one another.

The word *talent* also has biblical associations, thereby broadening, by means of metaphor, the context within which we might consider it. In the familiar parable Jesus relates to his disciples in Matthew 25:14–30, a master sets out on a journey and entrusts to his three servants a varying number of talents. In this context a talent is a unit of currency representing a significant amount of wealth. When the master returns, he finds that the first two servants invested their talents, doubling their value. The third servant, however, buried the single talent he received. This ensured it would not depreciate, which he feared, but it also ensured it would not increase in value. This parable has been interpreted in Christian tradition as an object lesson for followers of Christ: human beings are obliged to use their God-given gifts, whether material or gifts of the mind and spirit, in the service of the Master. The term *talent* is poetic in the sense that it uses a finite image, a coin, to gesture toward an infinite number of interpretive possibilities. As Tracy implies in his choice of this term, a gift for poetry is among those talents human beings are entrusted with and obliged to use, not bury.

The master in the parable denounces the servant who does not use his talent because he is "wicked and lazy," but also because he is afraid to take risks. As Milosz implies in "*Ars Poetica?*" there is a good deal of risk taking involved in exercising one's talent as a poet. This is where the virtue of hope is indispensable—and one might add the virtues of faith and love as well. Levertov suggests in her image of the poet's pilgrimage toward faith that the journey is made one step—and one poem—at a time; thus "every work of art is an 'act of faith' in the vernacular sense of being a venture into the unknown."[15] To engage in creation is to assert faith in one's talent, in the truth of the imagination, and in the value of one's craft.

In addition, to create is to acknowledge one's love of this gift or discipline and one's love of the world art serves to celebrate. Even given his dark disposition, Milosz acknowledges in his brief poem "Blacksmith Shop" that it is this enchantment with creation, in all of its finite particularity, that underlies and necessitates his own and every artist's work: "I stare and stare. It seems I was called for this: / To glorify things just because they are."[16] The young poet's compulsion to stare at the beauty of the world and to make something beautiful in response leads to this epiphanic moment, the discovery of his vocation, a "calling" to art that is analogous to a religious calling. Vocation entails a total commitment, a giving over of the whole self to the enterprise, yet it is hardly a matter of choice, for the called are chosen, marked by the gift of talent, capaciousness of imagination, and devotion to craft.

POETRY AND SACRAMENT

In his essay "Art and Sacrament," David Jones confirms the strong links forged between the artistic and the religious impulses and demonstrates the connection between the activity of artistic making and sacramental practice. Citing the root definition of the word *religion (religio)* as "that which binds man to God," Jones argues that art in its gesturing toward the infinite is inherently and "inescapably, a 'religious' activity." Grounding his observations in his reading of Aquinas and Jacques Maritain, he asserts the basic identity of man as Maker or Artist, a rational creature who differs from the animals in his possession of reason, volition, and the ability to engage in creating things that are both beautiful and gratuitous. The element of the gratuitous is very important. It sets human making apart from animal making, which is entirely functional and practical. Gratuitousness also allies art with the work of the divine since "the creation of the world was not a necessary, but a gratuitous, act."[17]

In the course of his essay, Jones expands the definition of both *art* and *sacrament*. Art includes not only the poem and the painting, but any object that is created or action that is performed with "significant intent." In other words, art is designed to say something beyond itself. The sign-making activity of artistic creation is of a piece with the sign-making that we typically think of when we hear the word *sacrament*. Sacramental activity engages the transcendent through the use of mundane materials: the priest employs water, chrism, bread and wine, while the artist uses paint, stone, wood, glass, film, ink and paper. Moreover, based on this similarity, Jones enables the reader to see the celebration of the sacraments as a kind of artistic making: the ritual of transubstantiation becomes an artistic act, as God transmutes wine into blood and bread into flesh through the agency of the priest. All sign-making becomes art, according to Jones's theory, and all artists the agents of the Divine, leading him to make the surprising statement "Calvary itself . . . involves *poesis*." This depiction of the crucifixion as art gives us a clear sense of the comprehensive nature of Jones's definitions of the sacramental, of poesis, and of the sacred quality of both. Artistic and religious endeavor become one, all of it manifesting the reality of grace.

THE CATHOLIC IMAGINATION

Though Jones himself is a devout Catholic and an artist, he makes no attempt in his essay to identify an explicitly Catholic imagination or to privilege Catholic artists over others. In fact he prefaces his argument with the statement "There are . . . no such things as the Catholic arts of painting and engraving or the Catholic art of writing prose or poems . . . [any more than there is] a Catholic science of hydraulics, a Catholic vascular system, or a Catholic equilateral triangle." Jones's approach is refreshing and compelling. It is instructive for a poet, teacher, or scholar to trace the similarities evident in the work of Catholic writers, painters, sculptors, and filmmakers. However, the work of Catholic artists also demonstrates great variety, a circumstance that renders claims for a single, monolithic Catholic imagination less and less tenable.

In addition, Jones argues well that all true art is, in some sense, "religious" (in his terms, that it gestures toward the divine). This religious orientation evident in poems and other works of art is often in keeping with the four presuppositions outlined earlier that resonate with Catholic tradition, regardless of a particular artist's practice. One certainly encounters religious poems written by Catholics, but one also finds religious poetry written by poets of other faiths and religious backgrounds, poets who profess no faith at all, and even poets who create art in opposition to institutional religion. Among the latter group is William Blake, a poet who firmly opposed the idea of Church and Creed yet is arguably one of the most profoundly religious writers who ever lived. All of his art is grounded in the belief that "everything that lives is Holy."[18] Few statements ring so true and resonate so thoroughly with Catholic tradition.

Thus teaching poetry in the context of the Catholic tradition entails comprehensive exploration of the small c catholic imagination, an engagement of poetry as a means of understanding and articulating the truths embodied in the finite expressions of the infinite Catholic faith, and a dedication to the process of facilitating the intellectual and spiritual journey students are invited to undertake.

CELEBRATION AND BURIAL: THE PARADOX OF POETRY

Nearly all of the poems and essays I have mentioned were written by Catholics, yet each has experienced Catholicism in a distinctive way: as male or female, religious or lay, cradle Catholic or convert, lapsed or observant. This variety, further evident in their nationalities (English, Irish, Welsh, and Polish), is representative of the diversity that characterizes both the world and the Church. Yet even amid their differences, these poets are united in essential ways: by the presence in their work of the four presuppositions outlined earlier (the goodness of creation, the infinitude of finitude, the power of the word, and creation as imitation of God), by their possession of the three qualities that enable them to flourish in their vocation (imagination, talent, and craft), and by a common devotion to the sacramental identity of art. Regardless of the content of their poems, whether they are writing about overtly religious subjects (Hopkins and Levertov) or writing about seemingly secular subjects in a religious way (Heaney and Milosz), these poets demonstrate their absorption of the Catholic tradition that has in turn informed their imaginations.

One final poem, by the American Catholic Josephine Jacobsen, directly addresses this subject of the sacramental function of art, conveying a vision that is deeply Catholic yet also deeply catholic, and thus singularly accessible to all. Jacobsen, who was a devout practitioner of her faith and daily communicant for most of her long life, was also a poet whose work was much valued by readers unfamiliar with her theological tradition, a fact evidenced by her election to the post of poet laureate. Some of Jacobsen's poems, such as *"Non Sum Dignus"* and "Ballad of the Four Saints," address Catholic subjects and bear clear witness to her religious identity, but she also devoted much of her writing life to finding a language that could communicate the truths she believed to non-Catholic readers as well. The title piece of her collected poems, "In the Crevice of Time," manages that minor miracle. Moving by indirection, the poem engages theological and aesthetic concepts grounded in earthy, anthropological reality. It depicts a prehistoric hunter-priest struggling to comprehend the death of one of his fellows:

> The thick gross early form that made a grave
> said in one gesture, "neither bird nor leaf."
> The news no animal need bear was out:
> The knowledge of death, and time the wicked thief,
> and the prompt monster of foreseeable grief.
> It was the tentative gesture that he gave.[19]

The hunter-priest intuits, quite without the help of theology or philosophy, that human life is different from vegetable or animal life. The sudden, dreadful comprehension of human death, accompanied by the compulsion to make something as a sign of this fresh-felt truth, manifests this special identity as Man becomes Maker before our eyes, demonstrating his kinship with the God he gestures toward but cannot name. Inevitably the reader becomes one with the prehistoric priest as he enacts the sacrament of art:

> In the abyss of time how he is close,
> his art an act of faith, his grave
> an act of art: for all,
> for all, a celebration and a burial.

The grave he makes, like the drawings scrawled on the cave wall, are all "tentative" gestures, sacramental signs that attempt to express the timeless through finite forms that cannot last. The rhythmic repetition of "his" and "for all," along with the powerful resonance of the final rhyme of "all" with "burial," acts as incantation, commands assent, and brings us inexorably into the strange light of that ancient cave. Through an act of imagination we become participants in the ritual "making" that acknowledges and insists upon the meaning of the individual human life even in the face of overwhelming mystery. Art is indeed an "act of faith," manifesting our belief in immortality, and bodies forth, all at once, our hope and our horror, our sorrow and our joy. It is both "celebration" and "burial"—words that describe the Catholic liturgy and its central sacrament, which commemorates both death and life, crucifixion and resurrection, human sin redeemed by the agency of divine Grace.

The language of poetry as used by Jacobsen, as well as by fellow poets Dante, Levertov, Hopkins, Heaney, and Milosz, is perfectly suited to convey the paradoxes of the Catholic tradition and of the art that emerges from it. It is fitting that their poems, conversant with the realms of the sacred and the secular, should serve as Virgils who lead poets and readers alike "around the spiral of hell and paradise," the pilgrimage of paradox we are all blessed to take, simultaneously alone and together.

NOTES

1. John Keats, *The Letters of John Keats,* edited by Hyder Edward Rollins, 2 vols. (Cambridge, Mass: Harvard University Press, 1958), 1:43.

2. John Ciardi, *How Does a Poem Mean?* (Boston: Houghton Mifflin, 1959).

3. Robert Frost, "The Figure a Poem Makes," in *The Collected Prose of Robert Frost,* edited by Mark Richardson (Cambridge, Mass.: Belknap Press, 2008), 132–3.

4. George Steiner, *Real Presences* (Chicago: University of Chicago Press, 1991), 143.

5. William Lynch, *Christ and Apollo* (Wilmington, Del.: ISI Books, 2003), 10.

6. Gerard Manley Hopkins, *The Major Works,* edited by Catherine Phillips (Oxford: Oxford University Press, 2002), 232.

7. Hopkins, *Major Works,* 129.

8. Hopkins, *Major Works,* 129.

9. Hopkins, *Major Works,* 128.

10. David Tracy, *The Analogical Imagination* (New York: Crossroad, 1981), 125.

11. Seamus Heaney, *Opened Ground: Selected Poems, 1966–1996* (New York: Farrar, Straus and Giroux, 1999), 3.

12. William Wordsworth, "Preface to Lyrical Ballads, with Pastoral and Other Poems (1801)," in *William Wordsworth: The Major Works,* edited by Stephen Gill (New York: Oxford University Press, 2000), 611.

13. Denise Levertov, *The Stream and the Sapphire* (New York: New Directions, 1997), 41–2; Czeslaw Milosz, *New and Collected Poems, 1931–2001* (New York: HarperCollins, 2001), 240.

14. Bede, *Ecclesiastical History of the English People* (New York: Oxford University Press, 1994).

15. Denise Levertov, "Work That Enfaiths," in *New and Selected Essays* (New York: New Directions, 1992), 249.

16. Milosz, *New and Collected Poems,* 503.

17. David Jones, "Art and Sacrament," in *Epoch and Artist,* edited by Harman Grisewood (London: Faber and Faber, 1952), 143–79.

18. William Blake, "The Marriage of Heaven and Hell," in *The Complete Poems* (New York: Penguin, 1988), 191.

19. Josephine Jacobsen, *In the Crevice of Time: New and Collected Poems* (Baltimore: Johns Hopkins University Press, 1995), 127.

SELECTED READINGS

Giles, Paul. *American Catholic Arts and Fictions*. Cambridge, UK: Cambridge University Press, 2008.

Greeley, Andrew. *The Catholic Imagination*. Berkeley: University of California Press, 2000.

Labrie, Ross. *The Catholic Imagination in American Literature*. Columbia: University of Missouri Press, 1997.

Lynch, William. *Christ and Apollo*. Wilmington, Del.: ISI Books, 2003.

Reichardt, Mary, ed. *Encyclopedia of Catholic Literature*. Westport, Conn.: Greenwood Press, 2004.

Tracy, David. *The Analogical Imagination*. New York: Crossroad, 1981.

7

Drama and Catholic Themes

Ed Block Jr.

PART OF THE challenge and satisfaction of teaching the Catholic intellectual tradition in literature comes from exploring and integrating developments in theology with literary studies of different genres. This essay uses key terms from Fr. Thomas Rausch's and Dr. Lawrence Cunningham's essays that reveal "some core elements of Catholic theology" together with insights from the dramatic criticism of Hans Urs von Balthasar and applies both to two highly acclaimed and eminently teachable plays: Robert Bolt's 1960 *A Man for All Seasons* and Brian Friel's 1990 *Dancing at Lughnasa*. Adapting Cunningham's view of theology's purpose, we might say that literature reflects imaginatively on both human experience and, analogously, religious experience. I explore human and religious experience in the plays by Bolt and Friel and analyze how these plays address the question Rausch poses: "What is the life that God calls us to?" or, put more simply, What constitutes the "good life"? Before approaching the two plays, however, it is helpful to review a bit of background on dramatic criticism.

By its nature, drama is the most "incarnational" of the literary genres. For its full realization, it needs to be "enfleshed" or "incarnated." That is, it requires literal, physical impersonation of the playwright's characters by live actors and actresses: real human beings, in a genuine space, speaking human language in dialogue, while their bodies move about the stage. Depending on the style and era of the drama, there will be more or less emphasis on historical place and time and on props meant to suggest the real world. Though the play on stage is itself, it is also a metaphor or sign of something beyond itself, something "self-transcending."

THEODRAMA

The late Swiss theologian and literary scholar Hans Urs von Balthasar entitled the second part of his great theological trilogy *Theo-Drama*. In it he argues that from a human and religious perspective, life needs to be understood as a drama of God's action in the world. Von Balthasar's Catholic anthropology is founded on a dialogical model that originates in the mother-child relationship and is related to Martin Buber's insights in *I and Thou*. *Theo-Drama* also emphasizes the tensions that exist between what is personal and what is societal or communal. This leads von Balthasar to highlight the roles we play as individuals and as members of society. He also calls attention to the different "horizons" within which human beings live and act: the finite or horizontal horizon and the infinite or vertical horizon.

The first volume of *Theo-Drama*, subtitled *Prolegomena*, is a long and sophisticated reading of Western drama from its origins to the late twentieth century. In it von Balthasar identifies key concepts and terminology which he then uses to construct a theodramatic theology. Though the book is too long to summarize, a few general insights from that *Prolegomena* are useful in analyzing how elements of the Catholic intellectual tradition play out in Bolt's *A Man for All Seasons* and Friel's *Dancing at Lughnasa*.

Von Balthasar first emphasizes the revelatory nature of drama: "In the theatre [the hu]man [being] attempts to [achieve] a kind of transcendence, endeavoring both to observe and to judge her/his own truth, in virtue of a transformation— through the dialectic of the concealing-revealing mask—by which s/he tries to gain clarity about her/himself. The human being beckons, invites the approach of a revelation about her/himself." Elsewhere he glosses this initial claim, saying, "In and through the temporal 'play' as such we can glimpse (but not seize hold of) an eternal meaning."[1] From a distinctively philosophical perspective he notes:

Nowhere is the character of existence demonstrated more clearly than in stage drama: we are drawn to watch it, and initially it is immaterial whether, in doing so, we are searching for or fleeing from ourselves, immaterial whether the performance is showing us the serious- or the play-dimension, the destructive or the transfiguring aspect, the absurdity or the hidden profundity of our life. Probably nowhere else but in this interplay of relationships (which is of the essence of the theatre) can we see so clearly the questionable nature and ambiguity not only of the theatre but also of existence itself, which the theatre illuminates.[2]

Both "clarity about oneself" and the interplay of relationships have central import in *A Man for All Seasons* and *Dancing at Lughnasa*. This self-knowledge is the "eternal meaning" to which von Balthasar refers. It often takes the form of a sense of wholeness that allows individuals to enter into relationship with God and their neighbor.

Von Balthasar finds particularly Catholic elements in a wide range of plays from the early modern period on. From the early modern period he cites Shakespeare and other Renaissance dramas, particularly the work of Pedro Calderón de la Barca. He has special praise for Calderón's *Three Retributions in One* and *Life Is a Dream*. He also finds Catholic elements in unlikely places throughout the drama of the eighteenth, nineteenth, and early twentieth centuries, from Goethe and Schiller to Ibsen and Shaw, and even in the likes of Bertolt Brecht, Eugene Ionesco, and Albert Camus's stage adaptation of William Faulkner's *Requiem for a Nun*.

In the early twentieth century the Catholic Renascence in France produced such writers as Georges Bernanos, Charles Péguy, and Paul Claudel. Claudel masterfully wove Catholic themes into his works, especially *The Satin Slipper*. Although in most situations it is far too long to produce or even read, *The Satin Slipper* remains a standard against which any Catholic drama may be measured.

Paul Claudel was a diplomat and world traveler whose horizon was nothing less than the terrestrial globe and the vault of heaven. Set in the Golden Age of Spain, the Age of Discovery, *The Satin Slipper* tells the tale of enduring love between Doña Prouheze and Rodrigo. Although Doña Prouheze acknowledges her love for Rodrigo, she refuses his advances. Instead of responding, she hangs her satin slipper on a saint's statue as a symbol of her desire to be holy. Unrequited, Rodrigo goes off to the New World to try to forget his love for Doña Prouheze, while Prouheze returns to her cruel husband, Don Camillo, and a marriage filled with suffering.

Rodrigo spends years in ambitious conquest, digging a canal from the Atlantic to the Pacific. He also attempts to rescue Prouheze from the coast of Africa, where her uncaring husband has imprisoned her. At the end of his life he is a prisoner on a ship run by a Carmelite nun. He is still in love with Doña Prouheze, who has died, and it is this abiding love that purifies Rodrigo's soul before he too dies. The play is full of Catholic pageantry and Catholic themes. Notes of courageous and kenotic love are struck early in the first act, with Rodrigo's Jesuit brother, who dies at sea, but they suffuse the entire play.

In writing *Murder in the Cathedral* and other plays in the 1930s, T. S. Eliot brought verse back to drama. Christopher Fry adopted Eliot's style and some of his sensibility, creating a number of religious dramas, including *A Sleep of Prisoners* and *The Lady's Not for Burning*. In the 1940s the French existentialist philosopher Gabriel Marcel wrote and produced such plays as *A Man of God* and *The Broken World* that placed Catholics in critical decision-making situations. In these works he explored the complexities of belief and relationship. At around the same time in the United States, Thornton Wilder wrote and produced a number of plays, including *Our Town* and *The Skin of Our Teeth*, that were imbued with a Catholic sensibility. Many readers and playgoers also find a Catholic sensibility in the almost nostalgic longing for the blessedness of everyday life implicit in Eugene O'Neill's only acknowledged comedy, *Ah! Wilderness*.[3]

A revival in British drama during the second half of the twentieth century brought to the stage a number of important plays dealing with belief, worship, and damnation. Notable among these are two plays by Peter Shaffer, *Equus* and *Amadeus*. In *Equus* a lonely and troubled adolescent, Alan Strang, fashions a strange religion that allows him to indulge his fascination with horses. The son of an atheist father and an Evangelical Christian mother, Alan devises a religion of Equus that is a complex protest against his parents, particularly their exaggerated responses to the divine. His religion also stands in stark contrast to the vacuity of mid-twentieth-century secular culture. Martin Dysart is Alan's empathetic psychiatrist. A man with an avocational interest in Greek antiquities, Dysart struggles to find meaning in his chosen profession. Even while helping Alan to regain "normalcy," Dysart is ambivalent about what he is doing. He envies Alan's "religion," which valorizes genuine passion and satisfies what Dysart admits is a primal human need for worship. Once he has put Alan on the road to improved mental health, he is haunted by the image and the mystery of Equus. In his final speech Dysart says, "I need...a way of seeing in the dark. What way is this?...*What dark is this?*...I cannot call it ordained of God: I can't get that far. I will however pay it so much homage."[4]

In *Amadeus* Shaffer portrays another "god-haunted" character, Antonio Salieri. Salieri is a contemporary and rival of Wolfgang Amadeus Mozart. While he is envious of Mozart's stunning musical abilities, he is also deeply angry with God for having favored this "spoiled child." The play is confessional in tone and is set at the end of Salieri's life. *Amadeus* dramatizes the many efforts Salieri made to undermine and destroy Mozart's career and the intense envy that fueled those efforts. At the end of his life Salieri rails against a God who could allow such transcendentally beautiful music to come from the likes of a "spiteful, sniggering, conceited, infantine Mozart." He offers a personal defense of sorts at the same time that he angrily accuses God: "Until this day I have pursued virtue with rigor. I have labored long hours to relieve my fellow men. I have worked and worked the talent You allowed me. [*Calling up*] *You know how hard I've worked!* Solely that in the end, in the practice of the art, which alone makes the world comprehensible to me, I might hear Your Voice. And now I do hear it—and it says only one name: MOZART!"[5]

A MAN FOR ALL SEASONS

During this time, Athol Fugard wrote two plays with subtle and compelling religious themes. In both *Sizwe Bansi Is Dead* and *MASTER HAROLD…and the Boys*, Fugard develops the underlying theme of long-suffering, kenotic love. But among these mid-twentieth-century plays, Robert Bolt's 1960 play, *A Man for All Seasons*, stands out. The play is set during several climactic weeks in the life of the martyr St. Thomas More, chancellor to King Henry VIII. Both the play and the later screenplay portray the Catholic sensibility "on trial."[6] The English agnostic Bolt was both a playwright and a popular screenwriter, perhaps best known for his screenplays of *Dr. Zhivago*, *Lawrence of Arabia*, *A Man for All Seasons*, and *The Mission*, a 1986 film about Jesuit "reductions" (missions) in South America during the eighteenth century.

While *A Man for All Seasons* hews close to the historical record,[7] it also develops the complexity of More's character, placing him in a variety of situations that reveal his "clarity about himself" and his courageous response to grace. But the play also starkly reveals the moral, spiritual brokenness or sinfulness of the characters with whom he interacts. Like *The Satin Slipper*, *A Man for All Seasons* maintains a strong sense of what von Balthasar termed the "vertical" horizon. More personifies a Catholic whose God is always present and active in both the private and public realms of his life.

Set in about 1530, when Lutheranism is spreading in England, the play opens at the death of King Henry VIII's chancellor, Cardinal Wolsey. Henry is seeking to have his marriage to Catherine of Aragon dissolved so he can marry his mistress, Anne Boleyn. In order to marry his brother's widow (Catherine of Aragon) in the first place, Henry had sought and received a dispensation from Rome. However, Catherine failed to provide Henry with a male heir, and it is on these grounds that he hopes to receive another dispensation. The death of Wolsey provides an unexpected opportunity to enhance Henry's position with Rome. He appoints his friend, Thomas More, chancellor and assumes that More will give "token acquiescence" to the dissolution of his marriage.

At the time the play takes place, More is at the height of his power, reputation, and influence. A member of Parliament, the author of *Utopia*, an international best-seller, and a friend of the famous, Thomas More is a rock star of his time. His home is an estate on the Thames River in Chelsea, a few miles by boat from London. There he lives, plays, and prays with his family and instructs his children, including his much beloved daughter Meg. On occasion More also welcomes Henry as his guest and entertains him with his witty conversation. When the play opens, More and his family are truly enjoying the good life, or what Cunningham terms the "graced life." Despite the difficulties that mount in the play and eventually envelop these characters, the grace in their lives endures.

The character of Richard Rich provides a dramatic counterpoint to the courage, grace, and self-knowledge we see exemplified in More. Rich is a young would-be courtier who seeks More's patronage and advancement at court. In discussing a bribe he refused, More warns Rich of the opportunities to accept even larger bribes that abound in London. As they converse, Rich begins to display the lack of self-knowledge and moral weakness that ultimately define him. Later in the play he implores More to hire him, but because More understands that such a position would put Rich in moral jeopardy, he refuses. As a way to avoid the temptations of court and public life, More instead urges Rich to accept a teaching position. In the climactic moment of a moving scene, More clearly identifies the weakness of character that Rich is unable to see in himself:

RICH: (desperately) Employ me!
MORE: No!
RICH: (moves swiftly to exit: turns there) I would be steadfast!
MORE: Richard, you couldn't answer for yourself even so far as tonight. (40)

Rich's character is clearly revealed in this scene. But so too is More's concern for a young man seeking his aid.

Henry VIII's secretary, Thomas Cromwell, appears in Bolt's play with a weak character and questionable morality. Cromwell is intensely ambitious. All that matters to him is protecting his position by providing "administrative convenience" for the king. Moral weakness coalesces in the play when Rich accepts an offer from Cromwell that provides a tempting opportunity to advance his career, but at great moral cost.

The crisis of Act I comes when Henry visits More in Chelsea and asks for his support in divorcing the queen. Once the king realizes he cannot persuade More to betray his conscience, the king backs off: "Your conscience is your own affair; but you are my Chancellor! There, you have my word—I'll leave you out of it. But I don't take it kindly, Thomas, and I'll have no opposition" (35).

In the conversations with his family that follow the king's departure, More makes it clear that he will rely on his God-given wits to thread his way through the mounting crisis. He hopes that by combining deft use of the law with silence on the matter of the king's divorce he will be able to save his family and himself.

More's decision to resign the chancellorship is a key scene in Act II. When the Duke of Norfolk announces that all the English bishops except one have accepted the oath of supremacy that makes Henry the head of the Church of England, More prepares to remove his chain of office. This act shows that More has great clarity about himself and how he relates to God. But it also underscores the extent to which he understands and values his relationships with those around him.

At first More asks his wife for help with the chain. Dame Alice fairly fumes, "God's blood and body *no*! Sun and moon, Master More, you're taken for a wise man! Is this wisdom to betray your ability, abandon practice, forget your station and your duty to your kin and behave like a printed book?" (55–56). Rebuffed, More turns to his daughter Meg, who helps him. Speaking up, the Duke of Norfolk says the resignation looks like "cowardice," but More responds that the king has "declared war on the Pope." In Norfolk's response he implies that the pope is just another political leader. More agrees, but says, "He's also the Vicar of God, the descendant of St. Peter, our only link with Christ" (57).

The duke scorns the "tenuous link" with Christ: "You'll forfeit all you've got— which includes the respect of your country—for a theory?" More, ever the lawyer, pauses and ponders. Then he says, "Why, it's a theory, yes; you can't see it; can't touch it; it's a theory. But what matters to me is not whether it's true or not but that I believe it to be true, or rather not that I *believe* it, but that *I* believe it. . . . I trust I make myself obscure?" With obvious irony Norfolk says "Perfectly!" More replies, "That's good. Obscurity's what I have need of now" (57). In this short exchange More demonstrates the depth and the source of his convictions and his integrity. Because his faith is utterly real to him, he is ready to give up all earthly wealth as well as "the respect of [his] country." But he is not eager for death. Rather he hopes to save himself by using his intelligence and knowledge of the law.

A bit later, an exchange with his future son-in-law, Will Roper, further clarifies the nature of More's action. Roper congratulates him, saying, "Sir, you've made a noble gesture" (58). More denies the claim energetically. Thumbing his nose, he says, "*That's* a gesture," and jerking up two fingers, "*That's* a gesture. I'm no street acrobat to make gestures! I'm practical." Roper responds, "You belittle yourself, sir, this was not practical; this was moral!" To which More replies, "Oh now I under-stand you, Will. Morality's not practical. Morality's a gesture. A complicated gesture learned from books—that's what you say, Alice, isn't it? . . . And you, Meg?" His daughter's response might apply to many in the audience as well: "It is, for most of us, Father" (59). More's words demonstrate that resigning his office is a genuine human action, deriving from his self-knowledge and necessitated by principles, conscience, and the reality to which his faith points. He knows his contextualized self and judges himself by his actions.

A short time later More dismisses part of his household because he can no longer afford so many servants. In this scene he once again reveals the clarity of his realism with respect to himself and others. He tells his steward, Matthew, that he will have to cut his wages and asks, "Will you stay?" When Matthew declines, More says, "I shall miss you, Matthew." Matthew demurs, "You never had much time for *me*, sir. You see through me, sir. I know that." But More gently repeats, "I shall miss you, Matthew; I shall miss you" (60).

When More leaves, the steward fumes, "*Miss* me?...What's *in* me for *him* to miss...?" The stage directions are "(*Suddenly he cries out like one who sees a danger at his very feet.*)" He then repeats More's words, "'Matthew, will you kindly take a cut in your wages?' 'No, Sir Thomas, I will not.' That's it and (*fiercely*) that's all of it!" More's expression of genuine love is too much for Matthew to acknowledge. Rather than accept More's love with its pain-filled possibilities, Matthew opts for an exclusively material interpretation that affords the protective emotional response of anger. This strategy is more than familiar to many twenty-first-century readers and audiences, and is similar to how More's family sometimes knowingly misunderstands his motives and actions. Matthew responds in anger, blind to his own self-worth and unable and unwilling to believe the lawyer's honest words of love.

Later More explains to his dear Meg and Roper his strategy for staying out of danger himself. He posits the strategy on the human being's God-given gifts:

God made the *angels* to show him splendour—as he made animals for innocence and plants for their simplicity. But Man he made to serve him wittily, in the tangle of his mind! If he suffers us to fall to such a case that there is no escaping, then we may stand to our tackle as best we can, and yes, Will, then we may clamour like champions...if we have the spittle for it. And no doubt it delights God to see splendour where he only looked for complexity. But it's God's part, not our own, to bring ourselves to that extremity! Our natural business lies in escaping. (78)

More's view of human nature is humble, shrewd, and biblical. In the ordinary course of life, human beings, made in the image and likeness of God, serve God best by using their minds. It is only in meeting an inescapable trial that the human being, More hopes, can measure up to the angels' "splendour." More reminds Roper that "it's God's part" to bring a human being to the "extremity" of confessing his beliefs and embracing martyrdom, if he has "the spittle for it." More cooperates with God's grace in living the good life and in living wisely by his wits. As clouds darken, he prepares to cooperate with God also in death, a task that in his case demands rather stunning moral courage.

In Act II More's fortunes are in decline, and he reveals himself to be cheerful even in poverty (69). He is detached. He says that his prison cell in the Tower of London is like any other place (86). When his daughter urges him to save himself and take the oath "and in your heart think otherwise" (87), More provides a final lesson that reveals both his self-knowledge and the depth of his faith: "When a man takes an oath, Meg, he's holding his own self in his own hands. Like water (*cups hands*) and if he opens his fingers *then*—he needn't hope to find himself again. Some men aren't capable of this, but I'd be loathe to think your father one of them" (87). In a few short sentences More affirms the conscience and selfhood of the individual person. In so doing he reminds the audience of the other characters in the play who "aren't capable of this," in stark contrast to him.

When More is finally brought into court, his final defense of conscience is also a defense of God's primacy in his life. In response to More's reference to "matters of conscience," Cromwell says he is "very used to hear it [the phrase] in the mouths of criminals." More responds with an analogy: "I am used to hear bad men misuse the name of God, yet God exists." He then returns to his defense: "In matters of conscience, the loyal subject is more bounden to be loyal to his conscience than to any other thing" (97). His final rejoinder applies as much in the twenty-first century as it did in an era of despotism: "What you have hunted me for is not my actions, but the thoughts of my heart. It is a long road you have opened. For first men will disclaim their hearts and presently they will have no hearts. God help the people whose Statesmen walk your road" (100).

Rausch observes that salvation is gained "not by fleeing from the world as something evil, but by living lives of faithful discipleship within it." The life of St. Thomas More, as depicted in *A Man for All Seasons*, manifests a very human attempt to lead a life of faithful discipleship even as the storm clouds of crises gather and threaten more and more people.

A Man for All Seasons can easily be read as a drama about how More gave up a temporal "good life" as Lord Chancellor and well-known gentleman of letters for an eternal "good life" with his Creator. More accepted this trade-off because of his conscience and his devotion to God and Church. Rausch reminds us, "Each of us must enter into the mystery of our own lives, in all our weakness and vulnerability, for it is precisely there that God's grace is to be found." In von Balthasar's terms, Bolt's play presents to readers and playgoers the drama of a person whose clarity about himself in relation to God and his fellow human beings is a witness to this "graced life." For More, life is as much graced in witty observations, good friends, esteem in the realm, and a loving family as in death.

DANCING AT LUGHNASA

For von Balthasar, Thornton Wilder's popular 1938 play *Our Town* is paradigmatic in another way that highlights clarity about self and understanding in relationships.[8] For von Balthasar, Wilder's stage manager is an analogy of God. But the character is also an actor who takes part in the action that the play presents. Through his relatively more objective eyes and comments, the audience is able to see how life, human existence, and its meaning unfold. The stage manager enables readers and playgoers greater clarity about themselves to form that sense of wholeness that von Balthasar so values in drama. Six years after *Our Town*, Tennessee Williams uses a narrator, Tom Wingfield, to introduce his memory play, *The Glass Menagerie*.[9] And almost fifty years after that, the dramatic use of the insider/outsider character is further developed by Brian Friel in *Dancing at Lughnasa*.

Friel was a schoolteacher in County Donegal, Ireland, in the 1950s before he began publishing short stories in the *New Yorker*. He also wrote radio plays and stage dramas. Around the time that Bolt wrote *A Man for All Seasons*, the British theatrical giant Sir Tyrone Guthrie invited Friel to work at his Tyrone Guthrie Theater in Minneapolis. From this residency came Friel's first international success, *Philadelphia, Here I Come!* In the next four decades he wrote almost two dozen plays, many of them concerned with Catholic Ireland and the Catholic worldview in which he grew up.

Dancing at Lughnasa (1990) plays deliberate variations on *The Glass Menagerie*.[10] Both are flashback or memory plays. Friel uses his character Michael in the same way Williams uses Tom, as both narrator and character. This external perspective also echoes the role of the stage manager in *Our Town*. In *Dancing at Lughnasa*, however, there is something more; Friel is trying to realize something like a von Balthasarian sense of wholeness that comprehends as it illuminates all of human existence, even its sufferings.

As current theory has pointed out, no artistic choice, especially the choice of narrator, is ideologically neutral. The choice of Michael in *Dancing at Lughnasa* is potentially nostalgic, but it also enables the von Balthasarian perspective. Even though the narrator's role occasionally spoils the suspense, one might view that role as Friel's way of unconsciously "enacting" God's absence and impotence (Rausch). Von Balthasar, and probably Friel, would accept the analogical relation between God (the "creative intelligence" behind the mystery of the universe, according to Rausch) and the artist, playwright, and narrator of the play.

Though *Lughnasa* is a memory play, the narrator stands above as well as within the play's actions. As a grown man, he is only mortal and cannot be completely sure which of his memories are real and which "illusory." But his response, both empathetic and yet detached, invites the audience and reader into a bittersweet sense of wholeness and an active acceptance, if not affirmation, of foggy remembrances. In this process, Friel affirms the power of two fundamental human faculties, memory and imagination, to "real-ize" or at least "re-cognize" the wonder and the marvel, as well as the pain, of our fallen world.[11] In his quasi-objective role, Friel's narrator, like Wilder's stage manager, also makes us aware of the tension between appearance and reality, the ideal and the actual, especially in the characters Kate, Father Jack, and the sisters Rose and Agnes.

As Williams does with *The Glass Menagerie*, Friel sets *Dancing at Lughnasa* at the height of the Depression, on the eve of World War II. Like Williams's play, *Lughnasa* also focuses on a marginalized family with one challenged sibling. Other similarities include period music and dancing, religious allusions, betrayal, and even implicit abuse of a disabled female by a more powerful male, but such comparisons carry us only so far.

The action of *Dancing at Lughnasa* takes place on two afternoons in the late summer of 1938, in and around the Mundy sisters' rural cottage near Ballybeg, County Donegal. The family—Kate, Maggie, Agnes, Rose, and Christina, along with Christina's illegitimate son, Michael—have been surviving on Kate's teaching salary and piecework knitting done by Agnes and Rose. Maggie and Rose also tend chickens, and Rose cares for a pet rooster. As the play opens, the sisters are talking about the annual celebration of Lughnasa, a harvest ritual associated with the ancient Irish god Lugh. Michael is building two kites.

The family's routine life is punctuated by music from a newly purchased radio (dubbed "Marconi"), the recent return of the sisters' brother, Father Jack, from missionary work in Uganda, and, in a climactic moment, the brief reappearance of Michael's father, Gerry Evans. In Act II, a few weeks later, Gerry returns to bid goodbye before leaving for Spain and service in the International Brigade. Rose is absent at the opening of Act II, but reappears after an unexplained tryst in the hills with a married man, Danny Bradley. The play ends with a picnic outside the cottage, during which Gerry and Jack exchange hats in a mock-serious ritual "swap" patterned on Ugandan tribal ceremonies.

Lughnasa, unlike *A Man for All Seasons*, appears to focus primarily on "the events of ordinary human lives," which Rausch tells us mediate God's presence. Like Bolt, however, Friel sets his play in definable historical time, which is an implicitly Catholic acknowledgment of the reality and value of the world.[12] Friel also asserts his objectivity as a playwright by setting the play against a historical and international backdrop. With the apparent inevitability of history, events unfurl: the end of colonialism, the advent of World War II, and the effects of international depression in Ireland.

It would be easy to cast the play as, on one level, a contrast between modernity and an unreflective, historically limited Catholicism of the 1930s. As with many a quality Catholic writer's work, the superficial evidence of Catholicism in *Dancing at Lughnasa* may seem thin and deceiving. Talk of modesty, obscenity, Pope Pius XI, and the pope's views on marriage might invite such a view. But the apparently conventional religiosity of the Mundy sisters stands out precisely because it is set against the pagan practices of the back hills peasant folks and what we learn of the pagan practices in Jack's Ugandan congregation. Even Gerry Evans's unreflective pop superstitions remind us of the place that primitive folk beliefs have in the experience of ordinary people. Thus, on closer scrutiny, we notice a number of similarities among the sisters' religiosity, the festival of Lughnasa, and the Ugandan fertility rituals of the goddess Obi about which Jack speaks. Curiously, all these rituals seek in their own way to affirm, to celebrate life.

The deeper worldview of Catholicism in the play, a world of intrinsic meaning, is taken for granted. This manifests itself in the sisters' love and care for each other, for Christina's child, and for Jack. Even the sisters' cautious charity and somewhat halting hospitality toward Gerry Evans reflects a Catholic worldview. The sisters' Catholicism can also help explain some of the choices they make that give further meaning to their lives. Christina does not leave with Gerry. Rose does not run off with Danny. The sisters care for Jack, trying to understand his attitudes and accept his "otherness."

Because some of the choices made by the family run counter to romantic, easy answers, the whole family and the whole play seem both contradictory and bathed in mystery. Family members avoid modern solutions, such as running off with a lover or treating Jack as the family dunce. But the Catholic culture or motivation is not referenced as a determining factor. One might interpret some of the family members' decisions, such as Agnes's and Rose's decision to leave the family and Ireland, as exile in large part occasioned by forces beyond their control. Or we may see it as self-sacrificial, and ultimately and unintentionally self-destructive.

Rausch observes that we cannot look directly at God.[13] To enable his readers and his audience to see what is not apparent, to see the mystery, Friel uses techniques of indirection. We catch a glimpse of God, or of mystery, out of the corner of our eye, as we would a fox disappearing in the tall grass at the edge of our yard. The celebration of Lughnasa and Jack's experience of Ugandan rituals remind us of the folly of trying to domesticate the divine.[14]

Rausch also refers to the "graced experience" from which all theological language arises. It is tempting to say that Friel, like all artists, seeks to call our attention to such graced experience, allowing us to glimpse the mystery that animates the scene, the situation, and the characters. As critics have noted, an artist like Friel seeks to express, if not "capture," an experience that may be difficult to put into words.[15] Friel seeks to embody the graced experience even as he points to its inevitable dissolution or loss. And what is that graced experience? It is the taste of the good life as experienced fleetingly but palpably by the members of a family in a small cottage in rural Ireland. It is graced because it points beyond itself to the ultimate good life of eternity. Yet behind and within these references to a transcendent reality, the fundamentally sacramental dimension of these people's lives can still be glimpsed.

The play abounds in paradox, reflecting the long-held Catholic belief that creation, including human nature, is, as Rausch reminds us, "both graced and flawed," "a world of damaged relationships" where human nature "under a veneer of civility and self-restraint still possesses those primitive instincts" that include "prejudice against the weak or the different." Another paradox concerns very ordinary features of the play. In *Lughnasa* plot, theme, and spectacle are unexceptional. Of the six classical parts of drama, however, it is music and spectacle that stand out. By giving greater prominence to music and spectacle than is currently fashionable in all but "musical theater," Friel actually achieves thematic complexity.[16] Much of the play's thematic richness as well as its ambiguity are carried by the songs and dancing. Aided by Friel's almost always lyrical prose, the dancing and the music transform other aspects of the play as well.

As might be expected from the title, the play's two acts are highlighted by a number of contrasting dances. After the elder Michael's long opening monologue, the action begins with the child Michael and three of the sisters involved in household tasks. Even in the midst of an ordinary day, primitive instincts are evident. Rose does a "bizarre" and "abandoned" dance as she sings "The King of Abyssinia" while feeding her chickens. Kate returns from shopping to relay the news from Ballybeg. It is here that we learn that the Sweeney boy was severely burned while celebrating Lughnasa. Kate also describes the delight in the eyes of the shop girl Sophia McLaughlin when she tells about the "supreme" Lughnasa dance: "You'd think it was heaven she was talking about" (11). In a very real sense it is. Abandonment to the ritual of the dance allows participation in a joy well beyond the reality of the moment. To Kate, Lughnasa is "like a fever." In her uptightness she seems positively life-denying. But suddenly the radio, "Marconi," starts broadcasting Irish dance music, and, one by one, the sisters get up from their tasks and start to dance.

This first dance in the play is full of ambiguity. Friel's stage directions (referring to "masks," "near hysteria," "parody," "caricature," and "defiance") suggest just some of the possible meanings that a production might emphasize or an audience construe. Maggie's "instant mask" does not conceal her "defiance," "aggression," or "crude mask of happiness." Perhaps a parodic reliving of the past, the dance has overtones of the pagan revelry taking place in the back hills. For Rose it is simple abandonment to the music. For Agnes the dance is a further revelation of her character, specifically her grace. Even for Kate the dance is an evocation or an embodiment "ominous of some deep and true emotion" (22).

Communal and yet personal, public or intensely private, it is probably fair to say that, for each of the characters, the dance has a special meaning. Their communal ritual of dancing together transforms the participants by knitting them together more closely. The ritual of the dance is not religious, but, as is true for a communal religious experience, it symbolizes, affirms, and encourages the participants even if it does not actually constitute solidarity and community.[17]

The first dance ends abruptly with each of the characters returning to her "ordinary self." Immediately the tensions and conflicts that had been suspended by the dancing reappear. But the memory of the ritual and its transformative power lingers. And yet the characters appear intent on denying whatever transcendent reality the dance embodied. Christina calls the radio a "bloody useless set," and this is picked up and exaggerated by Rose's parroting, "Goddam bloody useless" (22). Kate reasserts her authority, and the other sisters offer subtle rejoinders hinting at latent rebellion. It is Maggie who closes the scene by announcing the arrival of Gerry Evans.

Gerry Evans's first visit in thirteen months involves another series of rituals, ending in a second dance. Kate sounds the alarm. Gerry is not welcome; he has abandoned the woman he betrayed, along with the son she bore him, and Kate would have Christina "send him packing" (25). In time, charity—or is it only conventional, class-conscious hospitality?—prevails. Kate says, "Of course ask him in. And give the creature his tea" (25).

Gerry's dance with Christina (33) is formal, decorous, and as significant as the sisters' dance. It has many levels. Kate says, "He's leading her astray again." Maggie remarks, "Look at her face—she's easy led." To Kate, Gerry's "an animal," "a creature," and Christina "a fool." Yet even she admits that in their dancing "they're such a beautiful couple."

In the interplay of ritual and words Friel conveys subtlety and complexity in *Lughnasa*. While dancing with Christina, Gerry asks, "Do you know the words [to the song]?" She responds, "I never know any words." This response advances the play's paradoxical theme of words and wordlessness. Gerry then proposes marriage and Christina refuses, knowing that he would leave her again anyway. There is a sense of fatality in her response: "That's your nature and you can't help yourself" (33). Against his protestations, she says, "No more words. Just dance me down the lane and then you'll leave" (33).

After the dance Gerry leaves, and Jack enters, talking about Uganda, "ancestral spirits" (38), quinine addiction cured by a medicine man, and sacrificial rooster killing. As he tries to find the word ("exhibition," "demonstration," "spectacle"?) for "a sacred and mysterious…ritual killing," the theme of wordlessness or the unspeakable reappears in a new form. A bit later his words underline the fragility of language as he observes, "Coming back [from Uganda] in the boat there were days when I couldn't remember even the simplest words" (40).[18] Still, through the power of language, Jack is able to rename Michael's state. He is not "a child out of wed-lock," but "a love-child": "In Ryanga [his village in Uganda] women are eager to have love-children. The more love-children you have, the more fortunate your household is thought to be" (41). At the end of Jack's quasi-monologue, Kate reasserts her power and control by saying that, in Ireland, love-children "are not exactly the norm." The narrator's monologue that concludes Act I includes ominous news: a series of revelations, if not an anagnorisis.[19]

In Act II Jack, Gerry's return, and Rose's unexplained absence merely build suspense for the understated finale. The final scene, with its picnic and the comic exchange of hats, emphasizes the centrality of communal, as opposed to private or personal, values and actions. Nothing could be closer to the *koinonia* that is at the heart of Catholic reflection on the good life.[20] As Charles Taylor notes about the constituents of "the good life," "It is crucial to their being the goods they are that they be lived and enjoyed together, all the way from dance to conversation, to love, to friendship, to common self-rule."[21]

The final scene of the play takes place on one of the last warm, early autumn evenings. A Catholic sensibility is attuned to seasons, sacred and profane. Heightening the significance of the conclusion is its autumnal, elegiac tone. It would be straining to call the picnic "outside in the garden" (66) Eucharistic, but it does evoke prelapsarian contentment. Maggie offers sweet tea and caraway-seed and soda bread, with "only three eggs between the seven of us" (57), a possible allusion to the multiplication miracles in the gospels.[22]

What is it these characters desire from life? The inexpressible! As he flirts with Agnes and Maggie, for one moment Gerry is again the rooster in a flock of hens. And they? They have the attention of a man already related to them through Christina. Like the dance in a Shakespeare comedy, this one proposes a sense of failed unity and integration. And then Rose enters to announce the death of her pet rooster, perhaps killed by a fox. The rooster's fate is symbolic of the death that always hovers nearby, ready to disrupt the normal rituals of life, like picnics, dances, and the like. The rooster, the male principle, who makes the hens lay eggs, is dead: an ominous, wordless portent of the coming death of Jack and the departure of Michael.

Gerry notices Michael's now completed kites and their "garishly painted" faces, which are "crude, cruel, grinning faces...primitively drawn" (69). Whence comes that cruelty? It might express the redirected anger and frustration the boy feels. Alone, without a father, he is a "looker-on" of life. The kites may also express, by negation, what Michael wishes he had: a part in this final tableau. They also suggest the primitive forces, repressed as well as released, that are hinted at in the celebration of Lughnasa.

As the closing monologue suggests, the final scene is about the wordless mysteries of life. Jack, Gerry, and the Mundy sisters enact these rituals as a way to find meaning in their rapidly changing lives. The rituals and symbols point to a transcendent realm, beyond the mundane and painful reality of their Irish poverty. But it remains for us to catch the truth and hope for such transcendent meaning, much as we might try to retrieve a fleeting dream or a luminous vision. Friel's daughter, Judy, produced the play on a number of occasions. She quotes the famed critic Denis Donoghue to the effect that "a problem is something to be solved, a mystery is something to be witnessed and attested" (15).[23] This is the response to mystery that *Dancing at Lughnasa* elicits.

In an increasingly secular culture, it is almost a truism of literary criticism that authors find it difficult to portray human goodness. Unless a story or a film contains violence, sex, or some unspeakable form of evil, the attention of the audience often wanes. For this reason *Dancing at Lughnasa* may be too subtle for some, and this final scene might go past the inattentive reader or playgoer. Still this is a scene of relative plentitude, if not beatitude, before the forces of history, technology, and change, together with the consequences of personal decisions, disrupt the family. Its brief moments of qualified happiness suggest a glimpse of "the good life" that awaits us all in eternity.

Dancing at Lughnasa is witness to the Catholic belief that creation is graced, but damaged. The Mundy sisters are not a Holy Family in the clichéd sense, but they are a family that expresses its love in somewhat awkward and broken attempts at care and concern for each other. Few great plays (think of some by Brecht, or Elie Wiesel's *The Trial of God*) succeed as parables. But if *Dancing at Lughnasa* is a parable of anything, it is a parable of that *koinonia*, communion or fellowship referred to earlier. It is the parable of a humble, flawed familial community, attacked by change and temptation but, at least until the play's ending, united in flawed and fragile human care and love.

In the last moments of Lughnasa the play returns us to the question that focuses Rausch's chapter: "What is the life that God calls us to?" What is "the fullness of life," the *pleroma* to which God calls us?[24] It is not the narrated flight of Agnes and Rose, the death of Father Jack, or the revelation of Gerry Evans's multiple deceits that remains in the memory. Rather it is the picnic, a reminder of Eden and a preview of heaven. This meal together is an image of participation and communion. It symbolizes, intimates, or prefigures the ultimate graced experience referred to by Rausch of which we have all had some taste. In this way, rather than merely expounding a profound truth, it activates it.

The elder Michael's final monologue is in its own way mysterious, and it has elicited a variety of interpretations. As the characters assume "positions similar to their positions at the beginning of the play" (70), forming another tableau, Michael's memory is of dancing: "When I remember it, I think of it as dancing. Dancing with eyes half closed because to open them would break the spell. Dancing as if language had surrendered to movement—as if this ritual, this wordless ceremony, was now the way to speak, to whisper private and sacred things, to be in touch with some otherness" (71).

For some, this ending is unadulterated nostalgia. For others it is a final, wistful praise of a wordlessness that points toward the transcendent. The late poet Stanley Kunitz corroborates the truth intimated in Michael's epilogue: "There are forms of communication beyond language that have to do not only with the body, but with the spirit itself, a permeation of one's being."[25] A Catholic sensibility will see much more. Though the final scene has little to do with evil as such, one might be inclined to think of the things that will befall the Mundy sisters as unfortunate, sad, but at least realistic. In his book of aphorisms, *The Grain of Wheat*, von Balthasar makes a perceptive contrast between realism and grace, between a realistic way that evil has of looking at the world, and a way of looking that is informed by grace:

> Evil can deceive us with a convincing "realism": in its light, all things appear close up and stripped, in the true-to-life clarity of *verismo*, rescued from that blurry and hazy atmosphere that they have on "good" days. And yet the former is the illusion and the latter the truth; in the light of faith our real contour should indeed be hazy. A Christian existence without this atmosphere is as abstract as a surrealistic painting.[26]

Even after this close analysis of two plays, someone may wonder, Where is God in *Dancing at Lughnasa*? or even Where is God in *A Man for All Seasons*? Perhaps a von Balthasarian gloss on Buber provides a plausible answer. In the following passage, von Balthasar quotes and comments on passages from *I and Thou*:

> The "latency" of our relation to God, our "distance from God," the "pain of dryness"—these do not indicate that God is no longer there "but that we are

not always there" (*I and Thou* p. 99). It is the creature who must learn, through the "I-thou" relationship and "through the grace of its comings and the pains of its departures" (*I and Thou*, 33) to practice the presence of God, who is always there.[27]

I would suggest that in reading or seeing these two plays, we need to be "always there." We must be attentive to the mystery that surrounds the characters even when they are not. If we attend to both their words and the accompanying actions, we will more clearly understand their individual characters, the nature of their relationships, and the Catholic mystery that fills their lives and the plays themselves.

NOTES

1. Hans Urs von Balthasar, *Theo-Drama I: Prolegomena* (San Francisco: Ignatius Press, 1988), 12, 251.

2. von Balthasar, *Theo-Drama I*, 17.

3. O'Neill's tragedies, especially *Long Day's Journey into Night*, are also redolent with the fallen-away playwright's Catholic sensibility.

4. Peter Shaffer, *Equus* (New York: Penguin, 1974), 109.

5. Peter Shaffer, *Amadeus* (New York: Perennial, 1981), 59.

6. Robert Bolt, *A Man for All Seasons* (London: Methuen Drama, 1995).

7. Primarily William Roper's *Life of Sir Thomas More* in *Two Early Tudor Lives*, edited by Richard S. Sylvester and Davis P. Harding (New Haven, Conn.: Yale University Press, 1962).

8. In Wilder's play, a stage manager introduces two families and comments on the events of their lives (and deaths) that we see during two specific days in Grover's Corners, New Hampshire, at the start of the twentieth century.

9. I am not claiming that Williams consciously adapts Wilder's technique. The narrator and other metatheatrical devices have been around since the medieval theater. Some of Shakespeare's best-known plays employ such devices.

10. Brian Friel, *Dancing at Lughnasa* (London: Faber, 1990). Except for the embodiment of an alter ego in *Philadelphia, Here I Come!* or the use of techniques like the monologue structure from radio drama in *Faith Healer* and *Molly Sweeney*, Friel's plays, including *Lughnasa*, might seem hopelessly representational to the postmodern sensibility. The use of the narrator in *Lughnasa* therefore takes on even greater significance.

11. George Steiner speaks about the importance of "re-cognition" in *Real Presences* (Chicago: University of Chicago Press, 1989). On memory and imagination, see Monika Helwig, "The Catholic Intellectual Tradition in the Catholic University" in *Examining the Catholic Intellectual Tradition*, edited by Anthony J. Cernera and Oliver J. Morgan (Fairfield, Conn.: Sacred Heart University, 2000); Rudolfo Nicolás, "Depth, Universality, and Learned Ministry: Challenges to Jesuit Higher Education Today," presented at the conference Networking Jesuit Higher Education: Shaping the Future for a Humane, Just, Sustainable Globe, Mexico City, April 23, 2010.

12. On the philosophical significance of "ordinary life" since the Reformation, see Charles Taylor, *Sources of the Self: The Making of the Modern Identity* (Cambridge, Mass.: Harvard University Press, 1989), 13–16, 81–3, 211–47.

13. The Incarnation, however, made it possible for certain people, the apostles, to see God in the person of Jesus.

14. Even if we see "going native," either in Ireland or Africa, as a dangerous giving in to the power of divine energy, we should recognize in such phenomena the uncontrollable outbreak or incursion of the transcendent, the divine. See Ronald Rollheiser, *The Holy Longing* (New York: Doubleday, 1999), 22–31.

15. Martine Pelletier, "Whispering Private and Sacred Things: Field Day, Brian Friel's *Dancing at Lughnasa* and Seamus Heaney's *The Cure at Troy*," *Etudes irlandaises* 17, no. 1 (1992): 129–45.

16. No fewer than ten named musical pieces occur. Rose's "King of Abyssinia" (to the tune of "Coming around the Mountain"), the dance tune "The Mason's Apron" (21), "Dancing in the Dark" (32), "The Isle of Capri" (34) and "Everybody's Doing It" (37), both of which Kate refers to as "aul pagan songs," "Play to Me, Gypsy" (43), in Maggie's "usual parodic style," "O redder than the cherry" (46) by Jack, which he thinks might be Gilbert and Sullivan, Gerry's single line from "That daring young man on the flying trapeze" (54), and the final scene's "Anything Goes" (64) and "It's time to say goodnight" (71). Fellow playwright Frank McGuiness and script writer for the film version adds a musical setting of Yeats's "Down by the Salley Gardens," which is sung by all five sisters. Regarding spectacle, Aristotle refers to *opsis*, or what can be seen. Most critics, following Aristotle, narrow the concept of "spectacle" to those more or less obvious, or even sensational aspects of the play on stage, ignoring most ordinary entrances and exits and concentrating on significant actions on the stage. This would include the numerous dances in *Lughnasa*.

17. In *A Secular Age* (Cambridge, Mass.: Belknap Press, 2007), 46, Charles Taylor speaks of feasts, festivals, and Carnival as the medieval way of dealing with the presence of chaos that existed in tension with order (and repression). In this light, the sisters' dance, if not all the dances in *Lughnasa*, hearken back to such (mythic) outbursts.

18. Critics have pointed to the influence of George Steiner's linguistic thought on Friel's *Translations*. See George Steiner, *After Babel: Aspects of Language and Translation* (New York: Oxford University Press, 1998). Clearly, language, speech, and wordlessness are of the essence in *Lughnasa* as well.

19. *Anagnorisis* is the Greek term Aristotle employs to define the revelatory "reversal" in classical tragedy. By including the information in a monologue, Friel minimizes any sense of surprise or climax that might detract from the point that the final scene is meant to make.

20. Both Rausch in his essay in this volume and Scripture scholar Raymond E. Brown refer to the Catholic sense of community using this term. See Brown's *The Community of the Beloved Disciple* (New York: Paulist Press, 1979).

21. Charles Taylor, *A Catholic Modernity?* (New York: Oxford University Press, 1999), 113.

22. See Luke 9:10–17.

23. I think it is no accident that Donoghue's phrasing resembles von Balthasar's in *The Grain of Wheat: Aphorisms* (San Francisco: Ignatius Press, 1995), 21. *Speaking of Beauty* (New Haven, Conn.: Yale University Press, 2004), Denis Donoghue includes a response to Hans Urs von Balthasar, *The Glory of the Lord: A Theological Aesthetics* (San Francisco: Ignatius Press, 1986), the first of von Balthasar's trilogy.

24. St. Paul, in Colossians 2:9, refers to Christ as *pleroma tes theotetos*.

25. Stanley Kunitz with Genine Lentine, *The Wild Braid: A Poet Reflects on a Century in the Garden* (New York: Norton, 2005), 53.

26. von Balthasar, *The Grain of Wheat*, 104.

27. von Balthasar, *Theo-Drama I*, 635.

SELECTED READINGS

Block, Ed. "Drama and Religious Experience: or Why Theater Still Matters." *Logos* 8, no. 1 (2005): 65–89.

Bolt, Robert. *A Man for All Seasons*. London: Methuen Drama, 1995.

Friel, Brian. *Dancing at Lughnasa*. London: Faber, 1990.

Taylor, Charles. *Sources of the Self: The Making of the Modern Identity*. Cambridge, Mass.: Harvard University Press, 1989.

von Balthasar, Hans Urs. *Theo-Drama I: Prolegomena*. San Francisco: Ignatius Press, 1988.

8

Fiction and Catholic Themes

Paul J. Contino

NARRATIVE EMBODIMENTS ARE required by a Catholic imagination rooted in the Incarnation. The Catholic imagination is grounded in the story of God who became flesh and dwelt among us, who redeemed us within the contours of a particular time and place, and remains in relationship with us. At its best, Catholic fiction provides vivid images of Catholic faith and practice and opens readers' imaginations to the mystery of God's love. Such stories invite us to "live the questions" that arise in any life oriented toward the love of God and the love of neighbor, especially as those questions arise in limit situations that all humans face. For while fiction can edify, it does so in a form distinct from but complementary to that of theology and philosophy, as fiction presents "the particularity, the emotive appeal, the absorbing plottedness, the variety and indeterminacy" of lived faith, with all its "joys and hopes...griefs and anxieties."[1]

For those hoping to hand down the Catholic intellectual tradition in narrative form—in, say, a course entitled "The Catholic Imagination in Literature"—two great works, uniquely capacious in their vision, are indispensable: Dante's *Divine Comedy* (1321) and Dostoevsky's *Brothers Karamazov* (1881). The first two parts of this tripartite essay focus on these. At first glance, this may seem odd: *The Divine Comedy* is, after all, a long poem comprising one hundred cantos composed in terza rima. But Dante's masterwork *is* narrative. Further it records an emblematic journey of descent and ascent within the context of a Catholic vision as commodious as Chartres Cathedral. *The Brothers Karamazov* was written by a Russian who loathed Catholicism and saw Russian Orthodoxy as humankind's only hope, but Dostoevsky's novel reveals the "interior affinity" between the two traditions.[2]

Catholics do well to recall Pope John Paul II's insistence that the Eastern and Western theological traditions constitute the "two lungs" with which the Church breathes.[3] Indeed *The Brothers Karamazov* might now be regarded as an essential Catholic novel, with an encompassing vision embraced by Catholics ranging from Bernanos to Dorothy Day to Pope Benedict XVI.[4] But what of that abundance of Catholic fiction that demands consideration in such an essay—works by Greene, Bernanos, Undset, Waugh, Flannery O'Connor, Endo, and many others? In the third part of this essay I review a few of these works with particular attention to the way their endings shape a Catholic vision of abiding grace.

Each of the works I discuss confers narrative form to the three key facets of Catholic anthropology outlined by Thomas Rausch in his essay in this volume: (1) God, who is Love, is both transcendent and immanent. (2) Human beings are created in the image and likeness of God and, though fallen, remain free and are redeemed through Christ. God respects our freedom and calls us to cooperate with his own freely given grace so that we might reach our end: the fullness of eternal life in Him. (3) Grace builds on nature and is often mediated by flawed yet saintly persons. Indeed the Christian faith is sustained by such people.[5] Citing Cardinal Newman, Lawrence Cunningham suggests that the goal of a Catholic education is to become a saint. The saints most persuasively radiate and mediate God's gracious love to others. Every person is called to be a saint. And for a Catholic, "holiness" remains the best description of "the good life." Persistently Catholic fiction offers narrative images of saints or of persons oriented toward sanctity, and such images edify and enrich the imagination of any reader who embraces the universal call to holiness.

DANTE'S *DIVINE COMEDY*

From his first line Dante reveals his communal imagination and his desire that we join him in his journey to God: "Halfway along the road of this *our* life."[6] He uses the first-person plural purposefully, to situate his journey within the life that *all* of us share. In Dante's understanding, our life has a clear and common *telos,* or goal: to dwell in eternal beatitude with God and our fellow persons. We are made for Heaven, it is our home, and Dante would like to help us get there. In its mediatory and charitable purpose, his poem shares roots with its predecessor, St. Augustine's *Confessions.* In that fifth-century classic, the middle-aged Augustine, bishop of Hippo, tells his own story of sinful wandering and graced conversion. His point is not to flaunt the beauty of his prose or, as with the eighteenth-century Rousseau or modern TV's daytime confessionals, to display his faults before a perversely curious audience. Augustine aims to edify, not entertain; his express purpose is to "serve" his "fellow pilgrims" to enable their own turning to God.[7] In both *The Divine Comedy* and *Confessions*, an older, wiser man looks back upon a younger, more foolish self and represents the voices of both. In the course of Dante's journey, the voices of younger pilgrim and older poet draw closer, uniting in the end.

Dante the poet begins by describing to us the kind of person he was at the age of thirty-five, on April 7, Holy Thursday, 1300, the date his pilgrimage commences. At this time, to the eyes of his Florentine contemporaries, Dante must have appeared quite successful. He was married to Gemma Donati, a woman from a prominent family, had four children, was already an accomplished poet, and, on the eve of being elected to city government as one of its six priors, wielded political power. In reality he was lost. By 1300, less than two years after being condemned and exiled from Florence on trumped-up charges, he was bereft of his spiritual moorings, metaphorically isolated in a dark wood, contemplating self-destruction. In the ninety-nine cantos that follow the *Inferno*'s prologue, Dante the pilgrim, with the help of three indispensable guides, recovers his direction and progresses toward a vision of communal redemption. In the final canto of *Paradiso* he beholds the God within whom we have our being, the Trinity, and within it God's face made incarnate in Christ. Dante's fallen human will is restored, made integral with the will of God: fully free, his desire is moved like a wheel by the Love that moves the sun and the other stars. It was this purified, luminous Love that moved him to write his masterwork. Every step of the way the author calls us to accompany him on his journey and learn from it.

Like Augustine, who exhorts his readers, "Come down that you can ascend, and make your ascent to God" (IV.xii.19), Dante the pilgrim must descend before he goes up. In *Confessions* the older Augustine describes the younger, striving like a Platonist to scale the heights of divine knowledge in solitude, but failing: "My weakness reasserted itself, and I returned to my customary condition" (VII.xvii.23). Later, when Augustine humbly descends beneath a tree in a Milan garden and relies upon a child guide, he picks up and reads St. Paul's Letter to the Romans. In so doing he experiences his dependence on God's grace and so finds the strength to turn to God fully. Similarly Dante attempts to climb up and out of the dark wood but is stopped in his tracks by the successive appearance of three beasts: a leopard, a lion, and a she-wolf. Dante cannot do it alone either; he needs the help of other people. And the expansive Christian community responds to his plight. Divine love moves the Virgin Mary to help him. Mary asks Lucia, who petitions Beatrice, who commissions Virgil, and it is he who points Dante in the right direction. Dante must first descend into the infernal realm of damnation before he can ascend Mount Purgatory and rise to Paradise. Virgil, representing the best a human being can be when endowed by native reason but bereft of divine revelation, can take Dante only so far. In the Earthly Paradise atop the mountain, Dante will be reunited with his deceased childhood love, the saintly Beatrice, who takes Dante into Heaven. There it is St. Bernard of Clairvaux who mediates Dante's climactic vision of all-encompassing divine love.

Why must Dante go down before he goes up? In Canto 1 of *Purgatorio*, Virgil explains that Dante "seeks his freedom" (71), and "there was no other way" (62) to liberate him but to travel first through Hell. The pattern remains incarnational. As William Lynch writes in *Christ and Apollo*, a splendid guide to the Catholic literary imagination, "The great fact of Christology [is] that Christ moved down into all the realities of man to get to His Father."[8] Augustine exhorted his readers to take Christ's descent and ascent as their own model. Like the young Augustine, Dante the pilgrim does not fully understand sin for what it is and requires this knowledge if he is to be receptive to God's ever-available grace.

Pride, the capital sin, infects the will of every soul in Hell, such that each willfully *refuses* grace and *chooses* damnation. The denizens of Hell "[shove] themselves from that shore, one by one, / Like birds obeying signals from another bird's call" (3.115–17). No matter his or her assigned place, each soul in the Inferno has been deformed by narcissism and willful isolation. Hell is populous, but it's an image of anticommunity. Frozen and dumb, the perpetually chewing Satan, his three mugs a travesty of the communal Trinity, is Hell's final, fitting emblem.

With relief one climbs out of this pit, sees the stars again, and arrives at the gently lapping shores of Mount Purgatory. No Catholic educator should end students' journey with *The Inferno*! For only in his rigorous ascent of Mount Purgatory does it become clear that Dante's goal is freedom in cooperation with God's grace. Despite its beauty, Purgatory entails suffering, a kind of therapeutic pain that opens the heart to God and other people. This liberating pain stands in stark contrast to the unrepentant, suffocating suffering of Hell.

The opening cantos of *Purgatory* provide a vibrant contrast to Hell's absence of community. In the *Inferno* the souls embark on a boat rowed by a monstrous old man and curse God, their parents, and the entire human race (3.103–5). The souls in Purgatory arrive on a boat piloted by an angel, who leads the singing of Psalm 113 "together in a single voice": "*When Israel went forth from Egypt's land.*" As Dante told his Veronese patron, Cangrande della Scala, *The Divine Comedy* should be read in just the way this psalm has been read in the tradition of the Church: both literally and allegorically. Both poem and psalm describe a literal journey: the first, out of Egypt; the second, through the afterlife. Allegorically both depict individual and communal freedom from sin through grace. Given this promise of "infinite Goodness" (3.121–22), the *Purgatorio* is infused with hope: every person there knows that Heaven is their final destination. They address each other with courtesy: the newcomer's first word to Dante and Virgil is "please" (2.58). They kindly request the prayers of the living in the hope of "reducing their [own] wait for blessedness" (6.27).

Every creature in Purgatory awaits a nuptial union with the loving Creator in Heaven. Each ascends the three steps, the symbolism of which is crucial to an understanding of Purgatory's purpose and provides an emblem for the sacrament of reconciliation. The first white step symbolizes penitence; all souls in Purgatory are sorry for the sins they've committed, for the good they've left undone. The second step, rugged, purple-black, symbolizes confession; all souls in Purgatory have confessed and publicly acknowledged their sins. The third step is blood-red and represents satisfaction or penance, which is the purifying work each soul in Purgatory sets out to accomplish on the various terraces of the mountain.

But does not Christian theology teach that Christ's blood (his life, death, and resurrection) has *already* accomplished this work? Yes, but drawing upon the Catholic tradition, Dante depicts these souls as *desiring* to respond to and *cooperate* with Christ's redemption through their efforts. God in turn respects and fulfills the desire of his creatures. Thus these souls freely unite their sufferings with the salvific suffering of Christ.

If the purgative process liberates, so too does the process of learning. This is seen in Canto 16, where Marco Lombardo explains that human free will is the root of social malformation. In Canto 17, the very center of the cantica, and thus the heart of the *Commedia* itself, Virgil explains that love motivates every human act and is the organizing principle of Purgatory itself. Penance moves the souls toward Love, and each of the seven deadly sins calls for an apt penance. The prideful are brought low by the stones upon their back, and the envious are made blind to covetous desire. The wrathful walk through a smoky murk that images the way they let rage cloud reason. The slothful run; the covetous face down and grasp the earth; the gluttonous fast; and the lustful chastely embrace as they circle through a cleansing fire.

Each "working terrace" also offers a spiritual lesson depicted in scriptural and classical images. The description of each terrace commences with an image of Mary as model of the virtue that counters the vice being purged. She humbly accepts Gabriel's summons, empathizes with her hosts at Cana, mildly reproves her once missing twelve-year-old son, vigorously assists her pregnant cousin Elizabeth, gives birth in a poor Bethlehem stable, demonstrates concern for others rather than herself, and remains chaste. Dante meditates upon these images, and at least on the terraces of pride, wrath, and lust also suffers, suggesting that his own propensities are being purged.

But even after his passage through the flames, his purgative journey is incomplete. He beholds an elaborate pageant, which represents the Church at its best, namely, in the liturgical celebration of the Word and Eucharist. He also sees the Church at its worst, corrupted by temporal power. He is then reunited with Beatrice, who helps him engage in the saving instruments of the Church. She elicits from him penitence and confession. Given Dante's love for her, many readers are surprised at the martial severity with which Beatrice draws out Dante's confession. However, Beatrice is presented less as an object of courtly love than of sanctified *eros*, who turns her lover in the proper direction, toward God. As an image of Christ, she offers both judgment and mercy. Virgil, the dear father who departs at this juncture, is satisfied with Dante's progress. After emerging from the flames, perhaps a bit prematurely, Virgil declares that Dante's will is now perfectly erect and free. Only after his tearful confession before Beatrice and subsequent cleansing in the waters of the Lethe and Eunoe is Dante himself ready to enter Paradise.

Many students find *Paradiso* to be the most arduous stretch of the journey. In fact Dante warns his fellow pilgrims that they might do well to stop at this point, declaring, "No one has ever made a voyage like mine" (2.7). However, Dante continues, if we are eager to eat the "angel bread of wisdom" (2.11) by plunging into a study of theology, we should continue with him into this luminous realm. Though presented in narrative form, *Paradiso* is unapologetically and necessarily theological. But the mysteries it explores and the communal joy it images in variations of light, dance, smiles, and song lend it unsurpassed beauty and oceanic depth.

The theology lessons begin early, when Beatrice speaks of the analogical imagination and explains how the created world reflects its Creator:

> "All things," she began, "have places where they belong,
> And this is how the universe is formed
> Both by and in the semblance of Almighty God.
> This ordering is how the highest of creatures,
> Angels and men, can see God's print in all features
> Of goodness, which is why this ordering was done." (1.103–8)

Beatrice herself is analogous to Christ, much as Mary's face most resembles that of her Son (32.86). It is crucial, however, to remember that any human analogy of the divine indicates similarity, but an even greater dissimilarity to the divine. For Dante, Beatrice is an icon, not an idol. For example, when Dante's attention finally shifts from her to Christ (10.58–63), she smiles radiantly!

The *Paradiso* is rich in theological dialogue. When Dante meets the first soul in Paradise, Piccarda Donati, he questions the cosmic order. How, he asks, can she be content since she is placed in the lunar sphere seemingly so far from God? Where's the justice in a Heaven ordered by hierarchy? Piccarda responds and speaks for all of the souls in Paradise:

> The very essence of this blessed existence
> Is forever staying inside the realm of God's will,
> By which His will and ours can join as one.
> Every soul in all these circles is a joy
> To each and all, and everything is God's
> Delight, He who draws us to His will,
> For in His will we have our peace. He
> Is the sea to which all things will flow, whatever
> It creates and also what Nature makes.
> And then it was clear to me that Paradise
> Is anywhere in Heaven, although God's grace
> May fall in different ways in different places. (79–90)

People vary in the degree to which they are receptive to God's grace (29.64–6). Some, because of their human limitations, are less receptive than others. Yet all are *equally* in Heaven.

Dante's questions continue: Why did Christ have to die on the cross? Beatrice explains that the Fall required either human satisfaction or divine mercy. In Christ, God chose both means of atonement (canto 7). Can human beings conform to the self-emptying model that Christ presents? Yes: Dante hears St. Thomas Aquinas's story of Francis of Assisi, who weds Lady Poverty, founds an order, and bears Christ's wounds (canto 11). At first St. Francis mistakenly thought he was called to be a soldier. Indeed the proper discernment of gifts and vocation is one of *Paradiso*'s recurring themes (8.145–8, 13.72).

In one of the most moving sections of *Paradiso*, Dante's ancestor Cacciaguida foretells the poet's coming exile from Florence. Cacciaguida affirms Dante's vocation, whose "poema sacro" (25.1) will be both prophetic and sacramental: "If at the very first taste your words are disturbing, / Later they will supply much needed food, / After they are finally digested" (17.130–32). Dante wonders whether such foreknowledge entails predestination and a consequent stripping of human freedom (17.37–42). Later he raises the still timely question of religious pluralism: What of those who do not believe in Christ, what of the "man...born near the Indus River" (19.70)? If all the redeemed are saved through Christ, how can one fathom the surprising appearance of the Roman Trajan and the Trojan Ripheus (or, earlier, Cato) among the saints? Such moments anticipate Vatican II's declaration, "The Catholic Church rejects nothing that is true and holy in [non-Christian] religions. She regards with sincere reverence those ways of conduct and of life, those precepts and teachings which, though differing in many aspects from the ones she holds and sets forth, nonetheless often reflect a ray of that Truth which enlightens all men."[9] Might God's providence extend to Virgil, whom every reader of the *Commedia* has grown to love? Dare we hope that Virgil will be among those "gathered and bound / By love in a single volume, all we have found / On single pages, scattered through our world" (33.85–7)?

Near the conclusion of the *Paradiso* Dante discerns an astonishing image, a fiery point of light, upon which he learns "The Heavens and everything in nature / Depend" (28.41–2). Here his understanding of the cosmos is radically inverted. This point, the luminous, loving mind of God, and not that little threshing floor Earth, is the true center of the universe, the "hidden ground of love."[10] Dante's attention is increasingly drawn into that central point, until, through the loving mediation of the saints, the point reveals its Trinitarian and Incarnate form. At the moment in which Dante tries to fathom how our human image is inscribed within the Trinity, he becomes the author of the narrative we have just completed: "my mind and will whirling around / Like a wheel smoothly turning without a sound, / Spun by the Love that moves both sun and stars" (33.143–5). Wielding words with all their limitations, Dante offers the *Commedia,* a work motivated by Divine Love, as an act of love for his fellow pilgrims.

DOSTOEVSKY'S *BROTHERS KARAMAZOV*

In his final and greatest novel, Dostoevsky's stated aim was to *"force [his readers] to admit* that a pure ideal Christian is not an abstraction but a tangible, real possibility that can be contemplated with our own eyes."[11] Though written about the Elder Zosima, his words can be applied to that character's disciple and the novel's hero, Alyosha Karamazov. In the course of the novel, Alyosha grows in his capacity to accept Zosima's vocational charge to serve as a "monk in the world" (247).[12]

Alyosha is born into a fractured family. His father, Fyodor, is a lustful buffoon who forgets his three sons after they are born. The eldest, Dmitri, is betrothed to Katerina, but in violent competition with his father for the love of Grushenka. Ivan, the middle son, falls in love with Katerina, but detaches himself from others in his refusal to accept God's creation, blighted as he perceives it to be by the unforgiveable suffering of children. Alyosha, the youngest, is gifted with saintly attributes.

His earliest memory is being held before the icon of the Mother of God by his suffering mother. Alyosha's gracious presence, especially his face and, over time, his words, prove to be a balm to his father, his brothers, and their lovers. In the preface to the novel he is described as an "eccentric" hero who nevertheless "carries within himself the very heart of the whole" (7). Given the etymological meaning of *catholic* as "regarding the whole," one can call Alyosha a "catholic" hero.

Dostoevsky described himself as a "realist in the higher sense," who reveals "the man in a man."[13] For Dostoevsky the deepest self is called to conform to the model of Christ. In his discourse, Zosima claims, "On earth, indeed, we are as it were, astray and if it were not for the precious image of Christ before us, we should be altogether lost, as was the human race before the flood" (276). Indeed the salvific image of Christ is so much at the center of *The Brothers Karamazov* that Dostoevsky's "higher realism" might be called "Incarnational realism," grounded as his art is in what he believes is the Word made flesh. Thus the novel represents time as transformed by Christ's Incarnation. Throughout the novel are reflections on the image presented in the novel's epigraph, from John 12:24: "Except a corn of wheat fall into the ground and die, it abideth alone; but if it die, it bringeth forth much fruit." Like Dante's *Divine Comedy*, the novel reprises a Christological descent-ascent pattern, imaged most vividly in Zosima's kissing the earth before he dies and Alyosha kissing it after waking from his dream of the wedding feast at Cana. After kissing the earth, he rises up "a resolute champion." Certain that "someone visited [his] soul at that hour," he is poised to commence his "sojourn in the world" (312).

Early on, the narrator describes Alyosha as "a realist." Josef Pieper's Thomist definition of prudence as "the perfected ability to make decisions in accord with reality" helps situate Alyosha's realism.[14] In the course of the novel, he grows in prudence. But even from the start he has his feet on the ground; he does not waste time or fall into inertia, despite a series of failures in his interventions with others. When he has someplace to go in a hurry, he knows where to find a shortcut (93) and is wise enough to bring along a snack when he anticipates the long day ahead of him (154).

Alyosha's prudence is not simple efficiency. It entails perceiving and loving the image of God in the people he encounters and serves through his loving attentiveness. On his first day as a monk in the world, he is anxious to see Katerina but runs into Dmitri along the way. Listening to his brother, he "made up his mind to wait. He felt that, perhaps, indeed, his work lay here" (96). Alyosha flexibly revises his plan as he apprehends his brother's need for a listener, a confessor to hear his "confessions of an ardent heart," and thus makes a firm decision to stay.

However, Alyosha's first three days are not always marked by such receptive stillness. At the end of his first day, overwhelmed by family conflicts, he flees back to the monastery as an escape (139). On his second day, his prudence falters as he tries to circumvent uncertainty and the readiness of those he is trying to help. Neither his hastily proclaimed insight that Katerina's love for Dmitri is delusional and destructive (167–8) nor his ecstatic promise to give his own rubles to the poor father Snegiryov (182) prove helpful. In both cases Alyosha speaks the truth but his words lack authority because they lack prudence. He is inattentive to what at the moment his interlocutors, Katerina and Snegiryov, are able to bear. These efforts at active love prove to be *too* active, too assertive.

Active love, the foundational theme of the novel, is first articulated by Father Zosima when he advises a doubting woman that her faith in eternal life will be nourished

> by the experience of active love. . . . If you attain to perfect self-forgetfulness in the love of your neighbor, then you will believe without doubt, and no doubt can possibly enter your soul. . . . [Active love] is a harsh and dreadful thing compared with love in dreams. Love in dreams is greedy for immediate action, rapidly performed and in the sight of all. Men will even give their lives if only the ordeal does not last long but is soon over, with all looking on and applauding as though on the stage. But active love is labor and fortitude, and for some people too, perhaps, a complete science. (54–5)

With its emphasis upon the sheer hard work of love, and the renunciation of self, active love is consonant with the image of the kenotic, self-emptying Christ (Philippians 2) so vital to both Orthodox and Catholic traditions, and also the image of the corn of wheat in the novel's epigraph (John 12.24). Yet the chapter "An Onion" makes clear that active love includes both *agape* and *eros*. Such active love produces the synthesis of *caritas*, affirmed by Pope Benedict XVI in his first encyclical, *Deus Caritas Est*: "*Eros* and *agape*—ascending love and descending love—can never be completely separated. The more the two, in their different aspects, find a proper unity in the one reality of love, the more the true nature of love in general is realized."[15]

Dostoevsky works from an incarnational anthropology which understands the human person as created in the image and likeness of God. Sin distorts this image, but Christ's redemption restores and elevates both spirit *and* body. Faith in the Incarnation of Christ, and the sacramental sense of immanent grace that follows from that faith, fosters trust. David Tracy writes, "As grounded in that gift of trust, *eros* will be transformed but not negated by divine *agape*. That transformation is *caritas*."[16] In Dostoevsky's artistic vision, the person is drawn to and by beauty to restore the beauty of his own divinely endowed image.

In the chapter "An Onion," which transpires on Alyosha's third day as "a monk in the world," Grushenka and Alyosha become living icons for each other. But as the chapter begins, Alyosha's image is distorted: his face is irritable as his trust in the goodness of the created world has been shaken by the death and premature bodily decay of his beloved elder, Zosima. Like Ivan, Alyosha questions divine justice, and in a fit of *nadryv*—the Russian word that denotes a de-formative, infernal self-laceration in which one hurts oneself to hurt another, or vice versa—he allows Rakitin to lead him to the temptress Grushenka, willfully casting his spiritual discipline to the wind, as if into God's face. Alyosha, wary of sexuality, fears Grushenka, who, two days earlier, had used her sexual allure to humiliate Katerina before his eyes. When he arrives at Grushenka's, Alyosha expects to find Sodom, which is the image his brother Dmitri uses when he agonizes to Alyosha about the ambivalence of beauty: "I can't endure the thought that a man of lofty mind and heart begins with the ideal of the Madonna and ends with the ideal of Sodom" (98). To his surprise, however, Grushenka, twice described as "beautiful" (296), presents an image of the Madonna, the face that most resembles Christ's, to borrow words from Dante's *Paradiso*. Thus Grushenka points up the Manichaean falsity of Dmitri's Sodom/Madonna dichotomy; the Madonna, who bore Christ in her womb, cannot be reduced to an abstract, solely spiritual antithesis to fleshly disorder. Mary is herself body and soul, like her son, Jesus Christ.

Dante's *Commedia* tells the story of a man whose soul is risen from the depths by the mediation of a beautiful woman, Beatrice, whom Dante loves, body and soul. This is also Alyosha's story. At first, when Grushenka sits "beside Alyosha on the sofa," he notices a change in *her* face: "Her lips glowed, her lips laughed, but it was a good-natured, merry laugh. Alyosha had not expected to see such a kind expression on her face" (299). His expectations are further overturned when Grushenka "suddenly skipped forward and jumped, laughing, on his knee, like a nestling kitten, with her right arm about his neck. 'I'll cheer you up, my pious boy'" (300). When we look at this scene, I ask my students if there is any sexual attraction on Alyosha's part. "Oh no," an earnest student usually replies, and points to the text for support: even with flirtatious Grushenka on his lap, Alyosha "felt numb.... There was nothing in his heart such as Rakitin, for instance, watching him malignantly from his corner, might have expected or fancied. The great grief in his heart swallowed up every sensation that might have been aroused, and, if only he could have thought clearly at that moment, he would have realized that he had now the strongest armor to protect him from every lust and temptation" (300). But another student might point out that the next word is "yet." In that "yet" we see that active love in *The Brothers Karamazov* can be understood as *caritas*:

Yet in spite of the vague irresponsiveness of his spiritual condition and the sorrow that overwhelmed him, he could not help wondering at a new and strange sensation in his heart.... This woman, dreaded above all women, sitting now on his knee, holding him in her arms, aroused in him now a quite different, unexpected, peculiar feeling, a feeling of the intensest and purest interest without a trace of fear, of his former terror. That was what instinctively surprised him. (300, my emphasis)

Alyosha's pure and intense interest is sanctified *eros*. He is powerfully *drawn to* Grushenka's beauty, not only the beauty of her physical form, but that beauty of the form in which she responds to Alyosha, bound up as that response is with her truthfulness and kindness. Thus Alyosha's "eyes involuntarily [rest] on her with attention" (299).

Grushenka's beauty is manifested most fully in her *attentiveness* to Alyosha when she learns of Zosima's death: "'Good God I did not know!' She crossed herself devoutly. 'Goodness, what have I been doing, sitting on his knee like this at such a moment!' She started up as though in dismay, instantly slipped off his knee and sat down on the sofa. Alyosha fixed a long wondering look upon her and a light seemed to dawn in his face" (302). Grushenka feels and respects what she imagines Alyosha is going through, and empties herself of her desire to flirt—and the anxiety it cloaks—to attend to him. The gesture of crossing herself is apt as her self-emptying reflects Christ's *kenosis*. Reflecting Christ's image, she is iconic: she reveals the transfigured glory of that which seems forsaken, only "harsh and dreadful," to recall Zosima's description of active love. In this crucial scene, *kenosis*, the painful self-renunciation always entailed in active love, emerges as beautiful.

The radiant look on Alyosha's face—"a light seemed to dawn in his face"— suggests the transformative power of such beauty, the spiritual *metanoia* that the icon seeks to inspire in its beholder. The transformation is manifested in Alyosha's impassioned declaration that follows. His voice, broken before by *nadryv*, is now "firm" as he first implores Rakitin to "look at" Grushenka as a means of transforming his hardened heart. Alyosha's *metanoia* is then given form by his own confession: "I came here to find a wicked soul—I felt drawn to evil because I was base and evil myself, and I've found a true sister, I have found a treasure—a loving heart." Finally, he acknowledges the manifestation of grace in Grushenka as he tells her, "You've raised my soul from the depths" (302), possibly a reference to Psalm 130:1.

Grushenka tells Alyosha that she has only given him an onion, referring to a folk tale in which a guardian angel appeals to God on behalf of a woman condemned to Hell, reminding God that the wicked woman had once given an onion to a beggar woman.[17] Inspired by Alyosha's restored, iconic image, Grushenka also makes a confession and confides in Alyosha the crisis of decision she faces. Alyosha assists her in making her decision by respecting her freedom and attending to that which she herself most deeply wishes. In response to her declaration of love, he says, "I only gave you an onion"; the verbal echo sensitively recalls and affirms Grushenka's own imagining, through narrative, of her capacity for active love (307).

The onion is an apt image, not only because it suggests the earthy, humble reality of active love, but in the way its layers of skin illustrate what is so mysteriously beautiful about the form of *The Brothers Karamazov*. Scenes like this one, in which repetitions sound in slightly different keys, chime throughout the entire novel and lend the novel its resonance and beauty.[18] Students and their teachers perceive and are drawn to this beauty. Like Dostoevsky's contemporary readers, who said to the author, "We've become better people since we read *The Karamazovs*,"[19] they are often transformed by it.

A FURTHER SAMPLING OF CATHOLIC FICTION

In this final section, I would like to present a limited overview of classic Catholic fiction, along with some contemporary works.[20] In these works the emphasis is on the portrayal of characters oriented toward sanctity. These characters reflect the variety of possible forms that "the good life" of holiness can take, for in each work, the path to sanctity is particular to that character. A number of Catholic works focus on characters committed to the vocation of priest or nun, but who see themselves as falling short in their vocation. In Graham Greene's *The Power and the Glory*, the unnamed whiskey priest considers himself an utter failure but remains committed to the beleaguered poor of Mexico. Ultimately he gives up his life to provide the sacraments and sacramental presence that the oppressive government has forbidden. He is moved to do so because he sees the image of God in each person he serves. Imprisoned, he reflects, "When you visualized a man or a woman carefully, you could always begin to feel pity—that was the quality God's image carried with it. When you saw the lines at the corners of the eyes, the shape of the mouth, how the hair grew, it was impossible to hate. Hate was just a failure of the imagination."[21] Similar is Father Jerome Strozzi, the hero of Jean Sulivan's *Eternity, My Beloved*. For Father Jerome the divine image is present everywhere, as he explains to the narrator toward the end of the novel: "As I've often told you, I instinctively see Jesus, Son of God, in every human being. God has no other image except the face of a person, every person."[22]

By his acceptance of martyrdom for his faith, the whiskey priest stands in contrast to Father Rodrigues, the Jesuit missionary to Japan in Shusaku Endo's *Silence* (1966).[23] Rodrigues symbolically renounces his faith by stamping upon an image of Christ. Paradoxically he feels closer to Christ in the aftermath of his apostasy. Perhaps the most memorable example of a priest who feels he has failed yet remains attentive to others is the nameless hero of Georges Bernanos's *Diary of a Country Priest* (1936). The final words of his diary suggest a movement toward graced self-acceptance: "I am reconciled to myself, to the poor, poor shell of me. How easy it is to hate oneself! True grace is to forget. Yet if pride could die in us, the supreme grace would be to love oneself in all simplicity—as one would love any one of those who themselves have suffered and loved in Christ."[24] His final words echo St. Thérèse of Lisieux: "All is grace."

The tone of graced self-acceptance pervades the concluding scenes in stories of other religious. In J. F. Powers's "Lions, Harts, and Leaping Does," the dying Father Didymus finally discerns the saintliness of his simple caretaker, Brother Titus.[25] In Edwin O'Connor's *Edge of Sadness*, the recovering alcoholic priest Father Hugh Kennedy embraces his position at poor, declining Old St. Paul's parish and reflects, "I might, through the parish and its people, find my way not again to the simple engagement of the heart and affections [which he had found at previous parishes], but to the Richness, the Mercy, the immeasurable Love of God."[26] In Ron Hansen's *Mariette in Ecstasy*, the heroine speaks in similarly graced, accepting tones as she writes to one of the sisters she had known in the convent where, thirty years earlier, she had been sent away because her mystical visions were judged fraudulent and disruptive to the community:

> Christ reminds me, as he did in my greatest distress, that he loves me more, now that I am despised, than when I was so richly admired in the past.
>
> And Christ still sends me roses. We try to be formed and held and kept by him, but instead he offers us freedom. And now when I try to know his will, his kindness floods me, his great love overwhelms me, and I hear him whisper, Surprise me.[27]

Persistently the Catholic narrative imagination suggests the presence of grace in the passage through limitation, including the limits of our human sinfulness. Sigrid Undset's epic trilogy, *Kristin Lavransdatter* (1922), tells the story of a fourteenth-century Norwegian woman who, against her father's wishes, enters a troubled yet passionate marriage with the excommunicated Erland, bears him eight sons, and lives through her husband's death and some of her children's before she herself dies during the Black Plague of 1349. Near death, just before receiving the viaticum, Kristin gives away her wedding ring so that Masses might be said for a poor woman whom she had courageously defended from a violent mob. She perceives the imprint of the letter *M*, the symbol of the Virgin, on her finger, and reflects:

> She had been a servant of God—a stubborn, defiant maid, most often an eye-servant in her prayers and unfaithful in her heart, indolent and neglectful, impatient toward admonishments, inconstant in her deeds. And yet He had held her firmly in His service, and under the glittering gold ring a mark had been secretly impressed upon her, showing that she was His servant, owned by the Lord and King who would now come, borne on the consecrated hands of the priest, to give her release and salvation.[28]

Similarly Charles Ryder, the narrator of *Brideshead Revisited* (1945) and eventual convert to Catholicism, finally accepts a crucial fact: "The worse I am, the more I need God."[29]

Narrative images of saints often suggest the saint's participation in the suffering of Christ. In "Parker's Back" (1965), the story she wrote on her deathbed, Flannery O'Connor tells the story of O. E. Parker, who, to please his sternly religious wife, has an icon of a Byzantine Christ tattooed on his back, the only spot on his body bereft of a tattoo. For his trouble he is soundly beaten by his wife, who turns out to be vehemently iconoclastic and condemns any imaging of the divine as idolatrous:

> Parker was too stunned to resist. He sat there and let her beat him until she had nearly knocked him senseless and large welts had formed on the face of the tattooed Christ. Then he staggered up and made for the door.
>
> She stamped the broom two or three times on the floor and went to the window and shook it out to get the taint of him off it. Still gripping it, she looked toward the pecan tree and her eyes hardened still more. There he was—who called himself Obidiah Elihue—leaning against the tree, crying like a baby.[30]

Unexpectedly Parker emerges as an image of Christ. When he submits to his wife's beating, he embodies *kenosis*: he empties himself of the will to resist and defend himself. The "large welts that form on the face of the tattooed Christ" form, of course, on his own flesh and thus suggest his participation in the sacrifice of Christ, as does his later leaning and weeping against the "single tall pecan tree on a high embankment,"[31] itself an image of the cross.

In Oscar Hijuelos's *Mr. Ives' Christmas* (1995), the title character receives the grace that enables him to forgive his son's murderer and, in the novel's final scene, to discern the figure of the risen Christ, "placing his wounded hands upon Ives' brow."[32] In "My Parents' Bedroom," the final story in Uwem Akpan's searing collection, *Say You're One of Them* (2008), a Rwandan girl witnesses the horrific murder of her mother by her own father. She sees, in the end, her little brother "playing with the glow of the crucifix, babbling Maman's name."[33]

Catholic fiction sometimes represents the power of the sacraments, especially the Eucharist. In Larry Woiwode's *Beyond the Bedroom Wall*, Alpha Neumiller recalls her conversion to Catholicism and her First Communion: "She'd converted because of the feeling of light, a light she'd sensed but couldn't quite see. The more she studied the Bible and the catechism, the stronger the light became....Since her First Communion, the light had stayed."[34] In Andre Dubus's novella *Voices from the Moon*, twelve-year-old Richie Stowe has a similar reverence for the Eucharist and a strong calling toward the priesthood.[35] He begins his difficult day at Mass and concludes it lying in a baseball field, gazing at the night sky while holding the hand of the girl he loves. In the close of the novella, Richie learns that the *caritas* to which the Eucharist calls him includes both an acceptance of the cross, and all the renunciation that active love entails, and a grateful openness to the grace mediated by his girlfriend, Melissa. In a star-filled scene that recalls both Dante's final vision and Alyosha's descent to and embrace of the earth, Richie gratefully recognizes that he can love both Christ and Melissa.

CONCLUSION

As Rausch notes, "Catholicism traditionally says *both/and*. Not Scripture alone but Scripture and tradition; not grace alone but grace and nature; not faith alone but faith and works as well as faith and reason." Allow me to add another pairing: we pray in gratitude for God's kingdom that is both present and still to come. In this life, limited as we are within the constricted contours of time, place, and commitment, we nonetheless receive glimpses of eternal life, full union with God and each other, which is the *telos* to which all are called. At the end of *The Divine Comedy* Dante glimpses the communion of saints surrounding the Triune God of Love. But he must then return to his temporal existence in Italy to fulfill his authorial vocation. At the end of *The Brothers Karamazov*, just after they have celebrated a funeral Mass for a nine-year-old boy, Alyosha is inspired to speak to a group of twelve boys, to exhort them to remember their friend and the goodness and kindness that each of them in their grief is revealing at that moment. The eldest and most precocious of the boys, deeply moved by Alyosha's words, asks him if it's true that they will rise again after death. Alyosha, fulfilling *his* vocation as a monk in the world, promises them the joy of the resurrection: "Certainly we shall all rise again, certainly we shall see each other and tell each other with joy and gladness all that has happened!" And then he walks with them, "hand in hand," to a traditional funeral dinner of pancakes.

Alyosha had been taught by his Elder Zosima that paradise is present as soon as one makes oneself responsible to all and for all. In his talk with the boys, in the heartbreaking wake of another child's death, paradise is present. Indeed in every work discussed in this essay, characters glimpse the promise of eternity within the contours of their limited lives.

NOTES

1. See Martha C. Nussbaum, *Love's Knowledge: Essays on Philosophy and Literature* (New York: Oxford University Press, 1990), 46, for a helpful elucidation of the ways fiction must accompany moral philosophy if philosophy is to adequately gain "love's knowledge." *Gaudium et Spes*, 1, www.vatican.va/archive/hist_councils/ii_vatican_council/documents/vat-ii_cons_19651207 _gaudium-et-spes_en.html.

2. I draw this phrase from Pope Benedict XVI, *The Light of the World: The Pope, the Church, and the Signs of the Times: A Conversation with Peter Seewald*, translated by Michael J. Miller and Adrian J. Walker (San Francisco: Ignatius Press, 2010), 87. The Holy Father comments on the recent progress in ecumenical relations between the Western and Eastern Churches: "Despite all the differences that have built up over the centuries on account of cultural separations and other factors, it is important that we truly relearn to see and understand our inner spiritual kinship with each other. On this level, I think we are making progress. I do not mean tactical, political progress, but rapprochement on the level of our interior affinity. I find this very consoling."

3. Pope John Paul II, "Euntes in Mundum" (1988), www.catholicculture.org/culture/library/ view.cfm?recnum=3700.

4. In a letter to his fellow Catholic poet Czeslaw Milosz, Thomas Merton wrote, "The answer—the only answer I know—is that of Staretz Zossima in *The Brothers Karamazov*—to be responsible to everybody, to take upon oneself *all* guilt—but I don't know what that means. It is romantic, and I believe it is true." Thomas Merton, *Striving towards Being: The Letters of Thomas Merton and Czeslaw Milosz*, edited by Robert Faggen (New York: Farrar, Straus and Giroux, 1997), 55.

5. See Henri de Lubac's influential *Catholicism: Christ and the Common Destiny of Man* (San Francisco: Ignatius Press, 1988), 15, where he insists, "Catholicism is essentially social."

6. Burton Raffel, trans., *The Divine Comedy* (Chicago: Northwestern University Press, 2010). In my discussion I draw from parts of my introduction to that translation.

7. St. Augustine, *Augustine's Confessions,* edited and translated by Henry Chadwick (New York: Oxford Worlds Classics, 1991), X.iv.6.

8. William Lynch, *Christ and Apollo: The Dimensions of the Literary Imagination* (Wilmington, Del.: ISI Books, 2004), 23.

9 Pope Paul VI, *Nostra Aetate* (October 1965), www.vatican.va/archive/hist_councils/ii_ vatican_council/documents/vat-ii_decl_19651028_nostra-aetate_en.html.

10. The phrase is Thomas Merton's, the title of a collection of his letters: *The Hidden Ground of Love: The Letters of Thomas Merton on Religious Experience and Social Concern*, edited by William H. Shannon. (New York: Farrar, Straus and Giroux, 1985).

11. Fyodor Dostoevsky, "Letter to N. A. Lyubimov, June 11, 1879," in *Selected Letters of Fyodor Dostoevsky*, edited by Joseph Frank and David I. Goldstein (New Brunswick, N.J.: Rutgers University Press, 1987), 469–70.

12. Susan McReynolds Oddo, ed., *The Brothers Karamazov* (New York: Norton, 2011), 247.

13. See Donald Fanger, *Dostoevsky and Romantic Realism* (Cambridge, Mass.: Harvard University Press, 1965), 215.

14. Josef Pieper, "Prudence," in *The Four Cardinal Virtues,* translated by Richard Winston and Clara Winston (Notre Dame, Ind.: University of Notre Dame Press, 1966), 31. I develop my discussion of prudence in "The Prudential Alyosha Karamazov: The Russian Realist from a Catholic Perspective," in *Dostoevsky and Christianity: Art, Faith, and Dialogue*, a special volume of *Dostoevsky Monographs*, edited by Susan McReynolds and Jordi Morillas (St. Petersburg, Russia: Dmitriy Bulanin, 2012).

15. Benedict XVI, *Deus Caritas Est,* 2005, 7, www.vatican.va/holy_father/benedict_xvi/encyclicals/documents/hf_ben-xvi_enc_20051225_deus-caritas-est_en.html.

16. David Tracy, *The Analogical Imagination: Christian Theology and the Culture of Pluralism* (New York: Crossroad, 1981), 432.

17. See the discussion of "The Onion," in Hans Urs von Balthasar, *Dare We Hope That All Men Are Saved?* (San Francisco: Ignatius Press, 1988).

18. See Robin Feuer Miller's eloquent discussion of the onion image in *The Brothers Karamazov: Worlds of the Novel* (New Haven, Conn.: Yale University Press, 2008), 87–8.

19. See Dostoevsky's letter to his wife, Anna, cited in Miller, *The Brothers Karamazov*, 7.

20. For a helpful listing of Catholic fiction, see www.catholicfiction.net/catholic-fiction-reading-list/. See also these two excellent anthologies: Daniel McVeigh and Patricia Snapp, eds., *The Best American Catholic Short Stories* (Lanham, Md.: Sheed and Ward, 2007); John B. Breslin, *The Substance of Things Hoped For: Short Fiction by Modern Catholic Authors* (Garden City, N.Y.: Doubleday, 1987).

21. Graham Greene, *The Power and the Glory*, (New York: Penguin, 1991), 131.

22. Jean Sulivan, *Eternity, My Beloved*, translated by Francis Ellen Riordan (St. Paul, Minn.: River Boat Books, 1999), 125.

23. Shusaku Endo, *Silence.*, translated by William Johnston. (New York: Taplinger, 1980).

24. George Bernanos, *The Diary of a Country Priest* (New York: Carroll and Graff, 2002), 296.

25. J. F. Powers, *The Stories of J. F. Powers.* (New York: New York Review of Books Classics, 2000).

26. Edwin O'Connor, *The Edge of Sadness* (Chicago: Loyola Press, 2005), 637.

27. Ron Hansen, *Mariette in Ecstasy* (New York: HarperCollins, 1991), 179.

28. Sigrid Undset, *Kristin Lavransdatter III: The Cross*, translated by Tiina Nunnally (New York: Penguin, 2000), 422.

29. Cited in Paul M. Puccio, "Brideshead Revisited," in *Encyclopedia of Catholic Literature*, edited by Mary R. Reichardt (Westport, Conn.: Greenwood Press, 2004), 742. The two volumes of this *Encyclopedia* offer numerous discussions of Catholic fiction and offer a very good resource for anyone planning a course in Catholic fiction.

30. Flannery O'Connor, *The Complete Stories* (New York: Farrar, Straus and Giroux, 1996), 529–30.

31. F. O'Connor, *The Complete Stories*, 510.

32. Oscar Hijuelos, *Mr. Ives' Christmas* (New York: HarperCollins, 1995), 248.

33. Uwem Akpan, *Say You're One of Them* (New York: Little, Brown, 2008), 354.

34. Larry Woiwode, *Beyond the Bedroom Wall* (New York: Farrar, Straus and Giroux, 1975), 256.

35. Andre Dubus, *Selected Stories* (New York: Vintage, 1995).

SELECTED READINGS

Boyle, Nicholas. *Sacred and Secular Scriptures: A Catholic Approach to Literature*. Notre Dame, Ind.: University of Notre Dame Press, 2005.

Gandolfo, Anita. *Testing the Faith: The New Catholic Fiction in America*. New York: Greenwood, 1992.

Giles, Paul. *American Catholic Arts and Fictions: Culture, Ideology, Aesthetics*. New York: Cambridge University Press, 1992.

Labrie, Ross. *The Catholic Imagination in American Literature*. Columbia: University of Missouri Press, 1997.

Lynch, William F. *Christ and Apollo: The Dimensions of the Literary Imagination*. 1960; Wilmington, Del.: ISI Press, 2004.

Reichardt, Mary R. *Encyclopedia of Catholic Literature*. Vols. 1–2. Westport, Conn.: Greenwood Press, 2004.

9

Reading Christian Texts and Images

PART I.   CHRISTIAN LITERATURE IN A SECULAR UNIVERSITY

ROBERT KIELY

When the Widow Douglas decided that regular readings from the Bible might save Huckleberry Finn from damnation, Huck went along for a while: "After supper she got out her book and learned me about Moses and the Bulrushers; and I was in a sweat to find out all about him; but by-and-by she let it out that Moses had been dead a considerable long time; so then I didn't care no more about him; because I don't take no stock in dead people."[1]

The Bible is boring to Huck because it is an old book about people who no longer matter, a dead letter. From everything he had heard, the "Good Book" was bitter medicine, good for you, according to elders, but hard to swallow. He and many generations after him have been led to believe that the Bible was a list of negative instructions ("do nots") sent directly from God. If you find problems with them, inconsistencies, brutalities, that must be your fault for misreading them.

Whether they have read it or not, everybody has opinions about the Bible. Among those better educated than Huck, it seems that in order to make sense of the Bible you need to know Hebrew and Greek; if you expect to teach it to college students, you need an advanced degree from a divinity school. Because I had neither of these qualifications, I was a bit surprised some years ago when the chair of the Harvard English Department phoned to ask if I knew anyone who might want to teach the course (then required for English majors). The current professor was retiring and the course was about to be dropped from the curriculum.

Call it hubris, call it folly, or call it a "calling," but the next morning I woke up determined to teach the course myself. My doctorate was in English; my previous classes had all been in the nineteenth- and twentieth-century novel. I knew how to analyze a text; I knew narrative theory; and, as a lifelong Catholic, I had a friendly, if unschooled, relationship to scripture. I felt strongly that it would be a shame to drop from the English curriculum the one book that had a more pervasive and important influence on English and American literature than any other. I had certain negotiating points to make with the chair. The course must not be required. The Bible carries so much baggage—especially in the minds of those who have not read it—that I did not want to present it as a burden but offer it as an opportunity. I asked to choose a colleague from the Divinity School to supplement some of my lectures with historical background. I wanted to use the New Revised Standard translation for most of the books, reserving the King James for Psalms, Isaiah, Song of Songs, Ecclesiastes, and 1 and 2 Corinthians. Relieved to be rid of another headache, my colleague was happy to let me do what I wanted.

Two hundred students turned up for the first class. Christians, Jews, Muslims, atheists, agnostics—I never asked about religious affiliation, but as I visited discussion sections, most backgrounds became self-evident. I did ask how many had read some of the Bible before; about half raised their hand. So with many of these bright, curious, open-minded students, we were really beginning at the beginning. It was absolutely exhilarating. I told them that I was not a Bible scholar, but that I had spent my career analyzing texts and would do my best to teach them how. I said to them, as I often said to myself, "If the Bible is accessible to only a tiny group of scholars, the claims that scripture is revelation *for all* would be nonsense." Most people of the book, Jews and Christians, are not theologians or historians, and for generations most people have read the Bible in translation. (We all needed to understand that we were dealing with an English classic, not the original Hebrew or Greek. My colleague often explained the derivation of important terms, but we had to acknowledge that our texts were approximations of the original, not the original.) I also told them that if "Bible as literature" meant leaving God out of the picture, this would not be such a course. Without divulging a denominational tie, I made it clear that although I was not trying to convert anyone, I did take the religious claims of the texts seriously.

Maps, paintings, archaeological sites, secondary sources, and historical chronologies were posted on the course's website along with the following short introduction:

Methodology: In this course studying the Bible "as literature" does not mean ignoring its religious, ethical, and historical claims, but rather indicates an approach to English translations (New Revised Standard Version and King James) which emphasizes interpretation through close examination of literary genre, narrative and lyrical structure, imagery, and representation of character. Attention is given to the literary characteristics of chronicle, parable, proverb, psalm, prophecy, gospel, and epistle. Themes: The major topics covered in the first part of the course are Covenant, Wisdom, and Prophecy as markers in the history of the Hebrews and as conceptual constructs with distinctive symbolic and formal attributes. In the later part of the course, we look at the distinction between ethical teaching and divine revelation, Jesus the rabbi and Jesus the Messiah. Written work: Two formal papers are required in addition to short assignments, explications, definitions, and responses each week.

We started slowly with Genesis. In lectures I gave brief historical contexts, but I concentrated on careful, attentive readings of texts. As in any literature course, I asked students to pay attention to patterns, repetitions, images, perspective, shifts in tone and point of view, and treatments of time, place, and character. When theological questions emerged, as they often did (from all quarters), I directed students back to the text and their own analyses, asking them (gently) not to tell me what their "rabbi," "sister," or "professor" had told them.

With rare exceptions, student response was overwhelmingly positive. Those with no religious background or previous knowledge of scripture found unexpected drama and beauty. Everyone was impressed by the moral, psychological, and literary sophistication of the stories of Joseph, Saul, David, Solomon, Ruth, and Esther. I was particularly moved by Jewish students who had been raised in nonobservant families. Many came to office hours to tell me how much it meant to be reading "the history of our people" at last. Over the years many began attending services at Hillel, and three became rabbis. The Hebrew Bible was unfamiliar territory for many of the Catholic students; they were often puzzled (as who wouldn't be?) by the complications and ambiguities posed by the Lord's relation to Israel. The Evangelical Protestant students had trouble accepting the possibility that some of the narratives were legendary rather than historical. A group invited me to lunch to discuss Daniel in the lion's den as historical fact. Of course, I reassured them that they were free to believe what they wished (and the grade would not reflect their decision), but I did ask them whether it really made a difference to their faith if some of the narratives, like the parables of Jesus, were fictions. These students also had trouble keeping Jesus out of the Old Testament. I asked everyone to use historical imagination and not to anticipate events that had not yet occurred. When one student wrote an essay on Jonah as a Jesus figure, I asked him to rewrite the paper. He protested, but we reached an understanding when I said that I liked and indeed agreed with his interpretation, but was asking him to try to think what the story might have meant before Jesus entered history.

Theological questions arose from readings of the texts rather than as predetermined formulations superimposed on them: Why are there two creation stories? Why is the disobedience of Adam and Eve so crucial, and why is it often referred to as "the Fall" when "falling" is not part of the narrative? Why does God choose the Jews? Why does God harden Pharaoh's heart? Why is Saul rejected by God, while David is forgiven and rewarded? What is Job doing in Holy Scripture? Is God a God of Mercy or a God of Justice? Can God change His mind? How do we interpret the miracles of Jesus? Which is more important: the teaching of Jesus or the action of Jesus? Why does Jesus sometimes want to keep his teaching secret? Whose fault is it that Jesus is crucified? What is the central message of Jesus? Why does Paul put such emphasis on the Resurrection?

No teacher can provide easy or simple answers to these questions, and students did not expect me to. But they did expect me to help them persist reasonably, patiently, carefully, and with sensitivity to the details as well as to the spirit of the texts. I reminded them that asking difficult questions, as in a yeshiva, is an act of reverence, not disrespect. I was inspired by the seriousness and passion with which students of all backgrounds wrestled with questions that (unknown to them) Jewish and Christian scholars have raised and debated for centuries.

There are problems and limitations in reading scripture or any long and complex literature in one term, but one of the great advantages is that large patterns, faults, and shifts become clear, as if seen as part of a vast interconnected landscape: the constant references to and rethinking of the earlier texts in the later ones, Psalms recalling Exodus, Jonah recalling Genesis, Jesus quoting Isaiah. Most people who attend religious services know scripture in bits and pieces. One of my favorite assignments is to ask students to go home, sit down, and read the Gospel of Mark from start to finish. I think it is safe to say that none of them had ever done this with any gospel. The effect was powerful and, to many, surprising. Jews were surprised to find that Jesus was "so Jewish." Christians were surprised by how many rules Jesus broke. Everyone was struck by his combination of the traditional and radical. Reading Luke brought home to all the relevance of the parables of the Prodigal Son and the Good Samaritan. The mystical beauty and pathos of John appealed to the Buddhists and Hindus. For all, the incidental and chronological disparities among the gospels faded in importance next to the clarity with which Jesus emphasizes love of God and neighbor, compassion for the poor and marginal, faith in the Father.

I learned a great deal about ways of reading and teaching the Bible by visiting the weekly section discussions of fifteen led by graduate teaching fellows. I never failed to be impressed by the civility, intelligence, critical acumen, and sensitivity of the students. All of us on the teaching staff made it plain from the start that all questions and viewpoints were welcome, that each should be treated with respect, and that course grades would be based on knowledge and analytical skill, not belief. It became obvious quite quickly that in disconnecting the Bible from dogma—doctrinal rigidity and antireligious prejudice—we provided students with breathing room, a safe space to explore difficult and controversial questions, and a usable vocabulary with which to express nuanced and complex views. In the process the faithful were exposed to thoughtful skepticism and the skeptics witnessed intelligent faith. Not a small thing in the world we inhabit.

Encouraged by student response to the Bible course, I began to plan a lecture course that I would call Classics in Christian Literature. Perhaps a better title would have been Varieties of Christian Literature, since my intention was not to present an encyclopedic survey, but rather to choose a small, representative sample of some great literary texts. I posted the aims of the course as follows:

> The emphasis will be on how individual Christians have expressed their personal experiences and understanding of God and the teachings of Jesus. Though some attention will be given to historical context and doctrinal debates, the focus will not be on institutional history or systematic theology, but on the witness of individual Christians through a rich variety of literary genres, including autobiography, letters, sermons, legends, meditations, and lyrical poems. Questions to be considered will include: How does each author define what it means to be a Christian? Why is language—the word—so important to Christian writers? What is the assumed audience (readership) of each text? What is the relevance of these texts to a modern reader?

An obvious and perfectly rational way to structure such a course would be to assign readings in chronological sequence, but, for various reasons, I decided not to do this. I did not want to give a false impression of "coverage" of centuries of highly complex history. As in the Bible class, I provided essential historical and biographical contexts for each writer, but I wanted the focus to be on writings, not on dates of crusades, monarchies, papacies, or revolutions. Most important, I did not want broad and vague categories—Reformation, Counter-Reformation, Enlightenment, Modernism—to limit or prejudice the students' direct engagement with each text. I knew that in this class most of the students would be Christian (although all were welcome, and many came from other backgrounds), and I did not want to set up a simplistic, ready-made Catholic-Protestant polarity from the start. As everyone quickly realized, reform was on the Christian agenda for a very long time.

I hoped that students would discover the enormous range, creativity, color, and originality in Christian writing throughout the centuries, see the magnetism of

Jesus and the power of the gospels over time, and recognize the persistence of individuality within the commonality of faith. The course was organized by literary genre, but before we did anything else, I asked everyone to read or reread at least one gospel and the Nicene Creed. We then looked at spiritual autobiography: Augustine's *Confessions*, the *Autobiography of Teresa of Avila*, Martin Luther's *Preface to Latin Writings* and *Biblical Prefaces*. We then considered letters: Paul's Epistle to the Romans; letters of first- and second-century Christians; a letter of Gregory of Nyssa on what it means to be a Christian; the letters of Hildegard of Bingen and Catherine of Siena; Martin Luther's *Freedom of a Christian*; Dietrich Bonhoeffer's *Letters from Prison*; and Martin Luther King's *Letter from Birmingham Jail*. In the section on sermons, we read an early sermon by Clement of Rome, *The Rule of Saint Benedict*, *The Little Flowers of Saint Francis,* homilies of Saint Patrick, and selected sermons of Calvin, John Donne, and Newman. Next we looked at meditations: the *Divine Revelations* of Julian of Norwich, *Spiritual Friendship* by Aelred of Rievaulx, Kierkegaard's *The Difference between a Genius and an Apostle*, and Thomas Merton's *Monastic Peace*. We concluded with poets: George Herbert, Gerard Manley Hopkins, and T. S. Eliot.

Treating historical sequence this cavalierly risks leaving students a bit hazy about dates, but the benefit (a huge one, in my mind) is that they are free to experience a writer and a text with a sense of discovery and an immediacy that transcends centuries. I know perfectly well that a whole term or year could be spent on Augustine and his times, but I also know that for a nineteen- or twenty-year-old American college student, reading *The Confessions* for the first time without too much apparatus can be an extraordinarily powerful experience in itself and an incentive to learn more about the period and the scripture and philosophy that saturate the text. Everyone seemed to be fascinated by Augustine and to see in him something of themselves: restless intelligence, passion, idealism, self-absorption, ambition. They could see, with a little prompting from me, how much Catherine of Siena and Teresa of Avila were influenced by him, how much they resembled him intellectually and, in turn, how much they all prefigured Luther. Catholics and Protestants alike were surprised by Catherine's outspoken ways with popes and bishops and Teresa's difficulties in reforming the Carmelites while staying out of trouble with the Inquisition. Catholics tended to find much to agree with in the early Luther, though most felt he eventually went too far. Everyone, even the Baptists, loved Francis. One student invited me to lunch and asked me if I thought it was all right for a Baptist to pray to Il Poverello!

Letters, sermons, and poems were the catalysts; doctrine, theological controversy, and historical and personal circumstance emerged from them without forming an impenetrable wall around them. The Church is porous, the students learned, a land with many borders—some well-guarded, some not—a city with many gates, a ship with many portholes.

Naturally students saw differences among the writers as well as many broad similarities. Some had to do with temperament and voice, as, for example, between Hopkins and Eliot. Some had to do with organization, as between Benedict and Francis. Benedict's *Rule* was a total novelty for everyone; Catholic students were no exception. There were pleasing discoveries: for example, that slave and free were treated equally in the monastery; that the younger monks were listened to with respect; that a portion of wine was served at meals except during Lent and fast days. The emphasis on obedience was harder to accept until I asked how many in the class were on athletic teams or in the orchestra or glee club. Suddenly the idea that well-being and harmony might result from following the directions of a talented coach or conductor sounded plausible. It also was clear that a corrupt coach or a tone-deaf conductor could lead his or her followers to disaster.

Catherine of Siena and John Calvin startled and disturbed students. They appeared to represent in exaggerated form Catholic and Protestant stereotypes as imagined and feared by others. Catherine's brilliance and bravery were never in question, but her passionate exclamations, her frequent references to the body and especially the blood of Christ, her visions and trance-like states, her celibacy, her support of a weak pope whom she criticized but obeyed, her support of the Crusades—all these seemed to many students peculiarly "Catholic" oddities. Calvin, by contrast, seemed cool, detached, severe, and disembodied in his strict logic. His ideas about election and predestination cast a chill over Catherine's hot-blooded determination to rescue from damnation even the most hopeless of ecclesiastical and secular cases. Perhaps the most important discovery for students reading these writers was that, stereotypes notwithstanding, they forced them to revisit and reflect on their own attitudes and beliefs.

Familiar debates about faith and works, tradition and scripture, hierarchy and congregation, ornament and plain style, authority and freedom, free will and predestination, saintliness and saints took on fresh meanings and did not all fit into neat sectarian assumptions. Although Dietrich Bonhoeffer was a German Lutheran pastor, Thomas Merton a Trappist monk, and Martin Luther King an African American Baptist preacher, students found much in common among them and much to admire. All three lived in dangerous times; all three made radical choices informed by their faith in Christ; all three found comfort in solitude and prayer; all three gave their lives for their beliefs.

Obviously a course of this kind is not the same as one that might focus exclusively on Roman Catholic texts. But I think such a combining of works from the Western tradition of Christianity makes essential points that are often forgotten by Christians and are as important to Catholics as to Protestants and non-Christians. First, it is impossible to make sense of Christian writing and thinking without a knowledge of scripture, especially Genesis, Exodus, Psalms, Isaiah, the Gospels, and Paul's Epistles. (This was old and good news to the Protestants, but a jolt out of the blue to some Catholics.) Benedict's *Rule*, *The Little Flowers of Saint Francis*, the letters of Catherine and Hildegard are as steeped in scripture as the sermons of Luther and Calvin. Second, the Church—long before Luther—was anything but a battalion of unthinking drones in lockstep. Benedictines argued with Augustinians; Dominicans argued with Franciscans; Franciscans argued with themselves; the pope argued with bishops; the Jesuits argued with everybody. Much of the time these arguments had little to do with religion and everything to do with politics and power. They would have made Jesus weep. Christians hated and killed one another. But there were also genuine differences of opinion about how to live the Christian life, how to understand God's will, how to imitate Jesus. Third, although in the worst of times Christians fought one another; in the best of times they prayed together and spoke to one another. In a sermon preached in the 1620s John Donne spoke words that must have shocked both the Puritan "left" and Catholic "right" in his congregation or listening outside the church doors: "The Lord thirsted our salvation. . . . He desired the conversation of man, for man's sake. . . . The Lord became Christ to save man, to save man, all ways, in all his parts, and to save all men in all parts of the world."[2] The inclusiveness of this sentiment would still shock some Christians, but Donne's repetitions leave no doubt about what he meant by combining "conversation" with "salvation" as English Christians were on the verge of a religious war that would make dialogue, common prayer, and tolerance for different forms of worship anathema to each faction. Fourth, Catholics, Protestants, and non-Christians have nothing to fear (or lose) and everything to gain by talking to one another and learning from one another. Surely, to be Catholic (or Christian of any kind) cannot really mean being blind, deaf, and dumb to the beliefs, opinions, and values of others.

More and more of my students are from mixed ethnic, linguistic, and religious backgrounds. One American response to this is to try to blank out all traditions, to enter adulthood as a new version of a "Know Nothing," with plenty of prejudices and taboos but no knowledge, experience, or sympathy for any religious or cultural identity. Another response is to find a tight little island, a narrow orthodoxy of one kind or another that shuts out competing or confusing alternatives. But a little confusion combined with an intelligent curiosity and a good heart is not a bad thing for a nineteen-year-old. It is good to be knocked off balance in order to find out where you stand. And it is good to find brotherhood and sisterhood across boundaries that once were dangerous or impossible to bridge. Christians have more in common than some of our ancestors thought. On all sides and from all sides, persecutions have been imposed and suffered that must have pierced the Savior's heart. Conversion, as my students learned from Augustine and Bonhoeffer, Teresa and Eliot, Herbert and Hopkins, Francis and Luther, Kierkegaard and King, is both a solitary and a collective process, a lifelong conversation with Jesus and with one another, an adventure open to all, costing, as Julian of Norwich said, "not less than everything."

PART II.   THE VIEW FROM A CHURCH-RELATED UNIVERSITY

PAUL J. CONTINO

Robert Kiely begins his essay with Huck Finn's encounter with Moses. My essay begins with Moses' encounter with God. Among the first commandments God gives to Moses on Mount Sinai is this: "You shall not make for yourself a graven image, or any likeness of anything that is in heaven above, or that is in the earth beneath, or that is in the water under the earth" (Exodus 20:4).[3] Why, then, have images played such a vital role in the Christian tradition, especially in Catholicism and Orthodoxy? Professor Kiely teaches the books of the Bible and the writings of saints such as Augustine, Benedict, Francis, and Catherine of Siena. In his classes he has complemented his analysis of the words in these writings with images inspired by them. Vivid renderings by the Renaissance artists Giotto, Fra Angelico, Piero della Francesca, Tintoretto, Titian, Caravaggio, and others bring the viewer into a deeper, more sensuous appreciation of the scene described in the text. I've sat in classes in which Kiely has done this to memorable effect, and his sumptuously illustrated book, *Blessed and Beautiful: Picturing the Saints*, is the next best thing to sitting in class with him. For the past twenty years I've taught at two church-related schools, Valparaiso University (Lutheran) and Pepperdine (Churches of Christ), and like Kiely, have tried to integrate the Christian pictorial imagination with the study of texts. As a complement to his essay, I will describe some of my own work in this area.

Let us return to God's commandment to Moses. Do Christian depictions of Christ and the saints transgress the divine prohibition against images? I'm convinced that if we take the Incarnation seriously, the answer is no. The Word has become flesh, and scriptural witnesses claim to "have heard...seen with [their] eyes...looked at and touched with [their] hands" the incarnate Christ (1 John 1:1). In the eighth century, when St. John of Damascus defended images in the face of the Byzantine emperor Leo's iconoclasm, he used numerous arguments. Among these was the argument that the illiterate can "read" images and thus be edified by them, an argument Pope Gregory the Great made over a century earlier. But at the heart of John's argument is the reality of Incarnation: Christ's embrace of material existence removes the prohibition against using matter to represent the divine:

In times past, God, without body and form, could in no way be represented. But now, since God has appeared in the flesh and lived among men, I can depict that which is visible of God [for Christ is "the image of the invisible God" (Colossians 1:15)] .... I do not venerate the matter but I venerate the Creator of matter, Who became matter for me, Who condescended to live in matter, and Who, through matter, accomplished my salvation; I do not cease to respect the matter through which my salvation is accomplished.[4]

The Incarnation lends a renewed holiness to material reality. Twelve centuries after John's defense, a number of Eastern Orthodox icons—the Mount Sinai Christ Pantocrator, Rublev's Trinity, the Vladimir Madonna, among them—have found a treasured place in the spiritual lives of many Western Catholics, as have images by the Renaissance artists Leonardo and Michelangelo and the more modern artists Rouault and Sadao Watanabe.

In my classroom experience I have found that attentively viewing icons and other styles of Christian painting illuminates the literature we are studying. Paintings engage the sense of sight and appeal to our desire for beauty (one of the divine attributes). They invite the viewer into a deeper imagining of the narrative being explored. For example, whenever I teach Dostoevsky's *Brothers Karamazov*, I ask students to view the icon of Christ Pantocrator from St. Catherine's monastery, which, ironically, is situated at the foot of Mount Sinai. I invite the students to look attentively at the image, and then to imagine it in relation to that novel's Christian vision. For Orthodox believers—and increasingly for Catholics—the icon recalls the viewer to his or her vocation: to repent and return to God (*conversio*). It reminds believers that in our pilgrimage in this life, we are called to holiness, to become saints and thus icons of Christ for each other, much as Alyosha and his mentor, Zosima, are called in the novel. The Sinai Pantocrator, one of the earliest of icons, proves to be especially heuristic. It was painted in the sixth century, not long after the Council of Chalcedon forged the definitive statement on the Incarnation, that Christ is both man and God, finite and infinite, "without separation or confusion."[5] This icon imparts a vivid sense of what the Christian calling might mean.

Jesus' face in the icon is asymmetrical. His right eye is open, receptive. It gazes into ours with tenderness and merciful acceptance. Human beings in our fallenness are loved and redeemed. Here is the radically open Christ who acknowledges human openness and our capacity to change. This is "the Being" of whom Alyosha Karamazov reminds his brother, Ivan, when Ivan has insisted that no one dare forgive the torturer of an innocent child. Here is the "Being [who] can forgive everything, all *and for all*, because he gave his innocent blood for all and everything."[6] In contrast, Jesus' left eye challenges and insists on the necessity and eventuality of closure, the closure of

Christ Pantocrator, sixth-century icon (reproduced by permission of the Holy Monastery of Saint Catherine, Sinai, Egypt.)

decisive choice and final judgment. *We* are responsible for the violence that blights our world. Zosima articulates this challenge of responsibility in his last discourse, moments before he speaks of the "precious image of Christ": "There is only one means of salvation, then take yourself and make yourself responsible *for all* men's sins."[7]

Dostoevsky drew the phrase "for all" from the Eucharistic Prayer in St. John of Chrysostom's *Divine Liturgy*, and the phrase is crucial in understanding *how* the image of Christ is represented as salvific in the novel.[8] "For all" is the linguistic key that links two claims about reality: first, that Christ's redemptive work was accomplished *for all,* and second, that, in cooperative response, we must therefore work in active love *for all*. Christ forgives *for all* and yet we are responsible *for all*: How can the promise of salvation be simultaneously taken up and imposed by Christ?

The paradox grows clear a few lines later in Zosima's discourse: the only way in which we can accept and enact this imposition of responsibility is in conforming to the image of Christ, which stands before us as both model ("Go and do likewise") and gracious ground, the Word that creates, sustains, and enters the world, and thus provides the warrant for an analogical conception of being. In grace, "in touch with other worlds," we must by our responsible example challenge each other to be responsible. Responsibility entails active love, which Zosima starkly contrasts to the unrealistic "love in dreams" that is exemplified by fantasy, a denial of duration, and a greedy desire for immediate applause.[9] Active love is a "harsh and dreadful thing" and always entails work, endurance, and sometimes suffering. In such suffering we participate in the salvific suffering of Christ (Colossians 1:24). When we fail to love actively, we are called to articulate responsibility for our failure in confession—a complex but crucial practice in *The Brothers Karamazov*.[10] Thus the Sinai icon has a classically Catholic "both/and" quality: the viewer who longs to conform to its form must sustain *both* a belief in God's mercy and grace *and*, concomitantly, a commitment to personal responsibility and work.

In the centuries-old tradition of the Orthodox icon, the flesh that is depicted is always *transfigured*, radiant, no longer subject to the decay wrought by time or the passions. Beginning with Giotto in early fourteenth-century Italy, an "intense study of the human form…was further developed by a loving attention to the sheer physicality of Christ,"[11] and to the physicality of the saints, those who yearn to conform to Christ's image. In his Incarnation, Christ enters time, and the Italian Renaissance imaged Christ and the saints in particular moments, in specific places. The Orthodox tradition often takes exception to this development in religious art. Leonid Ouspensky, one influential commentator, contrasts a painting by Raphael (whose work Dostoevsky revered) with an icon of the Madonna and child, and finds Raphael deficient: "What is shown to us [in the icon as opposed to Raphael's painting] is not an individual interpretation or an abstract or more-or-less deteriorated understanding, but a truth taught by the Church."[12]

But the "incarnational theology" made possible by Christ and taught by the Church deeply animates the art of the Renaissance.[13] One of the most powerful experiences a fortunate student or teacher can have is to make a pilgrimage to Florence. Here it is possible to view for oneself the different artistic approaches to the Incarnation that so troubled Ouspensky. A first stop would be the Uffizi, where hang not only Giotto's palpably embodied rendering of the Madonna Ognissanti, but also beautiful Byzantine paintings of the same subject by Cimabue and Duccio. And nearby is the second stop, the Franciscan church of Santa Croce, where Giotto's late frescoes present the life of St. Francis of Assisi in pictorial narrative form. Giotto's work invites viewers to attend to the temporal, spatial realities of our

earth-bound lives, to which the Incarnation has lent a renewed honor. In its attentiveness to and appreciation of the human experience, Giotto's art bears affinities
to the literary work of his friend and fellow Florentine Dante Alighieri.

When invoking Giotto for illustration of religious themes in literature, I have asked
students to select one of the frescoes from the narrative life of Christ that he depicts
in the Scrovegni Chapel—the Nativity, Baptism, Last Supper, Crucifixion, or Resurrection—and compare it to the way that scene is represented in a traditional icon.
Students thus become more aware of the homely human realities that Giotto includes
in his pictures, and the way his work visualizes the slow transpiring of time.[14]

The Italian artists who followed Giotto took his realism even further. Robert
Kiely's *Blessed and Beautiful: Picturing the Saints* offers a rich introduction to these
successors, and what follows is a brief overview of the book.[15]

Kiely writes, "I was attracted and intrigued not simply by the extraordinary
beauty of much that I saw, but particularly by the enormous, astonishing, variety
of ways of depicting figures of supposedly orthodox—that is, consistent and
clear—significance. What I discovered were images often infused with tenderness,
exquisite sentiment, erotic vigor but also ambiguity, irony, even humor, *and not
necessarily less inspirational because of this*" (10, my emphasis). Kiely's book "link[s]
particular scriptural, literary, and theological texts with paintings of unique
beauty" (11) and provides a rich source for any student who wishes to understand
the way the Incarnation lies at the heart of the Catholic intellectual tradition,
especially as that tradition is embodied in art and narrative.

The saints recapitulate the image of Christ in particular ways. "Mary, like Jesus, is
often spoken of in terms of paradox: humble/regal; weak/strong; maiden/mother"
(35), but she "is not only 'like' Jesus; she contains, reveals, and reflects Jesus," especially as she is described by St. Bernard of Clairvaux in the final canto of Dante's
Paradiso or rendered in Piero della Francesca's Madonna of Mercy (38–9). In the
vivid, tactile art of Caravaggio, especially the *Madonna dei Palafrenieri*, Mary emerges
as "a figure of enormous dignity and beauty. In leaning slightly to support her son,
she reveals the full breasts of her womanhood. Her sexuality and sustaining presence
seem, for a precarious split second, in perfect balance" (45). Thus Mary is both "wom-
anly" and "holy," revealing "a healthy body and a perfect spirit"; she is "a flesh and
blood Mary with a gusto and pleasure that do not preclude reverence" (47).

All four gospels present Mary Magdalene as present at Christ's Resurrection,
and even as apostle to the apostles, though her noble stature has been diminished
by some Christian commentators. St. Ambrose of Milan read Jesus' words to Mary,
"Noli me tangere," as a prohibition against women teaching in church; John Calvin
read them as Christ's imperative to cease "the stupid and excited desire to keep
him here on earth" (89). Although there is no scriptural evidence of her sexual sin,

Donatello sculpts a penitent "wraith withering away from fasting," chastely draped by rags (98), in stark contrast to Titian's painting of a nubile nude with flowing hair. Most dramatic are renderings of the post-Resurrection meeting itself, in which Mary mistakes Jesus for the gardener, hears her name, recognizes her teacher, but is told not to touch him. In Fra Angelico's and Benozzo Gozzoli's versions of this scene in the Convent of San Marco, "the elegant postures and pleasant exchange of looks suggests a minuet in which each partner knows his or her role. This is not a shocking, disturbing scene in which Mary overreacts but a quiet beginning of a heavenly dance" (90). In contrast, Titian's version is markedly erotic, yet with "a theological as well as an aesthetic rationale, in keeping with Church teachings about the Incarnation and Resurrection, to the belief that the risen Jesus revealed his full humanity to individuals according to their needs and abilities to 'see': to Thomas through touching his wounds, to Peter and John through feeding them breakfast, to Mary Magdalene through exposing enough (not all) of his male flesh" (92–3). And in contrast with those Church fathers who ignored her feminine grandeur, Piero della Francesca and Sebastiano del Piombo, like the poets Donne and Greve, "recover some human dignity, pride and complexity for a woman who, through no fault of her own, lost her importance as a beloved friend of Jesus and her stature as 'apostle to the apostles'—not to mention her virtue—in the eyes of many men and women for centuries" (105).

St. Augustine provides an especially complex instance of incarnational tensions. In his *Confessions* he describes how he came to renounce the Gnostic dualism of the Manichaeans and recognized the limits of Platonic thought, in which he found the Logos but never the Logos made flesh. Yet Augustine consistently privileges spirit *over* flesh, even as he poetically, sensually renders the distracting plenitude of creation: "Even after his conversion to Christianity, Augustine never fully abandoned his dualistic habits of mind, but, in some of his greatest rhetorical and theological moments, he recognizes that in accepting the Incarnation, the taking of flesh by the Divine, he throws all neat dualistic categories into question" (181). A proto-iconoclast, Augustine did not believe that Churches should be decorated with images, "yet his experience of his own body and of himself as a rhetorician persuaded him that to be human was to be an embodied image-maker ever conscious of the need for mediation between that which is" and that which he longed to be (190). One of my favorite moments in *The Confessions* occurs when Augustine, writing in the present tense as the middle-aged bishop of Hippo, past the turbulent passions of youth, confesses his continuing tendencies toward distraction:

> I now do not watch a dog chasing a rabbit when this is happening at the circus. But if by chance I am passing when coursing occurs in the countryside,

it distracts me from thinking out some weighty matter. The hunt turns me to an interest in the sport, not enough to lead me to alter the direction of the beast I am riding, but shifting the inclination of my heart. Unless you [God] had proved to me my infirmity and quickly admonished me either to take the sight as the start for some reflection enabling me to rise up to you or wholly to scorn and pass the matter by, I would be watching like an empty-headed fool.... My life is full of such lapses, and my one hope is in your great mercy. When my heart becomes the receptacle of distractions of this nature and the container for a mass of empty thoughts, then too my prayers are often interrupted and distracted; and in your sight, while I am directing the voice of my heart to your ears, frivolous thoughts somehow rush in and cut short an aspiration of the deepest importance.[16]

One wonders whether Vittore Carpaccio had this passage in mind when creating his *Vision of Saint Augustine*. This painting depicts the saint gazing attentively out the window, but with a little dog on his left and a sheet of music on the floor, both "emblematic of the tendency of the best of human minds to wander" (196). Thus the artist, like Augustine, reminds us of the limits of our embodied existence this side of heaven, where our bodies and souls will be transfigured—and will remain eternally, lovingly attentive to the Creator. Yet here on earth we can give thanks for the blooming confusion of creation. As Kiely eloquently says in his conclusion to the chapter on St. Augustine:

Melodies and metaphors, toothaches, erotic dreams, naked feet, fistulas, finger-nail clippings and hair shavings, faithful dogs, and disobedient monks have not yet been transformed in the Maker's caldron and resurrected into a new and better life. While waiting for that day, the artist-theologian *fluctuates* between image and abstraction, body and soul, and in so doing, imitates, perhaps not altogether unconsciously or perfectly, the Mediator whom he struggled throughout his life to understand and love. (197)

Midway through *Blessed and Beautiful*, Kiely includes a chapter tangentially focused on St. Lawrence, but largely an appreciation of the art criticism of John Ruskin. Ruskin was raised evangelical but, when traveling in Italy, fell in love with Catholic art. In his finest observations, he attends to the margins of the painting he is studying. For example, he sings the praises of Fra Angelico's side portrait of St. Lawrence in his *San Marco Altarpiece*. Indeed Kiely's description of the way Ruskin looks at a painting can be applied to his own commentary on religious art: "The critic's moment of insight or identification is a sharing that is personal in tone and almost sacramental in its implications. Ruskin presents himself as a witness to the transformative power of art. His is an exemplary case of willing and disciplined susceptibility to that power. He challenges...the viewer and reader to study first and only then let the imagination see" (152). Ruskin's exemplary challenge is one we can propose to our own students.

Another lover of Fra Angelico's *San Marco Altarpiece* is Father John Saward. In *The Beauty of Holiness,* whose title aptly echoes Psalm 29, Saward perceives that the community of saints represented in that painting "pledge that their holiness is not a mere dream. From the altar they say, from this tabernacle, the Splendour of the Father showers His loveliness on the world."[17] The works of Saward and Kiely, along with many others like them, bear eloquent witness to a recent observation by Pope Benedict XVI: "Art and the saints are the greatest apologetic for our faith."[18]

Most of the students I teach are from the Protestant tradition, which, while historically suspicious of religious imagery, has not been consistently opposed.[19] For example, in the *Institutes,* Calvin adamantly rejects patristic arguments defending images and claims that in such "idols" "the majesty of God is defiled by an absurd and indecorous fiction, when he who is incorporeal is assimilated to corporeal matter."[20] But Calvin's argument does not attend to the central claim of St. John of Damascus, that the Incarnation, the Divine embrace of the corporeal, changes everything. Martin Luther was more measured in his response to images and harshly criticized religious leaders like Theodore Beza, who led a sixteenth-century reprisal of iconoclasm:

> I have myself seen and heard the iconoclasts read out of my German Bible. I know that they have it and read out of it, as one can easily determine from the words they use. Now there are a great many pictures in those books, both of God, the angels, men and animals, especially in Revelation and in Moses and Joshua. So now we would kindly beg them to permit us to do what they themselves do. Pictures contained in these books we would paint on walls for the sake of remembrance and better understanding, since they do no more harm on walls than in books. It is to be sure better to paint pictures on walls of how God created the world, how Noah built the ark, and whatever other good stories there may be, than to paint shameless worldly things. Yes, would to God that I could persuade the rich and the mighty that they would permit the whole Bible to be painted on houses, on the inside and outside, so that all can see it. That would be a Christian work.[21]

In the twentieth century Paul Tillich lauded the expressionist art of painters like Emil Nolde. More recently the work of the Catholic theologian Hans Urs von Balthasar has continued to assist Christians from various traditions to a deeper understanding of the vital role that beauty plays in our receptivity to God's goodness and truth.

Teaching Christian imagery for twenty years at two universities, each with roots in Protestant traditions, has provided me with rich occasions to discuss varied views such as these, to illuminate our reading of literary narratives, and to explore the role that images continue to play in our spiritual lives.

NOTES

1. Mark Twain, *Huckleberry Finn* (Boston: Houghton Mifflin, 1958), 4.

2. John Donne, "Sermon at Lincoln's Inn, Sunday After Trinity, c 1622," in *The Complete Poetry and Selected Prose of John Donne*, edited by Charles M. Coffin (New York: Random House, 1952), 480.

3. All Scriptural citations are from the Revised Standard Version.

4. From John of Damascus, *First Homily in Defense of the Holy Icons,* quotation on www.orthodoxresearchinstitute.org/articles/liturgics/scouteris_icons.htm.

5. This image can be viewed at http://campus.belmont.edu/honors/SinaiIcons/WIcons01.jpg.

6. Fyodor Dostoevsky, *The Brothers Karamazov*, edited by Susan McReynolds Oddo (New York: Norton, 2011), 213, italics in original.

7. Dostoevsky, *The Brothers Karamazov*, 276, italics added.

8. The Orthodox theologian Alexander Schmemann explains, "As we stand before God, there is nothing else we can remember and bring with us and offer to God but this self-offering of Christ, because in it all thanksgiving [the root meaning of Eucharist], all remembrance, all offering—that is, the whole life of man and of the world are fulfilled." Schmemann cites the Orthodox Eucharistic prayer:

> Remembering this commandment of salvation
> And all those things which for our sakes were brought to pass,
> The Cross, the Grave, the Resurrection on the third day,
> The Ascension into Heaven, the Sitting on the right hand,
> The Second and glorious Advent—
> Thine own of thine own we offer unto Thee,
> *In behalf of all and for all.*

Alexander Schmemann, *For the Life of the World: Sacraments and Orthodoxy* (Crestwood, N.Y.: St. Vladimir's Seminary Press, 1997), 41, italics added. I develop my analysis of the Sinai icon of Christ and its affinity to *The Brothers Karamazov* in "Incarnational Realism and the Case for Casuistry: Dmitri Karamazov's Escape," in *The Brothers Karamazov: Art, Creativity, and Spirituality*, edited by Pedrag Cicovacki and Maria Granik (Heidelberg: Universitätsverlag C. Winter Heidelberg, 2010): 131–158.

9. Dostoevsky, *The Brothers Karamazov*, 55.

10. Dianne Thompson writes, "In Dostoevsky's fiction salvation begins with confession." Dianne Oenning Thompson, *The Brothers Karamazov and the Poetics of Memory* (Cambridge, U.K.: Cambridge University Press, 2009), 110. I have written more fully about confessional dialogue in Paul J. Contino, "Zosima, Mikhail, and Prosaic Confessional Dialogue," *Studies in the Novel* 27 (1995): 63–86.

11. Lawrence Cunningham, *An Introduction to Catholicism* (Cambridge, U.K.: Cambridge University Press, 2009), 86.

12. Leonid Ouspensky, *Theology of the Icon* (Yonkers, N.Y.: St. Vladimir's Seminar Press, 1992), 1:184. It's interesting to note that a copy of a Raphael Madonna and child hung in the

study of the great Russian author Fyodor Dostoevsky, a gift presented to him by his more ecumenical friend, Vladimir Solovyov.

13. Robert Kiely, *Blessed and Beautiful: Picturing the Saints* (New Haven, Conn.: Yale University Press, 2010), 5.

14. For a helpful discussion of the role of pictorial narrative in Renaissance art, see Jules Lubbock, *Storytelling in Christian Art from Giotto to Donatello* (New Haven, Conn.: Yale University Press, 2006).

15. A fuller treatment of Kiely's book appears in Paul J. Contino, "Paradoxical Portraits," *First Things,* March 2011, 211: 63–4. Parts of the present discussion are drawn from this review. Page references are to Kiely, *Blessed and Beautiful*.

16. St. Augustine, *Confession,* translated by Henry Chadwick (Oxford: Oxford World's Classics, 1992), 212–13.

17. John Saward, *The Beauty of Holiness and the Holiness of Beauty: Art, Sanctity, and the Truth of Catholicism* (San Francisco: Ignatius Press, 1997), 111–12.

18. Pope Benedict XVI, "Meeting with Clergy" August 6, 2008, www.vatican.va/holy_father/benedict_xvi/speeches/2008/august/documents/hf_ben-xvi_spe_20080806_clero-bressanone_en.html.

19. See, for example, the work of David Morgan, especially *Icons of American Protestantism: The Art of Warner Sallman* (New Haven, Conn.: Yale University Press, 1996) and *Protestants and Pictures: Religion, Visual Culture, and the Age of American Mass Production* (Oxford: Oxford University Press, 1999).

20. John Calvin, *Institutes of the Christian Religion* (1536), translated by Henry Beveridge (Grand Rapids, Mich.: Eerdmans, 1962), 1:91.

21. Martin Luther, "Against the Heavenly Prophets in the Matter of Images and Sacraments" (1525), in *Luther's Works,* translated by Bernhard Erling, edited by Conrad Bergendoff (Philadelphia: Muhlenberg Press, 1958), 40:98.

PART I: SELECTED READINGS

Alter, Robert. *The Art of Biblical Narrative.* New York: Basic Books, 1983.
———. *The Art of Biblical Poetry*, New York: Basic Books, 1987.
Arnold, Eberhard, ed. *The Early Christians: In Their Own Words.* Farmington, Pa.: Plough, 1998.
Gerhart, Mary, and Fabian E. Udoh, eds. *The Christianity Reader: Textual Resources for the Study of Religion.* Chicago: University of Chicago Press, 2007.
Harris, Stephen. *Understanding the Bible.* New York: McGraw Hill, 2002.

PART II: SELECTED READINGS

Cole, Bruce. *Giotto: The Scrovegni Chapel, Padua.* New York: George Braziller, 1993.
Kiely, Robert. *Blessed and Beautiful: Picturing the Saints.* New Haven, Conn.: Yale University Press, 2010.
Pelikan, Jaroslav. *The Illustrated Jesus through the Centuries.* New Haven, Conn.: Yale University Press, 1997.
———. *Mary through the Centuries: Her Place in the History of Culture.* New Haven, Conn.: Yale University Press, 1996.
Thiessen, Gesa Elsbeth, ed. *Theological Aesthetics: A Reader.* Grand Rapids, Mich.: Eerdmans, 2004.
von Balthasar, Hans Urs. *The Glory of the Lord: A Theological Aesthetics.* 7 vols. San Francisco: Ignatius Press, 1989.

10

Political Theory and Catholic Themes

Jeanne Heffernan Schindler

A few years ago, in a *New York Times* op-ed piece entitled "Should Our Lives Be Unified?," the ever-provocative Stanley Fish set out to debunk what he called "the myth of the unified life," that is, "the idea that we all have, or should have, a set of core values to which we are responsive no matter what it is we happen to be do-ing—working, worshipping, playing, parenting, voting." The attempt to live con-sistently according to our deepest convictions, he cautioned, can get us into trouble, especially in a liberal democracy that requires moral neutrality in public life for the sake of accommodating pluralism. Social peace, the argument goes, demands a fragmentation of our identities. Thus Fish thinks it understandable, even commendable, when politicians bracket their moral and religious views in order to win an election or, more pertinent for our purposes, when a scholar assumes a radically different perspective in his research from that which orients his life outside the university. The postmodern professor bluntly recommends compartmentalizing one's life. He invites the reader to ask, "Must I be one person at home and in the sanctity of my church and another when I venture out into the world? The liberal state answers, Yes."[1] Fish concurs.

Fish's perspective should not surprise us; he is a product and partisan of the contemporary university whose basic assumptions were stated with breath-taking boldness by Max Weber as early as 1918. The academy then and now is all about fragmentation. Weber puts it quite starkly: the academic vocation entails narrow specialization according to an empirical, ostensibly value-free mode. Gone are the pretensions of earlier classical and Christian understandings of the intellectual life, "the 'way to true being,' the 'way to true art,' the 'way to true nature,' the 'way to true God,' the 'way to true happiness.'" For Weber, the rationalism of science dispelled all of these "illusions" and introduced a new paradigm of learning. According to its strictures, in Mark Schwehn's words, "questions of ultimate meaning and value *must not* be examined within the academy."[2] With this shift the academy became a different universe and, consequently, a different university.

It was a universe anticipated—and feared—by sensitive observers for over a century. John Henry Newman argued strenuously against it, recognizing how grave a threat Weber's disenchanted university posed to a genuine education. In Newman's context the threats arose from the twin impulses of utilitarianism and secularism. On the one hand, utilitarianism subjected the learning enterprise to a pragmatic calculus, imperiling those academic disciplines that for centuries had been central to liberal learning but the practical utility of which was doubtful. On the other hand, secularism directly undermined the theological foundation of higher education. Newman perceived both forces as a threat to the unity of truth and the integrity of the university.

For Newman, "all that is good, all that is true, all that is beautiful, all that is beneficent, be it great or small, be it perfect or fragmentary, natural as well as supernatural, moral as well as material, comes from Him."[3] The divine origin of all of reality, sacred and mundane, renders it worthy of study—for its own sake—and the insight that theology lends to this study is irreplaceable. Thus the burden of his *Idea of a University* is not only to defend the value of a liberal education against the short-sighted demands of the pragmatists, but also to defend the place of theology in the university curriculum. Liberal education, Newman insisted, is a good in itself (since knowledge is a good in itself), though it also has secondary benefits. A cultivated, enlarged, disciplined mind will be useful in any undertaking—social, political, economic, and so forth.

A liberal education must also include theological studies, for theological inquiry has its own distinctive contribution to the common stock of knowledge. In short, the discipline of theology has the singular capacity to answer foundational questions *presupposed* by the other fields of inquiry. Newman insisted that without theology's unique competence, every discipline would suffer. In particular, political science, the subject of this essay, would suffer because its foundation would be weak and its perspective restrictively narrow. Likewise theology without the assistance of political science would find itself bereft of important insights about how a community lives together well. There is an indispensable, though asymmetrical, reciprocity here.

Now this might seem a strange contention, especially today, when any intermingling of religion and politics provokes suspicion. But Newman is right. If the structure and curriculum of the university are not faithful to the unity of truth, education is lost. Thus if politics is studied, as it is in most colleges, as a field susceptible only to descriptive, putatively "scientific" analysis, it will never be understood. It will be rendered trivial and, in the end, fatally boring. When, in the spirit of Weber, the deepest questions about the highest things must be bracketed in favor of a "neutral" inquiry into the social scientific data, one has neglected the most compelling dimensions of political life, those that reckon with profound questions of truth, justice, freedom, and goodness. And in the spirit of Lawrence Cunningham's argument, when political inquiry is cordoned off from theology, it is deprived of theology's unique capacity (identified by David Ford) to affirm, critique, and transform it.

The only remedy for this problem is to recover the classical and Christian meaning of political philosophy, which escapes the sterility induced by the artificial disciplinary boundaries we've inherited. For the ancients and the Christians alike, political philosophy was, etymologically, the love of wisdom concerning the things of the polis. Now, for such luminaries as Plato and Aristotle, the search for wisdom about the city—that is, how we can live together well—was premised upon a certain anthropology. To make this concrete, the ancients considered justice to be the central political virtue, and they defined it as "giving to each man his due." This might seem simple and straightforward, a purely political question, until one considers that it implies prior knowledge about what a man is. And this requires enormous philosophical effort. The kind of inquiry typical of modern political science (focused on such apparently neutral things as elections or city planning or taxes) would not yield this insight. Even political philosophy alone is inadequate. Rather, many philosophical avenues of inquiry are required: metaphysics, ethics, philosophical anthropology, and epistemology, to name a few.

THE CLASSICAL POLITICAL TRADITION AND ITS RIVALS

Plato and Aristotle, whom the early Church fathers called "the protoevangelium," or precursors to the Gospel, invested their heart and soul into this comprehensive inquiry, and it yielded rich fruit, both for philosophy and political science. Since the Church's own thinking about politics is deeply indebted to the ancients, it is worth recalling their central insights. They recognized that man is qualitatively different from every other living being because he is possessed of an extraordinary power, reason, which, if used well, enables him to navigate the world and strive for happiness through the cultivation of virtue. But they also recognized that man is complicated. He is not only rational but is embodied and experiences a range of emotions. As Plato observed so memorably in *The Republic*, man's happiness depends crucially on the ordering of his soul, that is, on the way the rational, spirited, and desiring parts of his being relate. To enjoy happiness, he insisted, an inner harmony must be achieved, according to which reason governs the other elements of his person. Plato argued that the same principle held analogously for communal life.

Aristotle elaborated upon these Platonic insights, and it is helpful to recount his main theses in some detail given how influential his work has been for Catholic political thought. Far removed from modern assumptions, Aristotle perceived an intimate relationship between ethics and politics. Neither would be intelligible without the other; hence his startling claim in book 1 of the *Nicomachean Ethics* that statesmen are concerned above all with the character of their citizens, that they be good people who do fine actions. He lays the groundwork for such a startling claim early in the book when he observes that human nature is teleologically ordered to goodness, that the highest human good is happiness, and that the only way to achieve it is through the cultivation of virtue.

The happy or flourishing life is the one in which our thinking, feeling, and acting conform harmoniously to the good. But this is a high achievement, and it requires the support of a community animated by the same vision. One crucial source of this support is the statesman who enjoys a special prerogative when it comes to the moral and intellectual formation, and hence happiness, of the citizenry. He has the power of the law at his disposal, a power that should be used for the well-being of his people, never for self-aggrandizement. The law, with its unique power to compel, is an instrument in service to the end or telos of politics, namely, the flourishing of the citizens. As he notes in *The Politics*, cities come into being for the sake of mere life, that is, survival, but they remain for the sake of living *well*. The final cause of political life, then, is the well-being of the citizenry, comprehensively understood.

This vision of politics was challenged to its core in early modernity, which witnessed a veritable revolution in political theory. The main outlines of this revolution merit review here, since it challenged the central tenets of Catholic political thought so fundamentally and because modern political theory in the form of liberalism has determined the political and cultural ethos of our time. The first shots were fired by Machiavelli, who, in the dedicatory letter at the start of *The Prince*, boasts that he is adopting utility (rather, it must be implied, than truth or goodness) as his guide in formulating political advice. Taking history instead of philosophy as his touchstone, Machiavelli offers the reader not a sustained anthropology but rather myriad historical examples that testify to the ultimate criterion of success as the central political value. With extraordinary candor, he explicitly disavows the idealism and moral rigor of the classical tradition and substitutes usefulness in their place. In a passage that bears an uncanny resemblance to Fish's recommendation, Machiavelli insists that the successful statesman must learn to be good or not good according to circumstances. Directly contradicting Plato's defense of being over appearance and the purity of Aristotle's conception of virtue, the founder of modern political thought counsels the practice of deception, violence, and all manner of crimes if circumstances warrant it.

As Harvey Mansfield has noted, politics, according to the clever Florentine, becomes an autonomous sphere, not limited by anything above it—God, the Church, or ethics. Attempting to free the statesman from the strictures of classical and Christian morality, Machiavelli tries to persuade the reader that any means will be judged good in retrospect if, in the end, one's reign and territory are secure. To conceive of politics as a noble enterprise designed to promote the good life of one's citizens would now be the stuff of a bygone era. With Machiavelli, "political realism" makes its debut.

A century later Hobbes radicalizes his predecessor's proposals. Recall that Machiavelli self-consciously resisted philosophy, grounding his project historically instead. He provides little argument to justify his revolutionary notions; "the facts" of political success or failure are to speak for themselves. Hobbes, on the other hand, launches a frontal assault on classical and Christian metaphysics, ethics, and politics—in that order. A materialist, he denies the existence of an immaterial soul and offers a mechanistic model for understanding the human. Man is reduced to matter in motion, and his ethical convictions are likewise reduced to stimulus responses. What strikes the individual as pleasurable will be adjudged good; what strikes him as painful will be deemed evil. There is no right and wrong, noble and base in things themselves; there are only physiological states of pleasure and pain on the part of the judging subject.

What is more, there is no natural telos of human life and no objective moral order to which man's thinking, desiring, and acting should conform in order to yield happiness. As Hobbes puts it with characteristic bluntness, "The Felicity of this life, consisteth not in the repose of a mind satisfied. For there is no such Finis ultimus, (utmost ayme,) nor Summum Bonum, (greatest Good,) as is spoken of in the Books of the old Morall Philosophers." In a world of finite goods and unlimited desires, conflict inevitably arises, rendering life in the state of nature "solitary, poore, nasty, brutish, and short."[4] To avoid such conflict is precisely the rationale for entering the social contract, an agreement forged to ensure the security of the contracting parties who mutually forfeit a portion of their liberty so as to gain the protection of a sovereign with virtually unlimited power.

Among the most important powers vested in the Hobbesian sovereign is religious authority. Witness to both the Thirty Years War and the English Civil War and keenly aware of the divisive potential of religious difference, Hobbes subordinated the church to the state and conferred upon the sovereign the most elevated ecclesial office. He would stand not only as head of state, but as head of the church. As chief pastor, he would determine doctrinal matters, appoint bishops, set the biblical canon, settle theological disputes, decide what should be taught, and a host of other tasks traditionally taken to be episcopal, if not papal, in nature.

Hobbes took particular aim at papal authority, since the pope represented a rival sovereignty. A Catholic citizenry, he thought, would be a divided citizenry, with only a qualified allegiance to their political sovereign; their souls would be subject to a foreign power, a distant potentate in Rome with undue authority across the globe. Such a scenario, he argued, induces double vision. Since Hobbes's primary concern is political unity and stability, it is not surprising that he goes to great lengths to establish public religious uniformity as a political first principle. Men must experience simplicity in their allegiances, and unifying the church and state is one crucial vehicle for doing so. The alternative is a fractured body politic vulnerable to civil war.

Hobbes initiated the social contract tradition, and others within liberalism, from Locke to Rousseau to Rawls, adopted it with various modifications. Each of Hobbes's successors would temper the absolutism one finds in his doctrine of sovereignty. They propose, at least ostensibly, a more benign and limited state. Yet despite their differences with Hobbes, their vision of politics is decidedly modern and departs significantly from the classical and Christian political tradition. One finds in Locke's *Second Treatise*, for instance, two notions that characterize most liberal political theory: the contractual nature of human relations and the negative purpose of politics. For Locke as for Hobbes, the body politic was conceived according to the heuristic device of the contract. It was not, as it was for Aristotle, an organic development flowing from man's nature and his affinity for communal life. Rather man is portrayed as an individual in the first instance. It is only the "inconveniences of the state of nature," that is, of his atomized natural existence, that propels him into political society.

Man's political bonds are not the only relationship characterized primarily as private and contractual. Locke also views intimate relations, such as marriage, in these terms. He favorably entertains the notion that the marriage contract is limited and revocable. Its principal end being the procreation and rearing of

children, once the couple's offspring reach maturity the reason for the union disappears. And so Locke wonders why the conjugal bond might not be made, as he
puts it, "determinable, either by consent, or at a certain time, or upon certain Conditions, as well as any other voluntary Compacts, *there being no necessity in the
nature of the thing,* nor to the ends of it, that it should always be for life."[5] This contractual model has been overwhelmingly influential in the Anglo-American
political scene. So has Locke's conception of the purpose of politics. Again unlike
the ancients who envisioned a high task for the political order (indeed nothing less
than promoting the happiness of the polis through the cultivation of a virtuous
citizenry), Locke proposes a much more modest, not to say degraded role for
politics: to protect the individual and his property. Virtue in the classical sense
makes no appearance in the whole of the *Second Treatise.*

Continuing the liberal departure from classical and Christian political thought,
Rousseau, like Hobbes and Locke, undermines the independent foundation of civil
society and reduces the prime units of political community to the individual and
the centralized state. He heralds the state as a liberator, not from the brutishness
of the state of nature, but from the tyrannical conventions of society. Society, with
its artificial forms and statuses, breeds corruption, inequality, and disunity. Man
is delivered from these chains only by a radical dependence on the state. Total
individual freedom and unitary state power converge. The union is effected in the
General Will, a suprahuman expression of political intelligence that ostensibly
reflects the highest interests of the citizens, freed from narrow partisan attach-
ments. To be effectual the General Will must command the absolute obedience of
the citizenry, a collection of individuals beholden to no other association than the
state itself. Civil society cannot stand. As Robert Nisbet observes, in Rousseau's
political vision in order "to achieve a pure sovereignty, one which will be untrammeled by social influences, one which will encompass the whole of man's personality, it is necessary that the traditional social loyalties be abrogated."[6] And
abrogated they were via the legal assault upon the traditional social order com-
menced by the French Revolution (inspired, not incidentally, by Rousseau): the
abolition of guilds, the attempt to eradicate cultural localism, the weakening of the
family, and the pointed attack on the corporate Church.

The anthropology and political vision of the founding figures of liberalism have
decisively influenced American political thought. The rights-bearing autonomous
individual is the icon of contemporary politics, the central purpose of which is the
protection of his liberty. Whereas for the ancients the state's role was in the first
place educative, habituating citizens in the way of virtue, the modern state is supposed to be neutral regarding the good life. This neutrality reflects liberalism's
rejection of classical metaphysics and its corresponding social ontology. As John

Rawls famously insisted, justice in a liberal context is political, not metaphysical. At least putatively, politics, Rawls says, should not be guided by a robust conception of the good. The state must prescind from questions of ultimate value, remaining agnostic as to what is the good for man. Instead it must protect every citizen's right to decide this question for himself.

Nowhere is Rawls's approach stated more clearly in a judicial context than in the 1992 *Casey* decision, which reaffirmed the constitutional protection of abortion by appeal to individual freedom. "At the heart of liberty," the U.S. Supreme Court declares, "is the right to define one's own concept of existence, of meaning, of the universe, and of the mystery of human life. Beliefs about these matters could not define the attributes of personhood were they formed under compulsion of the State." The vision of freedom proposed here flows logically from the twin tenets of American liberalism, identified well by Michael Sandel as state neutrality and individual autonomy. The incoherence of this perspective becomes obvious when one considers the consequences of such a conception of autonomy. In absolutizing the perception and judgment of the individual, the Court has neglected the intrinsically social nature of man and has, ironically, undermined the basis of law and political authority. It is in distinct contrast to this perspective that Catholic political thought emerges as a coherent and compelling alternative.

CATHOLIC POLITICAL THOUGHT: BIBLICAL FOUNDATIONS

One best understands Catholic political thought against the backdrop of this contest between the ancients and the moderns. But in fact the tradition begins before the classical authors noted above. Its roots are biblical and can be found in the first place in the Hebrew scriptures, indeed in the first book of those scriptures. As Thomas Rausch notes, Genesis offers fundamental anthropological insights that inform a Christian view of the human person. These same insights form the foundation of Catholic political thinking. The first is the doctrine of creation, which illuminates the nature of being itself. The text is a celebration of the created world insofar as God blesses each aspect of his handiwork with the observation "[I]t was good."[7] In this pithy but triumphantly anti-Manichaean text, the goodness of matter is unqualifiedly affirmed. And the fact that creation is composed of so many and diverse forms indicates something about the nature of being, namely, that it is good and plenitudinous. (This will be important for understanding the nature of political authority and its positive foundation.)

Genesis also reveals several crucial things about man that bear directly on a Catholic understanding of politics. Recall that it was only after the creation of man that the Bible proclaims God's work "*very* good" (Genesis 1:31). This should not surprise us, for while it is true that man is a part of the created world, he is at the same time qualitatively different from every other part of it: he is uniquely made in the image and likeness of God. The text of the first, or Elohist, creation story conveys this directly. As Pope John Paul II remarks, "The creation of man is essentially distinguished from God's earlier works. Not only is it preceded by a solemn introduction, as if it were a case of God deliberating before this important act, but above all the exceptional dignity of the human person is highlighted by 'likeness' with God, whose image he or she is."[8] Genesis thus emphasizes the distinctiveness of man (that is, the human), as well as sexual difference, which suggests to the pope that there is a special dignity to being embodied as male and female, that being male and female is somehow intrinsic to bearing the *imago Dei*.

According to a Catholic interpretation of Genesis, the unique privilege of bearing the image of God as male and female is inseparably related to the fact that we were created by a Trinitarian God. The language of Genesis 1:26, what the pope calls the "solemn introduction" before the creation of man, hints at this unmistakably as it begins, "Let *us* make man in our image, after *our* likeness" (emphasis added). But to what are we *qua* male and female likened? To a God who is a loving communion of persons and whose communion reveals the importance of *activity*, *receptivity*, and *generativity*. The Father, the first person and "active principle" of the Trinity, so to speak, begets the Son in an outpouring of divine love, while the Son, the second person and "receptive principle" of the Trinity, gratefully receives his being from the Father, and the mutual love they share in turn generates the Holy Spirit. All of which shows what the sixth-century Church father Pseudo-Dionysius calls the self-diffusiveness of divine love; it pours itself out, generating new life.

This brings us back to Genesis, the very record of God's self-diffusive and generous love. For it was *out* of love and *for* love that the world was created. And, according to John Paul II, the human person testifies to this "design for love" precisely in his body. The body matters; it has an intrinsic meaning relevant to an investigation of political life. What the pope observes is that the body's design reveals man's intrinsic sociability. To make this case, he again goes back to the text, this time to the second, or Yahwist, creation account. In this story the pope is especially struck by what he calls the "original solitude" of the first man (*adam,* meaning "human"). Adam is unique among creation. He is vested with the power of reason and self-awareness, which enables him to name the animals, beings with whom he shares the earth but from whom he is importantly different. Adam enjoys a direct relationship with God. He converses with him, responds to his initiative, and is singularly capable of forging a covenant with his Creator. There is thus an important sense in which the first man—that is, the human as such—is alone, inhabiting a distinctive niche in the chain of being that is revealed to him through his observation of the visible world and his subsequent awareness that he is embodied in a way different from all the rest. Unlike the other animals he is a *person*, enjoying a unique way of relating to God and the world by virtue of his reason and will. But this personhood is not separate from his material existence; rather it is manifest precisely in his body. This is the first, and positive, meaning of what John Paul II calls "original solitude."

The second meaning stems from God's recognition that Adam, the human being, needs a partner like himself. With a tender awareness God acknowledges, "It is not good that the man should be alone; I want to make him a help similar to himself" (Genesis 2:18). And so God casts a deep sleep upon the man and, taking one of his ribs, fashions a suitable helpmate, woman. In the pope's gloss on this passage, he notes, "If one then supposes a certain diversity of vocabulary is significant, one can conclude that man (adam=human) falls into that 'torpor' in order to wake up as 'male' (is) and 'female' (issa)."[9] The differentiation into male and female, that is, the introduction of sexual difference, is directly intended by God. And it is experienced by Adam, now male, as a joyful discovery. Upon seeing Eve—embodied like him in recognizably human form, different from all the other animals, and, yes, different from him—he rejoices: "This time she is flesh from my flesh and bone from my bones" (Genesis 2:23). Adam recognizes Eve as another *person*, complementary to himself. The great significance of this differentiation is immediately apparent. Adam and Eve are made *for* each other; they are made for union. "Therefore," Genesis explains, "a man leaves his father and his mother and cleaves to his wife, and they become one flesh" (2:24). And this one-flesh union, like the love found in the Trinity, is designed to be fruitful, or, to use Pseudo-Dionysius's language, to be self-diffusive and generative. And so, by nature, it is. The uniquely complementary bodies of husband and wife enable a union so intimate that it can result in a miracle: the creation of new life, the two truly becoming one in the identity of the new child.

This too is recognized by Genesis and is given a narrative place of prominence. In the first creation account, after God makes man in his image as male and female, he bestows a blessing upon them and enjoins the couple, "Be fruitful and multiply" (Genesis 1:28). This is not an afterthought; it is not accidental to their creation as male and female persons; it is an essential purpose for their sexual differentiation. Moreover the command to be fruitful does not impose an onerous duty, as if the Creator anticipated the original sin and preemptively punished it. Instead it is the extension of a blessing, one that recognizes the creation of children by a man and a woman as an expression of similitude to God himself. Genesis thus recognizes that man is *intrinsically social*, designed for interpersonal communion and for community building.

The fact that Genesis portrays man as intrinsically social, created in the image of a relational God, forms one of the main points of contrast between a Catholic anthropology and that found in liberal political theory. The basic atomism underlying the latter becomes clear when one considers its central heuristic device, noted above: the social contract. The parties to the contract are individuals—not couples, not families, not kinship groups—who, before making their self-interested compact, view one another suspiciously as threatening to their lives and property. As the sociologist Robert Nisbet observed of liberalism's anthropology, it was inspired by the model of Newtonian mechanics, which prompted liberal theorists to envision man according to the terms of Enlightenment science: man as matter in motion, the self-sufficing and independent individual as the atom, the basic unit of social reality. Human associations would be considered secondary, derivative, and conventional. Those that were not the product of conscious agreement by contract were taken to be unnatural limitations upon human freedom. "A free society," in consequence, would be "one in which human beings were morally and socially, as well as politically, free from any kind of authorities and institutional functions." As Nisbet explains, "The ideal, insensibly, became one of a vast mass of individuals separated from one another in social terms, participating only through the impersonal mechanisms of the market and the legal state."[10]

Genesis, by contrast, portrays man as precisely designed for communion, both with God himself and with other human beings. The human communion to which he is first drawn is found in marriage and the family. The Church recognizes marriage as divinely ordained, endowed with essential attributes, such as permanence, fidelity, and fruitfulness, which reflect God's relationship with his people. It also recognizes the family as the first natural society and "the primary place of humanization for the person." It is the "cradle of life and love," in which children receive their human formation, first hearing the Gospel announced through the words and witness of their parents, learning the virtues, and experiencing what it means to love and be loved.[11] In contrast to the way liberalism characterizes family ties, a Catholic conception of the family emphasizes enduring bonds and duties that "are not limited by the terms of a contract."[12] The family is a crucial witness to the kind of relationships rooted in Christian love, relationships "lived in gratuitousness," which, in the words of *Familiaris Consortio*, "[take] the form of heartfelt acceptance, encounter and dialogue, disinterested availability, generous service, and deep solidarity."[13] As we will see, given the critically important role of the family, the Church considers it worthy of special protection and promotion by the state.

Genesis testifies to our basic sociability and indicates its initial expression in marriage and the family. The next book of the Pentateuch, Exodus, testifies to the natural breadth of that sociability, as it highlights the nature of Israel as a *people*.

While individual actors like Moses and Aaron are crucially important to the Exodus narrative, their actions are in the service of their community. Social bonds are depicted as extending beyond the intimate communion of husband, wife, and children; they reach even beyond kin to a vast congregation of people united by a common covenant. As Exodus 3 memorably records, God cares about this people; he has heard their cry and will liberate them so that they might worship him in freedom.

God seeks the well-being of the Jews *as a community* and to that end promulgates laws to guide their common life. But the Ten Commandments are not the only laws governing Israel. Moses institutes additional legislation addressing the specific needs of his community. As lawgiver and judge, he inhabits a role that participates in God's authority, and just as God governs for the good of his people, so did Moses as his deputy. Mosaic law thus cultivated the virtues worthy of a people chosen by God to be his own, virtues of holiness, justice, hospitality, purity, and so forth. Governed by law and regulated by judges, the community of Israel was in fact a *political* community, and its experience contradicted what is a commonplace in our culture, namely, the notion that religion is fundamentally a personal, private affair that concerns an individual and his relationship with God. Exodus tells a different story. It suggests that religion bears directly on the identity and practices of a community and that God cares about how the common life of his faithful is organized, which is to say that God cares about politics.

The New Testament confirms this line of development, even recognizing political authority as a divinely ordained service. St. Paul, for instance, exhorts his listeners to "be subject to the governing authorities. For there is no authority except from God, and those that exist have been instituted by God" (Romans 13:1), and he counsels the brethren to offer prayers of intercession and thanksgiving "for kings and all who are in high positions" (1 Timothy 2:1–2). Likewise St. Peter enjoins the believers to adopt an attitude of respect for the offices of politics, urging them to "[h]onor the emperor" (1 Peter 2:17). Such references are suggestive of what a Christian disposition toward political authority should be, but they do not constitute a developed concept of Christian citizenship or theory of the state. These elemental convictions about the origin of government and the respect it commands require elaboration.

ENRICHING THE CLASSICAL POLITICAL TRADITION

Catholic social and political thought, though it embraces much of the classical tradition, raises the stakes of the political enterprise as conceived by the ancients. It supplies irreplaceable information about the human person necessary to both phi-

losophy and politics. As noted above, St. Paul considers political authority ordained by God and charged with superintending the temporal—and, indirectly,
eternal—welfare of human beings, who are vested with a transcendent destiny:
union with a personal, loving God in a state of perfect happiness. As the encyclical
Evangelium Vitae (*The Gospel of Life*) expresses it, "Man is called to a fullness of life
which far exceeds the dimensions of his earthly existence, because it consists in
sharing the very life of God. The loftiness of this supernatural vocation reveals the
greatness and the inestimable value of human life even in its temporal phase."
"[Although] life on earth is not an 'ultimate' but a 'penultimate' reality," the text
continues, "even so, it remains a sacred reality entrusted to us, to be preserved
with a sense of responsibility and brought to perfection in love and in the gift of
ourselves to God and to our brothers and sisters."[14]

The knowledge that we are called to enjoy intimate communion with God himself is the fruit of revelation. It cannot be yielded by even the most penetrating
philosophical or political analysis. Unaided by revelation, reason can attain important theological truths, such as the existence of God. However, to know that
humans were created out of love and saved by Jesus, the God-man, who has suffered on our behalf so as to be reunited with us, requires the revelation of the
Gospel. This good news sheds a whole new light on the nature of man, which in
turn illuminates both the origin and the nature of the political enterprise.

While politics is commonly considered a remedy for human deficiencies or, as
Reinhold Niebuhr famously put it, "a necessary evil, required by the Fall of
man,"[15] the Catholic political tradition thinks otherwise. It affirms its intrinsic
goodness. As our reflections on Genesis and Exodus indicated, the Church recognizes man's sociability as a divinely given attribute and so maintains a high
regard for human communities. As Rausch puts it, "Catholicism's fundamental
ethos … is communitarian." Precisely because humans were designed for communal life, Catholic political thought considers political authority natural, part
of the created order in its integrity. In this vein St. Thomas Aquinas argued that
government would have been present before the Fall because "there could be no
social life for many persons living together unless one of their number were set
in authority to care for the common good."[16] Centuries later Pope John XXIII
reaffirms this view: "Since God made men social by nature, and since no society
can hold together unless someone be over all, directing all to strive earnestly for
the common good, every civilized community must have a ruling authority, and
this authority, no less than society itself, has its source in nature, and has, consequently, God for its author."[17]

This position might seem implausible to a modern audience accustomed to
seeing political authority primarily as an agent of coercion and punishment. But it

is a crucially important point. Yves Simon, a twentieth-century Thomist philosopher, helpfully explains that the essential function of political authority, namely, caring for the common good, stems not from human deficiency but from the plenitude of being that is instantiated in creation. As Simon observes, political authority is necessary to make decisions that promote the common good when the means to a given end are not univocal. Because of the abundant nature of being, this will frequently be the case, for the world is marked by the generosity and overflowing goodness of the Creator, which presents political authority with multiple, good possibilities.

An analogy might illuminate the matter. The world's great capitals exhibit very different personalities, expressed through their distinctive architecture and public monuments, the layout of their streets, the location and design of their parks, and so forth. The unique gestalt that is Paris, London, or Rome was born of multiple decisions by public authorities choosing among numerous possibilities of design and style. Because beauty is manifested in so many different ways, no one possibility can claim an exclusive prerogative. A decision is needed to select the design in question; someone must render an authoritative judgment. While independent owners, builders, and developers contribute enormously to the character of a city, they operate within codes or shared norms. In addition, every city is at least partly defined by its large public monuments and undertakings. Considered in its essential function, the decisions of political authority are of this kind, made necessary not by human deficiencies but by the bountiful character of the good.

Political authority concerns itself with much more than city planning, of course, and it also has the burden of reckoning with human sinfulness, which makes its remedial or punitive function necessary. What is more, human sinfulness can corrupt the exercise of political power itself. Augustine's concept of the two cities vividly illustrates this problem and is a crucial contribution to Catholic political thought. A keen observer of the human animal, he perceived two basic, competing allegiances in man, an allegiance to the self or to God, which he describes allegorically as a kind of membership in either the City of Man or the City of God. "The two cities," he explains, "were created by two kinds of love: the earthly city was created by self-love reaching the point of contempt for God, the heavenly city by the love of God carried as far as contempt of self." The love of self or the love of God bears directly on the way the two cities exercise power. "In the former," he writes, "the lust for domination lords it over its princes as over the nations it subjugates; in the other both those put in authority and those subject to them serve one another in love, the rulers by their counsel, the subjects by obedience."[18] For Augustine, the Christian ruler can be accounted good only if his reign reflects this

principle of service and is characterized by a dedication to the welfare of his people—a position central to Catholic political theology ever since.

The luminaries of the Church's political tradition, from Augustine to Aquinas to
the papal authors of the social encyclicals, uniformly insist that political authority
must be exercised with a view to the common good, a concept now understood
quite robustly as the sum total of social conditions that promote the integral
development of the person. In order for the state to govern in authentic accord
with the common good, its decisions must be rooted in the moral law from which
the positive law derives its obligatory force. In striking contrast to the epistemological and ethical relativism of the *Casey* decision, the Church holds that God has
fashioned the world with a deep ethical structure that is intelligible and accessible
to man and that man's happiness depends upon living in harmony with its requirements. Since the Church considers political authority to be vested with the high
purpose of promoting human flourishing, its decisions must foster the virtues of
its citizens. Politics, in other words, must be ethically formative, and it must be
animated by a concern for justice rather than partisan or private advantage. The
state's obligation to effect justice was, of course, recognized by the ancients. What
Catholic political thought contributes to the classical political tradition on that
score is an expanded circle of deserving recipients, since, in Rausch's words, "every
human person is sacred, an absolute value." The Church insists then that the state
exercise special vigilance to defend the dignity and protect the rights of the most
vulnerable members of society: the poor, the marginalized, the homeless, the
unborn child, the immigrant.

Beyond the minimum requirement to protect human rights, though, political
authority is charged with attending to its citizens' well-being, comprehensively
understood. In short, it must promote the good life. In seeking to promote the
good life of the community, the state will necessarily have a concern for the
material, social, and spiritual welfare of its people. This is not to say that the state
exhaustively, or even necessarily directly superintends each of these areas. To
the contrary, Catholic political thought recognizes a multiplicity of actors in its
social ontology. Though contemporary politics conceives of social life according to
an impoverished "individual-state-market grid,"[19] the social landscape of a Catholic
vision is richly populated by the institutions of civil society. Born of human solidarity, these associations—like the family, church, school, and trade organization—assist in the full development of the human person. As *Gaudium et Spes*
articulates it:

Man's social nature makes it evident that the progress of the human person
and the advance of society itself hinge on one another. For the beginning, the

subject and the goal of all social institutions is and must be the human person that for its part and by its very nature stands completely in need of social life. Since this social life is not something added on to man, through his dealings with others, through reciprocal duties, and through fraternal dialogue he develops all his gifts and is able to rise to his destiny.[20]

In specifying this social context, the Church underscores the importance of civil society as the connective tissue of a polity. "The social nature of man," *Centesimus Annus* contends, "is not completely fulfilled in the State, but is realized in various intermediary groups, beginning with the family and including economic, social, political and cultural groups which stem from human nature itself and have their own autonomy, always with a view to the common good."[21]

Political authority has the special task of ensuring the conditions within which the institutions of civil society can achieve their proper ends. As the Church conceives it, the state must relate to these institutions and to individuals according to the principle of subsidiarity. Subsidiarity holds that there are functions proper to each of the agents in the social ontology that should be given the liberty to fulfill their given functions. Likewise the principle holds that wherever feasible the smallest or least centralized authority (whether the individual, small social groups, or local government) should be allowed wide latitude in decision making so as to promote full human development. The principle reflects two fundamental convictions. First, God, though omnipotent, governs the universe in a way that grants freedom to his creatures. As the *Catholic Catechism* articulates it, "He entrusts to every creature the functions it is capable of performing, according to the capacities of its own nature."[22] Social life should reflect a similar respect for human freedom. The second, related conviction is that the nonpolitical organs born of human sociability, such as the family, church, and other associations of civil society, as well as the bonds of solidarity between them, do not owe their existence to the state and should not be suppressed by it. Their existence, as Pius XI would insist, is "a matter of private order and private right."[23]

Though always rooted in these two convictions, the principle of subsidiarity has been articulated in a variety of ways. Affirming the legitimate autonomy of individuals and associations, Leo XIII, for instance, argued that they should "be allowed free and untrammeled action as far as is consistent with the common good and the interest of others."[24] Forty years later his successor, Pius XI, authored what is considered the locus classicus on the subject. In *Quadragesimo Anno*, he wrote:

It is a fundamental principle of social philosophy, fixed and unchangeable, that one should not withdraw from individuals and commit to the community what they can accomplish by their own enterprise and industry. So, too, it is an injustice and at the same time a grave evil and disturbance of right order to transfer to the larger and higher collectivity functions which can be performed and provided for by lesser and subordinate bodies. Inasmuch as every social activity should, of its very nature, prove a help to members of the body social, it should never destroy or absorb them.[25]

In response to their respective political contexts, Leo XIII and Pius XI asserted the principle of subsidiarity against the menace of collectivism. Later formulations of the principle accent the positive role of the state. For instance, John XXIII, in addressing the question of private initiative and state intervention in economic matters, affirmed the legitimacy of the latter so long as it had a particular character, namely, one that "encourages, stimulates, regulates, supplements, and complements" the proper initiative of private actors.[26] Speaking more broadly, *Gaudium et Spes* enjoins public authorities to protect the rights and promote the proper activities of individuals, families, and the social and cultural associations that compose civil society, each of which enjoys its own sphere of autonomy.

Not surprisingly the Catholic political tradition has accented the importance of the Church among these institutions and has insisted, contra the claims of a Hobbes or a Rousseau, that the state respect its freedom to carry out its mission. With its eschatological horizon and the supernatural gift of grace at its disposal, the Church offers a version of the good life that surpasses that found within the bounds of the polis. The city cannot save us, and as Lawrence Cunningham aptly observes, Christian holiness exceeds Aristotle's *eudaimonia*. On the other hand, Catholic political thought does not denigrate the work of the state, though it recognizes it as an institution in the order of nature rather than grace. It sees the state as a crucial partner with the Church in advancing human well-being. The state has the distinctive juridical authority to ensure different elements of the common good (e.g., a living wage, environmental protection, safe working conditions). It also has an irreplaceable educative role insofar as the instrument of law has a powerful capacity to shape the character of its citizens. Since the cultivation of the natural virtues enables men to live out the infused virtues more easily, the Church highly regards the formative dimension of political authority. So elevated and weighty is the responsibility of fashioning good law, in fact, that Pope John Paul II describes it as "a task which brings man close to God, the Supreme Legislator."[27]

Few have understood more keenly the burden and privilege of the vocation to politics than St. Thomas More. His example is a striking counterpoint to Fish's proposal of a compartmentalized life. Unlike most of his peers, More recognized that to retain its integrity and authority the state must act in harmony with the natural law and divine law. Politics, in other words, cannot be considered an autonomous sphere with no higher point of reference; rather it is a service by which truly human goods, generously given by God, are fulfilled. More testified to the divine origin and end of these goods throughout his life as a public servant and for this reason is considered by the Church the patron saint of statesmen. His final words, uttered before his martyrdom, reflect an ordering principle at the heart of Catholic political thought and the only understanding that can genuinely guide a community in living together well: "I die the king's good servant, but God's first."

NOTES

1. Stanley Fish, "Should Our Lives Be Unified?," *New York Times,* February 18, 2007.

2. Max Weber, "Science as a Vocation," in Mark Schwehn, *Exiles from Eden: Religion and the Academic Vocation in America* (New York: Oxford University Press, 1993), 7, 10.

3. John Henry Newman, *Idea of a University* (Notre Dame, Ind.: University of Notre Dame Press, 1990), 50.

4. Thomas Hobbes, *Leviathan* (New York: Penguin Books), 160, 186.

5. John Locke, *Second Treatise of Government* (Cambridge, U.K.: Cambridge University Press, 1960), 321, emphasis added.

6. Robert A. Nisbet, "Rousseau and the Political Community," in *Tradition and Revolt: Historical and Sociological Essays* (New York: Random House, 1968), 20–1.

7. Author's scriptural references are from the Revised Standard Version (Catholic edition).

8. John Paul, II, *Man and Woman He Created Them: A Theology of the Body* (Boston: Pauline Books and Media, 2006), 135.

9. John Paul, II, *Man and Woman He Created Them,* 8:3.

10. Robert A. Nisbet, "Moral Values and Community," in *Tradition and Revolt*, 136.

11. John Paul, II, *Christifideles Laici,* December 1988, 40, www.vatican.va/holy_father/john_paul_ii/apost_exhortations/documents/hf_jp-ii_exh_30121988_christifideles-laici_en.html.

12. Pontifical Council for Justice and Peace, ed., *Compendium of the Social Doctrine of the Church* (Washington, DC: U.S. Conference of Catholic Bishops, 2004), 96.

13. John Paul, II, *Familiaris Consortio,* November 1981, 43, http://www.vatican.va/holy_father/john_paul_ii/apost_exhortations/documents/hf_jp-ii_exh_19811122_familiaris-consortio_en.html.

14. *Evangelium Vitae,* 2, www.vatican.va/holy_father/john_paul_ii/encyclicals/documents/hf_jp-ii_enc_25031995_evangelium-vitae_en.html.

15. Reinhold Niebuhr, *The Children of Light and the Children of Darkness: A Vindication of Democracy and a Critique of Its Traditional Defense* (New York: Scribner's, 1944), 91.

16. Thomas Aquinas, *Summa Theologiae,* 1a.96.4.

17. John XXIII, *Pacem in Terris,* 269, www.vatican.va/holy_father/john_xxiii/encyclicals/documents/hf_j-xxiii_enc_11041963_pacem_en.html.

18. Augustine, *City of God,* book 14, excerpted in *From Irenaeus to Grotius: A Sourcebook in Christian Political Thought,* edited by Oliver O'Donovan and Joan Lockwood O'Donovan (Grand Rapids, Mich.: Eerdmans, 1999), 142–3.

19. Mary Ann Glendon, *Rights Talk: The Impoverishment of Political Discourse* (New York: Free Press, 1991), 143.

20. *Gaudium et Spes*, 25, www.vatican.va/archive/hist_councils/ii_vatican_council/documents/vat-ii_cons_19651207_gaudium-et-spes_en.html.

21. *Centesimus Annus*, 31, www.vatican.va/holy_father/john_paul_ii/encyclicals/documents/hf_jp-ii_enc_01051991_centesimus-annus_en.html. These reflections on civil society were originally published in my essay in *Christianity and Civil Society: Catholic and Neo-Calvinist Perspectives* (Lanham, Md.: Lexington Books, 2008). They are reprinted here with permission.

22. *Catechism of the Catholic Church* (New York: Catholic Book Publishing, 1994), nn1883–5.

23. Pius XI, *Quadragesimo Anno*, 87, www.vatican.va/holy_father/pius_xi/encyclicals/documents/hf_p-xi_enc_19310515_quadragesimo-anno_en.html. John Courtney Murray, S.J., reminds us that this principle had been articulated centuries earlier by Gelasius I, who underscored the distinctive dispensation of the Christian era for Emperor Anastasius, asserting, "Two there are, August Emperor, by which this world is ruled on title of original and sovereign right—the consecrated authority of the priesthood and the royal power." "Are There Two or One?," in *We Hold These Truths: Catholic Reflections on the American Proposition* (New York: Sheed and Ward, 1960), 202.

24. Leo XIII, *Rerum Novarum*, 35, www.vatican.va/holy_father/leo_xiii/encyclicals/documents/hf_l-xiii_enc_15051891_rerum-novarum_en.html.

25. Pius XI, *Quadragesimo Anno*, 23, www.vatican.va/holy_father/pius_xi/encyclicals/documents/hf_p-xi_enc_19310515_quadragesimo-anno_en.html.

26. John XXIII, *Mater et Magistra*, 53, www.vatican.va/holy_father/john_xxiii/encyclicals/documents/hf_j-xxiii_enc_15051961_mater_en.html.

27. Jubilee of Government Leaders, Members of Parliament and Politicians, Address of the Holy Father John Paul II, November 4, 2000, 4, www.vatican.va/holy_father/john_paul_ii/speeches/2000/oct-dec/documents/hf_jp-ii_spe_20001105_end-jubilparlgov_en.html.

SELECTED READINGS

Grasso, Kenneth L., et al., eds. *Catholicism, Liberalism, and Communitarianism: The Catholic Intellectual Tradition and the Moral Foundations of Democracy*. Lanham, Md.: Roman and Littlefield, 1995.

O'Donovan, Oliver, and Joan Lockwood O'Donovan, eds. *From Irenaeus to Grotius: A Sourcebook in Christian Political Thought*. Grand Rapids, Mich.: Eerdmans, 1999.

Pontifical Council for Justice and Peace, ed., *Compendium of the Social Doctrine of the Church*. Washington, DC: U.S. Conference of Catholic Bishops, 2004.

Schindler, Jeanne Heffernan, ed. *Christianity and Civil Society: Catholic and Neo-Calvinist Perspectives*. Lanham, Md.: Lexington Books, 2008.

Simon, Yves R. *Philosophy of Democratic Government*. Notre Dame, Ind.: University of Notre Dame Press, 1993.

11

History in a Catholic Framework

Glenn W. Olsen

ANYONE WHO SPENDS his or her life working in an academic discipline likely senses the inadequacy and contingency of how academic fields are currently understood and practiced at colleges and universities. Partly this is because all fields have a history and carry the various twists and turns of this history with them to the present. Some fields have had to disown part of their ancestry, the modern chemist, for instance, being careful to distinguish what he or she does from ancient alchemy. Other disciplines, such as history, need to acknowledge the many senses in which the label for their field has been used, and then to declare an allegiance to or affinity for one or more of these senses.

At the least, most labels can signify a subject of study, a body of knowledge, and a methodology. To Herodotus (ca. 484–ca. 425), the first we know to have used the term, *historia* originally signified "research," with an unclearly defined methodology, or no single methodology (methodology per se tends to be a concern of the modern period), but emphasizing the primary act of consulting evidence to see what we can know of the past. Then was to follow an artful narration of what had been found in the evidence, in which the historian told an enjoyable story, or one from which a reader could benefit either in understanding or in moral growth. Eventually, in his distinction between poetry and history in the *Poetics*, Aristotle (384–22) codified this, arguing that history was a "narration of singulars," implicitly obligated to preserve the past in all its uniqueness.

Here the emphasis was on history as a method of presentation that does not abandon the uniqueness of each event in the quest for some generalizing law or pattern. Suspect was the kind of generalization the poet, philosopher, or—jumping to the modern period—social scientist engages in. The first obligation was for the historian to insist on all the ways one event is not like another. This does not mean that historians do not generalize or speak of "history teaching," but Aristotle thought that if one really wanted to understand the differences between areas of knowledge, history should be seen as a kind of narrative rather than a means of generalization. In fact most ancient historians thought of history as a subspecies of ethics. Consequently they heavily favored interpretations that, for instance, showed that states become strong through discipline and weaken with riches and the quest for pleasure.

From the first, historians understood that they could not present a narrative without some assumed framework or narrative line. For the ancients in the Mediterranean Basin this was usually political, the framework of the Peloponnesian War giving Thucydides (ca. 460–ca. 395) the story line or narrative he needed to tell his story, or the rise of Rome giving a frame for Livy's (59 BC–AD 17) presentation of Roman history. It is difficult to say what came first, narrative frame or research, and in an important sense they always coexisted in dialogue with one another, each modifying the other and making it more specific. But to repeat, the framework did not simply arise from the events examined, but in an important sense was assumed or chosen. To use a political framework, one had first to think of politics as central to human life and as therefore particularly important for describing humans in time.

INTERPRETATIVE FRAMEWORKS AS THEOLOGIES OF HISTORY

Thus the argument of Karl Löwith in his classic, *Meaning in History*, that in the modern period the frameworks have always been "theological." Ever since Judaism and Christianity came to influence a larger world, Jewish and Christian belief in a creator God working in time has influenced how history's story has been told, even by those such as Karl Marx (1818–83) who begin with the premise that God does not exist.[1] While they may deny that God exists, they write a secularized history that retains ideas historically associated with and dependent on the Jewish or Christian idea of a God directing history, so that ultimately history has a point and is moving in some single direction, such as the withering away of the state. The ways of retaining some such framework have been manifold: some (re)turn to politics or economics for their frameworks; some are Hegelian, that is, they see

History as being about the realization of freedom; some, as just stated, are Marxist and claim the priority of material configurations in shaping the rest of life; some are liberal and assert a doctrine of general progress, so that the story is about humankind's achievement of some general condition, perhaps peace or universal human rights; but all are theological, obtaining their narrative framework from a principle of selection by which some matters are included in one's story, and others excluded.

Christianity, according to Löwith, differs from Marxism here in its acknowledgment that its interpretive framework is theological. It is honest about what it does when it reads history. The history it tells is derived from Christian revelation, and not something that follows from the facts alone. According to Löwith, if we speak properly we acknowledge that the general frameworks for historical interpretation in the modern period have been theological in nature, not something deduced from the historical record, but something imposed on it. They express a theology of history rather than a philosophy of history. That is, they are derived from various secularizations of the Jewish or Christian idea of providence and are not the result of an examination of the historical record by an unaided reason. In fact in some obvious sense they may well go against the bare facts. The twentieth century was filled with wars, some of them arguably the worst the race has known, but a progressive historian might insist that, against all this evidence of human evil, history is really about a movement toward universal peace and brotherhood. Never actually achieved, this brotherhood is always in formation. It is a secular eschatology, suggesting that history has a direction. Although Christians themselves commonly speak of such things as "Augustine's philosophy of history," it would be better to speak of "Augustine's theology of history," and leave the word *philosophy* to describe such things as a given historian's notion of the nature of causation or social class, things open to reason.

THE ORIGINS OF THE CHRISTIAN IDEA OF HISTORY

Virgil (70–19) is not necessarily thought of today as a historian, but in some ways he was the Roman historian par excellence and the chief link between pagan and Christian ways of thinking about events in time. Although the story he had to tell, the founding of Rome, was political, it was also more than that and implicitly expanded history to being about more than politics to being about providence, and thus about something more basic than the political at the center of human life. Subsequently Christians expanded Virgil's Stoic sense of an impersonal destiny driving all things into the Christian sense of providence, in which God sees every bird fall and can number the hairs on one's head. Here the framework for history, already providential for Virgil, became explicitly theological, asserting a personal God at work in time. Or rather, a view long present in the history of Judaism walked onto a much larger, Roman stage. From the time of the first Christian historian, Eusebius (ca. 263–339), most Christian historians tried some form of the pagan way of composing history, both pursuing documentary research and building their histories around political mileposts. But these were suffused with a Christian theological understanding, in which ultimately history was about God's works in time, centering on preparation for the Incarnation of Christ, his coming, and the subsequent proclamation of his message to the ends of the earth.

A first instinct, dominating in Eusebius, was to write as if the historian's duty was the explication of what God was doing in time. This was closely tied to an ancient idea at the center of much Jewish thought: that in history God punishes evil and works for good. The corollary was that the historian could—and should— trace this, as if he (before the modern period there were very few women historians) were weighing historical events by a divine measure. If with Constantine (ca. 272–337), the emperor converted to Christianity, he was to be praised; if with Julian (331/32–363), whom the Christians called "the Apostate," the emperor departed from the faith, an early death was his just reward. Most Christian historians until the time of Bishop Jacques-Bénigne Bossuet (1627–1704) wrote as if the historian—of course guided by such things as the Bible—is privy to God's designs.[2] Today when Christians invoke "the signs of the times" they implicitly retain such a view: an individual or community is thought capable of telling what the Spirit is doing.

In ancient Christianity Augustine (354–430) represents a kind of minority report. Almost alone before the modern period, he considered the question of precisely what it means to write a Christian history, and decided that such a history could be written in only the most restricted sense. Augustine held that the Scriptures contain revelation that does make a public claim. That is, through the Holy Spirit the Old and New Testaments are witnesses to the "Great Things" done by God in history, of how salvation has been, so to speak, carried by certain saving events. Where the Scriptures are clear, the Christian historian may speak. Where they are silent, he or she may not. Augustine took this to mean that when the Scriptures chronicle the saving events, as in the biblical story of God's work from creation to Incarnation, one can say a good deal about how God has been at work in time, but that we have no privileged public way of knowing this after the close of the New Testament.

Augustine came to think that even with prayer and revelation none of his contemporaries could properly write the kind of history Eusebius had envisioned. The historian could not normally write an "inspired" history. Yes, where the Bible had made claims for God's calling or leading of his people, one could write a "salvation history," a narrative of the events down to the Incarnation and establishment of the Church by which God had intervened in history. But this was essentially an ex post facto history, a history of what God has revealed of what he has done in time. It ends with the closing of Scripture; the Bible portrays the Great Deeds by which we are saved, but provides little information (its prophecies are vague) on how God is working today, and "no one knows the hour when Christ will return." What is said in Scripture cannot be extrapolated in any precise way to the present or future. We can know what God asks of us ("Keep the commandments," "Love your neighbor"), and we may presume that God is present where his commandments are kept and neighbors are loved, but we do not precisely know how God works in events.

The Scriptures do not speak of the present in a way that it is so clear that, beyond such things as noting the spread of the Christian message, we can chart the work of the Spirit right now. We can know enough so that we often can see where we should take our stand or for what cause we should work, but we cannot confidently declare that we understand the movement of history. By faith Christians believe that God has been at work down to our times and is at work right now, but lacking a specific or personal revelation the historian simply has no method by which the history of what God is doing can be chronicled for our own times. Even if we agree with the theologian Hans Urs von Balthasar (1905–88) that in an important sense revelation is not just a past event, but something always happening, in the sense that saints continue to appear with missions for their age, discernment is difficult and the public status of such claims in doubt. Balthasar thought that one of the functions the saints performed was to confront each age with its limitations and to point some way forward.

One argument early Christians made was that the truth of Christianity was proved by its rapid expansion, both in the time of the martyrs, when Tertullian (ca. 160–ca. 220) claimed that "the blood of the martyrs is the seed of the Church," and after the conversion of Emperor Constantine to Christianity in 312. The Muslims later made a similar argument in regard to the truth of Islam. Such arguments seem implicitly to be arguments from success, in which the worldly success of a religion is taken to prove its truth. But a thoughtful Christian might ask—and Augustine did ask—whether either Christianity or history is really about success. First, success is a category largely determined by perspective. What might look like success from the perspective of the moment might look very different from the perspective of a century. At the least, we cannot presume that history is progressive, that it is a story of improvement or of things getting generally better. There are undoubtedly kinds of specific progress, such as in our accumulating knowledge of medicine, but there is no sanction either in Christianity or simply in consulting the historical record for a general notion of progress. Even in the case of alleged specific forms of progress, one can well ask whether each claimed progress does not contain something undesired.

Further, if we think about what it means that God-in-Christ himself was slain when he came to this world, his life is not in any usual way about categories of success. Though he conquered death, in some way the course of his life was a simultaneous descent to death and ascent or return to his Father. May we not conclude from this that the main historical category is something like struggle, with no promise of success in time? For the Christian, life is cloaked in deep mystery as to its final historical implications. One could argue that the more one understands Christianity as centrally about faithfulness to God, come what may, and not about success, the less likely a history premised on progress can be adequate to Christianity's message.

THE ENLIGHTENMENT REDEFINITION OF HISTORY

For centuries Augustine's stance was hardly known in Christendom, and a history writing more descendant from Eusebius was practiced. In an important sense, we must wait for the Enlightenment of the eighteenth century for the Eusebian view to be overthrown. But then, as the modern university began to appear and in the nineteenth century history departments were founded in research universities, it was the Enlightenment view of history more than any Christian view, Eusebian or Augustinian, that came to dominate. Enlightenment thought could have Christian and non-Christian forms, but generally both in some way marginalized God, leaving him out of the story, no longer presenting him as central to what was happening in time. The theological word for this is deism. Even when the Enlightenment historian was Christian, he likely thought of God as the Divine Clockmaker who set the mechanism of the world in movement but no longer intervened in it.[3] Just as did the natural scientists of the time, the Enlightenment-formed historian wished for a historical order with so much natural integrity that it could effectively be understood and chronicled without reference to God. The historian could then show how this is the cause of that, just as if he were a physician analyzing disease, a physician no longer looking for the bad spirits that earlier people thought caused the disease, but rather looking for the illness's observable natural antecedents.

The historian still needed a framework for his narration, and for this he could return to the political frameworks used before the appearance of Christianity, as did Edward Gibbon (1737–94). The result was a world much less mysterious and a history much more matter-of-fact and in human control than the medieval historian had known (cf. Rausch's discussion of "the mystery of the divine"). For the medieval historian history had been unpredictable, intruded on in disorienting ways by demons and disease, raised high by persons of extraordinary sanctity; history was God's threshing floor, as the early Christians had said. Right through the Middle Ages, as long as God was thought of as at every moment creating or working in time, the regularity and confidence about tracing real causal chains so desired by the Enlightenment historian was impossible.

Every new discipline that appeared within the emerging university of the nineteenth century was anxious to find some kind of self-grounding authority not external to itself. The natural sciences led the way, sometimes concocting such stories as there having been an age-old hostility between science and religion in order to assert science's independence of all external authority.[4] History never found its mandate in ecclesiastical authority in the way theology had, but like all fields, now was in search of some self-validating authority. Hence, as in other fields, historians more and more looked to the approval of other historians, and then to associations of historians, for validation of their work.

HISTORY IN CATHOLIC HIGHER EDUCATION TODAY

Today history in the Catholic college or university finds itself in a very mixed situation. In spite of the fact that among leading postmodernist thinkers, Christian or not, all or many of the Enlightenment premises are rejected, almost all the traditions of the Enlightenment in fact continue to flourish. In fact most Catholic historians work squarely within them. It is not that these historians no longer trace God's work in time in true medieval fashion, something I have suggested may be to the good. The problem is that few communicate any reservations about the Enlightenment framework of their historical presentation. We rarely find even a Christian humility in which the historian is full of doubts about what can be known and communicates this hesitancy to his or her students. More common is a confident narrative born of the Enlightenment in which it is assumed—but now in secular guise—that the historian has privileged access to the meaning of history, and that this meaning is a tale of progress.

The very meaning and propriety usage of the term *Catholic historian* is debated. Some think this is only a way of specifying a historian who happens to be Catholic. Others think there is such a thing as "Catholic history," something parallel to another contentious label, "Catholic philosophy."[5] In the marginalizing of God in

Enlightenment narrative, Satan and the forces of evil were ontologically banished from history. The contemporary historian cannot seriously—with the occasional exception made for a Hitler or for polluters of the environment—entertain the idea that a war between good and evil, between becoming Godlike and turning from God, is at the center of time, and that, as Augustine said, some of the forces involved are demonic. Priests preach from the pulpit, obviously with good intent, that one should never think of the spread of AIDS as a divine judgment on evil. Such pronouncements ironically at one and the same time arguably return us to the situation of the medieval historian. Speaking as a mind reader of the divine, these homilists also seem very removed from, say, especially what the Old Testament says about God's judgments in history as the Lord of Time (cf. Cunningham, "Jesus Christ, Only Son and Lord"). We have hardly a Catholic historian so liberated from Enlightenment premises as to share St. Anthony's fear of demons. When I asked a good friend, an ex-Jesuit with a mission to free Christianity from all belief in Satan, "But what then of the Angels?," he could only throw up his hands.

But what of the angels, that is, of a world whose story includes that of the angels and about which we can hardly ever speak confidently? What about the kind of universe sketched out in Augustine's *City of God*, a universe in which two Cities are forming, one composed of all created beings with a will, angels and humans, who choose for God, and one composed of all those who choose for themselves or the Devil? Is not the assertion that there is a titanic struggle going on at the heart of history something to catch the student's imagination, and a kind of relief from the banal categories of progress to which he or she has likely previously been exposed? If one asks current students "How is belief in progress going?" one might find that they both believe and disbelieve what they have been told. If one considers the Holocaust under the banner of historical progress, one might find belief in progress crushed, but shortly thereafter the same sobered student may well return to the assuring progressive perspectives American education has channeled deep into his or her psyche. Hoping that this is not a sin against hope, I assume that the history faculty at Catholic colleges and universities in the near future will be typical of the historical profession. As children of the Enlightenment, they will be held, if not captivated, by its mundane story. But an interesting book suggests that I may be wrong here.

John L. Allen Jr., in a book suggesting what the shape of "the future church" might be, has a good deal to say about the future return of beliefs long thought banished.[6] Allen believes that the future of the Church lies in what he calls Southern Christianity, the non–North American, non-European Christianity of roughly the southern hemisphere, where most Christians live. This is a Christianity less influenced by the Enlightenment than is the American and European North. It is also one in which the spiritual realm, including the demonic, is much more alive. Allen devotes a subsection to witchcraft, which in Southern Christianity is viewed as demonic but real. He cites a number of authorities on the point that belief in witchcraft is ubiquitous in Africa, one of the regions in which Christianity has been growing explosively. But it is also common in Mexico and India. One priest from Malawi insists, "Since Christ in the gospels encountered the devil, it is proper for Christians to accept the reality of witchcraft."[7] An African theologian points out that "the implicit Christology of many Africans is that of 'Christus Victor,' whose resurrection invested him with definitive power to vanquish the dark forces in the spiritual world."[8]

The North, still in the sway of the Enlightenment, regards all this as superstition. Commonly its priests, sent to minister in the South, doubt their own redemptive powers and are helpless. Should the concerns of Southern Christianity be taken seriously, should the concerns of Jesus as portrayed in the Gospels in struggle with the demonic ever be taken seriously in the North, one result would be a different "history" than we now have. It would be one much more concerned with the heroic and martyr themes that run throughout Christianity and one much less dismissive of, say, the bloody crucifixes of early modern Bavaria or the mimetic crucifixions of the Philippines today. Obviously should such an evangelical Christianity spread, it would present its own dangers, but it might also have the kind of radical edge attractive to some of the young. One of the really liberating things about being a Catholic is that, if you have given up on success, or see that success is in God's hands, not your own, you can say pretty much what comes into your head. Committed Catholics can have much more fun in life, because they likely have a very well-developed sense of the human comedy. Certainly this should be true of committed Catholic historians.

THE PROSPECTS OF THE NEAR FUTURE

Presumably the Catholic college or university of the near future will have to work with viewpoints still derived from the Enlightenment and professors still formed by Enlightenment practices. Some of these practices, including much that goes under the term *historical criticism*, the examination of primary sources in their historical context, were a great achievement by the Enlightenment. But some have reduced our sense of life's depths. Bernard Lonergan (1904–84) hoped for a "Second Enlightenment," in which the premises of the original Enlightenment would be reconsidered. Although he thought the First Enlightenment majestic in some of its achievements, he nevertheless believed that serious misjudgments had been made that ever since have distorted things human. One could hope that Catholic education would take up pursuit of Lonergan's Second Enlightenment and that this would ultimately influence the understanding and teaching of history.

Almost single-handedly the English Catholic historian Christopher Dawson (1889–1970) already pursued, so far as history is concerned, something like Lonergan's proposal. Dawson thought the long-established tripartite division of history into ancient, medieval, and modern profoundly misleading.[9] This division, derived from the Renaissance, has been strongly inclined to view the Middle Ages, that time in which Christianity especially dominated the Western story, as "in the middle." It is both a decline from what the ancient world had achieved and an indistinct hiatus between the ancient and modern worlds, in the latter of which the human progressive march begun by the ancients was resumed. Far better, Dawson thought, to abandon this tripartite division and see all history, Christian or not, as the history of culture, with each culture on its own time line.

Dawson thought that religion was at the heart of each historical culture, that culture is embodied religion. Greek history was about the history of Greek culture, about the history of the culture Greek religion formed, its origins, development, and passage into later history as one influence among others. Similarly Christian culture should be viewed as formed by many sources (Jewish and biblical, Greek and Roman); manifest in the coming of Christ; maturing in Patristic, "medieval," and all the later forms of Christian culture (Baroque, Romantic, etc.); and continuing in an apparently diminished form to the present. Here there is no ancient-medieval-modern, but so far as Christian culture is concerned, one continuing story not yet over. If the subject is the cultures of the world, it has many overlapping story lines. Dawson thought that in the Catholic school that for the most part has a lay audience, the study of Christian culture would be a much better preparation for life in the world than present curricula are. With the study of Christian culture, both as it had existed worldwide and within their own country, Catholic students could come to know the culture that had formed them, and then could form some sense of how to find their way in this culture.

What happened in the United States, on the contrary, was that an originally largely evangelical Protestant people formed an educational system outside and largely ignorant of the Catholic tradition. For a long time the schools and universities, both public and private, of this evangelical culture maintained an education heavily influenced by Protestantism. In spite of the efforts to secularize education by the likes of Horace Mann (1796–1859) and John Dewey (1859–1952), as late as 1950 Harvard University described its curriculum as that appropriate to the formation of a Protestant gentleman.[10] By this time Catholics had long since set up their own schools. Though they commonly thought of themselves as good

Americans, the very fact of a separate educational system witnessed to some degree of discontent with at least the incompleteness of what passed for education in the larger culture.

A generation later, the curriculum, inherited from Europe by American Catholic colleges and largely composed of the study of the Greek and Latin classics and philosophy, had largely disappeared. This was, in no small measure, the result of a widespread understanding in the United States of what the *aggiornamento* (updating) of the Second Vatican Council (1962–65) entailed. This curriculum in its own way communicated a solid knowledge of Catholicism. Until Vatican II the dominance of philosophy persisted, but after that Thomas Aquinas fell into considerable disfavor. In most schools the Catholic curriculum increasingly imitated what was studied in non-Catholic schools; that is, it lacked focus. Though there has been some reaction to this in recent years, by earlier standards most Catholic schools today, like most non-Catholic schools, present a slim core curriculum, a potpourri of elective courses, and an ever-enlarging number of courses devoted to majors. Now collegians take vocational courses in preparation for a career rather than studying the liberal arts in preparation for life and citizenship. This too is not likely soon to disappear, and like many of the developments chronicled, has benefits as well as liabilities. The question is how in such an environment history is to be taught. The proposal is that Dawson's ideas could be a solution.

POSSIBILITIES

A few relatively small Catholic schools have refused to one degree or another to accept the developments just described. Also a number of larger universities have had second thoughts about their participation in these developments and are trying to reassert a contemporary Catholic character of the form alluded to by Cunningham. Aside from these, we have a set of facts in place that in one way or another must be addressed.[11] The facts on the ground are too diverse to propose a single program of study for all. What seems more promising is to discuss the form that the study of history might take in such renewal. The concern is to describe general principles and approaches rather than a specific curriculum in detail. What follows can be adjusted to a wide variety of circumstances. It can be adapted to those schools that have retained Western civilization courses; it is also congenial for those institutions that, like most state schools, increasingly center on world history; it can be taken up by those schools that have diminished their core requirements as well as those that retain a good number of required courses.

First, either in a specific course on the nature of history, or more likely as a segment of some existing course, there might be several days dedicated to discussing the matters with which this essay began: the questions of interpretive framework, point of view, and the nature of Christian culture. Whether this is best done at the beginning of an existing course or later on is debatable. Often one understands more if a discipline is first practiced for some time and then reflected on. A good case can be made for an approach that raises various questions as they become relevant to the subject matter, that is, integrating discussion of theoretical questions into the narrative of the course. For instance, in history the study of Christian anthropology as described by Rausch might best be taken up when appropriate to the subject matter rather than at the beginning of a course.

In a Western civilization course, the optimism of ancient Greek anthropology might first be delineated with reference to Plato, and then the continuing optimism of Greek Christian anthropology defined and introduced as part of the discussion of the Greek Fathers. Augustine is the obvious choice for making clear the greater pessimism of the Western Fathers. Such specification of main varieties of anthropology would work especially well if the professor were already well grounded in Church history, but we cannot in many cases presume this. Therefore for some a more theoretical discussion of what the anthropological options are might well begin the course.

In any case, at some point the belief in general progress, the Whig view of history, should be discussed, along with the alternatives a Christian or anti-utopian reading of history entail. These alternatives insist that history is a dramatic story with no certain end other than the coming of a Kingdom that begins its story in time but is fulfilled after time. There should also be discussion of what follows if the nature of this Kingdom is as unsuspected as was the form the Messiah took in Jesus of Nazareth in terms of the messianic claims that preceded him. Almost all students will have brought to class a general belief in progress, and, as already suggested, the discussion might be whether in fact history is witness to such a progress. Likely one will want to read, or at least describe, the views of Hans Urs von Balthasar on the dramatic nature of history and the idea of Karl Rahner (1904–84) that Catholicism is eschatological rather than chiliastic, not expecting immediate transformation but working as an earthly leaven so that even now the will of God be done, and life—political, economic, and social—in some measure be transformed.[12] Here if not elsewhere there should be a discussion of Christian anthropology of the order proposed by Rausch, some discussion of the views of the Greeks, Romans, and others as to what humans are and what can be expected of them and what kind of history they can have. As Rausch explains, the important distinctions between the Christian anthropologies of the East, the Roman

Catholic Church, the Classical Protestant Reformers, and Christianity as recast in the Enlightenment must be specified.

The question of historical objectivity must be broached.[13] Explanation must be made that the traditional way in which objectivity has been demanded of the historian since the Enlightenment is impossible. This idea, carried into history from the natural sciences as they have developed, must be shown to be beyond humans, who must always write from some limited point of view that cannot see or consider all at once. It should be made clear that objectivity is possible only for God, the Judge of all-at-once, and in fact that its espousal was one more way in which recent centuries have attempted a secularized divinization of man. The historian was to play God, judging as if he could have sufficient information to make a decisive weighing of the evidence.

Much better, even in the natural sciences, is a quest for fairness, in which the ideal is never to lie about the evidence and always to try to be fair to all parties. It should be explained that one of the things asked of the historian is always to be empathetic, to try to put oneself into the world being described, but also to learn from postmodernism that a hermeneutic of suspicion is in order. That is, one is to be both empathetic and suspicious. One is to view Nazism in all its variety as the best Nazi theoreticians and apologists did, as a response to various problems of modern society, above all its rootlessness and destruction of community, and, that having been done, to ask what of this self-presentation is either self-deceiving or intended to deceive us.[14]

HISTORY IN ITS RELATION TO THEOLOGY

The relation of history to theology also must be discussed. In addition to what has already been said, one must ask: What are the implications of the Incarnation? Above all, does Christian revelation provide a center for the interpretation of history? This is a sensitive question. However, one must ask what the implications of the Incarnation are for understanding those cultures without a knowledge of Jesus Christ. What is implied by St. Paul's statement in Romans 1–2 that all have been given a "law written on their hearts," that is, a partial knowledge of the truth apart from revelation, a "natural law"? Here it is important to stress the Catholic belief that Christ has been present or working in all cultures, and that what humans know of truth, goodness, and beauty is more than what is contained in Christian revelation. It might be suggested that in all periods a question facing anyone who believes in revelation, that is, in a knowledge going beyond reason alone, is how this is to be related to all knowledge claims in place when the revelation appeared.

It can be suggested that there are always three alternatives: (1) the rejection of all previous knowledge claims in favor of the new revelation as the sole valid knowledge ("fundamentalism" or *Scriptura sola*, or Classical Protestantism); (2) the assertion that everyone is more or less talking about the same thing and that there is broad commonality between previous knowledge claims and the new revelation ("liberalism" or liberal Protestantism); or (3) the belief that in principle truth might be found in either the old or the new, and the Christian's duty is to "plunder the Egyptians," that is to take everything true in the old claims into the new religion. This third option is that which has generally been taken by Catholicism and carries a laborious obligation to sift through all claims, neither presuming that revelation is the full word on all subjects nor even that on some things revelation has something to say.

A couple of examples are in order of the Catholic belief that truth may be known outside revelation, and that therefore the Catholic should customarily be respectful in addressing those outside the faith, who presumably know something of the truth. Pope Innocent IV (ca. 1195/97–1254) was asked whether Christians have the right to attack Muslim peoples simply because they are Muslim. Innocent declared that Christians were not to initiate wars of conversion, for every people has institutions that participate in the good, and it would be unjust to destroy these. The Muslim practice of marriage, if incomplete, is witness to a natural good found in Islam. Earlier Alcuin of York (ca. 735–804) had argued against Charlemagne's (742–814) practice of conversion by the sword.

HISTORY AND THE CATHOLIC INTELLECTUAL TRADITION

As already noted, it would be good to describe and discuss the views of Christopher Dawson. Students coming from a significantly secularized society, in which religion no longer seems the center of life, might object against Dawson's view that every culture has an embodied religion at its center. It would be useful to consider whether, and to what degree, our culture is indeed secularized, and whether this secularization is a one-way street from which there is no exit or return to a more sacral form of life. Has the Western world, especially since the Enlightenment, been engaged in an attempt to remove God from life, and how has this gone? Is the West exceptional in this, as John Allen might argue? Might therefore secularization not be the last word? Could it be true that in our society—in all societies— secularization and sacralization take place simultaneously, one area developing with less reference to God and another reconnecting, or finding new ways, to God?

Here the question of modernism might be introduced, though that is a most slippery word and there are many ways of taking it. If modernism, as in art, be understood as an attempt to separate ourselves from the past in order to create a new cultural space, perhaps one free from God, what are we to make of such modernists as Constantine Brancusi (1876–1957)? Brancusi saw his art in the manner of his own Eastern Orthodox tradition, as through abstraction trying to penetrate to things as they really are.[15] Might there indeed be some justice in the Slavophile criticism of the Western Enlightenment as an overestimation of the powers of reason? Or, perchance, also in early twentieth-century artistic criticism of the Renaissance mimetic tradition? From a different vantage point Joseph Ratzinger (Pope Benedict XVI) noted that this had effectively reduced the presence of transcendence in life, representing life as locked in by a nature through which no icon could penetrate.[16]

In any case, the question might be posed: Where right now is the sacred found? And is the Christian still to work so that his or her society take on "the form of Christ"? Is Christ's command to mission, to spreading his Word to all peoples, still incumbent on Christians? Above all, what is a contemporary understanding of the Jesuits' belief that God is in all things and that all must be done to the Glory of God?

HOW CATHOLICISM ENLIGHTENS HISTORICAL SCHOLARSHIP

A certain number of students study history because they want to know more about some period or field of which they are little informed. As someone brought up a Protestant and with little knowledge of anything between the New Testament and Luther, this was my own situation, and is at least a partial explanation of why I chose medieval history for graduate study. In my first job, at a Jesuit university, one of my fellow history faculty was a Basque American who thought about everything he did in the light of his Catholicism, and consequently had the most interesting and unusual things to say. I had met pious, even intelligent Catholics before, but he was something else. He accepted virtually none of the commonplaces of our culture or of most American Catholics. Most of the Jesuits could barely tolerate him (a minority thought him just what the doctor ordered). At first, outside of noting in my lectures all the bad things that might be said against democracy and all the good things in favor of the Inquisition, my professional study of history was little affected by my adult conversion to Catholicism. That is, from the first I gave passionate lectures that sometimes resulted in the conversion of my students, but my research and writing pretty much proceeded along the lines I had learned in graduate school. I still believed in objectivity, for instance. Though from the first I published on Church history and had to deal with interpretive questions in that context, I did not generally think of my scholarly writings as "enlivened" by my faith. Clearly I tended to see things in a Catholic way, sometimes defending this or that pope against what some uncomprehending non-Catholic had written. I was told by others that I was fervently Catholic in the classroom, but I was perhaps a decade into my professional life before I began to urge views in my scholarly writings that were distinctly against the grain of the age, as I assume any genuinely Catholic views will be. In this case the views were in regard to how Scripture was to be read.[17] From trying to explain to moderns how differently people of earlier ages had looked at the world, I was slipping into thinking that, in regard to such things as whether Scripture had a spiritual sense, an earlier age had seen farther than we do. It was some years before I came to see why and how progressive views of history must be rejected, but already I could see that just because something was later did not mean that it was truer or better.

I came to hold that history is not a tale of general progress, but essentially tragic or dramatic, as von Balthasar had said. In every age God's will is being done and is not being done. In every age there are saints and sinners. We must hold our breath as to how it all will turn out. This said, though I could see some sense in counting churches built or communions taken as some kind of indication of where God is still working in time, I became very reluctant to think that as a Christian historian my primary task was to chronicle God's advance.

Though almost all Protestant thinkers have conceded to progressive categories of thought, seeing history itself as linear, I came to see that some Catholics still stand beside their Orthodox brethren in protesting the view of time and human development that has come to dominate the West. According to this now regnant view, time must take either a cyclical or a linear form, the latter presumptively being the Jewish and Christian preference because it expresses the idea that salvation has a history. But I understood that the view of the Church Fathers and of medieval thinkers such as St. Bonaventure was much more sophisticated than this. The fullness that had come in Christ was not something that would be surpassed, one stage in a tale of progress, but something available for acceptance or rejection in all historical moments. History, at least so far as a human can chronicle, does not have one narrative line for the simple reason that some accept Christ, some close in on themselves. Thus there is not one linear and irreversible direction in which the story of salvation, or human history itself, moves. All moments stand equally before God, and in them God's will is both being done and not being done.

The Orthodox Romanian student of religion Mircea Eliade (1907–86), in the very act of thinking of himself as vindicating the distinctiveness of a supposedly

Christian preference for linear views of time, fell into the trap of accommodating to the secularized Western notion that the Christian story is a progressive story.[18] It is hard to say whether Christianity here was a central cause of the secularization of the West, or whether the secularization of the West remade Latin Christianity. But to say that the Christian story or the human story is linear and progressive is ironically tantamount to removing God from history, for it gives a narrative story line such integrity and visibility that anyone can chronicle it. In the old view, the mystery of the drama of the struggle between good and evil, the drama of salvation, continued until the end of time and had no clear outcome within history. In the new view as the eighteenth century developed it, there was visible a story almost a fool could write, a story that made sense of secular experience and gave it an integrity apart from God.

Because there is a powerful egalitarian impulse in liberalism, liberals and liberal or progressive historians have tended to miss the great variety of human life, all the ways people are not equal and differ. One could almost describe liberal historiography as tedious, as tending to flatten all the ways we differ from one another. It is probably better at catching the ways people are bad than the ways they are good. How different is a Catholic sensibility, nurtured, say, on the lives of the saints in their unending variety and aware that God intends every human for a life different from every other. Before the "metaphysics of clarity" beloved of the Enlightenment and then of liberalism, the saint's life, especially its masculine form (witness St. Francis of Assisi), was centered on the idea of the conversion of the soul, of abrupt and radical change, of at one moment being one thing, at the next another. In this pre-Enlightenment view, with its central theme of conversion, history was subject to supernatural intervention and conversion was often not gradual, but abrupt. William Butler Yeats declared that saints are never Whigs, people who believe in general progress: the Whig makes the world impervious to the adventure that is Christianity.

A view nourished by study of the saints tends to anticipate great variation, finally great variation in holiness, in the people it studies. Further, because it does not consider humans to be as rational as the Enlightenment drew them, it is willing to see all the ways human life is enveloped by mystery and hardly ever turns out as one might have expected. I suppose that this latter sensibility is fostered by the Christian idea that, though we are cooperators with God, He is the final author of history, a heresy to all forms of rationalist historiography. There is another consideration here. Because Enlightenment historiography is the product of a commercial or bourgeois culture, it is interested in the things such a culture is interested in. This means that religion tends to be slighted in most liberal historiography. If religion is at the center of life, but life today lacks a center, this means almost by definition that taking history seriously in the way Christianity does is likely to make one question the commonplaces of the day and incline to some kind of countercultural history. If one is not up to this, one ought probably to go into some other field. But of course the larger point is that by conventional standards, being Catholic is almost certainly going to complicate any life.

NOTES

1. Karl Löwith, *Meaning in History: The Theological Implications of the Philosophy of History* (Chicago: University of Chicago Press, 1949).

2. There were important countercurrents: Avihu Zakai, *Jonathan Edwards's Philosophy of History: The Re-Enchantment of the World in the Age of Enlightenment* (Princeton, N.J.: Princeton University Press, 2003).

3. Mark Noll, *America's God: From Jonathan Edwards to Abraham Lincoln* (New York: Oxford University Press, 2002).

4. See the various writings of Edward Grant and David C. Lindberg on the inadequacy of such views.

5. See George M. Marsden and Frank Roberts, eds., *A Christian View of History?* (Grand Rapids, Mich.: Eerdmans, 1975); Glenn W. Olsen, "Christian Philosophy, Christian History: Parallel Ideas?," in *Eternity in Time: Christopher Dawson and the Catholic Idea of History*, edited by Stratford Caldecott and John Morrill (Edinburgh: T & T Clark, 1997), 131–50.

6. John L. Allen Jr., *The Future Church: How Ten Trends Are Revolutionizing the Catholic Church* (New York: Doubleday, 2009), especially 35–7.

7. Allen, *Future Church*, 37.

8. Allen, *Future Church*, 37.

9. In addition to the republication of Christopher Dawson's *The Crisis of Western Education*, with an introduction by Glenn W. Olsen (Washington, DC: Catholic University of America Press, 2010), see the following, all by Glenn W. Olsen: "The Maturity of Christian Culture: Some Reflections on the Views of Christopher Dawson," in *The Dynamic Character of Christian Culture: Essays on Dawsonian Themes*, edited by Peter J. Cataldo (Lanham, Md.: University Press of American, 1984), 97–125; "The Meaning of Christian Culture: An Historical View," in *Catholicism and Secularization in America: Essays on Nature, Grace, and Culture*, edited by David L. Schindler (Notre Dame, Ind.: Communio Books, 1990), 98–130; "Deconstructing the University," *Communio: International Catholic Review* 19 (1992): 226–53; "Why and How to Study the Middle Ages," *Logos: A Journal of Catholic Thought and Culture* 3, no. 3 (2000): 50–75; "Humanism: The Struggle to Possess a Word," *Logos: A Journal of Catholic Thought and Culture* 7 (2004): 97–116; "Why We Need Christopher Dawson," *Communio* 35 (2008): 115–44; *The Turn to Transcendence: The Role of Religion in the Twenty-First Century* (Washington, DC: Catholic University of America Press, 2010).

10. On this and the following, see Glenn W. Olsen, "The University as Community: Community of What?," *Communio* 21 (1994): 344–62. It can be read in longer form in *Ideas for the University*, edited by Ed Block Jr. (Milwaukee, Wisc.: Marquette University Press, 1995), 29–60. On Dewey see also Glenn W. Olsen, "The Quest for a Public Philosophy in Twentieth Century American Political Thought," *Communio* 27 (2000): 340–62.

11. My two daughters attended the University of Notre Dame (the boys went to Jesuit schools), studying in the Program of Liberal Studies, and I note in a recent solicitation for

donations that one could choose to contribute to "Catholic Mission." On March 16, 2010, the Cardinal Newman Society of Manassas, Virginia, established the Center for the Advancement of Catholic Higher Education, dedicated to the renewal of Catholic identity at Catholic colleges and universities: www.CatholicHigherEd.org.

12. The writings of von Balthasar are not easy to understand; the work to be studied might be his *A Theology of History* (1963; San Francisco, Ignatius Press, 1994).

13. Peter Novik, *That Noble Dream: The "Objectivity Question" and the American Historical Profession* (Cambridge, U.K.: Cambridge University Press, 1988).

14. I have discussed the desired relation of empathy and a hermeneutic of suspicion in Glenn W. Olsen, "Marriage, Feminism, Theology, and the New Social History: Dyan Elliott's Spiritual Marriage," *Communio* 22 (1995): 343–56, and have considered Nazism in chapters 2, 3, and, especially 5 of Olsen, *Turn to Transcendence*.

15. Again, I have discussed modernism in chapter 3 of Olsen, *Turn to Transcendence*.

16. Joseph Cardinal Ratzinger, *The Spirit of the Liturgy* (San Francisco: Ignatius Press, 2000).

17. I will not go into this here, but see most recently my "The Spiritual Sense(s) Today," in *The Bible and the University*, edited by David Lyle Jeffrey and C. Stephen Evans, Scripture and Hermeneutics Series (Grand Rapids , Mich.: Zondervan, 2007), 8:116–38.

18. On the following, see Glenn W. Olsen, "Problems with the Contrast between Circular and Linear Views of Time in the Interpretation of Ancient and Early Medieval History," *Fides quaerens intellectum* 1 (2001): 41–65.

SELECTED READINGS

Gleason, Philip. *Contending with Modernity: Catholic Higher Education in the Twentieth Century*. Oxford: Oxford University Press, 1996.

Hart, David B. "Christ and Nothing." *First Things* 136 (October 2003): 47–57.

Marsden, George M. *The Soul of the American University: From Protestant Establishment to Established Nonbelief*. New York: Oxford University Press, 1994.

Olsen, Glenn W. *Beginning at Jerusalem: Five Reflections on the History of the Church*. San Francisco: Ignatius Press, 2004.

———. "The Two Europes." *The European Legacy: Toward New Paradigms* 14, no. 1 (2009): 133–48.

12

Mathematics, Reality, and God

Paul A. Schweitzer, S.J.

BEAUTY AND ESTHETICS IN MATHEMATICS

Mathematical beauty is the principal virtue that attracts people to mathematics. There are various ways of expressing why some mathematical objects, figures, and proofs are beautiful, but simplicity and symmetry are among the reasons. A certain completeness is perceived, so that no part can be removed without its absence being felt as a flaw. There is a necessity; the mathematical object must be as it is, if it is not to be damaged. This beauty has an innocence and purity that suggests its divine origin. Let us see some examples.

As a first example, consider the golden mean, φ, the ratio of the base to the height of a rectangle pleasing to the eye. If a square of the same height is removed and the remaining rectangle is rotated 90°, it will have the same proportion (see figure 12-1). If the height is 1, then the length of the base is φ. If we remove the large square on the right side of figure 12-1, the base of the remaining rectangle will be $\varphi - 1$. Then the basic property of φ states that φ is to 1 as 1 is to $\varphi - 1$, that is, $\varphi/1 = 1/(\varphi - 1)$. Thus $\varphi^2 - \varphi - 1 = 0$, so the quadratic formula gives $\varphi = (\sqrt{5} + 1)/2$. The value of the golden mean φ is approximately 1.6180339887. A rectangle with these proportions is aesthetically pleasing in either horizontal or vertical form, so it is the shape usually used for the frames of paintings. Repeatedly cutting off squares with inscribed circular arcs produces a lovely spiral in figure 12-1. The golden mean also occurs in three different ratios of segments in the pentagram,

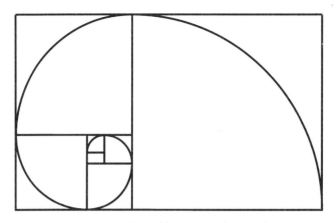

FIGURE 12.1 The golden mean and its spiral.

the regular five-pointed star. In figure 12-2, the ratios of the segments AD:AC, AC:AB, and AB:BC are each given by the golden mean.

The golden mean φ is also related to the sequence of Fibonacci numbers, named after the Italian mathematician Leonardo da Pisa (1171–1249), "figlio de Bonacci," that is, "son of Bonacci." The sequence is 1, 1, 2, 3, 5, 8, 13, 21, 34, 55, 89,..., each term being the sum of the preceding two terms. If we denote the nth term by a_n, so that $a_1 = 1$, $a_2 = 1$, $a_3 = 2$, $a_4 = 3$, and so on, then the ratios a_{n+1}/a_n of successive terms

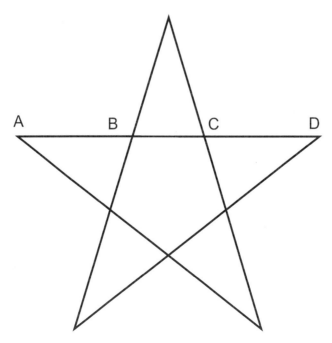

FIGURE 12.2 The golden mean in the five-pointed star.

converge to φ as n tends to infinity. This sequence occurs in nature in the spirals visible in the core of the sunflower, as in figure 12-3, where the numbers of clockwise and counterclockwise spirals in the sunflower are the Fibonacci numbers 34 and 55, respectively.

The feeling for mathematical beauty is a quality shared by outstanding mathematicians. Leonhard Euler (1707–83) appreciated the beauty of his formula, $e^{\pi i} + 1 = 0$, which brings together in impressive harmony the five most important numbers: 0, 1, e, π, and i. The prolific but eccentric Hungarian mathematician Paul Erdös (1913–96) liked to talk about "The Book," in which God (whose existence he doubted) would have gathered together all of the most beautiful, surprising, elegant, and simple proofs in all of mathematics. I remember fondly how one of my mathematics professors at Princeton University, Salomon Bochner (1899–1982), after writing some especially beautiful part of mathematics on the blackboard, would turn around to the class, beaming with an intense and contagious delight.

The aesthetic sense of what is fitting and beautiful guides research in physics as well as in mathematics. In 1928 the eminent physicist Paul Dirac (1902–84) arrived at his celebrated equation describing the electron and similar particles because it was so beautiful. Its symmetry suggested the possibility of the existence of a particle similar to the electron, but with negative energy. This was the positron, the antiparticle of the electron, discovered in 1932.

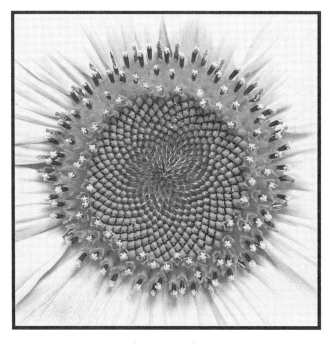

FIGURE 12.3 The Fibonacci numbers in the sunflower.

The theory of general relativity of Albert Einstein (1879–1955), explaining the gravitational field as the curvature of the four-dimensional continuum of space-time, is convincing because of its simplicity and beauty. In 1919, after the theory was confirmed during an eclipse of the sun observed in Sobral and Principe, Einstein was asked what would have been his reaction if the observations had not confirmed his theory. He replied, "Then I would feel sorry for the dear Lord. The theory is correct anyway." The theory was so elegant that its correctness could not be doubted.

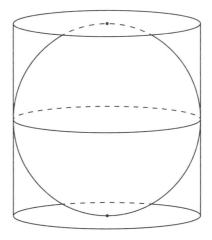

FIGURES 12.4A and 12.4B Archimedes' sphere and circumscribed cylinder. *Cicero Discovering the Tomb of Archimedes,* painted in 1797 by Benjamin West (1738–1820).

In *On the Sphere and Cylinder,* Archimedes (287–212 BC) proved the beautiful theorem that the ratio of the volumes of a sphere and the cylinder circumscribed about it is 2:3, and the ratio of their areas is the same. Plutarch (AD 45–120), in *Parallel Lives,* says of Archimedes, "Although he made many excellent discoveries, he is said to have asked his kinsmen and friends to place over the grave where he should be buried a cylinder enclosing a sphere, with an inscription giving the proportion by which the containing solid exceeds the contained."[1] Cicero (106–43 BC) recorded that when he was quaestor in Sicily in 75 BC he managed to track down Archimedes' grave. It was a small column with the sphere and cylinder above it almost covered by bushes, but after the brush was cleared away, Cicero was able to read what was left of the inscription. In his reverence for the great mathematician and scientist, he donated funds to restore the tomb (see figure 12-4).

The musical scale is another example of beauty linked to mathematics. An octave in the musical scale has seven tones and five half-tones, making a total of twelve half-tones. An octave corresponds to doubling the frequency of a tone. Consequently, in the tempered scale, each half-tone corresponds exactly to a ratio of frequencies equal to the twelfth root of 2. By a marvelous coincidence, the powers of this twelfth root of 2 are very close to fractions with a small numerator and denominator. For example, the fourth power, which is approximately 1.25992 (corresponding to the interval from do to mi), is very close to 5/4 = 1.25, and the seventh power, approximately 1.49831 (corresponding to the interval from do to sol), very close to 3/2 = 1.5. The harmonies of the overtones of a fundamental frequency are therefore close to powers of the twelfth root of 2, contributing to the perceived harmony. The slight differences between these values are what determines the qualitative difference among the various keys of musical compositions. The intimate relationship of music to mathematics was recognized in higher education in the Middle Ages, when music was one of the four disciplines of the quadrivium, along with arithmetic, geometry, and astronomy, to be studied after the trivium, which consisted of grammar, logic (then called dialectic), and rhetoric.

After all these instances of how beauty is everywhere present in mathematics, let us ask what the significance and meaning of this beauty may be. There is a pristine quality of mathematical beauty that avoids the blemishes and faults that seem to appear in the material universe and in human society. The poet Edna St. Vincent Millay (1892–1950) wrote, "Euclid alone has looked on Beauty bare." Mathematics has escaped from original sin; we seem to be viewing the framework of existence before any defects have appeared. This unsullied beauty is a reflection of the beauty of the Creator and of his original creation. The transcendental categories of being—one, good, true, and beautiful—can be seen in mathematics, and they display the marvelous qualities of the absolute Being, our creator God. Just as when the beauty of the lilies of the field, the songs of birds, or the smile of a child overwhelms us, in the contemplation of mathematical beauty a window opens onto eternity and one can sense the holy presence of our loving God.

MATHEMATICS IN RELIGIOUS ART

The Catholic Catalan painter Salvador Dalí (1904–89) painted two famous paintings that mix mathematics and Christian faith: *Crucifixion—Corpus Hypercubus* and *The Sacrament of the Last Supper*.[2] In "Corpus Hypercubus," the cross has the form of the three-dimensional surface of a four-dimensional hypercube, unfolded so as to fit into three-dimensional space (figure 12-5). To understand this, consider how one can make a three-dimensional cube out of a sheet of construction paper cut into the form of a cross composed of six squares, four of them vertical and one on each side, as in figure 12-6. By folding the paper along the edges separating the squares, as many children know, the result will be a three-dimensional cube with six squares as faces.

FIGURE 12.5 *Corpus Hypercubus*. ©Salvador Dalí, Fundació Gala-Salvador Dalí / Artists Rights Society (ARS), New York 2011.

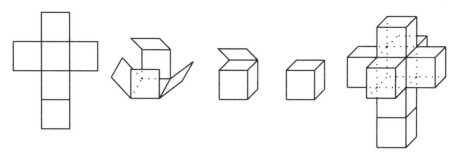

FIGURE 12.6 The hypercube and the cube, both unfolded.

Dalí's painting is based on the analogous construction in one higher dimension. In four-dimensional Euclidean space, endowed with coordinates (x_1, x_2, x_3, x_4), the hypercube is formed by the points whose coordinates x_i are each between 0 and 1, for i = 1, 2, 3, 4. This is analogous to the way that a three-dimensional cube in three-dimensional space with coordinates (x, y, z) is obtained by restricting the values of each of the coordinates $x, y,$ and z to lie between 0 and 1. Just as the cube has six squares as faces, corresponding to making each coordinate either 0 or 1, the hypercube has eight cubes as faces, corresponding to making each of the four coordinates x_i equal to 0 or 1. We can imagine the boundary of a hypercube to be unfolded into a shape of three-dimensional construction paper cut into eight cubes, four in a vertical sequence with one on each side, left and right, and two others, front and back, as in figure 12-6. Looking at *Corpus Hypercubus*, we see that it is exactly this unfolded hypercube that Dalí has portrayed as the cross. The eighth cube, in front, is merely outlined by the four nails, in order not to hide Christ's body.

What is the message of this four-dimensional hypercube in Dalí's painting? The reference to the fourth dimension evokes Einstein's special theory of relativity, in which the fourth dimension, time, is joined to the three spatial dimensions to form the four-dimensional space-time continuum. Dalí places the crucifixion of Christ at the center of all of space-time, as the pivotal event in the history of the whole universe. Christ's body floats in space, freed from suffering and death by the resurrection. The woman in the painting contemplates Christ in the full Paschal mystery of our faith: the crucifixion, death, and resurrection of the Lord, which opens for us the way of grace and salvation.

Dalí's painting *The Last Supper* also uses a geometrical image to express the meaning of Christ's farewell dinner with his apostles in which he instituted the Eucharist (figure 12-7). The frame of the room is clearly a 12-sided regular polyhedron, the dodecahedron, the fourth of the Platonic solids portrayed in figure 12-8. In the section below on numerology and symbolism, we shall see that the numbers

FIGURE 12.7 *The Last Supper.* ©Salvador Dalí, Fundació Gala-Salvador Dalí / Artists Rights Society (ARS), New York 2011.

7 and 12 connote fullness and plenitude. The twelve apostles united around the Lord are going to preach the Gospel to the whole known world; their mission and the one who sends them bespeak totality and plenitude. Dalí associates them symbolically with the faces of the dodecahedron. Their cowls even have a pentagonal shape. The fullness, beauty, and symmetry of the dodecahedron are evoked by Dalí to symbolize the completion of Christ's own work on earth, to be continued by the Twelve and their successors. The arms of Christ are spread above, inscribed in the dodecahedron, as they will soon be spread on the cross, suggesting blessing with the fruits of the cross and the sending of the Holy Spirit, recalling Christ's promise "I shall be with you always, until the end of the world" (Matthew 28:20).

Dalí's use of mathematical symbols to express profound religious realities is an example of what Thomas Rausch refers to as the "sacramental imagination" of Catholicism. The young and handsome Christ in both paintings suggests his victory

FIGURE 12.8 The five Platonic solids, the regular polyhedra.

over evil, sin, and death. The first light of dawn in the Crucifixion and the horizon opening out onto the world in *The Last Supper* symbolize that victory as it spreads out over the whole earth and even to all of space-time.

MATHEMATICS AS SCIENCE

Mathematical discoveries date from the early ages of human civilization. The Pythagorean theorem, which states that the area of the square on the hypotenuse of a right triangle is the sum of the areas of the squares on the two legs, was apparently used by the builders of the pyramids in ancient Egypt. The Rhind papyrus, an Egyptian scroll copied by the scribe Ahmes from an earlier work dated around 1850 BC, has solutions to various mathematical problems.[3] Cuneiform baked clay tablets from ancient Babylonia (ca. 1900–1600) contain multiplication tables, probably used by children learning their lessons.[4]

Since these ancient times mathematics has investigated and studied a great variety of numerical and geometrical problems. In the third century before Christ, Archimedes made significant advances in geometry and used mathematics to study statics. In the late Middle Ages there were advances in the solution of polynomial equations. At the dawn of modern science toward the end of the sixteenth century Galileo introduced precise mathematical measurements into his studies of physics, and mathematics became the language of science. The Nobel Prize physicist Eugene Wigner, in his fascinating essay "The Unreasonable Effectiveness of Mathematics in the Natural Sciences," analyzes the surprising human capacity to describe and understand natural phenomena through mathematics.

As a science, mathematics attains the highest degree of precision because arithmetical calculations can be exact. Measures of weights, lengths, and volumes are only approximations, to a greater or lesser degree of accuracy, but counting a number of objects can give a precise answer. Even though arithmetic is abstracted from experience of nature and daily life, it reaches a degree of absolute precision that no other domain of human activity can rival.

AXIOMATIZATION OF MATHEMATICS

A new dimension of logical structure was introduced into mathematics by Euclid around 300 BC, when in *Elements of Geometry* he described a system of axioms and postulates and used them to prove many basic theorems about geometric figures in the plane. Somewhat earlier, in the fourth century BC, Aristotle had introduced principles of logic. Many of the theorems of Euclid were already known facts, but the logical structure of giving cogent proofs for them in a logical order, starting from the axioms and postulates, was an important advance.

It later turned out that Euclid's assumptions—his axioms and postulates—were not complete. A thoroughly formal presentation of geometry requires axioms dealing with the order of points on a line and of the location of points inside or outside of a polygon. For example, the fact that the bisector of the angle at one vertex of a triangle meets the opposite side between the other two vertices is clear from our geometrical intuition, but it does not follow from Euclid's assumptions. There is also an amusing (but false!) proof that every triangle ABC is isosceles (i.e., has two sides, AB and AC, equal in length). First, suppose that the bisector AE of the angle A meets the perpendicular bisector DE of the opposite side, BC, *inside* the triangle at the point E (see figure 12-9, for which I thank my colleague Fabio Souza).

If one argues that the triangles BDE and CDE are congruent, so that BE = CE, then the triangles AEB and AEC are congruent (using the angle-side-side argument, which is valid in this case since the angles AEB and AEC are both obtuse), so that AB = AC. The fallacy lies in the fact that if the sides AB and AC have different lengths, then the intersection point will actually lie *outside* the triangle. It was only in 1899 that the great German mathematician David Hilbert (1862–1943) published a complete set of axioms for planar Euclidean geometry, including axioms involving order of points on a line and the location of points on one side or the other of a line.[5]

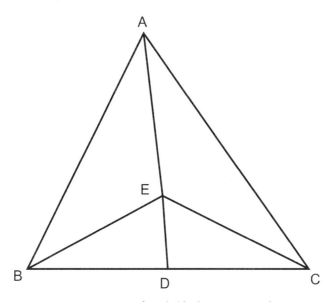

FIGURE 12.9 A triangle with false bisectors AE and DE.

There were two important advances in the axiomatization of mathematics in the nineteenth century. First, non-Euclidean geometry was discovered by Carl Friedrich Gauss (1777–1855), Janos Bolyai (1802–60), and Nikolai Lobachevsky (1792–1856), who showed that there was a logically consistent geometry, now called hyperbolic geometry, that did not satisfy Euclid's fifth postulate. For centuries mathematicians had tried without success to prove the fifth postulate, also known as the parallel postulate, from Euclid's other axioms and postulates. It states that if two straight lines meet a third one so that the sum of the interior angles on one side of the third line is less than two right angles, then the first two lines will meet on that side, provided that they are extended sufficiently far. In 1733 the book *Euclides ab omni naevo vindicatus* (Euclid freed from every blemish), written by the Jesuit priest Girolamo Saccheri (1667–1733), was published. In it he proved many results that follow from supposing the parallel postulate to be false. He concluded that the results were so counterintuitive that Euclid's parallel postulate would have to be accepted. His conclusion about the parallel postulate was wrong, but his theorems were correct. In fact he had discovered many of the most basic properties of non-Euclidean geometry. Almost a century later, when Gauss realized that this non-Euclidean hyperbolic geometry was logically consistent, he hesitated to publish this conclusion for fear of being ridiculed. The method by which the three geometers Gauss, Bolyai, and Lobachevsky showed that hyperbolic (or Lobachevskian) geometry is as logically consistent as Euclidean geometry was to construct a model of hyperbolic geometry inside Euclidean geometry. It follows that if there is no inherent contradiction in Euclidean geometry, then there is no contradiction in hyperbolic geometry. It is interesting to note that the underlying geometry used by Einstein in his general theory of relativity is a version of non-Euclidean geometry.

The second advance in axiomatization of mathematical theories was in mathematical analysis, the branch of mathematics that grew out of the differential and integral calculus discovered by Isaac Newton (1643–1727) and Gottfried Leibniz (1646–1716) in the second half of the seventeenth century. Problems and basic questions arose in the late eighteenth and early nineteenth centuries: Exactly what properties should be supposed to hold for a numerical function? When should an infinite sequence of numbers be said to converge? When should an infinite series (or sum) of terms have a limiting value? It was necessary to decide exactly what were the assumptions, because different assumptions would lead to different conclusions. This led to the creation of systems of axioms for the real numbers, which correspond to the points on the line and form the basis for mathematical analysis.

Since the end of the nineteenth century mathematics has been organized like Euclid's geometry, around systems of axioms that reflect properties of the structures that are being studied. From the axioms new statements, called theorems, are deduced by strict rules of logic. This procedure is so precise and secure that there is essentially no disagreement about what results follow from the axioms, although there are different positions concerning which axioms should be assumed. The process of proving theorems in a formal system is very precisely determined. Determining which sequences of propositions constitute a proof—the syntactic aspect of the theory—can be checked without any need for creativity. It can be completely mechanized and done on a computer. On the other hand, discovering which propositions are true and finding proofs of them requires intelligence, sometimes even genius!

The precision of mathematical argument can function as an incentive and as a goal to strive for in other sciences and in other branches of human thought. It is obviously desirable that rational discourse and arguments have criteria by which their validity can be analyzed and decided. Nevertheless it is clear that most judgments in many fields of thought, as well as in the decisions of daily life, do not admit criteria as clear and precise as in mathematics. The rules for arguments in theology and humanities have to be very different in nature from those of mathematics. Every social science must have its own criteria and means of verifying its conclusions. Even in the physical sciences such deductive arguments as in mathematics are often not possible. In mathematics one argues that if the axioms A, B, C, and D are assumed, one can prove theorems J, K, and L, and rigorous proofs are given. The process of induction in physics and other empirical sciences, on the other hand, goes in the opposite direction: if J, K, and L are known to follow from A, B, C, and D, then when J, K, and L are observed in a sufficient number of experiments, this is interpreted as support for affirming A, B, C, and D. Observing that the conclusions are satisfied in sufficiently varied laboratory experiments gives credence to the hypotheses. Even though the precision and deductive certainty achieved in mathematics are positive qualities, they cannot be required in the same degree in other disciplines. One should not reject arguments in philosophy and theology, for example, because they do not exhibit mathematical rigor; they must be judged by their proper principles and methods.

LIMITATIONS IN MATHEMATICAL DISCOURSE

Although mathematics has demanding requirements of precision in discourse and proofs, these requirements have intrinsic limitations even in their application to mathematics itself. This amazing discovery from the 1930s has far-reaching implications.

The axiomatization of mathematical theories in the nineteenth century and the development of set theory as a foundation of mathematical theory led naturally to the hope of finding an axiomatic basis for all of mathematics. This was the goal of Alfred North Whitehead (1861–1947) and Bertrand Russell (1872–1970) in their enormous three-volume work, *Principia Mathematica*, published in 1910, 1912, and 1913 and in a revised second edition in 1927. Despite their heroic effort, Kurt Gödel (1906–78), in 1931 a young Austrian mathematician, proved their goal to be unattainable. His paper "On Formally Undecidable Propositions of *Principia Mathematica* and Similar Systems,"[6] was one of the most important intellectual advances of the twentieth century, even of the whole history of human thought. Gödel showed that if a finite set of axioms is sufficiently powerful to be able to deal with the basic properties of arithmetic, then it must be either inconsistent or incomplete. This means that if there is no proposition such that the proposition and its negation can both be proven from the axioms (consistency), then there must be a meaningful proposition in the system—one that must either be true or false in any interpretation of the axioms—such that neither the proposition nor its negation can be proven from the axioms (incompleteness). Hence mathematical thought must always look beyond the axioms to the basic insights behind them. Furthermore there will always be new questions in mathematics that have not yet been answered. Mathematics in itself reveals an opening to the infinite, to the transcendent, to a tendency that reaches beyond all its conquests. Intuition can never be replaced by formalism, even in this most formal of fields, and certainly not in any other field, such as the social sciences, philosophy, and theology. This is not a flaw, but a fundamental limitation of human thought, an invitation to contemplation.

Gödel's idea is so brilliant that we should take a moment to see how it works. He assigned numbers to propositions and to proofs. Then he constructed a proposition, let us call it P, that asserts that the proposition assigned a certain number n cannot be proven from the axioms. (The construction of P, which depends on the set of axioms chosen, is lengthy and complicated.) When we calculate the number assigned to the proposition P, we discover that its number is n. Thus in a certain sense, P asserts that P itself cannot be proven! Now if the system is consistent and P could be proven, it would be true, so it could not be proven—a contradiction! Hence if the system of axioms is consistent, P cannot be proven. But then what P affirms is true. Thus P is a meaningful proposition that is true but cannot be proven from the axioms. In particular, neither P nor its negation can be proven from the given axioms. We could add the true proposition P as a new axiom, but then Gödel's construction would give a new proposition P' to which his argument would apply.

In 1937, a few years after the appearance of Gödel's paper, another epochal work in the same direction, "On Computable Numbers, with an Application to the

Entscheidungsproblem," was published by a young English mathematician, Alan Turing (1912–54).[7] In this paper Turing invented a kind of computer, now called a Turing machine, capable of performing any calculation that could be explicitly and completely described. The machine has a finite tape for memory, but the tape can be extended as far as the calculation requires in both directions, so that arbitrarily large computations can be carried out. All contemporary digital computers are fundamentally Turing machines, so in a certain sense he was the inventor of the computer. He showed that there exists a universal Turing machine, which can do all the calculations that any other Turing machine can do. A fundamental question about the calculation done by a given Turing machine with a given input is whether the machine will ever stop, or whether it will keep on computing forever. Turing showed in his article that the stopping question is undecidable, thus giving another version of Gödel's theorem extended into the field of computability. During the Second World War, Turing, an extraordinarily brilliant man, invented machines that decrypted intercepted messages of the German armed forces, thus contributing significantly to the defeat of Hitler's Germany. Unfortunately his important contributions to winning the war were not sufficient to avoid his prosecution for being openly homosexual; he was subjected to an invasive treatment with hormones and tragically took his own life in his early forties.

Perhaps one can see a tragic flaw of pride (the hamartia of classical Greek theater) in the definitive failure of Whitehead and Russell's project, as shown by Gödel's theorem. With a surprising lack of modesty they took their title, *Principia Mathematica,* from *Philosophiae Naturalis Principia Mathematica*, the title of Newton's great work in which he created the calculus and presented his theory of gravitation. Implicitly they put their work on the same level of importance as Newton's. But however we may judge the intentions of Whitehead and Russell, the failure of their undertaking teaches us a clear lesson. Formal logical arguments from axioms are not sufficient to decide important questions in mathematics, let alone in other fields. Intuition and reasoning transcend the possibilities attainable by formal axiomatic arguments. We must respect the varied nature of different forms of human reasoning and not try to limit them to a mathematical form. Every type of rational discourse must be judged according to its own procedures and limitations. Decisions involving common sense cannot be reduced to syllogisms. This conclusion is especially important when we deal with fundamental questions of values and religious truths, where the basic premises are much more difficult to reach.

A further example of the limits of axioms in mathematics is a proposition called the "continuum hypothesis." It states that any infinite set S of real numbers must either be enumerable (i.e., there must exist a one-to-one correspondence between the natural numbers and the elements of S) or have a one-to-one correspondence with the set of all the real numbers (expressed by saying "S has the cardinal of the continuum"). Gödel and Paul Cohen (1934–2007) showed that the continuum hypothesis is independent of the other axioms in the usual (Zermelo-Frankel) axiomatization of set theory, which remains equally consistent if either the continuum hypothesis or its negation is added as a new axiom. In other words, the continuum hypothesis can neither be proven nor disproven within Zermelo-Frankel set theory. Nevertheless Gödel considered this an open problem that may be decided some day by new mathematical insights. Perhaps someone will discover a new proposition that will be generally recognized as true, and such that adding it to the Zermelo-Frankel axioms makes is possible to prove the continuum hypothesis (or its negation!). In Gödel's view, here again mathematics passes beyond the limits of the axiomatic method.

THE SOURCE OF MATHEMATICAL OBJECTS

If mathematical truths cannot simply be reduced to a set of axioms, then we must ask what mathematical objects are and where they come from. This question cannot be evaded. Generally speaking, mathematical concepts had their origin in abstraction from the perception of reality. The counting numbers, now known as the "natural numbers," arose at the dawn of human consciousness, to make it possible to number the oxen in a herd, the number of coins in a purse, or the number of people in a tribe. Thus numbers were abstracted from concrete reality.

Systems of representing numbers also were developed very early on. Already mentioned are Sumerian clay tablets with multiplication tables. In ancient Sumer numbers were measured in multiples of 60, a custom that has left its traces in contemporary measures: an hour has 60 minutes, a minute has 60 seconds, an angle of an equilateral triangle has 60 degrees. In ancient Israel and Greece letters had numerical values on the base ten, a consequence of counting on one's fingers. Some learned rabbis know the Old Testament text by heart, so they can recite lengthy lists of numbers for hours on end by interpreting the text numerically. In Greece, α' represented 1, β' was used for 2, γ' for 3, and so on. Then ι' was used for 10, $\iota\alpha'$ for 11, $\iota\beta'$ for 12, then ρ' for 100, σ' for 200, and so on. Three obsolete letters were also used, since the later Greek alphabet had only twenty-four letters. For thousands, a prime was put on the lower left rather than on the upper right, so numbers up to 999,999 could be represented. Archimedes (287–212), the great mathematician and scientist from Syracuse in Sicily, created a new system of numbers of astronomical size in his essay "The Sand Reckoner."[8] This permitted him to calculate the approximate number of grains of sand that would be needed to fill up the whole visible universe! He did this to show that the expression "as infinite as the number of grains of sand on the beaches of the sea" did not make any sense, since that would be only a very large but still finite number.

The invention of the numeral zero, 0, in India, transmitted to Europe by the Arabs, made our modern positional notation possible and greatly simplified calculations. (Zero and positional notation were invented independently in the pre-Columbian Mayan culture in Central America, but they used the base twenty, apparently since in their tropical climate they used both fingers and toes for counting.) The binary system, with only 0 and 1 as numerals, was fundamental in the development of digital computers, where components have only two positions (on and off) and most computations are carried out in binary. Just as in the decimal system 269 represents 9 units plus 6 tens plus 2 hundreds, counting from the right, so in the binary system 10011 represents 1 plus 2 plus 16, giving 19 (with 4 and 8 omitted because of the 0s in their positions). The binary cases have the values 1, 2, 4, 8, 16, 32,..., counting from the right. Each case has as its value the double of the case to its right.

Fractions, known as "rational numbers," were necessary to measure quantities that are not given by whole numbers, such as the result of dividing two loaves of bread among five people, so that each one receives two-fifths of a loaf, or measuring lengths, volumes, or weights to a reasonable approximation.

There are also "irrational numbers" that cannot be expressed as the quotient of two whole numbers. For example, the square root of 2, $\sqrt{2}$, which is the ratio of the length of the diagonal of a square to its sides, cannot be written as p/q. (If it could be so represented, then we could choose p and q so that at least one of them would not be even. Then p^2/q^2 would be 2, so $p^2 = 2q^2$, and consequently p must be even, say p = 2k. But then we would have $4k^2 = 2q^2$ and so $q^2 = 2k^2$, and q would also be even, contrary to assumption.) Ancient historians relate that when this was discovered and disclosed by a member of the Pythagorean school in the fifth century BC, it was such a scandal that he was put to death. The story is probably fictitious, but it shows a possible motivation for the term *irrational*. In any case, to measure lengths—or areas, volumes, or other continuous sizes—we need what are called "real numbers," which correspond to all the points on a line once we have marked two points as 0 and 1. Every point on the line, like every real number, can be represented by an infinite decimal expansion. For example, 1/3 = 0.33333..., where the 3s repeat infinitely often, and 2 = 2.0000... and 16/7 = 2.2857142857..., where the block 142857 is repeated ad infinitum. A real number will be irrational if there is no such eventually repeating block in its decimal expansion. The golden mean φ is such an irrational number.

In the late Middle Ages "complex numbers" of the form $a + bi$ ("*a* plus *b* times *i*"), where *i* is an "imaginary number" satisfying $i^2 = -1$ and *a* and *b* are real numbers, were invented to provide solutions of certain equations with no real solutions. Today complex numbers are extremely important in almost all branches of mathematics and their applications. Many fields of physics, such as electromagnetic theory and quantum theory, use complex numbers in an essential way. It is fascinating to note that the creation of imaginary numbers to provide solutions for unsolvable equations ended up as a fundamental advance in mathematics, without which modern technology would not be possible.

Geometrical figures and spaces are also abstracted from observations of reality, but in this case from the spatial relations between objects. There were many advances in Babylonia, Egypt, and Greece leading up to the organization and axiomatic presentation in Euclid's *Elements*. In the seventeenth century Fermat (1601?–65), Descartes (1596–1650), and other mathematicians discovered that each point in the plane could be represented by an ordered pair of real numbers (x,y), using the horizontal x-axis and the vertical y-axis. These "coordinates" x and y made it possible to translate geometric statements into algebraic ones, relating y to x and leading to great progress in geometry. It is also possible to represent a point in three-dimensional space by an ordered triple (x,y,z), and so spatial geometry can also be translated into algebra and mathematical analysis. It was a natural further step to consider spaces of four, five, or even n dimensions. A point in n-dimensional Euclidean space is defined to be an ordered sequence of n real numbers $(x_1, x_2, \ldots, x_n)$. The geometrical properties of figures in n-dimensional space, such as lengths and angles, can then be formulated in terms of the coordinates $x_1, x_2, \ldots$, and x_n. As was the case for complex numbers which were created as extensions of other mathematical numbers but not abstracted from reality, the creation of n-dimensional space has led to extremely important practical and theoretical applications. Here we see a dimension of nobility in human rationality; the human mind shows that it is in the image of God as it creates these new mathematical objects (see Genesis 1:26–27).

THE EXISTENCE OF MATHEMATICAL OBJECTS

As we have just seen, mathematical objects arise in human thought by abstraction from observations of reality. Yet most practicing mathematicians consider them to have some kind of existence in themselves, since they are not amenable to mathematicians' desires and do not yield to our wishes. The question of whether a certain conjecture is true is an objective question that must be investigated to be decided, independently of whether one would like it to be true or false. In what sense, then, can mathematical objects like numbers, sets, and geometrical figures be said to exist?

Plato (428/427–348/347 BC) thought mathematical objects, like other ideas, had a real existence in some ideal world. St. Augustine (354–430) gave a Christian interpretation of Plato's position by claiming that Platonic ideas exist in the mind of God. For the believing Christian, this claim yields two possible implications: either numbers are inherent in any possibility of existence, before God created anything, or else they are in God's mind as creator. Perhaps these two positions are just two facets of the same basic belief, for God is the creator of all that is except himself. All created reality existed in the mind of God prior to its creation, and God is pure existence (*summum esse*, as St. Thomas Aquinas expresses it). All that exists is derivative from God, numbers and other mathematical objects as well.

An interesting application of the belief that numbers exist in some objective sense is the way they are being used in the Search for Extra-Terrestrial Intelligence (SETI). The prime numbers 2, 3, 5, 7, 11, 13, 17, 19, . . . , those positive whole numbers (excluding 1 itself) that cannot be factored into whole numbers greater than 1, are fundamental in studies of arithmetic. Because it is difficult to imagine any process not due to intelligent beings that could produce the ordered sequence of prime numbers, this list has been radioed into outer space in hopes that another intelligent civilization may observe it and send back some similar reply. (Unfortunately, if there are intelligent extraterrestrials, they are probably hundreds or thousands of light-years away, so no quick reply can be hoped for.)

ANALOGIES BETWEEN MATHEMATICS AND THEOLOGY

Mathematics advances with an enormous dynamism. A research mathematician is often asked by people who have never encountered advanced mathematics how it is possible to do research. "Haven't all the problems been solved by now?" In reality, as old mathematical problems are resolved, many more new ones keep appearing. The proliferation of new questions and ideas has also been taking place in Christian theology throughout its history. There were times when many people thought that the essential problems of our faith had been solved, and there were only secondary questions to be attacked. Yet as Blessed Cardinal John Henry Newman (1801–90) explained in his revolutionary work, *An Essay on the Development of Christian Doctrine*, the Holy Spirit keeps giving new insights to help theologians advance in understanding the Christian faith. The way both mathematics and theology keep advancing and deepening their understanding is a first common trait.

A second similarity in the progress of mathematics and theology is the strong interlinking of their various subordinate disciplines. Perhaps this unity is easier to understand in theology, where there is a common focus on God's salvific action in the world. In mathematical research, on the other hand, new theories and domains are constantly appearing. One would expect that these theories would diverge and become independent of each other, but that is not what happens. The history of mathematics is full of surprising connections between what were thought to be independent fields. The studies of the young French mathematician Evariste Galois (1811–32) on permutation of roots of polynomial equations led to the concept of a group that has since become a unifying structure in essentially all branches of mathematics and science. The Atiyah-Singer index theorem, proven in various versions in the 1960s, showed that deep invariants in the algebraic topology of manifolds and in the analysis of differential operators were actually the same! The examples can be multiplied without end. Despite the expansion of mathematical research into new and apparently divergent fields, they often come together and form one closely integrated field of study.

Not only are mathematics and theology integrated disciplines in themselves, but a third similarity is that they both perform a function of integrating widely different areas of human thought. Throughout the Middle Ages theology was considered the "queen of the sciences," though the word *science* meant organized knowledge and referred to all domains of human thought, and not just empirical science, as we use the word today. All forms of learning were integrated in the almost universal belief in a God who created everything and gave human beings the intelligence to study and understand all of creation in all its aspects.

In contemporary secular society, it is now mathematics that is considered the queen of the sciences, and science is now understood to be the empirical study of nature. The physical and social sciences all depend on mathematical measurement and analysis. This common dependence on mathematics makes it the "language of science." It has become a common structure that relates and integrates all forms of precise reasoning.

A fourth fundamental analogy between mathematics and theology can be seen in the observation of the Jesuit theologian Gerald O'Collins, cited in Lawrence Cunningham's chapter, that there are "three fundamental strands of contemporary theology: academic, practical and contemplative." Cunningham quotes O'Collins's observation, "We might contrast faith seeking scientific understanding with faith seeking social justice and with faith seeking adoration." These three strands have analogous lines of force in mathematics. Like theology, mathematics seeks scientific understanding in resolving open problems and organizing the discoveries in coherent and simple theories. The practical applications of mathematics as the language of science serve other branches of science and technology, thus contributing significantly to social organization and advance. Finally, there is a dimension of mathematical activity that shares the humble and unselfish attitude of contemplation of God. The pursuit of understanding and new advances in mathematics seeks insight and knowledge for its intrinsic value in itself, rather than for applications or other advantages. There is a dimension of unselfish asceticism in the long hours and struggles of research. Just as faith seeking adoration reaches out to God himself, so mathematics—as viewed in St. Augustine's version of Platonic philosophy—seeks to contemplate the mind of God.

NUMEROLOGY AND SYMBOLISM

From ancient times, numbers have had a certain symbolic significance, although today they have lost their aura of mysticism. Let us consider the traditional symbolic significance of several numbers and how that symbolism is reflected in Judeo-Christian faith. *One* represents unity and existence, and is affirmed of God in the profession of Israelite faith, the Shema Yisrael prayed daily by pious Jews: "Hear, O Israel: the Lord our God, the Lord is one" (Deuteronomy 6:4). But *one* also denotes solitude and seeks a partner, leading to *two*, a couple. In Christian theology, God the Son proceeds from God the Father. Then the love of *two* generates a third, as the Holy Spirit proceeds from the Father and the Son, or as sexual relations procreate a child. But *three* exhibits some incompleteness, lacking the eightfold symmetries of the four points of the compass, the symmetries of the square and mandala. So *three* leads to *four*, which represents fullness or completeness. *Three* and *four* put together by addition and multiplication give *seven* and *twelve*, numbers that suggest totality or plenitude, as in the seven cardinal virtues, the seven gifts of the Holy Spirit, the seven sacraments, the twelve tribes of Israel, and the twelve apostles. Today the symbolic values of numbers have lost their importance. Perhaps we might suggest that cultivation of this mystical dimension of numbers is analogous to the contemplative life of prayer and meditation that opens our consciousness to profound and mystical aspects of reality and of our relationship with God.

Number theory is still one of the most popular and attractive branches of mathematics. It has received the attention and contributions of many of the greatest mathematicians through the centuries. Gauss, considered the greatest number theorist of all time, referred to number theory as the "queen of mathematics." The oldest unsolved mathematical problem is a question from number theory: Does there exist an odd perfect number? A natural number is said to be *perfect* if it is equal to the sum of all its divisors, except itself, such as $6 = 1 + 2 + 3$ and $28 = 1 + 2 + 4 + 7 + 14$. The even perfect numbers are known to be precisely the numbers of the form $2^{p-1}(2^p - 1)$ where $2^p - 1$ is a prime number, but the conjecture that no odd perfect numbers exist remains unproven after at least two and half millennia of efforts.

There is an interesting anecdote about the Cambridge and Oxford don G. H. Hardy (1877–1947) and his collaborator Srinivasa Ramanujan (1887–1920), both eminent number theorists. When Hardy visited Ramanujan in a hospital, he disagreed with Ramanujan's statement that every number was interesting, asking what was special about the number of the taxicab that he had taken, 1729. Ramanujan answered immediately that it was the smallest number that could be expressed as the sum of two cubes in two different ways, $1{,}729 = 9^3 + 10^3 = 12^3 + 1^3$. Upon hearing of this incident, another famous number theorist and collaborator of Hardy, J. E. Littlewood (1885–1977), commented, "Every positive integer is one of Ramanujan's personal friends."

MATHEMATICS AND PROOFS FOR GOD'S EXISTENCE

The pristine beauty of mathematical figures and structures can be seen as a reflection of the beauty of the Creator, as I have said. Harmony and symmetry in nature have a similar impact. In contemplating many aspects of nature we are led to believe in the presence of God. But in this section we shall consider two classical philosophical proofs of God's existence to see whether mathematics can shed some light on them. Christians usually do not believe in God the Father and in Jesus Christ because of formal logical proofs; nevertheless proofs are important and deserve our attention. We shall comment on the second and third ways of showing God's existence proposed by St. Thomas Aquinas (1225–74) and also on the ontological argument as reformulated by Gödel.

Aquinas's second and third ways of proving God's existence use arguments from efficient causality and from contingency and necessity. He argues that an infinite regression does not give a sufficient explanation (*Summa Theologiae*, Iᵃ, q. 2, a. 3). Sometimes his argument is criticized by saying that it would be possible to have an infinite regression of efficient causes, say $C_1, C_2, C_3, \ldots, C_n, C_{n+1}, \ldots$, such that C_{n+1} is the cause of C_n, C_n the cause of $C_{n-1}, \ldots, C_3$ the cause of C_2, and C_2 the cause of C_1, as if Aquinas had not considered this possibility. The causes would have an ordering like the negative numbers. This criticism is based on a misunderstanding of his argument. He explicitly recognized the logical possibility of a universe that had always existed, so that there could be an infinite regression of generations of men or other organisms, but he discarded this possibility because of the Christian belief that God created the universe, which he interpreted as necessarily a creation at a determined moment in time. (Today I think that there would be no theological difficulty in holding that God's creation may have been before time, from all eternity. Furthermore, in the standard model of cosmology, no one knows what might have existed "before" the big bang—if it makes any sense to talk about "before"!) Aquinas's argument is not about partial efficient causes, but about the total cause of the existence of a being. He claims that if C_3 is the total cause of C_2 and C_2 is the total cause of C_1, then C_1 depends for its existence directly on C_3, since the causality exercised by C_2 on C_1 depends totally on C_3. However one judges the validity of Aquinas's metaphysical argument, the mathematical possibility of a sequence of causes or events in an infinite regression did not escape his notice. It is not a refutation of his argument. Bringing in the mathematical concept of infinite ordered sets sheds no light on the question. For Aquinas, not only does the existence of a nonnecessary being require an efficient cause at the onset of its existence, but the continuing action of such a cause is necessary as long as the being continues to exist. The same analysis applies to the third way, which argues from necessity and contingency.

If mathematics does not disprove Aquinas's five ways, it does shed some light on the ontological argument for God's existence, first formulated by St. Anselm of Canterbury (ca. 1033–1109), taken up by Leibniz, but rejected by Aquinas, Kant, and most other philosophers. Anselm considered "that than which nothing greater can be conceived" (*id quod magis cogitari nequit*) and argued that such an existing being would be greater than one that did not exist. His argument was rejected by Gaunilo, a monk who was his contemporary. Descartes based his philosophy on an argument analogous to Anselm's. In recent decades there has been considerable interest in variations of the ontological argument.

After the death of the great mathematician, physicist, and logician Gödel, an unpublished version of the ontological argument that he had composed was found among his papers; it has been published in his *Collected Works*.[9] Gödel had discussed his argument with several logician colleagues and considered it to have value. According to his widow, he read the Bible every morning, but apparently he hesitated to publish his argument because he did not want to be known as a religious person. Since he was arguably the greatest logician in human history, his argument carries weight, so we shall briefly examine it.[10]

The argument uses modal logic, the logic of possibility and necessity. Gödel considers what he calls "positive properties," and the essence of God is to have all positive properties and no others. According to Gödel, there can be no incompatibility among different positive properties. In particular, a property and its negation cannot both be positive. Necessary existence is a positive property, as is the property of being God-like. For any property P, if P is positive, then being necessarily P is positive. The final result is that, necessarily, the property of being

God-like is exemplified; that is, there necessarily exists a God-like being, a being with all positive properties. Thus God exists!

There is not enough space to give the complete argument, much less to analyze it in depth. The logic seems to be correct, if one accepts the axioms of modal logic that Gödel uses. There is room for disagreement in the premises, the axioms that he assumes. Nevertheless, in an age when many people think that God's existence has been disproved, that science leaves no room for God, that there is an irreducible conflict between science and religious faith, we should remember that one of the greatest scientists and mathematicians of the twentieth century constructed a logical proof for the existence of God that he apparently considered to be valid.

NOTES

1. For an English translation and the Greek text, see Bernadotte Perrin, ed., *Plutarch's Lives*, 11 vols. (New York: G. P. Putnam's Sons, 1917), 5:480–1. See also Professor Chris Rorres's website, www.math.nyu.edu/~crorres/Archimedes/Tomb/Cicero.html.

2. Color reproductions of Salvador Dalí's paintings *Crucifixion—Corpus Hypercubus* and *The Sacrament of the Last Supper* are easily accessible via Google Images. The originals are in the Metropolitan Museum of Art in New York and the National Gallery of Art in Washington, respectively.

3. For information about the Rhind papyrus, see http://library.thinkquest.org/25672/areasand.htm; www.math.tamu.edu/~don.allen/history/egypt/node3.html; www-history.mcs.st-andrews.ac.uk/HistTopics/Egyptian_papyri.html.

4. Jöran Friberg, "A Remarkable Collection of Babylonian Mathematical Texts," *Notices of the American Mathematical Society* 55 (October 2008): 1076–86.

5. David Hilbert, *The Foundations of Geometry* (1899; Chicago: Open Court 1980).

6. Kürt Gödel, "Über formal unentscheidbare Sätze der Principia Mathematica und verwandter Systeme," (1931) in *Collected Works* 4 vols. (Oxford: Oxford University Press, 1986), 1:30–5.

7. Alan Turing, "On Computable Numbers, with an Application to the Entscheidungsproblem," *Proceedings of the London Mathematical Society* 42 (1936): 230–65; correction *Proceedings of the London Mathematical Society* 43 (1937): 544–6.

8. Archimedes, "The Sand Reckoner," in *The Works of Archimedes,* translated and edited by T. L. Heath (London: C. J. Clay and Sons, Cambridge University Press, 1897), 221–32.

9. K. Gödel, "Ontological Proof," in *Collected Works,* 5 vols. edited by S. Feferman (Oxford: Oxford University Press, 2001), 3:403–4. There is an excellent introduction by R. M. Adams (388–402).

10. For a good discussion of the ontological argument, a detailed analysis of Gödel's argument, and recent references, see G. Oppy, "Ontological Arguments," *Stanford Encyclopedia of Philosophy,* http://plato.stanford.edu/entries/ontological-arguments/.

SELECTED READINGS

Goldman, David. P. "The God of the Mathematicians." *First Things,* no. 205 (August–September 2010): 45–50.

Hofstadter, Douglas. *Gödel, Escher, Bach: An Eternal Golden Braid.* Vancouver, Wash.: Vintage Books, 1979.

Huntley, H. E. *The Divine Proportion: A Study in Mathematical Beauty.* Mineola, N.Y.: Dover, 1970.

Smullyan, Raymond. *Gödel's Incompleteness Theorems.* Oxford: Oxford University Press, 1992.

Weyl, Herman. *Symmetry.* Princeton, N.J.: Princeton University Press, 1983.

Whitman, Andrew P. "Mathematics: The Language of Astronomy and the Mind of God." In *The Heavens Proclaim—Astronomy and the Vatican.* Vatican City State: Vatican Observatory, 2009.

Wigner, Eugene. "The Unreasonable Effectiveness of Mathematics in the Natural Sciences." In *Symmetries and Reflections.* Bloomington: Indiana University Press, 1967.

13

Catholic Themes in Art and Music

Charles Scribner III

IN HIS CHAPTER Lawrence Cunningham calls attention to the particular emphasis the Old Testament authors placed on God as Creator. He goes on to say that some theologians even go so far as to describe creation as a kind of "primordial sacrament": "Both Judaism and Christianity resist identifying creation as divine; it is created. However, creation reflects the work of the creator."

The notion that creation mirrors its creator has special resonance for Catholics; it has long been at the heart of our tradition, both explicitly and implicitly. It even has provided a basis of proof for the existence of God, the so-called cosmological argument proposed by the great Thomas Aquinas a millennium ago. The idea of a spontaneous creation ex nihilo without any agent, that is to say, without a Creator, is difficult for most mortals to imagine, however plausible it may be in principle to contemporary cosmologists. It runs counter to human experience. Our first appreciation of God, as we gaze up to the heavens, is of God as an Artist. Whatever else the universe may hold, its infinite variety and reflected glory suggest a vast canvas comprising a multitude of masterpieces.

The theme of creation has given rise to some of the greatest achievements by human creators in the realm of art. Arguably the most famous sacred work of art in Christendom is Michelangelo's great Sistine Chapel ceiling, known to students and tourists alike long before they see it in the flesh. In his television series *Civilisation*, Kenneth Clark said, "It is possible to interpret the whole of the Sistine Ceiling as a poem on the subject of creation." Thanks to its thorough cleaning and restoration two decades ago, it may now be experienced afresh, as it was when first unveiled to the impatient Pope Julius II. After five centuries of grime, candle smoke, and clumsy touch-ups were dissolved and wiped away by the Vatican restorers, the ceiling is once again ablaze with color; no longer is it seen "through a glass darkly," in the vivid words of St. Paul, but "face to face."

If one individual, and only one, could be chosen to epitomize artistic genius it would be Michelangelo. Not only does he personify the Renaissance man as a *Bildung*, to invoke Cunningham's elegant term—well rounded, like a classical sculpture—but he towers over the history of art just as his youthful *David*, the marble embodiment of heroic virtue and virility, has loomed over Florence for half a millennium.

Michelangelo was a prodigy. Yet unlike the prodigies Bernini and Mozart, the source of his technical prowess has remained shrouded. Both Bernini and Mozart had professional artist or composer fathers to instruct them from the time they could walk. Michelangelo's father, too patrician to labor and too poor to provide any meaningful support, failed even to offer encouragement to the aspiring artist. "I sucked in chisels and hammers with my nurse's milk" is the only explanation Michelangelo was to offer in later years. As an infant he had a stonecutter's wife for his wet nurse. A teacher, Henry Adams once wrote, can never know the full extent of his influence: "A teacher affects eternity." That anonymous instructor who taught Michelangelo to wield a chisel indeed made a vital contribution to Western art.

Michelangelo was destined to live an extraordinarily long and productive life: eighty-nine years, almost two generations beyond the normal expectancy for that time. Yet what if our Florentine prodigy had survived no more than Mozart's thirty-five? He would still have left behind enough masterpieces to guarantee his preeminence in the annals of art. Among these one would find the Vatican *Pietà*, the *Bacchus*, the *David*, and most of the Sistine ceiling. The last would surely then be viewed as his Requiem, the masterpiece that, reluctantly undertaken, hastened the demise of its creator, who had protested in vain that he was a "sculptor, not a painter." (Fortunately Pope Julius was unconvinced.)

Vita brevis, ars longa. In Michelangelo's case, both life and art were long—and of enduring significance. It is nigh impossible to overestimate his influence on later artists. Rubens and Bernini are the Castor and Pollux of the Baroque age, but it is difficult to write about them without regularly invoking the name of Michelangelo, as did Rubens and Bernini in both word and work. (A biographer of Rodin would say no less.) Arriving in Rome for the first time in 1601, the twenty-four-year-old Rubens proceeded to sketch figures from the Sistine ceiling, rendering Michelangelo's heroic forms as sensuously and vividly as though they had been drawn from studio models, not copied from century-old frescoes some sixty feet overhead. A few years later the painter Annibale Carracci advised the ten-year-old Bernini to study Michelangelo's *Last Judgment* for a full two years in order to get a firm grasp of anatomy.

"He was a good man, but he did not know how to paint"—El Greco's appraisal represents the minority. The founding fathers of the Baroque—Carracci, Caravaggio, and Rubens—owed Michelangelo an incalculable debt, and paid him homage with their brushes. Poussin, Velazquez, even Rembrandt may be cited among the beneficiaries of "the Homer of painting," as he was dubbed by Sir Joshua Reynolds, president of the Royal Academy. In his last discourse in London to his fellow academicians, in 1790, Reynolds concluded, "I should desire that the last word which I should pronounce in this Academy, and from this place, might be the name of Michelangelo." A few years earlier the German poet Goethe confessed in his *Italian Journey* that he had become so enthusiastic about Michelangelo that he had lost all his taste for Nature, since he could not see her with the same eye of genius. Sir Thomas Lawrence, the British portraitist, supplied in 1819 a more biblical explanation: "God gave the command to increase and multiply before the Fall, and Michelangelo's is the race that might have been."

Steeped as he was in Neoplatonic philosophy, which to the Renaissance mind was wholly compatible with Christianity, Michelangelo pictured mankind and divinity alike in idealized human form. "His people are a superior order of beings," concluded Reynolds. The prototype is Original Man, naked Adam, that sensual revision of a classical river god who reaches out, languidly, to receive from his Creator the spark of a divine soul. Yet the artist's mind that gave immortal form to that perfect male remained conflicted and tormented, a soul yearning to escape the shackles of human flesh.

"L'amor mi prende e la beltà mi lege" ("Love seizes me and beauty binds me")—so Michelangelo described in verse, as in stone, his soul's struggle against its earthly chains. We are reminded of his unfinished marbles, those human forms that barely emerge from the confines of stone. Surely no artist in history has bequeathed so many unfinished masterpieces to the world. Far from being depreciated, those incomplete metamorphoses reveal, as no polished *Pietà* could reflect, the lifelong psychic conflict that fueled his creativity. Such pain was the touchstone of Michelangelo's artistic growth. It was the process of creation, not the finely chiseled product, that progressively engaged his fertile imagination. In the Sistine ceiling he gave the very subject of Creation, beginning and end, its definitive epic form for our eyes to behold. These he did complete.

But Michelangelo was not alone in recomposing Creation. Almost three centuries later he was answered in the thunderous chords, evocative harmonies, and soaring lines of an oratorio, *The Creation* by Franz Joseph Haydn. Composed by the prolific maestro well into his sixties, it represents Haydn's response to Handel's *Messiah*, which so overwhelmed Haydn upon his first hearing it in 1791 at Westminster Abbey that he wept during the "Hallelujah Chorus." "He is the master of us all" was Haydn's verdict. Yet six years later he began to compose his own sacred masterpiece of comparable scope and power. A prequel of sorts to *Messiah*, Haydn's *Creation* sets to music an assemblage of texts derived, by an unknown librettist, from Milton's *Paradise Lost*. Then in Vienna that great patron of Baroque music Baron Gottfried van Swieten (who had earlier introduced Mozart to the music of Bach and Handel) provided a German translation for Haydn to set arguably the greatest music he ever wrote. He told his biographer, "I was never so religious as during the composition of *The Creation*. Daily I fell on my knees and asked God for strength."

The oratorio was hugely successful from first hearing—so much for the mistaken notion that all great art must go unrecognized by contemporary society—and was repeated countless times throughout Europe. Haydn's last public appearance was at a performance in 1808 in Vienna—his former pupil Beethoven was among the listeners—shortly before he died. At the climactic moment of Creation, the thunderous, exalting *fortissimo* of chords that accompany and overwhelm the words of God's command "And let there be light," Haydn was himself so deeply moved that he confessed, "It was not I, but a Power above who created that."

Ever since I was a schoolboy soprano, my favorite chorus in all music was Haydn's triumphal setting of the opening of Psalm 19, the climax of part 1 of his *Creation*: "Die Himmel erzählen die Ehre Gottes, und seiner Hände Werk zeigt an das Firmament" ("The heavens declare the glory of God, and the firmament proclaims his handiwork"). Almost fifty years later this music still conveys, as no mere words alone can, the Creator behind creation, just as Handel's soprano solo in *Messiah*, "I know that my redeemer liveth," redeems the suffering of Job as well as our own and points forward, as an aural prefiguration, to Christ our Redeemer, our Messiah. As the Composer in Richard Strauss's opera *Ariadne auf Naxos* rightly proclaims, "Musik ist eine heilige Kunst"—Music is a Holy Art. But Music is, fortunately, in good company with her sister arts.

When my elder son, Charlie, was two years old I took him to kneel before the crèche set up for Christmas at our parish church of St. Vincent Ferrer. Gazing in wonder over the finely carved figures of the Holy Family, the shepherds, and the Magi gathered at the manger along with attendant animals, he sang out, "Ee— eye—ee-eye—oh." My son may have mistaken the ownership of the farm, but he had no problem with animal iconography! Images speak with immediacy to the very young, as to us all.

One is reminded of another Charles, the narrator of Evelyn Waugh's most Catholic novel, *Brideshead Revisited*, magnificently translated to film for television a generation ago (and now available on DVD). In one early, idyllic summer scene on the terrace of Brideshead, Charles challenges his eccentric and much beloved new college friend Sebastian over the latter's troublesome convictions as a Catholic. Charles, played to the hilt by Jeremy Irons in the television series, dismisses it as "an awful lot of nonsense," but Sebastian retorts:

> "Is it nonsense? I wish it were. It sometimes sounds terribly sensible to me."
> "But, my dear Sebastian, you can't seriously believe it all."
> "Can't I?"
> "I mean about Christmas and the star and the three kings and the ox and the ass."
> "Oh, yes, I believe that. It's a lovely idea."
> "But you can't believe things because they're a lovely idea."
> "But I do. That's how I believe."

What brings Catholics to the Manger, time and again? To the Mass? To faith? What about Sebastian's claim to believe something because it is a "lovely idea"? Is that nothing more than the intellectual equivalent to his beloved teddy bear, Aloysius (named after the young Jesuit saint)? Is truth more likely to be lovely? A theological argument might be fashioned in favor of this "lovely idea" based on the claim in St. John's gospel that God is both absolute Truth and absolute Love—an equation, as it were, that supports Sebastian's point. In retrospect over the two millennia of Christianity, it appears that the Church implicitly adopted this notion insofar as it encouraged and commissioned artists to present its stories and theological claims in the most attractive and "lovely" fashions. By the time Christianity emerged free into the light of the Roman Empire, it decked itself and its core beliefs in the splendid raiment of visual art: architecture, painting and sculpture.

St. Luke, evangelist and author of the book of Acts, was considered a physician and hence became the patron saint of doctors and surgeons—as well as butchers and students, an arresting combination! But he was also the patron saint of artists, owing to an old tradition, unsupported by fact, that he painted the first icon, from life, of the Virgin Mary. Hence the many artists' guilds of St. Luke down the centuries. But that honor perhaps should have gone to the Apostle Paul, for it was Paul's wildly successful mission to the gentiles throughout the Roman Empire that ultimately converted that empire and brought Christianity into the realm of its painters and sculptors, something that would have appeared alien to the first Jewish Christians, steeped as they were in the iconoclastic tradition of Judaism and its prohibition of graven images (a tradition that later took root in Islam and in the stricter sects of Protestantism).

The first known Christian paintings date from two centuries after the death and resurrection of Jesus; they were found in the house church at Dura Europas in present-day Syria. There we see beautifully preserved frescoes from the year 235, of Jesus as the Good Shepherd—the oldest image of that most popular Early Christian symbol—along with miracle scenes of Peter healing the paralytic and Jesus walking on water, and the Three Marys at the empty tomb of Jesus on Easter morning, among others. But the first full flowering of Christian art would have to wait another century and a major military victory, that of the Emperor Constantine at the Milvian Bridge in 312.

Before battle Constantine had a vision of a huge cross appearing in the sky along with a Greek inscription: "By this, conquer" (later rendered in Latin *In hoc signo vinces,* "By this sign you shall conquer"). He ordered his troops to display on their shields the Christian insignia of *chi-rho* (the first two Greek letters for "Christ"). The next year the grateful, victorious emperor issued an imperial decree of tolerance, the Edict of Milan, for Christians throughout his empire, an end of persecution, and the restoration of confiscated property; in time he went further, declaring Christianity its official religion. The Catholic Church had finally become Roman, beyond all dreams.

During his transformative reign over both empire and Church, Constantine not only presided over the Council of Nicea, which adopted the Creed recited today at Sunday Mass, but also sponsored a huge program of magnificent church building, from St. Peter's in Rome to the Church of the Holy Sepulcher in Jerusalem. These huge basilicas—the term comes from the Greek word for king, *basileus*—provided splendid gathering places for the Christian faithful, now liberated to worship aboveground. The catacombs along the Via Appia Antica had small chapels decorated sparingly, if poignantly, by frescoes of Christ and his saints, but the basilicas of Constantine spared no expense in celebrating the once-persecuted faith that had become the official religion of Rome and her sprawling empire. The new temples of the Christian God represented, in effect, the pagan temples of classical antiquity (think of the Parthenon) turned inside out.

Those pagan temples, reflecting ancient worship, proclaimed their sacredness externally: the exteriors, facing the public, were sheathed in marble columns and adorned with relief sculpture brightly painted. The Christian basilicas, by contrast, were designed to house congregations that assembled inside to worship their God in a participatory fashion. Hence the rows of magnificent marble columns were moved inside to reinforce the ceremonial procession from entrance to altar, while the wall surfaces were dematerialized by glowing mosaics and frescoes and punctuated by windows to illuminate this New Jerusalem, a symbolic Heaven on Earth.

Imperial trappings of royal power were transferred to the worship of the new King of Kings. The emperor's throne room became the hall of the New Emperor, Christ. Whereas Roman emperors sat under a baldachin at the rear of the hall, filled with adoring subjects, Christ appeared, liturgically, in the Sacrament under the baldachin or marble *ciborium* (an architectural term referring to the permanent vaulted canopy over the altar) at the altar at the climax of each Mass. Altar replaced throne for this new heavenly emperor, who ruled from a cross. Lest there be any doubt, monumental images of Christ now appeared in apses, from Santa Pudenziana in Rome to San Vitale in Ravenna, wherein Christ was bedecked with full imperial regalia: Christ as Emperor, Pantocrator, Ruler of the World. At the same time the pope, his vicar on earth, likewise assumed imperial trappings as Pontifex Maximus and over time assembled a ceremonial court that would rival, and ultimately outlast, the secular emperor's, thus sowing the seeds of perennial conflict between Church and state down the ages to its climax in Napoleon's attack on the papacy. But that lay many centuries in the future.

The crowning glory of Early Christian celebrations of Christ as Emperor are still preserved today in the mosaics of Ravenna, the seaport town on the Adriatic that for one brief shining moment served as capital of the Roman Empire in the West. Unrivaled in splendor and glittering detail, its fifth- and sixth-century mosaics— from San Apollinare Nuovo, to the Baptistry, to San Vitale and the mausoleum of Galla Placidia—belie any erroneous notion of artistic decline in the period of the early Dark Ages.

Even in the West, where the Pax Romana of a bygone empire had long given way to tribal warfare and warlords had little use for architects and artisans, civilization, that is to say, the classical heritage of Greece and Rome, was preserved for later revivals by those diligent monks in Iona in western Scotland and in Ireland, who kept vast libraries of ancient manuscripts and piously copied them while adding their own illuminations of fantastic decorative shapes and colors. (For a lively and unabashed treatment of this thesis, see the persuasive view offered by Kenneth Clark in *Civilisation*.) The epitome of these manuscripts is *The Book of Kells*, now preserved at Trinity College in Dublin and visited by countless tourists. Its maze-like geometric patterns foreshadow the art of Frank Stella, the American abstract painter and sculptor who was influenced as a college student in Princeton's Department of Art and Archaeology by such early medieval art.

On Christmas Day in the year of our Lord 800, the pope crowned Charlemagne—or Karl der Grosse, or Carolus Magnus, depending on one's preferred tongue—emperor (Imperator Augustus) of a revived Roman Empire in the

West to rival the Eastern emperor enthroned in Constantinople, the former Byzantium. Charlemagne is rightly considered the father of both the German and French monarchies, but also in a larger sense the father of a united Europe. His palace in Aachen stands as a magnificent medieval successor to the sixth-century emperor Justinian's San Vitale in Ravenna, which Charlemagne saw and admired on his way back from Rome. His reign marked the first artistic renewal in the West, a consciously classical revival known as the Carolingian Renaissance.

Charlemagne presented several relics to the Abbey of St. Sernin in Toulouse, which immediately established it as a worthy site for pilgrims to visit en route to Santiago de Compostela in Spain, which housed the head of the apostle James and lay at the hub of pilgrimage routes in Europe. Three centuries later, in 1120, the abbey church of St. Sernin was completed, only forty years after it was begun in 1080. It rises as a magnificent monument to the style known as Romanesque, its towering nave crowned with a barrel vault—think of an inverted half-pipe in Olympic snowboarding competition—supported by massive round columns directing the thrust of tons of stone downward to earth. It is called a basilica, but it bears little resemblance to those of Rome. Rather it epitomizes the "pilgrimage plan," a practical arrangement of side chapels radiating off a semicircular aisle behind the high altar and apse, to accommodate queues of passing pilgrims gaining valuable indulgences through their veneration of relics—a spiritual World's Fair pavilion. Two years into construction, the architect, or his best pupil, began work on the new Spanish pilgrimage church of Santiago de Compostela at the end of the line.

But high noon in the Middle Ages was yet to come, along with the full flowering of the Gothic style epitomized in France by the cathedral of Chartres, begun in 1194. The technical innovation of rib vaults and flying buttresses directs the downward forces outward, beyond the exterior walls, as well as downward. These advances allowed builders to scale new heights and to dematerialize the walls with luminous stained-glass windows. Kenneth Clark called Gothic cathedrals "hymns to the divine light." High Gothic was, in every aspect of the word, all about light, the Shadow of God. It achieved and reflected in all media, fully coordinated, a parallel spiritual universe, a retreat from the mundane world, a vision of Heaven on Earth.

Gothic cathedrals have been evocatively dubbed "sermons in stone" and "frozen music." Nowhere are they better described and explained than in Emile Mâle's *The Gothic Image*. But others too have captured the magic. In *The Power of Myth*, Joseph Campbell muses about Chartres, "I'm back in the Middle Ages. I'm back in the world I was brought up in as a child, the Roman Catholic spiritual-image world, and it is magnificent.... That cathedral talks to me about the spiritual information of the world. It's a place for meditation, just walking around, just sitting, just looking at those beautiful things." As Albert Finney, playing an architect, says to Audrey Hepburn, his wife in the 1967 film *Two for the Road*, "Nobody knows the names of the men who made it. To make something as exquisite as this without wanting to smash your stupid name all over it.... All you hear about nowadays is people making names, not things." *Plus ça change...*

By the fourteenth century, the twilight of the Middle Ages offered a glimmer of a new dawn, the Renaissance. Heralded in Italy by Giotto, it rose to new heights of humanism in the late fifteenth and early sixteenth centuries in the art of Leonardo, Michelangelo, and Raphael. "Man is the measure of all things," that famous proclamation of the ancient Greek philosopher Protagoras, became a new credo for artists and architects alike, as the ideal of the human body was revived from classical antiquity and applied to architectural theory as well: buildings should evoke bodies. The new basilica of St. Peter's in the Vatican, designed to replace the now crumbling Constantinian original, was to be crowned by a dome symbolizing the Head, or Crown, of Christendom.

The Renaissance life of the mind brought forth countless treatises on humanistic theory, which spelled out a Christian humanism wholly compatible with Catholic faith. Just as there was at that time no "Da Vinci" (he was always called Leonardo), there also was no "Da Vinci code" needed to reinterpret the new humanism in the light of modern secularism. Any contemporary passerby would have recognized (from countless Early Renaissance precedents) the young, beautiful disciple with long tresses beside Christ in the Last Supper as the future evangelist John, the "beloved disciple." But they would surely not have posited, like perennial schoolboys, so many erections beneath the folds of drapery in images of the Dead or Resurrected Christ. Brilliant scholar though he was, Leo Steinberg illustrated (in his *Sexuality of Christ in Renaissance Art and in Modern Oblivion*, cited in Thomas Rausch's chapter) the pitfalls of post-Freudian interpretations that conjure up overly erotic readings of such drapery folds and of Christ's "slung leg" over his Virgin mother's lap (another salacious Steinberg inference) in Michelangelo's *Pietà*.

It may not be necessary to *be* a Catholic in order to understand faithfully the masterpieces of Christian art, but it is necessary to think like a Catholic and to shun anachronisms that obscure our understanding of the masters. The model here is D. W. Robertson's classic *A Preface to Chaucer,* wherein the great scholar applied the lessons of medieval iconography to reinterpret the satire and sense of the *Canterbury Tales* in the light and context of their time, not ours. Fidelity to the author or artist is as essential to today's scholars and teachers as fidelity to the composer is to conductors and singers. However challenging and contrary to our contemporary notions of spontaneity and creative deconstruction, it is required.

Within a few years of the unveiling in 1512 of Michelangelo's Sistine ceiling, the high noon of the Renaissance was eclipsed by storm clouds: in 1517 Martin Luther nailed his ninety-five theses to the door of the Castle Church in Wittenberg. Though no one, least of all Luther, would have foreseen it at the time, this act was to set in motion a full-scale revolution; the Protestant Reformation engulfed the Church and eventually most of Europe. A decade later, in 1527, Rome was brutally sacked by imperial troops and German Protestant mercenaries. The religious crisis sparked a parallel crisis of faith among artists, who soon retreated into fantasy and a style we now call Mannerism. Self-conscious to the extreme, Mannerism was a progressively trendy style that divorced art from nature in the works of Pontormo, Rossi, Parmigianino, and their northern Flemish followers Goltzius, Spranger, and Cornelis van Haarlem. But as in the case of postwar Abstract Expressionism four hundred years later, it was only a matter of time before a counterreaction took root, a return to basics, in this case a return to nature and naturalism that followed in the wake of the Catholic Counter-Reformation.

As a deliberate response to the wave of iconoclastic Protestants who stripped Catholic churches and cathedrals of their altarpieces, sculptures, and stained-glass windows, the Council of Trent called upon the Church to enlist an army of artists to defend doctrine through the alluring propaganda of their creations. As in the Middle Ages, art was once again to be the handmaid of the Faith. The Age of the Baroque, the zenith of overt Catholic spirituality in art, was about to dawn, and where more appropriately than in Rome?

No single artist did more to revolutionize and reform religious art than Michelangelo Merisi da Caravaggio (1571–1610). He was literally a "second Michelangelo" and aware of the weight of his Christian name. He did not disappoint. This powerful genius from northern Italy broke into Roman art at the dawn of the Baroque like a bolt of lightning, electrifying his age and sending a current down through the art of the entire seventeenth century. He lived only thirty-nine years, his career confined to two decades and a few dozen major commissions; he had no workshop, no students or studio of assistants. Yet he left an indelible imprint on Rubens, Rembrandt, and Velázquez, to name just three artists who in the coming years were to become the brightest lights.

Caravaggio was controversial. In a *Who's Who* of painters his police record would take first place; his antisocial behavior ranged from throwing a plate of artichokes at a waiter to killing a man on a tennis match (for which he had to flee Rome and travel in exile from Naples to Malta to Sicily). He was equally controversial in his art; few painters have provoked such extremes of praise and condemnation from their contemporaries. No major religious painter had so many altarpieces rejected, but then snatched up by some of the most discriminating connoisseurs of the day. He was praised and damned for the same thing: his bold and often brutal naturalism, his revolutionary aim to paint the people and objects of the natural world as he saw them; to do otherwise, he claimed, would be but "bagatelles, child's play." He was admired, but begrudgingly, considered a useful reformer who restored naturalism to art, who brought it back down to earth after decades of flights of Mannerist fantasy. Yet for some of his admirers he was a revolutionary who went too far.

The seventeenth-century biographer and critic Gian Pietro Bellori labeled Caravaggio a mere "imitatore della natura," an imitator of nature who often "degenerates into low and vulgar forms." Among the paintings Bellori singled out as "failing in decorum" is the masterpiece painted in 1601, *The Supper at Emmaus*, today in the National Gallery in London, a tour de force of technique and innovation by the artist approaching thirty years of age. Bellori castigated "the rustic character of the two apostles, the Lord who is shown young and without a beard, the innkeeper's failure to remove his cap, and a basket of fruit out of season" (for a biblical scene that took place the day after Easter, in springtime). Yet three centuries later the American abstract painter Frank Stella (one of the few with a degree in art history) wrote in the *New York Times*, "Abstraction today wants to make sure it can have everything Caravaggio served up in *The Supper at Emmaus*, a painting filled with projective gesture, psychological presence, and pictorial import."

Caravaggio followed St. Luke's account of the post-Resurrection appearance (24:13–35) and the Venetian artistic tradition of showing the startled disciples recognizing Jesus at the moment he blesses the bread at their evening meal in an Emmaus inn—a pictorial variation and condensation of Leonardo's famous *Last Supper* in Milan. The resurrected Christ's far-reaching gesture of benediction is framed by the thunderstruck disciples, the right one flinging his arms outward in the form of a cross, as though to exclaim, "But Lord, you were crucified!" The Renaissance theorist Leon Battista Alberti wrote that the movements of the body reflect those of the soul, and therefore thought and feeling should be conveyed through outward gesture by artists. Here Caravaggio already reveals himself as a master of psychological and dramatic rhetoric: his gestures speak louder than words.

But what of Bellori's complaints? Let's cross-examine him. First: the youthful beardless Christ, so unlike the familiar face of Jesus. (The great Bernard Berenson called him "against all tradition and precedents, a boy preacher startling the yokels out of their wits.") Yet this face of a resurrected Christ who does not look like himself reveals Caravaggio's brilliant solution to the mystery of why these disciples had failed to recognize him, an original solution based on scripture. St. Luke never fully explains why the disciples failed to recognize Jesus after he joined them along the walk to Emmaus; he mentions only that "their eyes were kept from recognizing him." But at the end of St. Mark's gospel there is a brief reference to the appearance (16:12) that is both explicit and explanatory; he states that Christ appeared to the disciples *in alia effigie*, as the Vulgate renders it, "in another likeness."

Evidently this single phrase suggested to Caravaggio a solution to the problem of recognition. It also offered a biblical sanction for showing Christ in a different guise, *in alia effigie*, as the Evangelist describes him. Yet by following Mark's lead and adopting a new face for Christ, Caravaggio intended not only to rationalize the miracle of recognition but also to *sacramentalize* it. This appearance at supper was traditionally interpreted by theologians as a confirmation not only of Christ's physical resurrection but also of his bodily presence in the Eucharist, a doctrine of paramount importance to the Church of the Counter-Reformation. The doctrinal controversy between Catholics and Protestants over the nature of Christ's identification with the sacrament had by this time led to an intensified Catholic emphasis on the centrality of the Eucharist, explained in part by the traditional Church teaching of Transubstantiation. The Church reaffirmed this tenet of faith by every available means, including artistic representations of Eucharistic subjects such as the Supper at Emmaus. In the Jesuit book of engravings, Geronimo Nadal's *Evangelicae Historiae Imagines* (1593), the Supper at Emmaus is illustrated as a prefiguration of the Mass, wherein Christ, as Priest, distributes the broken bread to his two disciples. Caravaggio intended his version to be no less sacramental; he merely sought a more visually persuasive way of conveying the same idea.

For Caravaggio, the disciples' recognition of Christ is achieved solely through the Eucharist. To underscore this point he deliberately removed all other clues to Christ's identity; we look in vain for the nail prints or the side wound (later revealed to the doubting Thomas). His hands are so arranged that it is impossible to determine whether the wounds are there or not, and the garments cover his side. Most striking of all, Christ's face is not that of the Crucified, even at the moment of recognition. That recognition therefore is the result of his gesture alone, the extended hand blessing the bread, an allusion to the priest's act of blessing at the consecration of bread into the Body of Christ during the Mass. (Beside the loaf of bread are the vessels of water and wine, as on an altar.) Christ's sacramental gesture becomes the sine qua non of his self-revelation to his disciples, as if to stress that only through the Eucharist does Christ reveal himself physically and spiritually to the faithful, now as then.

The particular likeness Caravaggio chose for this *alia effigies* harks back to the earliest type in Christian art, young and beardless, as found on the Junius Bassus sarcophagus, unearthed in Rome in 1595. The Early Christian status of this Apollonian type (as distinct from the later, mature and bearded Zeus-type that took hold in art) provided historical justification for its adoption here at a time when the Counter-Reformation Church engaged in a general revival of Early Christian sources to buttress its historical and sacramental claims and to counter Protestant assertions that they, the anti-Catholics, were the true heirs to the Early Christians. This type was revived occasionally during the Middle Ages and Renaissance; two important examples may have served as actual sources for Caravaggio. One was a devotional painting (Galleria Borghese, Rome) based on a lost Leonardo of the *Salvator Mundi*. Now attributed to Marco d'Oggiono, but then thought to be by Leonardo himself, it hung in the bedroom of Pope Paul V as his most cherished painting. Like his counterpart at Emmaus, the young Savior of the World is shown in the act of blessing, a gesture of salvation with clear sacramental overtones. This iconic image of an eternally youthful Christ offered to Caravaggio an esteemed prototype for his Savior at Emmaus, one who likewise reveals himself in a gesture of blessing.

According to Catholic doctrine, salvation is inseparable from the Resurrection and the Second Coming of Christ. So it is singularly appropriate that an even more famous source for Caravaggio's Christ was the most prominent scene of Resurrection and Judgment in Rome. This is the one painted by his namesake Michelangelo in the Sistine Chapel fresco, where high above the altar Christ appears at the end of time as a youthful beardless deity. The two images share not only the facial type but also their crucial, contrapuntal gestures. In Michelangelo's fresco Christ's right arm is raised while the left and less active one reaches across his side as if to point to his side wound. Caravaggio lowers the dramatically extended right arm as he transforms a gesture of judgment into one of blessing. But the left arm, relatively unaltered, recalls what is no longer visible: the side wound. These formal allusions to Michelangelo's Christ of the Last Judgment suggest a deeper link between the two subjects: the idea that Christ's appearance to his disciples at Emmaus anticipates, proleptically, his final appearance to all mankind. Both artists represented the Resurrected Christ as epiphanies.

Caravaggio had three primary sources for his Christ *in alia effigie*: the Early Christian type, the Leonardesque *Salvator Mundi*, and Michelangelo's Judge. They all share a common referent: the image of the eternal, divine Savior; not the earthly, historical Jesus but the heavenly, glorified Christ of the Second Coming. To answer another of Bellori's complaints, the innkeeper has failed to remove his cap in the Lord's presence precisely because he remains outside this miraculous revelation, illumined by metaphysical light, the light of enlightenment. Yet his head casts a symbolic shadow, a negative halo, so to speak, above Christ's head, where we might expect to find a more traditional halo. Through this clever motif—a telling shadow of doubt—Caravaggio suggests that even those ignorant of Christ may yet honor him unconsciously. Likewise the basket of fruit, admittedly "out of season," is richly symbolic with Eucharistic grapes, the apple of Adam's fall, and a pomegranate, an emblem of resurrection. Perched precariously at the table's edge, it casts a shadow in the form of a fish, the ancient symbol for Christ (since the letters of the Greek word for fish, *Ichthus*, are a Greek acronym referring to "Jesus Christ, Son of God, Savior"). These symbolic shadows reinforce the metaphysical nature of Caravaggio's chiaroscuro, the juxtaposition of light and shadow, recalling the Latin maxim *Lux umbra Dei*, "Light is the Shadow of God."

The disciples are deliberately rustic, common humanity realistically rendered but dignified in their humility. One wears a cockleshell, symbol of a pilgrim, as though to say, We are all, even the lowliest of us, pilgrims on the way to Emmaus. Caravaggio was repeatedly criticized for populating his religious pictures with such ordinary people. Most scandalous was the claim that he used the body of a drowned prostitute in Rome for the model of the Virgin Mary in his later altarpiece *The Death of the Virgin*. (One cosmopolitan connoisseur recently quipped that he was sure Caravaggio would feel right at home on the New York subways.) Yet Caravaggio infused sacred subjects with power and conviction, a humanity that is confrontational but reasonable; the disciples, after all, were simple folk, unlike the high priests and Pharisees, the Establishment in Roman-occupied Palestine.

In his first *Supper at Emmaus*, Caravaggio reinterpreted a favorite subject of Renaissance art as a vivid confirmation of the Resurrection and the efficacy of the Eucharist. Basing his deceptively "unorthodox" representation of Christ *in alia effigie* on a verse in St. Mark's gospel, he fused in one image the earliest visual expression of Christ's divinity, the *Salvator Mundi*, and the Christ of the Second Coming, whose triumphant revelation is accompanied by a stark reminder of the Crucifixion. To achieve this translation of doctrine into drama, he juxtaposes two expansive gestures that break into the viewer's own space. Here, in one of his very rare miracle scenes, Caravaggio confronts us with nothing less than an affirmation of salvation.

Among the artists in Rome who experienced Caravaggio's groundbreaking work firsthand was a young Fleming named Peter Paul Rubens. Like so many others from the North, he had journeyed to Italy to finish his training as a painter. He arrived in Rome in 1601. The timing could not have been more propitious. The Eternal City was being transformed by the Counter-Reformation popes into the artistic capital of Europe, a propagandistic assertion of their spiritual primacy. Caravaggio was completing his wall paintings of St. Matthew's life for the Contarelli Chapel in San Luigi dei Francesi, an overpowering public debut of his dramatic chiaroscuro, which was to leave its mark on Rubens. An early sheet of sketches (Getty Museum, Los Angeles) for a *Last Supper* by Rubens reveals quotations from Caravaggio's *Calling of St. Matthew* as well as from his *Supper at Emmaus,* as the young Rubens (six years Caravaggio's junior) compiled his vast visual vocabulary. Whether Rubens actually met Caravaggio in the flesh must remain conjectural; what is certain is that he was profoundly impressed by his art and translated it into his own idiom, a blend of Italian and Flemish sources.

Upon his return home, Rubens transformed his Netherlandish heritage with reflections of antiquity, Michelangelo, Tintoretto, and Caravaggio in the first of his two great Antwerp triptychs, the *Raising of the Cross*, commissioned in 1610. Rubens broke the triptych boundaries as his heroic Crucifixion extends beyond the central panel to embrace the two flanking wings in his dramatic affirmation of redemptive suffering. His second triptych, begun a year later for the Harquebus-iers (or Musketeers) Guild altar in the cathedral, was the *Descent from the Cross*. By contrast, and in keeping with its biblical subject, it expresses a stately serenity, poignancy, and classicizing equilibrium. As in the *Raising*, that famous ancient sculpture of *Laocoön* provides the central quotation from antiquity, as Rubens here adapted the figure of the suffering Trojan priest to the Priest/Victim Jesus being lowered from the cross by his disciples. (Even in death Jesus' body thus evokes Laocoön's heroic suffering, while the faithful Nicodemus on the ladder in the *Descent* is a visual quotation of Laocoön's elder son.)

The wings illustrate the *Visitation*, on the left, and the *Presentation in the Temple* on the right, while the outside shutters illustrate the medieval legend of St. Christopher and the Hermit. The unified iconographic program celebrates the guild's patron saint, Christopher. (The holy giant is based on an antique sculp-ture, the *Farnese Hercules*.) In keeping with the meaning of his Greek name, Chris-tophoros ("Christ-bearer"), he is shown carrying the Christ Child across a river at night, illumined by a lantern held by a hermit. Each of the three biblical subjects on the inside panels likewise illustrates the bearing of Christ. In the *Visitation*, the Virgin carries Christ in her womb as she visits her cousin Elizabeth. In the *Presentation*, the high priest Simeon holds the Christ Child as Mary raises her arms to receive him, a gesture poignantly varied in the central panel, wherein as Mater Dolorosa she reaches up to hold her dead Son. Together the three panels present a gradual rightward descent in counterpoint to the central leftward low-ering of the dead Christ along a suspended sheet of incomparable whiteness. At first viewing, Sir Joshua Reynolds commented, "None but great colorists can venture to paint pure white linen near flesh." A century later Eugène Fromentin summed up, "Everything is restrained, concise, laconic, as if it were a page of Holy Scripture."

The central Eucharistic doctrine of the Counter-Reformation had affirmed both the reenactment of Christ's sacrifice in the Mass and the physical presence of Christ in the sacrament received by the faithful at the altar. Nowhere were those beliefs conveyed with such conviction and pathos as in Rubens's triptych that opened over an altar in Antwerp's cathedral, where it still bears eloquent witness today.

After the Eucharist, the sacrament of penance, which is the ritual confession and absolution of sins, was of foremost concern to Catholics during the Counter-Reformation. The rejection of sacramental confession by Protestants led to an insistent promotion by Catholics through sermons, treatises, and the visual arts. Following the doctrine's reaffirmation at the Council of Trent, images of penitent saints proliferated in altarpieces, prints, and paintings for private devotion. In his brilliant *Christ and the Penitent Sinners* (Alte Pinakothek, Munich), the work that first converted me as a college student to this artist, Rubens combined two of the most popular penitents, Mary Magdalene and St. Peter, together with the less frequently illustrated Good Thief and King David in a *sacra conversazione* of extraordinary grace and lyricism. This glowing picture represents the culmination of the artist's Antwerp decade (1609–20) of religious paintings for public commissions and private patrons.

Recalling the previous juxtaposition of the two figures in the *Descent from the Cross*, the composition is defined by the diagonal S-curve of the radiantly blond Mary Magdalene kneeling before the Risen Christ. In both, Rubens emphasized the Magdalene's long Titianesque tresses, with which she had dried the Savior's feet before the Passion. Christ is presented in classical perfection, like a Greco-Roman god, a combination of Apollo and Jupiter. His brilliant red toga contrasts with the Magdalene's yellow-white garment. Arms crossed over her breasts, she is identified as the woman taken in adultery whom Jesus saved and admonished to "go and sin no more." Behind Mary stand three biblical penitents, bridging both testaments and beckoned by Christ. Closest to the Savior, Peter, weeping and with hands clasped, reenacts his repentance for thrice denying his Master. The background rock symbolizes Christ's promise to him, "You are Peter and upon this Rock I shall build my church," an image and text invoked by the Roman Church in defense of the primacy of its first bishop and his papal successors. Identifiable by his crown is David, the king, psalmist, and penitent adulterer. At the far left, holding a cross parallel to Christ, is the Good Thief, to whom Jesus at the Crucifixion promised a place in Paradise. His pose is an evocative quotation of Michelangelo's statue of the *Risen Christ* in the Roman church of Santa Maria sopra Minerva.

Rubens's emphasis on the encounter between Christ and Mary Magdalene derives from the iconography of the *noli me tangere* ("Do not touch me"). In the

Risen Christ's first appearance to the Magdalene on Easter morning, as recounted by the Evangelist John, Mary wants to grasp Jesus (to prevent him from departing), but, close as they are, they do not physically touch. Rubens's stress upon the visual experience reaffirmed the function of religious art as prescribed by the Council of Trent: to evoke a lively sense of faith in the beholder. Here Rubens's emphasis is not so much on the act of penance as on the receptive gesture of the Risen Christ, a confirmation of Job's faith: "I know that my Redeemer liveth." Rubens combines heroic forms and sensuous surfaces to affirm, most invitingly, even seductively, his own affirmation of salvation.

Nowhere does Rubens offer more inventive variations on a religious theme than in his several Adorations of the Magi, a series of Epiphanies that reach a High Baroque climax in the 1624 altarpiece for the Norbertine (Praemonstratensian) Abbey of St. Michael's in Antwerp. His first version, also his first major commission, in 1609, upon his return to Antwerp from Rome, was for the Staatenkammer (Chamber of States) in the town hall. A nocturnal procession with shades of Caravaggio, Elsheimer, and the Venetians provided a stately backdrop for the signing of the Twelve Years' Truce between the two Netherlands, North and South. For the high altar of St. Michael's, where Rubens had earlier provided an altarpiece for his mother's tomb, he shifted the time to midday for his most joyous and liturgical interpretation of the biblical subject. Rubens is said to have painted it in a week, surely an exaggeration. Yet the lively brushwork reveals a new fluidity and breadth, as though he had adapted the style of a spontaneous oil sketch to a full-scale painting. However rapid the execution, the composition was carefully prepared by an oil *modello* (Wallace Collection, London), wherein he introduced a powerful centripetal grouping around the visually arresting Moorish king. The host of worshippers descends in a reverse S-curve from camels that, as Julius Held noted, allude to the liturgy for the Feast of the Epiphany: "Multitudes of camels shall cover thee, dromedaries of Midean and Epha" (Isaiah 60:6).

Rubens's language of images reflects the liturgical function of the altarpiece as backdrop to the celebration of the Mass. Unlike the artist's earlier versions and his preliminary *modello*, the foremost king no longer offers gold; he is now robed in splendid ecclesiastical vestments, as though he were a priest kneeling before the sacrament on the altar. The Virgin is rotated to a frontal view as she displays the body of Christ, whose reclining pose prefigures a *Pietà*. The close association of nativity and death was common throughout early Netherlandish altarpieces, which likewise employed "disguised symbolism" in the straw (bread), the ox (sacrifice), and the wooden crate with white cloth (altar), together alluding to the Eucharistic sacrifice of the Mass.

Rubens's Counter-Reformation imagery extended to the original marble frame and sculptures, dismantled two centuries later but still preserved today in the parish church of St. Trudo (Groot Zundert, Netherlands). The pediment was originally crowned by three alabaster statues designed by Rubens, each symbolizing the triumph over evil and heresy. St. Michael defeats Satan; the Virgin crushes the Serpent underfoot; St. Norbert stands victorious over the prostrated heretic Tanchelm, who already in the twelfth century had denied the Eucharist, church hierarchy, the paying of tithes, and ritual. It is precisely these proto-Protestant denials by Tanchelm that Rubens reversed in his resolutely Catholic epiphany. In the painting Ancient Rome is personified by two soldiers beside a Corinthian column entwined with ivy, symbolizing its supplanting and renewal by the Church. The universality of the new Roman (Catholic) Empire is embodied in the assembly of witnesses—including an African, an Indian, and an Asian—from the knight on horseback to the beggar below him. In this Flemish Baroque feast for the eyes Rubens reorchestrates his Netherlandish heritage and Italian influences with operatic grandeur. Centuries later we can almost hear Handel's joyous chorus from Messiah, "For unto us a Child is born," resounding through the paint.

Rubens is an artist's artist; his influence down the centuries is legendary: Van Dyck, Jordaens, Watteau, Boucher, Fragonard, Gainsborough, Delacroix, and Renoir each paid him homage with their brushes. Even such unlikely heirs as Cézanne and Matisse studied him and painted copies of his masterpieces. Yet the painter's Rubens represents but one side of this multifaceted genius. His contemporary and friend General Spinola said of him, "Of all his talents, painting is the least." Renowned throughout Europe as a diplomat, Rubens negotiated peace between England and Spain, for which he was knighted by both kings. He was also a dedicated scholar and Christian humanist, a learned classicist and antiquarian, a prodigious correspondent (in several languages), an amateur architect—in short, a true Renaissance man. His nephew described his life as "but one long course of study." The court chaplain at Brussels eulogized him as "the most learned painter in the world."

Rubens was also a devout Catholic, loyal subject of the Spanish Hapsburgs, devoted husband, father of eight children, a prosperous, energetic, life-loving, thoroughly balanced man who lived in harmony with his society and, we may assume, with himself. No one could be further from the modern conception of the struggling artist who, in order to exert his genius, pays dearly, economically, spiritually, and socially. Admittedly the very qualities with which Rubens was blessed tend to detract from his popular appeal today. Modern society prefers to find genius in a tormented Michelangelo, a rebellious Caravaggio, a withdrawn and introspective Rembrandt. Hollywood has yet to project Rubens's exemplary life onto the big screen.

There is another issue. Rubens was, like so many Christian artists down to the nineteenth century, a literary artist, that is, a visual artist who faithfully interpreted and translated texts into images. The modern student who would strive to understand his achievements within the Catholic tradition must at least be biblically literate. One need not have a graduate degree in theology, but one must know both Testaments as well as the fundamentals of the faith: the core beliefs, the saints, the liturgy, and basic Church history and structure. These are the very things that fifty years ago every Catholic school pupil knew before receiving confirmation. Times have changed, but the groundwork required for an educated appreciation of timeless art has not. One cannot read French poetry without knowing French; one cannot read an Old Master religious painting without having a basic literary and religious knowledge.

As impresario of vast decorative programs and multimedia productions, Rubens was without peer in northern Europe; for his equivalent one must look south, a generation later, to the great Italian maestro Gian Lorenzo Bernini. Bernini personified the Baroque style and era, and he dominated the seventeenth century. His audience comprised Europe's leading patrons, prelates, and princes, but Rome was his very ample stage. Bernini's monumental presence throughout the Eternal City remains as resonant as the ancient ruins. In marble, travertine, bronze, stucco, and gilt; in paint, through glass and shimmering water, sculptured space and channeled light, Bernini left his imprint on the Catholic capital, the indelible stamp of genius. Within its walls he created another realm, one of imagination incarnate, which centuries later still shapes our experience of Rome and transfigures it.

According to his earliest biographers, Bernini was "the first to attempt to combine architecture, painting and sculpture in such a way that together they make a beautiful whole (*un bel composto*)." To this end he would "bend the rules without actually breaking them." This unification of the arts was his own concept. Though he wrote no treatise, he left a brilliant illustration of his theoretical views and their fulfillment in a small chapel of the church of Santa Maria della Vittoria in Rome. There, in 1647, Cardinal Federigo Cornaro commissioned a memorial chapel for his illustrious Venetian family, which had supplied six cardinals and a doge; five years later Bernini's most famous, and telling, masterpiece was completed.

Cornaro's close ties with the Discalced Carmelites and his special devotion to their founder gave rise to the central subject, St. Teresa's vision of an angel piercing her heart with the flaming arrow of Divine Love. The white marble altarpiece, executed by Bernini's own hand, is enshrined within polychrome decoration that transforms the shallow chapel into a multilevel depiction of heaven. Bernini has grouped the eight Cornaro figures four on a side. The eight interlocutors, spanning two centuries, are shown discussing and meditating about an apparition set deliberately beyond their sight lines: "Blessed are they that have not seen, yet believe." These animated, marble "donor portraits" are set against illusionistic reliefs of colonnaded and vaulted transepts (or perhaps heavenly corridors; they are surely not theater boxes, as so often described) directly above the wooden doors of Death.

Two colorful roundels of inlaid marbles in the pavement below show skeletons arising from the crypt. In the vault, overhead, frescoed clouds and angels spill over the architectural fabric of the chapel and stucco illustrations of Teresa's life. Bernini's heavenly perspective is both a metaphysical intrusion into the viewer's space as well as a fusion of the long intense life of holiness. The heavenly aura, painted by Bernini's collaborator Abbatini, is realized below by sunlight passing through tinted glass before materializing into gilded bronze shafts. These descend upon the cloud-borne Teresa and angel in a metamorphosis of reflected light, "the Shadow of God." The bronze altar relief of the *Last Supper* at the worshipper's level marks the Eucharistic significance of this re-created miracle, as the transubstantiation of earthly matter into divine substance completes the meaning of Bernini's *bel composto*.

Sculpture and painting are complemented architecturally by the tabernacle in which Teresa's transverberation is exposed, suggesting a gleaming Host suspended in a bejeweled monstrance. With its hidden source of filtered light, this miniature temple anticipates Bernini's full-scale oval church of San Andrea al Quirinale, "the work which displeased him least," where Bernini himself used to pray each day to find peace and solace. Through the interplay of concave and convex shapes, the pediment of heaven's portal bows outward as if in response to the spiritual force within. The divine text, recorded by Teresa and here spun into the timeless shape of illusion, is inscribed on a banderole suspended by angels above the entrance: *Nisi coelum creassem ob te solam crearem* ("If I had not created heaven I would create it for you alone").

Within the columned aedicule of variegated marbles, Bernini admits the viewer to an intimate vision of this sixteenth-century Spanish mystic: the moment at which the beautiful young angel has withdrawn his golden arrow from Teresa's breast. Filled with the love of God, Teresa swoons, unconscious, elevated on a cloud, her lips parted, her limp hand dangling at her side. As befits the founder of the Discalced (unshod) Carmelites, she is barefoot. But there is nothing naturalistic about the flood of drapery that expresses the turbulence of her soul, while the angel is dematerialized in folds that crackle like flames. (Bernini, the loving father, modeled the pure spiritual angel after his firstborn son!) Nor do Teresa's features conjure up that indefatigable founder of sixteen convents, who declared, "God walks among the pots and pans." There is nothing mundane about Bernini's depiction of her mystical transport; his hard marble achieves an irresistible seduction of the senses.

Bernini's artistic combining of the spiritual and the sensual has elicited mixed responses down the centuries, especially from the neoclassicists and prudish Victorians. Taine and Stendhal raised critical eyebrows at what they considered unabashed eroticism. Even in his own day an anonymous diatribe accused Bernini of "dragging that most pure virgin not only into the third heaven, but into the dirt, to make a Venus not only prostrated but prostituted." Yet the great majority of the clergy applauded his achievement wherein he "conquered art." Those who were scandalized simply missed the point: Bernini has faithfully translated into three dimensions the saint's own words in her autobiography, which had been read aloud at her canonization ceremony in St. Peter's:

> Beside me, on the left, appeared an angel in bodily form. . . . In his hands I saw a great golden spear, and at the iron tip there appeared to be a point of fire. This he plunged into my heart several times so that it penetrated to my entrails. When he pulled it out I felt that he took them with it, and left me utterly consumed by the great love of God. The pain was so severe that it made me utter several moans. The sweetness caused by this intense pain is so extreme that one cannot possibly wish it to cease, nor is one's soul content with anything but God. This is not a physical but a spiritual pain, though the body has some share in it—even a considerable share.

Since the time the early Church fathers allegorized the Old Testament's erotic "Song of Songs," the vocabulary of earthly love was understood as the best approximation of the incomparable, ineffable ecstasy of mystics in total communion with God. Just as such an encounter was couched in physical terms, so Bernini fused in the sculptural ensemble of angel, saint, and billowy cloud (all carved from a single block of stone!) several layers of meaning drawn from episodes in Teresa's life. His three key innovations in representing Teresa were her reclining pose, her elevation on a cloud, and the infusion of sensuality. Each novelty of the sculpture alludes, as Irving Lavin has shown, to her death ("in ecstasy," as reported), her frequent levitations (usually following communion at Mass), and her mystical marriage with Christ (whom she addressed, in her last words, as "spouse"), respectively. Bernini's literary source was penned by no less an author than the late pope, his patron, Urban VIII. The pope's liturgical hymns to Teresa called her transverberation "a sweeter death" and the saint herself a "victim of love" who heard "the voice of her Spouse" beckoning her to "the wedding feast of the Lamb," where she was to receive her "crown of glory." It was left to Bernini, who credited God alone as the author of his inventions, to merge traditional iconography, orthodox theology, and human experience into a unified image of Divine Love.

Bernini returned to the theme of a full-length marble figure of a holy woman in ecstasy a quarter-century later, in a commission for another small chapel, this time a combined funerary monument and altar work: the *Blessed Ludovica Albertoni* (San Francesco a Ripa, Rome). Ludovica was an ancestor of the reigning pope, Clement X (Altieri). A widow, she had devoted her life to prayer and to serving the poor. At her death in 1553 she was granted an ecstatic vision, which Bernini staged above her altar in the family's burial chapel. Conceived in 1671, following her beatification, the work was finished in 1674.

Ludovica lies on her deathbed and at the threshold of eternity. Carved in the form of a sarcophagus, the marble altar is wedded with the tomb sculpture in a luminous apparition at the end of the small, dark chapel. The walls converge as though wings of a huge triptych have been opened to reveal Bernini's most painterly tableau. With head thrown back, in extremis, lips parted and eyes upturned, she clutches her breast. Physical agony and metaphysical "movements of the soul" resonate through the folds of her dress. White cherubs float like snowflakes down streams of daylight from concealed side windows; at the top of the vault the dove of the Holy Spirit hovers as its symbolic source. Behind Ludovica, Bacciccio's paradise painting of the *Virgin and Child with St. Anne*, to whom the chapel was dedicated, provides a window into Ludovica's vision.

The day before her death from fever Ludovica received the sacrament and then ordered everyone out of her room. When her servants were finally recalled, "they found her face aflame, but so cheerful that she seemed to have returned from Paradise." The intimacy, if not the spiritual intent, of the scene to which Bernini admits the viewer was appreciated by the novelist Aldous Huxley, to whom Ludovica's experience seemed so private "that, at first glance, the spectator feels a shock of embarrassment." Allusions to both her physical death and her mystical dying (her ecstatic transport of the previous day) coalesce in a single image, and her consummation of death through divine love is shared sacramentally by all who partake of the Eucharist at her altar tomb.

A comparison with the *St. Teresa* illuminates the artist's profound revisions over a quarter-century. A tactile apparition has modulated into an ineffable transfiguration—from body into soul. Architectural isolation (Teresa's monumental tabernacle) yields to dramatic immanence as Ludovica's jasper pall cascades toward the spectator like the overflowing stage of Bernini's play "The Flooding of the Tiber." His special effects anticipate DeMille's or Spielberg's as diagonals are resolved in sustained horizontals. No family effigies are here introduced as eternal witnesses. Even the choir of cherubs is reduced to a chamber ensemble. Blessed Ludovica is the embodiment of "the good death," to which Bernini devoted his final meditations six years later, and in this sculpture she is contemplated by the viewer alone. "Eternal rest grant unto them, O Lord, and let perpetual light shine upon them." This is Bernini's *Requiem*.

The next year, for the Holy Year (1675), Bernini completed his most widely visited chapel, the Sacrament chapel in St. Peter's, Rome. Flanked by two exquisite, larger-than-life bronze angels kneeling in prayer, Bernini here provides for all time a vertically staged drama: Christ's sacrifice, symbolized by the crucifix, is liturgically reenacted at the altar during the Mass; directly above, a level higher, we see the gilded bronze tabernacle—the symbolic site of his burial and resurrection. A masterpiece of miniature architecture, its ribbed dome is a revised reduction of Michelangelo's at St. Peter's. Crowned by a gilded statuette of the Risen Christ (in lieu of a cupola), its drum is encircled by a rhythmic ring of Corinthian pilasters; at the front, two dark windows flank a sunburst of the Holy Spirit (recalling Bernini's miracle in stucco, amber, and light above the *Cathedra Petri* in the apse of St. Peter's). The gold and lapis columns of the portico are surmounted by bronze statuettes of the twelve apostles, "pillars of the Church," while Faith and Religion take their place over the main portal. The richly symbolic form of the tabernacle, epitomizing Bernini's architectural ideal for churches, refers both to the Early Christian *Anastasis* formerly erected over Christ's tomb at the Church of the Holy Sepulcher in Jerusalem and to Bramante's *tempietto* outside San Pietro in Montorio, Rome, on the nearby Gianicolo. As in his first great altar work for St. Peter's, the towering bronze *baldacchino* over the main altar, Bernini has fused references to Christ and his first Vicar in a sculptural hybrid: Jerusalem has been spiritually transferred to Rome.

"If you want to see what a man can do, you must give him a problem," Bernini once said. Here he confronted an "obstacle," Pietro da Cortona's background altarpiece, and exploited it by converting it into an integral part of his composition. In this final reconciliation of painting and sculpture, Pietro's colorful angels now frame the heavenly dome of Bernini's tabernacle (which symbolically eclipses Pietro's globe), while Bernini's sculptured angels are coordinated in scale and placement with the Trinity in the painted heaven, their implicit source. Twice human-scale, these exquisite apparitions, modeled by the maestro himself, direct the worshippers to the sacred mystery they embrace. One turns in rapture toward the tabernacle while the other beckons the viewer to partake of the eternal.

In his first altar work for St. Peter's, Bernini had raised a huge, sculptural baldachin over an altar, itself above a tomb (of the Apostle Peter). Now in his old age he retranslated sculpture into miniature architecture, a bronze tabernacle in the form of a tomb and elevated above an altar. Form and function are equated in this late work that radiates its creator's faith. Bernini repeatedly credited God as the source of his ideas; nowhere did he offer more inviting evidence of this belief. The striking realism of the former child prodigy was transfigured, in the end, by the ethereal vision of a genius for whom life and art were as inseparable as fact and faith.

George Bernard Shaw wrote, "You use a glass mirror to see your face; you use works of art to see your soul." But for the Catholic tradition, the works of art—or more precisely, their *medium*—may shift over time. By the end of the seventeenth century, that is to say, after the death of Bernini, the rich tradition of Baroque religious art, wherein the depth of meaning matched the height of illusion, took off into a late flight of decorative fantasy: the Rococo of the eighteenth century. Kenneth Clark aptly titled this chapter of *Civilisation* "The Pursuit of Happiness." From the pilgrimage church of Vierzehnheiligen near Bamberg, which is a wedding cake of delicious confections in gilded stucco and paint, to the Venetian frescoes of Tiepolo, the last painter in the "grand style," who rendered every Virgin Mary a queen, the visual arts sought to delight the senses but rarely to stir the soul with any profound insight. Yet despite the dawning of the secular and skeptical Age of Reason, the Catholic tradition remained vital in the realm of music.

The greatest music of the eighteenth century was religious. Though he was a Lutheran, Johann Sebastian Bach composed sacred masterpieces in the Catholic tradition that reveal a musical equivalent to the Sistine ceiling. His monumental biblical oratorios, the *St. Matthew Passion* and *St. John Passion*, rival the most profound altarpieces of all time. Indeed that impeccable German soprano Elisabeth Schwarzkopf, who called herself an *Augenmensch* (a visual person), said she would picture in her mind Grünewald's famous *Crucifixion* from the *Isenheim Altarpiece* while singing the *Matthew Passion* in order to convey in sound its true feeling and colors. In addition to so many cantatas (sung to perfection by Schwarzkopf in her early recordings), he also composed the magisterial Mass in B Minor; it has no peer. Compared with that seasonal favorite, Handel's *Messiah*, Bach's *Christmas Oratorio* is more ecclesiastical than operatic; it glows with the flickering of church candles, not the blaze of chandeliers or footlights. There is a magic to Bach that never stales; it becomes more miraculous at each hearing. He is the master of all sacred music.

But Bach was not without worthy successors. The masses of Haydn and Mozart rank high in the heavens of sacred sound. The devoutly Catholic Haydn has never been underestimated in this realm. His *Seven Last Words of Christ,* originally composed as instrumental counterparts to the biblical readings on Good Friday and later reworked as a choral piece, may indeed offer the last word on this theme. But Mozart was not so fortunate. What bad luck, illness, and a tragically untimely death (at age thirty-five) did not do, modern authors have wrought with a vengeance. Will future generations be able to picture this genius as other than the crude caricature of Shaffer's play and film *Amadeus*? A drunken imbecile with a God-given talent and a dippy wife? The common wisdom used to be that Mozart's religious music was merely "for hire," something he knocked off to earn a living so that he could write the operas, symphonies, and chamber pieces he really loved. What a surprise, then, to read that his widow, Constanze, said that his favorite genre of all was church music.

A close study of Mozart's sacred music confirms Constanze's claim. For instance, his *Vesperae Solennes de Confessore*, with its twilight "Laudate Dominum," was as carefully composed as anything he ever wrote, and reveals that he paid close attention to the texts of the psalms and canticles that comprised the chanted sequences of these vespers. They should be heard in their liturgical context, ideally in an Austrian Rococo church by candlelight. His glorious *Coronation Mass* in C Major offers a telling footnote and glimpse into Mozart's creative process. The soprano's hauntingly beautiful "Agnus Dei" calls to mind its later recapitulation (and reworking) for the countess's poignant aria in Act 3 of *The Marriage of Figaro*: "Dove sono i bei momenti?" ("Where have all the sweet moments of love gone?") So much for the myth that Mozart recycled bits of opera for his church music; here it was precisely the opposite. Both arias begin sorrowfully (as befits the "Lamb of God, who takes away the sins of the world") and then are suddenly transformed into a joyful conclusion. For Mozart, the peace of "dona nobis pacem" is not passive, not the absence of pain or conflict, but the consummation of joy.

In the nineteenth century, the Romantic century, artists took to the garrets and with rare exception painted no longer for church or court but for private collectors, and for themselves. Their doctrine of "art for art's sake" took root and replaced the idea that art was the medium for conveying religious truths. (How many Rodins or Monets are to be found in churches?) But the Catholic tradition continued to flourish in music, through Beethoven's *Missa Solemnis*, Schubert's richly melodic Masses, Berlioz's *Te Deum* and *Requiem,* down to the Masses and triumphant *Te Deum* of the late Romantic (and profoundly Catholic) Anton Bruckner at the close of the century.

Even the anticlerical Verdi was not immune. His *Requiem*, performed and recorded in modern times perhaps more than any other composer's, has rightly been proclaimed his greatest opera. Yet its "Dies Irae" captures in sound the impact and *terribilità* of Michelangelo's *Last Judgment* more faithfully and powerfully than anything before or after. Its history is one of musical resurrection. As originally planned, it would have been but a fragment of the eventual masterpiece. After the death of Verdi's operatic predecessor Rossini in November 1868, Verdi proposed as a memorial to that great Italian composer a Requiem Mass to be composed sequentially by a group of Italy's leading musical lights. Verdi's own contribution was the *Libera Me*, that impassioned prayer for absolution: "Libera me, Domine, de morte aeterna in die illa tremenda, quando coeli movendi sunt et terra, dum veneris judicare saeculum per ignem" ("Deliver me, O Lord, from eternal death in that awful day, when the heavens and the earth shall be shaken, when thou shalt come to judge the world by fire"). But the project was scuttled by administrative bickering, and Verdi's contribution lay in limbo for several years.

In May 1873 the great Italian novelist Manzoni, author of *I Promessi Sposi*, died. Verdi considered him not only "one of the finest [novelists] of all ages" but also "a comfort to humanity." As a heartfelt memorial to his literary hero and friend, Verdi completed the *Requiem*, adding all the liturgical movements that lead up to his concluding *Libera Me*. Performed at the first anniversary of Manzoni's death, on May 22, 1874, at the Church of San Marco in Milan, it was then repeated at a packed La Scala. The opera house venue permitted wild applause and encores that would have been unseemly in church; at the end Verdi was given a silver crown.

The Austrian poet and opera librettist Hugo von Hofmannsthal once wrote of art, "Depth must be concealed. Where? On the surface." ("Die Tiefe muß man verstecken. Wo? An der Oberfläche.") That insight has aptly been applied to the deceptively simple and delightfully "superficial" yet profound masterpieces of Mozart. Yet it may also explain the enduring achievement of Verdi's *Requiem*. It all rings true, right up to that hushed final repeated prayer "Libera me . . . Libera me." With a subtle stroke of genius, Verdi has the orchestra end quietly on a C Major chord, as if to affirm that the prayer has not been in vain. The late music editor and author George Marek summed it up best: "The *Requiem* is one of those rare religious compositions which are loved both by the faithful and the agnostic. It is also one of those pieces of music which appeal both to the musically literate and the musical beginner. Its beauty lies deep and on the surface."

A word about recordings. I am not surprised to find that I own more recordings of Verdi's *Requiem* than any other piece of music. There is such room here for a variety of interpretations, and a cornucopia of records to prove it. All the great conductors tackle this work. Yet after decades of listening I find myself drawn closest to that of an Italian maestro. But it is not the obvious one, Arturo Toscanini, who recorded it several times. Rather it is Carlo Maria Giulini, who recorded it with Elisabeth Schwarzkopf's definitive rendition of the soprano's *Libera Me*. In the words of the priest and critic Alec Robertson, "Toscanini's unforgettable interpretation was, at any rate in the 'Dies Irae' and 'Libera Me' full of the visionary fervour and fire of an Old Testament prophet. Giulini's belongs to the New Testament. There are stern words in the Gospels about the Last Judgment but the keynote of this [Giulini's] less austere interpretation is compassion—the compassion of Christ."

The musicologist Richard Osborne adds: "It is not necessary to be a practising Catholic in order to conduct Verdi's sacred music supremely well, though in Giulini's case a fiercely held faith has always been a factor to reckon with, the gentle manner disguising the fires stoked up within." Dame Elisabeth Schwarzkopf, who had earlier recorded, to my ears, the consummate *Nozze di Figaro* under Giulini's baton, commented to me just a few months before she died, "I liked him [Giulini] very much. We all know he fought great battles inside himself to make it right, you see, to find the expression; you could feel it—that he was giving his utmost to do the right thing and never felt safe that it was the right sound; he battled for it all the time, and that brings forth great expression from a human being."

A decade later Verdi composed the most hauntingly plaintive *Ave Maria* in the history of music: Desdemona's bedtime prayer, charged with the foreboding of danger, indeed doom (just moments before she is strangled by her jealous husband) in his late opera *Otello*. It conjures up in sound the Blessed Virgin with more power and presence than any spoken prayer or painted altarpiece. Music and words are here perfectly matched to evoke beauty and simple faith, a pair of velvet gloves. There is an irony here that must be faced: so often Verdi is described as fiercely anticlerical and agnostic, and indeed he often presented himself this way. Yet his final work, composed when he was approaching eighty-five, was his *Quattro Pezzi Sacri* ("Four Sacred Pieces") that included along with two a cappella hymns to the Virgin (*Ave Maria* and *Laudi alla Virgine*) his late masterpieces of choral writing, the *Stabat Mater* and *Te Deum*. Compared with the equally "operatic" version of the *Stabat Mater* by Rossini, Verdi's is distinctive in his care to underscore with meaning every phrase of that thirteenth-century medieval poem about the Crucifixion. The poem itself is uneven, and Rossini had farmed out to an assistant those verses he considered weaker: the result is an operatic alternation of arias and choruses. Verdi's is one seamless garment of intense narration, bringing into focus the heroism and horrors of the Crucifixion that begins with Jesus' Mother standing full of grief by the Cross on which her Son has been hung ("Stabat Mater dolorosa / Juxta crucem lacrymosa / Dum pendevat Filius") and concludes its long sequence of images and prayers with the intercession "When my body shall die, grant that my spirit may be given the glory of Paradise. Amen." ("Quando corpus morietur / Fac ut animae donetur / Paradisi gloria. Amen.") The prayer is full of drama, but equally of divine compassion and humanity. The series of four pieces ends with the thunderous and glorious *Te Deum*, which Richard Osborne rightly claims as the "*Requiem's* true sequel, a setting which ponders the heights, and scales the depths, of human yearning."

How, then, are we to describe, if not explain, Verdi: brilliant agnostic or ultimately, if paradoxically, Catholic composer? The question is as old as St. John's account of the Doubting Thomas, and as modern as those complex characters in the novels of Graham Greene (especially the "whiskey priests" of lost faith in his novel *The Power and the Glory* and his play *The Potting Shed*). How often those very people who believe they have lost belief end up praying and giving witness, perhaps more persuasively through the power of doubt, to the last word of faith. Often they end up being the ones who offer others the greatest inspiration, especially if they are touched by divine genius. Like Leonardo, another famous doubter, Verdi gave precise instructions for his Catholic burial. In his case, "one priest, a candle, a cross."

What of the next, our immediate past, century? Religious painting and sculpture offer a few exceptions that prove the rule: the sacred oils of Rouault evoking stained-glass images of devotion and the minimalist *Stations of the Cross* by Matisse at the Rosaire chapel he designed in Vence. As the twentieth century traveled through Expressionism and Cubism to Abstraction, the Catholic tradition seemed left behind. Even in music, despite the occasional choral work of merit—above all, Poulenc's soul-searing opera *The Dialogues of the Carmelites*—the tradition has waned. Think of the much touted *Mass* by Leonard Bernstein that opened the Kennedy Center in 1970 and brought its composer to tears. It is really a theater piece, a "deconstructed" Mass, complete with doubt-ridden celebrant. It fit the times to a T. Where, then, is the Catholic tradition to be sought? In the century's new medium: film. Ours is the age of new technology and electronic recordings; perhaps these will provide new media for transmitting the tradition.

One masterpiece that stands head and shoulders above all biblical films is Pasolini's *The Gospel According to Saint Matthew* (1964). It is stark, minimal, haunting, and hypnotic. The controversial communist and agnostic director cast a Jesus who was utterly convincing, unlike so many Hollywood fantasies. In the bleakness and aridness of the black-and-white setting, Pasolini's Jesus conveys a gaunt, frail physicality charged with spiritual magnetism. His Christ is both real and Reality. The moment of his nailing to the cross is pure pain distilled by acceptance and love, unbearable to watch but impossible to ignore. The grand Technicolor epics of Hollywood do not come close to capturing the faith conveyed by that self-proclaimed doubter director. Only a Graham Greene could have put it into words. But the simple subtitles of Matthew's own text already said it all.

As for audio recordings, the past century has at least succeeded in preserving for posterity the masterpieces of music (just as film, and now digital technology, has preserved the visual arts of both past and present). These recordings are themselves works of art, performing art. Arguably the most prolific and painstaking in recorded classical vocal art, the late Elisabeth Schwarzkopf once described her many long sessions at the EMI studios a matter of "sculpting in sound." In that she proved the vocal successor to Michelangelo and Bernini. She set a standard, just as artists and composers have done in the visual arts and music. As for the present state of the arts, it is hard to be optimistic, yet one must remain hopeful. In the words of John of Salisbury, "We are dwarfs standing on the shoulders of giants." Yet our artistic, as well as spiritual, mantra must surely remain "Onward."

A NOTE ABOUT NOTES

Because this chapter represents a personal overview, an essay rather than an academic treatise, I have decided to forgo endnotes. Yet I owe the reader a few signposts. For more on Michelangelo, see Hibbard (below); for Haydn and Mozart, I am especially indebted to H. C. Robbins Landon, from his record notes on Haydn's *Creation* (for Vanguard's Everyman Classics, 1967) to his brilliant book of myth-breaking, 1791: *Mozart's Last Year* (New York, 1990). My full study of Caravaggio's *Supper at Emmaus* may be found in chapter 6 of *Art, Creativity and the Sacred* (below). My discussion of Rubens and Bernini is largely drawn from my two books below, which contain the relevant source notes. The best analysis of Bernini's *Ecstasy of St. Teresa*, together with a brilliant study of that artist's creation of the Baroque *Gesamtkunstwerk*, remains, three decades later, Irving Lavin's master-piece of art historical scholarship, *Bernini and the Unity of the Visual Arts* (Oxford: Oxford University Press, 1980). George Marek's notes for the 1954 recording (for RCA, under Toscanini) offer an inviting introduction to Verdi's *Requiem*, with further insights by Richard Osborne found in the current CD set of the 1964 Giulini recording by EMI. My repeated citations—always forte, never piano—of the late soprano Dame Elisabeth Schwarzkopf admittedly reveal a personal prejudice; they may indeed be colored by this author's affection, but she was my vocal standard of perfection long before she became my friend and, some might claim, obsession.

SELECTED READINGS

Apostolos-Cappadona, Diane, ed. *Art, Creativity, and the Sacred*. Revised ed. New York: Continuum, 1995.

Clark, Kenneth. *Civilisation*. New York: HarperCollins, 1990.

Graham-Dixon, Andrew. *Caravaggio: A Life Sacred and Profane*. New York: Norton, 2011.

Hibbard, Howard, *Michelangelo*. New York: Harper & Row, 1985.

L'Orange, H. P. *Art Forms and Civic Life in the Late Roman Empire*. Princeton, N.J.: Princeton University Press, 1971.

Mâle, Emile. *Religious Art: From the Twelfth to the Eighteenth Centuries*. Princeton, N.J.: Princeton University Press, 1983.

Scribner, Charles. *Bernini*. New York: Abrams, 1991.

———. *Rubens*. New York: Abrams, 1989.

PART THREE

Religious Themes Related to the Sciences

14

Psychology in a Catholic Framework

Jeffrey B. Adams

LAWRENCE CUNNINGHAM POSES the question "What impact should theology have on the generic Catholic student?" His response sets a challenge to his readers: we as Catholic educators should not be content to turn out well-rounded students; instead our goal should be the formation of persons who seek a life of holiness. Cunningham's essay focuses on theology's role in achieving this goal. However, lasting development of students' attitudes toward life's meaning and purpose must take place in multiple contexts well beyond required theology courses. All disciplines must lend a hand in achieving this aim. This essay discusses psychology's potential contributions to helping "make holiness more intelligible and appealing" to students and the issues faith-oriented psychologists face in carrying out this task.

From a psychological perspective, the goal of educating students toward a Catholic conception of a life well lived is essentially an issue of social influence. That is, increasing the likelihood that material offered in the classroom will take root in our students' minds is achieved by understanding the dynamics between factors involved in this process. As educators, we build our expertise and carefully craft our presentations, understanding that our material needs to be accessible and sufficiently compelling for thoughts to germinate. However, social influence suggests that no matter how high the level of professors' knowledge and presentation quality, learning will take place only when properly combined with additional factors. Social influence theory describes this process as involving subtle and complex interactive patterns among four primary elements: the communicator, the message, the communication method, and the audience: who says what, in what way, to whom. Applying these elements to the issue at hand, this essay focuses on who and what students studying psychology will encounter that will influence whether they accept the overall message that a truly satisfying life is one that is God-centered.

THE AUDIENCE: COLLEGE STUDENTS, RELIGION, AND SPIRITUALITY

To begin, consider the audience. What does social science research tell us about the current student population entering our classrooms? In particular, what is their attitude toward religion? How receptive are they likely to be to the proposal that their lives will be fuller and happier if they live in relationship with God?

It is axiomatic that college is a time of transition and challenge. Poised between childhood and adulthood, students have recently passed through rapid physical, cognitive, and emotional development. Regarding religion in particular, complex abstractions required by maturity have challenged youth's basic, concrete religious conceptions.[1] As a result young adulthood is the least religious time in individuals' lives. College-age students consistently score lower than older adults on measures of beliefs about God, heaven, and sin and on assessments of their participation in traditional religious activities, such as formal services, prayer, and volunteerism.[2]

In addition to being the least religious group, research over the past two decades indicates that a significant portion of the college population is developing a distinct attitude toward religion. A 2004 survey by the Higher Education Research Institute at UCLA offers a glimpse into this issue.[3] These researchers surveyed more than 112,000 students at 236 colleges and universities. At first glance the findings are encouraging for the goal of engaging students in conversation about a life of holiness: over 75 percent of the students surveyed reported that they search for meaning and purpose in life, and similar numbers reported believing in the sacredness of life and having an interest in spirituality. Looking deeper, however, one sees the elements of a growing trend in young adults' approach to religion: a movement to reject religion, considered institutional, static, dogmatic, and coercive, in favor of a personalized, dynamic, accommodating spirituality. Even more telling about their attitude toward religion is that 83 percent of the respondents reported believing that most people can grow spiritually without being religious.

The movement away from religion toward spirituality alone started receiving attention in the social science literature in the 1980s. Robert Bellah and his colleagues labeled the phenomenon "Sheilaism," a term they selected from an interview that they felt captured a common attitude toward religion and spirituality they were observing: "I believe in God. I'm not a religious fanatic. I can't remember the last time I went to church. My faith has carried me a long way. It's Sheilaism. Just my own little voice."[4]

Research indicates that the trend away from institutional religion and traditional religious authority is growing, roughly averaging 25 percent of college students self-labeling as "spiritual but not religious." Of course the percentage of students describing themselves as solely spiritual varies widely depending on the college or university sampled. Percentages as high as the upper 30s have been reported at secular institutions, while spiritual-only groups at Christian colleges account for percentages only in the low single digits. Proportions of students self-identifying as spiritual-only at Catholic colleges appear to vary widely between campuses. Two recent studies involving six Catholic colleges in the northeastern United States found spiritual-only students accounting for between 11 and 39 percent of the students at the campuses surveyed.[5]

What does it mean to be spiritual but not religious? How might these students compare with the majority of their peers, the 50 to 66 percent who label themselves both spiritual and religious, in terms of attitudes and behaviors traditionally associated with a search for holiness? One basic belief difference between the groups is their image of God. A substantial majority of spiritual and religious students conceive of God as transcendent and personal. In contrast, the spiritual-only majority believe that what we call God is either a transcendent aspect of human nature or an illusory, though useful myth. In terms of principles guiding their search for meaning, spiritual-only students are significantly less likely than their religiously oriented counterparts to agree with statements such as "My faith gives my life meaning and purpose," "My faith is a way of life," "My faith is an important part of my individual identity," and "My faith guides my whole approach to life." Behaviorally spiritual-only students report that they are significantly less likely to attend any type of formal religious or spiritual service, meditate or pray outside of a formal setting, and read material or seek advice from specialists concerning spirituality or religiousness.

These belief and behavior characteristics of spiritual but not religious students have led Christian Smith and Patricia Snell of the Center for the Study of Religion and Society at the University of Notre Dame to suggest that the literature greatly overestimates the number of college-age students who are truly spiritual-only. Smith and Snell suggest that true spirituality involves actively seeking the transcendent of life, "not some free-floating experience of individualistic interiority and self-exploration."[6] They speculate that a significant portion of those identifying with the spiritual-only group on surveys are doing so because saying they are not spiritual implies they have no interest in their own subjective, interior life, a characterization contrary to their overall self-image. Instead of describing these students as spiritual-only, Smith and Snell suggest that these emerging adults are better portrayed as either "selective adherents," individuals who take a pick-and-choose approach to religion by ignoring customary beliefs and practices considered irrelevant to their personal lives and choosing what they feel is useful, or "religiously indifferent," young adults who are able to appreciate religion as a moral guidance system but who simply do not care enough to invest in its beliefs and practices.

Smith and Snell's religious type system further suggests refinement of the spiritual and religious group classification. Their research leads them to propose that the number of emerging adults who strongly embrace religious faith, a group they call "committed traditionalists," accounts for only about 15 percent of the population. As with the spiritual-only group, the less committed spiritual and religious students are also better described as being selective adherents or religious indifferents, the two groups they found making up the majority (55 percent) of emerging adults with whom they worked. In support of Smith and Snell's reclassification, Adams and Freitas found that only 25 percent of the students in their survey who self-identified as both religious and spiritual described themselves as being strongly religious.[7] The remaining 75 percent were split between labeling themselves slightly or moderately religious.

These surveys portray the student audience as holding varied attitudes toward religion, with roughly 33 percent being split between those highly committed to religion and those who rebuff it. The highly committed are likely open to receive messages regarding a God-centered life, and those rejecting religion are likely to be hostile to such communications in any form. Research indicates that the character of the majority in between, the group traditionally attended to because of their capacity for change, has been moving toward rejecting traditional religion in favor of an individualized spirituality. Only a minority of this group, though growing in number, indicates a desire to totally dissociate from institutional religion and religious authority. However, the moderately weak commitment the remaining students have to both religion *and* spirituality makes it arguable that neither religion nor spirituality is of primary interest to them. In other words, the majority of students Catholic educators encounter in the classroom will likely not be enthusiastically receptive to a traditional religious justification for living a life of holiness, particularly when proposed by communicators identified as religious authorities. Instead, to engage this audience, at least initially, the message will need to take on a different form presented by communicators from a variety of disciplines.

What sources of information are college-age audiences likely to find compelling? Smith and Snell's emerging adults say they are convinced by those who provide "proof," and proof to them primarily comes from two sources: what they learn from personal experience and the evidence provided by science. It is students' implicit belief in the integrity of this second source's knowledge claims that opens the door for psychology to act as an important communicator in forming students' conceptions of the good life.

THE COMMUNICATORS: TRUSTING IS BELIEVING

William Kilpatrick, an educational psychologist formerly of Boston College, begins his book *Psychological Seduction: The Failure of Modern Psychology* with a description of a lasting memory he took away from church one Sunday morning:

> The priest was delivering a sermon, and to buttress his message he referred to the authority of John's Gospel, the Epistles of Saint Paul, the writings of Saint Augustine, and so on. The congregation seemed unmoved. The man to my left yawned. A woman in the next row was checking the contents of her purse.
>
> "As Erich Fromm says..." the priest continued. Instantly a visible stir of attention rippled through the crowd as it strained forward to catch every nuance. The yawning man closed his mouth, and the lady shut her purse; both came alert. Erich Fromm. Of course! If anyone knew the answers to the riddles of life, it would be Erich Fromm.
>
> It seemed two kinds of faith prevailed in that congregation: faith in God and faith in psychology. It was hard to say which was the higher faith.... The real problem is telling them apart at all.[8]

For a message to be influential, its source must be perceived as credible. As Kilpatrick's scenario depicts, today's audiences, including those motivated enough to attend church services, are less inclined to have confidence in the expertise of religious authorities than in that of psychologists, even when the message involves a topic traditionally associated with religion. Confidence in psychologists' competence is rooted in the field's association with science. Our culture has placed great credence in scientists and their knowledge since the 1950s, to the point that today trust in scientific understanding is a conviction young adults accept as common sense. To many, scientists generate knowledge that is factual, rational, and objective. In contrast, nonscientific knowledge sources tend to be associated with subjectivity and opinion. As Gregory Peterson describes it, "To be a scientist is to be a producer of truth; the rest of us who are not scientists must have our claims to producing knowledge greeted with suspicion."[9] And though historically science and religion have been deeply intertwined, the past half-century has witnessed increasing doubt in religion as a source of truth about human nature and purpose. Instead, like Kilpat-rick's congregants, students increasingly turn to psychology and its representatives for answers to their questions about the riddles of life. As troubling as these devel-opments may be, they indicate that religious psychologists are in a unique position to engage an often skeptical audience in discussions regarding a life of holiness.

In addition to channeling students' intuitive confidence in scientific knowledge, psychology affords Catholic educators an excellent position of influence because the field commands an exceptionally large audience. Psychology departments do not worry about drawing students into their classes or majors into their programs. If anything, departments are more concerned with capping classes at a reasonable size and limiting the numbers of majors they accept. Student interest has resulted in psychology's being the second most popular undergraduate major in the United States, according to the *Princeton Review*.[10] In addition, the U.S. Department of Education states that the number of undergraduate psychology majors increased by an average of 19.7 percent each year between 2000 and 2006, with continued growth expected for the foreseeable future.[11]

While psychologists' position as influential communicators opens the door to faith-oriented educators, it also exposes students to a population noted as being among the least religious in academia. In fact many individuals whose professional writings (e.g., texts, research articles, commentaries) students will be assigned hold significantly less positive attitudes toward religion than does the general population in the United States. Two recent surveys report that while 55 percent of the general population says religion is important or very important to them, only 21 percent of psychologists share this attitude.[12] Conversely 48 percent of psychologists say that religion is not at all important to them, compared with only 15 percent of the general population. Only 32 percent of psychologists believe God exists, compared with 90 percent of the general population.

Given this mix of psychologists' attitudes toward religion, what images of reli-gion and religion's role in students' personal formation are students likely to encounter during their psychological studies? In other words, will psychology's messages be a help or a hindrance in attracting students toward a life of holiness? The answer is potentially both.

THE MESSAGE: IT DEPENDS

An often surprising feature of psychology about which students quickly learn is that the field encompasses multiple and diverse perspectives. Psychology is composed of numerous, discrete specialties (e.g., clinical, cognitive, physiological, social) taught in divergent courses with a distinct theoretical orientation (e.g., behavioral, humanistic, psychodynamic, social-cognitive), often favoring either a research or an applied focus. What confuses and sometimes frustrates students when confronted with the discipline's extensive diversity is the multiple accounts psychologists voice when explaining human behavior. Many students expect ordered, concrete facts similar to what they encounter in math, chemistry, and physics, but instead are regularly exposed to an assortment of empirical findings and theoretical assertions—some unique, some similar, some complementary, some conflicting—all presented with equal conviction.

Psychology's diversity of perspectives is illustrated in the field's descriptions of the good life and the role religion can play in individuals' search for meaning and purpose. Some psychologists take the stance that their discipline has nothing to say about religion, while others see the two as intimately entwined. Some speak of religion being a source of personal growth and greater life satisfaction for individuals; others describe religion as leading people to infantilism, dogmatism, and prejudice. Where some see religious communities as providing social support and a secure environment aiding personal growth and development, others perceive demands of conformity, subservience, and brainwashing.

Essentially students will encounter three message types within the psychological literature regarding religion and the role it plays in people's well-being.

Separatism: Islands unto Themselves

Separatism is arguably the dominant view of religion within academic psychology, and so is a perspective to which all students will be exposed. It represents the view that science and religion are non-overlapping disciplines that study independent aspects of human life. Separatism's message is that psychological science addresses solely empirical issues and can describe only "what is." Religion, on the other hand, considers what "might be" or "should be." Values and questions about meaning and purpose are the purview of religion; they are matters separatists believe science simply does not, and cannot, address. Because of this orientation, textbooks for courses in standard psychology curriculums seldom reference religion, except perhaps as an example of a historical misinterpretation of abnormal behavior causes or as an event illustrative of dysfunction, like the mass suicide at Jonestown in Guyana. The same absence of religion is true within mainline journals and many trade books students are likely to be assigned. As a result, majors can pass through a psychology curriculum without ever reading about or being asked to consider potential interactions between psychological material and religious conceptions of life.

The growth of separatism and its powerful influence within psychology can be seen in the field's historical relationship with religion. During the late nineteenth and early twentieth centuries, a time when the newly recognized discipline of psychology was just beginning to get its legs, the role religion played in people's lives was a prominent area of interest for psychologists. The subject captured the attention of the period's most renowned psychologists, as evidenced in works such as Edwin Starbuck's *The Psychology of Religion*, William James's *Varieties of Religious Experience*, and Sigmund Freud's *The Future of an Illusion*.[13] Even one of psychology's first professional journals, the *American Journal of Religious Psychology and Education*, was dedicated to this area.[14] However, following this initial period psychology became dominated by behaviorism, a theoretical orientation known for its push to identify psychology as a science, strictly interpreted. The result is a large gap in the literature stretching from the late 1920s to the early 1950s, indicating a time when little work connecting psychology and religion took place. Religion slowly began to be reinstated as a valid topic of study in the 1960s and 1970s, and since that time the psychological literature on religion has grown significantly, with increasing numbers of psychologists supporting perspectivalism, the third message type, to be discussed shortly. However, separatism remains a strong influence, relegating religion's return to being chiefly a specialty topic subject.

Robert Kugelmann's account of the fate of the American Catholic Psychological Association provides another illustration of separatism's effect within the field, in this case the tension Catholics in particular experienced between their faith and their professional roles.[15] After World War II psychology experienced rapid growth within the academy and especially within applied occupations. Recognizing this growth and perceiving bias against their religious affiliation, a group of Catholics gathered during the 1947 American Psychological Association convention and founded the ACPA. Their intent was to seek assimilation of Catholic psychologists and Catholic university psychology departments into the mainstream and to find ways to integrate the science of psychology with the Catholic faith and with Catholic philosophical thought. The first goal was achieved by the early 1970s; the second was not. Instead just the opposite occurred. The ACPA disbanded in 1975, fueled by strong dissent between its science-oriented and philosophy-oriented members, and it became an ecumenical subdivision of the APA: Psychologists Interested in Religious Issues. Pushed further still by separatists' interests, PIRI changed its title in 1993 to the Psychology of Religion, defining itself as a division that "promotes the application of psychological research methods and interpretive frameworks to diverse forms of religion and spirituality."[16]

In all, students' views on religion and the good life are not likely to be challenged by messages separatist faculty bring to their classrooms. This necessitates that faculty wishing to engage students in dialogue about psychology, religion, and a life of holiness must take the initiative to generate this conversation, either creating new courses acceptable to their department or finding ways to insert coverage of these issues in courses they already offer.

Finally, it should be noted that a separatist approach implicates neither psychologists' personal views on religion nor their conceptions of the good life. It is equally possible for both devout believers and atheists to perform professionally within psychology without ever revealing their personal faith or philosophical position to students and colleagues. In fact because graduate training in psychology also is dominated by a separatist orientation, it may be the case that young Catholic faculty believe it is not their place to introduce these topics in the psychology classroom. In this case it falls to administrations to create an atmosphere supporting and even encouraging cross-disciplinary integration. Only when faculty feel confident that their efforts at integration do not threaten their academic standing will they be able to provide students with an all-important model of a faith-oriented scientist.

Religious Oppositionism: Psychology's Bid to Define the Good Life

Interaction between religious and psychology programs will encounter resistance from those supportive of psychology's second message regarding religion. Religious oppositionism presents an unabashedly antagonistic message: that religion is harmful to psychological health and should be replaced with more realistic, rational alternatives. To oppositionists, belief in a supernatural God equates to an obsessional neurosis, the childish looking for a big daddy in the sky, or a misguided surrender of self-integrity and control in exchange for feelings of belonging and protection.[17] The mind and a sense of free will, previously regarded as evidence of humans' uniqueness in the animal kingdom as well as the outward manifestation of the soul, are explained as cognitive illusions, byproducts of neural networks shaped and molded by an adaptive drive to maintain perceived control in life. Virtues and values, meaning and purpose are reduced to evolutionary drives fashioned by cultural demands. Because religion is delusional, oppositionists set themselves the tasks of explaining how these irrational belief systems developed and educating individuals in more logical and advanced belief systems.

Students may not directly encounter oppositionism's message in their studies. The literature is there, but more available in the public realm than in traditionally assigned classroom material. For those attuned to these issues it may be difficult to believe that the recent positive media coverage afforded individuals like Michael Shermer and Steven Pinker can be missed, but in an academic setting their work is likely to be restricted to specialty courses. Some of psychology's most influential early figures, such as Sigmund Freud, Abraham Maslow, Erik Fromm, B. F. Skinner, and Albert Ellis, also can be found among the ranks of those delivering the religious oppositionists' message, but again their works directly commenting on religion are likely limited to specialty courses.

What most psychology majors will encounter are not oppositionists' denunciations of religious conceptions of a life well lived, but the secularist views with which oppositionists replace them. Within psychology, oppositionists' conceptions of what constitutes the good life principally take the shape of descriptions of the healthy personality. Having rejected religious conceptions of human motives and purpose, oppositionists construct a naturalistic view of well-being in its place, embedded in seemingly impartial, medical language. Oppositionists have turned issues previously considered characteristics of virtue and maturity into descriptive statements of positive functioning and mental health. The highest good for human beings has become the healthy psyche, alternatively described by oppositionists as one directed by rational, objective assessment of physical and social reality or one focused on achieving self-actualization, an idealized image of humans that sets self-love (high self-esteem) as the main criterion for mental health.[18]

Oppositionists' views are deeply embedded in personality theory and applied psychology, highly popular topics in the psychology major. As a result, students are likely to learn oppositionists' proposals of the good life without recognizing the theories' secularist roots or their implications for religious conceptions. An even more difficult issue religious faculty must confront is that students find oppositionists' views intrinsically attractive. This is in part because many oppositionists' proposals of well-being are highly influenced by humanistic psychology, an orientation that concurs with students' individualistic approach to life.

Perspectivalism: The Whole Is Greater than the Sum of Its Parts

Perspectivalism's message represents psychology's alternative to separatism's and oppositionism's dismissal of religion. In contrast to separatism's isolation of each discipline and oppositionism's claim of psychology's supremacy, perspectivalism proposes that both fields provide accurate, complementary knowledge that best benefits an understanding of human life when integrated.

Perspectivalism is best explained by an analogy. Imagine that you are sitting at the center of an athletic arena, watching a familiar contest take place. Up above the highest section of seats far to your right is an enormous screen displaying video highlights from the game. You glance up at the screen occasionally and see instant-replay close-ups of dazzling moves and spectacular shots. You see these plays, you understand what they mean, and they are thrilling to watch.

While watching the video screen you imagine yourself being lifted up into the air and then slowly, gently moving closer and closer to the screen. As you draw nearer, the picture becomes difficult to see. Closer still you find that what you thought was a single screen is actually thousands of small lights rapidly changing intensity, illuminating and dimming, creating a breathtaking light show. You continue your movement toward the lights until you can actually see into one of the bulbs. The filament glows with heat, quickly cools, and then burns once again. Suddenly your vision becomes telescopic, and you can now see molecules dancing through a vast space.

For a perspectivalist, several key principles emerge from this analogy. The first is that the situation involves but a single reality. Reality changes its appearance and meaning, however, depending on the vantage point from which it is viewed. It is understood that the screen is composed of flickering bulbs, but this need not eliminate, nor can it fully explain, the validity and significance of the picture's moving images. Instead, altering the viewpoint creates genuine attributes, emergent properties, which are not characteristic of the system's parts.

A second principle that emerges from the analogy is that each viewpoint perceives a "truth" about the object being observed. If properly applied, each viewpoint's methodology is capable of accurately understanding aspects of the object available to that vantage point. At the same time, one perspective's methodology, though highly useful and productive on its own level, is simply insufficient for understanding all aspects of reality.

A contemporary philosopher whose work bears on this issue is Alasdair MacIntyre.[19] MacIntyre proposes that people involve themselves in systems of activity that he labels "social practices." Each social practice involves highly complex interactions between individuals who work toward established goals and whose behavior is governed by standards of excellence that are appropriate to and definitive of that practice: "Tic-tac-toe is not an example of a practice in this sense, nor is the throwing of a football with skill, but the game of football is, and so is chess." Within any practice one can be judged to perform well or poorly, skillfully or ineptly. However, the criteria used to judge quality in one practice may not transfer effectively to another practice, nor need they. Using MacIntyre's parameters, it is possible to regard both science and religion as practices. As such, the appropriate standards used to judge scientific knowledge are not the same criteria used to evaluate religious knowledge. Failure to meet the standards of excellent scientific practice is a failure only if one is engaged in the practice of science, not if one is engaged in the practice of religion. Of course, the same assertion applies to religion.

A third principle a perspectivalist would take from the video analogy is that no perspective takes precedence over another. As David Myers describes it, "An evolutionary explanation of universal incest taboos (in terms of the genetic penalty offspring pay for inbreeding) does not replace a sociological explanation (which might see incest taboos as a way of preserving the family unit) or a theological one (which might focus on moral truth)."[20]

Applying these three principles to the relationship between psychology and religion results in the perspectivalists' message that both science and religion are unique and valid vantage points from which to study human thought, feelings, and behavior. Each contributes true knowledge that is not accessible to the other, but is necessary to a complete understanding of humans. Therefore accepting the findings of one perspective (e.g., science) need not necessitate, or even imply, rejection of the other's (e.g., religion).[21] "Mind and brain are not seen as separate entities, but the same set of events viewed from two perspectives, from within and from without. Purpose and mechanism are not mutually exclusive; they are alternative ways of analyzing the same system. An act is free when described in actor-language and determined when described in spectator-language."[22]

As indicated earlier, psychological literature on religion written from the perspectivalist viewpoint has been growing over the past thirty years. Strong indicators of this trend are the appearance of several professional journals to manage increased research efforts (e.g., *International Journal for the Psychology of Religion*, *Journal of Psychology and Theology*, *Psychology of Religion and Spirituality*) and the publication of books addressing religion and spirituality by the American Psychological Association, such as William Miller and Harold Delaney's *Judeo-Christian Perspectives on Psychology: Human Nature, Motivation, and Change* and Edward Shafranske's *Religion and the Clinical Practice of Psychology*.[23] Additional evidence for increased interest in the area can be found in the fact that psychology of religion courses are being offered at colleges and universities in increasing numbers, including several graduate programs, religious and secular, that offer doctoral-level training in the psychology of religion. At the same time it should be noted that psychologists' engagement with religious issues does not necessarily indicate support for a Christian worldview. What perspectivalism does provide to students, however, is the vitally important message that committed scientists believe a dialogue between psychology and religion is possible *and* desirable, and the individuals engaged in this work provide students with personal embodiments of these beliefs.

Despite psychologists' increased attention to religious issues, students' chances of being exposed to perspectivalists' material still are not high. It takes a determined effort on faculty's part to bring these ideas to their classrooms and to draw students to their courses. As discussed earlier, faculty motivation toward these ends also is likely to occur only in an academic culture where interdisciplinary approaches are openly encouraged and supported.

In summary, psychology students can encounter within their courses three different messages regarding religion. Separatism portrays psychology as unrelated to religion and spiritual issues, religious oppositionism depicts psychology as inherently hostile to a religious worldview, and perspectivalism approaches psychology and religion as complementary views whose knowledge, when combined, provides a richer understanding of human beings. Of these messages, perspectivalism is the sole supporter of conversation between psychology and religion and therefore the perspective through which religious psychologists can contribute to making "holiness more intelligible and appealing" to students.

While these three perspectives describe psychology's direct commentary on religion, there remains a viewpoint deeply entrenched not only in psychology but in our society that perspectivalists, if not all religious educators, must address before having any hope of instilling in students a desire for holiness. This viewpoint is scientism.

SCIENTISM

As addressed earlier, belief in the authority of science is a key factor in psychology's ability to influence students. However, this same belief in excessive form is a major impediment to students' seriously considering perspectivalism and to a religious worldview in general. This attitude has been labeled scientism. Scientism is an all-inclusive life philosophy whose tenets include science being deemed exclusively capable of accurately describing reality.[24] It tends to emerge publicly in connection with controversial topics such as evolution, stem cell research, abortion, and euthanasia, often juxtaposed with equally radical forms of religion. Regarding religion, its message is quite clear: religion and science are fundamentally incompatible. Scientism supports this claim by portraying religion as devoid of reason, based exclusively on blind, unquestioning faith in a nonexistent spiritual authority. Individuals must choose between science and religion, between being rational, clear thinkers or "dyed-in-the-wool faith-heads."[25]

The primary obstacle to accepting perspectivalism posed by scientism lies in the confusion of science, the epistemological methodology, with scientism, the worldview. This confusion creates the misperception that to support science and its findings necessitates loyalty to the principles of scientism. Convincing students of perspectivalism's adequacy therefore involves having students critically examine the assumption that genuine scientists need to be scientistic and demonstrating that a viable worldview advocating for both science and religion exists between the polarized interpretations of scientism and religious fundamentalism.[26]

Immediate evidence for the fact that there are scientists unsupportive of scientism's principles can be found in two of psychology's three perspectives on religion. Separatism and perspectivalism use the term *science* solely to denote an epistemological method, a system of inquiry created to gather information about the observable world. To these perspectives, science is but one of the many possible methods available in the search for knowledge. Oppositionism, on the other hand, extends the meaning of science beyond methodology into a scientistic worldview, applying the philosophical assumptions of science's methods (e.g., materialism, reductionism, determinism) to account for all of reality. While separatism and perspectivalism advocate that science is, to use MacIntyre's terminology, a practice whose internal standards limit its interpretations and conclusions exclusively to descriptive knowledge, oppositionism freely extends science's epistemic authority into prescriptive, moral authority.[27] This scientistic perception of psychology poses a particularly difficult barrier to individuals attempting to understand the role religion plays in defining a life well lived because it affords oppositionist psychologists a perceived level of authority and a degree of influence far beyond the legitimacy afforded to them by science. The result is an unjustified ready acceptance of psychologists' prescriptive speculations, leading some authors to contend that divisions of psychology are no longer science, but religion.[28]

A second important supposition for students to consider is scientism's depiction of science as the paradigm of rationality and objectivity, the exclusive generator of fact. While steadfastly defending science's strengths as an epistemic method, perspectivalists question the degree of objectivity obtainable by scientists given that science is a human endeavor. As such, human values inevitably penetrate scientific practices. Within psychology, for example, occurrences of values' influence can be shown in psychologists' attraction to their profession and subdisciplines, their selection of research topics, the language they choose in labeling constructs, their interpretations of data, and their definitions of mental illness and mental health.[29]

Scientism's declared incompatibility between science and religion also can be used to illustrate the influence of human values within scientism. Embedded in every worldview, be it scientific, religious, or atheistic, are philosophical presuppositions foundational to each view's conception of the world. These assumptions profoundly affect science's theories, methodologies, and interpretations. It is disagreement over these assumptions and not conclusions based on empirical evidence that leads scientistic scientists to repudiate religion. However, presuppositions are, by definition, truths taken for granted, accepted without proof. Scientism therefore is clearly self-contradictory since it does not conform to its own principle. That is, scientists, remaining within the parameters set by their practice, cannot use their methods to account for their presuppositions. Scientific evidence cannot "prove" correct any of scientism's premises regarding the nature of reality or of the humans inhabiting it; neither can it prove religion's assumptions wrong. Instead scientism's premises are completely taken on faith.

Again the existence of three identifiable, distinct psychological perspectives on religion helps illustrate this issue within psychology. These perspectives exist not as the result of theory built on experimental evidence, but because their proponents do not share fundamental assumptions. For example, separatists take a dualistic approach to reality, believing that reality involves both material and supernatural aspects. Oppositionists disagree, assuming that nothing other than matter exists. Perspectivalists circumvent this conflict by proposing that matter and spirit are aspects of a single reality, representing the appearance and character of reality that is available to observers as they alter their vantage points.

A final example of subjectivity within science is recognizing the role values play in influencing attraction to any worldview, including scientism. Accepting a worldview indicates belief in an authority and that authority's ability to accurately describe reality. Returning to social influence terminology, an audience accepts an authority's message only when it perceives the communicator to be credible. Credibility can be established in multiple ways, but ultimately belief in any authority is preceded by a very human emotion: trust.[30] All individuals—including students and professors—often accept knowledge claims based on trust in others, not because they have personally conducted in-depth investigations into each and every assertion.

Given the importance of an audience's trust in communicators, students' willingness to consider the perspectivalists' message strongly depends on their witnessing faculty grappling with integrating their own scientific and religious viewpoints into personal worldviews, modeling for students what David Myers calls "faith-rooted rationality."[31] The availability of such role models is of course dependent on a college's or university's commitment to bringing faith-oriented academics into their faculty. In psychology in particular, institutions will need to be strongly dedicated to this goal given the relative shortage of perspectivalists in the field and the lack of graduate programs training scholars from within this orientation. Also, as stated previously, faculty are likely to bring their perspectivalist viewpoint into the classroom only when they are confident that their behaviors will be supported by both their colleagues and their institution.

AN EMPIRICAL REFLECTION ON A LIFE OF HOLINESS

What remains is a quick examination of perspectivalists' investigations into the relationship between religion and the good life. Since the return of religion and religious issues as acceptable topics of study within mainstream psychology, a small but significant body of research has been growing within the discipline examining aspects of oppositionist and perspectivalist proposals concerning religion's effect on psychological well-being. As with all empirical endeavors, this research has undergone, and continues to experience, growing pains, chiefly due to the complex nature of the issues being investigated. Foremost has been the difficulty of satisfactorily defining both religion and human well-being and then developing reliable and valid measures meeting psychology's psychometric standards. Measures have greatly progressed, but still remain controversial and limited in their ability to assess what many believe to be principally nonempirical constructs.

Of particular interest to this essay is any research related to Cunningham's proposal that "a fuller happiness or satisfaction lies in the ongoing graced attempt to live in relationship to the Holy One revealed in Christ." The religious attitude Cunningham describes goes well beyond a simple question of whether individuals consider themselves religious and/or spiritual. Instead an "ongoing graced attempt" refers to a person's degree of commitment to pursuing a life of holiness.

The importance of commitment within religiousness research can be traced back to the work of Gordon Allport.[32] Allport proposed differentiating between two general approaches individuals could take to religion. He labeled one perspective the intrinsic religious orientation. Intrinsic religious individuals hold religion as their master motive in life, bringing other motives into harmony with their faith. Intrinsics actively commit to creating comprehensive and integrated philosophies of life centered on their faith. They live their religion. Individuals with an extrinsic religious orientation develop other needs that serve as their master motives. For extrinsics, religion serves as a means to other ends: to provide security and solace, self-justification, and status. Their religious beliefs tend to be lightly held or shaped to fit personal needs. Extrinsics use their faith pragmatically. Allport's intrinsic/extrinsic religiousness distinction had a huge impact on research in psychology and sociology of religion. A variety of measures distinguishing individuals' degree of religious commitment are used in much of the work being conducted today.[33]

Attempts to empirically measure the second issue in Cunningham's proposal, "a fuller happiness or satisfaction," strongly illustrate the limitations of the scientific method when applied to human beings, and in turn support perspectivalism's appeal for cooperative communication between psychologists and colleagues of other disciplines. As one might expect, the abstract and value-laden natures of the terms *happiness* and *satisfaction* have led to multiple and varied measures. As indicators of individuals' well-being researchers use measures such as the presence or absence of psychological dysfunctions; involvement with risky behaviors, such as premarital sex, alcohol consumption, and drug use; quality of relationships with family and peers; frequency of giving and volunteer behaviors; personal life satisfaction ratings; and purpose in life. Appraisal of how well these measures represent a fuller happiness or satisfaction, a life well lived, is left to interpretation and debate.

Quickly summarized, the pattern emerging from research regarding the relationship between religion and well-being indicates that young adults who are strongly committed to their religious and spiritual quest tend to score higher on measures of positive life outcomes than their less committed or nonreligious peers. In other words, students who make an ongoing attempt to live a life of holiness tend to have happier and more positive and purposeful lives. It should be noted that these are general patterns describing average relationships. Examples contradictory to this pattern exist on an individual level. There are weakly committed and nonreligious students whose lives evidence many positive outcomes, and there are those committed to their religion struggling through difficulties. However, differences between groups are consistent enough for researchers to conclude that the general patterns are real.[34]

SUMMARY

This essay has considered the role psychology can play in facilitating student interest in and commitment to a God-centered life of holiness. Many psychologists will have little or nothing to say about this issue. Courses that dominate most undergraduate curriculums likely will not mention religion in their material, nor are they likely to discuss conceptions of a life well lived. "It's not on their radar," as our students might remark. It is not that these individuals consider psychology's knowledge inapplicable to religious issues; it is simply that they identify themselves and their work with a strictly controlled science. Individuals interested in religious issues are welcome to utilize psychology's discoveries if they wish, with the qualification that these individuals must not violate the scientific integrity of their findings.

A second observation is that this separatist view does not represent all of psychology. Instead two substantial factions within the discipline are vocal on religion and conceptions of the good life: oppositionists and perspectivalists. There are significant differences between the two in what they have to say and in how they frame their comments, however. The more dominant group, oppositionists, is antagonistic to religion and religious interpretations of the ideal life. Instead of outwardly attacking religion, however, most oppositionists have relied on the building cultural attitude of scientism to support their secular models, mixing epistemic authority with moral authority and promoting with scientific and medical terminology their prescriptive ideas of how people should live. Students will encounter these models chiefly within applied courses, psychology's most popular offerings, and are not likely to recognize the negative implications of these models for Christian conceptions of the good life.

Unlike oppositionists, perspectivalists do not believe that scientific and religious perspectives inherently conflict. Instead they advocate many religious conceptions of human life and promote open dialogue between psychology and religion. They share separatists' boundary views on science, but avoid the need to isolate science from religion by conceptualizing the two disciplines as complementary practices, each using methodologies designed to gather valid knowledge useful to a complete picture of a life well lived. Perspectivalism best fits the Catholic view of religion's relationship with science and would be the orientation most conducive to attracting students into considering a life of holiness. However, it is the least visible perspective in psychology. As a result it will take a concerted effort from faculty and their departments to make this view available to students.

Student confidence in science places perspectivalist psychologists in a strong position of influence. However, even when their messages are brilliantly constructed, the content is insufficient by itself to persuade students to pursue a life of holiness if the audience is not initially receptive. Educators have traditionally faced students with widely varied responses to religion. There have always been students who are highly committed to religion and those antagonistic to its message. Today these two groups appear to equally compose roughly a third of the students at many colleges and universities. The orientations of the remaining two-thirds appear to be unlike those of past students, however. While the majority wish to identify as both religious and spiritual, a growing minority identify as spiritual only, distancing themselves from traditional religious beliefs and practices. Even those continuing to identify as religious do not hold religion as a central guiding principle in their lives. Instead they approach life and the knowledge it offers with a naïve scientistic attitude. Educators in all disciplines, particularly the social and natural sciences, must confront the polarizing nature of this attitude and themselves exemplify faith-rooted rationality if they desire to convince students that a life centered in God will be happier and fuller than any of the alternatives.

NOTES

1. For readings on religious and faith development, see James W. Fowler, *Stages of Faith: The Psychology of Human Development and the Quest for Meaning* (San Francisco: Harper and Row, 1981); David Elkind, "The Origins of Religion in the Child," in *The Psychology of Religion: Theoretical Approaches*, edited by Bernard Spilka and Daniel N. McIntosh (Boulder, Colo.: Westview Press, 1997), 97–104.

2. Ralph W. Hood Jr., Peter C. Hill, and Bernard Spilka, *The Psychology of Religion: An Empirical Approach*, 4th ed. (New York: Guilford Press, 2009), 109–39.

3. Higher Education Research Institute at UCLA, "The Spiritual Life of College Students: A National Study of College Students' Search for Meaning and Purpose," accessed on May 24, 2009, at www.spirituality.ucla.edu.

4. Robert N. Bellah, Richard Madsen, William M. Sullivan, Ann Swidler, and Stephen Tipton, *Habits of the Heart: Individualism and Commitment in American Life* (Berkeley: University of California Press, 1985), 221.

5. See Jeffrey B. Adams and Donna Freitas, "Alternate Measures of Religiousness and Spirituality in College Samples," unpublished raw data, 2009, SPSS file; Vincent L. Bolduc, "Measuring Catholicity on Campus: A Comparative Sample at Four Colleges," *Journal of Catholic Higher Education* 28 (2009): 125–45.

6. Christian Smith and Patricia Snell, *Souls in Transition: The Religious and Spiritual Lives of Emerging Adults* (New York: Oxford University Press, 2009), 295.

7. Adams and Freitas, "Alternate Measures."

8. William K. Kilpatrick, *Psychological Seduction: The Failure of Modern Psychology* (Nashville, Tenn.: Thomas Nelson, 1983), 13.

9. Gregory R. Peterson, "Demarcation and the Scientistic Fallacy," *Zygon: Journal of Religion and Science* 38 (2003): 760.

10. "Top Ten College Majors," *Princeton Review*, accessed on June 3, 2009, at www.princetonreview.com/college/top-ten-majors.aspx.

11. National Center for Education Statistics, "Digest of Education Statistics," retrieved on July 12, 2010, at http://nces.ed.gov/programs/digest/d08/tables/dt08_314.asp.

12. See Mark R. McMinn, William L. Hathaway, Scott W. Woods, and Kimberly N. Snow, "What American Psychological Association Leaders Have to Say about Psychology of Religion and Spirituality," *Psychology of Religion and Spirituality* 1 (2009): 3–13; Harold D. Delaney, William R. Miller, and Ana M. Bisono, "Religiosity and Spirituality among Psychologists: A Survey of Clinician Members of the American Psychological Association," *Professional Psychology: Research and Practice* 38 (2007): 538–46.

13 Edwin D. Starbuck, *The Psychology of Religion* (New York: Scribner's, 1899); William James, *The Varieties of Religious Experience: A Study in Human Nature* (1902; Cambridge, Mass.: Harvard University Press, 1985); Sigmund Freud, *The Future of an Illusion* (1927; New York: Norton, 1989).

14. As cited in Raymond F. Paloutzian, *Invitation to the Psychology of Religion*, 2nd ed. (Boston: Allyn and Bacon, 1996), 39.

15. Robert Kugelmann, "American Catholic Psychological Association: A Brief History and Analysis," *Catholic Social Science Review* 5 (2000): 233–49.

16. "Psychology of Religion," Division 36 of the American Psychological Association, accessed on July 24, 2010, at www.apa.org/about/division/div36.aspx.

17. Freud, *Future of an Illusion;* Abraham Maslow, cited in David M. Wulff, *Psychology of Religion: Classic and Contemporary Views*, 2nd ed. (Oxford: Wiley, 1997), 605; Erich Fromm, *Psychoanalysis and Religion* (New Haven, Conn.: Yale University Press, 1950).

18. An intriguing controversy currently taking place in psychology involves the question of whether a rational, objective view of self or a biased, self-bolstering view is better for one's mental health. Traditionally the former has been the model of choice within clinical psychology. However, research connecting mildly skewed positive self-images and overly optimistic views of one's future with higher levels of self-esteem and behavioral functionality (i.e., successful lifestyle) has led some theorists to propose that clinicians and counselors would better serve their clients by helping them avoid an accurate picture of their lives. See Shelley E. Taylor, *Positive Illusions: Creative Self-Deception and the Healthy Mind* (New York: Basic Books, 1991).

19. Alasdair MacIntyre, *After Virtue*, 2nd ed. (Notre Dame, Ind.: University of Notre Dame Press, 1984), 187.

20. David G. Myers, *Social Psychology*, 4th ed. (New York: McGraw-Hill, 1993), 5.

21. Psychology's perspectivalism message corresponds well with the Catholic Church's view on the relationship between religion and natural science as voiced by the Dialogue Group of Scientists and U.S. Bishops: "Despite occasional tensions and disagreements, there can be no irreconcilable conflict between religion and science.... The Church does not propose that science should become religion, or religion science. On the contrary, unity always presupposes the diversity and the integrity of its elements.... The unprecedented opportunity we have today is for a common interactive relationship in which each discipline retains its integrity and yet is radically open to the discoveries and insights of the other." National United States Conference of Catholic Bishops, "Science and the Catholic Church," retrieved on March 18, 2009, at www.usccb.org/shv/publications.shtml.

22. Ian G. Barbour, "Ways of Relating Science and Theology," in *Physics, Philosophy, and Theology: A Common Quest for Understanding,* edited by Robert J. Russell, William R. Stoeger, and George V. Coyne (Notre Dame, Ind.: University of Notre Dame Press, 1988), 7.

23. William R. Miller and Harold D. Delaney, *Judeo-Christian Perspectives on Psychology: Human Nature, Motivation, and Change* (Washington, DC: American Psychological Association, 2004); Edward P. Shafranske, *Religion and the Clinical Practice of Psychology* (Washington, DC: American Psychological Association, 1996).

24. Michael Shermer, founder of the Skeptics Society, defines scientism as "a scientific worldview that encompasses natural explanations for all phenomena, eschews supernatural and paranormal speculations, and embraces empiricism and reason as the twin pillars of a philosophy of life appropriate for an Age of Science." Michael Shermer, "The Shamans of Scientism," *Scientific American*, June 2002, 35.

25. Richard Dawkins, *The God Delusion* (Boston: Houghton Mifflin, 2006), 5.

26. "Scientistic" refers to any person or perspective that adheres closely to scientism.

27. From a perspectivalist view, oppositionists, particularly those in psychology's applied fields whose work necessarily involves value judgments, commit what Gregory Peterson labels a border-crossing violation when they use science's standards to judge other systems of belief. Naturally the same principle applies to religious interpretations. That is, perspectivalists would consider religion to be overstepping its practice boundaries if its practitioners attempted to refute scientific theory based solely on knowledge gained through religion's epistemological methods.

28. See Paul C. Vitz, *Psychology as Religion: The Cult of Self-Worship* (Grand Rapids, Mich.: Eerdmans, 1977); Don S. Browning and Terry D. Cooper, *Religious Thought and the Modern Psychologies,* 2nd ed. (Minneapolis: Augsburg Fortress, 2004).

29. David G. Myers, *Social Psychology*, 9th ed. (Boston: McGraw Hill, 2008), 9–13.

30. See James D. Proctor, "In __ We Trust: Science, Religion, and Authority," in *Science, Religion, and the Human Experience* (New York: Oxford University Press, 2005), 87–108.

31. David G. Myers, *A Friendly Letter to Skeptics and Atheists: Musings on Why God Is Good and Faith Isn't Evil* (San Francisco: Jossey-Bass, 2008), 17.

32. Gordon W. Allport and J. Michael Ross, "Personal Religious Orientation and Prejudice," *Journal of Personality and Social Psychology* 5 (1967): 432–43.

33. See Peter C. Hill and Ralph W. Hood Jr., *Measures of Religiosity* (Birmingham, Ala.: Religious Education Press, 1999).

34. See Smith and Snell, *Souls in Transition*.

SELECTED READINGS

Allport, Gordon W. *The Individual and His Religion*. New York: Macmillan, 1950.

Kilpatrick, William K. *Psychological Seduction: The Failure of Modern Psychology*. Nashville, Tenn.: Thomas Nelson, 1983.

Myers, David G. *A Friendly Letter to Skeptics and Atheists: Musings on Why God Is Good and Faith Isn't Evil*. San Francisco: Jossey-Bass, 2008.

Paloutzian, Raymond F., and Crystal L. Park. *Handbook of the Psychology of Religion and Spirituality*. New York: Guilford Press, 2005.

Smith, Christian, and Patricia Snell. *Souls in Transition: The Religious and Spiritual Lives of Emerging Adults*. New York: Oxford University Press, 2009.

15

Evolutionary Biology in a Catholic Framework

Oliver Putz

TO ASK WHAT the Catholic intellectual tradition has to offer the biological sciences may seem like asking the wrong question. Yes, the history of biology is full of great names linked in one way or another to the Church. Albertus Magnus and Hildegard of Bingen come to mind, and of course in more recent times Gregor Mendel and Teilhard de Chardin. And undoubtedly their faith played a vital role in which research questions they pursued. But ultimately the life sciences are not dependent on theological insights whatsoever. The reverse, however, is not at all the case. A theology that ignores biological explanations will inevitably misconstrue not only creatures such as the human being, but also the process of creation as well as God the Creator. It therefore appears more pertinent to ask what biology has to offer the Catholic intellectual tradition.

But tradition is more than theology, and so the question of how Catholic thought might constructively offer biology valuable insights cannot be dismissed out of hand. It has been argued that Christianity in fact significantly prepared the ground for modern-day biology. For one, Christians have always advocated the notion of linear time flowing irreversibly forward, thus making possible the evolution of new life forms by natural selection. Moreover the Aristotelian monism adopted by medieval scholastics, according to which mind and body are not two separate substances, but rather two aspects of one being, provides a workable metaphysical foundation for numerous biological phenomena, including those studied by contemporary neurobiology. Finally, the medieval realist notion that what a thing is can be deduced from how it acts (*agere sequitur esse*, "action follows being"), justifies observations and empirical inquests into the nature of living things. At least historically, then, Catholicism played an instrumental role in the development of modern biology.

At no point, however, did Catholic thought contribute either method or data to biology. Rather it supplied metaphysical concepts regarding the nature and meaning of being as such that shaped an overall interpretation of living things. So to be quite exact it would be best to ask how the Catholic intellectual tradition can help reconcile theology and biology into one coherent and comprehensive worldview. This question is of interest not only for the Catholic biologist, but for all believers who acknowledge the necessity of a functional relationship between theology and science.

One area in which such an appropriate relationship between theology and science is absolutely mandatory is the treatment of so-called limit questions. What characterizes these questions is that they transcend the scope of the discipline in which they arise. Consider, for example, the ethical questions that arise in modern medicine or questions about divine action in a freely evolving universe. By default, limit questions require interdisciplinary approaches that situate an area of intellectual inquest into a broader context. Catholic thinkers have repeatedly offered metaphysical responses to specific limit questions emerging from the life sciences, thereby generating constructive and innovative ways to integrate theology and science into a comprehensive interpretation of human existence.

This chapter takes a closer look at Karl Rahner's response to limit questions raised by biology. It also submits a constructive proposal for a cosmic theodicy in response to evolutionary suffering. More often than not, Catholics who engage evolutionary biology do so by turning to the Jesuit and paleoanthropologist Teilhard de Chardin. No one can dismiss Teilhard's fundamental contribution to either the Church or theology and science in general. Nevertheless Rahner's approach to integrating creation theology and evolutionary biology is metaphysically and methodologically more robust, which is why it is the focus of this essay.[1] In particular, I will concentrate on his treatment of biological anthropology, mainly because few other topics in the dialogue between theology and biology have had such profound implications for believers and unbelievers alike. For theological anthropology, human existence is grounded in the unique personal relationship with God, which constitutes "humanness" and gives it meaning. With human evolution as its central theme, biological anthropology specifies humanity's relationship to the rest of nature, thereby challenging long-held ideas of human uniqueness. How to respond to limit questions prompted by biological anthropology in light of theological anthropology is doubtless one of the most challenging and pressing issues in religion and science today.

ANTHROPOLOGY: THE HUMAN WORD ABOUT THE HUMAN BEING

That anthropological limit questions are of such profound importance to so many is in all likelihood due to the simple fact that by definition anthropology concerns itself with human self-understanding. As its Greek etymology suggests, anthropology is the reflective human "word about the human being," the never-ending attempt to answer the question that the human being itself poses. It is the study of humanity in all its diverse aspects, aiming at understanding the full sweep and complexity of human being across cultures and history. The results of anthropological research thus bear relevance for everyone regardless of creed or race.

Magnus Hundt first introduced the term *Antropologium* in 1501, but of course as self-reflective beings humans have always asked about the origin and meaning of their existence in some form or other. Already Paleolithic *Homo sapiens* addressed the anthropological question implicitly in creation myths, religious cults, and animistic art possibly more than 150,000 years ago. With the dawn of civilization the human question was asked more explicitly.[2] Socrates deemed the unexamined life "not worth living" and declared the ancient Apollonian imperative *Gnothi seauton* (Know thyself), of which Thales said that it was the most difficult of tasks, the goal of his philosophy—though not without simultaneously insisting that the only thing man can know is that he does not know anything. Medieval anthropology, creatively appropriating Platonic and Aristotelian ideas, took on a distinctly theological nature, viewing humanity as part of a hierarchical order of being that has its origin in God. By the time Hundt coined his *terminus technicus*, anthropology had already undergone a lengthy evolution.

One might say that modern anthropology had its origin in the work of Otto Casmann, who in *Psychologia anthropologica* (1594) divorced medieval anthropology from its Aristotelian metaphysical foundation and thereby opened the door for the budding natural sciences to partake where heretofore philosophy and theology had ruled alone. In 1928 Max Scheler wrote that the answer to the question "What is the human being?" emerges from the tension among three circles of ideas: the Judeo-Christian tradition (humanity created in the image of God), the Hellenistic tradition (self-consciousness elevates humanity to unique status), and the natural sciences (humanity as the product of evolution).[3] Though much has changed in theology, philosophy, and the natural sciences since then, the overall problem

Scheler faced remains the same: whether the three anthropological horizons—
theological, philosophical, and biological—can be coalesced into one coherent idea
of the human being. If so, the path to synthesis must involve an integration of
theological anthropology and biological anthropology catalyzed by philosophical
anthropology and metaphysics. Hence this essay addresses both the theological
and the biological anthropological endeavors before identifying several limit questions and presenting Rahnerian responses to them.

Theological Anthropology: Humanity vis-à-vis a Personal Creator God

A fundamental assumption of Judeo-Christian anthropology is that humanity is
in a special salutary relationship with God, a relationship characterized by the
God-given human uniqueness and a particular divine interest in the salvation of
human kind. Tradition has anchored this idea theologically in a short, somewhat
enigmatic Bible passage (Genesis 1:26–28), according to which God created the
human being in the divine image. For millennia theologians have grappled with
the possible meaning of this obscure text and proposed a plethora of possible readings. Most of them can be subsumed under one of three broad categories, each
highlighting the specific emphasis of its interpretations. Substantive interpretations view the divine image as a trait or property of the human being. In functional
interpretations it reflects our actions, particularly our dominion over the earth.
And in relational interpretations the image is found in the relationship with others
and with God. Virtually all proposals agree that the human being is the result of a
particular divine creation, which elevates humans above all other life in their
extraordinary relationship with God.

Roman Catholic teaching traditionally has favored an amalgamation of all three
readings. According to *Gaudium et Spes*, humanity is created in the divine image
insofar as humans are unities of body and soul capable of knowing and loving their
creator, thereby being elevated above all other creation, animate or inanimate.[4] By
means of its self-consciousness and reason, the human being shares in "the light
of the divine mind" and, as such, is capable of accepting the always already graciously extended divine invitation for unity with God. Only in this ultimate
personal relationship, the text continues, can humanity live according to truth
and find its fulfillment. This orientation toward communion as a human constitutive the conciliar document sees already expressed in the fact that humans were
created as women and men. Human reason not only elevates humanity over all
other creation, but also is the means by which, when in proper communion with
God and others, humans come to understand their responsibility toward the rest
of creation. To be created in the image of God, then, means to have cognitive and

affective capacities (substantive) that enable us to respond to God's invitation to communion (relational) and to act as God's stewards on Earth (functional).

As Thomas Rausch points out in his essay in this volume, humans are in a personal relationship with an absolutely transcendent and equally totally immanent God, who is pure, self-subsistent Being, forever mysterious, yet ever-present in unsurpassable nearness. This God not only created the cosmos out of nothing (*creatio ex nihilo*), but also maintains it in being (*creatio continua*). As such, God acts in the world in each and every moment, is deeply connected to the universe, and partakes in the life of all creatures within it. Like all creation, the human being is thus utterly dependent on God, even in its fundamental freedom to either accept or reject divine love. But free we are nevertheless. And with freedom, says *Gaudium et Spes*, comes a propensity for sin. The document insists that humanity has more often than not rejected God as the ultimate ground of being and thus disturbed the relationship with God. The doctrine of original sin traces this inclination to the very beginnings of humanity. For Rausch, the biblical story of the Fall hints at the selfishness that as a part of our biological inheritance subsists in us, inclines us toward evil, and requires salvation. Adam, as the first human, thus symbolizes the ambiguity of human nature as both graced yet flawed, which is overcome in Jesus of Nazareth as the new Adam, in whom the mystery of divine Love and humanity's ultimate calling is revealed and salvation is found.

Biological Anthropology: Homo sapiens as the Result of Evolution

Some biological anthropologists may share this theological assessment of being human, but they surely would not make exegesis or fundamental theology part of their investigation. Theirs is a professional commitment to a branch of biology that is concerned with the adaptations, variability, and evolution of human beings and their living and fossil relatives (figure 15-1). Consequently their method is empirical and, as such, reductionistic. The theoretical underpinning of their research project is Darwinian evolution.

Generally speaking, evolutionary theory explains biological diversity of species as the outcome of a gradual process of descent with modification from a common ancestor. Two opposing forces significantly drive this change in the frequency of heritable traits across one or more generations. On the one hand, novel variations in traits are constantly and randomly introduced to populations through genetic (mutations, recombination) and epigenetic (gene-environment interaction altering gene expression) changes. On the other hand, natural selection increases the frequency of beneficial characteristics while eliminating detrimental ones. The selection pressure prevents less successful variants from reproducing, thus allowing

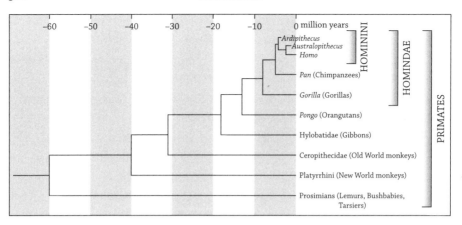

FIGURE 15.1 Primate phylogeny. Biological anthropology studies human beings in relationship to all other primates. Anthropological research places a particular emphasis on hominid evolution, including studies of extinct ancient species (paleoanthropology), as well as comparative investigations into behavior of extant species (cognitive ethology).

better adopted individuals to pass on their traits to future generations, thereby shaping the distribution of a trait within a population. As a directed process, natural selection produces adaptations that are well designed to function in a given ecological context. As Francisco Ayala once put it so eloquently, natural selection leads to design without a designer.

However, natural selection is only one mechanism of evolution, and therefore must not be conflated with evolution per se. Organisms are replete with structures that lack any discernable beneficial function, and yet they arose in the same evolutionary process. Adaptationists commonly view these as vestigial features that once evolved by natural selection to serve a purpose in an ancestral species. While this explanation certainly has merit in some instances (e.g., pelvic girdle in whales), in many other cases it amounts to little more than the untestable speculation that there was once an unknown function in an unknown environment. Another way to explain these features is to think of them as byproducts of the evolution of other traits, not unlike how spandrels in medieval basilicas result from the intersection of two rounded arches at right angles rather than the architect's decision to provide space for artistic decoration. An example of such a trait with significant evolutionary importance is human language, which many biologists consider the byproduct of the evolution of other cognitive capacities, primarily recursive thought.

The exact evolutionary history of humanity is shrouded in scientific mystery. Most paleoanthropologists agree that humans originated in Africa, but therein ends the consensus. For the past thirty years two conflicting theories have domi-

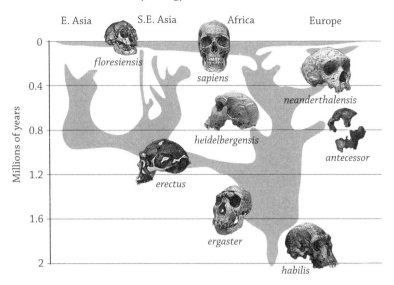

FIGURE 15.2 Temporal and geographical distribution of *Homo*. The genus *Homo* originated in Africa some 2.5 million years ago and subsequently migrated out of Africa repeatedly. At about 40,000 years ago, up to five *Homo* species may have lived side-by-side, resulting in limited interbreeding, at least in Europe.

nated the paleoanthropological debate. Proponents of the regional continuity model argue that the variation between modern humans is the result of an early and middle Pleistocene radiation of *Homo erectus* from Africa. Accordingly humanity evolved as a single, continuous human species over the past 1.7 to 1.9 million years, with local differentiation forming regional populations and gene flow preventing speciation. Advocates of the replacement model (also called the "Out of Africa" model) contend that *Homo sapiens* evolved once from an African ancestor (most likely *Homo heidelbergensis*) between 200,000 and 150,000 years ago and then, some 50,000 years ago, migrated via the Levant into Asia and subsequently into Europe and Australia (figure 15-2). There they replaced local populations of *Homo erectus* and other hominins such as the Neandertals (*Homo neanderthalensis*). In this scenario hominin evolution involved the coming and going of numerous species in at least two, possibly three genera (figure 15-3).

While substantial evidence supports the replacement model, recent fossil and DNA analyses favor a third model, known as the assimilation model. The replacement model predicts that due to their earlier divergence, African populations of *Homo sapiens* should exhibit the greatest genetic variation and show distinct frequencies for particular genes. Moreover the earliest fossils of *Homo sapiens* should occur in the continent of origin, Africa, whereas the youngest records should be found at the peripheries of the radiation. Empirical evidence so far

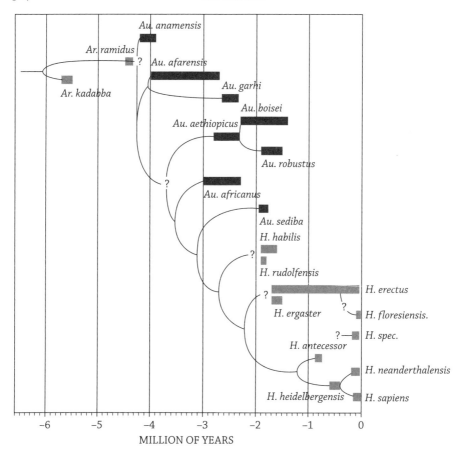

FIGURE 15.3 Possible evolutionary relationships and temporal distribution of three hominid genera. Biological anthropologists continuously debate the exact phylogenetic relationships among hominid species. The phylogenetic tree presented here divides the Hominini into two distinct genera, *Australopithecus* and *Homo*. Alternative analyses propose a third genus, *Paranthropus*, comprising three species (*P. aethipicus, P. boisei, P. robustus*). The present tree also presupposes either the replacement model ("Out of Africa") or assimilation model of human evolution, according to which *Homo sapiens* evolved from an ancestral species, most likely *Homo heidelbergensis* (sometimes also referred to as *H. rhodesiensis*).

supports both predictions. Recent studies have shown that the genetic difference between two Bushmen of the Khoisan community of the Kalahari Desert in South Africa is, on average, greater than between a European and an Asian individual. The oldest fossils of *Homo sapiens* were found in Africa and date back to some 160,000 years ago. Nevertheless analysis of the newly sequenced Neandertal genome shows that Europeans and Asians, but not Africans, share 1 to 4 percent of their nuclear DNA with Neandertals, suggesting that some interbreeding must have taken place when anatomically modern humans migrated into Europe from Asia about 80,000 years ago. At least in the case of Neandertals, then, *Homo sapiens* did not merely replace other humans, but to some extent assimilated them. And while DNA studies on other human species (e.g., *Homo erectus* and an unknown *Homo spec.* that lived in southern Siberia until 40,000 years ago) indicate no interbreeding, the Neandertal data clearly show that neither the regional continuity model nor the replacement model in the strict sense accurately captures human evolution.

Underlying the question of human evolutionary origins is a more fundamental issue of evolutionary biology, namely the problem of defining and recognizing species. Contrary to what a nonspecialist might think, what characterizes a species is notoriously difficult to say. In fact instead of one species concept evolutionary biologists operate with at least twenty-two distinct concepts. They all more or less share the notion that species are taxonomic ranks comprising individuals of similar distinguishing features. But morphological similarities alone are not good enough. Dogs, for example, come in many shapes and sizes, yet they still constitute the same species.

Ernst Mayr introduced the biological species concept, which defines a species as "a reproductive community of populations (reproductively isolated from others) that occupies a specific niche in nature."[5] Although this definition works well in many situations, it nevertheless fails in such cases of asexually reproducing organisms, ring species, or chronospecies.[6] Others therefore view species as statistical phenomena, where a species is defined as a separately evolving lineage that forms a single gene pool. Such issues indicate that a pressing question of evolutionary biology today is whether "species" is actually an ontological category or an epistemological one. Either way, the question for paleoanthropologists is at what point one can truly speak of "humans."

ANTHROPOLOGICAL LIMIT QUESTIONS: ASKING BEYOND THE SCOPE OF BIOLOGY

In light of theological anthropology, the biological description of the human being raises a variety of questions transcending the scientific realm. First are those regarding creation. How can divine creation and human evolution be compatible? One might say that if God created humanity, God did so through evolution. But this merely begs the question of how to envision the divine concurrence in the biological process. Underlying this specific question is the more general one of how God acts in an evolving world. What is needed to respond appropriately is a metaphysical account of becoming that integrates theological concepts with biological ones.

Second are questions about the nature of the salvific relationship between the human being and God. Christian anthropology insists on the uniqueness of the human being insofar as no other creature is in the same type of personal relationship with the divine. Given the biological data, one might ask: Which human being? Up to about 40,000 years ago *Homo sapiens* may have lived side-by-side with as many as four other human species. Were they all in the same personal relationship with God? And if so, why did they go extinct, possibly replaced by anatomically modern humans who outcompeted them in the struggle for resources?

This brings up the third set of questions, which address the issue of natural evil. Why does biological evolution bring with it such immense suffering? From a theological perspective, this limit question can be put thus: How could an omnipotent, omniscient, and most of all omnibenevolent God responsible for the creation of humans through evolution let some of these humans go extinct? And why choose evolution, a process involving disease, pain, death, and even natural catastrophes, as the means by which to create the diversity of life, human or nonhuman?

The following presents Rahner's proposal for answering the first two sets of questions. It also includes my attempt to answer the third set of questions in a theodicy that operates from within a Rahnerian perspective.

HOMINIZATION: BECOMING HUMAN THROUGH ACTIVE SELF-TRANSCENDENCE

Initial Catholic responses to Charles Darwin's *On the Origin of Species* (1859) were ambivalent at best, ranging from open-minded interest (e.g., Cardinal Newman, M. D. Léroy) to condemnation in no uncertain terms (Provincial Council of Cologne in 1860). Overall, however, the Church was reluctant to make any authoritative pronouncements on the issue. In the 1950 encyclical *Humanis generis* Pope Pius XII finally declared the study of evolution completely in accordance with Catholic teaching, so long as it is done by "men experienced in both fields" (i.e., theology and evolutionary biology) and "inquires into the *origin of the human body coming from pre-existent and living matter*" only.[7] Concerning the creation of the soul, Pius merely restated the long-held opinion that as a spiritual substance it could not originate in matter and instead must be created immediately by God. Not surprisingly, this decoupling of matter and spirit inasmuch as their origins are concerned was problematic for those who argued for the substantial unity of body and soul.

For Rahner, such a "moderate evolutionism," which explores the biological origins of the human being while abstaining from comprehensive statements about ultimate human reality, is hardly an adequate solution to the anthropological problem. He asks how we can speak of soul and body in such a way that, unlike *Humani generis*, it does not sound like a "lazy compromise between a theological and scientific statement."[8] His own proposal of a theology of becoming begins, therefore, with a dual-aspect monist description of spirit and matter. Pointing out that for Christianity everything that is, material and spiritual, has its origin in God, he concludes that all observable diversity is united by similarities rather than divided by differences. The world as a whole has *one* origin, *one* self-realization, and *one* determination. Matter and spirit are not disparate entities, but two aspects of the same reality. What is evolving, then, is spirit-matter as a unity in difference.

At work here is the Aristotelian-Thomistic theory of potentiality and actuality, according to which every substance has an informing principle, the substantial form, which actualizes the substance's primary matter and thus makes it what it is. By itself the primary matter is no more than a possibility-of-being that is empty and undefined. Every concrete being, humans included, is the actualized being of a particular possibility-of-being, or, as Rahner puts it, *beseelter Leib und leibhaftiger Geist* (spirited body and embodied spirit). The evolution of new being thus does not simply refer to change as the natural sciences would describe it—for example, the evolution of *Bauplans* or the developmental changes during ontogenesis—but more precisely the emergence of substantially new being as such.

Taking a cue from the scholastic notion of the *scala naturae* (great chain of being), Rahner sees evolutionary becoming as an increase in being. Being, he holds, is less a distinctly determinable entity than a progression of actualization of self-presence. What characterizes the intensity of being of a thing is dictated by its ability to be present to itself in self-knowledge. In other words, the more self-conscious a being, the more fully being is actualized in it. Thus a stone has less self-presence than a dog, which in turn is less fully actualized being than a human. At the end of this succession is absolute being, which constitutes the perfectly perfect union of being and knowledge that is entirely self-present without any interaction with others. Such a being without any limit and total independence is of course no other than God. Evolutionary becoming for Rahner is the transition from one degree of actualized being to a greater one. It is the evolution of spirit-matter in an increasing actualization of self-presence.

While biology finds no directionality in the evolutionary process, this metaphysical account assumes as much on the basis of the nature of being and the constant movement from the earliest form of spirit-matter to complex life forms capable of conscious self-reflection. However, it is important to point out that this direction is not toward the human being per se, but rather toward self-consciousness, and thus toward spiritual beings in personal relationship with the divine. This is what Rahner means when he says that matter by virtue of its inner constitution develops toward spirit. In this process of becoming, spirit-matter assumes a greater fullness of being, which constitutes simply an increase in self-presence. To Rahner, this becoming is true self-transcendence, where in surpassing itself a being actively achieves its own fullness. How are we to envision this active self-transcendence, and what is God's role in it?

Pivotal to Rahner's solution are two scholastic principles. One is the idea that every becoming of new being in the world is always the actualization of a new form that heretofore had been present only potentially in an already existing being, a notion expressed in the formula *eductio e potentia materiae*, the drawing forth from the potentiality of matter. The other is the concept of the *concursus divinus*, the divine concurrence, which points to the fact that God as the transcendent constitutive enables the finite being to actively assume fuller actualized being. Therefore becoming in the world is always the bringing forth of a new substantial form through the actualization of that which is potentially already present in the subjacent by means of both creaturely and divine agency (figure 15-4).

In its original form, the *eductio* suggests that a substantially new principle of being present in a finite concrete being as potentiality is actualized efficiently under the influence of an internal or external finite agent. What makes this idea problematic is that it implies vitalism and that it reduces divine action to just

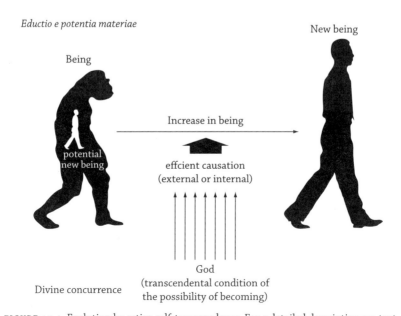

FIGURE 15.4 Evolution by active self-transcendence. For a detailed description see text.

another efficient cause. The reason Rahner nevertheless thinks the concept helpful is its emphasis on becoming as an increase in being. Moreover it implies that in becoming a finite being actively surpasses itself and assumes a new substantial reality. Yet this active self-transcendence cannot come about solely by the powers of the becoming finite being, or else the finite being would give more than it possesses, violating the principle of causality. To resolve this issue, Rahner casts the divine concurrence in a transcendental fashion, where the divine absolute being acts immanently in the finite being as the necessary condition of the possibility of its self-transcendence.

It might help to follow Rahner's reasoning regarding the actual nature of the divine participation that enables active self-transcendence. Simply put, the challenge is to maintain the free act of the finite being under the influence of divine grace, while simultaneously affirming its dependence on divine grace in the first place. It is the same question that in the sixteenth century dominated the controversy about efficacious grace between the Dominican Domingo Bañez and the Jesuits Luis de Molina and Francisco Suárez. For Bañez and his followers, God as highest cause moves every finite cause to its proper acts. While this assures divine agency, in Rahner's opinion here the freedom of the individual is little more than mere postulate. Molina and Suárez, in contrast, argued that divine action cooperates with creaturely efficient causation to produce the overall outcome. Here divine agency neither precedes the acts of a creature nor gives it any directionality, so that the individual freedom of the finite being is safely in place. The problem is that this view violates the principle of causality. By regarding divine action as the underlying necessary condition of active self-transcendence, Rahner opts for a both-and rather than an either-or.

The notion of divine concurrence as necessary condition presumes that God as pure act precontains all reality and belongs to the constitution of the finite cause *as such*, without being its *intrinsic constituent*. God gives the UV radiation that brings about a gene mutation being, but God is not part of that radiation. Therefore it takes both, God as ultimate and UV radiation as efficient cause, to prompt a gene mutation that in turn actualizes the heretofore only potential new being of an organism.

Rahner summarizes his philosophy of becoming in four ontological theses. First, becoming is always, by its very constitution, a self-exceeding and not a replication. Second, this self-transcendence is made possible by the absolute being immanently at work within the becoming finite being as fundamental cause and ground of this becoming. Third, the essence of the self-transcending finite being does not limit what can become through this self-transcendence. It does, however, show that something more has to become, and moreover that the starting point of this movement limits the possibility of what can become immediately of the self-transcending finite being. Fourth, these principles can be applied to the developing of matter toward spirit.

With his concept of active self-transcendence, Rahner has managed to provide a metaphysical perspective that allows him to wed Aristotelian essentialism with biological evolution while avoiding dualism (matter and spirit as separate entities), reductionistic materialism (spirit or consciousness emerges from matter), or vitalism (life as the result of an extrinsic principle). This, in and of itself, is a major achievement. But more to the point, Rahner shows how becoming and ensoulment can be reconciled in a comprehensive metaphysics rather than a lazy compromise. That is, he has answered the first limit question: how we are to envision creation and evolution in an integrated fashion. Which brings me to the second limit question: What constitutes the salvific personal relationship between God and creature, and what creatures are in fact in such a relationship with the divine?

SALVATION THROUGH A PERSONAL RELATIONSHIP WITH GOD

One can summarize Rahner's theological project thus: Rahner seeks to explore the nature of the personal relationship between God and human being as the very core of our being and our salvation.

As Rahner sees it, this relationship is characterized first and foremost by the always present divine self-communication, an ontological act of grace in which God gives Godself to the human being and thereby instills in him the desire for union with God. It is not a relationship that takes place only in religious practices, like prayer and communion, but because it is so much an intrinsic part of who we are unfolds in every moment of our existence. Hence, whether we realize it or not, we are always already related to God. One might say, therefore, that Rahner creatively appropriates the view of the thirteenth-century Franciscan Duns Scotus that God created the universe in order to communicate Godself and that creation exists to receive God's free self-gift. By asking how this relationship plays out, and moreover how the ontological structure of human cognition constitutes the precondition for its possibility, Rahner makes anthropology the starting point and heart of his theology.

As self-conscious beings, humans ask the question about the nature and meaning of their existence and that of all beings. They do so not out of mere intellectual curiosity or because they have nothing better to do, but because asking the question about being as such (the *Seinsfrage*) in order to find meaning in their existence is an inescapable aspect of the human ontological constitution. To be human, Rahner argues, is to reach beyond the concrete objects of one's sense experiences toward the underlying "beingness" as it applies to all things, oneself included. In fact, that we ask about the meaning of our own being is no less than the result of personal self-reflection on what Rahner calls the "original experience" of our very concrete self in the world. But the human capacity to ask about our own existence in a self-conscious, self-present way is somewhat peculiar: no answer is ever exhaustive and instead conjures up only more and larger questions. We are literally to ourselves an infinite horizon of questions that expands with every answer to the *Seinsfrage* we may put forward. In Rahner's eyes, the ability to question everything, to always reach beyond all that can be expressed in one way or another, is evidence that we are embodied spirits and reveals our transcendental constitution.

When Rahner calls the human being the transcendent being it is because of our never-ending openness toward more being with which we question what is before us. In fact all human knowledge and conscious actions are grounded in this preapprehension (or, as Rahner calls it, *Vorgriff*) with which we reach for the beingness of all beings. We can grasp the concrete beings we encounter only against the underlying infinite horizon of absolute being. Unlike the twentieth-century philosopher Martin Heidegger, Rahner insists that the whereunto of the preapprehension cannot be nothingness—the final result of a life lived toward death—but rather absolute being. Hence he concludes that the *Vorgriff* goes unto God.

It follows that every concrete, categorical experience embraces a second, transcendental experience of absolute being that results in an unthematic knowledge of God. This is such a radical move on Rahner's part that it deserves repeating. With every experience of a concrete object in the world—be it a coffee mug, the family dog, or ourselves—we are brought before the Holy Mystery that is God. In order to articulate this transcendental experience, one has to use symbolic representation and, ultimately, language. But of course such an attempt to capture the absolute transcendent in categorical terms is bound to fail; for one, because our language is insufficient to articulate the ineffable, but also because any such categorical expression would immediately be scrutinized by our preapprehension. Every reflection on the content of transcendental experience glimpses God as a receding horizon that, though always ever-present, nonetheless remains ultimately unreachable. God is present to us in every moment of our life, yet remains shrouded in mystery.

One cannot help but notice how for Rahner self-consciousness is closely entangled with being transcendentally conditioned and therefore being aware of God. This transcendental consciousness that leads to an unthematic knowledge of the divine is part and parcel of any being capable of inquiring about the meaning of its existence and placing itself in question. However, Rahner disagrees with thinkers such as Henri de Lubac, for whom transcendental consciousness, and with it the human orientation toward God, is a natural existential that could have come about through biological evolution. Rather he insists that the grace of God acts by instilling the desire for the union with God on human *natura pura*. To be sure, Rahner holds that this grace is never withheld nor given only after a person has proven herself worthy by living a virtuous life. It is always already present from the very moment an individual comes to be. Thus, phenomenologically speaking, there is no difference between de Lubac's and Rahner's proposals; in either case, human being is always laced with divine grace.

Rahner sees the ontological act in which God makes Godself the constitutive element of human being at the very beginning of every human life as the expression of the personal relationship between God and human being and calls it the divine self-communication. It is the gratuitous unowed self-gift of God that instigates within the human being the desire for union with God not as a natural, but as a *super*natural existential. It is precisely because of God's free act on our *natura pura* that quasi-formally causes us to be ordered toward God that the desire for unity with God becomes a human existential. In other words, just as a form informs the being of a thing, so God informs our being to desire God. The significant difference is that God maintains absolute freedom and independence, as opposed to becoming part of human being, as a substantial form in the strict sense would. Hence Rahner envisions the divine self-communication as being a quasi-formal cause for the supernatural existential, which can therefore be seen as the divine self-communication in the form of offer. This is what Rahner means when he says that the human being is the "event of God's self-communication." To bring it to the point, the personal relationship between a self-conscious subject and God rests in the divine self-communication as the quasi-formal cause of creaturely desire to be in union with God, which in itself is the necessary condition for a subject's openness for revelation both in the transcendental experience as well as in history. All beings in personal relationship with God, then, are events of God's self-communication.

Rahner's answer to the second limit question identifies salvation first and foremost with the personal relationship between self-conscious creature and God as an event of God's self-communication. But as was pointed out earlier, the movement of cosmic and biological evolution is not directed to *Homo sapiens* per se, but to all self-present life. The problem of which human species was the first one to be in a personal relationship with God comes down to the question of which human species was self-conscious. Space limitations prohibit a detailed answer, but let it suffice to say that archaeological evidence overwhelmingly suggests that this was true for all *Homo* species. Moreover empirical evidence suggests that even some nonhuman animals possess self-cognizance at the level of conscious self-reflection. If one adopts Rahner's transcendental approach, it follows that all these species are in their very own, species-specific way events of God's self-communication.[9]

What does this say about the nature of God? Of the ten or so *Homo* species, only *sapiens* is still extant; nine species are extinct. Given the likelihood that earlier hominins like the *Australopithecines* and *Ardipithecines* were also self-conscious, the number of extinct species that once were in personal relationship with the divine increases. Aside from the suffering that is intrinsic to the evolutionary process, this outlook raises the very disturbing question of why an all-powerful, all-knowing, and all-loving God would allow for those events of divine self-communication to suffer extinction.

EVOLUTIONARY SUFFERING: NATURAL EVIL AND AN ALL-LOVING GOD

For the believer, the theory of evolution doubtless exacerbates the problem of evil in a world created by a benign, loving God, who is in personal relationship with every one of us. It is an undeniable fact that the suffering of innocent life is not only unavoidable but also necessary for life to exist and evolve. Predation, diseases, genetic mutations, earthquakes, and supernovae—all are absolutely indispensable for life to emerge and subsequently assume greater complexity. Given the traditional Christian belief in an all-loving and all-powerful God who is concerned compassionately with the agony of even the lowest of creatures, this seems quite scandalous. If God is infinitely powerful, God must be able to abolish all natural evil; if God is perfectly good, God must want to eradicate evil. But because evil exists one must ask with Epicurus and Hume: Whence natural evil?

A common response to this question is exemplified by Francisco Ayala's theodic proposal, which casts natural evil as the inevitable outcome of a trade-off between cosmic creativity and creaturely suffering.[10] A creative, evolving universe, the argument goes, is simply fundamentally more desirable to God than an unchanging one. Yet God could not have created a world that is both creatively developing *and* devoid of the struggle and ordeals that mark nature. Hence, all things considered, the universe we live in is the best possible world, even with the immense suffering of innocent life.

Another, equally common approach views evolutionary suffering as the price for the possibility of love. Most love defenses address the issue of moral evil, arguing in an Augustinian vein that in order for an agent to make virtuous decisions there has to be freedom of choice, and consequently the not unlikely possibility of moral agents choosing wrongly.[11] Others, like John Hick in his famous thesis of "soul-making," reason that it is in the encounter with all kinds of suffering, including natural suffering, that humans can surpass themselves and develop truly virtuous qualities, first and foremost the ability to love others and God.[12] In other words, for Hick natural evil exists as a necessary means to the end of human virtuousness. The problem with these two models is that one contradicts common concepts of God, whereas the other undermines its original objective by being overly anthropocentric. Ayala's model implies that for God the welfare of the universe outweighs that of the individual being, which is diametrically opposed to the traditional notion that God is invested in the existence of every creature, whether animated or not, sentient or nonsentient. And in Hick's utilitarian developmental defense all creaturely agony serves only one purpose: the spiritual growth of humanity. In a final analysis, both theodic avenues fail to achieve their goal and leave us with equally, if not more severe problems than we set out with.

An alternative love defense could be one that radically accentuates love as the divine principle and sees suffering as a necessary condition of the possibility of the full actualization of love.[13] To avoid misunderstandings, such a transcendental approach suggests neither that love requires suffering to exist, nor that one should seek out suffering in the hope of a greater capacity for love. Instead it holds that suffering can deepen love and facilitate its growth to its fullest potential. Thus the good that comes at the price of natural evil is neither the universe nor human morality, but love itself.

How to envision this fuller actualization of love? The answer to this question rests in the multiple dimensions of love. Hellenistic philosophy differentiated between *eros*, the ascending, longing love that is drawn by someone or something, and the descending, giving, and kenotic love called *agape*.[14] Though distinctly different, *eros* and *agape* are nevertheless inseparable aspects of all love. As Pope Benedict XVI points out in his first encyclical letter, the more the two find a proper unity, "*the more the true nature of love in general is realized.*"[15] Ergo, love is fully actualized only when both *agape* and *eros* are thoroughly present and in a healthy balance, with the former informing the latter. It is in achieving both that suffering can play an intricate role.

That said, an interesting problem concerning the relationship between creation and the full realization of love arises. *Eros* as genuine love of the other requires a wholly other as the object of its passion; without that other, *eros* cannot be. This implies that prior to the creation of the world as the object of God's passionate love, the divine *eros* existed merely as potentiality. Only in the self-giving act of

God creating the cosmos out of nothing is *eros* actualized for the first time. This, then, could be the foundation of a cosmic theodicy that goes right to the core of natural evil, namely the most basic physical makeup of the universe.[16] In order for the other to be truly *other*, God had to release creation into freedom, that is, active self-transcendence. Without that, the cosmos would be little more than a creation in which God is focused on God's own creativity instead of the other's self. This would be neither *eros* nor *agape*, but a form of divine narcissism, an attribute incompatible with Christian doctrines of God. Instead the efficient causes that bring forth new being (emergent realities realizing their potential) are, so to speak, set up to achieve this freedom and allow for cosmic evolution to produce the wholly other necessary for *eros* to emerge and love to assume fuller actuality.

But how does suffering factor into the equation? Releasing creation into free self-fulfillment constitutes a painful separation, which analogically speaking is very much like the grief parents suffer as they allow their children to grow into independent people. Parents are fully aware of the potential dangers that await children on their journey into adulthood, and with helpless realization of their own diminishing control they cannot but permit their children to explore their path freely. To interfere at any point of potential hazard will prevent this process from unfolding and essentially stifle love before it can flourish. In an analogical sense, God creates the world so that it can shape itself through a process of true becoming, but this act of infinite love is associated with the painful awareness that there will be hardships on the way. To quote John Taylor, "The bewilderment is greater for the one who is walking away but the pain is almost certainly worse for the one who, out of love and knowing the hazards, lets go."[17] But let go God must, just like any other parent, or else love as the true union between God and creature as wholly other is forfeited. Therefore divine suffering is indeed the necessary precondition for love to grow into something more full and rich than it was prior to the existence of the wholly other.[18]

With the emergence in cosmic evolution of self-conscious beings, sentient love enters the picture and the question becomes how suffering can help sentient love to become more fully realized. For Hick, suffering is the way sentient beings become aware of God and grow spiritually, but if one adopts Rahner's view of the human transcendental constitution, we always already are spiritual and in relationship with God. Hence self-conscious beings do not have to suffer in order to become capable of love, but rather to transform their initially *eros*-dominated love into a balanced love informed by *agape*. What renders sentient love substantially marked by *eros* is the structure of consciousness. No matter how much one extends oneself to another, one always experiences pleasure and personal fulfillment. Self-love is thus always a potential aspect of sentient love. Yet under circumstances challenging sentient beings existentially either in their personal being or in their relationship with others, love can deepen through a transformative strengthening of the agapic over the erotic element. In such times of suffering, what assures that love is more fully actualized is the conscious choice on the part of the sufferer for love despite the risk of further impending pain. Think, for example, of the transition from "being in love," a mostly *eros*-dominated passion, into "loving" as a more mature and agapic love, a process that usually is marked by crisis painfully experienced as the loss of the blissful ease of young love. In that sense, then, suffering signifies the passage into the proper unity of love, in which the true nature of love can be more fully realized, just as Pope Benedict XVI suggested.

This movement from *eros* to *agape* seems to be the underlying theme of all sentient existence that finds its completion only in the final moment of its earthly existence. Popular imagination sees death as the grim reaper tearing us violently from life into nothingness, but for Rahner it constitutes the ultimate salvific moment. It is in death that we are left with nothing but the freedom to submit to God in absolute trust and love, thereby committing the final act of self-actualization. This final act of freedom that completes us in God seems to me to be nothing less than the final transition of human love from *eros* into full *agape*. It is this salvific instance of giving ourselves not for our sake, but for the sake of love as the divine all-encompassing principle, that we are taken up into divine love. Love has now come full circle and is finally actualized to its fullest potential.

No theodicy ever succeeds in explaining evil sufficiently, and the same holds true for the love defense presented here. Nevertheless the present proposal might at least help to shed some light on how the existence of evolutionary evil can be meaningfully reconciled with a God who created life to communicate to creatures the fullness of divine love. Species extinction as much as individual death in this context is not something God chooses, but something that results from the intrinsic freedom of the system (the *eductio e potentia materiae*) and something God has to allow in order for love to be. Only in fully actualized love is salvation of all being guaranteed and creation brought to full union with God.

CONCLUSIONS

In this chapter I set out to investigate how the Catholic intellectual tradition can contribute to a synthesis of theological and biological anthropology. I singled out Karl Rahner's transcendental theology as a particularly fertile approach that on the one hand maintains the methodological independence of both disciplines, and on the other hand integrates them philosophically into a new understanding of human existence vis-à-vis a personal Creator God.

Rahner's concept of becoming as active self-transcendence maintains premises absolutely fundamental to evolutionary biology, such as the potential open-endedness of the process (*Homo sapiens* still evolves), the essential role scientifically quantifiable efficient causes play in the becoming of new being, and the lack of a predetermined outcome in the strict sense. Simultaneously it preserves important theological and philosophical axioms like the absolute transcendence and immanence of God, the salvific nature of the personal relationship between God and self-present being, and the directionality of cosmic becoming as the unfolding of a divine plan (i.e., Dun Scotus's notion of creation). Many scientists may not share Rahner's metaphysical presuppositions and therefore find his overall proposal less than appealing, but those who do agree with him on the nature of being will easily see the potential his proposal holds.

Much more can and should be said regarding the work of other Catholic thinkers and their influence on contemporary biology. My concern in this essay, however, has been to present one particularly fruitful perspective that opens up avenues for future research. Here Rahner's transcendental approach is exceptional and his perspective offers a path into some of the most difficult issues in religion and science today.

But his is more than just a powerful model of interdisciplinary thinking that may generate research questions in theological anthropology. Rahner's integration and its metaphysical underpinnings could also shape research questions in behavioral and evolutionary biology. More than anything, his proposal hints at the directionality of the evolutionary process toward the complexification of self-cognizance and the emergence of self-consciousness. This directionality should not be narrowly conceived as moving from earliest life forms toward human beings, but toward self-conscious beings as events of God's self-communication. If true, this overall movement of becoming should be detectable by the biological sciences. The fact that a form of self-consciousness is present in nonhuman primates and some other animals suggests that self-consciousness is indeed the product of convergent evolution. Rahner may have more to offer biology than biologists currently suspect.

NOTES

1. Among others, three problems stand out in Teilhard's integration of theology and science. First, his Omega Point concept conflates theology and science methodologically, thereby committing a category mistake that is ultimately problematic. Second, the notion that the physical universe is developing toward the Omega Point (i.e., Christ) has panentheist undertones that jeopardize the transcendence of God and are in conflict with traditional doctrines

of God. Third, his approach is a form of mysticism rather than a systematically and formally developed theology. Rahner's integration of theology and science maintains the methodological independence of both disciplines, stays clear of any panentheist tendencies, and succeeds in providing a comprehensive worldview to which both fields contribute equally. For Teilhard's perspective, see primarily P. T. de Chardin, *The Human Phenomenon* (Eastbourne, U.K.: Sussex Academic Press, 2003); P.T. de Chardin, *Christianity and Evolution* (New York: Mariner Books, 2002).

2. Given this essay's objective, I focus first and foremost on the Western tradition. Of course, quite similar developments took place in other cultures, as illustrated by the Indus Valley civilization of western India and or Chinese Mohism.

3. Max Scheler, *Die Stellung des Menschen im Kosmos* (1928; Bonn: Bouvier Verlag, 2007), 9.

4. *Gaudium et Spes*, chapter 1, in *Vatican Council II*, vol. 1, *The Conciliar and Post Conciliar Documents*, new revised ed., edited by A. Flannery (Northport, N.Y.: Costello, 2004).

5. Ernst Mayr, *The Growth of Biological Thought: Diversity, Evolution, and Inheritance* (Cambridge, Mass.: Belknap Press, 1982), 273.

6. Ring species are species with a geographic distribution that forms a ring and overlaps at the end. Adjacent populations are capable of interbreeding and producing fertile offspring, except for the extreme ends of the range. Assuming the biological species concept, where would one draw the line between new and old species? Similarly chronospecies present a problem for the biological species concept. These are species that change over time so that at one point the ancestral originator of the lineage can no longer be considered the same species as its direct descendent. At what point in time, then, can one speak of a new species?

7. Pius XII, *Humani Generis: On Evolution and Other Modern Errors* (1950), 36, www.papalencyclicals.net/Pius12/P12HUMAN.HTM, my emphasis.

8. Karl Rahner, "Die Hominisation als theologische Frage," in P. Overhage and K. Rahner, *Das Problem der Hominisation: Über den biologischen Ursprung des Menschen, Questiones Disputatae* 12/13 (Freiburg i. Br.: Herder, 1961), 56, my translation. (Boston: Pauline Press, 2006), 135, footnote 1.

9. O. Putz, "Moral Apes, Human Uniqueness, and the Image of God," John Paul, II, *Man and Woman He Created Them*, 2006), 159. *Zygon* 44, no. 3 (2009): 613–24.

10. F. Ayala, "Darwin's Gift to Science and Religion: Commentaries and Responses," *Theology and Science* 6, no. 2 (2008): 179–96.

11. St. Augustine, *On Free Choice of the Will*, translated by Thomas Williams (Indianapolis: Hackett, 1993).

12. J. Hick, *Evil and the God of Love*, reissued 2nd ed. (Houndmills, U.K.: Palgrave Macmillan, 2007).

13. O Putz, "Love Actually: A Theodicy Response to Suffering in Nature. In Dialogue with Francisco Ayala," *Theology and Science* 7, no. 4 (2009): 345–61.

14. Eros, of course, includes physical but also many other forms of love. What characterizes all erotic love is its ascending nature, that is, that the love is drawn toward a person or thing. Agape, on the other hand, is a love that desires to empty itself for the benefit of the beloved. The erotic love referred to here is obviously not love of a physical, but nevertheless of a passionate nature.

15. Benedict XVI, *Deus Caritas Est*, encyclical letter, part 1, 2006, 7, www.vatican.va/holy_father/benedict_xvi/encyclicals/documents/hf_ben-xvi_enc_20051225_deus-caritas-est_en.html, my emphasis.

16. The reason biological evolution can result in increasingly complex organization instead of deteriorating into complete disarray (entropy) is that organisms are local *open* systems. As such, they lose energy to and have to take up energy from their environment. The necessity for predation therefore is already built into the physical laws of the universe, particularly the second law of thermodynamics, which states that the entropy of an *isolated* system that is not in equilibrium will tend to increase over time.

17. J. V. Taylor, *The Christlike God*, 2nd ed. (London: SCM Press, 2004), 190.

18. Whether or not God can suffer is a long-disputed question of Christian theology. Some consider God impassible and immutable, which precludes any notion of divine suffering. For them, the suffering of God is not a helpful theodic perspective, but rather one that seems to undermine the total transcendence of God. According to thinkers like Johann Baptist Metz, suffering is not a sign of love, but of the inability to love. Moreover the idea of a suffering God is not helpful psychologically, insofar as it simply does not justify the existence of evil and suffering. Rahner certainly did not subscribe to the notion of a suffering God. Others, however, find it impossible to envision God to be entirely unmoved by human acts. Their argument is that love is by no means a one-way relationship, and that if God is indeed love, the beloved too must affect God, particularly when the beloved suffers. Thus a love that remains unaffected by the beloved is hardly worth being called love, and the one who cannot suffer cannot love. The notion of a suffering God reemerged dramatically in the theological responses to the horrific wars of the nineteenth and twentieth century.

SELECTED READINGS

Edwards, Denis. *The God of Evolution: A Trinitarian Theology*. New York: Paulist Press, 1999.

Haught, John F. *God after Darwin: A Theology of Evolution*. Boulder, Colo.: Westview Press, 2000.

O'Leary, Don. *Roman Catholicism and Modern Science: A History*. London: Continuum, 2007.

Rahner, Karl. *Hominization: The Evolutionary Origin of Man as a Theological Problem. Questiones Disputatae* 13, translated by W. J. O'Hara. New York: Herder and Herder, 1965.

Zycinski, Jozef. *God and Evolution: Fundamental Questions of Christian Evolutionism*. Washington, DC: Catholic University of America Press, 2006.

16

Environmental Studies in a Catholic Framework

Elaine C. Grose

BOTH CATHOLICS AND non-Catholics draw on the Catholic intellectual tradition as a source of knowledge, faith, and the reflections of believing communities. The tradition is a rich resource and a storehouse of understanding and insight. As such, it provides a solid foundation for building honest societies and guiding people and institutions in the wise use of resources.

The important theological and philosophical insights inherent in certain components of the Catholic tradition have particular implications for higher education and learning and provide a foundation for better understanding the contribution modern science makes to our world. These include (1) commitment to the continuity between faith and reason, (2) respect for the cumulative wisdom of the past, and (3) attention to the community dimension of all human behavior.[1] Theology and philosophy also help us understand the strengths and limits of science in the human quest for knowledge and truth. The focus in this chapter is on the responsibility society has to harbor, preserve, and nurture natural resources for future generations.

Essential to our tradition is the conviction that the world makes sense and the human mind has the capacity to understand it. Through faith, reason, and education, people find meaning in God's creation and understand God's revealed world, which then leads to a greater love of God and all things of God.

As Lawrence Cunningham noted in his essay, early Christian doctrine held that God was the author of two texts: the Book of God (the Bible) and the Book of

Nature. The two sources of revelation were completely compatible, meaning that, given the right interpretative tools, the eternal truths of God's design, legible in nature, did not contradict the Bible, nor did the revelation about the way God acted in special ways with Israel and through his Son, Jesus Christ, do violence to nature. In a spiritual reflection, Basil Pennington, a Trappist monk and priest, observed, "The whole of creation bespeaks its Maker. As the Greeks would say, the whole of creation is full of logoi, little words... it all speaks of God, gives expression to the Word."[2]

The medieval world understood nature as the direct work of God. For them, the stars in the sky and the leaves on the trees were signs and symbols that signified the Creator's absolute authorship. Writing in the twelfth century, Hugh of St. Victor reminded his contemporaries that the true Christian continually seeks understanding. Much as modern scientists try to uncover general laws that apply to much of the physical universe, Hugh said Christians should seek deeper meaning in nature. They should seek to penetrate the outward appearance of things in order to recover God's meaning. A divine plan could be discovered, perhaps more clearly with the centuries, because for Hugh and his contemporaries the whole visible world was a book written by the finger of God, created by divine power.

Hugh of St. Victor reflected a long Christian tradition in which St. Augustine (354–430) stands as a towering figure near its beginning. Augustine, a great reader and writer of books, encouraged the faithful to be good readers of a book that was all around them. "Look above you! Look below you! Note it. Read it," he said. "God, whom you want to discover, never wrote that book with ink. Instead He set before your eyes the things that He had made. Can you ask for a louder voice than that?"[3]

Many centuries later Martin Luther, adhering closely to Augustine, his theological mentor, said, "All creation is the most beautiful book or bible, for in it God has described and portrayed Himself."[4] In Catholic spirituality we are taught to see God in all things. What is insufficiently emphasized is that seeking God in all things means exploring the true nature of things. Whether or not they believe in God, scientists seek the deeper laws in nature, the common ways in which chemicals, cells, oceans, and celestial bodies interact. For Christians, such discoveries do not undermine God's plan; rather, the laws of nature that are constantly being refined by scientists often help us to better appreciate the scale and magnitude of God's plan.

Environmental studies is one of the youngest of the academic fields at the university level. Because it embraces a number of other disciplines in the natural, social, and spiritual sciences, it is an academic field rather than a particular discipline. It seeks to explain the conditions under which the environment changes, develops, and sustains itself. No such thing as Christian environmental studies exists, nor is it being proposed in this essay. Nevertheless, like the other sciences, environmental studies is important for all Christians because it helps people understand the Book of Nature.

BIBLICAL CONCERN FOR THE ENVIRONMENT

Environmental studies begins by describing the world in terms of atoms, elements, compounds, and matter. But in order to explore the many feedback relationships that exist in the environment, environmental scientists rely on results from various branches of science. They develop complex mathematical models to explore the capacity of various approaches to explain how the environment has developed until now and how it will likely unfold in the future. All this is done without any explicit reference to creation.

Because environmental studies necessarily considers the past and the ways Earth's environment has developed over hundreds of millions of years, it draws on various models of evolution. For at least fifty years most theologians have deemed scientific evolution to be compatible with Catholic doctrine, though for many years scientific evolution was separated from Catholic understanding of creation. Over the past several decades, however, Catholic theologians have sought ways to take seriously an evolutionary framework and explain how Catholic theology is compatible with such a worldview. John F. Haught, a Roman Catholic theologian at Georgetown University, has explored this area in several recent books and essays. He writes, "Evolutionary science has changed our understanding of the world dramatically . . . and so any sense we may have of a God who creates and cares for this world must take into account what Darwin and his followers have told us about it."[5] He argues that evolutionary theory is actually a gift to theology because the very vastness of evolution in time, space, and energy prods theologians to appreciate the vast initiative involved in creation. Indeed evolution prods theologians to examine once again, with the benefit of a modern understanding of the development of the world, the implicit metaphysics embedded in the Bible's account of God's creative acts.

For Haught, the conversation between religion and evolutionary theory is mutually beneficial. A theological perspective, he believes, clarifies the directionality one finds in evolution's story of "life's long journey," from simple to complex, from the inanimate to living and finally to self-conscious creatures. Theology can enlarge evolution's story to make better sense of "the emergence of the most obvious experience any of us has, namely, the sense of our own selves as experiencing subjects."[6]

Environmental studies is a broad platform on which many disciplines coexist. It encompasses health, political science, theology, justice, law, literature, history, ethics, and, most important, many scientific disciplines. The study of the environment and ecology is vital to our understanding of relationships among humans, animals, plants, and ecosystems. At this stage in the development of the academic field of environmental studies, it appears that the interdependence and interaction among various components of the environment are delicate or, more accurately expressed, finely calibrated. That is, relatively small environmental changes, while not necessarily destroying the environment, make an impact that renders it either deleterious or downright inhospitable to various life forms, including human life.

Humans inhabit two worlds, physical and cultural. The relevant components of the physical world are soil, plants, animals, fossil fuels, air, and water; and technology, institutions (religious and secular), economics, and political organizations are the salient cultural institutions. Both worlds are essential to living, but integrating them successfully can cause tensions. In order for humans to prosper over the long term, the tensions between both worlds must be actively managed.

Our world is supported by biodiversity. Because the plethora of species and ecosystems supplies the world with fuel, medicine, food, materials, and water, it is important to understand how species function and in particular how they prosper or die. Besides supporting the world, biodiversity provides a unity to the world. Seen through a Catholic lens, the Trinity embraces loving community, and Trinitarian theology provides unity to all biodiversity: plant, animal, and human species. They all stem from God, the Creator of the universe. In the Christian tradition Jesus is the Word; that is, he is the prism for understanding both the Bible, which is the book of God's love, and the book of nature. Finally, the Holy Spirit animates all things. The Spirit is the essence through whom all species are created, and the Spirit leaves a divine trace or image in each created thing.

In time and space every species has a unique essence and purpose, which constitutes its value. Species have both instrumental value and intrinsic value. Instrumental value is what a species offers its own and other species, such as food, building materials, and medicine. Intrinsic value inheres in a species merely because it exists. Its essence and existence come from God, and for this reason any animal, plant, or thing has value. A forest of trees in the mountains plays a useful role in purifying the environment, but the forest is beautiful to the eye and by its way of being can stimulate humans to think about God.

Close to two million known and described species populate the world. However, the estimated total number of species is closer to fourteen million. Plants and insects, the richest in number of species, are found throughout the world, although the tropical rain forests are the most prolific areas. It is estimated that between the year 1642 and 2001 approximately 631 species and subspecies went extinct in North America alone due to colonization or human activities. Each year 3,000 to 30,000 species are disappearing, "an all time high for the last 65 million years."[7] This is up to 82 species per day, between 1,000 and 100,000 times the natural rate.[8] At the same time, new species arise every day. How many of these species are genuinely new and how many have been around for generations but are now newly discovered is as yet unknown. What is clear and exciting is that many new species are being discovered in tropical rain forests, and everywhere many new amphibians and plants emerge annually to be recorded by scientists.

The five main reasons for species extinction are habitat destruction, invasive species, pollution, overexploitation, and increase in population. All of these reasons are connected to human endeavors. Habitat destruction is the primary cause of species loss and is responsible for 36 percent of known extinctions. Many species are "specialist" species and thus adapted to a specific habitat, diet, and climate. Unlike humans, these animals and plants cannot be successfully relocated; destroying their habitat destroys them. The introduction of invasive species, air and water pollution, population increases, and overexploitation are human endeavors that constantly threaten other species.

What the Church says about creation has two primary sources: the Book of Genesis and the Gospel of St. John. The first three chapters of Genesis offer the traditional account, which over thousands of years has been plumbed for deeper messages. The Gospel of John adds a heightened realization of the implication of Jesus as Son of God. The beginning of this gospel places Jesus with the Father and the Spirit at the very beginning of the world. Let us examine first the important messages in Genesis relative to human beings and the environment.

With respect to creation, Genesis makes two central assertions. The first is that, made in the image and likeness of God, man and woman share in God's authority. As God has dominion over all creation, God gives to man and woman dominion over all animals (Genesis 1:26–27). The second statement that is vital to our view of the environment occurs just a verse later, when God says to Adam and Eve, "See, I have given you every plant yielding seed that is upon the face of all the earth, and every tree with seed in its fruit; you shall have them for food. And to every beast of the earth, and to every bird of the air, and to everything that creeps on the earth, everything that has the breath of life, I have given every green plant for food" (Genesis 1:29–31). Genesis then adds the affirmation that God looked at everything he had created and found it was very good. This account of creation is followed by a second creation account, in which Adam is the first living being created, after which the animals are made, and then Eve is formed from the rib of

Adam. In this account God sets Adam and Eve in a beautiful garden, which is to be their home. They are innocent and apparently in a warm climate since they wear no clothes. They are to be happy, till and care for the garden, and have amiable conversations with God when he takes his daily stroll in the evening, in the breezy part of the day. This is the idyllic beginning of the human race.

Scripture scholars tell us that one of the central messages in the early chapters of Genesis is not that God made the world in six physical or metaphorical days. Rather the central messages focus on God, his relationship to men and women (as represented by the first members of the human race), and the directives God gives to Adam and Eve. Scripture scholars also inform us that two questions motivate the creation stories: Why should Jews keep the Sabbath holy? and How did evil enter the world? The story of the first sin highlights the fact that sin entered through the free decision of Adam and Eve. God did not create moral evil, but he does allow it to happen. God is more directly involved in physical evil (suffering, senescence, death, and decay), a topic treated at length in chapter 15 of this volume.

Genesis says four very important things about human beings. First, although human beings are finite and God is infinite, they are made in such a way that God can speak to them and they can understand him. Humans can reply to God and God understands whatever language they speak. Second, because men and women exercise dominion over all living and nonhuman things, they are a bit like God, who exercises dominion over the entire universe, since he created it. But their dominion initially is limited. They are to organize the animals as they see fit, but the only living things they are permitted to eat are the leafy things. (Only after the flood are Noah and his offspring permitted to eat certain types of animals.) God does not say exactly what dominion entails; rather he assumes man and woman are smart enough to figure it out. Third, God likes beautiful things, and he knows man and woman like beautiful things as well. The Garden of Eden is a place of beauty, and God tells the man and woman that they should till the garden and care for it. That is, they have the intelligence to understand how to preserve the beauty in creation. Fourth, they are commanded not to eat of the fruit of the tree of the knowledge of good and evil. They can eat the fruit from any of the other trees or bushes, but not of the tree of the knowledge of good and evil. One purpose of this restriction is to indicate that men and women can be perfectly happy even though there are some modest constraints on their freedom, constraints that come from God.

Modern society is focused on economic productivity and the consumption of goods and services. In the human eagerness to produce and consume goods, people often forget the beauty of creation. Similarly people often act as if in exercising dominion over nature they need only concern themselves with the present and the near future. That is, humans are insufficiently concerned about the long-term sustainability of all living things on the planet. Earth is used and abused by humans rather than reverenced. Many people also misinterpret the word *dominion*. Out of context, dominion might appear to imply freedom to do anything we want with the creatures subject to us. However, the context of Genesis is that, once God creates something, he passes judgment that what was created was good. God does not grant men and women dominion to destroy good things forever. Rather they are given dominion to enable future generations ("increase and multiply") to be able to enjoy creation, just as early humans did. Responsible dominion or stewardship calls human beings to the practice of ecologically appropriate virtues such as compassion, humility, moderation, detachment, and gratitude.

In the Book of Numbers the meaning of *dominion* is clarified in an important way. The early part of chapter 35 in Numbers identifies crimes in which human blood is intentionally shed; the penalty for these crimes is death. However, a connection is made between the shedding of blood and the desecration or pollution of the land on which it took place. Through Moses God says to the Israelites, "You shall not desecrate the land where you live. Since bloodshed desecrates the land, the land can have no atonement for the blood shed on it except through the blood of him who shed it. Do not defile the land in which you live and in the midst of which I dwell; for I am the Lord who dwells in the midst of the Israelites" (Numbers 35:33–34).

Desecration or defilement of the land occurs when innocent blood is shed. The emphasis here is on the role played by human blood in particular, although many other passages warn human beings not to consume the blood of animals. Blood was considered the carrier of life. A reasonable interpretation of such passages is that humans should not despoil the land. Such defilement occurs when humans rob the land of its ability to support life, be it animal or human life. Responsible human beings should be concerned lest they pollute the land and waters of Earth. Through deforestation, oil spills, and water and air pollution, people kill wildlife and deny life its sustaining elements, even at times to the point of the extinction of a species. When this is done, not only is the land defiled but humans act contrary to the will of God, who created all being.

As was pointed out earlier, the account of creation in Genesis gives men and women dominion over the animals. In addition, they are to till the garden and be good stewards of it. The presumption is that men and women, because they are rational animals, understand how to exercise the responsibilities given them. Their ability to figure out how to exercise their responsibilities requires discernment and wisdom. Wisdom, often referred to in the Bible as "she," is an unfailing treasure for the person who seeks it. More precious than gold and silver is knowledge about "the organization of the universe and the force of its elements, the beginning and the end and the midpoint of times, the changes in the sun's course and the variations of the seasons. Cycles of years, positions of the stars, natures of animals, tempers of beasts, powers of the winds and thoughts of men, uses of plants and virtues of roots—such things as are hidden I learned and such as are plain. For Wisdom, the artificer of all, taught me" (Wisdom 7:7–22).

This passage from the Book of Wisdom confirms the ability of human beings to understand the general patterns of how the world operates. It also implies that understanding the way the world functions shares in divine wisdom, since it was God who made the world. Undeniable is the fact that, compared to modern scientists, the author of the passage had a modest understanding of how the world functions. But the author was wise enough to understand the important ways in which the world reflects divine order, beauty, and abundance. If society a thousand years hence is chosen as the standard, even scientists today will be deemed deficient in their technical understanding of the world. Human understanding of the Book of Nature gets more precise and comprehensive over time. Indeed a novelty of our own age is the very study of the environment as a complete ecological system. The new science reveals that nature is neither endless nor inexhaustible.

At a casual glance, some catastrophic events suggest that human beings need not be concerned about the environment. For instance, Earth may experience an even greater calamity than the one suffered some 65 million years ago, when, scientists believe, the planet was struck by a large meteor or meteorite shower that radically altered its ecosystem. The Bible also suggests that no matter what humans or nature does, God can handle it. The final chapter of the Book of Revelation begins by speaking of a new heaven and a new earth: "Then I saw a new heaven and a new earth. The former heaven and the former earth had passed away, and the sea was no more. I also saw the holy city, a new Jerusalem, coming down out of heaven from God, prepared as a bride adorned for her husband" (Revelation 21:1–2). It appears that if this earth and the other heavenly bodies are to pass away, human beings need not be so concerned about conserving the present earth.

It is true that both Paul (1 Corinthians 15 and other letters) and Revelation refer to a new reality after the resurrection of the dead. Our bodies and our world will be radically transformed by God. We will become like Christ in his resurrected body, the one experienced by the early disciples when Jesus appeared to them. Earth and the universe as we know it will also be changed dramatically. These changes are to take place at the end of the world and at God's initiative. Until the world ends, men and women labor under the command of Genesis to be proper stewards of creation. If a natural catastrophe occurs, God will handle it. In all other eventualities, humans should make reasonable plans to preserve the fruitfulness of the earth and its ecosystems for future generations.

In a sense humans destroy part of themselves when they destroy any part of the ecosystem. Humans cannot abdicate their responsibility, nor can they separate themselves from the fullness of creation. Early anthropocentric views of the earth and humanity, the incredible abundance of energy and goods produced by the earth, and the relatively small human population until about a hundred years ago led people to believe that they did not have to be concerned about the future of nature. Humans considered themselves to be above and separate from the plants and other creatures. Reason and the ability to plan and execute large projects made people believe they were apart from nature and not subject to its constraints. Somehow plants, animals, energy, and the atmosphere would always be clean and wholesome; they would flourish, no matter what humans did. However, human neglect and abuse of nature and natural resources have revealed the interconnectedness and interdependence of all ecosystems within the biosphere. Destruction of nature by human beings will eliminate the possibility of future human beings.

STRENGTHS AND CHALLENGES

As was noted earlier, environmental studies is a relatively new and broadly encompassing academic field. Within the field itself are many issues about which scholars disagree. Some of these are purely technical and empirical, while others are mixed because they engage scientific, political, and philosophical perspectives. As is analogously true for other chapters in this volume, there is no academic discipline that can even approximately be termed "Catholic environmental studies." Rather Catholics and others make judicious choices from the findings of environmental scientists and then incorporate these findings in a reasonable way both into their general outlook on life as well as in their specific practices.

Drawing upon the Catholic intellectual tradition, Catholics have available to them several perspectives that enable them to take seriously the results of environmental science and link them to their beliefs. The process of integrating a new academic discipline into the broader Catholic intellectual tradition often takes several decades. Often what initially appear to be fruitful theological or philosophical approaches to a new academic area have various weaknesses that prevent the approach from embracing all the important scientific and social components of the new discipline. The very newness of environmental studies encourages a tentative, probing path to uncover the best ways to account for the strengths of environmental studies.

In the second half of this essay I identify four important components of environmental science. I then select some prominent theological approaches in the Catholic intellectual tradition and analyze the capacity of each theological approach to integrate the four important components or results of environmental studies.

The following components are stated in fairly broad terms, and for this reason most scholars working in the area would accept what follows.

FOUR COMPONENTS OF ENVIRONMENTAL SCIENCE
Ecosystems Are Interactive

Ecosystems are interactive complexes of communities and the nonbiological elements affecting them in a particular area. For example, a forest, a beach, and a park are ecosystems. Many plants and animals depend on each other to maintain the health of their ecosystem. Within the ecosystem live producers, consumers, and decomposers that compose trophic levels, food chains, and food webs.

When such systems fail, the consequences may be severe. Because ecosystems supply organisms with food, destruction of a highly productive ecosystem, such as a tropical rain forest, can have devastating effects on its populations. Deforestation daily destroys habitats, thus causing extinction of species. Deforestation also adds carbon dioxide, a greenhouse gas, to the atmosphere. Often ecosystems can reclaim themselves, but it depends on the extent of the damage they have sustained. Raging forest fires in the Rocky Mountains destroy thousands of acres a year; however, the forest can repopulate itself to its original fullness through primary and secondary succession. The problem is that repopulation takes up to a hundred years. However, clear-cutting in a forest destroys the land forever, turning it into a totally different ecosystem.

Deleterious Effects of Humans on Ecosystems

Natural, regenerative processes within an ecosystem can be disrupted by destructive activities of human beings. Industry, technology, restructuring the landmass, housing, highways, a desire for new energy sources, pollution, climate change, and overpopulation can significantly disturb an ecosystem. Humans depend for our well-being on the goods and services, or ecosystem capital, that ecosystems provide. Our continual consumption and destruction of various ecosystems are what impairs or obstructs the natural ability of ecosystems to regenerate. For millions of years ecosystems have existed to sustain structures, processes, and biota. But the recent surge in world population has caused humans to appropriate approximately 40 percent of the world's primary productivity (oceans, plants, forests, land) to support human activity, even though humans constitute only 5 percent of the planet's biomass.

Life Is Competitive

At all levels various forms of life compete with each other. Species competition can be intraspecific, when members of the same species compete with each other, or interspecific, between or among different species. Most intraspecific competition is territorial or for basic resources. When species compete for scarce resources, one or more species may become extinct through natural selection.

Interspecific competition occurs in all ecosystems. Often the competition is for food, water, space, and habitat. This occurs between animals and humans. This type of competition leads to battles or even wars. Territorial wars happen more often between humans and animals than among animals themselves. Many ecosystems support numerous species. However, when humans intervene and destroy natural habitats, animals are forced to adapt, migrate, or gradually die out. The number of species that die off annually merely as a result of competition is unknown.

In the distant past, species extinction rates were most often influenced by climate change, plate tectonics, and asteroid impacts. Recent extinction rates are attributable to habitat loss, climate change, invasive species, overpopulation, overexploitation of natural resources, and pollution, all of which are human interventions.

Human Ingenuity and New Energy Sources

In the short time humans have populated the planet they have been successful in finding new sources of energy when traditional sources no longer fulfilled the needs of a growing population. Prior to the discovery of electricity, people heated their homes and cooked with wood, coal, kerosene (oil), peat, and dried manure. They used horsepower and foot power for travel prior to the discovery of the engine. Many people in developing countries still use these sources of energy.

During the Industrial Revolution the fossil fuels of coal, oil, and natural gas provided the energy for the new machines and products that were produced. Natural resources that took millions of years to form were used with little attention given to depletion, pollution, or consequences for the environment and ecosystems. The current challenge is to replace these nonrenewable fuel sources with renewable sources. Sources of renewable energy such as solar, wind, water, tides, waves, geothermal, hydrogen, and biofuels are readily available. The problem is to

develop economically efficient ways to tap these resources on a scale commensu-
rate with current use of nonrenewable energy sources.

   Human ingenuity is the most valuable human resource because it can devise
ways to allow for continued productive development without drawing down nonrenewable sources of energy. Humans need to discover ways to fuel their massive
transportation grids, to provide electricity using renewable resources, and to
create products that do not rely on plastics made from oil. Certainly we have the
intelligence and creativity to accomplish these tasks. The question is whether we
have the political and moral resolve.

THEOLOGICAL APPROACHES TO ENVIRONMENTAL STUDIES

The Catholic intellectual tradition affirms the compatibility of faith and reason.
Therefore the components of the religious tradition should be compatible with the
findings of the science. At the same time, one can reasonably expect that the religious tradition can offer some insight into the larger projects men and women
desire or should desire to undertake.

   The Catholic intellectual tradition offers three general approaches to the environment. It is instructive to briefly identify the various strands of the tradition
and then explore how adequately they integrate the four general findings of environmental science outlined above. The three general Catholic approaches are (1)
solidarity or kinship with creation, (2) caution with and deference to most life
forms, and (3) common ownership of the environment for all generations. These
approaches are not mutually exclusive, but each offers a different focus as well as
distinct religious justifications.

   Before exploring the strengths and weaknesses of these approaches, it is helpful
to recall two aspects of the Catholic intellectual tradition that are shared by all
three approaches. The first is that creation is God's work. As stewards of creation,
our prime responsibility is to God. Of course, such responsibility includes being
our brother's keeper, but the focus is on rendering to God the respect and reverence due something that is God's work. Indicating that all creation mirrors God's
goodness, St. Thomas Aquinas noted, "[God] brought things into being in order
that His goodness might be communicated to creatures and be represented by
them; and because His goodness could not be adequately represented by one
creature alone, He produced many and diverse creatures; that what was wanting to
one in the representation of the divine goodness might be applied to another."[9] If
all creation mirrors God's goodness, then we are obliged to honor and reverence all
creation as we honor and reverence God.

Another outstanding example of treating creation as God's special gift to human beings is visible in the life and writings of St. Francis of Assisi. Part of his appreciation of the environment appears in his "Canticle of the Sun," which expresses love of and appreciation for Brother Sun, Sister Moon, Mother Earth, and Brother Fire. That is, Francis sees all of God's creation personified and integrated into a single family. The realities that drive the human ecosystem are viewed as relatives of human beings. In his "Canticle of the Sun" Francis sings God's praises for the different components of creation:

> Be praised, my Lord, through Sister Moon and the stars; in the heavens you have made them bright, precious and beautiful.

> Be praised, my Lord, through Brothers Wind and Air, and clouds and storms, and all the weather, through which you give your creatures sustenance.

> Be praised, My Lord, through Sister Water; she is very useful, and humble, and precious, and pure.[10]

The second common aspect of Catholic approaches to creation is their attention to the beauty of the created world. Some parts of creation may be terrifying (tornadoes, hurricanes, ugly bugs), but even these can be understood as belonging to a divine plan that humans will never completely uncover in their life on Earth. What touches humans most deeply is a profound, expansive, and inexplicable beauty that is found in all parts of creation.

St. Bonaventure, also a Franciscan, emphasizes that Francis saw beauty in nature as a reflection of Beauty in God himself. Using various metaphors, Bonaventure explains how Francis reaches God through nature:

> In beautiful things [Francis] contuited [co-intuited] Beauty itself and through the footprints impressed in things he followed his Beloved everywhere, out of them all making himself a ladder through which he could climb up to lay a hold of him who is utterly desirable. With an intensity of unheard devotion he savored each and every creature—as in so many rivulets—that fontal Goodness, and discerned an almost celestial choir in the chords of power given to them by God, and like the prophet David, he sweetly encouraged them to praise the Lord.[11]

Because all things and creatures image God, Bonaventure spoke of creation as theophanic, meaning that God appears in all creatures. This theophanic nature of creation is at the heart of Franciscan ecotheology. The whole of creation in its truest form is an expression of the love, truth, glory, and goodness of God.[12] A good point to make to students studying the environment is that each aspect of creation has intrinsic value, not merely instrumental value. Acknowledgment of this induces people to be compassionate, reverent, and caring for Earth because, like all things, people are interconnected with the triune God.

In sum, each of the three theological approaches have in common an emphasis that creation is God's work and that the beauty human beings see, feel, and intuit in creation are reflections of God's beauty. Because each theological approach has a distinct perspective, it has its own strengths and weaknesses. The following sections explore these differences and comparative advantages.

Solidarity and Kinship

Solidarity and kinship with nature is based on the way humans interact with animals and plant life. Progress by human beings began by recognizing the solidarity of humans with nonhuman animals. Animals taught humans how to fly, how to hunt, how to make food, how to keep themselves sheltered, and how to care for their young. Although animals do not have the ability to reason, they have the instinctual ability to strive for survival, as humans do.

St. Francis of Assisi is the best known proponent of the solidarity approach to creation. Francis had a glorious admiration for the nonhuman aspects of God's creation. Throughout his life he grew in awareness and consciousness of the interconnectedness of all beings and nonbeings. The Franciscan intellectual tradition recognizes this interconnectedness that validates God's indwelling in all creation.

Because St. Francis recognized God's indwelling in all creation, many of the stories that surround his life deal with his love for animals. Perhaps *Fioretti* (*Little Flowers*),[13] a collection of legends and folklore that sprang up after the saint's death, is the most well known. It is said that, one day, while Francis was traveling with some companions, they happened upon a place in the road where birds filled the trees on either side. Francis told his companions, "Wait for me while I go to preach to my sisters the birds." The birds surrounded him, drawn by the power of his voice, and not one of them flew away.

Another legend from the *Fioretti* tells that in the city of Gubbio, where Francis lived for some time, was a wolf "terrifying and ferocious, who devoured men as well as animals." Francis had compassion for the townsfolk and went up into the hills to find Brother Wolf. After speaking with Brother Wolf and then with the townspeople, Francis worked out an agreement whereby the townspeople would feed the wolf and keep the dogs away from it, and the wolf would no longer threaten the townspeople.

A more modern version of Francis's kinship with animals and all creation is articulated by Teilhard de Chardin, the Jesuit paleontologist and theologian. Teilhard espoused the continuing evolution of the biosphere and all creation, with which our fate here on Earth is intimately linked: "There is a communion with God, and a communion with the earth, and a communion with God through the earth."[14] He joined the two creation stories, the story of creation in the Bible and the story of evolution from Darwin, into a new creation story. In Teilhard's opinion, the creation story is never ending because of the evolutionary process. What God created has evolved through the millennia and is still evolving. The world as we know it is not stagnant but constantly in motion, constantly evolving, through living beings, the geology of the earth, and human consciousness and awareness. As species become extinct and new species evolve, all creatures and life partner with God to continue the creative process. It is a cooperative process combining knowledge, spirituality, and communion.

Teilhard postulated that the universe is an organism that is "fundamentally and primarily living."[15] Environmental studies must consider the universe as a whole and Earth as a living biosphere where all living entities, animals and plants, contribute to the continuation of the genesis and biogenesis of life.

The solidarity and kinship approach fits well with the analysis of all creation as an ecosystem that is finely calibrated but that can be damaged by the irresponsible action of human beings. However, it says little about the sometimes violent competition that characterizes animals in nature. Also, although not opposed to the use of natural resources, this emphasis is silent about the amount of such resources that should be used by any one generation. By stressing the common lot of humans with all created things, this approach arouses sympathy for disappearing species. However, it does not seem capable of setting guidelines about where feelings of kinship should stop and prudential judgment about what types of development to allow or promote should begin.

Caution and Deference

Blessed John Duns Scotus, another Franciscan, emphasized the diversity and distinctness of each created thing. The created world was such a vast diversity of life that Scotus believed it was God's free gift of love. Each creature and plant is defined by its uniqueness. Scotus refers to this unique individuation as *haecceitas,* or "thisness." This-ness differentiates a thing from everything else in the universe, so that no two things are exactly the same. *Haecceitas* defines how people are to think of nature. When speaking of biodiversity, we often refer to various species and express concern about species extinction. But Scotus wants people to reverence not just the species but the individual being. Thus in Scotus's view there can be no insignificant being. For example, one should not say that because the mosquito is small and bites people it therefore does not matter if it becomes extinct. Although humans do not adequately grasp what the Creator's intent was in creating the mosquito, we know that the mosquito is a source of food for spiders, birds, and frogs. This-ness calls people to have a profound reverence for all life because of the individuation conferred on each being by God.[16]

For Scotus, the created world and all things that are in it are good, and thus there is great hope for humans and all creation. In an ecologically threatened world, humans need to follow their affection for justice and inclination to live in mutual relation with all creation. This requires humanity to value each aspect of creation as sacred.[17]

The approach of Scotus encourages humans to defer to the individualness of each entity, not just each of the tens of thousands of species in the world. Scotus wants to reverence the role of individual humans, but not at the expense of other entities in God's creation. In modern society, Scotus might say, an anthropocentric view of the world is dangerous because it makes it easy to forget that humans are simply one small part of God's creatures. A lack of humility about human status in creation causes humans to be destructive and insensitive to God's creation.

In agreement with this, James Nash introduced the idea of "ecological sin," which he defines in part as "the arrogant denial of the creaturely limitations imposed on human ingenuity and technology, a defiant disrespect or a deficient respect for the interdependent relationships of all creatures and their environments established in the covenant of creation, and an anthropocentric abuse of what God has made for frugal use."[18] When humans believe they are better than all the rest of creation, they are being egotistical, arrogant, and prideful. It is this state of pride that rules the destruction of other species for the "greater good" of humans. Walter Rauschenbusch states it best:

> Beauty that ages have fashioned and that no skill of man can replace is effaced to enrich a few persons whose enrichment is of little use to anybody.... For any long-range care of nature capitalism is almost useless.... The avarice induced by our economic system *sacrifices the future of the race* to immediate enrichment. From the point of view of a religious evolutionist that is one of the greatest of all sins. God and nature are always supremely intent on a better future.[19]

One implication of Scotus's *haecceitas* approach is that humans must abandon the notion that the rest of creation is theirs to own, plunder, or destroy. Related to this, because each entity enjoys status as God's creation, humans should be obedient to other creatures, "our brothers and sisters." Humans are not superior to animals and plants. We need to understand that we cannot use and abuse creation for our own self-interests but must put the well-being of all involved into perspective.

Caution and deference (even obedience) to the rest of creation highlights the interconnectedness of creation and therefore the damage that can be done if the focus of human beings is primarily on their own welfare. In a good sense, this approach questions the normal assumptions about human beings occupying the pinnacle of creation. It both startles and motivates people to be cautious in undertaking actions that harm other created entities.

On the negative side, the deference approach seems to suggest that any human action that harms any other entity, much less an entire species, is suspect and possibly sinful. But this does not take into account the good that can accrue to humans by "reasonable interventions," nor does it acknowledge that even though one source of energy may eventually be depleted, other sources of energy are likely to be unveiled in the future.

Common Ownership by All Generations

Papal statements appear to favor the approach that emphasizes that nature in all its facets belongs to all humankind, past and present. It should be used wisely and not wastefully. In his 1990 World Day of Peace message, Pope John Paul II said, "Today, the dramatic threat of ecological breakdown is teaching us the extent to which greed and selfishness—both individual and collective—are contrary to the order of creation, an order which is characterized by mutual interdependence."[20] Every creature is the word of God, every creature has a purpose, and all creatures, even humans, are interdependent one with another. Fairness requires that human beings take into consideration the needs and opportunities of all creation, not merely human beings.

In his encyclical *Caritas in Veritate*, Pope Benedict XVI speaks of the Church's responsibility toward the environment. The Church itself, he says, must play a constructive role in the public sphere.

[The Church should defend] earth, water, and air as gifts of creation that belong to everyone. She must above all protect humankind from self-destruction. There is need for what might be called a human ecology.... The deterioration of nature is in fact closely connected to the culture that shapes human coexistence: when human ecology is respected within society, environmental ecology also benefits.... The book of nature is one and indivis-ible: it takes in not only the environment but also life, sexuality, marriage, the family, social relations: in a word, integral human development. Our duties towards the environment are linked to our duties towards the human person.[21]

Like St. Thomas, Bonaventure emphasizes that all creation shares in the existence of God. For Bonaventure, the universe is like a book reflecting, representing, and describing its Maker, the Trinity, at three intensities of expression: trace, image, and likeness. The aspect of trace is found in every creature; the aspect of image, in the intellectual creatures or rational spirits; the aspect of likeness, only in those who are God-conformed. In this approach human beings are given a clear priority, but they must also act to protect all of God's creation. If they act only for selfish reasons, they are not God-conformed. Thus all creatures are related to their Cre-ator and depend upon Him. All creatures, no matter the degree to which they par-take of being, have God for their Principle. All rational beings, however little they may partake of light, are intended to grasp God through knowledge and love. All righteous and holy souls possess the Holy Spirit as an infused gift.[22]

The common ownership approach appears to balance nicely the connectedness of life, its competitive features, and the drive to improve the human situation. It appears to regard the ecosystem as fairly robust but still needing appropriate attention. The only component of environmental studies not addressed directly is the ability of humans to discover new sources of energy for their plans.

On the negative side, the common ownership of all generations, past and future, is hard to make practical with clear principles of action. For this reason, this approach also lacks the motivating force both of solidarity and kinship as well as of caution and deference.

CONCLUSION

As a relatively new academic field, environmental studies still lacks consensus about how the environment works. It lacks precision in analyzing how ecosystems react to small or large disruptions. Similarly, it cannot quantify the potential the environment offers in terms of its ability to support large populations that draw down many current natural resources. Despite the present limitations on this academic field, the subject offers many opportunities for a faculty member to offer students ways to understand how the particular aspect of the environment being considered in a course connects with much broader issues of religious belief and practice.

The theme of respect for the environment is articulated in various national cultures. For this reason, many students taking courses in environmental studies approach the subject with both interest and awe. Students live the awe, but it is important for them and their future to explore the source of their wonder and concern for the environment. This essay highlights the source of awe in the creative act of God. God made the world out of love, and it was his plan to have the world and all the creatures in it flourish under the guidance, management, and stewardship of human beings. God is the one who made the world awesome and put awe in human beings so they could appreciate the beauty and full extent of creation.

During this past century a greater appreciation has emerged among humans for both the vastness of the universe and the delicate balance among life forms and inert elements that make up the planet. At the very least, human beings are more aware of maintaining a proper balance. Much more scientific work needs to be done to indentify specific features and magnitudes of that balance. As that work continues, humans will hone more carefully the approach to stewardship that most faithfully takes into account the findings and projections of science.

Environmental studies through all its disciplines proclaims the beauty of the earth (culture), the *haecceitas* or "this-ness" of all beings (spirituality), and the knowledge (education) that all of creation witnesses to God. Everything is a source from which one can distill a higher and more celestial knowledge that is both valid and useful. In the Nicene Creed Christians profess God as "maker of heaven and earth, all that is seen and unseen." The vision and values of the Catholic intellectual tradition resolutely affirm the inherent value of human beings as "created in the image and likeness of God" (Genesis 1:27) and the intrinsic goodness of the created world that participates in the goodness of God. Anthony J. Cernera and Oliver J. Morgan explain:

> This is a deeply Catholic, sacramental view which integrates learning and faith, spirituality and scholarship. God is present and working in all of creation: in nature, in history, in culture, in each human person and creature. Because every element in creation and every valid method for learning about the created world is worthy of study, exploration, and contemplation, the impulse to a mission of education and learning is never far away from Catholic faith. The inner dynamic of Catholicism moves inevitably toward intellectual exploration and verification.[23]

Environmental studies taught in Catholic colleges and universities has a faith-based mandate to educate students not only in the facts of pollution, climate change, biodiversity, chemical use, and human population growth, but also in the

spiritual aspects of the created world and the role of responsible human beings in
it. Ecological accountability calls humans to perceive Earth and the entire cosmos
as a God-given home. For humans to have any lasting, positive effect on preserving
the goodness of Earth and its future, they must believe deeply that Earth is to be
reverenced and shared with all creation with which human beings are everlastingly
interconnected.

NOTES

1. Monika Hellwig, "The Tradition of the Catholic University," in *Examining the Catholic Intellectual Tradition*, edited by Anthony J. Cernera and Oliver J. Morgan (Fairfield, Conn.: Sacred Heart University Press, 2000), 7.

2. From Basil Pennington, *Lectio Divina,* quotation on www.bookofnature.org/library/ngb.html.

3. From St. Augustine, "Book of Nature," in *De Civitate Dei,* book 16, 1, quotation on www.bookofnature.org/library/ngb.html.

4. Martin Luther, *World of Thought*, translated by Martin H. Bertram (St. Louis, Mo.: Concordia, 1958), 179.

5. John Haught, *God after Darwin: A Theology of Evolution* (Boulder, Colo.: Westview Press, 2000), 7.

6. Haught, *God after Darwin,* cited by Peter Steinfels in "A Catholic Professor on Evolution and Theology: To Understand One, It Helps to Understand the Other," *New York Times*, August 20, 2005, www.nytimes.com/2005/08/20/national/20beliefs.html.

7. David S. Woodruff, "Declines of Biomes and Biotas and the Future of Evolution," *Proceedings of the National Academy of Sciences* 98, no. 10 (2001): 5471.

8. Dr. Andrew Balmford, Cambridge University Zoology Department. The natural background rate is only between 0.1 and 1 species a year, per million species. See www.healthy-world.org/species.html.

9. St. Thomas Aquinas, *Summa Theologica*, I 47.1, http://biblestudy.churches.net/CCEL/A/AQUINAS/SUMMA/FP/FP047.HTM.

10. "The Canticle of the Sun," also known as "Laudes Creatorum" ("Praise of the Creatures"), is a religious song composed in the Umbrian dialect of Italian. It is believed to be among the first works of literature, if not the first, written in the Italian language.

11. Ilia Delio, *Simply Bonaventure: An Introduction to His Life, Thought, and Writings* (Hyde Park, N.Y.: New City Press, 2001), 62.

12. Dawn Nothwehr, *Franciscan Theology of the Environment: An Introductory Reader* (Quincy, Ill.: Franciscan Press, 2002), 195.

13. See Otto Karrer, ed., *St. Francis, The Little Flowers, Legends, and Lauds*, translated by N. Wydenbruck (London: Sheed and Ward, 1979), 244.

14. Pierre Teilhard de Chardin, *Writings in Time of War* (New York: Harper and Row, 1968), 14.

15. Pierre Teilhard de Chardin, *Christianity and Evolution* (New York: Harcourt Brace Jovanovich, 1971), 62.

16. Teilhard, *Christianity and Evolution*, 288.

17. Teilhard, *Christianity and Evolution,* 290.

18. James Nash, *Loving Nature: Ecological Integrity and Christian Responsibility* (Nashville, Tenn.: Abingdon Press, 1991), 119. Published nineteen years ago, this book became a powerful text in the emerging field of ecotheology.

19. Walter Rauschenbusch, *Christianizing the Social Order* (New York: Macmillan, 1912), 253–4.

20. Pope John Paul II, *Message for the Celebration of the World Day of Peace,* January 1, 1990, www.vatican.va/holy_father/john_paul_ii/messages/peace/documents/hf_jp-ii_mes_19891208_xxiii-world-day-for-peace_en.html.

21. Pope Benedict XVI, *Caritas in Veritate,* www.vatican.va/holy_father/benedict_xvi/encyclicals/documents/hf_ben-xvi_enc_20090629_caritas-in-veritate_en.html.

22. St. Bonaventure, *On the Trinity,* chap. 12, 1–2, www.catholic.uz/tl_files/library/books/Bonaventure_breviloquium/.

23. Anthony J. Cernera and Oliver J. Morgan, "Implications and Future Directions," in *Examining the Catholic Intellectual Tradition*, edited by Anthony J. Cernera and Oliver J. Morgan (Fairfield, Conn.: Sacred Heart University Press, 2000), 203.

SELECTED READINGS

Dalton, Anne Marie. *A Theology for the Earth. The Contributions of Thomas Berry and Bernard Lonergan.* Ottawa: University of Ottawa Press, 1999.

Delio, Ilia. *A Franciscan View of Creation: Learning to Live in a Sacramental World.* Franciscan Heritage Series 2. St. Bonaventure, N.Y.: Franciscan Institute, 2003.

Delio, Ilia, Keith Douglass Warner, and Pam Wood. *Care for Creation: A Franciscan Spirituality of the Environment.* Cincinnati, Ohio: St. Anthony Messenger Press, 2007.

Nash, James A. *Loving Nature: Ecological Integrity and Christian Responsibility.* Nashville, Tenn.: Abingdon Press, 1991.

Nothwehr, Dawn. *Franciscan Theology of the Environment: An Introductory Reader.* Quincy, Ill.: Franciscan Press, 2002.

17

Physics and Astronomy in a Catholic Framework

William R. Stoeger, S.J.

A CLEAR TRADITION within Catholic teaching extends back through the Fathers of the Church to the Old and New Testaments, emphasizing the basic compatibility between what nature reveals and what is contained in divine revelation. Despite this tradition, the climate today is rife with narratives and myths highlighting the essential opposition of science and revelation. This essay explores the underlying sources of those serious misunderstandings. More important, it outlines the fundamental insights that have emerged in the past several decades and compellingly reinforce the perennial conviction that science and revelation share deep concerns and yet have distinct approaches. As long as each realm is properly understood and interpreted, science and revelation cohere well.

The bases for this fundamental compatibility between the findings and perspectives of the natural sciences and the central conclusions and insights of Catholic theology (and of most philosophically mature Christian and monotheistic theologies) have already been implicitly, and in some ways explicitly, discussed in Lawrence Cunningham's and Thomas Rausch's contributions to this volume. Cunningham refers to the "two books" of nature and divine revelation as the principal sources of theological reflection. Later he writes that "the Catholic theological tradition has always taught that we learn something about God from the sheer fact of creation [and that] some theologians have insisted that creation is a kind of primordial sacrament, a visible sign that mediates grace (God's love) to us." A proper understanding of God as Creator and of creation as God's gift thus will be consistent with whatever is reflected in our scientifically based knowledge of nature, correctly interpreted.

Correlatively, many of the fundamental principles of Christian anthropology that Rausch highlights are intimately connected with and supportive of the inherent coherence between Catholic and Christian teaching and the findings and understandings of the natural sciences. God as transcendent and immanent, God's creation as both flawed and graced, the key insight that grace builds on nature, and the realization that God always respects our freedom are also fundamental for a thorough appreciation and understanding of this consonance and compatibility.

In this chapter I explore these foundations for the mutually enriching relationships between theology and science. I compare and contrast theology and the sciences in some detail, with an emphasis on their particular competencies and their limitations. Then, using important results from the natural sciences, I examine key features of nature that are philosophically and theologically relevant. Finally, I show why a traditional portrayal of creation and God as Creator is thoroughly compatible with a proper scientific understanding of the laws of nature, the Big Bang, and biological evolution. As Catholics, Christians, and scientists, we need not be reluctant believers or half-hearted scientists. We have plenty of evidence and very good reasons to "believe in" both the Big Bang and divine creation as well as in both divine creation and biological evolution!

Before embarking on this journey, it is important to survey the academic climate in that region of the intellectual universe where the natural sciences abut the disciplines of philosophy and theology. It appears as if the weather there has been foggy for decades, if not centuries. The reason is that because of a plethora of basic misunderstandings and misinterpretations, many people today conclude that Christian theology and the natural sciences are in irreconcilable conflict, or alternatively that there is an unbridgeable gulf between them. And even though many Catholics strongly affirm the inherent compatibility of natural sciences and divine revelation, there are some very devoted Catholic scientists who are skeptical about the extent to which they are reconcilable. It is striking that so many intelligent people who are well disposed to the Catholic faith have contrary views. What, then, are the basic reasons for this frequently encountered perception of fundamental incompatibility?

THE PRESENT CLIMATE OF PERCEIVED CONFLICT
BETWEEN SCIENCE AND RELIGION

The origins of this misunderstanding are to be found on both sides of the relationship. One partial explanation points to popular accounts of science and religion. People's attitudes to the natural sciences are influenced by popular and semipopular scientific writing, mass media, and general education lectures and materials. A strong current of scientism runs through all these communication streams. Scientism is the belief that the natural sciences provide the only valid form of knowledge. As represented in popular culture, scientism preaches that philosophy, theology, the arts, and the humanities are incapable of providing people with anything more than narrative, imaginative, and symbolic representations of that for which we wish and hope. According to scientism, the humanities offer stories, but nothing about reality as it actually is.

In scientism the bias is toward the facts and provable theories. Philosophy and particularly theology affirm nonfactual or at the very least nonverifiable truths about God, Creation, or Jesus, for example. Because they are empirically nonverifiable, such assertions are either discounted or dismissed by scientism. An important distinction to remember, however, is that scientism is not a conclusion of any of the natural sciences. Rather it is itself a philosophical position to which many (although certainly not all, or even most) scientists and scientifically inclined citizens subscribe. The difficulty is that oftentimes under the guise of a scientific finding some prominent scientists and proficient popularizers strongly promote this view. Indeed they occasionally hawk scientism and atheism as a combined package.

On the side of religion and faith there are also problems. Some groups of Christian believers are literalist readers and interpreters of the Bible. Particularly in the United States, a number of influential Christian fundamentalist groups strongly insist on an uncompromising literalist interpretation of the Old and New Testaments. Their energy is particularly focused on the creation accounts in Genesis, and they discount all scientific conclusions (such as biological evolution) that seem to contradict the details and the obvious consequences and inferences from an overly literal and historical reading. Like the popularizers of scientism, biblical literalists are often enthusiastic and effective evangelizers of their point of view. They want everyone to be literalists, and they produce media that promote this message. This fundamentalist approach obstructs critical discussion of what the authors of these accounts originally intended. As a result basic theological truths in important biblical passages are obscured. Of course, such approaches often implicitly reject major conclusions not only of biology, but also of astronomy, paleontology, cosmology, physics (particularly various isotope-dating methods, such as carbon dating), and geology.

Because Christian fundamentalists are consistent in their biblical literalism, they knowingly sweep away centuries of understanding and interpreting the Bible in a capacious way. The early Fathers of the Church, including Augustine, who is revered by many fundamentalists, cultivated many ways to interpret biblical passages. The Fathers were neither idealists nor literalists; rather they recognized that the Scriptures cannot be treated as a single literary genre. Indeed in many important instances, to treat certain biblical passages literally is to misinterpret them.

The revealed truths contained in the Old and New Testament are not primarily historical or scientific, but theological. Such theological truths are vital for Christian faith and practice. However, they are often expressed in narrative and symbolic styles that are unfamiliar to popular understanding and therefore require historical, cultural, and literary analysis.[1] The Catholic Church has been in full agreement with the need for nuance and context in the interpretation of biblical texts, as is obvious from recent and not so recent Church documents and papal statements on theology and science.[2]

The two extremes, of scientism on one side and biblical literalism on the other, are by no means the only factors promoting the perception of incompatibility between theology and the natural sciences. A number of other, more subtle but still very powerful factors contribute to the antagonistic relationship.

In the area of science and the philosophy of science, a few dominant research agendas indirectly buttress the incompatibility narrative. Two of these are causal reductionism and determinism, neither of which is a scientifically based finding. Rather each is a philosophical position claiming some scientific support. Causal reductionism maintains that the only real causes, indeed the only real entities, are those found among the basic constituents of matter. According to this idea, higher functions are reducible and completely explained by more basic realities. The causal reductionist would explain mind, spiritual experiences, and noble aspirations as chemical changes or biological processes. For the causal reductionist, lower level organization and activity provide both necessary and sufficient conditions for all that happens at higher levels. A more catholic approach would acknowledge that lower level organization and activity are necessary conditions, since one needs a functioning brain to process spiritual feelings and have spiritual thoughts. But by insisting, for example, that the brain is both necessary and sufficient, causal reductionists reduce spiritual experiences to chemical or biological ones. It then naturally follows that causal reductionists deny there are any spiritual realities. Because people have chemical, not spiritual, experiences, it is not possible for them to have thoughts of God or any other spiritual reality. Causal reductionists assert that experiences of God or other spiritual realities are actually chemical experiences that people arbitrarily interpret (because they are historically conditioned) using spiritual language.

Determinism gives another slant on physical or physiological phenomena in humans. Determinists maintain that the behavior of higher level systems, including the moral identity of a human being, is really completely specified (determined) by what happens at lower levels, within the system itself and within the environment or context within which it exists. Human beings really make no genuine choices; free choice is simply an illusion stemming from an imperfect knowledge and understanding of reality. Both causal reductionism and determinism strongly reinforce the perception that the sciences and faith or theology are incompatible.

From the natural sciences themselves as well as from philosophical reflection on scientific findings, a very strong body of evidence now exists demonstrating that both determinism and causal reductionism are unsupportable by scientific analysis. Already at the levels of physics and chemistry, as well as biochemistry and biology, chemical and biological processes indicate a nonreductionist universe. For instance, on the basic level of physics, quantum indeterminacy is obviously inconsistent with determinism. At the levels of biochemistry and higher systems, the information contained in DNA, RNA, and proteins as well as the functions they code for and execute are simply not causally reducible to the sequences of nucleic acids and amino acids.

Even in science, history and environment count. The functional and structural relationships DNA has with the history of the layers of environment and with the chain of organisms within which they were selected are essential to the information DNA conveys and the roles it carries out. The detailed work in recent years on the general class of phenomena referred to as "emergence" reinforces this nonreductionistic conclusion.[3] Basically emergence is the process by which lower level systems organize themselves (or undergo organization and development) into more complex systems. The new organisms or systems have properties and behaviors that are qualitatively different from those of the component subsystems. Obvious examples are the emergence of living systems such as the cell from nonliving systems and the emergence of consciousness in higher level organisms.

Misinterpretations also occur in theology, both in popular literature as well as in specifically theological publications. Serious misunderstandings still exist among some theologians about a handful of fundamental scientific-theological issues. Misunderstandings and misplaced emphases center around who or what God is, what creation is, and how natural and moral evil and imperfections are consistent with Christian belief. These questions will be examined later in the chapter, but at this point it is important to reiterate a basic theological assertion that has been constant in the Catholic theological tradition but especially emphasized by Thomas Aquinas and his theological followers. In speaking about God, words like *cause* and *being* have to be interpreted carefully. In fact it is a fundamental mistake to imply or envision God as another being or cause in the universe. Even if we upgrade God to a "superbeing" who is more powerful, knowing, imaginative, and loving than all other humans combined, this constitutes a misunderstanding of Catholic and Christian doctrine about God. The difficulty with this approach is that we amplify the impact of the being, but we still envision God acting in or complementing other natural causes. The Christian God creates ex nihilo: he creates something out of nothing. God wills it into being; there's no work involved and no material. There are no scientific theories that can analyze how God creates.

Another framework error is to consider creation simply as an event in the past or as the origin of this world at a particular initial moment. Rather divine creation is an ongoing relationship of ultimate dependence. Also, God empowers and enables creation to act freely according to its God-given nature. Thinking of God instead as simply controlling or channeling creation is a serious distortion that generates enormous theological problems relating to the presence of evil and God's action in the world. More will be said about this later.

COMPARING AND CONTRASTING THE NATURAL SCIENCES AND THEOLOGY

When addressing issues that involve both God and nature, it is important to outline clearly what the natural sciences do and what theology does and how they go about their business. Having a clear idea of their distinctive competencies, commonalities, differences, and limitations is essential to avoiding misunderstandings.

The natural sciences are disciplines oriented toward a detailed qualitative and quantitative understanding and modeling of the regularities, processes, structures, and interrelationships that characterize aspects of material reality. They rely on rigorous, repeatable, empirical analysis and experiment. The phrase "regularities, processes, structures, and interrelationships that characterize aspects of material reality" is really equivalent to "laws of nature" in the broad sense.

The sciences have been enormously successful in their pursuit of understanding natural phenomena. At the same time it is important to note that this success has been bought with blood, sweat, and tears and often comes after countless failures. Seemingly promising research follows twisting and turning streets. Unfortunately in a good number of cases, the hope for positive results disappears when the research project hits a dead end. Many, many researchers over the centuries have been engaged in the endeavor, and, God willing, such research will continue for centuries to come. Despite clear scientific norms and the efforts and skills of so many researchers, the extraordinary competencies of the natural sciences are matched, as we shall see, by notable limitations. One limitation is either total blindness or severely impaired perception of crucial areas of reality.

A classical definition of theology relates faith to understanding. What is faith? According to the American theologian Avery Cardinal Dulles, faith is the positive ongoing response in discernment and commitment to perceived divine revelation.[4] The ongoing response includes thought, prayer, and action. It deepens or weakens in light of further discernment based on the personal and communal experience of trying to live out one's religious beliefs. In its ongoing adjustments to changes in one's relationship with God, faith is very much like a deep personal relationship with a spouse or with a good friend. Faith definitely involves discernment, which means candidly figuring out what God wants of one. Because faith requires discernment as well as trust and loving interaction, it resembles the relationship between friends or spouses.

The classic description of theology alluded to above was first articulated succinctly by St. Anselm of Canterbury as "faith seeking understanding."[5] Theology is the discipline directed toward understanding God, the presence and action of God in our world, and our response to that transcendent reality. Its primary source is Scripture, which is God's word to human beings. But theology must critically evaluate all realms of human experience, knowledge, and understanding. Thus theology must be radically interdisciplinary, not in the sense that it should somehow include the concerns of the sciences and other disciplines, but simply in the sense that it is called to take their basic, well-supported findings, perspectives, and understandings into critical consideration as its pursues its quest for understanding God and God's relationship to us and our world.

Religion is distinct from faith, but closely related to it. Motivated by faith and guided by at least an implicit theology, religion focuses on the establishment and expansion of a faith community. As is the case for any community, it entails social institutions, prescribed patterns of behavior, restrictions and obligations, authority, and rituals. Because religion involves communication with and praise of God, its rituals are usually more extensive than those in many other human communities.

Religion, or the faith community, yields benefits because at their best the institutions and practices of religion solidify and support faith, promote continuity, and authenticate and advance expressions of faith in concrete personal and social living. However, institutions within a religious group can also end up compromising faith and obstructing its growth, priorities, and practices. This happens when particular persons or religious institutions wind up serving primarily worldly goals instead of promoting praise of God and love of neighbor. At its best, religion mediates and focuses faith's purifying and constructive critique of society and culture and their institutions.

These descriptions of science, faith, theology, and religion clearly reveal the differences between the natural sciences and theology. First, sciences and theology have very different foci and interests as well as very different types of questions they seek to answer. The sciences focus on modeling and understanding in great detail the structures, interrelationships, and processes that characterize physical, chemical, and biological systems. Theology, on the other hand, concentrates on the relationship between God and human beings, as revealed in both nature and human history. In many ways these two disciplines could not be more different from one another!

Both disciplines also have distinctly different presuppositions. For instance, theology assumes there is reality beyond what is observed and measured, and that at least to some extent that reality can be known and understood. It also assumes the existence of divine revelation in Scripture as well as the validity of at least some religious experiences people have. Theology assumes that religious experiences have an impact on religious faith. The natural sciences do not share these presuppositions or assumptions. They do, however, have their own assumptions about reality and about our ability to know and understand it. In particular they assume a tight relationship between causes and effects, the validity of logic, their criteria for truth, and the objective independence and ordering of nature. Of course, these assumptions are strongly supported by our prescientific experience, and even more by the fruitfulness of scientific investigation itself.

By and large many of the assumptions the natural sciences make with respect to empirical reality are also made by Catholic and Christian theology. In addition, however, theology relies on assumptions and presuppositions that transcend those shared with the sciences. Much as the assumptions of the natural sciences are experientially supported, so too critical reflection on our individual and communal experiences of religious belief strongly supports the truth of theology's assumptions. And as is the case for scientific assumptions, the theological presuppositions also have shown themselves to be very fruitful over time.

Other differences between theology and the natural sciences emerge from these presuppositions. The two groups differ markedly in their "data," their methods of collecting data, the criteria used to validate findings and conclusions, the type of knowledge and understanding generated, the tangible products yielded by their findings, the communities they nurture, and the respective cultural impacts.

Although they are rarely discussed, obvious similarities also exist. Probably the most fundamental common ground that science and theology share is that they are both sources of knowledge and understanding. Each is oriented toward discovering the truth, though admittedly different aspects of the truth. One reason to compare natural sciences with theology (rather than with faith or religion) is to conduct the discussion on the same epistemological or disciplinary level. Both the natural sciences and theology pursue greater knowledge and understanding. Knowledge is communal, and both natural sciences and theology are practiced in communities of researchers and scholars. Moreover such communities are partially overlapping, since there are a number of scientist theologians in the world.

Philosophy is an independent discipline, but it serves both theology and the natural sciences. Without a philosophy adequate to both realms of experience, theology and science cannot be related in any reliable way. Philosophy, especially the branches of epistemology (the philosophy of knowing) and metaphysics (the study of being), is needed as an interlocutor to bridge the two very different universes of discourse represented by the natural sciences and theology.

THE COMPETENCIES AND LIMITATIONS OF THE SCIENCES AND THEOLOGY

Many people who have studied the history of the relationship between theology and the natural sciences have pointed out that the conflicts that have arisen are in large part traceable to the failure of one side or the other to recognize adequately its own limitations and to respect the competencies of the other. Interestingly, it happens that the competencies of the sciences in many ways neatly complement the limitations of theology and vice versa.

As already noted, the dynamic interplay of well-informed hypotheses and focused experiment and observation enables the natural sciences to produce striking advances. Such results yield detailed knowledge and understanding of the structures, regularities, and processes in nature on all scales and levels. In addition they generate ever-improving, technologically sophisticated products. Theology, of course, is not interested in or capable of quantitatively and qualitatively modeling and understanding systems, organisms, and their properties and behavior. Whenever theology has unwittingly or even intentionally ventured into these areas or pontificated about them, it has stumbled badly and distracted people from the real gifts theology yields when properly pursued.

Theology is oriented toward understanding God, the presence and action of God in nature and in history, the origin and destiny of human beings in God, God's revelation to humans, and guiding a person's or community's response to those fundamental and transcendent realities. The natural sciences are simply not capable of or interested in pursuing such questions. (Simply as human beings, however, many scientists engage theological issues as they seek to understand the full reality of their lives.)

The natural sciences reveal aspects of nature and raise questions about reality that indirectly influence how theological issues are framed. Scientific perspectives on these issues help theology hone its understanding of God, especially God's relationship with nature and human beings. Consider the caution with which theologians now speak of God's ongoing activity in the world. Careful theological language results from taking into account the way science now understands how the world operates. For example, theologians no longer speak of God as if he completely controls or micromanages nature and history. Nor do theologians describe God as creating each species individually, separately, and "directly," as if God somehow operates outside of the evolutionary process, which God oversees and sustains. Thanks to the natural sciences, theologians now assume that human beings were created from other hominoids, who evolved from the rest of the biological world. All these developments are due to the overwhelming empirical evidence gathered and marshaled by the natural sciences.

Despite these impressive scientific achievements, the natural sciences are very limited in their capacity to deal with some very important aspects of human experience. Science addresses some large, expansive questions, but neglects other significant questions that are outside their realm of inquiry. Consider, for example, the question, Why is there something rather than nothing, or Why is there this type of order rather than some other type of order? These questions expand far beyond the natural sciences. Although the natural sciences can investigate how something emerges from something else, they cannot deal with ultimate origins. In particular they cannot probe the ultimate source of the regularities, relationships, and processes found in nature.

The natural sciences are equally inept at dealing with personal, moral values or things that endow our lives with worth, orientation, and meaning. Pursuing scientific research and study presupposes certain values, orientations, and meanings, but the natural sciences do not and, adhering to their capabilities and methods, cannot directly justify such values, orientations, and meanings. A related limitation is that the natural sciences cannot handle the concrete and singular, that is, one-time events. Using their regular procedures, they cannot explore events or experiences that cannot be subsumed under a general law. This is a striking and unfortunate deficiency, since it is often the particular and unique that is the source of meaning and orientation in persons' lives.[6] Unlinked to other academic disciplines, the natural sciences rarely increase meaning in our lives, though they may sustain meaning through medical and other innovations. In fact some critics object that the natural sciences diminish meaning because they suggest that laws or patterns, not individuals, are significant. Science may forecast the future of groups or communities, but they have no interest in whether such groups either survive or thrive.

A particular incident of the helplessness of science in handling individual events is its inability to deal in any significant way with personal relationships. It is striking that the sciences have nothing to say to individuals as particular persons. To the extent that divine revelation is personal or involves nonmaterial communication, the natural sciences cannot critically examine or evaluate such experiences. Manifestations of the transcendent may leave traces in particular experiences of individuals or groups, but the natural sciences can evaluate only a small component (the material facet) of such experiences. A corollary of the inability to handle particular occurrences is that we should not expect natural scientists to aid in our understanding of personal miracles, unless the scientist is willing to think outside the scientific box.

Philosophy and theology are far from adequate in dealing with individual experiences or fundamental nonscientific topics. Nonetheless, with help from the sciences and other disciplines, theology and philosophy gradually sift out inadequate understandings in these areas. By focusing on how genuine communication and change occur in and among individuals, philosophy and theology offer insights that help people interpret their individual religious and nonreligious experiences.

A central limitation of the natural sciences pertains to their ability to reveal and model the structures, regularities, processes, and relationships manifested in nature. Expressed more succinctly, the natural sciences find it difficult to situate the laws of nature. They have difficulty fitting their models and theories into a larger framework that includes God, values, personal experiences, and other universes that could exist.

Many scientists believe the laws of nature are indeed the structures, regularities, processes, and relationships within reality as they actually function. In fact the natural sciences reveal our limited and provisional description and understanding of the "laws of nature." The way science understands and models nature is always provisional and incomplete. Large segments of nature (think of the health sciences) are still not modeled, explained, or understood. For hundreds of years to come the general situation of significant scientific ignorance about large swaths of reality handled by the natural sciences will likely persist. Scientists will have their "laws of nature," but they will be distinct from and at best a distant approximation to the "laws of nature as they actually function in reality." These go far beyond what "our laws of nature" describe.[7] Though the natural sciences have gifted us with wonderful, amazing, and humbling visions and understandings of our world and our universe, we need to remind ourselves frequently that those constitute merely the tip of the iceberg in terms of the mystery of reality as it actually is evolving and functioning.

THEOLOGICALLY RELEVANT FEATURES
OF THE SCIENTIST'S UNIVERSE

Certain central features of reality are very relevant to theological reflections. Putting aside the detailed scientific and specialized knowledge gained through science, a scientist interested in religious issues readily singles out important and striking properties of physical, chemical, and biological reality that are building blocks for his or her theological reflections. The following scientific features are fundamental and revelatory of who God is and what creation, including ourselves, is in relation to God.

The central feature uncovered by science is that the world is changing and evolving on all scales and has been doing so since the beginning of creation. Generally speaking, it has been developing from more simple systems to more complex and highly differentiated systems. Eventually these ongoing processes yielded beings who are conscious, rational, and creative and who communicate in words and other symbols. This has happened and continues to develop through the God-given processes and dynamisms within nature itself. This feature of the universe may appear almost pedestrian to many moderns, but two hundred years ago this was not what most people thought.

This feature asserts that God has endowed creation with intrinsic dynamisms and with relative autonomy. Given the intrinsic order and processes of nature, which ultimately originate and are held in existence by God as Creator (see below), there is neither need nor evidence for control, micromanagement, or intervention of these processes from "outside." Nature and the universe at large manifest what has been called "formational and functional integrity."[8] Once certain forces exist, nothing else is needed *at the level of explanation and understanding that is capable of being probed by the natural sciences.*

Paired with the striking characteristic of the self-sufficiency of nature (as viewed by scientists) are the unity and solidarity of nature and the universe. Everything is related and connected with everything else, albeit in highly intricate, complex, and different ways. Everything in the universe acts according to the same fundamental laws of physics, chemistry, and biology. And everything that has emerged has proceeded from something else according to those same regularities and processes.

None of this should be interpreted to mean that God is no longer creating nor deeply involved in the operation of evolutionary processes, or that God absented himself from significant developments for a few billion of the total 13.7 billion years the universe has existed. God is the origin of the processes, laws, and beings, and God continually holds them in existence. In some limited ways the processes reflect God's goodness, beauty, and love, and they embody God's purposes. Without God the processes, laws, and beings would not exist. In an active way God continues to create in and through all the laws of nature. All the processes, regularities, relationships, and vicissitudes of the cosmos and of nature, including chance and uncertainty, depend on God for their functioning.

Features of nature that are closely connected to the self-sufficiency, unity, and connectedness of the universe are the transience and fragility of the beings that exist within it. Stars, planets, and mountains eventually undergo destruction and decay, even as new stars, planets, and mountains emerge.

"Contingency" has two rather different aspects. The first facet is that, aside from God, everything we see or can think of depends completely on something else for its existence and capabilities. Nothing is "necessary." Nothing, except God, has to exist. Thus everything in nature and the universe, including human beings, is contingent. Transience and fragility are clear manifestations of that contingency. Nothing lasts forever; everything we know and understand eventually undergoes disruption, dissolution, and demise. The continual emergence of new and more complex systems and organisms is evolution. But it clearly depends on the decay and break-up of earlier systems and organisms. In fact a very good case can be made for the absolute necessity of fragility and transience in an evolving universe. Evolution would quickly come to a halt if everything that emerged were eternal.

A second but closely related aspect of contingency is that events in nature involve some chance. Were it possible to measure things perfectly, every event could be assigned a numerical probability. Less quantitatively, natural scientists know that what actually happens is never completely certain or inevitable, even when we take every reasonable action to ensure a given outcome. Despite such local randomness, chance always operates within a larger framework of dynamic order and fixed patterns of relationships.

Another obvious feature of nature, which is automatically presupposed by scientists and others, is that all reality manifests a profound order and intelligibility. Although this is taken for granted, it is not the only way to imagine the universe. The sciences cannot explain that order. Nor can they explain why that order, despite its complexities, is simple enough to be modeled in a way that explains its internal structures and relationships.

As we investigate the universe it becomes obvious that reality is organized in levels of complexity nested within one another. This can be called its "hierarchical structure." For example, the human body or any multicellular animal is composed of many organs, all working together and each composed of different types of structures. Each structure within an organ and within the body as a whole functions the way it does because of the different types of cells (muscles, blood, nerve and brain, bone, heart, kidneys, etc.) of which it is composed. But each of those cells is itself a very complicated functioning unit in its own right, with many different components. Furthermore each of the tens of thousands of different molecules that make up cells or that cells produce has its own basic structure and special ways of interacting with other molecules. The type of interaction depends on the structure and the properties of the various types of atoms that constitute the molecule, and particularly on the relationships among the atoms. If one magnifies one's investigation sufficiently, one eventually arrives at the stage of the fundamental particles, the protons, neutrons, and electrons. Scientists still do not understand completely the constituents of these particles and the ways they interact.

Hierarchical structure highlights the pervasiveness and importance of relationships. Simply expressed, relationality is a striking feature of reality. The internal and external relationships among components of systems interact with key aspects of their environment across space and time. The sum of these functional, spatial, historical, and compatibility relationships makes things what they are. These connections are often referred to as "constitutive relationships." They identify key aspects of the formal cause of each system, entity, and organism.[9]

Water offers a good example of positional variables at a very fundamental level. It is not simply the atoms and properties of hydrogen and oxygen that make water water, although they are necessary components. It is rather the relationships among the two atoms of hydrogen and the single atom of oxygen that constitute water and are responsible for its properties. The position and interaction of the hydrogen and oxygen atoms make the properties of water distinctly different from the properties of hydrogen or oxygen alone.

One can describe relationality over a range of systems, varying from very simple to highly complex entities. As one moves from uncomplicated molecules, to cells, to organs, to bacteria, to viruses, and on to various types of animals, more levels of relationships are necessary to describe how the entity functions. Furthermore as changes are introduced in RNA and DNA, environmental history becomes an important explanatory relationship. Interestingly, the central role of relationality in the ongoing development of reality at all levels mirrors the central importance it has in what Christian faith tells us about God. God is a Trinity of Persons, each of which and all of which are constituted through their ongoing relationships with one another. The self-related God who is one also creates, and in so doing establishes relationships with the beings He creates.

Directionality revealed by the natural sciences is another obvious feature of the universe and all systems within the universe. The universe has been continually evolving toward cooler, lumpier, more complex and highly differentiated configurations over the past 13.7 billion years. The systems and organisms within it have also been gradually evolving from simpler to more complex. In the case of systems and organisms a clear, smooth, inevitable ascending trend is not the norm. Rather it happens by fits and starts, often punctuated by significant reversals. But gradually ever more complex and behaviorally advanced systems and organisms have emerged from simpler systems and organisms. This occurs via natural selection, as entities and organisms undergo modifications in continual interaction with their environments.

Directionality exists both at the local and the global level. But it remains only a direction; it is not specified by a fixed end point toward which a system, organism, or the universe itself evolves. Rather for any particular system or organism within a particular environmental context, there is an orientation toward a well-defined, limited range of proximate outcomes. The possible outcomes are based on the conditions at the present time and the processes, regularities, relationships, and constraints to which it and its environment are subject.

It appears as if the universe and nature itself is fine-tuned for complexity. In particular this complexity results in rational human beings who are conscious and transcend their given environment. This orientation toward an environment that is favorable to humans is often referred to as "the anthropic principle." If the values of any of the various fundamental constants of nature (such as the gravitational constant) that dictate the strength of the fundamental forces (gravity, electromagnetism, the two nuclear forces) were just a bit different, complexity at any level would not have been possible. Findings from physics, cosmology, and chemistry affirm this. The same would be true if any of the other key parameters characterizing the structure and history of the universe were just a little bit different. And without complexity, there would be no life. For instance, the rate of the expansion of the universe and its physics had to be just right for stars to form. Without stars there would have been no chemical elements heavier than hydrogen, helium, and a little bit of lithium, that is, no carbon, oxygen, phosphorus, iron, or anything else. Thus without stars there would be no chemistry to speak of and no possibility of life. From the strictly scientific point of view we do not know how to account adequately for this apparent fine-tuning.

In recent years, instead of a "universal explanation" more cosmologists have suggested a multiuniverse explanation. That is, this universe can be better explained if there were a really existing collection of many universes, what is called a multiverse. These different really existing universes would represent a wide range of possible values for the fundamental constants and parameters. Then, from this multiverse that consists of many parallel universes, the only universe humans get to see and experience is the one in which humans actually live.

Such a multiverse, if it exists, provides an intuition for the seeming serendipity of winding up with a universe well disposed toward life in general and human life in particular. At the ultimate level of explanation, however, the sciences cannot provide an answer to the important question, Why is this universe, within this multiverse, the way it is, such that life and consciousness have emerged within them in at least one location? A really existing collection of universes cannot provide an explanation for the existence of this universe, the mulitverse itself, or the intrinsic order of this universe.

The basic characteristics of the universe explored in this essay are obviously interrelated. The formational and functional unity and integrity of nature, along with its evolution toward complexity and life, are enabled by the critical roles of relationality, hierarchical organization, directionality, transience and fragility, and emergence. From the perspective of Catholic and Christian theology, these must in some way reflect who God is and is not, both as Creator and Lord. This leads us to the concluding discussion on the theology of creation and its relationship to Big Bang cosmology, biological evolution, and other overarching natural processes revealed by the natural sciences.

THE BIG BANG AND DIVINE CREATION

A pertinent, simple, and helpful exposition of the profound essential compatibility between the contemporary findings of the natural sciences and Catholic theology is a careful contrast between Big Bang cosmology and divine creation as traditionally understood in Catholic theology. An accurate contrast requires a correct understanding of the earliest stages of the universe. Also needed are clear accounts of the ongoing divine act of creation, which necessarily involves describing what is meant by God the Creator. The basic points from this example can be extended to considerations of biological evolution and divine creation, as well as to the more difficult issues of the origins of life and consciousness. What has already been presented provides part of the groundwork for our exploration.

The earliest stages of the universe are summarized by what is referred to as "Big Bang cosmology." The essence of what cosmologists have discovered through data collected over the past eighty years or so is that hotter, denser, and simpler prevailing conditions characterized increasingly early stages of the development of the universe. In fact according to models based on at least three or four completely independent and very reliable sources of evidence, about 13.7 billion years ago the universe was so hot that all the laws of physics we presently know (gravity, electromagnetism, the nuclear forces) were unified in a single "superforce." Even space, time, and matter were very different, if not completely hidden, in an extreme quantum-gravitational condensate.

Under those unimaginably extreme conditions a very different form of physical reality and a much simpler set of physical laws existed. Once the temperature had cooled down enough, these initial conditions gave birth to the space-time-matter complex and the laws of physics that rule the universe. This threshold for the emergence of the laws of nature occurred much less than one second after whatever triggered the expansion and cooling. This unknown condition (it was not really an event) is known as "the Big Bang." The era before the emergence of the gravity and space-time we have now is "the Planck era." The laws of physics other than gravity emerged very shortly after the Planck era, though still well within one second of the Big Bang.

For the first 300,000 years the universe was expanding and cooling, but it was very boring. It was too hot for stars or galaxies, and there was no chemistry to speak of. Because there were no stars, none of the elements heavier than hydrogen, helium, and lithium had been manufactured. After 300,000 years it became cool enough for structures to begin to emerge, and stars, galaxies, and clusters of galaxies began to form. However, these entities were not formed quickly; it probably took several million years for the ancestral overdensities to gradually break away from the cosmic expansion, collapse, and coalesce. These overdensities were regions of slightly higher density than the cosmic background density and formed from quantum fluctuations during the initial very rapid expansion of the universe. They are clearly seen in the cosmic microwave background radiation and were the seeds out of which clusters of galaxies, galaxies, and stars formed. Once stars formed, of course, the heavier elements were gradually produced, and the universe began to evolve chemically, which was absolutely essential for the eventual emergence of life.

Two key points are essential to contrast the Big Bang and divine creation. The first point has already been noted, that the Big Bang is not an event. Certainly it should not be thought of as an event before which absolutely nothing at all existed. Such a description in no way is supported by the physics, the cosmology, or the philosophical reflection on what physics and cosmology give us. The Big Bang refers primarily to the very hot, dense, simple undifferentiated quantum state of the universe before it began to expand and cool. Because all laws of physics we presently know with confidence break down when such an extreme configuration is encountered, physicists and cosmologists often simply point to that state, since they have not yet explained or adequately modeled it. The conditions in the Big Bang cannot be reproduced or studied directly in particle accelerators, since the temperatures far exceed their energetic capabilities.

Despite the lack of direct experimental and observational access and of an adequate theoretical model, much research is currently being done by quantum cosmologists and other quantum gravity (e.g., superstring) theorists to fill these lacunae and to identify indirect indicators of what that "initial" state was like. As a result they have finally developed some provisional and partial descriptions of it.

Although no direct experiment or observation can test the physics of the Big Bang state itself, there are relics present in the universe that give us some information about it. From those and from what we know from quantum field theory and how gravity must mesh with it, we can venture well-informed scenarios that suggest what that primordial state of the universe was like and how it evolves. Similarly work has been done on how the universe began to expand and cool and eventually yield our universe. Further work in quantum cosmology promises to provide an indirectly well-supported description of the universe prior to the Big Bang as well as its transition to the expanding, cooling universe that gave birth to life. A key criterion for any such description is that it must yield the physics we know and love when the temperature (energy) of the universe cools enough for space, time, and gravity to emerge. That is, there must be physical continuity between our universe and that primordial configuration.

As far as the second point is concerned, some physicists claim that physics is capable of completely explaining the creation of the universe. They base this assertion on their conviction that researchers will one day develop a coherent explanatory model of the characteristics that preceded the Big Bang. This future model can then be used to describe the physical processes that generated our universe from that pre–Big Bang state. This is very likely an attainable goal.

Physicists convinced that they can explain creation often correctly claim that the initial, pre–Big Bang state was some sort of vacuum. From there, however, they mistakenly say that modeling the transition from the vacuum state shows an account of "creation from nothing." But that is far from what divine creation is! A vacuum state in physics is not absolutely nothing; it is simply a state without particles. But this is not nothing. In a vacuum, fields exist and there is a definite physics of the vacuum. A vacuum is a state of potentiality, and it can evolve into other, much richer states through the physical processes that are possible within it. The only way physics could completely explain creation is if it were capable of explaining ultimately the existence of physical reality itself, including the primordial vacuum and its physics.

To account for "creation from nothing," philosophically understood, we must speak about beginning with absolutely nothing: no vacuum, no energy, no physics, nothing at all. The challenge is to show how to get from absolutely nothing to something. One also has to explain how the particular regularities, processes, and relationships that characterize any level of physical reality were chosen and instantiated, and why the universe has this particular physics rather than another. Clearly physics will never be able to provide such an explanation. In fact it is not the way physics as a discipline is conceived or operates. Physics and cosmology, like all the natural sciences, presume something exists and has a definite order. Then they try to describe and model what exists, and to describe with qualitative and quantitative precision the laws of nature that pertain to it. Physics and cosmology can thus describe how earlier systems and configurations generate new, more complex systems and configurations through the operation of those laws of nature. But they are incapable of explaining and modeling the ultimate origin of their existence and of their properties.

The limits of physics and cosmology with respect to physics are now apparent. The next issue is to consider the essential characteristics of divine creation as it has been developed over the centuries. Particular emphasis here is given to the formulation by St. Thomas Aquinas and then refined and challenged by Christian philosophers and theologians since Thomas.

The Christian and Catholic concept of divine creation, which is also shared with much of Jewish and Islamic traditions, is often referred as "creation from nothing" (*creatio ex nihilo*). The heart of *creatio ex nihilo* is ultimate dependence of everything upon God for existence and order, not merely initially at the moment of creation, but always. This means that *creatio ex nihilo* is also *creatio continua* (continuing creation), God sustaining or conserving all things in existence and order.

Although most people associate creation with a starting moment, in the Christian tradition divine creation is not essentially about a beginning in time. Rather it refers primarily to what may be called an "ontological origin," the ultimate foundation of existence, which is God the Creator. There may have been a "beginning in time," but that is an issue separate from what is basic to the philosophical and theological concept of divine creation. Another helpful image of creation is that given by Aquinas; he refers to it as participation in God's being. "Participation" points to the ongoing sharing in being that results from individual entities being connected to and dependent for their being upon infinite being. With participation the shift is away from a starting point and toward an ongoing sharing. According to the Christian understanding, creation is an ongoing relationship with the source of all being and order: God. Creation is the relationship that endows all that is with its existence, order, and dynamism.

Because creation is an ontological origin and a sharing in God's being, it is apparent that divine creation is compatible with Big Bang cosmology. The natural sciences in general and Big Bang cosmology in particular are simply not capable of revealing a physical or scientifically accessible characteristic that provides the ultimate ground of existence and order. As was mentioned earlier, everything physical in this world is contingent. Nothing physical in the universe is self-sustaining or exists of absolute necessity. Nothing material or physical can be the ultimate foundation and ground of existence and order.

Divine creative action or causation is very different from any other kind of action or causation we encounter in the world. This is why God's universal creative action is often referred to as "primary causality." All other action or causation is "secondary causality," which is the main causality people and researchers deal with in their lives. When the terms *action* and *cause* are applied to God it is important to recall that the terms are not being used in the way they are understood in daily or academic life. They are being used analogically, which means that they denote something like action and cause in the way they are normally understood, but there are still big differences. Significant adjustments are required to apply these concepts to God.

God is radically different from anything else, including any other actor or cause. God is not just another object or cause in the universe. One reason is that God cannot be located, he cannot be "found" as a separate entity within the universe. Even though people feel close to God in nature, God is not in nature; rather, as David Burrell points out in chapter 5 of this volume, nature participates in God. The beauty and freshness of nature remind us of God's beauty and his constant renewal of human beings. But God is not in nature. God is beyond and transcends everything else that exists. Because God as Creator knows no boundaries, he is also profoundly and actively immanent (present) in each nook and cranny of the universe, not, however, as an object or a person to be found, but as Creator. He remains the source of being and order. As Creator, however, he maintains an ongoing, highly differentiated, creative relationship with everything in reality.

God as Creator has deep respect for what is created. Each creature receives its dignity by God because God gives each creature the autonomy and capability of being a cause in its own right. God endows and empowers each thing to be what it is and to act freely according to its nature. God as primary cause does not substitute for, interfere with, countermand, or micromanage the natural (secondary) causal structures of nature and of history, despite the fact that God is the ultimate ground and source of all being. Some people might object, "What difference, then, does God make?" God is the ground of all Being. As such, God makes all the difference in the world, because without God, nothing at all would exist except God.

What results from this discussion of Big Bang cosmology and divine creation is the clarity of a fundamental Catholic teaching: there is no essential conflict between the two *if each is properly understood.* On the contrary, there is deep compatibility and complementarity between the two accounts of origins. Divine creation outlines more clearly the ground of our being, and it suggests the complete otherness of God. God is not just a Being, or the sum of other beings, or a Being more powerful than any other being. God is Infinite Being and the source of all being. Big Bang cosmology and the scientific perspective that flows from it describe the amazing story of how physical reality unfolded through the processes, relationships, and regularities that God empowers and enables and through which God works. Much more could be said. For example, it is clear from this discussion that a similar compatibility and complementarity exists between biological evolution and divine creation.

What God reveals to us through the Scriptures and Tradition, reaching fullness in Jesus Christ, and what God reveals to us through our increasing scientific knowledge of nature is and must be coherent, compatible, and complementary. This is true as long as each is properly understood. Any apparent contradiction or conflict between them is the result of misrepresentation or misunderstanding of one or the other.

NOTES

1. See, for instance, R. J. Clifford, "Creation in the Hebrew Bible," in *Physics, Philosophy and Theology: A Common Quest for Understanding,* edited by Robert J. Russell, William R. Stoeger, and George V. Coyne, 2nd ed. (Vatican City State: Vatican Observatory, 1995), 151–70.

2. See, in particular, Pope John Paul II, "Message of His Holiness Pope John Paul II to the Reverend George V. Coyne, S.J., Director of the Vatican Observatory, from the Vatican, June 1, 1988," in Russell et al. *Physics, Philosophy and Theology,* www.vatican.va/holy_father/john_paul_ii/letters/1988/documents/hf_jp-ii_let_19880601_padre-coyne_en.html.

3. See Nancey Murphy and William R. Stoeger, eds., *Evolution and Emergence: Systems, Organisms, Persons* (Oxford: Oxford University Press, 2007), 378. See particularly chapter 4 by Terrence Deacon.

4. Avery Dulles, "The Meaning of Faith Considered in Relationship to Justice," in *The Faith That Does Justice*, edited by John C. Haughery (New York: Paulist Press, 1997), 10–46.

5. Anselm of Canterbury, *Proslogion,* preface (Prooemiium), in *St. Anselm's "Proslogion" with "A Reply on the Behalf of the Fool" by Gaunilo and "The Author's Reply to Gaunilo,"* translated by M. J. Charlesworth (Oxford: Clarendon Press, 1965), 101–5.

6. See Albert Borgmann, *Technology and the Character of Contemporary Life* (Chicago: University of Chicago Press, 1984), 302.

7. William R. Stoeger, "Contemporary Physics and the Ontological Status of the Laws of Nature," in *Quantum Cosmology and the Laws of Nature: Scientific Perspectives on Divine Action*, edited by Robert John Russell, Nancey Murphy, and C. J. Isham (Vatican City State: Vatican Observatory, 1993), 209–34.

8. These terms were first coined and thoroughly discussed by Howard J. Van Till, *The Fourth Day: What the Bible and the Heavens Are Telling Us about Creation* (Grand Rapids, Mich.: Eerdmans, 1986). The idea of the functional and formational integrity of nature goes back to Basil of Caesarea (*Hexameron*) and Augustine (*De Genesi ad Litteram*), as Van Till emphasizes.

9. Cf. William R. Stoeger, "The Mind-Brain Problem, the Laws of Nature, and Constitutive Relationships," in *Neuroscience and the Person: Scientific Perspectives on Divine Action,* edited by Robert John Russell, Nancey Murphy, Theo C. Meyering, and Michael A. Arbib (Vatican City State: Vatican Observatory, 1999), 129–46.

SELECTED READINGS

Barr, Stephen. *Modern Physics and Ancient Faith.* Notre Dame, Ind.: University of Notre Dame Press, 2003.

Carroll, William E. "Divine Agency, Contemporary Physics, and the Autonomy of Nature." *Heythrop Journal* 49, no. 4 (2008): 582–602.

Harrison, Peter, ed. *The Cambridge Companion to Science and Religion.* Cambridge, U.K.: Cambridge University Press, 2010.

Haught, John F. *Science and Religion: From Conflict to Conversation.* Mahwah, N.J.: Paulist Press, 1995.

Murphy, Nancey, and William R. Stoeger, eds. *Evolution and Emergence: Systems, Organisms, Persons.* Oxford: Oxford University Press, 2007.

Russell, Robert John, William R. Stoeger, and George V. Coyne. *Physics, Philosophy and Theology: A Common Quest for Understanding.* 2nd ed. Vatican City State: Vatican Observatory, 1995.

PART FOUR

The Good Life in the Professions

18

Economics and Business in a Catholic Framework

John J. Piderit, S.J.

Economies involving millions of people generate many complicated but reasonably predictable feedback relationships. In addition, agents in growing economies—consumers, producers, investors, and governments—create unpredictable feedback because they are endlessly resourceful in developing new desires, products, approaches, and policies. In order to analyze how such complicated economies operate, one must make simplifying assumptions. Assumptions make a model more manageable by illuminating how certain variables move in response to exogenous (that is, not formally in the model) shocks to the system. Clarity comes at a price because such models are also less realistic. Nonetheless the simplifying assumptions do not vitiate the usefulness of the model. Abstract models provide economists with three types of benefits: theoretical insights into what causes variables to change, empirical models that predict future values of economic variables, and laboratories or virtual spaces in which economists explore the potential ethical impact of policies on economic environments.

These three benefits justify examining some models and their assumptions to clarify where Christians can or should make their economic mark. The focus in this essay is not on how economists use models, but rather on how individuals with Catholic religious convictions see themselves fitting into typical economic models. The general point is that Christian believers, as consumers, producers, workers, traders, financiers, or innovators, have important religious convictions they should make effective in their economic decisions. They also have important ethical views, most linked to religious perspectives. This chapter highlights how religious views should rely on good economic theory and solid empirical results in order to become operational.

Oftentimes Christian convictions are at variance with assumptions made in traditional economic models. However, with only a few exceptions, it is assumed here that behavior motivated by specifically Christian convictions does not have a major impact on the way the economy functions. In an economy of 100 million people it makes little analytic difference if the assumptions of 5 million of them differ slightly or markedly from the simplifying assumptions made by economists. To be precise, the assumption is that Christian behavior will have only a minor impact on the analysis in the model, on the model's predictive ability, and on policies that promote fairness and social justice. Nonetheless it is vitally important that individuals with Christian convictions understand how their convictions differ from the conventional assumptions used by economists. In particular, if via baptism Christians are supposed to have died to this world, one would expect them to have an economic strategy reflecting that conviction. Just being good cultural citizens in a secular society does not cut it for Christians.

One way to understand what this essay does is to visualize a white piece of paper. In the center is the drawing of a large shape with smooth borders; the drawing covers most of the paper. The large shape with the smooth borders represents an economic model, either for a particular market, some aspect of a market, or an entire economy. The smoothness of the border represents simplifying assumptions made about the group of people active in the particular market or economy. Economists understand that their model, the smooth shape, exists as part of a larger universe, which is either the whole piece of paper or an entire sheaf of papers. Depending on the market one is considering, there is always some room outside the shape, which indicates people not involved in the particular market or economy being examined. For example, if one is looking at gross national product, young children are not usually included in the model. They are members of families, but their "economic activity" is not being directly modeled; their parents' activities are.

Within the smooth border, imagine that there are millions of small colored dots. Each color indicates a different type of conviction or worldview for distinct participants in the market. Suppose green represents people or firms with typical Catholic beliefs, practices, or convictions. Note that by letting one color represent a large class of people, another simplifying assumption is made, namely, that people who identify themselves as Catholic are virtually indistinguishable from one another with respect to their religious beliefs and practices. In effect all Catholics are assumed to have certain types of assumptions or behaviors.

In most neoclassical models economists effectively disregard the many different colored or religiously tinted points within the smooth border. They make simplifying assumptions for all consumers and producers, no matter their religious conviction, ethnic background, educational achievement, or any other distinction. All consumers are assumed to be utility maximizers; all producers and investors are profit maximizers; all banks want a reasonable trade-off between risk and return on assets. Economists understand that each consumer is different, as is each producer. Nonetheless they make simplifying assumptions so that assumptions about individual consumers generate an overall community preference function (with the mathematic quality of continuity and strict concavity) that captures the total effect of all individual consumers. Similarly in order to simplify religious considerations it is assumed that various beliefs and practices are equally important in the lives of all Catholics. In this essay a number of Catholic or Christian convictions, beliefs, and practices are invoked and applied to particular economic circumstances.

BASIC RESULTS FROM THE NEOCLASSICAL MODEL

In intermediate microeconomics students learn the main assumptions made by neoclassical economists concerning consumers and producers. Economists realize how numerous and fairly demanding these assumptions are. In order eventually to appreciate a Catholic perspective, it is helpful to list a few of the assumptions of the neoclassical model.

Consumers:

C1. Consumers have well-defined preferences over all goods and services.

C2. Consumers prefer more goods or services rather than fewer, but the more a consumer has of a certain type of good or service, the less satisfaction each additional unit brings. This property generates concave utility functions and convex iso-utility (indifference) curves or surfaces.

C3. Consumers who borrow money do not default on their obligations.

C4. Consumers do not generate externalities.

C5. Consumers attempt to maximize the utility they get from all goods in which they have an interest.

C6. It is possible to aggregate the preferences of consumers to generate a social preference function with the characteristics listed in C1–C4.

Producers of any particular good:

P1. The technically efficient way to produce the good is known to all producers, and if there are improvements in production methods, they are quickly learned by any producer.

P2. The producer purchases labor, capital, land, and any other factors of production and inputs in perfectly competitive markets. That is, factor prices (wage rates and the rental cost of capital) are not influenced by any producer's purchase of a factor.

P3. No producer supplies such large amounts of product to the market that the producer has a discernible impact on the price.

P4. Producers always fulfill their contracts, and corporate bankruptcies do not occur.

P5. Producers do not generate externalities.

P6. Every producer maximizes profits.

If these assumptions, plus several more, are made, one can prove the following:

The Fundamental Theorem of Welfare Economics: In an economy characterized by consumers and producers adhering to the assumptions listed above, the resulting equilibrium of goods produced and exchanged is Pareto-efficient; that is, in this equilibrium no resources are wasted.

Although this theorem does not presume the existence of money, money is the best way to facilitate exchange between producers and consumers in the economy because money is a means of exchange. Its purchasing power is determined by the amount of money in circulation, the speed of circulation, and the quantity of goods produced. According to economists, money is neither good nor bad; it is simply functional. But it has consequences. Even though money, assets, and debt raise important issues for Christians, in this essay they are treated as background variables.

Under much less stringent assumptions than those used to prove the Fundamental Theorem of Welfare Economics, a second theorem can be proved:

The Static Gains from International Trade Theorem: In all economies differing according to their relative endowments of factors of production, every economy benefits from free trade.

The International Trade Theorem does not ensure that in any given country every producer or worker will gain from trade. For example, a country that has a lot of capital relative to labor when compared to another country will export goods that use a lot of capital (relatively speaking); as a result, owners of capital will benefit from trade, while laborers will not. The Static Theorem claims that the gains from trade are positive for the overall economy and the gains are such that, were it feasible for those who gain from trade to compensate the losers, both groups would come out ahead as a result of trade.

Finally, although it has been proven only for very restricted circumstances, most economists in developed countries endorse the following statement:

> The Dynamic Gains from International Trade Theorem: If new methods of production or new products are regularly generated by one or more countries in an international system, all countries benefit from free trade over time. "Benefit" means that per capita GNP in each country increases more under a system of free trade than under either a system of managed trade or no trade.

In less technical language, competitive markets and international trade generally yield efficient results, even though they may generate an income distribution that, for good reasons, people in the economy consider unfair. When a consensus exists among citizens that the income distribution is unfair, introducing income and corporate taxes or some system of production and consumption taxes can ameliorate the disparity in incomes to some degree. Taxes do introduce inefficiencies, but they are still feasible and can make good sense. A trade-off exists between a fair distribution of income and an efficient (no waste) economy. In a growing economy the trade-off between fairness and efficiency is more pronounced in the long run.

Just as there are trade-offs between efficiency and taxes that modify the distribution of income, so individual consumers and producers choose their own trade-offs. Such trade-offs mean that particular consumers or producers, for religious or other reasons, may not conform to the assumptions listed above. In particular they may not adhere to a conventional understanding of maximizing utility or maximizing profits. But as was indicated earlier, unless there is a large proportion of such Christian or religious producers or consumers and their behavior is markedly different from that described in the assumptions above, the impact on the overall economy is likely to be small in the short run, though more pronounced in the long run.

As Thomas Rausch notes, grace-filled actions build on nature. One implication of this is that committed Catholics should incorporate good economics in their plan to follow Christ in the Church, which is the main focus of this essay. While economists often evaluate fairness, for Christians fairness is not enough because it should be linked to their commitment to Christ and loving concern for their neighbor.

CHRISTIAN PRIORITIES

Consider a married Christian with a family. Whether a consumer and a worker or a consumer and a producer, the Christian wants to provide for the well-being of his family. However, this is not the first priority of a believer. Jesus tells the parable of the pearl of great price: "The Kingdom of heaven is like a merchant searching for fine pearls. When he finds a pearl of great price, he goes and sells all that he has and buys it" (Matthew 13:45–46). The Kingdom of God was the focal point of the preaching of Jesus.[1] Therefore Christian belief and practice are the highest priority, even higher than the family. Jesus affirms this in many ways. At one point the disciples tell Jesus that his mother and brothers and sisters are outside and want to speak with him. Jesus replies, "Who is my mother, and who are my brothers?" Pointing to his disciples, he says, "Here are my mother and my brothers. For whoever does the will of my Father in heaven is my brother and sister and mother" (Matthew 12:48–50). So even family considerations must yield to the will of God, which is the highest priority.

Jesus himself gave witness to his determination to obey the will of the Father by submitting to death on the cross: "[Jesus] emptied himself, taking the form of a slave, coming in human likeness; and found human in appearance, he humbled himself, becoming obedient to death, even death on a cross. Because of this, God greatly exalted him and bestowed on him the name that is above every name, that at the name of Jesus every knee should bend, of those in heaven and on earth and under the earth, and every tongue confess that Jesus Christ is Lord, to the glory of God the Father" (Philippians 2:7–11). St. Paul and the fathers of the Church describe Jesus as the new Adam, who by his perfect obedience redeems the first Adam and all who receive the Holy Spirit in baptism.

It may seem that fair profits, wages, and property should be the next priority, since a man or woman has to be concerned about providing for the family in a well-organized economy. But following the will of the Father means adhering to the norms set by Jesus for his followers, those who want to be with Christ in his Kingdom. While fulfilling all the particular prescriptions of Torah is no longer necessary for a Christian, Jesus set an even higher bar. When responding to a question about what is the greatest commandment, Jesus said, "You shall love the Lord, your God, with all your heart, with all your soul, and with all your mind. This is the greatest and the first commandment. The second is like it: You shall love your neighbor as yourself. The whole law and the prophets depend on these two commandments" (Matthew 22:37–40).

The most elemental way to love God is to conform to the way he made us. Both Lawrence Cunningham and Rausch cite the importance of the Book of Nature as part of God's natural revelation to human beings. They note the centrality of the first creation story in Genesis. At the conclusion of this account God says, "'Let us make man in our image, after our likeness. Let them have dominion over the fish of the sea, the birds of the air, and the cattle, and over all the wild animals and all the creatures that crawl on the ground.' God created man in his image; in the divine image he created him; male and female he created them. God blessed them, saying: 'Be fertile and multiply; fill the earth and subdue it. Have dominion over the fish of the sea, the birds of the air, and all the living things that move on the earth'" (Genesis 1:26–28).

The Catholic tradition has emphasized two aspects of this divine reflection on God's creation. The first is that "in his image" includes the fact that man and woman are rational. More precisely it means that man and woman have an intellect, both practical and theoretical. Memory and imagination also belong to the faculty of the intellect. Hence when men and women use their intellect to analyze things, to imagine things, or to recall things, they imitate God. When they plan things carefully, as we imagine God planning creation, they imitate God. Another similarity with God is the human ability to construct things. God, of course, is able to bring things to life and to create things out of nothing, abilities beyond human capabilities. Nonetheless humans can construct things using the goods and materials of creation. When such goods are useful, beautiful, fun, relaxing, or simply imaginative, provided they are not used for evil ends they conform to God's plan. Thus although humans are made of flesh and bones and are finite, they imitate God through a variety of intellectual and physical acts.

Divine reason infinitely transcends human intelligence, but the account of Adam and Eve in the Garden of Eden confirms that human beings are such that they can speak and reason with God. God has an infinitely grander perspective, but human beings flourish in accordance with God's will when they use their human reason to figure out how best to exercise dominion over the earth, sea, and air, how to fill the earth and subdue it. At the very least this means that when people correctly use their reason, memory, and imagination, they do not go against God's plans for them. God frequently does not allow plans conscientiously devised by human beings to be fulfilled, but he wants people to try to figure things out. Also the account of what transpires in the Garden of Eden suggests that man and woman are given great latitude in arranging things. Indeed in the Garden of Eden they are given only one specific thing they are not allowed to do: eat the fruit of the tree of the knowledge of good and evil (Genesis 2:17). Adam and Eve had to conform to other laws of their nature (do not kill, do not steal, do not bear false witness, etc.), but the focus in the Garden of Eden is on their innocence, openness to God, and freedom. They were to take reasonable steps to exercise dominion and to increase, multiply, and populate the earth.

The sin of man and woman in Eden does not change the central responsibility given them. They are to use their reason and freedom to develop their relationship with God and to exercise dominion over the earth for the benefit of all, not just themselves. These are the most basic ways they are obedient to God. Obedience to the will of God involves freedom and human ingenuity, guided by human reason. The primary obedience God desires cannot therefore be properly described as blind obedience. As was indicated above, some activities, such as killing people or telling lies, are off limits in attempts to subdue the earth. But aside from a limited group of prohibited activities, humans are supposed to use their freedom and imagination to both praise God and love others. By arranging and building things, they are a bit like God and they conform to God's plans for them, provided they use well the things they produce.

The most basic requirements for fair dealings are made explicit in Commandments 4 through 10 of the Decalogue. According to the Catholic system of counting the commandments, number 4 is to honor your father and mother, number 5 is not to kill, number 6 is not to commit adultery, number 7 is not to steal, number 8 is not to bear false witness (that is, tell the truth), number 9 is not to covet your neighbor's wife, and number 10 is not to be desirous of your neighbor's goods. Although the commandments are given in the Torah (Deuteronomy 5:16–21), the Catholic Church interprets them as applications of the natural law to the situation of the Jews. That is, a version of the commandments with a more inclusive formula for Commandments 1, 2, and 3 is a general requirement of all people.[2]

Having fair dealings with a neighbor, however, is not the same as loving your neighbor. In the parable of the Good Samaritan, both a priest and a Levite who are traveling on the road to Jericho pass by a man who had been beaten and robbed. They see him, but they do not even speak to him. The next person to encounter the badly injured stranger is a Samaritan, belonging to a group despised by Jews. It is the Samaritan who goes out of his way to help the disadvantaged person: "But a Samaritan, who was on a journey, came upon him; and when he saw him, he felt compassion, and came to him and bandaged up his wounds, pouring oil and wine on them; and he put him on his own beast, and brought him to an inn and took care of him. On the next day he took out two denarii and gave them to the innkeeper and said, 'Take care of him; and whatever more you spend, when I return I will repay you'" (Luke 10:33–35). The parable highlights three points. First, the person in genuine need (the one who was robbed and beaten) determines who counts as a neighbor. Second, effective love is shown in actions, less so in words. Third, special love is shown when a person offers an abundance of time and resources to a stranger. This parable provides guidelines for all followers of Christ.

Jesus also emphasizes the importance of loving action for those in need when he speaks about inviting people to a feast: "When you hold a lunch or a dinner, do not invite your friends or your brothers or your relatives or your wealthy neighbors, in case they may invite you back and you have repayment. Rather, when you hold a banquet, invite the poor, the crippled, the lame, the blind; blessed indeed will you be because of their inability to repay you. For you will be repaid at the resurrection of the righteous" (Luke 14:12–14). Clearly Jesus is telling his followers to care for those in need. But how to do that effectively in a world with over a billion people in need is a critical issue for a Christian consumer or producer.

Although not normally included in the list of neoclassical assumptions for consumers and producers, adhering to Commandments 4 through 10 and reaching out to love one's neighbor clearly make a material difference in how an economy operates, if a sufficient proportion of the population adheres to these norms. If honoring one's parents includes taking care of them in their old age once they can no longer care for themselves, a society that generationally abides by this norm is more likely to generate greater satisfaction and lower transaction costs than one that does not. Similarly if people regularly lie or steal, the costs of running a business are going to be considerably higher than in an economy in which most people tell the truth and respect both the private property of others and commonly shared property, such as sidewalks, streets, parks, and beaches.

Assumptions C3 (consumers do not default) and P4 (producers fulfill their obligations to producers and consumers; that is, they do not go bankrupt) are among the more important assumptions. When they are not fulfilled on a regular basis, it is no longer possible to count on efficiency in a perfectly competitive economy. But if economic agents regularly lie, the likelihood of personal or corporate bankruptcy is very high. The reason is that lying agents are prone to take delivery of goods without ever paying for them, and lying producers are inclined to generate batches of goods and then renege on their commitment to pay their factors of production. Christians who put a high priority on fulfilling basic moral injunctions according to the natural law are more likely to generate an economy in which the minimal conditions for economic efficiency (in the Pareto sense) are fulfilled.

Taking stock of a partially articulated Christian model, the following responsibilities are priorities for Christians: (1) doing the will of the Father; (2) according to the account of creation, subduing and developing the earth in freedom, with an eye to enabling all people to flourish as human beings; (3) adhering to the ten commandments; (4) attending to the genuine needs of one's family and relatives; and (5) taking effective action to help nonrelatives in genuine need. The first priority, doing the will of the Father, should be the primary concern of each Christian. Priorities 2 through 5 are particular ways to fulfill the Father's will. But each Christian should seek guidance in prayer about the particular way in which God wants him to live his commitment to Christ.

The challenge to obey the commandments and attend to the needs of one's family requires considerable virtue. Given the reality of sin in the world, Christians need more than good intentions to consistently obey the commandments and fulfill the needs of their family. They need a strategy.

CHRISTIAN CONSUMERS: BONDAGE AND FREEDOM

In his Letter to the Romans, St. Paul articulates the moral struggle in which human beings are involved. Some people are blithely unaware of the difficulty, and for them there is little struggle. However, most people regularly experience the reality Paul depicts. Describing himself as a slave to Christ, Paul first bemoans his own struggle and failures when he was without belief in Christ: "We know that the law is spiritual; but I am carnal, sold into slavery to sin. What I do, I do not understand. For I do not do what I want, but I do what I hate" (Romans 7:14–15).

Earlier in this epistle Paul spoke bluntly to the Romans about their former slavery to sin and their current status as slaves to righteousness: "Do you not know that if you present yourselves to someone as obedient slaves, you are slaves of the one you obey, either of sin, which leads to death, or of obedience, which leads to righteousness? But thanks be to God that, although you were once slaves of sin, you have become obedient from the heart to the pattern of teaching to which you were entrusted. Freed from sin, you have become slaves of righteousness" (Romans 6:16–18). That is, their faith has prompted the Christians in Rome to become slaves to Christ, who has redeemed them from sin. By their faith in Christ, which has been confirmed and made effective in baptism, and through participation in the liturgy of the Christian community, Roman and all other Christians are justified.

Even though via baptism Christians die to a former way of life, it is always possible to slip and fall into sin. To avoid this Christians have to be vigilant and take reasonable steps to avoid becoming once again slaves to sin. Sins happen because the flesh is weak; Christians lose their focus, yield to their passions, and forget their goal. As a result they lapse in their commitment to Christ and his Church.

Aside from a master ruling over human slaves, bondage takes two forms: organic and psychological. Organic slavery is slavery to some substance and is more commonly called an addiction, since in this case some organs of the body develop elevated needs for certain chemicals. Psychological bondage occurs if a person becomes very accustomed to engaging in a particular activity and as a result regularly spends excessive amounts of time in this activity, such as watching television, eating too much food or too much of particular types of food, drinking certain nonalcoholic drinks, gambling, playing with computer games, or even reading certain types of novels.

A third type of bondage does not involve an addiction, or if so, it is of a mild variety. This very modern penchant involves an otherwise mature adult who accumulates material things or services but only very infrequently uses them. Certain types of clothes, electronic gadgets, household goods, books, recreational equipment, tools, toys, cars, and many other goods may be the focus of a soft addiction. The items themselves are unobjectionable; the difficulty is that they are seldom used by the particular consumer. The consumer is basically warehousing the items, not making good use of them either for fun or for his benefit or the benefit of others. The common term for this is consumerism, a malady of developed societies. Consumerism affects not only the wealthy or upper-middle class; it is an equal-opportunity affliction. In a sense consumerism is the inverse of the normal type of addiction: whereas addicts compulsively purchase and use the same good over and over again, consumerists buy an excessive amount of a variety of goods and then underutilize them.

The reason for raising the specter of sin and bondage in general, as well as the sin of consumerism in particular, is that Christian consumers have to at least entertain the possibility that when it comes to making decisions about what to purchase, they are not truly free. Alternatively some Christian consumers may have to review the pattern of purchases and ask guidance of the Holy Spirit whether such purchases are consistent with what happens in baptism, when one dies to the old way of life and begins a new life in Christ.

Christians rejoice at baptism in being released from the bondage of sin, but they should be intent lest they fall into sin in the future. It is true that through the sacrament of reconciliation the Catholic Church offers forgiveness to its members. Nonetheless the goal should be to avoid sin. Indeed in the act of contrition used in the sacrament of reconciliation the penitent says that he will avoid the "near occasions of sin" in the future. That is, a wise Christian, realizing that in certain circumstances he often sins, that is, falls back into the way of life associated with the "world," develops a strategy for avoiding such lapses. If he is prone to consumerism, he may decide never to shop without a list of the things he needs to purchase. He might further decide to check with a friend or relative in making the list to assure it's a list of needs rather than wants.

A similar approach could be adopted with a particular psychological addiction spreading throughout American society: the addiction to pornography. Over the past ten years the Internet has increased the availability of pornography many times over and also made it far easier to access, establishing a trend that seems likely to continue unabated. Someone inclined to pornography on the computer needs to develop personal rules that help him resist the penchant for succumbing to pornography's siren song. He might, for example, decide to use his computer only in public or semipublic places.

A Christian receives a calling to follow Christ and is expected to give daily witness to Christ's message of love in word and action. Figuring out how to do this, given the Christian's unique abilities and inclinations, requires prayer, reflection, and discussion with others. For example, a young couple may consider how many children, with God's cooperation, they wish to have. Suppose the couple feel they will be good parents and also feel that it would be good for their children to have a number of brothers and sisters. The couple might also be motivated by a desire to follow Christ by acting against the prevailing consumerism in their society. By choosing to aim for four or five children rather than one or two, they put pressure on themselves to reduce the amount of consumption and focus instead on doing activities together as a family. Another couple might come to a different decision about children. Whatever their approach, all Christians are called to challenge selfish norms of secular society and give witness to the priority of the Kingdom of God in their lives, living their faith both on Sundays and throughout the week. They should make time available for prayer and sharing the Good News, and they should also have a plan for how they intend to assist the less fortunate. These are minimal requirements for leading the Christian life.

The issues in this section relate to consumer preferences. In the normal neoclassical approach, consumer preferences are taken as given. A person has a certain array and contour of preferences, and it is of little concern to the economist how those preferences are developed or molded. Most economists believe preferences are influenced by advertising, though the extent of the influence is unknown. The main reason economists believe advertising is effective is that they believe firms act rationally. Corporations are not likely to spend money on advertising if they are convinced it has practically no impact on consumption patterns.

Christians are subject to the allure of advertising, but with the gift of the Holy Spirit they are supposed to critically form consumer preferences. People cannot be true Christians if all their preferences for goods and services are indistinguishable from those of unbelievers. When they are children, Christians most likely accept the preferences of their parents, and because they judge their parents to be good and faithful people, they might well adopt their preferences as their own over time. And they might be quite correct in doing so. However, the Christian calling is personal. Christians have the responsibility to align their religious convictions with the talents and skills they have acquired. God may be calling the son or daughter to something different from what the parents chose. As an adult, the only way to discover this is through prayer and careful consideration, not by blindly accepting established parental norms. True Christian adults align their preferences with Scripture and the communal experience of the Catholic tradition. In the context of prayer, they consider the best approach to take to goods and services, and based on this approach they allot their time and money.

The emphasis in this section has been on avoiding sin and rejecting consumerism. One practical impact on a person's indifference curves is that, other things being equal, the nonconsumerist reaches a satiation point more quickly than the person who enjoys having many goods.

CHRISTIAN PRODUCERS

In economic models producers constitute another generic economic agent. The first responsibility of Christian producers should be to bring to market only items and services that promote the common good, that is, that conform to proper dominion and stewardship of creation. Goods and services are used to pursue important human values. Some goods cannot be reconciled with the legitimate pursuit of any fundamental human value, and a Christian producer should not manufacture them or play a role in making them available to consumers. For example, it would be seriously wrong for a Christian producer to be involved in the production of addictive drugs, since they easily lead to incapacitating dependence. Also goods and services such as pornography, prostitution, and anything that causes harm to other people are incompatible with a Christian commitment. If an instrument or drug is used primarily in the provision of abortions, a Christian cannot in good conscience assist in its production. Where a good can be used for either legitimate or immoral purposes, the producer has a responsibility to take reasonable steps to discourage the use of the good for immoral purposes.

This also applies to workers at firms that produce goods used mainly for immoral purposes. Christians cannot satisfy themselves with the claim that "it's just a job." The job has to plausibly promote some good in society. At the end of a pay period, workers and owners must be able to say that they are pleased with their work because it positively contributes to society. They have to be able to take legitimate pride in assisting in the production of the goods made with their cooperation.

No separate analysis of the role of financiers in modern society is undertaken in this essay. Nonetheless many of the comments in this section apply equally to financiers and to how people invest their money.

Not all goods have to serve the physical health and welfare of people. Any society rightly produces goods that, though not essential, are both an expression of human ingenuity and also an aid to participating more fully in genuine human values. In general, therefore, goods and services promote the health, safety, and education of people and also enable them to pursue human values in more advanced ways. A society in which most people can travel by airplane is not clearly better than a society in which only a limited number of people can do so. However, the "air travel society" affords people the ability to travel to other countries to see beautiful things and learn about how people in other countries order their lives. Similarly if space travel becomes accessible to families sometime in the future, this can be a very positive development, other things being equal. At the very least, it would give people a new perspective on the planet and open up to them new ways to appreciate the grandeur of God's creation.

Developing new goods and services, finding more efficient ways to produce ordinary goods, and creating things that are beautiful or fun to use, even if they are not obviously useful, all are very human things to do and not activities that need be rejected by Christians. When production plans are undertaken to help people take greater delight in God's creation, God himself takes delight in human ingenuity.

Catholic owners of corporations and CEOs have a responsibility to identify or locate the "goodness" of their factories, firms, or corporations within the realm of human activities. For example, the Catholic head of the Widget Corporation should spend time explaining to employees and perhaps also to shareholders the benefits of producing more or better widgets for modern society. It is far too easy for people to become careless about the types of goods they produce, especially if they do not reflect on the true benefits they bring to society. Making efforts to share with workers and others the good reasons for producing something helps CEOs attend to what their Christian commitment requires of them in the marketplace.

Making sure goods pass moral muster is a task for each Christian. An economist can look solely at the market and examine how the equilibrium price gets determined. But for the Christian, more important than the price is the benefit the good brings to people in society. (Depending on the good and the circumstances, the price can be a reasonable reflection of the benefit yielded to society by a particular good.) Christians should not be involved in the production or consumption of goods that are used predominantly in immoral ways. But a particular Christian can maintain an even higher standard. As a result of prayer and discernment, an individual Christian may choose to eschew working for a particular corporation because its products make only a trivial contribution to society.

Jesus often seemed to praise an innovative spirit of production, though his main interest in these instances was in having his disciples be resourceful in spreading the good news about the Kingdom of God. In the parable of the talents, Jesus praises the creativity of the two successful businesspeople who made the talents entrusted to them work for their master: "After a long time the master of those servants came back and settled accounts with them. The one who had received five talents came forward bringing the additional five. He said, 'Master, you gave me five talents. See, I have made five more.' His master said to him, 'Well done, my good and faithful servant. Since you were faithful in small matters, I will give you great responsibilities. Come, share your master's joy'" (Matthew 25:19–21). The main point of the parable is that we should be as resourceful in spreading the Gospel as good businesspeople are entrepreneurial in generating wealth for themselves and others.

As the master was generous in his reward to the two "good and faithful" servants, should producers and employers be particularly generous to their workers? The parable of the workers in the vineyard suggests this approach. In this parable, the worker who worked only a single hour is paid the regular daily wage given to all workers in society. The main points of the parable (Matthew 20:1–16) are that God the Father chooses to be generous to some, and that some people who are last here on Earth will wind up first in the Kingdom of God. Nonetheless the parable asks the hearer to applaud the generosity of the owner of the vineyard. Should Christian employers in American society be generous in a similar way?

In the neoclassical model, the employer takes the wage rate as given and hires as many people as he can reasonably afford at this wage rate. Presumably were the employer to pay workers a bit more he would hire fewer workers. So in the sense that a higher wage comes at the cost of fewer workers, there is no free lunch. Were the employer to both pay each worker more and maintain the same number of workers and do this consistently over a longer period of time, this would eventually result in lower profits and attract less investment in the firm. In the case of regular employment, a trade-off of something good for current workers with something bad for potential but unknown workers is unavoidable.

Nonetheless, as depicted in the powerful Last Judgment story told by Jesus, every Christian has a grave responsibility to be generous: "Then the king will say to those on his right, 'Come, you who are blessed by my Father. Inherit the kingdom prepared for you from the foundation of the world. For I was hungry and you gave me food, I was thirsty and you gave me drink, a stranger and you welcomed me, naked and you clothed me, ill and you cared for me, in prison and you visited me.'…'Amen, I say to you, whatever you did for one of these least brothers of mine, you did for me'" (Matthew 25:34–36, 40).

Jesus generally approved of generating a surplus. The surplus he emphasized was made visible in tangible things, such as the abundance of wine at the wedding feast of Cana, the surplus of bread and fish at the multiplication of the loaves and fishes, and the person who throws a banquet to which he invites many people. However, these physical manifestations of abundance point to an abundance of love, care, and concern that characterize those who participate in the Kingdom of God. For the Christian, the Kingdom has already arrived in the Church, and especially in the Eucharist. For both producers and consumers, the Eucharistic meal is a participation in the life of Christ and the Kingdom that will eventually be revealed in power.

MANAGING THE RISK OF SALVATION

Judging from the parable of the talents, Jesus does not appear opposed to people profiting from being resourceful in their investments. However, his statements about rich and poor in a variety of parables and incidents offer caution about generalizing his views in a simple way. Consider the poor widow: "When [Jesus] looked up he saw some wealthy people putting their offerings into the treasury and he noticed a poor widow putting in two small coins. He said, 'I tell you truly, this poor widow put in more than all the rest; for those others have all made offerings from their surplus wealth, but she, from her poverty, has offered her whole livelihood" (Luke 21:1–4). In the parable of the rich man and Lazarus, after his death Lazarus is at Abraham's side, while the rich man suffers torments (Luke 16:19–31).

Although in the Old Testament wealth was often considered a sign of God's favor, Jesus told his disciples that they participate in the Kingdom of God only through a willing surrender to God and through no reliance on wealth. This is yet another instance of how Jesus reveals himself as the new lawgiver, the new Moses: "Jesus looked around and said to his disciples, 'How hard it is for those who have wealth to enter the kingdom of God!' The disciples were amazed at his words. So Jesus again said to them in reply, 'Children, how hard it is to enter the kingdom of God! It is easier for a camel to pass through the eye of a needle than for one who is rich to enter the kingdom of God.' They were exceedingly astonished and said among themselves, 'Then who can be saved?' Jesus looked at them and said, 'For human beings it is impossible, but not for God. All things are possible for God'" (Mark 10:23–27).

A wealthy person who wants to remain faithful to Christ and the Church needs a good strategy that will keep him relying completely on God and not on his personal wealth. By not having a good strategy a Christian risks no longer acting as a Christian. Unfortunately a Christian can become like the husband who spends too much time on his business and thereby endangers his commitment to his wife and children. Christians can become too preoccupied with less important things.

Compared with over one billion people worldwide living in abject poverty, all Americans, even those considered poor, are somewhat wealthy. This is one reason that so many people from other countries want to come to the United States. They understand that this country offers a path out of poverty and bondage and toward freedom and well-being. So the wealthy Christians of the United States, both those deemed so by American standards and those considered so in comparison to others around the world, are called to rely completely on God. Given that, what counts as a good, risk-averse strategy for American Christians, the wealthy ones of the world?

As Jesus himself indicates, his followers are to place their trust completely in God, not in goods, services, insurance policies, opulent homes, or other forms of accumulated wealth. They also have to use their wealth both to promote the Kingdom and to help poor people, their brothers and sisters in Christ, wherever they are.

Jesus, of course, did not systematically explore how economies function, but Christians now have the benefit of economic analysis. With regard to eliminating poverty and promoting economic development, economists and politicians have tried different policies. Despite disagreements, economists and businesspeople now know that some policies promote high growth over the long term and are effective ways to get large numbers of people out of poverty. They also know that, no matter what is done in terms of governmental policy, many people will suffer severe setbacks due to changes in the economy. At times of crisis these people will need assistance in getting goods and services for their families. Even very good social safety nets do not catch everyone who falls down in an economy. So individuals have to be ready to contribute in particular cases.

The poor are God's children, placed in our midst as reminders that, no matter their health, natural talents, or financial circumstances, all people are God's children. Jesus expected that his followers would take effective action to assist the poor and less fortunate in their need. If he had lived in a world in which he knew about billions of poor people around the globe, he would have spoken powerfully on their behalf and against those who refuse to help. Given these two realities, risk-averse Christians who follow in the footsteps of Jesus Christ should not be timid disciples who are barely recognizable as Christians. Blessed with reason and imagination, Christians should have two general strategies for the poor: one for general generosity that focuses on the large number of poor in the world, and the other for particular generosity, which responds to poverty at the local level. In addition the very wealthy need a family strategy to remind themselves and their families that their confidence is in God, not in their abundant wealth.

Any general strategy to help the masses of poor people around the world should be well conceived, in accordance with sound economic models and with a high likelihood of succeeding if the policies are adhered to consistently over a period of twenty or thirty years. Any large endeavor involving many countries of necessity must rely on decisions taken by governments of poorer countries. One cannot compel countries to adopt an economic policy or adhere to it over several decades. Nonetheless the norm for the policy should be that the benefits are sufficiently obvious that the poor country perceives the benefits, even though some groups in the poor country may have to make considerable adjustments.

Scores of policies would satisfy the criterion for improving the lot of the poor, provided both the developed countries and the poor countries themselves adhere to whatever is being asked of them. Out of all these policies, two possibilities are presented here to highlight the freedom Catholics have to choose a policy they deem reasonable. Each policy is conveniently associated with a U.S. political party.

The first global policy to fight poverty (A) invites all countries to participate in free trade, that is, in importing and exporting goods without government constraints. More precisely, within a time period of four or five years, all countries would ideally agree to eliminate all taxes or subsidies, direct or indirect, on traded goods. Economic analysis, econometric studies, and case studies suggest that all participating countries would benefit immensely from such a general commitment to free trade. For people in poor countries the substantial downside is that the wealthy countries would also profit from such a free trade regime. That is, in a world with free trade the rich continue to get richer. More important, however, is that within ten to fifteen years many poor countries would experience substantial growth in per capita GNP. In order for a Christian to count this as her policy, she would have to take effective action to elect people who would commit to pushing for such a policy.

An alternate general policy (B) would be to impose some percentage tax on countries whose per capita GNP is above a certain level. These annual taxes would be funneled to an agency that would invest the funds in world health and education projects in poor countries. Such a plan has weaker theoretical and econometric support in large part for two reasons. First, it is not designed to promote self-sufficient economic production in poorer countries; second, research shows that whatever international organization is in charge of the distribution of the funds, it is prone to distribute proportionally equal funds to all countries, no matter the merits of proposals from individual countries. Despite these disadvantages, for a variety of reasons many people in developed countries would more readily support B than A. For a Christian to consider B as his policy to combat global poverty, all other things being equal, he would have to endorse candidates for office who support plan B.

Whether a Christian endorses strategy A, B, or some other strategy, he has an obligation to use his influence, organizational talents, and imagination to promote the strategy. And if it eventually appears that some other strategy is more likely to gain general support and will also substantially improve the well-being of the poor, the Christian should be flexible and support that policy.

Consider now a policy for particular (or local, neighborhood) generosity. Jesus, who is our model, focused his comments on both actual and imaginary (Lazarus) poor people. But the goal was always to get his followers to assist actual poor people in the communities in which they live. So in order to be good followers of Christ, Christians either have to give effective help and loving care to poor people they meet on the street or who live in their neighborhoods, or they have to donate money to worthy groups (there are thousands of them in the United States) who work with the poor both to improve their lives and to comfort them. Some Christians may refuse to give money to poor people they suspect will not spend the money properly. That's a defensible position. But in that case a Christian should contribute to an organization that he feels effectively helps the poor in his town or neighborhood.

Jesus regularly encouraged his followers to ask the Father anything they wanted. Every Christian must be concerned for the poor, pray for the poor, and offer them loving service. Writing a check is good but insufficient, just as saying prayers for the poor is not enough. Christians are called to offer resources, prayers, and loving service. This requirement is a simple application of grace building on nature.

Finally, a wealthy family must make clear to themselves as well as to other members of the Christian community that their primary wealth is in Christ and the practice of the faith. A good, risk-averse, rich Catholic family knows they need a strong family culture that emphasizes generosity and the correct use of goods so that they fulfill Jesus' criteria for being members of the Kingdom of Heaven. There are many ways for a wealthy family to do this, but all ways should reinforce to both parents and children that excellent clothes, wonderful gadgets, several beautiful homes, and lots of cars are not part of their way of living. The family need not dispose of its financial wealth, since it can make sense to store up wealth either for starting a new corporation or for committing the money to support a major charitable undertaking. However, their lifestyle and prayers should make it clear to them and to others that their trust and joy are in the Lord.

CONCLUSION

This chapter explored where Christian commitment fits into the standard economic model of production and exchange. Economic theories provide a foundation for understanding which policies and institutions promote efficient, productive societies. They also provide a framework for the individual Christian both to critique a secular understanding of society and to explore what Christ calls a modern Christian to do. According to norms in economics and business, signs of a well-ordered society include efficiency, profitable businesses, and a high per capita GNP. A properly motivated Christian evaluates consumption, production, and distribution in terms of Christ's call to promote the Kingdom of God. The chapter suggested areas in which a committed Christian can be economically astute and at the same time faithful to the Gospel.

NOTES

1. In the Gospels Luke refers to the "Kingdom of God," while Matthew, writing primarily for Jews, prefers "Kingdom of Heaven."

2. More generally Commandment 3 requires that some day, whether Saturday or another day consistent with one's religious tradition, be set aside for rest and praise of God. Similarly Commandments 1 and 2 can be formulated so that they require praise and honor of a Supreme Being, not specifically Yahweh.

SELECTED READINGS

Barrera, Albino. *God and the Evil of Scarcity: Moral Foundations of Economic Agency*. Notre Dame, Ind.: University of Notre Dame Press, 2005.

Cavanaugh, William T. *Being Consumed: Economics and Christian Desire*. Grand Rapids, Mich.: Eerdmans, 2008.

Clegg, Samuel. *The Commercial Society: Foundations and Challenges in a Global Age*. New York: Roman and Littlefield, 2007.

Finn, Daniel K. *The Moral Ecology of Markets: Assessing Claims about Markets and Justice*. Cambridge, U.K.: Cambridge University Press, 2006.

Piderit, John. *The Ethical Foundations of Economics*. Washington, DC: Georgetown University Press, 1993.

How beautiful are the footsteps of those who bring good news. —Romans 10:15–17

19

Education in a Catholic Framework

Melanie M. Morey

THE PRIMARY SERVICE performed by college and university schools and departments of education is preparing future teachers and school administrators. This common mission requires that they focus on developing the knowledge and skills of would-be educators for the sake of tomorrow's students and society. A Catholic approach to education endorses this common mission but expands and infuses it with a particular sensibility rooted in Catholic, rather than secular, philosophy and anthropology.

Anthropological concerns are at the heart of the educational enterprise. At its most basic level education shapes the growth and development of individual human beings within a cultural framework. Cultural attitudes about the origin, nature, and destiny of human beings and the meaning of the good life influence educational aims, pedagogy, and curriculum. But education itself is also preeminently a cultural activity. It is the primary means by which cultures perpetuate themselves. As James Quillen pointed out in 1954, "The school is concerned with the transmission, conservation, and extension of culture. Cultural transmission and personality formation are perhaps the two most important functions of the school."[1]

All educators operate out of some kind of foundational anthropology, whether or not they are aware of it or examine it in any depth. The operational anthropology informing most American educators and educational theorists today is influenced by two things: scientific positivism and a secular cultural norm that increasingly relegates religion to the private sphere. Any anthropology used to diagnose current educational theory and practice necessarily combines elements of scientific anthropology and philosophical anthropology. If it aims to analyze the education of the entire person, however, that anthropology should also include theological elements. Yet this dimension is formally absent from the approach usually taken in graduate schools of education. Such truncated anthropologies pose serious problems for conscientious educators desiring to fulfill their responsibility to transmit American culture to whole persons encountered in actual classrooms.

Religion is not only an important component of the worldview of most American students, but it is also at the heart of American culture. It was religious belief and the desire to practice religion freely that brought our forebears to these shores. And religious convictions played a significant role in shaping the kind of nation our founding fathers and mothers set out to establish. Until very recently strong religious strains permeated American culture. They were also part of the cultural legacy transmitted in public schools. Even today many educators and educational theorists are themselves religious. They teach and do their scholarly work in what by Western standards is still a very religious country. Although the number of Americans claiming to be religious is declining, most students are nurtured in backgrounds that are at least religiously tinted. It is also true that the majority of Americans claim to be believers. Religion plays a significant role in American culture, and yet in schools of education throughout the country religion is generally ignored as a factor in student development.

Traditionally in Catholic educational circles things have been different. A Catholic approach to education flows from and is grounded in a foundational anthropology that is deeply theological. It reflects what the believing community understands about who we are as human beings and how God relates to us and we relate to God. In his book *Recovering a Catholic Philosophy of Elementary Education*, Curtis Hancock reminds us that Catholics approach education by first "recalling our metaphysical and theological heritage, by recalling who we are, how we got here, where we are going, and why we are going there."[2] Invoking a metaphysical and theological heritage, as Hancock does, may seem quaint and almost medieval. Educators might claim that schools of education no longer have a tradition in metaphysics. In fact, in this situation "metaphysics" is shorthand for "critical analysis of educational foundations." Without this educational metaphysics, critical thinking is at best shallow.

As Hancock further notes, education and schooling are not just about discovering the new. They also require remembering what human beings have already learned and yet find so easy to ignore or forget. By invoking a Catholic anthropology in a way that makes sense for students today, individual educators can make present and engage the collective wisdom of past centuries and apply it critically in their current circumstances.

PRESENT REALITIES

For centuries Catholics have been educating children, adolescents, and young adults. In the process they have produced a vibrant educational legacy and body of thought. Strangely the Catholic educational approach and enterprise often go unexamined in the very places dedicated to the study and exploration of education: college schools and departments of education. This is certainly true in the United States, where any serious and thorough consideration of Catholic education, be it empirical or analytical, is rare. Of course there are instances when Catholic education is the focus of scholarly discussion, study, and debate, but even in these instances the exploration is often flawed because it sidesteps Catholic education's theological underpinnings.

When Catholic education, or any religiously inspired educational approach for that matter, is stripped of the religious belief that animates it, it is robbed of its defining character. Equally important, whatever contribution the resulting educational theory can make to modern educational practice is occluded. In his chapter on music and art in this volume, Charles Scribner takes issue with how most nonbelievers approach the masterpieces of Christian art. "It may not be necessary," Scribner points out, "to *be* a Catholic in order to understand faithfully the masterpieces of Christian art, but it is necessary to think like a Catholic and to shun anachronisms that obscure our understanding of the masters." A similar claim could be made about attempts to examine and explore Catholic education. Being Catholic is not a requirement for understanding the Catholic approach to education. However, having a grasp of how Catholics think is. And what Catholics think is shaped by specific religious beliefs.

The unwillingness of college and university schools and departments of education to attend to the religious dimension of religiously inspired education is a serious omission. It impoverishes educational theory, practice, and debate in this country. It artificially constricts the range of material that can be explored in courses and constrains both students and teachers who might hope to integrate their own faith and learning. It leaves would-be educators ill prepared to address the religious and ultimate concerns of their future students.

In secular terms, however, the most trenchant criticism of the benign neglect of Catholic education is that it is insufficiently critical. Omitting religious considerations impedes the ability of critical thought to reach down to foundational issues.

Furthermore, although being dismissive of a religious approach may be popular, it certainly is not inclusive. Neither is it hard-hitting or profound.

Given this reality, Catholic colleges and universities have a unique opportunity to offer something different and a special responsibility to do so. These institutions assert that faith and reason are mutually enriching, and they commit themselves to taking religious faith seriously in the classroom as well as in the chapel. If Catholic colleges and universities do not shun the "anachronisms that obscure [a full and rich] understanding" of a Catholic approach to education, and if they fail to embrace a robust intellectual engagement with the faith that defines faith-based education, who will?

At the moment, however, most programs at Catholic institutions mirror those at all other American colleges and universities. Professors and programs at these Catholic colleges and universities rely on the same truncated anthropology as their secular colleagues and pay little attention to the distinctive Catholic anthropology that has shaped Catholic educational thought and practice for centuries. Schools and departments of education at Catholic colleges and universities are shaped more by current scholarly realities, trends in education, and the demands of state licensure than by anything distinguishably Catholic. But this does not have to be the case. These institutions could offer a program that would be more interesting for students, more illuminating for a society struggling with how to fix its educational system, and of greater service to the educational mission of the Church in whose name they operate. Juxtaposing Catholic educational approaches with secular American models would provide an interesting point of comparison and contrast that surely could provoke greater interest in and scrutiny of both.

Each of the central components of Catholic anthropology that Lawrence Cunningham and Thomas Rausch explore in their essays contributes in different ways to shaping a distinctively Catholic approach to education. What follows is a brief exploration of what some of these theological themes mean for various components of the educational experience. In highlighting the differences between a Catholic and a predominantly secular American approach to education, this short essay offers a peek at what could be in store for undergraduate education students if Catholic belief and educational thought and practice were more fully integrated into their courses.

THE GOOD LIFE AND EDUCATIONAL AIMS

The good life for Catholics is holiness, and it is to that end that an education that is truly Catholic must be directed. "Like the Holy One who called you, be holy yourselves also in all your behavior; because it is written, 'You shall be holy, for I am holy'" (1 Peter 1:15–16). This holiness for which human beings are destined by their Creator is the eternal sharing in relationship with the Triune God in whose image we are created. Cunningham reminds us that the notion of the graced or holy life as the good life is a long-standing notion in the Catholic tradition taught both by Augustine and Aquinas.

Holiness means becoming what God wants us to be. In Gospel terms that means each person should use the five talents given to make five more (Matthew 25:14–30). God gives to each individual a unique array of capacities and longings and is delighted when they are used well and harmoniously. But people are social beings as well as individuals. They are created by and in the image of a relational God and are made for relationship with God and with each other. Ideally each person is conceived, nurtured, and educated in love and in a community of loving individuals. People do not come to know God alone and on their own. For this reason Cunningham points out that the holiness to which all human beings are called is not purely personal. No one goes to God alone.

If the ultimate goal of each person is personal holiness and holiness in communion with others, then education properly understood should help people achieve this goal and contribute positively to what Cunningham describes as "the ongoing graced attempt to live in relationship to the Holy One revealed in Christ."

For Catholics God is the beginning and the end of human life and all education: "I am the way, the truth, and the life. No one comes to the Father except through me" (John 14:6). Holiness is the goal of Catholic education. For some, such an educational goal seems incompatible with cultivating critical thinking. However, this very approach has educated millions of students. It has helped them learn to write well, think imaginatively and precisely, and achieve a fluency in mathematics that eludes many other students. Holiness aims at developing the whole person. Adding religion and religious themes to the educational endeavor helps motivate students in Catholic schools to perform. This approach is not simply about inserting more material into the already crowded curriculum; rather it is about including themes that influence how material is presented.

While holiness and the search for truth is the aim of a Catholic education, the aim of secular education is quite different. Complete consensus about secular educational aims does not exist in this country. Nevertheless one very important thrust of American education is decidedly democratic. As American society has become more diverse and pluralistic over time, a shared view of the good life has been supplanted with a view of the "good process" which allows the society and culture to continue over time. This shared commitment to political process is reflected in educational theory and practice. As Amy Gutmann points out in her book, *Democratic Education*, Americans "disagree over the relative value of freedom and virtue, the nature of the good life, and the elements of moral character. But…we are committed to collectively re-creating the society that we share. Although we are not collectively committed to any particular set of educational aims, we are committed to arriving at an agreement on our educational aims. The substance of this core commitment is conscious social reproduction."[3] As a result the goal of public education is defined in terms of democratic virtue and the creation and cultivation of "ideal" citizens who are prepared to sustain and enhance American democracy into the future.

In a Catholic approach education is teleological, and its end point is relationship with God. Speaking of a deep human longing for God, St. Augustine in his *Confessions* famously wrote, "Our hearts are restless, until they find rest in Thee."[4] In a democratic approach, education is committed to an ongoing democratic process, not to a specific aim. There is no truth beyond the truths the society agrees to at the moment and no purpose beyond the continuation of the democratic society.

Educational aims set the stage for how the practice of education unfolds in educational institutions. Different aims of necessity produce at least some variations in educational practice. But it is also true that more than one type of practice can bring about the same goal. The political approach of American secular education, for instance, is not intended to produce holy people. But surely there will be many holy graduates of public education participating in the joys of eternity. Arguing symmetrically, it is also quite true that a commitment to producing good citizens is not the province of secular or public schools alone. American Catholics have long believed that their faith was compatible with the ideals and practices of American democracy, and Catholic schools have enthusiastically encouraged their students to cultivate civic virtue. Nevertheless a distinctly Catholic education is a different cultural experience, or at least it should be if it has integrity. That means that although some aims, goals, rationales, and practices in the Catholic and democratic educational approaches are mutually shared and/or congenial, others simply are not. Without the differences, the distinction between the two approaches would be meaningless.

Thomas Lickona points out, "Down through history, all over the world, education has had two great goals: To help students become smart and to help them become good."[5] Modern democratic education carefully constrains the meaning of *good* to be applicable primarily to participation in the democratic process. Nonetheless most educators, regardless of where they teach, readily identify "useful" or "important" skills students acquire. In practice educators establish goals for students at all grade levels that lead to broader attainment of school aims. Included among these goals are the following important areas:

1. Personal skills (moral, social, concentration, motor, and artistic skills)
2. Real-world knowledge
3. Creative, playful, and speculative appreciation and capacities
4. Critical reasoning and imagination

Regardless of whether the educational approach is democratic or Catholic, teachers and administrators work in developmentally appropriate ways to help students reach these goals. In a Catholic approach to education these general goals are modified by theological understandings that inform Catholic anthropology. In a Catholic approach the goals are focused or reimagined in the following way:

1. Personal skills are best developed by imitating Jesus Christ, the fullest expression of human flourishing.
2. Knowledge of the real world tells us things about God, since the real world is made and sustained by God.
3. Creative, playful, and speculative appreciation and capacities are not only fun and satisfying, but they reflect and share in the creative impulse of God, who made us in His image and likeness.
4. Critical reasoning and imagination should make full use of all available human knowledge, including personal, objectively empirical, historical, and analytical knowledge, and all sources of beauty and inspiration.

The Catholic slant on educational goals appears at first to narrow the focus to Jesus Christ and the Catholic Church. But because secular goals are delimited by those needed to participate constructively in a democratic society, Catholic educational goals are actually more expansive and embracing. As was noted earlier, they also offer Christian students powerful motivation to master material.

A Catholic approach to education provides an integrated Christian vision of reality. Therefore it requires some adjustments in educational method or strategy. A Catholic approach to the development of cognitive and emotional intelligence utilizes most teaching methods employed in a secular setting, but it also distinguishes itself by invoking four sources of understanding and authority and presenting them as such to students:

1. Scripture
2. The Church, including sacraments and liturgy
3. All of creation, which in its evolution reflects the Creator
4. Christian culture as it has developed over time, which preserves religious heritage and helps students understand and live out religious commitment

PEDAGOGY AND PRACTICES

As was noted earlier, all education is a cultural activity. Teachers and schools transmit culture to the next generation, and they do so primarily by means of practices. Teachers employ practices every day in order to help their students attain the general goals that their schools establish. At first blush the term *practice* sounds rather mechanical and uninteresting. What comes immediately to mind is the old saying "Practice makes perfect," which suggests endless repetitions of a basic activity that is more numbing than inspiring. But the term *practice* refers to a vast array of activities and rituals, some of which are rote and others that are more creative, exciting, engaging, and inspiring. Classroom practices include recitations, individual work and group projects, singing, art and modes of imaginative expression, the particulars of classroom etiquette, the choreography of movement (such as standing, sitting, lining up, moving about), recess, lunchtime rituals, assemblies, story hours, and countless other activities that engage students in classrooms all over the country every day. Teachers develop signature ensembles of educational practices that are compatible with their own style and personality. They choose varied activities that will maintain student interest. They also develop patterns of repetition they believe will be most conducive to student development.

Practices are the major components of the educational process, but they do not operate alone; they are embedded in a persuasive framework of understanding that is aimed at keeping students engaged. Within this framework practices are justified to students by three features linked to the practices: narratives, norms, and benefits. When brought together these components help students understand why any particular practice makes sense. They constitute the spin educators deftly employ to motivate their students to meet educational goals.[6]

Narratives explain why certain practices are important and how they fit with other practices. They also make a connection with the ways students understand other important things in their lives. Narratives establish a cultural context and connect the activities of the present with those of the past. All teachers use narratives. Occasionally they simply give their students directions about what to do, imparting cultural information regarding "how things are done around here." But far more frequently practices are introduced and reintroduced to students by means of narratives designed to persuade.

Norms are cultural standards. They are markers—positive and negative—that convey to students how practices ought to be undertaken, in what context, and with what frequency. Clearly some norms are negative, cultural "thou shalt nots." But more important and far more often norms are positive standards that illuminate cultural values. For example, teachers still teaching penmanship prob-ably tell students to make sure they put a crossbar through the vertical part of the *t* so that it cannot be confused with the letter *l*. They also likely remind students to be neat when writing because it enhances readability. This is a simple example in which a teacher reinforces both a positive and a negative norm for the students and at the same time emphasizes a general cultural value of neatness.

Benefits are consequences students value that result when they perform prac-tices properly. A teacher employing the practice of daily quizzes in at least one subject will surely be greeted by a chorus of groans from her students. (Indeed the teacher may join the student chorus with a silent internal groan at the prospect of correcting the daily quizzes!) Students quickly realize this practice means there always will be an immediate price to pay for skipping homework. The teacher will encourage compliance and maybe a bit more enthusiasm if she allows the quiz scores to count double when averaging the students' grades. Not only will the stu-dents benefit generally by not falling behind in their work, but they can also take advantage of the opportunity the quizzes present to improve their overall grade in the class. That is especially helpful for students who tend to clutch when faced with major tests or exams. There are many times when students avoid or prefer to avoid things they have to do in school. Describing and demonstrating the benefits they accrue by engaging in practices help motivate them.

In most circumstances, practices, narratives, norms, and benefits operate together as part of a sound pedagogical approach that students experience count-less times every day. Of course, practices may reinforce a wide variety of important skills for students. For example, a teacher might ask students in the lower grades to clear their desks and sit quietly in preparation for story time. The teacher explains that being calm and attentive will enhance their enjoyment of the story and help them remember it as well. In this example the practice is to clear desks and sit quietly. The norm is obvious: students should be calm and quiet as they prepare to hear or read a story. The benefit is greater enjoyment and retention.

Narrative, norm, and benefit work together to persuade students to engage in practices in a particular manner. If in the teacher's estimation one narrative, norm, and benefit ensemble fails, he makes modifications either on the spot or the next time the practice is employed. For example, on another occasion a teacher might make the following narrative modification. "We all like stories because they are exciting and tell us about interesting things and interesting people. But it is easy to get distracted or to distract others when desks are cluttered and people are chat-ting. In order to fully enjoy the story, you have to be prepared to pay attention and listen carefully. So first clear your desks. Then, think about the one person you would most like to write about if you were writing a story. While you are doing that you will quiet down and get in a 'story'" mood. This slightly different array introduces a step related to stories that will help the students settle themselves.

In *The Challenge to Care in Schools*, Nel Noddings discusses a set of components she believes are essential to the process of moral education.[7] Although her comments are primarily about moral education, the components themselves have wider application. They also are implied in the persuasive pedagogical framework of practices, narratives, norms, and benefits. One of the components is practice itself, but the others—dialogue, confirmation, and modeling—enrich the persuasive framework already identified.

Dialogue is embedded in the concept of narrative, which is surely more than just an oral presentation. In most cases a narrative is also an invitation to some deeper conversation. This is particularly true as students mature. Narratives are intended to impart information and make sense of things. When a particular norm does not make sense to students, one or more of them will probably object. The teacher then has to respond and perhaps provide a more convincing narrative. At times students also suggest adjustments to practices that make them more educationally effective or beneficial. And students are almost experts when it comes to figuring out what benefit they will get out of things. They can often identify benefits teachers miss.

Noddings also points out the importance of *confirmation,* which is an integral part of establishing norms. As indicated earlier, norms are not always or even usually negative; in most cases they are positive expectations. When students are developing skills it is important to confirm their progress. Confirmation helps people move farther along the path to achieving a goal. It is grounded in a positive assessment that people really want to achieve standards and perform. When that is the case, a confirming comment can provide that all-important boost that keeps students going. It also serves to demonstrate to others what the norm really looks like when it is being lived out.

Finally, Noddings points out how important *modeling* is when educating and forming young people. Teachers have to show students how to do the things they want them to do and how to be the kind of people they want them to be. This means that educators must themselves be true to the things they are asking of their students.

Practice, narrative, norm, and benefit ensembles are pedagogical tools with great creative potential. Some teachers use them more artfully than others, some more consistently. But in all settings teachers employ a variety of practices they persuasively embellish with narratives, norms, and benefits to help their students develop skills. Part of the process includes repeating many practices over and over again until they can be performed with ease and proficiency.

THE CATHOLIC DIFFERENCE

There are two distinctions between how this approach is employed in a democratic approach to education and how it is used in a Catholic approach. First, the range of practices in the Catholic approach is broader because of the inclusion of religious belief in the mix. Second, the persuasive framework in which practices are imbedded includes a Christian perspective and appeals to Christian authority and cultural understanding.

Three examples of a regular school practice embedded in the context of a Catholic-nuanced narrative, norm, or benefit will help illustrate these important distinctions. The first example is minor. A teacher in a Catholic school could choose to use it or some variation on it, or not bother. Much would depend on the personal preferences and goals of the teacher. The second example is more substantive and deals particularly with the academic arena of school life. The third example represents a significant difference in the Catholic approach to education in terms of character development.

A Minor Preschool Practice

For the minor example, consider a "tidying" practice that might take place in any pre-K class. At the end of the day the teacher will ask all of the children to join in putting all the supplies, toys, and books back in their storage cubbies. As part of a narrative she might tell the children that keeping their classroom neat and orderly will help them find what they need the next day. It is also the best way to make sure that none of the supplies gets lost or broken. Finally, working together will make the chore go quickly because many hands make light work. A Catholic school teacher could do exactly the same thing, but she might choose to amplify the narrative by including a religious dimension: she could remind the children that everything we have is a gift from God. She might say, "God loves and cares for everything he made, and we should too. One way we can show God we love the things he has given us and are grateful for them is by taking care of them and treating them with respect. God is delighted when we take good care of things. Remember the story about creation? God made everything and put it in its proper place. The fish were in the sea and the birds were in the air. When God works, everything is in order. We should try to follow what God did and make sure things in our classroom are in order too."

This example is focused on a specific activity with very young students, but it is intended to be suggestive of an entire of range of possible religious narratives, norms, and benefits that can be employed. In parochial schools religious themes are used to promote various educational goals; here the themes include a focus on Christ and the Creation story as well as the importance of Scripture, the Church, sacraments, and Christian culture. Each theme can be developed in scores of ways, and any of these ways can be used by an imaginative, religiously motivated teacher to develop effective narratives, norms, and benefits.

In Catholic schools some practices are distinctly religious, such as prayer, reading Bible stories and parables, and reading literary encounters with saints and sinners both real and fictional. Others, such as helping those in need, are practices that most teachers, whether in public or Catholic schools, employ. In a Catholic approach these practices are enhanced by narratives, norms, and benefits emanating from the Catholic themes mentioned earlier. For instance, one particular practice for elementary school children could employ contributing some of their spending money toward Haiti orphan relief. The Christian narrative certainly would emphasize that the suffering Haitian children and the students are brothers and sisters in Christ. It would also reference Scriptural accounts of Jesus' unceasing message of love and mercy and the miracles he performed to alleviate suffering. The beatitudes and parables, such as the parable of the Good Samaritan, would enrich supporting narratives. The tradition of almsgiving that extends back to the very early Church and the readiness of monasteries and convents to assist the poor would also be helpful connections to make with students. Stories about saints and holy people such as Dorothy Day and Mother Teresa, who gave their lives in service to the poor, also create a Catholic cultural context for what might otherwise be a purely secular practice.

Knowledge Skills

The second example focuses on students in algebra class learning how to graph functions, especially equations of lines. If the students can already multiply and divide quickly and without hesitation, graphing equations is pretty straightforward. Figuring out the slope of the line and its y-intercept is not difficult, but at first it can be confusing. In fact the confusion is an important part of the learning process. Clarity replaces confusion for most students once they can graph many different equations and are able to look at a graph and figure out what the equation must be. But getting to this point requires work. A ninth-grade algebra teacher knows what it takes for algebra students to become proficient. He will structure assignments so that over a two- or three-week period the students will graph at least sixty or seventy equations. Working with many different examples gives students the opportunity to sort out their confusion and begin to see patterns. They develop their graphing skills, and as a result their confidence grows significantly.

But this math moment can suggest something more revelatory, and a Catholic school teacher helps students by making the connection. The teacher could well tell struggling algebra students, "Graphing functions at first is rather mysterious, seeming almost unintelligible. However, by focusing your mind acutely and patiently and persistently working on problems, you begin to understand more. You make progress and then encounter setbacks when confusion reigns again. But eventually you became adept at graphing and begin to recognize patterns that you could hardly imagine when you started. And with this comes some sense of awe, deeper understanding, and now a different kind of mystery, deeper, richer, and more intriguing. A relationship with God plays out in a similar way. God is infinite, way beyond comprehension, but He is not unintelligible. He communicates with people. But in order to understand 'God's language' you have to patiently and persistently focus your mind on God and talk to God in prayer. It is work, but it's worth the effort. At first the whole thing is confusing, but working through confusion to greater understanding is a life skill mature people must develop. It takes time to know God, just as it takes time to understand equations. Growing in relationship with God requires patience. God gave us the ability to learn about equations and graphs and to analyze the world. What students do in algebra is God's work and it will help you come to know God better."

Personal Moral Skills

To set the stage for the last example, consider what Thomas Lickona says. He succinctly states the twofold purpose of education: helping students to be smart and to be good. How is the latter goal understood in a secular approach to education and in a Catholic approach? What are the differences?

One way to help students be good is to nurture their development of moral skills. In the public forum teachers, educational theorists, and politicians discuss whether public schools should even try to develop students' moral skills. Helping students become good citizens is one of the political aims of public education. But being good citizens is not the same as being moral persons and, as Gutmann points out, Americans "disagree over...the elements of moral character."[8] If Americans cannot agree on what constitutes moral character, they certainly cannot help students achieve it.

Gutmann gets around this difficulty by focusing on educating for "democratic" character rather than moral character, and she therefore attends to the attainment of democratic skills rather than moral skills. She claims that schools are not very good at teaching the morality of principle. This she defines as doing what is right and good not for its democratic utility or because authorities demand it, but just because it is right and good. While schools can help students move beyond the morality of authority that belonged to early childhood, she does not think that in a democratic society schools can help students become morally principled: "What the most successful schools seem to teach is not the morality of principle but rather the morality of association: the willingness and ability to contribute and to claim one's fair share in cooperative associations." The morality of association is marked by the virtues of "empathy, trust, fairness, and benevolence."[9] Undergirding this approach is a view of freedom that leans toward *negative* liberty, the view that no one should interfere with a person's pursuit of what he wants as long as it does not limit the freedom of others. But in her analysis Gutmann puts a stopper on negative liberty. She maintains that in its extreme form it takes toleration and mutual respect too far, thereby undermining the ideal of democratic justice.

Offering a utilitarian justification for her approach, Gutmann notes, "Teaching the morality of association marks great moral progress over teaching the morality of authority.... Schools that teach the cooperative virtues are uncommonly successful and minimally problematical." She says that moral education "begins by winning the battle against amoralism and egoism. It ends—if it ends at all—by struggling against uncritical acceptance of the moral habits and opinions that were the spoils of the first victory."[10] In the democratic model there are some truths that support democracy, but no ultimate truth. This model harbors a certain suspicion of authority and emphasizes individualism and democratic process, an embrace of multicultural recognition and appreciation, and an expanded view of the value of tolerance.

While Gutmann puts some limits on toleration and mutual respect in her analysis, she admits that in practice moral neutrality is often the norm in democratic education. Values clarification is the form that character development takes in a broad swath of American public schools. This approach stresses the importance of helping students define their own moral principles by developing moral reasoning skills and the capacity to make choices. However, it also clearly maintains that there is no such thing as a right set of values that can be passed on in schools.

Because the range of skills necessary to be good citizens is limited and the democratic approach to moral formation is confined to dealing only with these skills, it cannot take a stand on many pressing moral issues that affect society and also vex students. Whether young people should view pornography, whether students should treat those in authority with respect, what students should do to become good friends, spouses, and parents as opposed to good citizens, whether there is a moral reason for studying hard—all these issues, if they are treated at all, are underspecified in the public school framework of public virtue.

Since the scholastic philosophers of the thirteenth century Catholics have relied on a well-articulated natural law approach to morality, and it is this approach that identifies the contours of the good life. According to this approach, all human beings, regardless of whether or not they are religious, have an innate sense of what is right and what is wrong in terms of certain basic or fundamental values. This way of approaching morality is articulated quite well in the words of the American Declaration of Independence: "We hold these truths to be self-evident, that all men are created equal." But Catholics believe that natural law is only one component of three that contribute to moral character and behavior. Christian belief and practice based on the revelation of Scripture are the two additional components that reinforce moral teaching and also provide assistance to Catholics in their acquisition of moral skills.

The normative source of Christian belief is Scripture, but it is augmented by authoritative interpretation that comes from the lived experience of the believing community over time and is annunciated by the teaching authority of the Church. Catholics also believe that religious practice combined with belief will enhance and reinforce moral skills. A Catholic approach to education helps students to be good by relying on Scripture, belief, the practice of the faith, and attentiveness to the lived cultural experience of Christian communities. The experience of the Christian community living the faith is what leads to the development of moral skills.[11]

The theological implications of the account of creation in Genesis combined with the teaching of Jesus that every human being is called to a loving, personal relationship with him and the Father, through the Holy Spirit, yield a powerful, motivating story for students. Human beings all enjoy a common dignity precisely because they come from God and are made in his image and likeness. Human creation is specific, not generic. All individuals are given special gifts, which God wants them to develop and share with others.

Being "made in the image of God" means that people can use their human reason to understand the world and that to which God is calling them. Given the ability of reason to understand, Catholics believe in Truth with a capital *T*. Truth is a norm that God puts in each human being. This truth-norm means the scope of tolerance has limits that keep it from tipping into relativism. For Catholics, tolerance means respecting the right of each individual to his or her opinion. It does not hold that all opinions have equal value. Cultivation of the virtue of prudence, which is the ability to judge wisely, is also important in a Catholic approach to moral education.

The view of human freedom operative in a Catholic educational approach leans strongly in the direction of a *positive* freedom to do as we *ought* to do. There is a clear recognition that although human beings are good and graced creatures,

something in how we behave and operate is awry. Sin is a part of human experience. St. Paul in his Epistle to the Romans hauntingly describes his frustration at
a perverse part of human nature that we all experience: "What I do, I do not understand. For I do not do what I want, but I do what I hate" (Romans 7:15). But for
Catholics, sin never is the last word. Through his passion, death, and resurrection,
Jesus Christ redeemed humanity from the power of sin. Redeemed by grace, we
are truly free to respond to God's grace or turn away.

The Catholic model for desiring to do the right thing in life is Jesus Christ.
Natural law is used to sort out the important issues and figure out what should be
done. Prayer and a focus on Christ should give us the strength to do what we know
we ought to do.

Corrective Packages

In order to help students develop moral character, teachers and schools must confront students when they do something wrong. They do this by means of "corrective packages" that include practices, norms, narratives, and benefits. The practice
in this case has both a restorative and a readjustment component. By performing
the practice, the student attempts to set things right. The narrative, norm, and
benefits of the practice clarify why the punishment fits the crime, so to speak. It
also offers a rationale for why the corrective package is fair. The norm identifies
what the student did that was wrong. Together with the narrative it explains why
it is wrong and how seriously wrong it is. The benefit for the student may include
both the fact that he satisfies what the school requires of him and that he partially
makes up for the wrong he has committed. If the narrative and norm are well
stated, the student sees how the corrective package offers him a way to get back on
track. Regaining his equilibrium is at best a dubious benefit for the student, though
in time he may come to a greater appreciation of the corrective action. Having to
make amends is difficult. Because discipline is painful but also a necessary part of
character formation, it must be done lovingly. Therefore the thrust of the encounter
with the student should be finding a better way for the future.

Plagiarism is a serious problem in American education and one that has become
all the more common with the growth of the Internet. Suppose that a teacher discovers that one of the juniors in his class has plagiarized a major section of her
research paper. After confronting the student, let us suppose that the teacher—
regardless of the school—tells the student that she will receive a grade of zero on
the paper she plagiarized and that she will have to do another written assignment
whose grade will be averaged with the zero she received for the original assignment. Chances are that the corrective package presented to the student would

differ widely across schools, but to keep things simple, let us suppose the practice is the same regardless of the school. The only part that differs in the corrective package is the justification: the narrative, norm, and benefit.

In a public or nonsectarian (democratic) school, the teacher would clarify what the student did that was wrong. He might begin by saying, "Plagiarism is a form of stealing, and it is simply not fair to take someone else's work and claim it as your own. Besides which, when you plagiarize you cheat yourself because you are not learning anything. If you get caught plagiarizing down the road, the consequences can be very serious. People can lose their jobs and their careers can be ruined if they are caught plagiarizing." That said, the teacher would present the corrective package.

In a Catholic school the teacher would employ a different justification for the corrective package, pointing out that plagiarism is a serious offense against God that hurts you and also wounds the community. (After all, as the theologian James F. Keating points out, a central truth of Christianity is that everything we see and everything we are is a gift, a spontaneous and generous gift from God.) "When you plagiarize, you are using someone else's work to make yourself appear more than you are. It is both stealing and a lie. It is also a slap at God, who gives us all that we have. We show our gratitude to God by celebrating the giftedness of others. Citing someone else's work recognizes that person's giftedness and celebrates it by pointing it out for others to see and appreciate. It also recognizes and praises the giver of all good gifts, God Almighty. When you plagiarize you lie about yourself and what you are capable of doing. You refuse to use and develop the gifts God has given you and you steal the just praise someone else has earned. God gives each of us special gifts that we have to develop. Plagiarism short-circuits this process." The teacher might also say that the student has done something seriously wrong and that she will have to do some things that show God and the community that she has learned an important lesson. He might finish by saying to the student, "God gave you a voice and you need to find it and use it to the best of your ability. If you do this next assignment well and tell God that you are sorry for what you did, you can get back on the right track. We all know you have something to say that is worth saying, and we all want you to succeed. But part of success is being honest with yourself and fair with others. It is also admitting what you have done wrong."

In a Catholic worldview the intention of the student counts. So it is important for teachers to find out the student's motivation in plagiarizing. Perhaps the student wanted to meet the deadline but ran out of time, so she decided to add a segment she found on the Internet. As I indicated earlier, corrective narratives need to fit the crime, and the wealth of narratives in the Catholic tradition provides teachers with a lot of flexibility. In this case, the student who was pressed for time cut corners. The teacher will certainly confirm the student's good intentions, but he will also clarify the adjustments that can restore the student to good standing in the school community. The teacher could remind the student of the parable Jesus told of the general who, with 10,000 troops, went out to meet an enemy of 20,000 troops. A good general with only 10,000 troops would sue for peace and pay a penalty rather than have his troops die (Luke 14:31–33). Jesus says that, in the same way, Christians have to plan ahead; if they do not, they will suffer the consequences.

In this example it is easy to see how distinct the two justifications are for an identical corrective package. The Christian justification reminds the student that, as one of God's creatures and a follower of Christ, she is expected to obey the commandments and also love other people and be generous. The Catholic school teacher has the option of including some of the points made by the democratic school teacher. It is also possible that the democratic school teacher can adapt the Catholic narrative, norm, and benefit by stripping it of its specifically religious content and emphasizing basic moral principles instead ("Always tell the truth," "A wise person never cheats," "It is important for people always to be fair," "Be true to yourself," etc.). Along with the democratic way and the comprehensive religious way, such general ethical principles offer a third path for teachers to promote good moral behavior: the path of general moral principles.

MOVING FORWARD

As I stated at the beginning of this essay, the primary job of college and university schools and departments of education is to prepare future teachers and school administrators. In fulfilling their primary mission, Catholic education schools and departments can and should offer a program that is distinctively Catholic. These are the departments and schools best positioned to examine, explore, and further a distinctively Catholic approach to education for the benefit of their students, society, and the Church. There are many ways to go about doing that; Catholic schools and departments of education must consider their unique capacity and responsibility for preparing the teachers and administrators who will serve in Catholic schools in the future.

The challenge is significant. In a survey she conducted in 1999, Sister Mary Traviss, O.P., found that only twenty-six Catholic colleges and universities offered specific programs for the preparation of Catholic school teachers and administrators. She also found significant differences among their programs. Some offered only an elective in the teaching of religion; others referred generally to emphasizing an unspecified "Catholic tradition"; and some indicated their preparation courses were open to all students regardless of where they intended to teach. Traviss concluded that there was a real problem that needed to be addressed: "If the Catholic schools are to continue to be staffed by prepared personnel, the bishops, superintendents, Catholic colleges and universities will have to cooperate in working on this apostolic challenge. It is a need that will not resolve itself."[12]

Education schools and departments are demonstration projects wherein classroom practice either reinforces or undermines what is being taught. This means that the only way Catholic education schools and departments can prepare educators who take a distinctively Catholic approach to education is by actually using the approach themselves. What students experience in these learning laboratories will influence their own educational practice in the future. This unique circumstance places particular demands on departments that claim a Catholic identity and mission. If they are going to graduate teachers who take faith seriously and engage it deeply, their students will have to experience something other than religious tokenism in their education courses. That means they must be exposed to how Catholics think and what that thinking means for how they understand education. Students will also have to encounter faculty members at Catholic education schools and departments who take seriously both faith and the theological foundations of Catholic educational thought and practice. Finally, over the course of their studies students at these institutions must encounter some Catholic faculty members who are personally committed to the faith, are well informed about what a Catholic approach to education entails, are willing to integrate that knowledge appropriately in their courses, and witness to the faith.

NOTES

1. James Quillen, "An Introduction to Anthropology and Education," in *Anthropology and Education*, edited by George Dearborn Spindler (Stanford: Stanford University Press, 1955), 2.

2. Curtis L. Hancock, *Recovering a Catholic Philosophy of Elementary Education* (Mount Pocono, Pa.: Newman House Press, 2005), 10.

3. Amy Gutmann, *Democratic Education* (Princeton, N.J.: Princeton University Press, 1987), 39.

4. St. Augustine, *Confessions,* book 1, chapter 1, www.leaderu.com/cyber/books/augconfessions/bk1.html.

5. Thomas Lickona, *Character Matters* (New York: Simon and Schuster, 2004), xxiv.

6. For a more in-depth discussion of this model of pedagogy, see John J. Piderit, S.J. and Melanie M. Morey, *Renewing Parish Culture* (New York: Rowman and Littlefield, 2008).

7. Nel Noddings, *The Challenge to Care in Schools: An Alternative Approach to Education* (New York: Teachers College Press, 2005), 21–7.

8. Gutmann, *Democratic Education*, 39.

9. Gutmann, *Democratic Education*, 61.

10. Gutmann, *Democratic Education*, 61–2.

11. For a more thorough discussion of Catholic morality and moral skills development see, John J. Piderit, S.J., *Sexual Morality: A Natural Law Approach to Intimate Relationships* (New York: Oxford University Press, 2012).

12. Cited in Thomas C. Hunt, Ellis A. Joseph, and Ronald J. Nuzzi, eds., *Handbook of Research on Catholic Education* (Greenwich, Conn.: Information Age, 2004), 143.

SELECTED READINGS

Buetow, Harold A. *The Catholic School: Its Roots, Identity, and Future*. New York: Crossroad, 1988.

Greeley, Andrew. *The Catholic Imagination*. Berkeley: University of California Press, 2000.

Hancock, Curtis L. *Recovering a Catholic Philosophy of Elementary Education*. Mount Pocono, Pa.: Newman House Press, 2005.

Hunt, Thomas C., Ellis A. Joseph, and Ronald J. Nuzzi. *Catholic Schools in the United States: An Encyclopedia*. Westport, Conn.: Greenwood, 2004.

Piderit, S. J., John J., and Melanie M. Morey. *Renewing Parish Culture*. New York: Rowman and Littlefield, 2008.

20

Medicine, Health, and Catholic Themes

Myles N. Sheehan, S.J., M.D.

PROMINENTLY DISPLAYED IN the atrium of Loyola University Chicago's Stritch School of Medicine is a quotation from the twenty-fifth chapter of Matthew's Gospel: "I was ill and you cared for me." The words come from Jesus' prediction of the final judgment, in which he lists care of the sick as one of the criteria by which humans will be judged for entry into God's kingdom. The message for the students at this Catholic medical school is clear: care for the sick is a fundamental mission of Catholicism and the motivation for a Catholic medical school. The Catholic intellectual tradition provides fertile ground for those who seek a career in the health care professions. Medicine, nursing, physical and occupational therapy, and other health care–related disciplines all encounter critical questions of life and death, the meaning of illness, the presence or absence of God, as well as issues about the nature of the human person. Catholicism engages these questions, and the insights it provides give meaning and grounding for health care professionals.

In this chapter I focus on medicine because of my experience as a physician and a medical school educator, but this emphasis does not exclude nursing or any other health care profession (physical therapy, occupational therapy, etc.). Nursing and other health care professions constitute a medical team at many health care institutions. Each health care profession has a distinctive role that is both complementary to and different from that of the physician, and the contributions of Catholic theology and religious practice offer similar and valuable insight and motivation to the full range of health care professionals.

All facets of Catholic health care flow from the mission of the Catholic Church. Although the mission motivates, it does not ensure better health care. It is tendentious and false to claim that Catholic health systems or Catholic health care professionals are better, more caring, or more worthy than their non-Catholic counterparts. The practice of medicine and the care of the sick are found in every culture and are part of every human tradition, religious or not. The universality of our limited human life span, the reality of illness, disease, and death, and the desire to be relieved from suffering and not abandoned to the experience of illness go beyond any one tradition. These universal human experiences speak to basic claims made by Catholic theology. Medicine and health care are important places to explore the meaning of Catholic faith.

The thesis of this essay is that just as worship and liturgy are part of theology in its role of faith seeking understanding, the health care professions provide a vital arena for believing Catholics to understand issues basic to Christian anthropology, Christology, the nature of the Church, and the life of the Christian in the world. Catholicism and theology provide fundamental insights for physicians, nurses, and other health care professionals because of the tradition's fuller and more developed anthropology than the alternate, pragmatic anthropology relied upon at secular health care facilities. Catholic anthropology is fuller and better articulated because it benefits from centuries-old experience in health care.

Students who come to medical or nursing school may well experience disconnects between their chosen discipline and their faith experience. That is largely because the nature of the human person, the value and dignity of life, and questions of meaning and sickness are far removed from the concerns of science that dominate their professional training. Premedical studies in the United States, for instance, require two years of chemistry, two years of biology, a year of physics, and a year of mathematics, along with the other requirements necessary for a bachelor's degree. The emphasis on science, experimental evidence, and a reductionist approach to life are part of the professional formation physicians and nurses receive. However, expertise in molecular genetics, biochemistry, and statistics may not be what best equips students either to face persons in their illness or deal with their own reactions to the tensions and tragedies they encounter in medicine.

Health care is based in science, and therefore medicine and the other health care professions must emphasize objectivity in examination, diagnosis, and prognosis. But health care also deals with persons and thus encounters human subjectivity. The Catholic tradition, with its focus on love and service, has much to offer in this realm.

The Catholic tradition views human life partially as mystery. Sick or concerned patients in particular are aware of the mystery of their own lives as well as how they relate to God and other persons. The physician in the Catholic tradition is called to respect this mystery and even cherish it. Life is not simply molecules, chemical reactions, and neurotransmitters. Catholicism teaches that both objectivity and an acknowledgment of mystery are needed in health care. Would-be doctors and nurses are called to a life of meaning, depth, and encounter with some of the most profound mysteries, joys, and disappointments of life. By sharing these with their patients, health care providers have a privileged opportunity to encounter God.

Medicine has a broad frontier where innovations take place. Basic sciences, such as biology, chemistry, and physics, provide the underlying insights that lead to new discoveries. Medical advances occur when new discoveries in basic science are applied to remedying defects, diseases, and physical problems in human beings. While it is not the primary intention of scientists, the sciences provide insights into what it means to be human and how humans are similar to and different from other species. Science even studies human consciousness, and the results constitute part of the data of medicine.

Medicine also has an impact beyond medical ethics. In fact the impact goes beyond ethics. New medical techniques often raise ethical issues; however, the more significant impact of new medical advances is in terms of how we understand ourselves. For Christians, the advances continually refine how we understand the statement in Genesis that human beings are made in the image and likeness of God. In this way medical advances refine Christian anthropology by uncovering the most basic physical and psychological structures of human beings. These structures allow for change and also prompt questions about what is essential in human beings, what can but should not be modified, and what by all means should be changed, enhanced, and improved.

For believers who are in health care or involved in teaching or health sciences research there are challenges in living at the frontier of human progress. One is incorporating the living of the Catholic faith into the scientific or medical project itself. The Christian message contains themes that depict the great distance between God and humanity as being foreshortened in Jesus Christ. In the words of the Creed recited each Sunday at Mass, Jesus is "God from God, Light from Light...who by the power of the Holy Spirit was born of the Virgin Mary and became man." In continuity with the Jewish tradition, Jesus preached trust in the God he called Father, the necessity of prayer, and the requirement of care for one's neighbor. Christians, following the teaching of Christ, attempt to live a life of prayer, service, hope, and worship of the One who died and rose from the dead.

In their faith and daily activities Christians in health care experience positive aspects of the human frontier, places where God interacts with human beings.

However, they also encounter bleak challenges that are not as friendly to the faith. Christian health care workers and researchers are surrounded by a reductionist view of humanity that leaves no room for spirit, soul, or God. More immediately than academics in other areas of the university, Christian academics in the health sciences live out their faith in the midst of determined materialists who see only principles of chemistry and physics that leave no room for God. In this milieu they encounter places where God interacts with human beings. In their healing ministry and through the story of Jesus these Christians experience a calling to divine life.

In the past century the reductionist approach to human life gained great traction, with a broad swath of academics claiming that human reason and a focus on physical reality are all we need. While this approach is satisfying to many, in my experience it is often found wanting by those who work in health care at Catholic institutions. Theology can play a vital role here. In exploring and addressing the concerns and desires of Christian believers working in the health sciences, theology can show how Christian faith incorporates, lives with, challenges, and ideally assimilates the data of the basic sciences in medicine. Theologians can also highlight the many deficiencies of a reductionist approach. Even more important, theology explores and elucidates the lived experience of those in medicine and science who strive to integrate faith and science.

MEDICINE AS A VOCATION

In his essay exploring Catholic anthropology and the good life, Thomas Rausch offers fruitful perspectives on the question "What is the life God calls us to?," but they are general, not specific to medicine and nursing. Deciding to be a doctor or a nurse is not simply a decision to enter a profession that provides satisfaction, prestige, and financial rewards. Medicine is a vocation, a calling from God. As the quotation in the atrium of Stritch School of Medicine testifies, caring for the sick is part of Jesus' charge to the disciples. A vocation to health care is a call to a critical mission of the Church. Care for the sick is central to Christianity. Becoming a health care professional beckons Christian believers to follow the example of Jesus Christ.

Following the Example of Jesus

In the Christian tradition healing the sick is a sign of the inbreaking of the Kingdom of God and a manifestation of Jesus as the Christ, the Messiah of God. Christian anthropology holds that the God who created the universe has taken on a human nature. The nearness of God is seen and experienced in Jesus. Jesus reveals God's presence in his teaching and proclamation, but also through miracles. In the words of the Book of Revelation, Jesus makes all things new (Revelation 21:5).[1] The new creation that Jesus begins in his ministry includes curing leprosy, bringing sight to the blind, restoring physical integrity to the crippled, and expelling demons whose manifestations appear to the modern eye to be remarkably similar to epilepsy and severe mental illness. Not limited to the healing of illness, the miracles of Jesus even include the restoration of life to those who are dead: the son of the widow of Naim, the daughter of Jairus, and best known of all, Lazarus.

Jesus' miraculous cures are certainly a sign of his power and evidence of an extraordinary relationship to God. But they are also manifestations of who God is, what God does, and how God relates to humanity. Illness in Jesus' time was seen as punishment for sin. Specific illnesses rendered a sick person not only miserable due to a lack of effective health care, but separated from the community, since in many cases the sick person was unclean according to Mosaic law. The leper, for example, was ritually impure and not allowed to be near others. Another poignant example of social separation is the woman with a hemorrhage who touched Jesus' cloak in an effort to find relief after years of suffering. In addition to suffering and embarrassment, she had squandered her resources on doctors who could not cure her. Not simply another healing narrative, Jesus' miracle rendered him impure because he was touched by a woman with vaginal bleeding. Her knowledge of her infectious ritual impurity explains her fear when Jesus turned to her and asked what she had done. As is revealed in this miracle and in others, Jesus is not concerned with becoming impure by contact with the sick. In healing their physical and mental ailments, not only does Jesus restore people to health; he also leads them from the margins of society and restores them to God's community, the people of God. Because of Jesus' activity in restoring health and healing sin, He is often referred to by the early Church Fathers as the Divine Physician.

Jesus' encounter with the Canaanite woman, most vividly recounted in the Gospel of Matthew (15:21–28), provides a clear example not only of the challenges encountered on the frontier of healing, but also of how one can experience vibrant, living faith. In this story Jesus travels outside the territory of Israel, seemingly to sidestep some of the mounting opposition to him from religious leaders. As he walks with his disciples, he is accosted by a Canaanite woman, a Gentile. Somewhat impetuously she approaches and beseeches him to heal her daughter, whom she believes is possessed by a demon. Perhaps tired and likely preoccupied with the problems he is facing, Jesus says nothing. He might have thought to himself, "Here I try to get away from the hostility of the religious establishment, and my dear Father sends me this loud demanding woman." The woman is in his face demanding a cure. He and his disciples move on, but the woman does not yield. She follows them, calling Jesus to do something for her.

Aspects of this scene, including what happens before the direct encounter with the woman, are repeated daily in health care centers around the world. Physicians and nurses, overworked and stretched beyond their limits, are often ambushed by a demanding family member. Jesus is the love of God in our midst, but he was also human, and his empathy with the Canaanite woman at that point may have been minimal. Practically forced to speak with her, he is at best aloof, if not downright cold and hostile. He restates the priority of his mission to Israel. But the woman makes a plea for help. In human terms it seems at this point that Jesus just wants to move on. However, he may have deliberately said something harsh to test her faith or to probe why she expects good things from a Jew. In any event, referring to the fact that she is not Jewish, he says something shockingly harsh to her: "It is not fair to take the children's food and throw it to the dogs." Unfazed, the woman continues to negotiate with Jesus. But she does so with faith and a self-deprecating wisdom that reveals her only care is for her daughter: "Yes, Lord, but even the dogs get the crumbs that fall from the master's table." In this resilient, witty, and clever response Jesus perceives a deep faith that moves him beyond his own human limits as a Jew whose main mission is to heal and elevate the Jewish people. In his humanity he realizes the power of God beyond the frontiers of Israel and his own culture. He answers, "Woman, great is your faith! Let it be done for you as you wish." The story concludes, "Her daughter was healed instantly."[2]

The experience of Jesus with the Canaanite woman speaks to all health care providers. The story recounts a brief but deep encounter that Jesus has with a foreigner. Of course, health care providers are usually dealing with people who are foreigners to sickness and disease. Confronted with serious sickness in their loved ones, they do not know what to do. But they see capable, loving people around them in the hospital. In their desperation they want the nurse or physician to do something now to rid their loved one of this sickness, this infirmity. They may plead, importune, and make demands on nurses and physicians, but their motivation is the love of their sick relative or friend. So a first fruit of this story is that health care providers should recall how blessed they are to have the gift and expertise of healing, given to them over many long years of study and mentorship. Yes, they are besieged, but so was Jesus. Jesus was gifted far beyond health care providers, but health care providers have impressive gifts.

In all they do, health care providers should keep their eyes resolutely fixed on Jesus. His example as the Divine Physician is not simply one who heals and preaches. His healing ministry stretches the limits of his human understanding.

Encountering the faith of those he meets, Jesus is changed in his humanity even as he heals and exercises his divine and human powers. That is especially true when he encounters those who are seemingly beyond the limits of what culture and tradition say are the boundaries of God's power and being.

A third part of the story reveals something especially wonderful for health care providers: the woman's daughter is cured immediately. Jesus is the full-satisfaction nurse and physician! Health care providers want success, not for themselves but for their patients. Also, Jesus directed his disciples that, in curing others, they should freely give what they have freely received (Matthew 10:8). Modern health care, including Christian health care, costs so much, but in imitation of Jesus, by being alert and responsive to concerned relatives, together with their healing expertise Christian health care providers offer without cost their additional love, concern, and prayers. This is both a compelling package and also a good evangelical strategy for Christian physicians and nurses.

Jesus' example of curing and restoration of the sick as a sign of the Kingdom of God is taken up by his disciples after the Resurrection. It is seen as authoritative evidence that the work Christ began continues in his followers in the Church. After Jesus was arrested by the Jews, Peter denied him three times. But several weeks later, after the experience of Pentecost, Peter boldly heals people in the name of Jesus. The Acts of the Apostles also presents other leaders of the Church as not only preaching the new faith, but as powerfully witnessing to it by their authority over illness. Legend suggests that one of the evangelists, St. Luke, was himself a physician, and referred to by St. Paul as the "dear and glorious physician."

What else does Jesus' example imply for Catholic health care practitioners? It is a call not simply to care for the sick but also to give particular attention to those on the margins of society. It is a call to risk reputation and even life for those who are suffering, and to do so with the faith that providing personal, expert care is part of how God cares for his children. Christian physicians and nurses are called by faith to do the work of the Church and to fulfill a mission of the Church. In this way they cooperate with the Holy Spirit and enable Christ's healing and care to continue in the world. Understood correctly and practiced with love, health care is a sign that the Kingdom of God is coming. Through nurses and physicians God is making things new. The Kingdom of God comes even in the contemporary world. It comes when Christian health care practitioners are pushed by encounters with extreme situations that seem far removed from their own faith experience. It comes when doctors and nurses, like Jesus with the Canaanite woman, move beyond their own comfort and confront the need for God in those for whom they care.

Healing as a Mission of the Church

The tradition of healing was central to the life of Jesus and is a critical component in the life of the Church. Just as the Church proclaims and teaches, sanctifies and governs, so too the Church cares for the sick. She does so not only in obedience to the command "I was ill and you cared for me," but as a manifestation that the Spirit of Christ is alive and powerful in those who follow him.

Beginning in the fourth century the monks in the Egyptian desert and later those in the large monasteries founded in Europe combined prayer and loving service. Specifically they took in the sick and cared for them. Monasteries were known not only for prayer, contemplation, and learning, but also as places where the sick would be provided with care and comfort. In the Middle Ages and the Renaissance religious communities and lay persons in confraternities cared for the sick. They did so through epidemics of the plague and the scourge of syphilis introduced to the New World. They cared for those made ill by poverty, infirmed by old age, and wounded in battle. From the very first, medical schools were part of the great universities of Europe and flourished alongside faculties of philosophy, law, and theology. Hospitals grew as institutions from the roots of the medical care religious communities provided to sick brothers and sisters and their neighbors. These institutions thrived and grew in nineteenth-century America, primarily because of Catholic sisterhoods. The sisters made heroic sacrifices to establish Catholic health care in the new country, where they and their faith were often greeted with suspicion at best and hatred and violence at worst. And their hospitals cared for all who came to them, frequently providing an example of charity and benevolence on the frontiers of the expanding West.

In the United States Catholic health care is a major presence among health care providers, with about 16 percent of hospital beds in the country under Catholic auspices. The Catholic Health Association works with and for Catholic health care in advocacy, ethics, and issues of mission and identity. It describes Catholic health care as continuing the healing ministry of Jesus Christ. Like his ministry, Catholic health care and its mission of caring for the sick are sacramental, signs of the coming of God's kingdom.

The miraculous cures of Jesus' time and the early days of the Church are less evident today. However, the sign of Jesus and his followers who care for those who are sick, separated, alienated, and in need of comfort and healing remains present in Catholic hospitals and health care organizations. This is not simply because good medical care is available in Catholic hospitals. Indeed, as indicated earlier, it may be that equally good or better technical care is available in other institutions. Rather the importance of Catholic health care is that it is a ministry, service done explicitly in the name of Jesus, as a mission of the Church. The ministry of Catholic health care differs from other providers; it is obliged to care for the poor and to give particular attention to those who are old and facing the end of life. Catholic health care also must combine physical healing with pastoral care and provide sacraments and spiritual services to those who come for relief from their illness.

The story of Catholic health care in the United States and Canada is really two stories. It is a story of heroism in expanding health care and hospitals in difficult conditions, in primitive regions, often in the face of hostile persons, persecutions, epidemics, limited supplies, and material hardships. It is equally a story of prayer, witness to Christ, lives rooted in religious commitments, and profound sacrifice on the part of the religious women who created Catholic health care. Religious women, sisters in a variety of congregations, would personally tend the sick as nurses, clean the hospital, prepare the food, gather in prayer around the dying, and worship together in a community celebrating the Eucharist and engaging in common prayer. They also provided a distinctive witness of dedication to Christ in the care of the sick and the example of their lives. Of course, not every sister was a wonderful example of heroic virtue, but many were. Even in this time of greatly decreased religious vocations, the vigor of Catholic health care speaks to the legacy of the sisters' example. The number of sisters has greatly decreased, but their example underscores that caring for the sick is part of a vocation, a calling from God to care for those who are ill, just as Christ did. This vocation requires education, hard work, technical skill, and discipline. But the lives of the sisters are also exemplary witnesses of the centrality of prayer to health care in the Catholic tradition, and now many Christian nurses and physicians carry on the religious mission of Catholic health care centers.

The historical realities of Catholic health care and the ongoing work of Catholic hospitals and health care practitioners are visible signs of what the Church is called to be: the continuing presence of Christ in the world, a sacrament of the reality of God's Word spoken to those who are sick and suffering.

THEOLOGY AND THE FORMATION OF HEALTH CARE PROFESSIONALS

Forming individuals who will continue the ministry of health care, whether as practitioners in a Catholic hospital or working in another setting, is an important mission for a Catholic university. Although theological ethics plays an important role in helping health care providers understand Catholic ethical theory and practice in medicine, in the Catholic tradition ethics relies primarily on the natural law. That is, it does not directly engage the message of the Gospel. A Christian is someone embraced by God, saved by Christ, and elevated through Christ and the Church to participation in the divine life of the Trinity.

The example of Jesus and historical examples of how faith and health care have been mutually supportive are both potentially strong motivators for health care workers. So too is the commitment of Catholic health care over the centuries to providing care for the uninsured, the illegal alien, the unborn, and the chronically ill and dying. However, to remain true to the Catholic mission in a demanding profession, modern health care workers require more than an awareness of social justice or a short Bible or history lesson. They need practical theological analysis to help motivate the loving care they should be or are already providing. Theology is traditionally described as faith seeking understanding. The pointed question in this context is: What does Catholic faith reveal to those desirous of careers in health care?

The Creed and Health Care

As noted by Lawrence Cunningham in his essay, the heart of Catholic theology is the Creed, with its proclamation of a triune God known as Father and Creator, Jesus Christ, the only son and Lord, and the Holy Spirit. For those who spend their professional life in medicine and health care, their practice and experience reveal this triune God in unique ways. At the Last Supper Jesus admonishes his disciples to "Love one another as I have loved you" (John 15:12). One of the ways Jesus loved was by curing the faithful; therefore health care is both a manifestation of God's love and a path for fulfilling our responsibility as followers of Christ. Care for the sick is not simply a miraculous charism, but a healing that goes beyond physiological restoration. It should bring people back into community, more loving as a result of their encounter with infirmity. Care for the sick should also draw in those whom society reviles. Catholic health care institutions should risk scorn and disapproval in order to restore to health and holiness those whom society sees as pariahs. As Jesus taught us, the God of creation is close to the poor and less fortunate; they are the lost sheep whom the shepherd seeks out. The Parable of the Good Samaritan also shows the neighbor to be one who is wounded and left abandoned, the person who first of all needs attention and salve for his wounds. But this requires someone with the generosity to abandon current plans and tend to the person in need.

Theology for future doctors and nurses can also lead students from the proclamation of the triune God to the concluding phrases of the Creed: the Church, the communion of saints, the forgiveness of sins, the resurrection of the body, and the life of the world to come. A sign of the Church is its continuity with the apostolic tradition, a tradition that is manifest in its teaching, its faith, its origin, and its practice. The same Spirit that brought the Church into being at Pentecost guides the Church today. In its infant years Peter and others manifested the ongoing power of the Gospel by healing the sick. Catholic health care providers continue that tradition. The continuity with all those who have faith in Christ is part of what it means to be a member in the communion of saints.

The experience of physicians in caring for the sick is usually not miraculous. Indeed the healings of Jesus may seem very distant from how physicians practice. But there are some constants. Just as Jesus experienced the reality of evil and sickness in the people who approached him for cures, Catholic nurses and physicians also experience the reality of physical evil in the suffering of their patients. Like Jesus ("He did not work many mighty deeds there because of their lack of faith"; Matthew 13:58), health care providers are dejected when they are unable to cure. Working with people who experience great failure requires great strength. An alcoholic who is not able to stop drinking, a drug addict who cannot stop using, a prisoner who has hurt others and is now shot and dying, a thoroughly obnoxious and entitled patient, a neurotic and demanding businessman, and all the other examples of patients who are not easy to care for—in all these cases the physician experiences the reality of sinful humanity and the need to confront sin with love. In their own anger, occasional lack of caring, episodes of hubris, and instances of poor judgment, physicians discover a personal reality of sin. Not all health care is marked by miracles, healings, and joyful encounters between a caring physician and a suitably grateful patient. A Catholic physician needs to know about sin in its various forms—personal, systemic, and social. He or she must also believe that the triune God proclaimed earlier in the Creed is the only source of ultimate healing and forgiveness.

Cognizance of the image of Jesus as Divine Physician can be not only an inspiration but a challenge for health care practitioners. It is professionally frustrating and personally heart-wrenching to work intensely to cure someone who is critically injured or seriously ill only to have him die despite one's best efforts. In the Gospels Jesus is able to confront illness and death and then transform it. He cures infectious diseases, blindness, paralysis, deafness, inability to speak, bleeding, withered limbs, mental illness, epilepsy, and other conditions.

Extremely common among excellent physicians and nurses is the conviction that in almost all cases they can cure and transform the lives of the sick and suffering. This is not evidence of delusional behavior; rather it signifies an overabundance of self-confidence. Of course, all physicians and nurses have to rely on intelligence and other natural gifts, but hubris can cause overconfidence in genuine but limited talents. The reality of failure stalks the lives of all who care for the sick.

Living the life of medicine and nursing in humility, recognizing failures and disappointments, being grateful for wonderful cures, happy births, and suffering alleviated—all these experiences can bring the Catholic health care practitioner to a new maturity and self-understanding in the light of Christ the Divine Physician. The cures and miracles of Jesus were not about himself. They were based on a personal authority that was fully grounded in his relationship with the Father. The experience of miraculous cures and healings helped Jesus see more clearly what was being asked of him by the Father as he moved closer to his own suffering and death. The challenge for mature Christians in health care is to see their practice as an extension of their relationship with God, not as an opportunity for ego boosting or self-aggrandizement. Physicians and nurses have received talents directly from God and also through parents, mentors, and friends. They now share their gifts and presence with the sick person; they are willing to be with the person who is ill in the way that God is willing to be with us. Just as Jesus in his humanity was drawn ever more deeply into the reality of human frailty, suffering, and evil, the example of the Divine Physician calls physicians and nurses to compassionate care, even when there is no cure possible. In imitation of Christ, they ponder what next to do with the patient, they are attentive to the frailty of those for whom they care, and, from time to time, they experience personal suffering when their patients die or simply in the exhaustion of working long hours. And, yes, they are at times also exasperated and disgusted with health care systems that seem unable to offer the care that a child of God deserves.

The Divine Physician entered into the experience of illness, suffering, and death and conquered it. Although our society often denies death, medicine in the Catholic tradition cannot. And yet health care in the United States is sometimes justly criticized for its emphasis on technology and an inherent promise that all conditions are curable. This leads to a view that death is a failure for the physician and therefore something to be forestalled even when there is no realistic chance of recovery. Theology can inform those who would be physicians that our belief in the resurrection of the dead and the life of the world to come are not simply pious phrases but fundamental to belief and practice. A Catholic physician believes there are limits to human life and that death comes to everyone. The Creed, with its first statement of belief in God the Father Almighty, creator of heaven and earth, and its last statement of belief in the life in the world to come, has profound importance for Catholic health care. The Father has created us for something beyond sin and death; we are created for life with God, for holiness. As John Paul II wrote, "Life on earth is not the ultimate reality but a penultimate reality.... We are created with a supernatural vocation to life in God."[3]

In the final phrase of the Creed the believer states, "I believe in the communion of saints, the forgiveness of sins, the resurrection of the body, and the life everlasting. Amen." Death is not the end of community; the body that is the object of such care and attention by doctors and nurses is not forgotten. The sorrow of personal failings and even wickedness is overcome by the joy of forgiveness. Life continues in an enhanced, but still hidden mode. Catholic hospitals are places where these realities are made visible through the sacraments. Physicians and nurses call for the priest to anoint the sick person, to provide the care that comes with the Sacrament of the Sick. Holy Communion, viaticum, is given to provide food for the soul of those who are dying, to supply the nourishment to attain the life in the world to come. The Mass offered in the hospital chapel recalls Christ's death and ongoing presence as Risen Lord. Catholic hospitals and health care give a glimpse of faith that is lived in a liminal setting: at the boundary of life and death, sickness and recovery, tragedy and joy. The life of the believing doctor and nurse is lived in the midst of mystery, a frontier between the life we know and the life we are called to in faith.

Many fine hospitals and practitioners are not Catholic or religious. But Catholic hospitals offer something distinct and valuable. The local Catholic community and Catholic hospitals create the locus where a believing health care practitioner can live the Creed and have it be life-shaping, a place where the shared assertion "I believe" modifies health care that it is thoroughly human and spiritual. This creedal health care is clearly in the present but with roots in the past and hopes in the future; it is fully immersed in the reality of sin, suffering, and evil but also alive to grace, redemption, and the power of goodness.

Theology and Self-Understanding for Health Care Professionals

Theology has a role in forming and informing Catholic health care practitioners not only by illuminating the dogmatic statements of the Creed but by assisting individual physicians and nurses in answering the basic questions of human existence and meaning: Who am I? What am I doing? Who am I becoming by my actions? These are cyclical questions that arise, get partial answers, disappear, and then reappear. For months or years many practitioners are too busy to ponder these questions, but the questions always return because the self seeks understanding and direction.

Catholic doctors and nurses have a variety of callings in their lives: to be husbands, wives, parents, friends, good citizens. Yet they spend most of their active hours each day in the health care profession. In his essay Rausch describes the contemporary situation as a postmodern culture that denies the transcendent, that is, being and reality that transcends normal human experience. For physicians and nurses and those studying to become physicians or nurses, this denial is usually part of their training as well as part of the milieu in which they practice. That this is not a new phenomenon is evidenced in remarks made by Blessed John Henry Newman to the faculty of the Catholic Medical School of Dublin: "Morals and Religion are not represented to the intelligence of the world by intimations and notices strong and obvious, such as those which are the foundation of Physical Science.... The world is a rough antagonist of spiritual truth: sometimes with mailed hand, sometimes with pertinacious logic, sometimes with a storm of irresistible facts, it presses on against you."[4]

Medical training and the requirements for medical or nursing school are heavily scientific and rooted in a belief that what is real is what is measurable, verifiable, and physical. Many physicians and would-be medical students lack the intellectual background to appreciate that subjectivity is not specious or to understand that the basic sciences rest on premises that are themselves not demonstrable. (For example, it is impossible to provide a scientific argument that what is real is only that which is empirically verifiable.)

Doctors and nurses today are overwhelmed by scientific requirements for medicine and engaged in technologically sophisticated practices, and they live in a society not particularly open to the idea that there is a God, much less a God who has become personally involved with the life of humanity. It is no wonder that they might view their role as skilled and highly trained technicians who, by manipulating and controlling the determinants of disease, attempt to reverse the biological origins of illness. Catholicism has a different view. Individuals are called to respond to God's invitation to participate in God's own life. As Rausch notes, "What God offers, finally, is...a sharing in the divine life as self-gift. This is what Catholicism understands by the good life, following Jesus, living in communion with the Triune God." The example of Jesus and the tradition of health care in the life of the Church call health care professionals to offer holistic care—physical, spiritual, and emotional—to those seeking their assistance.

Theology is important in health care because the nature and quality of health care is at stake. Practitioners who view their role as skilled technicians take a different view of illness than those who see the personal care they provide to their patients as participating in God's life. The implication is not that nonbelieving physicians lack compassion or are uniformly unconcerned with the existential reality of the people who are their patients. Indeed I have seen some atheists who are extraordinarily compassionate and some loudly Catholic physicians who are mean and pompous. Rather by baptism in the Holy Spirit a believer participates in God's life. The believer's daily life should manifest God in this world. God works through the believing health practitioner who makes present God's love in a personal way. Rausch notes, "Without denying the reality of sin, with the damage, exploitation, even violence that it brings into our relationship and into our world . . . we live in a world in which grace abounds." Viewing her life in medicine as a response to grace, a physician-believer follows Christ in the Spirit by being obedient to the Father. She approaches her patients offering three-dimensional healing—in body, spirit, and emotions. By all means conscious of personal failings and sin, she lives the transcendent dimension in her life and makes it visible to those for whom she cares. In health care the ultimate theological question is whether illness is healed by technological means or by something more profound. If "something more profound" focuses on God's love, the believer lives this truth and also makes true healing possible by participating in and sharing the Spirit.

Doctors and nurses are called to be holy. Because "saint" is a synonym for "holy one," the vocation of health care providers certainly is to be saints. All practical vocational choices are secondary to the primary vocation to enter into eternal life with God. As noted by Cunningham, Cardinal Newman in his *Idea of a University*, which includes an essay on medicine, saw the ultimate end of education as leading the student to sanctity. Education for health care professionals shares this end. Caring for the sick is an immersion in mystery, it engages the nurse or physician in the deepest moments of life, and it leads to holiness, provided the gift is recognized and accepted.

Cunningham observes, "There is no meaningful concept of holiness unless it is seen in relationship to the One who is holy: God." For the woman or man open to that relationship, medicine provides a rich encounter with the Holy One. Rausch lists four fundamental principles of Catholic theological anthropology: "God is transcendent and immanent, God's creation is both flawed and graced, grace builds on nature, and God always respects our freedom." Each of these principles stems from human experience. The experience of health care provides extraordinary confirmation of these principles, as is evidenced in the following examples.

- The transcendence of God is revealed in the mystery of birth and death, sickness and recovery. God's "close transcendence" can be seen in the love of parents for a newborn as well as in the comfort and care given to an individual facing death.
- The knowledge of creation both flawed and graced is the stuff of health care. The beauty of creation is seen both in a healthy baby and in the recovery from illness. Medicine often must work with a flawed creation: leukemia in a young person, the development of dementia, or the self-destructive actions of an addict.

- Grace builds on nature in many ways in health care. First, God transforms nonbelieving physicians and nurses into believers, who then cooperate in transmitting God's grace to others.
- The believing nurse or physician also encounters grace every day. The body is the medium of medical care and it is the way the Spirit encounters humanity. One admires the courage and determination of a stroke victim undergoing physical therapy. In an intensive care unit, one is touched by forgiveness and reconciliation as a family grapples for meaning in the midst of tragedy. Responding to a diagnosis indicating death, a person humbly accepts the prospect with courage and faith.
- God's respect for freedom means patients make big choices. In the emergency room one often confronts the terrible violence people inflict on each other. A physician, nurse, or orderly feels the pain and confusion surrounding a patient and family as they perceive death approaching. These moments highlight genuine freedom. For some, these moments are excellent reasons to deny God's existence. For others, it is a moment to perceive the awesome freedom given to humans.

Encountering the holy is insufficient to make saints out of doctors and nurses. Contemplation of God in the action of health care should evoke a response of love. This love should imitate the love of God by looking outward to embrace all people. Practically speaking, for nurses and physicians this means surrounding all patients in the facility with expert physical care, heartfelt prayers, and spiritual encouragement and witness.

Service to the sick is part of the mission of the Church, and it is most intensely provided by physicians, nurses, orderlies, assistants, administrators, and other health care professionals. In this way the Church practices mercy and compassion and also shows concern for human society. Health care providers informed by the Catholic tradition, however, also have another crucial role in the Church: assisting Catholicism to learn about the world. In words addressed to medical students at the Catholic University of Dublin, Blessed John Henry Newman describes medicine and Catholicism as having mutually supporting roles.[5] Newman emphasizes the role of the Church as the teacher of truth and values to medicine. The hierarchy is not well positioned to do this for medicine. Indeed the Church can do this only through its members, and Newman highlights the need for physicians at the university to be the links between religion and science.[6]

Taking up themes sounded by Newman, John Paul II, in his World Day of the Sick message for 2001, affirmed the Church's historical care for the sick for two thousand years as well as its defense of ethical values and human dignity. He also noted the "invaluable service" that committed Catholic physicians and nurses can provide to the Church: "Physicians and other health care practitioners with an understanding of theology and basic competence in its methods and sources can provide invaluable service to the Church and to theology by sharing their experience with theologians and those who have the task of governance in the Church." He said that health care practitioners are positioned on terrain where basic values such as life and respect must be emphasized in order to protect and promote human flourishing. Then he called on biomedical researchers and health care professionals to work to advance knowledge to limit suffering and promote improved health care.[7]

During a visit to a hospice in Vienna in 1998, John Paul II spoke about the frontier between life and death. In particular he criticized a manipulative view of life that allows "human beings to be disposed of at will."[8] By themselves papal statements do not create or perceptibly strengthen a culture of life, so the Church has to rely on its most knowledgeable and dedicated followers to endorse and protect life.

Beyond the specific issue of protecting life, the key for theology is to work with physicians and nurses who have a lived, faith-infused experience of the limits of human life. Caring for older persons as a geriatrician, my personal experience is seeing men and women becoming increasingly frail, losing their ability to perform various tasks, and experiencing their body sending strong signals that their life is coming to a close. (In this situation the body communicates to the spirit of the person.) Though there is no cure for old age, a physician can still provide good care. The task of medicine in these cases is to limit suffering, avoid doing harm, attend to the person and his or her family, and be frank about the limits of modern health care. Death is a reality that ultimately cannot be avoided and, at the proper time, should be embraced. A Catholic health care practitioner works with people at this other frontier of human experience. Observing their reactions and listening to their experiences, the Catholic nurse or physician understands new ways to practice faith in our time.

The Catholic university, especially academic theology, needs the lived truth of believers involved in the health sciences and in providing health care. But Catholic health care, especially believing nurses and physicians, need understanding that comes through Catholic theology.

Enhancing communication among the health sciences, theology, and those who care for the sick are worthwhile tasks. Near the end of his essay Cunningham writes, "Theology can learn from all disciplines, and all other academic disciplines can learn from theology." He also states, "The Church is the community of people who praise God in Christ, who help make known the revelation of God, and who provide loving service to others." Medical and nursing schools are part of Catholic universities. Indeed Newman found it crucial to have a Catholic medical school as part of his project to create a Catholic university in Dublin. Not only do these schools benefit from the work of theology, but academic theology, as well as other academic departments, is enriched by dialogue and collaboration.

Universities are big places, and although academic departments collaborate, most work is done within departments. In my experience in a Catholic medical school I have seen that the physicians and students engaged in biomedical research, teaching, and patient care are not particularly aware of the work of the theologians in the university; likewise theologians rarely seem to consider the dramatic ways in which the transcendent God is powerfully present at the medical school and medical center. Too often what dialogue does occur focuses on controversial ethical issues rather than deeper issues about how medical practice enables believers to see more clearly how God presents himself in our lives. Ethics is important, but ethics rests on a prior understanding of what it means to be human in the presence of God. Being has priority in our effort to understand human action. Medicine and the other health professions exist at a number of frontiers of what it means to be human, embodied, and alive. By exploring these frontiers jointly with medical practitioners, theologians can enrich the understanding of themselves, practitioners, patients, and other Christians.

Ideally the Catholic university facilitates the education of physicians and other health care practitioners by sharing theological learning with nurses and physicians who are experts in how body and psyche function. Substantive contact between theology and health care will not happen if it relies only on the goodwill and serendipitous interests of individuals. The Church needs individuals who understand biomedical science and research, and humanity needs the Catholic faith to illuminate the practice of medicine and health care. Theology also needs the experience of health care if it is to remain in touch with human experience.

To satisfy mutual academic and ecclesiastical needs, the Catholic university should go beyond bioethics as a place of collaboration and establish centers for theological study and reflection within the health sciences. Having academic theologians whose expertise goes beyond moral theology and who do their work at the medical center would be an important bridge for mutual collaboration. Medical students, who frequently obtain degrees in public health as well as doctoral degrees in basic sciences, could have the opportunity for advanced study in theology as part of their medical training. Similar opportunities should be developed for those in nursing. Equally important, experienced researchers and practitioners should also have the opportunity to take time for study and research in theology.

The difficulty of establishing these programs is twofold: they would be new and innovative and they would require funding. For both reasons, they can come about only under bold and inspired leadership. The academic silos that keep disciplines locked away from each other are not easily connected. Lack of contact between disciplines in universities is not new, but the degree of specialization in different disciplines is making the separation more difficult to bridge. A task for the Catholic university that wishes to remain true to the universal dimension of its vocation is to be daring. It can do this by establishing meaningful pathways for study, dialogue, and mutual growth with the academic pursuit of health care. Health care sciences are on the frontier of much of how we understand our humanity. Academic theology would do well not to neglect the opportunity for faith to seek understanding in this vital arena.

NOTES

1. Quotations are from the New Revised Standard version.

2. I am indebted for my understanding of the encounter of Jesus with the Canaanite woman to Brendan Byrne, *Lifting the Burden: Reading Matthew's Gospel in the Church Today* (Collegeville, Minn.: Liturgical Press, 2004).

3. John Paul II, *Evangelium Vitae* 2, www.vatican.va/edocs/ENG0141/__P2.HTM.

4. John Henry Cardinal Newman, *Newman Reader*, chapter 13, p. 390, www.newmanreader.org/biography/ward/volume1/chapter13.html.

5. John Henry Cardinal Newman, *The Idea of a University* (London: Longmans, Green, 1947).

6. David Fleischacker, "John Henry Newman's Vision of the Catholic Medical School," *Newman Studies Journal* 4 (Fall 2007): 21–30.

7. John Paul II, *Message for World Day of the Sick*, 2001, www.vatican.va/holy_father/john_paul_ii/messages/sick/documents/hf_jp-ii_mes_20000822_world-day-of-the-sick-2001_en.html.

8. John Paul II, *Message to the Staff and Residents of the Rennweg Hospice*, Vienna, Austria, June 21, 1998, www.vatican.va/holy_father/john_paul_ii/speeches/1998/june/documents/hf_jp-ii_spe_19980621_austria-infermi_en.html.

SELECTED READINGS

Bernardin, Joseph Cardinal. *A Moral Vision for America*. Washington, DC: Georgetown University Press, 1998.

Mohrmann, Margaret E. *Medicine as Ministry*. Cleveland, Ohio: Pilgrim Press, 1995.

Parsi, Kayhan, and Myles N. Sheehan. *Healing as Vocation: A Medical Professionalism Primer*. Lanham, Md.: Rowman and Littlefield, 2006.

Pellegrino, Edmund D., and David C. Thomasma. *For the Patient's Good: The Restoration of Beneficence in Health Care*. New York: Oxford University Press, 1988.

Sulmasy, Daniel P. *The Rebirth of the Clinic: An Introduction to Spirituality in Health Care*. Washington, DC: Georgetown University Press, 2006.

21

Law in a Catholic Framework

Patrick McKinley Brennan

SO SATURATED IS our culture with the appearances of law that law itself seems an inevitability. But no matter how much Leviathan pushes, shoves, and enacts to the contrary, we must remember that human law is the artifact of an actualized capacity. Moreover the human capacity to make law, as Friedrich Hayek famously remarked, "has justly been described as among all inventions of man the one fraught with the gravest consequences, more far-reaching in its effects even than fire and gun-powder."[1] And like fire and gunpowder, "law" in some of its forms can be destructive. Considering law as violent is not fanciful. "Our modern dictators are masters of legality," Heinrich Rommen observed. "Hitler aimed not at revolution, but at a legal grasp of power according to the formal democratic processes."[2]

What counts as law? Do enactments that emerge from formal democratic processes yet are destructive of humans and what is good for them rise to the level of law? Some influential voices say yes; whatever the sovereign enacts is law, regardless of its content and consequences. Others counter that justice, not mere sovereign will, is necessary for an enactment to be accounted as law. To the extent a "law" is unjust, it is no law at all. The basic question, then, is: What is a necessary foundation for law?

Catholics come to the topic of human law from within a tradition that recognizes law long before enactments of the sort that concerned Hayek and Rommen. The Bible is permeated with the Hebrew concept of *Torah*, translated into Greek as *nomos* and into Latin as *lex*: law. Drawing in addition from Greek, Roman, and

Neoplatonic philosophical sources, the Church Fathers and later the Scholastics developed theories concerning the "law of nature," or natural law, law that in principle is knowable by all human beings. Natural law emerges from a consideration of the "eternal law," which St. Augustine defined as "the divine reason or the will of God commanding the natural order to be preserved and forbidding its disruption."[3] St. Thomas Aquinas, whose account of law is the principal resource in this essay, defined the eternal law as "nothing else than the type [ratio] of Divine Wisdom directing all actions and movements."[4]

In the development from Augustine's definition of the eternal law to Thomas's, a not so subtle shift occurs that foreshadows a cleavage that runs to this day through the tradition. While Augustine gave pride of place to both reason and will, his successors gave ever greater emphasis to will. By giving less emphasis to reason, the voluntarist approach (voluntas is Latin for "will") treats law as a sort of force majeure. Thomas, on the other hand, understands all law as a thing of reason or intellect. And although he recognizes that the ruler promulgates the law through his will, he never even mentions the will in his definition of the eternal or of any other kind of law.

Thomas expounded his intellectualist account of law in many writings, but most systematically in questions 90–106 of the Prima-Secundae of the Summa Theologiae, a handbook for confessors assisting sinners in their quest for the good life and the afterlife. It is important to underscore that in the section of the Summa in which he takes up the topic of law in a systematic way, Thomas's concern is "man, inasmuch as he too," like the Creator, "is the principle of his actions, as having free-will and control of his actions" (Prol. to I-II q. 90). In this context his particular object of investigation is the extrinsic principles by which God moves human beings to the goods that are the natural ends of humans: grace and law.

The project of modernity situates the origins and limits of human law in the agreement of the people to be commanded by a sovereign individual or group. It then defines law as whatever is commanded by that individual or group. By contrast the Catholic tradition of law recognizes that before agreement or disagreement is reached on anything, groups and individuals are always already under a higher law, the natural law. Only on the basis of this received natural law can any subsequent law properly be defined, framed, and judged. According to this tradition, the natural law is nothing less than our human participation in the eternal law, that is, the divine mind disposing all created things to their ends. Human law, therefore, far from being the arbitrary result of agreement and command, receives its warrant through the natural law and the eternal law of which it is a sharing. By giving practical effect to the norms of natural law, human law shares in the divine providential governance of the universe. Natural law first makes human law a practical possibility. Unless that higher law is acknowledged and articulated, humans' commands to one another are bound to be just so many arbitrary assertions.

In contemporary jurisprudential debates, natural law is a commonplace, but also something of an ideological football. The term is used in mischievously many ways. But in this essay, by adhering to the meaning that St. Thomas and his followers give it, it is possible to sketch the characteristically Catholic approach to human law and governance. Such a perspective in turn provides a framework to address a crucial problematic of contemporary legal practice and jurisprudence, namely, how best to handle what is intended by the term *natural rights*.

This essay follows St. Thomas, offering a particular theory of natural law and contrasting it with other theories of law. But before going forward, it is important to note that there are various accounts of natural law. John Finnis, an influential advocate of a rather different account of the natural law than the one pursued here, has noted that the various theories or accounts *of the natural law* are just that: theories or accounts that purport to be about some *thing*. Any hope of taking the natural law seriously depends on not vaporizing it into so many theories or motives.

THE REQUIREMENT "OF LAW"

By professional vocation lawyers interpret the law and contribute to its creation by applying it to real human situations. The Fifth Amendment (adopted in 1791) of the Constitution of the United States provides that "no person … [shall] be deprived of life, liberty, or property, without due process of law." The Fourteenth Amendment (adopted in 1868 as part of the post–Civil War Reconstruction) adds, "Nor shall any State deprive any person, of life, liberty, or property, without due process of law." These limitations on the authority, respectively, of the national and state governments are universally understood to impose the requirement of some kind of process—due process—before government takes a person's life, liberty, or property.

A challenging question much controverted in the U.S. Supreme Court today is whether either or both of these two amendments also impose a requirement of another sort. The first, uncontroversial requirement is known in the jargon as "procedural due process." The second, disputed requirement is known under the apparent oxymoron "substantive due process." The opponents of the latter sort of requirement, sometimes dubbed "due substance," highlight the language of the amendments. The plain terms of the Constitution require process, not substance, before government deprives a person of life, liberty, or property.

Jurists more solicitous of "substantive due process" counter, however, that the Constitution's language just as plainly requires the due process "of law." They then add that this implies that the putative law in question must meet certain substantive requirements. In other words, a procedurally proper enactment is insufficient. For an enactment to meet the Constitution's requirement "of law," it must pass not just a pedigree test but also a substantive test. This, they argue, is what the framers of the Fifth and Fourteenth Amendments meant and intended by including the words "of law." Because meaning is what counts, this meaning "of law" must be given effect. This perspective is frequently referred to as the "original intent" view of the Fifth and Fourteenth Amendments.[5]

Other jurists also friendly to "substantive due process" defend it not merely on the ground of original intent; they add that the nature of law itself implies a substantive requirement. According to this natural law argument, nothing is truly law unless it meets certain substantive requirements. That is, even if those who use the term *due process* intend to deny that it denotes a requirement of substance, law in fact requires substance of a particular sort. On this account, when a "law" attempts to take something from a person that it truly *should not take*, the requirement of due process "of law" cannot be met, no matter how many procedural bells and whistles the government provides, for the simple but profound reason that *law* is not at work. Many institutions of law may be engaged, but in this case the "law" is not law. This is the view associated with Thomas Aquinas.

The broad potential impact of this account of law can be seen by illustrating the grounds on which constitutional challenges are framed in court. Under the U.S. Constitution the most straightforward constitutional challenges occur when a plaintiff alleges that some "law" violates a right of hers enumerated in the Constitution, such as the right to free exercise of religion (First Amendment) or the right to keep and bear arms (Second Amendment). A more complex question arises when a plaintiff claims an injury by a "law" that touches a right not enumerated in the Constitution, such as the right to procure an abortion or engage in homosexual sex. To the consternation of some, the U.S. Constitution has long been interpreted to protect a whole range of such unenumerated rights. Furthermore these rights are frequently justified on the ground that an individual unenumerated right provides the "due substance" of "substantive due process." What is compelling in this approach is that if a "law" were to take away from a person something to which the person indeed has a right, no amount of process can reverse the injustice done. That is, in this case, the "law" fails in its substance, not its procedure.

But there is also a crucial difficulty with this approach, since in most cases it sets up a conflict or opposition between "right" and "law." This is true regardless of the basis of the right and irrespective of whether it is enumerated or unenumerated. A state or federal enactment can either be invalidated or not applied (and which of those two actions a court takes makes a big difference, as will be seen below) on the ground that it violates a right protected by the Constitution. When this is done, the stated reason usually is that the "right" trumps the "law." One can express the decision of the court in a more nuanced way that avoids the verbal conflict between right and law. Nonetheless the underlying reality remains, and the account offered here presents the conceptual and practical difficulties that pits rights and law against each other.

The Thomistic approach avoids this problem by drawing the implications of the true but usually unstated relationship between law, on the one hand, and rights, on the other. On this analysis, when the "law" in question tramps on a true protected right, it sheds its claims to be a law at all. To take a seemingly easy example, if a state required compulsory sterilization of the mentally disabled by statute, the "law" should not be followed, for the simple reason that, though perfectly pedigreed, it is not law at all. The appearance of law does not guarantee the predicates of law.

CARRIE BUCK BEFORE THE SUPREME COURT

The previously cited seemingly easy example was indeed easy for the Supreme Court of the United States, but in the other direction. By an 8–1 vote, the Court gave legal effect to a Virginia state statute that allowed compulsory sterilization of the mentally challenged, Carrie Buck. In *Buck v. Bell* (1927), Justice Oliver Wendell Holmes Jr., writing for the eight-member majority, invoked frustration with imperfection as partial justification for the ruling:

> It is better for all the world, if instead of waiting to execute degenerate offspring for crime, or to let them starve for their imbecility, society can prevent those who are manifestly unfit from continuing their kind. The principle that sustains compulsory vaccination is broad enough to cover cutting the Fallopian tubes [citing a 1905 Supreme Court precedent upholding compulsory vaccination]. Three generations of imbeciles are enough.[6]

Holmes's prose may have been even more expansive in earlier drafts of his opinion for the Court. Writing to his friend Harold Laski, Holmes referred to *Buck v. Bell*, "I wrote and delivered a decision upholding the constitutionality of a state law for sterilizing infants the other day—and felt that I was getting near to the first principle of real reform."[7]

The lone and silent dissenter from this force majeure approach to law was the one Catholic on the Supreme Court at the time, Justice Pierce Butler, who is said to have attended daily Mass.

If *Buck v. Bell* offends current moral sensibilities, it is merely an especially ugly application of a widespread modern account of what human law is. The towering English jurisprudent John Austin (1790–1859), writing just a little before Holmes, had announced that law amounts to the command of the sovereign backed by the threat of punishment, and in this he more or less echoed Thomas Hobbes's account of law of 150 years earlier. What was referred to at the beginning of this essay as the voluntarist or force majeure side of the Western tradition has been amply represented in Anglo-American legal theory and practice.

Intoning a note of optimism, Jean Porter has recently observed, "Almost no one today would be prepared to argue (as some early legal positivists did) that the law rests on arbitrary commands."[8] If almost no one is willing to argue that the sovereign's arbitrary commands can create law, Holmes nonetheless embodied a well-respected strand of legal tradition when for the Supreme Court of the United States he gave conclusive and compulsory effect to the Virginia legislature's enactment without raising the question of its morality or immorality.

In contemporary legal theory, more common than the concept of voluntarism is the concept of positivism. Positivism is a normative theory of law. According to positivism, something counts as law if two conditions are fulfilled. First, the lawgiver passed or enacted the purported law according to the procedures required in the jurisdiction, and, second, people recognize the legislation or enactment as the law of the jurisdiction.

Positivism has many conscientious proponents today. Indeed it is the dominant theory of law, in part because the theory has some attractive features. Positivists note that law is supposed to be a guide to conduct, and only what is posited can reliably serve this role. Nearly all other nonpositivist jurists share this view, however, and natural lawyers are certainly among them. Who will deny that law, if it is to bind, needs to be promulgated or posited? Some may claim that positivism is an amoral or immoral account of law. But positivists correctly reply that particular laws sometimes incorporate the requirement that legal officials enact or enforce moral norms. This is known as inclusive or incorporationist legal positivism, and there are indeed working examples of it. But Porter points out that what is essential for the positivists is that law must have a certain independence or separateness. For them law is not reducible to the contents of other normative ordering systems. It can be recognized solely by its pedigree and without regard to its moral status.

Before elaborating the reasons for a natural law approach, two observations are important. First, requiring law to be moral does not entail or even recommend that all morality should be enacted into law. Rather, this requirement is simply a recognition of the pre-positive fact that a necessary condition of human law is its morality. It simply requires that laws passed or enacted not directly conflict with accepted morals. For morality to be enforceable as human law, it must be enacted by the competent civil authority, and not all morality is ever enacted. The second observation is that legal positivists often seek to avoid the morality issue by hiding it in the way the law is interpreted. They do this by assigning the judiciary the task of "interpreting" enactments in such a way as to avoid doing what would be "iniquitous." Of course, "iniquitous" has substantive meaning only when used against the background of a moral system. In the fabled New York case of *Riggs v. Palmer* (1889), for example, where an heir would otherwise have taken possession of an estate that became distributable just because he had murdered the testator (his grandfather), the court interpreted the testamentary statute's language so as to avoid this result, doing so in derogation of the statute's clear terms. With only a single dissent, New York's highest court reasoned that if the legislators had foreseen this situation, they would have exempted it from the coverage of the statute. The judges in the *Riggs* majority operated under the influence of a doctrine known since Greek times as *epikeia*, since the Latin Middle Ages as *equitas*, and today in Anglo-American legal practice as equity, though it hardly has a fixed meaning even in Anglo-American law, let alone across the centuries. An approach of this sort is sometimes sound, as is illustrated below.

In the *Buck v. Bell* case, however, it is hard to see how such a doctrine of *epikeia* or equity can be invoked other than in an ad hoc fashion. The enacted legislative will was unfortunately clear, and the facts revealed no exceptional circumstances that would potentially implicate the doctrine of *epikeia*.

If the people have in fact endowed the court with the capacity to disregard statutes the court finds disagreeable, the facts of the case change dramatically. (It is very problematic, however, if a court is given license arbitrarily to ignore an enacted law.) If instead it is more plausibly assumed that the people have assigned the courts the job of following, perhaps with the benefit of *epikeia* in appropriate cases, what the legislature enacts, then the court's refusal to follow what is enacted would be action in defiance of the law.

The only way to avoid this conundrum is to claim that what has been enacted is no law at all, and this is what the natural law approach does. In contrast to positivism, natural law requires that the law conform both to procedural and substantive standards. The two necessary and sufficient conditions advocated by positivists only examine procedure and the populace's acceptance of the results of procedure.

FIRST IN THE ORDER OF BEING

If law is conclusively defined as what the legislature enacts, any argument that the statute at issue in *Buck* is not law is doomed. But legal positivists typically define law in just this way. When the positivist inquires whether a putative law is in fact a law, he does so with no more than what the influential positivist H. L. A. Hart referred to as the particular jurisdiction's "rule of recognition" to guide him. On this view, law is whatever the particular legal system recognizes as law according to its agreed upon conventional rules. In the natural law tradition, however, as we have already begun to see, when we come to the question of whether a putative law is in fact a law, we do so from within a context in which law is already at work. We are always and already possessed, we might say, of a higher rule of recognition, one that is not merely conventional, and it is this, the natural law, that vouchsafes that the project of saying that what law is cannot amount simply to definitional fiat or linguistic archaeology. The Thomistic tradition puts an end to dueling definitions of law by providing an ontological justification for what counts as law.

As Russell Hittinger explains, "St. Thomas himself makes it clear that the definition of natural law is not arrived at simply by examining the meaning or concept of law." It is arrived at instead by attending to what is first in the order of being, the divine governance:

> In *Summa Theologiae* I-II, 91.1, where he first outlines and defines the various laws, the existence of the eternal law (in reference to which the natural law is defined in 91.2) follows from the supposition that divine providence rules the entire community of the world....Law is nothing but a dictate of practical reason issued by a sovereign who governs a complete community. Granted that the world is regulated by divine providence...it is evident that the entire community of the universe is governed by the divine mind.[9]

Thomas's argument, then, runs as follows. *Granted* that divine providence rules the entire world through an ordinance of reason promulgated by him who has care of the world (God), for the common good, this is the eternal law, and it provides the pattern or definition of any other law, including the natural law: "an ordinance of reason for the common good, made by him (or them) who have care of the community, and promulgated" (I-II 90.4c).

The natural law is defined by reference to the law that is first in the order of being: the eternal law. But what exactly is this natural law that is thus defined? Thomas is unequivocal on this point. Responding to the objection that the presence in the human person of a natural law would be redundant because we are adequately governed by the eternal law, Thomas replies, "This argument would hold, if the natural law were something different from the eternal law: whereas it is nothing but a participation thereof" (I-II 91.2 ad 1). He elaborates:

> Law, being a rule and measure, can be in a person in two ways: in one way, as in him that rules and measures; in another way, as in that which is ruled and measured, in so far as it partakes of the rule or measure. Wherefore since all things subject to Divine providence are ruled and measured by the eternal law, ... it is evident that all things partake somewhat of the eternal law, in so far as, namely, from its being imprinted on them, they derive their respective inclinations to their proper acts and ends. Now among all others, the rational creature is subject to the Divine providence in the most excellent way, in so far as it partakes of a share of providence, by being provident both for itself and for others. Wherefore it has a share of the Eternal Reason, whereby it has a natural inclination to its proper act and end: and this participation of the eternal law in the rational creature is called the natural law. (I-II 91.1c)

The first chapter of Genesis speaks of man and woman being made in the image and likeness of God. One of the ways that man and woman are like God is that they can reason and understand. As is evidenced in the story of Adam and Eve in the Garden of Eden, man and woman can speak to God and they can understand God. Even though God is infinite, man and woman are made similar to God in that they can reason and understand divine things. In this same passage, Thomas explains how human reasoning to discover what humans ought to do is the way humans participate in the Divine Plan.

> Hence the Psalmist after saying (Ps. iv. 6): *Offer up the sacrifice of justice*, as though someone asked what the works of justice are, adds: *Many say, Who showeth us good things?* in answer to which question he says: *The Light of thy countenance, O Lord, is signed upon us*: thus implying that the light of natural reason, whereby we discern what is good and what is evil, which is the function of the natural law, is nothing else than an imprint on us of the Divine light. It is therefore evident that the natural law is nothing else than the rational creature's participation of the eternal law. (I-II 91.1c)

In sum, all rational humans are by nature possessed of a real law of divine origin, a "rule and measure" of human conduct that is a true participation in the divine mind under the aspect of the eternal law.

The thoroughly intellectualist character of Thomas's account of law starts at the top. It is an ordinance of reason, given by one mind to another. Strictly speaking, law is only "in" the mind, first of the lawgiver, then of the ruled. In the case of all of creation except rational creatures, God through and in the eternal law exhaustively governs by causing things, such as carrots and cows, to achieve the ends for which they were created. Such creatures "experience" the divine ruling providence as an instinct, appetite, or passion. Nonhuman creatures are not free; they are not the intelligent self-moving principles of their own acts. The eternal law rules such creatures in the mode of a force both greater than them and also within them (what can be called a force majeure), not in a rational manner. For this reason Thomas concedes that "there is no participation of the eternal law in them, except by way of similitude" (I-II 91.2 ad 3).

Humans too in their biological reality are the patients of God's causation. Humans, though, are not exhausted by their biological reality. Their biology enables them to reach beyond themselves, to have self-awareness, and to realize that they are called by God to realize themselves. God appeals to them in their freedom through the reasonableness of the precepts of the natural law, which is an intellectual sharing or participation in the divine governance. He invites the human person, as Thomas says, to be "provident both for itself and for others" by seeking and doing what is good. For Thomas, the first precept of God's law for humans is "that good is to be done and pursued, and evil is to be avoided" (ST I-II 94.2c). Thomas is careful to say that this ordinance "is the first precept of law"; it is not merely a principle of practical reason. Rather it is a sharing in the governance of a higher and ordering mind, the divine mind.

According to St. Thomas, then, human morality is legal, linked to God's eternal law via the natural law of which it is a sharing. Thomas's theory of natural law is a morality of the good life, for the morality of the natural law takes shape from the divine precept that we are to seek and perform what is good for us as humans (and to avoid what is not good for us). The good life for humans is attained by seeking the ends to which humans are naturally inclined: "Wherefore according to the order of natural inclinations, is the order of the precepts of the natural law" (I-II 94.2c). Thomas groups these goods, at the highest level of generality: to be, to live, and to know. "All these precepts of the law of nature have the character of one natural law, inasmuch as they flow from one first precept" (I-II 94.2 ad 1). The achievement, as circumstances allow and require, of the goods at which these precepts aim is the stuff of divine natural law and, correlatively, of the good and happy life for humans.[10]

NATURAL LAW AND HUMAN LAW

Once the natural law, its precepts, and the aim of the good life are in focus, the next question is how to make that law effective in human community. No sphere of human life is exempt from the natural law, but the natural law is made effective in different ways. In families it can work by counsel, encouragement, and rebuke. In small communities somewhat larger than families it can work through custom and friendship.

Although all humans are under the natural law, Thomas does not take human law for granted. Interestingly, because natural law enables humans to see that all humans are by nature equal, one human being, without further status or justification, cannot make law for others (II-II 104.5). The power to make laws requires authoritative designation as the political authority, that is, an authoritative entrustment from the people (or, as in the case of King David, a divine decree) with the responsibility for the common good of the community. It is in fact the distinguishing mark of a properly constituted political authority that it can make law for the community. As is clear, this leadership is not a matter of "sovereign" self-assertion, but of making the natural law effective in the community's living. Thomas notes that whoever is involved, enacting laws is a high calling: "Legislation is the epitome of participation in the eternal law, for it is in issuing the ordering-judgment that we are most imitative of God, who spoke such a word to his creation."[11]

The human lawmaker "derives" human law from the natural law. "Every human law has just so much of the nature of law, as it is derived from the law of nature. But if in any point it deflects from the law of nature, it is no longer a law but a perversion of law" (I-II 95.2c). Human law is "derived" from the natural law in two ways. According to the first way, it is as a conclusion from premises. Thomas's example is the rule that one must not kill (innocent) persons. According to the second way, it is by way of specification, and here Thomas's illustration is the fixing of a punishment. The natural law requires punishment for crime, but it is silent on how the criminal should be punished. Something needs to be made specific. Thomas says unfortunately little about the means or method of derivation, but he is emphatic that all human law derives from the eternal law by way of the natural law (I-II 95.2; 93.3).

Although Thomas offers little detail about the process of derivation, he does provide two foundational principles. The first concerns the freedom of the legislator. Unlike some later political thinkers of the Enlightenment, Thomas does not imagine that laws can be framed and people governed in some mathematical fashion. Instead, he explains, "rulers imposing a law are in civic matters as architects regarding things to be built."[12] Lawmaking and politics are "free" not in the sense that they can be pursued (as mathematics and geometry can) in isolation from everything else, but in the sense that they are social art that aims to preserve the goods of the people's tradition while adapting it and opening it to new ones. Like architecture, law has to fit the environment and the tradition.

The second foundational principle, prudence, is closely connected to the first. Whereas art has as its object things made, the virtue of prudence has as its object things done. Thomas distinguishes several species of prudence, including individual prudence (for directing one's own actions) and domestic prudence (for ordering a family). The kind of prudence necessary to translate the natural law into effective human law he refers to as regnative prudence. While *regnative* refers in its root to kingly rule, Thomas recognizes that the virtue is necessary for and applicable to all rightful forms of government (II-II 50.1 ad 2). And he denominates such prudence the "best" form of prudence, (II-II 50.1c; 50.2 ad 1) because its exalted task is to allow the ruler to achieve the common good, not just individuals' goods or the goods of partial societies such as families.

Recognizing that lawmaking is an art requiring regnative prudence on the part of the lawmaker, we can add more detail to the job description of the human lawmaker. First, the charge given to the lawmaker is to enact ordinances for the common good. So if the lawmaker should promulgate an ordinance for his private advantage, it would fail to be law (I-II 90.2). "The nature of law," as one commentator notes, "is not simply that the individual be subject directly to the will of the governing powers, but that both are subject to the requirements of the good of society."[13] Second, the good and stable order of the community is the first and indispensable requirement of the common good, for without it common life is not possible (I-II 95.4; 98.1). This in turn requires, third, that the laws be just. They must not only observe the requirements of commutative justice (fair exchange of goods and properties), but they must also conform to distributive justice, or the notion that the structure of society is such that each person receives his due. Adhering to this norm ensures an equitable distribution of benefits and burdens among the citizens according to function and merit (I-II 96.4; 100.2). A generally just distribution of goods is the hallmark of a polity ruled in accordance with the common good.

As Thomas notes, because the common good comprises many things, the law should take account of many things with respect to persons, matters, and times (I-II

96.1c). If unruly citizens prowl about disrupting good order or violate the terms of distributive justice, the common good is imperiled. Ordinances properly framed for the common good have as their intent and effect making citizens good (I-II 92.1).

Sometimes this last point is misconstrued as committing Thomas to the view that the lawmaker should use law to repress every whiff of vice. But Thomas's position on this matter clarifies the nature of law. He explicitly denies that human law should repress all vice, and he justifies this proposition on the ground that laws are framed for the multitude, many of whom are not virtuous. If the law were to demand too much of the nonvirtuous, they would break out into even greater evils (I-II 96.2 ad 2). Regnative prudence determines the speed, so to speak, at which the lawgiver can lead his subjects to the virtue necessary to promote the common good and pursue the good life. The virtuous, for their part, do not need to depend on human law in the same way for their own happiness (I-II 96.5c).

LEGAL ART AND PRUDENCE

Thomas's teaching on the limits of law's role in repressing vice exemplifies the larger point that law, while taking account of "many things," should be suitably general. As we saw above, Thomas conceives of all law as a "rule and measure," and he recognizes that "if there were as many rules or measures as there are things measured or ruled, they would cease to be of use, since their use consists in their being applicable to many things" (I-II 96.2 ad 2). The artful and prudent lawgiver, then, navigates between the generality necessary for law to have its characteristic breadth, on the one hand, and its appropriate particularity, on the other.

Some legislators may be in a privileged epistemic position vis-à-vis the natural law, but, with a qualification to be mentioned below, this is only because they are artful and prudent. Mastery of the political art and consummate regnative prudence do not, however, dissolve the human situation of uncertainty, change, and the unexpected. That is, even the most artful legislators have to deal with surprises. And, Thomas notes, many legislators to varying degrees are lacking in art or prudence. He therefore confronts the situation of laws that fail. As one might expect, he does so on the basis of his fully intellectual account of law, not on the basis of ad hoc "policy" choices that charm today's legal academicians. Thomas has things to say about what citizens should do in the face of what they regard as unjust laws, but here our focus is mostly on judges confronted with an arguably unjust law, as in *Buck v. Bell*. One can distinguish three kinds of cases.[14]

In a first sort of case (Case 1), a judge knows that the defendant he is called upon to sentence according to law has been convicted on false testimony. Is the

judge permitted to ignore the sentencing law and to innovate procedure in order
to avoid pronouncing the sentence? To focus on the main issue, assume that the
law in question is not contrary to the natural law and, further, that the judge has
done all that is legally available to avoid this result (appeals, etc.). Is the judge allowed to resort to "innovative sentencing"? Thomas answers no. "In matters
touching his own person," he explains, "a man must form his conscience from his
own knowledge, but in matters concerning public authority, he must form his
conscience in accordance with the knowledge attainable in the public judicial
procedure" (II-II 67.2 ad 4).

Case 2 concerns an ordinance that the gates of the city must be closed during a
siege in order to protect the city. May they be opened to save the lives of citizens
pursued by the enemy? Thomas does not indicate that this question is to be
answered by the judge's consulting the natural law directly. Rather the judge is to
look to the ordinance and apply *epikeia* or equity. As Hittinger notes, Thomas contends that it would be sinful for the judge not to grant equity.[15] But it is essential
to be clear about what equity is and is not. Equity is not the permission or duty to
act contrary to the law. The question Thomas asks is whether the judge should
judge outside the letter of the law. And his answer is yes, because the judge must
obey the law that is, strictly speaking, in this case only in the mind of the legislator, not in the statute books. In any legitimate judgment of equity, the judge
always "follow[s] the intention of the legislator" (I-II 96.6 ad 2). As we have seen,
the lawmaking enterprise can succeed only if the lawmaker can make standing
rules of general applicability. Unforeseen circumstances sometimes arise, however. In such circumstances the granting of *epikeia* is on the basis of what the judge
can conjecture the lawmaker would have intended had he foreseen the situation.

In Case 2 the law is materially but not morally deficient. A special circumstance may
call for the application of *epikeia*, but *epikeia* does not violate the natural law. A different sort of case (Case 3) arises when the laws in question do violate the natural law, as
by requiring murder or theft—or *perhaps* compulsory sterilization. What is a judge to
do in the face of a case presenting laws that violate the natural law? Thomas answers,
"Judgment should not be delivered according to them" (II-II 60.5 ad 1). This is because,
Thomas explains, "such documents are to be called, not laws, but rather corruptions
of law." Notice what Thomas does not say. He does not say that the judge is entitled to
make a new law. What he says is that the judge is not to proceed to judgment.

For Case 3 Thomas distinguishes two ways in which a law can be morally defective. If the "law" is defective by being opposed to the divine law (that is, in this context, the law of the Covenant or of the Gospel), Thomas holds that it "must nowise
be observed." If instead the "law" is defective by being opposed to the "human good"
by being ordained to a private good, by being enacted by one who has usurped

ruling authority, or by unjustly distributing benefits and burdens, it "do[es] not bind in conscience, except perhaps to avoid scandal or disturbance" (I-II 96.4c).

When, then, a putative law is defective in this second way, by being opposed "merely" to the human good, the citizen qua citizen can under certain circumstances ("to avoid scandal or disturbance") obey the "law." But can a *judge* proceed to judgment on the basis of such a "law"? Hittinger explains why Thomas's answer is no: "If the legislator cannot make unjust laws bind in conscience neither can the *iudex*. And if the sentence of a judge is not binding, it is no sentence at all. That is to say, he has not judged as a judge."[16]

CARRIE BUCK BEFORE A THOMISTICO SUPREME COURT

Oliver Wendell Holmes Jr. was a theorist of law, but also a judge, a man possessed of the power to enforce final judgments. It is widely acknowledged that Holmes was openly and notoriously engaged in nothing short of a revolt against the natural law and natural rights. He wrote to his friend Laski, "You respect the rights of man—I don't, except those things a given crowd will fight for." On an earlier occasion, he wrote to Laski, "All my life I have sneered at the natural rights of man." A right, in Holmes's estimation, was "only the hypostasis of a prophecy—the imagination of a substance supporting the fact that the public force will be brought to bear upon those who do things said to contravene it." Natural law, as Holmes boasted in a famed law review article, was no more than a person's "can't helps."[17]

According to the Catholic natural law tradition, however, natural law is exactly about what we can and are obligated to help. The natural law identifies norms people can freely obey or disobey. Because the norms promote the good life, disobeying them leads humans away from human fulfillment, not closer to it—but humans are "free" to do either.

The preceding analysis shows what nuances are needed to apply natural law to the complicated enterprise of human law. Indeed it is a far more challenging task than what is suggested by the usual rhetoric of Supreme Court nomination hearings, which often focus on originalism versus "judicial activism." It remains to sketch what a carefully calibrated natural law approach would yield in a case such as *Buck v. Bell* in a U.S. Supreme Court faithful to the principles of natural law expounded here, but faithful also, where possible, to the modalities of interpretation that are accepted in the U.S. constitutional tradition. The issues are complex, and space limitations allow only an outline that will necessarily leave some questions unanswered or incompletely addressed.

As a preliminary matter, what would be the answer if the following question were posed: Does a legislative enactment that permits or requires compulsory sterilization (of the "retarded") violate the natural law? If one is tempted to answer straightaway yes, one then has to ask what the legislators in Virginia were thinking when they enacted the statute that was brought to bear on Carrie Buck. Virginia was only one among many states that enacted such statutes during the decades when the eugenics movement was at its stride. Be that as it may, if there is something morally objectionable about such a statute, most people would probably justify this conclusion in terms of its violating a person's natural rights rather that its violating the natural law. Rights talk is the coin of the realm in the contemporary public square and the stuff of Supreme Court doctrine, but, as the reader will have noticed, no indication has yet been given where "rights" fit in Thomas's moral theology, a topic that will be addressed below.

Consider now the *Buck* case. What should the Supreme Court do with respect to it in a properly presented case? The issue is not only the statute's moral status, but also what the Court as a historically constituted judicial institution is allowed or required to do to rectify a possible injustice. As was noted earlier, *epikeia* is of no avail here, since the legislature's intent is clear in the statute. Furthermore, on Thomas's analysis, if the enactment violates the natural law (Case 3), *epikeia* is not available as a tool to correct that deficiency.

One possible judicial approach, as has already been observed, is for the Court to recognize an unenumerated right to, say, bodily integrity, and then on the basis of that positive law predicate either strike down or refuse to apply the statute on the ground that it violates "substantive due process." In this approach rights trumps "laws." When the right at issue is unenumerated, such an approach reasonably invites charges of "judicial activism." But whether such charges are probative is another question. It is enough for the moment to observe again that this is a not uncommon approach in federal courts.

A second possibility takes seriously the requirement of due process "of law," and asks: Does this Virginia statute violate the natural law? If the answer is yes, it thereby ceases to be law. Assuming for the moment that the answer to the question is yes, this is a situation like Case 3, which means that the Court may not proceed to judgment. It also means that the Court may not strike down the statute. On Thomas's account, judges do not have the power to invalidate legislative enactments solely on the ground that they violate the natural law.

A third possibility, however, is to return to and call into service the argument from "original intent." On this line of analysis, the original intent of the amendments' drafters would empower judges not just to deny effect to the statute (as in the second possibility), but to invalidate it or strike it down, that is, to declare it a nullity, if they concluded that it violated the natural law. The natural law itself does not confer on judges the power to invalidate iniquitous legislation. But even if natural law does not confer that right, it may be that the framers of the Constitution allowed the Supreme Court to make that determination.

The course pursued by the Court will be determined by resolving the underlying central issue: Does compulsory sterilization violate the natural law? The enactment and subsequent defense in court of the Virginia statute and ones like it suggest that there is nothing approaching agreement on this question. The Catholic Church, however, teaches with magisterial authority that, except for limited therapeutic reasons, sterilization is a violation of the natural law. Not accidentally, one of the Church's most focused teachings on the question appeared just four years after *Buck v. Bell*, in Pope Pius XI's encyclical, *Casti conubii* (Denz. 3722–23), which condemned *eugenicum*.

NATURAL LAW AND "RIGHTS"

The last comments we have from St. Thomas on the natural law are as follows: "Now although God in creating man gave him this law of nature, the devil oversowed another law in man, namely, the law of concupiscence.... Since then the law of nature was destroyed by concupiscence, man needed to be brought back to works of virtue, and to be drawn away from works of vice: for which purpose he needed the written law."[18] Thomas does not mean that the natural law ceased to exist; after all, it is our participation in the Divine Mind, which does not change. His point is that our sinfulness wiped out the natural law's efficacy in us, and for this the written law of the Covenant was given as a remedy. Explaining why it was right for God not to promulgate the New Law, the law of the Gospel and of grace, from the foundation of the universe, Thomas emphasizes that men and women had to realize they were in need. "It behoved man first of all to be left to himself under the state of the Old Law, so that through falling into sin, he might realize his weakness, and acknowledge his need of grace" (I-II 106.3c). Law and grace are the two extrinsic principles by which God leads his rational creatures to their ends. Law and grace are alike in that humans are "free" to defy them. Grace builds on nature, but neither law nor grace strong-arms free human beings.

The Church shares the grace of the sacraments with the lay faithful, and the Magisterium of the Church teaches the faithful and others the demands of the divine moral law, including the natural law. Thus if particular judges are in a privileged epistemic position vis-à-vis the natural law, it could be because they are graced to be taught by the Church. And this is just the sort of worry that animated opposition to the election of John Fitzgerald Kennedy in 1960. When natural rights are invoked, agreement often seems imminent. If instead natural law is the context, conflict is conjured. Nonetheless the validity of the natural law is not a function of its popularity.

Why have natural rights been so scant in the Thomistic account of natural law? First, the place of rights in the thought of Thomas is a highly contested question. My own position, equally subject to objection is that, while he does indeed recognize a version of what we contemporary Americans refer to as individual (or subjective) rights, his overwhelming focus is on law and, derivatively, on the right (*ius*, in Latin), not rights. By *ius* or "the right" Thomas means the relationships that properly obtain in a given social context when the moral law has been given effect. It is, in other words, a state of affairs in which justice (both commutative and distributive) generally obtains, and which may include an individual's having a justified claim on others in the community (II-II 57.1 and 2). The right consists in giving each one what is his or her due under the moral (and the valid positive) law.[19]

According to this account, there can be no true conflict between law and right (or even "rights"). It is law's task to give effect to the right (distribution of goods), and "law" that fails in this is no law at all.

Knowing the right is no easy task. Although every person lives under an indefeasible natural law obligation to make the natural law effective in his or her living, fulfilling this obligation requires extensive deliberation and cooperation. A people (or a sovereign) must set up government and then discipline it, and, in both phases, determine who is best situated—the legislature, the judge, or (to complete the picture) the administrator—to say what the right is and therefore what is or is not law. The assignment of roles has an empirical basis, which is sure to vary from time to time and place to place. What does not vary, though, is the requirement that those called upon to render judgment must look into the goodness and right of the putative law on the basis of which they are asked to render judgment. The practice sometimes called "judicial review" is not optional. And in order to determine whether a particular putative law rises to the level of law it is sometimes necessary to look into the eyes of the person whose shot at the good life is under judgment.

CODA

In 1980 a Virginia official found Carrie Buck still alive. She was living near Charlottesville with her sister Doris, who had also been sterilized. Carrie was found to be a woman of normal intelligence; she died in 1983 at the age of seventy-six. Behind the masks of the law, Catholics affirm, are persons who were created for the good life.

NOTES

1. Friedrich Hayek, *Law, Legislation, Liberty,* vol. 1, *Rules and Orders* (Chicago: University of Chicago Press, 1973), 72.

2. Heinrich Rommen, *The State in Catholic Social Thought: A Treatise in Political Philosophy* (St. Louis, Mo.: B. Herder, 1945), 212.

3. St. Augustine, "Contra Faustum: Reply to Faustus the Manichaean," in *Nicene and Post-Nicene Fathers,* translated by Richard Stothert, book 22, sec. 27, vol. 4, p. 283, www.sacred-texts.com/chr/ecf/104/1040104.htm.

4. St. Thomas Aquinas, *Summa Theologica* I-II 93.1. Most further citations to the *Summa Theologica* (also known as the *Summa Theologiae*) will be made parenthetically in the text. Quotations from the *Summa* are generally from the translation by the Fathers of the English Dominican Province.

5. Other so-called originalist views of these amendments deny that the original meaning of "law" as used in these amendments imports a requirement of substance.

6. 274 U.S. 200, 207 (1927).

7. Quoted in Albert Aschuler, "From Blackstone to Holmes: The Revolt against Natural Law," 36 *Pepperdine Law Review* 491, 504 (2009).

8. Jean Porter, *Ministers of the Law: A Natural Law Theory of Legal Authority* (Grand Rapids, Mich.: Eerdmans, 2010), xiii.

9. Russell Hittinger, *First Grace: Recovering the Natural Law in a Post-Christian World* (Wilmington, Del.: ISI Books, 2003), 61.

10. On the topic of Thomas on the good life, see Herbert McCabe, *The Good Life: Ethics and the Pursuit of Happiness* (London: Continuum, 2005).

11. Hittinger, *First Grace,* 100.

12. Thomas Aquinas, *In Decem Libros Ethicorum,* VI Lect. 7, par. 1197.

13. John Mahoney, *The Making of Moral Theology: A Study of the Roman Catholic Tradition* (Oxford: Clarendon Press, 1987), 241.

14. My account here tracks in most particulars that of Hittinger in *First Grace,* 104–11.

15. Hittinger, *First Grace,* 106 (citing II-II 120.1 ad 1).

16. Hittinger, *First Grace,* 109.

17. All quoted in Aschuler, "From Blackstone to Holmes," 497–504.

18. Quoted and discussed in Russell Hittinger, "Natural Law and Catholic Moral Theology," in *A Preserving Grace: Protestants, Catholics, and Natural Law,* edited by Michael Cromartie (Grand Rapids, Mich.: Eerdmans, 1997), 1, 7.

19. See Clifford G. Kossell, "Natural Law and Human Law," in *The Ethics of Aquinas,* edited by Stephen J. Pope (Washington, DC: Georgetown University Press, 2002), 169, 179–80.

SELECTED READINGS

Finnis, John. *Natural Law and Natural Rights.* Oxford: Oxford University Press, 1980.

Hittinger, Russell. *First Grace: Recovering the Natural Law in a Post-Christian World.* Wilmington, Del.: ISI Books, 2003.

Maritain, Jacques. *Man and the State.* Chicago: University of Chicago Press, 1951.

Porter, Jean. *Ministers of the Law: A Natural Law Theory of Legal Authority.* Grand Rapids, Mich.: Eerdmans, 2010.

Rommen, Heinrich. *Natural Law.* 1945; St. Louis, Mo.: B. Herder, 1998.